"In this exceptional theological commentary on the Bible's most foundational book, Alexander sets forth several biblical-theological trajectories for themes that run across the canon, climax in Christ, and consummate in the new garden-city of God. While some will disagree with his handling of certain critical issues, this commentary offers robust whole-Bible theology and rightly celebrates the hope of the coming offspring of Eve, Abraham, and Judah, who will defeat the serpent and restore God's blessing to the world."

—**Jason S. DeRouchie,** *research professor of Old Testament and biblical theology and Rich and Judy Hastings Endowed Chair of Old Testament Studies, Midwestern Baptist Theological Seminary*

"Desmond Alexander's commentary on Genesis is refreshing and insightful. Clearly written by a seasoned Old Testament scholar, his careful and judicious analysis of the text, chapter by chapter, will be a great benefit to students, pastors, and laypeople. The commitment of the series to a high view of Scripture and to the unity of Scripture is reflected throughout Alexander's commentary, enabling the reader to trace key themes across the canon and to interpret Genesis within the grand narrative of Scripture. Alexander masterfully achieves the goal of the series, and he does it with exegetical precision and theological insight. I highly recommend this commentary."

—**Carol M. Kaminski,** *senior professor of Old Testament, Gordon-Conwell Theological Seminary*

"Finally! A Genesis commentary that holds a high view of Scripture, is exegetically robust yet accessible, and prioritizes the theological themes that hold Genesis together and connect it to the rest of the Bible. It is this latter feature that sets Alexander's commentary apart. His explanation of the rich theological themes in Genesis and how they are developed in subsequent biblical books helps readers make sense not only of Genesis but the Bible as a whole."

—**Catherine McDowell,** *chair of biblical studies and professor of Old Testament, School of Ministry, Palm Beach Atlantic University*

GENESIS

GENESIS

Evangelical Biblical Theology Commentary

General Editors

T. Desmond Alexander, Thomas R. Schreiner, Andreas J. Köstenberger

Assistant Editors

James M. Hamilton, Kenneth A. Mathews, Terry L. Wilder

T. Desmond Alexander

Genesis
Evangelical Biblical Theology Commentary

Copyright 2025 T. Desmond Alexander

Lexham Academic, an imprint of Lexham Press
1313 Bay St., Bellingham, WA 98225
LexhamPress.com

You may use brief quotations from this resource in presentations, articles, and books. For all other uses, please write Lexham Press for permission. Email us at permissions@ lexhampress.com.

Unless otherwise noted, Scripture quotations are the author's own translation or are from the the Christian Standard Bible® (CSB), Copyright © 2017 by Holman Bible Publishers. Used by permission. Christian Standard Bible®, and CSB® are federally registered trademarks of Holman Bible Publishers.

Print ISBN 9781683598244
Digital ISBN 9781683598251
Library of Congress Control Number 2025935887

General Editors: T. Desmond Alexander, Thomas R. Schreiner, Andreas J. Köstenberger
Assistant Editors: James M. Hamilton, Kenneth A. Mathews, Terry L. Wilder
Lexham Editorial: Derek Brown, John Barach, Kelley Mathews, Mandi Newell
Cover Design: Fanny Palacios
Typesetting: Justin Marr

25 26 27 28 29 30 31 / IN / 12 11 10 9 8 7 6 5 4 3 2 1

For Derek Johnston
and in fond memory of his wife Heather

CONTENTS

GENERAL EDITORS' PREFACE

In recent years biblical theology has seen a remarkable resurgence. Whereas, in 1970, Brevard Childs wrote *Biblical Theology in Crisis*, the quest for the Bible's own theology has witnessed increasing vitality since Childs prematurely decried the demise of the movement. Nowhere has this been truer than in evangelical circles. It could be argued that evangelicals, with their commitment to biblical inerrancy and inspiration, are perfectly positioned to explore the Bible's unified message. At the same time, as D. A. Carson has aptly noted, perhaps the greatest challenge faced by biblical theologians is how to handle the Bible's manifest diversity and how to navigate the tension between its unity and diversity in a way that does justice to both.[1]

What is biblical theology? And how is biblical theology different from related disciplines such as systematic theology? These two exceedingly important questions must be answered by anyone who would make a significant contribution to the discipline. Regarding the first question, the most basic answer might assert that biblical theology, in essence, is *the theology of the Bible*, that is, the theology expressed by the respective writers of the various biblical books *on their own terms* and *in their own historical contexts*. Biblical theology is the attempt to understand and embrace *the interpretive perspective of the biblical authors*. What is more, biblical theology is the theology of the *entire* Bible, an exercise in *whole-Bible theology*. For this reason biblical theology is not just a modern academic discipline; its roots are found already in the use of earlier Old Testament portions

[1] D. A. Carson, "New Testament Theology," in *DLNT* 810.

in later Old Testament writings and in the use of the Old Testament in the New.

Biblical theology thus involves a close study of *the use of the Old Testament in the Old Testament* (that is, the use of, say, Deuteronomy by Jeremiah, or of the Pentateuch by Isaiah). Biblical theology also entails the investigation of *the use of the Old Testament in the New*, both in terms of individual passages and in terms of larger Christological or soteriological themes. Biblical theology may proceed *book by book*, trace *central themes* in Scripture, or seek to place the contributions of individual biblical writers within the framework of the Bible's larger overarching *metanarrative*, that is, the Bible's developing story from Genesis through Revelation at whose core is *salvation* or *redemptive history*, the account of God's dealings with humanity and his people Israel and the church from creation to new creation.

In this quest for the Bible's own theology, we will be helped by the inquiries of those who have gone before us in the *history of the church*. While we can profitably study the efforts of interpreters over the entire sweep of the history of biblical interpretation since patristic times, we can also benefit from the labors of scholars since J. P. Gabler, whose programmatic inaugural address at the University of Altdorf, Germany, in 1787 marks the inception of the discipline in modern times. Gabler's address bore the title "On the Correct Distinction between Dogmatic and Biblical Theology and the Right Definition of Their Goals."[2] While few (if any) within evangelicalism would fully identify with Gabler's program, the proper distinction between dogmatic and biblical theology (that is, between biblical and systematic theology) continues to be an important issue to be adjudicated by practitioners of both disciplines, and especially biblical theology. We have already defined biblical theology as whole-Bible theology, describing the theology of the various biblical books *on their own terms* and *in their own historical contexts*. Systematic theology, by contrast, is more topically oriented and focused on contemporary contextualization. While there are different ways in which the relationship between biblical and systematic theology can be construed, maintaining a proper distinction between the two disciplines arguably continues to be vital if both are to achieve their objectives.

[2] The original Latin title was *Oratio de iusto discrimine theologiae biblicae et dogmaticae regundisque recte utriusque finibus*.

The present set of volumes constitutes an ambitious project, seeking to explore the theology of the Bible in considerable depth, spanning both Testaments. Authors come from a variety of backgrounds and perspectives, though all affirm the inerrancy and inspiration of Scripture. United in their high view of Scripture and in their belief in the underlying unity of Scripture, which is ultimately grounded in the unity of God himself, each author explores the contribution of a given book or group of books to the theology of Scripture as a whole. While conceived as stand-alone volumes, each volume thus also makes a contribution to the larger whole. All volumes provide a discussion of introductory matters, including the historical setting and the literary structure of a given book of Scripture. Also included is an exegetical treatment of all the relevant passages in succinct commentary-style format. The biblical theology approach of the series will also inform and play a role in the commentary proper. The commentator permits a discussion between the commentary proper and the biblical theology it reflects by a series of cross-references.

The major contribution of each volume, however, is a thorough discussion of the most important themes of the biblical book in relation to the canon as a whole. This format allows each contributor to ground biblical theology, as is proper, in an appropriate appraisal of the relevant historical and literary features of a particular book in Scripture while at the same time focusing on its major theological contribution to the entire Christian canon in the context of the larger salvation-historical metanarrative of Scripture. Within this overall format, there will be room for each individual contributor to explore the major themes of his or her particular corpus in the way he or she sees most appropriate for the material under consideration. For some books of the Bible, it may be best to have these theological themes set out in advance of the exegetical commentary. For other books it may be better to explain the theological themes after the commentary. Consequently, each contributor has the freedom to order these sections as best suits the biblical material under consideration so that the discussion of biblical-theological themes may precede or follow the exegetical commentary.

This format, in itself, would already be a valuable contribution to biblical theology. But other series try to accomplish a survey of the Bible's theology as well. What distinguishes the present series is its orientation toward Christian proclamation. This is the Evangelical Biblical Theology Commentary series! As a result, the ultimate purpose of this set of volumes is not exclusively, or even primarily, academic. Rather, we seek to relate biblical theology to our own lives and to the life of the church. Our desire is to equip those in Christian ministry who are called by God to preach and teach the precious truths of Scripture to their congregations, both in North America and in a global context.

The base translation for the Evangelical Biblical Theology Commentary series is the Christian Standard Bible (CSB). The CSB places equal value on faithfulness to the original languages and readability for a modern audience. The contributors, however, have the liberty to differ with the CSB as they comment on the biblical text. Note that, in the CSB, Old Testament passages that are quoted in the New Testament are set in boldface type.

We hope and pray that the forty volumes of this series, once completed, will bear witness to the unity in diversity of the canon of Scripture as they probe the individual contributions of each of its sixty-six books. The authors and editors are united in their desire that in so doing the series will magnify the name of Christ and bring glory to the triune God who revealed himself in Scripture so that everyone who calls on the name of the Lord will be saved—to the glory of God the Father and his Son, the Lord Jesus Christ, under the illumination of the Holy Spirit, and for the good of his church. To God alone be the glory: *soli Deo gloria.*

ACKNOWLEDGMENTS

This commentary is the fruit of many years of researching and teaching the book of Genesis. My first forays into the academic world of Genesis began nearly fifty years ago when, in 1977, I embarked on postgraduate research on the Abraham narrative under the insightful supervision of Dr. Gordon Wenham. Engaging with the prevalent academic climate of the late 1970s, my PhD thesis challenged the suitability of the Documentary Hypothesis to explain the composition of Genesis 11:27-25:11. For his mentoring and friendship over many years, I am deeply grateful to Gordon Wenham. His two-volume commentary on Genesis is a masterly contribution to our understanding of this book. From these initial explorations of chapters 11:27-25:11, over the intervening decades, my interest in Genesis has expanded to include the rest of the book. My appreciation of this ancient text has grown significantly as the years have passed.

A vital contribution to my understanding of Genesis has come through the collaborative process of supervising various PhD theses that have engaged with all or some of Genesis. I am exceptionally grateful to James McKeown, Paul Williamson, Samuel Goh, Sarah Dalrymple, Rita Cefalu, Paul Twiss, and Mary Schieferstein for sharing invaluable insights, which have helped me see the riches of Genesis more clearly and in more depth. In addition, over the years, numerous scholars, through their writings, have challenged my thinking and sharpened my understanding of what Genesis says. It is impossible to acknowledge these authors here, and they go beyond those mentioned in the footnotes and bibliography of this volume. If I see things more clearly, it comes from standing on the shoulders of others. For assisting me in doing this by providing access to numerous resources, I am indebted to several generations of librarians at the Queen's University of Belfast and Union Theological College. My sincere thanks go especially to Joy Conkey and Margaret Ollivier for helping me complete this commentary. Their efficient contribution to running the library at Union Theological College is highly valued by staff and students.

Why, you might ask, write another commentary on Genesis when so many already exist? Hopefully, this volume offers new insights and a fresh reading of the text. In particular, I have endeavored to provide an interpretation of Genesis that views the book as a carefully composed and unified literary work centered on a unique patriline. Regrettably, many commentaries on Genesis approach the text as merely a collection of short stories that can be read largely in isolation from each other. The episodic nature of Genesis and its division into chapters and verses fosters this way of reading the text. Yet, such an approach must be firmly rejected in favor of a reading that takes seriously the thematic unity of the book. In addition, some scholars inappropriately affirm that Genesis is incoherent and cannot be read as a unified work of literature. However, this conclusion reflects a widespread failure in modern scholarship to understand and appreciate the literary techniques used to compose it. Consequently, many writers have not adequately grasped this ancient text's overarching message. Despite initial appearances, Genesis is a more coherent text than is often assumed.

The present commentary covers only some of what could be said about Genesis. No author could hope to engage comprehensively with all that has been written about Genesis in one book. Numerous monographs and essays have already been produced on Genesis or selected portions, discussing the text from differing perspectives and using various methodologies. Adopting a more focused approach, in line with the objectives of this commentary series, the present commentary distills what is most important for understanding Genesis as the opening book of the Christian Bible. Genesis lays a foundation that underpins the rest of the Bible. For this reason, it is unique within the Bible. Given this foundational role, understanding Genesis is not just beneficial but essential for grasping the rest of Scripture. A flawed reading of Genesis will likely result in a misreading of other parts of the Bible.

Every commentator on Genesis must make challenging decisions regarding the interpretation and meaning of the text. Others will not necessarily agree with my choices. My fellow series editors, James Hamilton and Kenneth Mathews, graciously recommended this volume for publication even when they would adopt a different approach on some issues. I hope that the final version does not disappoint them too much. I am solely responsible for the opinions expressed here; it should not be assumed that the series editors support everything written here.

I am deeply indebted to Lexham Press for agreeing to publish this commentary on Genesis. Derek Brown oversaw this book through the early stage of production in his role as an academic editor. As a copyeditor, John Barach has done an excellent job of identifying numerous minor mistakes in my initial manuscript. To them and other staff at Lexham Press, I am exceedingly grateful.

Finally, I cannot emphasize my family's support enough, which extends well beyond their encouragement for writing this commentary. Anne has been a loving and faithful partner for over forty years, prayerfully upholding me in everything I do. Her companionship has enriched my life more than words can express. I have also benefited enormously from the love of our children, Jane and David, their respective spouses, Ross and Alana, and our grandchildren, Martha, Maggie, and Gregor. Being surrounded by such a supportive family is a great blessing. I pray that they will find abundant and everlasting life in knowing the savior-king, divinely promised in the book of Genesis. With appreciation for their friendship over many years, this book is dedicated to Derek Johnston and in fond memory of his wife Heather.

SOLI DEO GLORIA

LIST OF ABBREVIATIONS

Miscellaneous

ANE	Ancient Near East(ern)
c.	circa, approximately
ch(s).	chapter(s)
CSB	Christian Standard Bible
ed(s).	edited by, editors(s), edition
Eng.	English
esp.	especially
ESV	English Standard Version
JPS	Jewish Publication Society Old Testament (1917)
KJV	King James (Authorized) Version
LXX	Septuagint
MT	Masoretic Text
NAB	New American Bible (2010)
NASB	New American Standard Bible
NET	The New English Translation Bible
NIV	New International Version, 2011 ed.
NJB	New Jerusalem Bible
NJPS	Jewish Publication Society Tanakh (1985)
NLT	New Living Translation
NRSV	New Revised Standard Version
NT	New Testament
OT	Old Testament
p(p).	page(s)
RSV	Revised Standard Version
SamP	Samaritan Pentateuch
SBL	Society of Biblical Literature

v(v).	verse(s)
Vg	Vulgate

Journal, Reference Words, Series

AB	Anchor Bible
ABD	D. N. Freedman (ed.), *Anchor Bible Dictionary*, 6 vols., New York: Doubleday, 1992
ASOR	American Schools of Oriental Research
AUSS	*Andrews University Seminary Studies*
BA	*Biblical Archaeologist*
BASOR	*Bulletin of the American Schools of Oriental Research*
BBR	*Bulletin for Biblical Research*
BHS	K. Elliger and W. Rudolph (eds.), *Biblia Hebraica Stuttgartensia*, 2nd ed., Stuttgart: Deutsche Bibelstiftung, 1977
Bib	*Biblica*
BibInt	*Biblical Interpretation*
BSac	*Bibliotheca sacra*
BZAW	Beihefte zur Zeitschrift für die alttestamentliche Wissenschaft
CBQ	*Catholic Biblical Quarterly*
CH	Code of Hammurabi
EvQ	*Evangelical Quarterly*
FAT	Forschungen zum Alten Testament
FOTL	Forms of Old Testament Literature
GKC	E. Kautzsch (ed.), *Gesenius' Hebrew Grammar*, rev. and trans. A. E. Cowley, Oxford: Clarendon, 1910
HALOT	L. Koehler and W. Baumgartner, *The Hebrew and Aramaic Lexicon of the Old Testament*, tr. M. E. J. Richardson, Leiden: Brill, 1994–2000
HTR	*Harvard Theological Review*
IBHS	B. K. Waltke and M. O'Connor, *Introduction to Biblical Hebrew Syntax*, Winona Lake: Eisenbrauns, 1990
IBS	*Irish Biblical Studies*
ICC	International Critical Commentary
IDB	G. A. Buttrick, T. S. Kepler, J. Knox, H. G. May, S. Terrien and E. S. Bucke (eds.), *Interpreter's Dictionary of the Bible*, 4 vols., New York: Abingdon, 1962

Int	*Interpretation*
JAOS	*Journal of the American Oriental Society*
JBL	*Journal of Biblical Literature*
JBLMS	Journal of Biblical Literature: Monograph Series
JBQ	*Jewish Bible Quarterly*
JETS	*Journal of the Evangelical Theological Society*
JJS	*Journal of Jewish Studies*
JNES	*Journal of Near Eastern Studies*
Joüon	Joüon, Paul. *A Grammar of Biblical Hebrew.* Translated and revised by T. Muraoka. 2nd ed. Subsidia Biblica 27. Rome: Pontifical Biblical Institute, 2006.
JSOT	*Journal for the Study of the Old Testament*
JSOTSup	Journal for the Study of the Old Testament, Supplement Series
LHBOTS	Library of Hebrew Bible/Old Testament Studies
NAC	New American Commentary
NIBCOT	New International Biblical Commentary Old Testament
NIDOTTE	W. A. VanGemeren (ed.), *New International Dictionary of Old Testament Theology and Exegesis*, 5 vols., Grand Rapids: Zondervan; Carlisle: Paternoster, 1997
NSBT	New Studies in Biblical Theology
OTL	Old Testament Library
PRSt	*Perspectives in Religious Studies*
RB	*Revue biblique*
SBJT	*Southern Baptist Journal of Theology*
TDOT	Theological Dictionary of the Old Testament
Them	*Themelios*
TOTC	Tyndale Old Testament Commentaries
TynBul	*Tyndale Bulletin*
VT	*Vetus Testamentum*
WBC	Word Biblical Commentary
WTJ	*Westminster Theological Journal*
ZAW	*Zeitschrift für die alttestamentliche Wissenschaft*

INTRODUCTION

Genesis is one of the most important books in the Bible and yet possibly one of the most misunderstood and misused. It is a foundational text for understanding our world, explaining how a divinely created planet that fills us with awe and wonder can at the same time be a place scarred by the terrible consequences of natural disasters and human immorality. As both good and evil impact our lives, Genesis offers a profound insight into why this is a universal experience. More importantly, highlighting the ultimate source of our ills, Genesis points to a cure, encouraging us to embrace God's solution to our personal shortcomings and perverse behavior.

Genesis is a book of striking contrasts. We see the evil of human nature exposed in a multitude of ways, most noticeably in the heinous violence of fratricide. We encounter some of the most punitive actions of God against human sinfulness (a great flood; the destruction of Sodom and Gomorrah). Yet, although Genesis records some of the most negative assessments of human nature in the Bible, it also highlights the grace and mercy of God as he acts to redeem a world controlled by the powers of evil. In Genesis the hope of restoration to a harmonious relationship with God is set against a background of intense darkness. This hope is like the sun rising in the morning, dispelling the blackness of a moonless night.

The English name "Genesis" is derived from the title given to the book by the earliest Greek translators in the third century BC. The Greek term γένεσις *genesis*, which means "birth/family line/genealogy," is regularly used to translate the Hebrew word תּוֹלְדוֹת *tôlĕdôt*.[1] As we shall see

[1] The Greek expression αἱ γενέσεις *hai geneseis* comes in 6:9; 10:1; 11:10, 27; 25:12, 19; 36:1, 9; 37:2; ἡ βίβλος γενέσεως *hē biblos geneseōs* comes in 2:4; 5:1.

below, this Hebrew term comes in headings that structure the contents of Genesis to highlight the existence of a special patriline that stands at the heart of God's plan to restore a dysfunctional world. Genesis, meaning "family line," is a very apt title for the book, capturing its central feature. The Jewish title for Genesis, which is derived from the book's opening Hebrew word, is *Bereshit/Bereshith*, meaning "In the beginning." Unfortunately, due to the Hebrew title, some scholars misinterpret the Greek term γένεσις (*genesis*) to mean "beginnings/origin." Genesis is a book of beginnings, but, as we shall see, there is much more to it than merely beginnings. At the heart of Genesis is a unique patriline that will ultimately lead to Jesus Christ.

I. How To Read Genesis

When it comes to reading Genesis, many people lose sight of the forest for the trees. It is commonplace for the text of Genesis to be fragmented into pieces that are read in relative isolation from the literary context in which they are placed. Many readers work with the assumption that passages within Genesis can best be understood independently of the whole or as part of a reconstructed source that is the result of a scholarly hypothesis that speculates on how Genesis was composed. Many commentaries and studies on Genesis assume that an appreciation of the whole book is hermeneutically unimportant for understanding every passage that composes Genesis. Yet, when a passage is freed from its literary mooring, all kinds of interpretations become possible. Context provides an important constraint in the process of reading any passage in Genesis.

Various factors account for the fragmentation that detracts from understanding Genesis as a coherent work of literature. The episodic nature of the book's contents creates passages that give the appearance of being self-contained units. The division of biblical books into chapters and verses has fostered in Christian circles a piecemeal reading of Genesis both in public and in private. Most readers engage with only a short section of Genesis at any one time.

Another significant driving force behind this fragmented approach to understanding the text of Genesis is the widely held belief that the book was composed from earlier sources and this ought to be the focus of attention when interpreting the text. While there is good reason to think of Genesis as a literary collage, created through combining preexisting materials, this does not justify ignoring the present coherence of the book. Even if the process of composition could be recovered—an unlikely possibility given the absence of preexisting source documents[2]—we should assume that the final author/compiler of Genesis created a coherent narrative. Importantly, every element within Genesis is part of a communicative process that involves the entire book. If we are to read Genesis through the eyes of its creator, we need to take every part into consideration. This is challenging for readers, who invariably find it easier to concentrate on a few verses in isolation from the rest of the book. Yet, every word and sentence within Genesis is set within the context of the whole book. This context shapes how each part ought to be read. Studies that ignore this book-wide context run the risk of misinterpreting what the author/compiler of Genesis intended to communicate.

The designation "author/compiler" is used to avoid two misunderstandings. First, the term "author" by itself conveys to most modern readers the idea of an individual who creates a work that is largely homogeneous in style. Moreover, every modern author is expected to avoid plagiarizing what others have penned. These factors are not true for Genesis. Genesis is far from homogeneous in style. If it is entirely the product of a single author, it is an astonishing work of literature, given the disparate literary forms that it contains. This would require rare literary genius, unlike any other in the ancient (or modern) world. More likely, however, Genesis consists of material, written by various authors, that was taken over by its author/compiler to produce the variegated text that we now possess. As we shall observe, however, these disparate materials have been brought together to form a literary work that, despite initial appearances, forms a unified narrative from beginning to end.[3] The

---

[2] Raymond F. Person and Robert Rezetko, "Introduction: The Importance of Empirical Models to Assess the Efficacy of Source and Redaction Criticism," in *Empirical Models Challenging Biblical Criticism*, ed. Raymond F. Person and Robert Rezetko, AIL 25 (Atlanta: SBL, 2016), 1–35, offer an insightful critique, challenging the usefulness of source and redaction criticism as practiced by some biblical scholars. See also Joshua A. Berman, *Inconsistency in the Torah: Ancient Literary Convention and the Limits of Source Criticism* (New York: Oxford University Press, 2017); Matthias Armgardt, Benjamin Kilchör, and Markus Zehnder, eds., *Paradigm Change in Pentateuchal Research*, Beihefte zur Zeitschrift für Altorientalische und Biblische Rechtsgeschichte 22 (Wiesbaden: Harrassowitz, 2019).

[3] See David W. Baker, "Diversity and Unity in the Literary Structure of Genesis," in *Essays on the Patriarchal Narratives*, ed. A. R. Millard and Donald J. Wiseman (Leicester: Inter-Varsity Press, 1980), 189–205.

compiler of Genesis has creatively chosen and arranged its contents. In this sense he is the book's author.

Second, the person responsible for shaping the present text of Genesis may have done more than simply arrange in a particular order preexisting materials that he has collected. These materials may have been changed through editing in the process of being compiled together. Since we do not have independent access to the earlier documents, we have no way of knowing how the compiler handled his sources. In a culture where plagiarism was not prohibited and the concept of copyright did not exist, authors/compilers had no reservations about duplicating with minor or major changes what others wrote.[4]

Scholarly assessments of Genesis have tended to view the book as so fragmented that it cannot be read as a coherent narrative. Yet, even among those scholars whose primary interest is in the process by which the book was composed, it is acknowledged that the text displays some evidence of unity. Out of early theories that viewed Genesis as composed of numerous fragments, there arose the Documentary Hypothesis of Wellhausen, Kuenen, and Graf.[5] This theory contends that Genesis comprises three sources that can be traced throughout the book, like three intertwined strands in a cord. The Documentary Hypothesis recognizes some degree of literary unity in each of the three sources than appear throughout Genesis, but contends that these sources can be distinguished from each other.

More recently some source critical studies have rejected the existence of three parallel documents in Genesis, favoring preexisting blocks of material that were subsequently linked together. These larger blocks of material originally existed independently of each other but were gradually combined to form Genesis.[6] One such block is the account of the life of Jacob in chapters 25–33. Erhard Blum suggests that we should no longer speak of this material as a "cycle of tales," but rather consider it to be "a major integrated story with themes of its own."[7] Blum's reassessment

---

[4] A comparison of Kings and Chronicles provides ample evidence of this. For an assessment of the Synoptic Gospels, which share much material in common, see Joseph A. Weaks, "Limited Efficacy in Reconstructing the Gospel Sources for Matthew and Luke," in Person and Rezetko, *Empirical Models Challenging Biblical Criticism*, 331–54.

[5] For a fuller account, see T. Desmond Alexander, *From Paradise to the Promised Land: An Introduction to the Pentateuch*, 4th ed. (Grand Rapids: Baker Academic, 2022), 233–58.

[6] For a summary of this approach, see Alexander, *From Paradise to the Promised Land*, 286–93.

[7] Erhard Blum, "The Jacob Tradition," in *The Book of Genesis: Composition, Reception, and Interpretation*, ed. Craig A. Evans, Joel N. Lohr, and David L. Petersen, VTSup 152 (Leiden:

is welcome, but he omits chapter 26 from this "integrated story" and sees chapters 34–35 as "rather loosely connected episodes and notes."[8] The account of Joseph's life provides another example of an "integrated story." There is a widespread recognition that chapters 37–45, excluding possibly chapter 38,[9] form a unified narrative that consists of closely linked episodes.[10] A similar case for an integrated story can be made for the episodes that compose the account of Abraham's life.[11] While the task of source critics is to decompose Genesis, even they recognize in different ways links that bind episodes together.

In a perceptive assessment of the current state of Pentateuchal studies, Jeffrey H. Tigay recognizes that some scholars have allowed their quest for sources to diminish their appreciation of the literary value of the received text. He writes:

> We have also seen that in recent decades scholars have recognized the importance of the final product and begun to recognize that redaction was not simply a mechanical process of cutting and pasting—though that was part of it—but involved careful thought and both theological and artistic judgment and that the final product was designed to describe a coherent history and a theological message and to do so in an aesthetically pleasing way. In this way, scholars are "remaking" the tradition and finding in the Torah a kind of literary integrity that transcends the signs of multiple authorship that abound in it.[12]

Brill, 2012), 182.

[8] Blum, "The Jacob Tradition," 181.

[9] The inclusion or exclusion of Gen 38 as part of the so-called Joseph Story continues to be a matter of debate. There are good reasons to view ch. 38 as an integral and necessary part of the narrative that is recorded in chs. 37–50. See Comments on ch. 38.

[10] See R. Norman Whybray, "The Joseph Story and Pentateuchal Criticism," *VT* 18 (1968): 522–28; George W. Coats, *From Canaan to Egypt: Structural and Theological Context for the Joseph Story*, Catholic Biblical Quarterly Monograph Series 4 (Washington: Catholic Biblical Association of America, 1976).

[11] See T. Desmond Alexander, *Abraham in the Negev: A Source-Critical Investigation of Genesis 20:1–22:19* (Carlisle: Paternoster, 1997).

[12] Jeffrey H. Tigay, "The Documentary Hypothesis, Empirical Models and Holistic Interpretation," in *Modernity and Interpretations of Ancient Texts: The Collapse and Remaking of Traditions.*, ed. J. Ikeda (Kizugawa-City, Kyoto, Japan: International Institute of Advanced Studies, 2012), 132–33. For a helpful corrective to Tigay's own approach to source analysis, see Person and Rezetko, "Introduction," 1–35.

Tigay's assessment reflects developments from the 1970s onwards. Recent decades have witnessed a growing interest in the topic of Hebrew poetics, the study of the rhetorical techniques used by ancient writers to compose their narratives. This has resulted in fresh evaluations of biblical texts, with some scholars being highly critical of ongoing attempts to discern the process of composition. Meir Sternberg is especially outspoken when he comments on "two hundred years of frenzied digging into the Bible's genesis." He writes, "Rarely has there been such a futile expense of spirit in a noble cause; rarely have such grandiose theories of origination been built and revised and pitted against one another on the evidential equivalent of the head of a pin; rarely have so many worked so long and so hard with so little to show for their trouble."[13]

Sternberg's disdainful appraisal of scholarly attempts to explain the compositional history of biblical texts arises out of a recognition that source-oriented critics confront an enormous challenge. He writes:

> The reading lot of the geneticist is perhaps the hardest of all, because the task of decomposition calls for the most sensitive response to the arts of composition. How else will one be able to tell deliberate from accidental roughnesses and identify the marks of disunity in unity through a text whose *poesis* covers the tracks of its *genesis*? It is this enforced movement from discourse to source by way of interpretation that allies genetic criticism with that branch of acrobatics known as lifting oneself up by one's bootstraps. But then it's either acrobatics or nothing.[14]

Sternberg highlights the challenge of unravelling the process by which ancient texts were composed. Acknowledging this difficulty, William H. C. Propp candidly says, "We must disabuse ourselves of the conceit that we will ever know exactly how the Torah came to be."[15] With this in view, he contrasts an important difference between synchronic and

---

[13] Meir Sternberg, *The Poetics of Biblical Narrative: Ideological Literature and the Drama of Reading* (Bloomington: Indiana University Press, 1985), 13.

[14] Sternberg, *Poetics of Biblical Narrative*, 16–17.

[15] William H. C. Propp, *Exodus 19–40: A New Translation with Introduction and Commentary*, AB 2B (New York: Doubleday, 2006), 734. In a similar vein, R. Norman Whybray, "Genesis," in *The Oxford Bible Commentary*, ed. John Barton and John Muddiman (Oxford: Oxford University Press, 2001), 39, remarks regarding Genesis, "About the process or processes by which the diverse material was combined to form a single literary work there is at present no consensus of opinion." Kris Sonek, "The Abraham Narratives in Genesis 12–25," *CurBR* 17

diachronic readings of Pentateuchal texts. Propp writes, "The *harmonizing* reader may at least recreate the editors' understanding of their product. But the *atomizing* reader posits and analyses literary materials whose existence is highly questionable."[16] As scholars begin to understand better the rhetorical techniques of biblical writers, the criteria for discerning sources have diminished.[17]

As we explore the book of Genesis many centuries after it was first created, it may be helpful to recall the distance that separates us from this text both chronologically and culturally. As Alter observes, writing about the Hebrew Bible in general:

> One might imagine the Bible as a rich and variegated landscape, perfectly accessible to the observer's eye, but from which we now stand almost three millennia distant. Through the warp of all those intervening centuries, lines become blurred, contours are distorted, colors fade; for not only have we lost the precise shadings of implication of many of the original Hebrew words, but we have also acquired quite different habits and expectations as readers, have forgotten the very conventions around which the biblical tales were shaped. Philological research in recent decades has made admirable progress in recovering the likely nuances of many particular words, but that is only a first step. The reconstruction through careful analysis of the literary procedures that govern biblical narrative can serve us, at the immense remove from which we view these ancient texts, as binoculars to bring much that seems hazy into focus.[18]

(2019): 163, writes, "Attempts to explain the origin, formation, and final editing of Genesis are numerous, complex, and often contradictory."

[16] Propp, *Exodus 19–40*, 734.

[17] Even advocates of the recently proposed Neo-Documentary Hypothesis recognize the shortcomings of distinctive vocabulary, style of writing, and theology as criteria for source analysis. According to Joel S. Baden, *The Composition of the Pentateuch: Renewing the Documentary Hypothesis* (New Haven: Yale University Press, 2012), 29–30, the all-important factor for source analysis is "narrative continuity." Baden maintains that due to "plot contradictions," "the Pentateuch is fundamentally unreadable" (Joel S. Baden, "Why Is the Pentateuch Unreadable? Or, Why Are We Doing This Anyway?" in *The Formation of the Pentateuch: Bridging the Academic Cultures of Europe, Israel and North America*, ed. Jan. C. Gertz et al., FAT 111 [Tübingen: Mohr Siebeck, 2016], 251). Unfortunately, Baden's approach to "narrative continuity" fails to consider sufficiently the rhetorical style of ancient writers. For a brief evaluation of this approach, see Alexander, *From Paradise to the Promised Land*, 295–97.

[18] Robert Alter, *The Art of Biblical Narrative* (New York: Basic, 1981), 185.

To this end, it is important to recognize that Genesis is best viewed as a literary collage. Different forms of writing have been placed side-by-side. The repetitive, majestic prose of Genesis 1, which describes the creation of the world, differs markedly from the down-to-earth prose account of Adam and Eve's creation in the Garden of Eden. The linear genealogies of Genesis 5 and 11, which are not quite identical in form, contrast sharply with the prose report concerning Noah and the great flood (6:9–9:17). The concise description of Esau's offspring in Genesis 36 has little in common with the extended account of Jacob's offspring that runs throughout Genesis 37–50. Jacob's deathbed pronouncement of blessings upon his sons stands apart stylistically from the prose narrative within which it is embedded. Some episodes are short (e.g., 11:1–9; 21:22–34); some are long (e.g., 24:1–67). Some appear to be reasonably self-contained (e.g., 12:10–20); others are heavily dependent on a knowledge of earlier material (e.g., 20:1–18).[19] Viewed alongside modern literary compositions, Genesis does not exhibit the homogeneity that we have come to expect in a literary work penned by one individual.

At first sight, this lack of homogeneity may suggest that Genesis is not a unified composition, but this argument rests on a misconception of what constitutes literary unity. Unity depends not on homogeneity, but on how the disparate parts complement each other. In the tale of the blind men of Hindustan, unable to see the whole animal, they perceived the elephant to be a curious assortment of unrelated objects. In truth, an elephant is far from homogeneous, but it is nevertheless a unity. Genesis may consist of very differing parts, but this does not automatically mean that it cannot be a unified literary work. As we shall observe in more detail below, the author/compiler of Genesis has with great skill composed this book to highlight the existence of a unique patriline that will lead to a future king who will bring God's blessing to the nations of the earth. This unifying factor, however, has proved elusive, especially given modern expectations regarding literary unity and the trend toward atomizing the text.

Regardless of how many writers were responsible for composing the contents of Genesis, less-than-homogeneous materials have been compiled together to create a unique narrative, that, while varied in style and

[19] See T. Desmond Alexander, "The Wife/Sister Incidents of Genesis: Oral Variants?," *IBS* 11 (1989): 2–22; T. Desmond Alexander, "Are the Wife/Sister Incidents of Genesis Literary Compositional Variants?" *VT* 42 (1992): 145–53.

form, nonetheless forms a coherent story. Moreover, we must recognize that Genesis, as a literary work, is much more than the sum of its parts. The atomization of the text has undermined our ability to appreciate the message of the book as a whole. As Polzin astutely observes, "Traditional biblical scholarship has spent most of its efforts in disassembling the works of a complicated watch before our amazed eyes without apparently realizing that similar efforts by and large have not succeeded in putting the parts back together again in a significant or meaningful way."[20]

Unfortunately, in the past two centuries, scholars have largely disdained the authors/compilers responsible for creating biblical books. Dismissed as merely editors, their compositional skills have been ignored. Scholars have disregarded their voice, favoring the hypothetical voices of reconstructed sources. Swept along on the tide of diachronic studies, commentators have struggled to appreciate what the author/compiler of Genesis wished to communicate.

When reading Genesis, we need to appreciate how episodes, which have been skillfully combined, to varying degrees presuppose what has gone before and anticipate what is still to come. Individual episodes may be read in isolation, but we should recognize that each episode is placed within a larger literary context that constrains and informs how we should interpret it. Unfortunately, critical methods that fragment the text of Genesis automatically undermine the importance of attempting to read the book as a coherent work of literature. As G. Geoffrey Harper observes, "Sequential reading is necessary for any narrative in order to derive the maximum benefit from the internal development of plot and character and for understanding the intrinsic logic of the whole."[21]

As we shall observe in more detail in the commentary section, features in an episode may take on added significance when viewed as part of a larger literary work. God's directive in Genesis 1 that humans should govern other earthly creatures on his behalf (1:26, 28) has a bearing on the events recorded in Genesis 3, where Adam and Eve fail to exercise authority over the serpent, one of the "wild animals" (3:1). Ignoring the voice of the Creator, the human couple embrace

---

[20] Robert Polzin, "'The Ancestress of Israel in Danger' in Danger," *Semeia* 3 (1975): 82–83.

[21] G. Geoffrey Harper, *"I Will Walk among You": The Rhetorical Function of Allusion to Genesis 1–3 in the Book of Leviticus*, BBRSup 21 (University Park: Eisenbrauns, 2018), 17. Jerome T. Walsh, *Old Testament Narrative: A Guide to Interpretation* (Louisville: Westminster John Knox, 2009), 15, uses the term "linearity" to describe this characteristic of narrative art.

the deceitful advice of a creature. Their action needs to be understood against the special status that God bestows on humans in Genesis 1, not merely the prohibition that is given in 2:16–17. If chapter 3 looks backward, presupposing chapter 1, it also looks forward, setting the agenda for later developments. God's pronouncement in 3:15 that the offspring of the woman will overcome the serpent plays a crucial role in shaping the plot that extends throughout Genesis.[22] These observations illustrate the importance of a sequential reading of Genesis. Many more examples could be added.

A sequential reading of Genesis reveals that later passages often presuppose the existence of earlier passages in different ways. The interconnected nature of the episodes in Genesis is reflected in how some episodes may assume a knowledge of earlier episodes to avoid repeating narrative details. The events described in 20:1–2 make sense only to those who have already read 12:10–13. A knowledge of 12:10–13 is essential for understanding why Abraham says that Sarah is his sister in 20:2. Similarly, God's remarks in 26:2–5 presupposes that readers are already familiar with the events of 22:1–18, in which Abraham demonstrates his obedience to YHWH and is rewarded through the giving of a divine oath that guarantees God's promises to the patriarch. The wording of 26:2–5 echoes what is said in 22:15–18. In similar fashion, God's words to Jacob in 35:11–12 recall what is said to Abraham in 17:1–8. This confirms that the divine covenant of circumcision is now established with Jacob, an important statement toward the end of the narrative section on Isaac's offspring (25:19–35:29). The careful reader of Genesis needs to be alert to intertextual connections that underline the book's narrative unity.

II. Structure of Genesis

One of the hallmarks of Genesis is the repeated use of a distinctive formula to introduce new sections of the book. This formula involves the Hebrew expressions אֵלֶּה תּוֹלְדוֹת (*ʾēlle tôlĕdôt*) (2:4; 11:10, 27; 25:12, 19; 36:1,

[22] See especially Todd L. Patterson, *The Plot-Structure of Genesis: "Will the Righteous Seed Survive?"* in the *Muthos-Logical Movement from Complication to Dénouement*, Biblical Interpretation Series 160 (Leiden: Brill, 2018). Cf. T. Desmond Alexander, "Genealogies, Seed and the Compositional Unity of Genesis," *TynBul* 44 (1993): 255–70; Alexander, *From Paradise to the Promised Land*, 25–38.

9; 37:2) and the variant spelling אֵלֶּה תּוֹלְדֹת (ʾēlle tôlĕdōt) (6:9; 11:10).[23] The KJV adopts the translation, "These are the generations of ..." The CSB opts for the rendering, "There are the family records of ..." A variation to this formula comes in 5:1: זֶה סֵפֶר תּוֹלְדֹת (*zeh sēper tôlĕdōt,* "This is the document containing the family records of ..."). The repeated use of this *tôlĕdôt* formula in Genesis is noteworthy, especially given its function in marking the start of new sections within the book.[24]

Everything about the formula suggests that it has been deliberately chosen by the author/compiler of Genesis as a device for structuring the entire book. This is especially evident when we appreciate that this distinctive heading is used to introduce a wide variety of materials within Genesis. It creates a sense of unity to sections that might otherwise appear unrelated. Moreover, as Matthew A. Thomas observes, these headings provide "continuity with the preceding material while presenting new material that will be the subject of the following section."[25] The author/compiler of Genesis uses the *tôlĕdôt* formula to place an expectation on readers: "we are expected to have read and/or heard earlier sections of the narrative and not to have simply begun reading at the *toledot* heading."[26]

An overview of Genesis reveals that the *tôlĕdôt* headings perform an important function in narrowing the reader's vision by focusing on selected individuals. Like the zoom lens of a camera, they pick out an individual who has been one of the figures that appeared in the preceding section. As Thomas remarks:

> Through the series of *toledot* headings, the narrative does not wander aimlessly, but according to a certain pattern. On the macro scale, this pattern takes the reader from the heavens and earth (creation) at the beginning of Genesis to Jacob (Israel) at the end of Genesis. Thus, within 36 chapters (2 to 37)

---

[23] The LXX translates the term תּוֹלְדֹת/תּוֹלְדוֹת (*tôlĕdōt/tôlĕdôt*) with either γενέσεις (*geneseis*) or γενέσεως (*geneseōs*), both of which are derived from γένεσις (*genesis*), meaning "family line/genealogy." This is the term from which the English title Genesis is derived.

[24] For fuller discussions, see Matthew A. Thomas, *These Are the Generations: Identity, Covenant, and the Toledot Formula*, LHBOTS 551 (London: T&T Clark, 2011); Jason S. DeRouchie, "The Blessing-Commission, the Promised Offspring, and the Toledot Structure of Genesis," *JETS* 56 (2013): 219–47; Sarah Schwartz, "Narrative Toledot Formulae in Genesis: The Case of Heaven and Earth, Noah and Isaac," *Journal of Hebrew Scriptures* 16 (2016): 1–36; Jared M. August, "The *Toledot* Structure of Genesis: Hope of Promise," *BSac* 174 (2017): 267–82.

[25] Thomas, *These Are the Generations*, 37.

[26] Thomas, *These Are the Generations*, 36.

> the reader's focus has been drawn from the entire universe to a small tribe wandering around the Levant and Egypt. A survey of the sections defined by the *toledot* headings will reveal an overall trajectory toward narrowing.[27]

Apart from the initial formula in 2:4, the remaining formulae almost always center on an individual (see Table 1).[28] Every person mentioned in these headings is related, belonging to the same line of descendants. However, not everyone is of equal importance. As we shall observe, the *tôlĕdôt* headings involving Ishmael and Esau introduce short sections that function like cul-de-sacs, providing limited information before the author/compiler returns to focus fuller attention on a younger sibling.[29] The author/compiler deliberately contrasts the shorter *tôlĕdôt* sections about the descendants of Ishmael and Esau with the longer *tôlĕdôt* sections about the descendants of their younger brothers, Isaac and Jacob, respectively.

Table 1

	Subject of Heading	**Type of material**	**Main characters**
Gen 2:4	heaven and earth	narrative	Adam and Eve; Cain, Abel and Seth
Gen 5:1	Adam's offspring	linear genealogy	List of descendants from Adam to Noah, via Seth
Gen 6:9	Noah's offspring	narrative	Noah and his family
Gen 10:1	Noah's sons' offspring	mainly genealogical material leading to the creation of nations	Descendants of Japheth, Ham, Shem
Gen 11:9	Shem's offspring	linear genealogy	List of descendants from Shem to Terah
Gen 11:27	Terah's offspring	narrative	Abraham, Sarah, Ishmael, Esau
Gen 25:12	Ishmael's offspring	mainly genealogical material	Ishmael's descendants
Gen 25:19	Isaac's offspring	narrative	Jacob and Esau
Gen 36:1	Esau's offspring	mainly genealogical material	Esau's family in Canaan

---

[27] Thomas, *These Are the Generations*, 42.

[28] The one exception comes in 10:1, where the three sons of Noah are named.

[29] The genealogical information about Cain's descendants in 4:17–24 functions in a similar way. The narrative returns in 4:25 to Adam and Eve's third son, Seth.

Gen 36:9	Esau's offspring	mainly genealogical material	Esau's descendants in Edom
Gen 37:2	Jacob's offspring	narrative	Jacob's sons, with a particular focus on Joseph and Judah

The one *tôlĕdôt* section that does not narrow the reader's focus is 10:1–11:9. The heading itself intimates this by naming Noah's three sons. This section provides a panoramic view of humanity but is immediately followed by a *tôlĕdôt* section (11:10–26) that focuses on a unique line of Shem's descendants, some of whom have already been mentioned in 10:21–31. With its emphasis upon the clans and nations of the world, 10:1–11:9 sets the scene for the role that Abraham will fulfill in bringing God's blessing to "all the peoples on earth" (12:3). As we shall observe in more detail later, Abraham's calling to be the spiritual father of many nations (17:4–5) is set against the background of the events described in 10:1–11:9.

The *tôlĕdôt* headings have the effect of narrowing the scope of Genesis. As a whole, Genesis brings together two contrasting movements. On the one hand, it highlights the growth of the human race, beginning with Adam and Eve and, after the flood, with Noah's sons. On the other hand, against this background of a growing human population, Genesis focuses on a single line of descendants that is traced from Adam and Eve, through their third-born son Seth, to Noah, and then onwards through Noah's son Shem to Abraham, Isaac and Jacob (see Figure 1 on the next page). Importantly, this unique patriline will impact positively the nations of the earth.

Through the *tôlĕdôt* headings and the contents of each section, the author/compiler of Genesis traces a unique patriline. This process involves the inclusion of genealogical material within the text of Genesis, sometimes in the form of linear and segmented genealogical lists that are introduced using *tôlĕdôt* headings[30] and sometimes within narrative sections (e.g., 4:17–24; 22:20–24; 25:1–4; 46:8–27). As Robert D. Robinson helpfully observes:

> The genealogies work in concert with the narrative to establish the genre of the work. It is a remarkable fact that, thanks to the

[30] Linear genealogies come in 5:1–32 and 11:10–26. These name only one individual in each generation. Segmented genealogies come in 25:12–18 and 36:1–6, 9–30. These list the names of all (or most) immediate descendants.

genealogies, virtually every character in Genesis can be related to every other by specific degrees of kinship—grandson, cousin, nephew. ... On the broadest plain, the level of Genesis as a literary whole, all the characters in Genesis are related as members of one extended family. ... In Genesis, narrative and genealogy come together in a common focus on the family.[31]

Figure 1

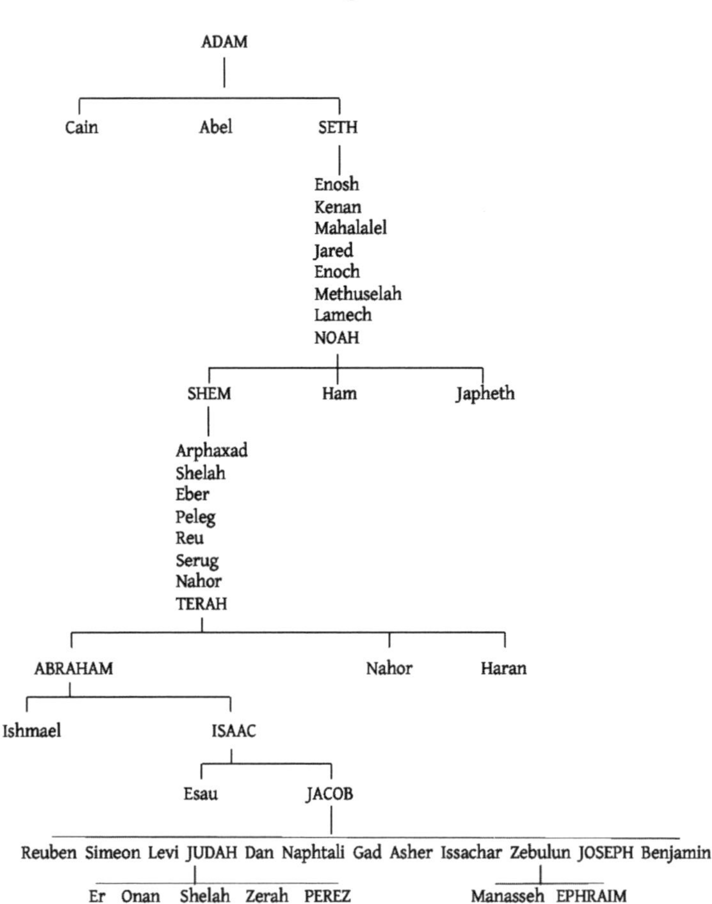

[31] Robert D. Robinson, "Literary Functions of the Genealogies of Genesis," *CBQ* 48 (1986): 601. Cf. T. Desmond Alexander, "From Adam to Judah: The Significance of the Family Tree in Genesis," *EvQ* 61 (1989): 5–19; Alexander, "Genealogies, Seed and the Compositional Unity of Genesis," 255–70; Alexander, *From Paradise to the Promised Land*, 25–38.

When the *tôlĕdôt* headings and genealogical materials are taken into consideration, along with the contents of all the episodes, it is no surprise that many scholars observe in the structuring of Genesis a carefully planned movement that directs attention to the nation of Israel. Michael A. Fishbane notes that the genealogies in Genesis 1–11 "provide a coherent, consecutive chain from Adam to Abram. They link narratives and determine the basic movement of the entire cycle. ... The movement is intentional and deliberate: from Adam to Abram, from the father of mankind to the father of one historical people."[32] In a similar way, Thomas claims, "Linear genealogies move the story of Genesis along toward its focus on Israel. These genealogies are not concerned with personages outside a narrow range of key figures in the story, but rather with the main lines of descent."[33]

There is some truth to these assessments, but they are insufficiently nuanced. Fishbane's claim that the movement is "from Adam to Abram, from the father of mankind to the father of one historical people" fails to embrace the idea that God intends Abraham to be "the father of many nations" (17:4–5). The narrowing movement in Genesis is not about the creation of Israel as a nation, although that is part of the message of Genesis. More importantly, Genesis is structured to highlight the existence of a unique patriline that will eventually exist within Israel. This lineage ends in Genesis with attention being drawn to Perez and Ephraim, the sons of Judah and Joseph respectively. The story beyond Genesis will focus on their patrilines (see Biblical and Theological Themes §1).

Remarkably, throughout Genesis 12–50, the unique patriline is frequently associated with a younger son, who receives the birthright of the firstborn. Viewed as a whole, the book of Genesis establishes a line of human ancestry that runs continuously from Adam to Jacob/Israel. The *tôlĕdôt* headings, in conjunction with the linear genealogies in Genesis 5 and 11, structure the whole of Genesis around this unique patriline, which has an important role to play in God's redemptive plan. Ultimately, this patriline leads to Jesus Christ.

---

[32] Michael A. Fishbane, *Text and Texture. Close Readings of Selected Biblical Texts* (New York: Schocken, 1979), 28.

[33] Thomas, *These Are the Generations*, 94.

III. Genesis and Its Immediate Literary Context (Genesis–Kings)

Although Genesis provides a selective account of past events, the book as a whole is oriented toward the future. As we shall discuss more fully in Biblical and Theological Themes §1, its disparate contents highlight a unique patriline that will eventually lead to a king who will mediate God's blessing to the nations of the earth. To this end, Genesis introduces multiple divine promises, but these remain unfulfilled when Genesis comes to an end after recording the death of Joseph (50:26). Even Joseph himself looks toward the future when he says to his brothers: "When God comes to your aid, you are to carry my bones up from here" (50:25).

With its future orientation, Genesis forms the first volume in a series of closely interconnected books (Genesis–Kings) that together compose one of the most significant metanarratives in the ancient world. The divine promises to Abraham and his offspring play a major part in shaping this metanarrative, announcing that Abraham will be the father of many nations, an expectation that includes his biological fatherhood of the nation of Israel (17:4–8). Whereas this latter expectation comes to fulfilment within the books of Exodus to Kings, the promise of international fatherhood remains unfulfilled by the end of Kings. Although the last chapter of Kings recounts the Babylonian destruction of Jerusalem in 587–586 BC and the deportation of Zedekiah, the Davidic king, to Babylon, the hope is not extinguished that the royal line, descended from the patriline at the heart of Genesis, will yet bring to fulfilment God's promise concerning the blessing of the nations.[34] This expectation remains alive in the postexilic period, producing what would later be designated the "messianic" hope.

An overview of the metanarrative in Genesis–Kings reveals that the divine promises introduced in Genesis shape the larger narrative. Genesis 15, with its emphasis upon Abraham's descendants taking possession of the land of Canaan, anticipates the Israelites being oppressed in a foreign land before they return to take possession of Canaan. The metanarrative account of their deliverance from

---

[34] See Stephen G. Dempster, "The End of History and the Last Man," in *The Seed of Promise: The Sufferings and Glory of the Messiah: Essays in Honor of T. Desmond Alexander*, ed. Paul R. Williamson and Rita F. Cefalu, GlossaHouse Festschrift Series 3 (Wilmore: GlossaHouse, 2020), 113–41.

slavery in Egypt and their settlement in the promised land runs across the books of Exodus to Samuel, with David's capture of Jerusalem from the Jebusites marking the end of the process.[35] While the final chapters of Genesis highlight the patrilines of Joseph/Ephraim and Judah/Perez, the books of Joshua and Judges recount how Joshua, an Ephraimite, successfully leads the Israelites into the promised land, only for subsequent generations of Ephraimites to turn away from God. Consequently, God removes future kingship from the tribe of Ephraim, giving it to the tribe of Judah.[36] The divine rejection of Ephraim is also reflected in the relocation of the central sanctuary from Shiloh to Jerusalem/Zion (see Ps 78:60–68).

As an integral part of the Genesis–Kings metanarrative, Genesis in its present form is a fitting introduction to what follows. With its future orientation it offers hope to the survivors of the Babylonian destruction of Jerusalem that God's promises, guaranteed through the covenant of Genesis 17, will yet be fulfilled. With good reason, the apostle Paul contends that the divine promises to Abraham and his singular offspring find their fulfilment in Jesus Christ (Gal 3:16). Importantly, for Paul, these promises, which offer hope to the nations, pre-date by centuries the covenant made at Mount Sinai. In the face of opposition to his mission to the Gentiles, Paul fervently maintains that the Sinai covenant does not annul the divine promises given to Abraham that the nations will be blessed through one of his descendants.

IV. Genesis and Its Ancient Near Eastern Background

Apart from observing the literary context of Genesis within the Old Testament, it is also important to consider the cultural context within

---

[35] In lists involving the inhabitants of Palestine, the Jebusites always come last (Gen 15:19–21; Exod 3:17; 23:23; 33:2; 34:11; Deut 7:1; 20:17; Josh 3:10; 9:1; 12:8; 24:11; Judg 3:5; one exception is Josh 11:3). Nahum M. Sarna, *Exodus*, JPS Torah Commentary (Philadelphia: Jewish Publication Society, 1991), 14, writes, "The fact that the Jebusites invariably appear in the final position may be an intimation of David's capture of Jebusite Jerusalem, which was the culmination of his conquests."

[36] This transition is reflected in the epilogue to Judges (chs. 17–21) and the book of Ruth. See J. Derek Johnston, "Setting the Book of Ruth in Its Literary Context with Special Reference to the Epilogue of the Book of Judges," *IBS* 27 (2009): 156–62; James McKeown, "Messianic Trajectories in Ruth—A Redeemer and Great Name," in Williamson and Cefalu, *The Seed of Promise*, 74–89.

which it was composed. Genesis is an ANE document that was penned for people who lived in a culture far removed from that of the modern world. We must exercise great caution that we do not misread Genesis by failing to appreciate the environment within which it was composed. Anyone who has spent time living in a foreign country will recognize something of the difficulty of understanding another culture.

In the light of this challenge, it is no surprise that contemporary scholars often draw on recent archaeological discoveries to inform their reading of Genesis and other biblical books. While this is to be welcomed, it comes with a danger warning. Given the limited and fragmented nature of the ANE evidence, much of which originates from outside the Levant, two related dangers exist.

First, there is the danger of failing to identify accurately the ANE parallels that may shed light on the text of Genesis. In the mid-twentieth century various biblical archaeologists proposed that the patriarchal traditions in Genesis reflect early second-millennium customs. However, this position was challenged in the 1970s by Thomas L. Thompson and John Van Seters, who argued that the stories concerning the patriarchs had no links with the second millennium BC.[37] While some of their criticisms of how extrabiblical parallels were used to support the historicity of patriarchal traditions were justified, some scholars rightly challenged their view.[38]

The difficulty of determining the cultural environment of the patriarchal narratives may be illustrated from proposals regarding the account in Genesis 23 of Abraham's acquisition of a burial tomb for Sarah at Hebron. In 1953, Manfred R. Lehmann proposed that the report of Abraham's purchase reflected an intimate knowledge of Hittite law and customs

---

[37] Thomas L. Thompson, *The Historicity of the Patriarchal Narratives*, BZAW 133 (Berlin: de Gruyter, 1974); John Van Seters, *Abraham in History and Tradition* (New Haven: Yale University Press, 1975).

[38] See A. R. Millard and D. J. Wiseman, eds., *Essays on the Patriarchal Narratives*, (Leicester: Inter-Varsity Press, 1980); A. R. Millard, J. K. Hoffmeier and D. W. Baker, eds., *Faith, Tradition, and History: Old Testament Historiography in Its Near Eastern Context* (Winona Lake: Eisenbrauns, 1994); James K. Hoffmeier, *Israel in Egypt: The Evidence for the Authenticity of the Exodus Tradition* (New York: Oxford University Press, 1997), 77–106; Kenneth A. Kitchen, *On the Reliability of the Old Testament* (Grand Rapids: Eerdmans, 2003), 343–52; Richard S. Hess, "Second-Millennium BC Cuneiform from the Southern Levant and the Literature of the Pentateuch," in *Exploring the Composition of the Pentateuch*, ed. L. S. Baker et al., BBRSup 27 (University Park: Eisenbrauns, 2020), 66–72.

from the second millennium BC.[39] Lehmann contended that the bargaining between Abraham and Ephron involved obligations to the local king, which were linked to ownership of the land. Ephron wanted to pass these obligations on to Abraham, but Abraham wished to avoid this. Drawing on several statutes from a Hittite law code found at Boghazköy in Asia Minor, Lehmann concluded:

> We have thus found that Genesis 23 is permeated with intimate knowledge of intricate subtleties of Hittite laws and customs, correctly corresponding to the time of Abraham and fitting in with the Hittite features of the Biblical account. With the final destruction of the Hittite capital of Hattusas about 1200 BCE, these laws must have fallen into utter oblivion. This is another instance in which a late dating must be firmly rejected. Our study again confirms the authenticity of the "background material" of the Old Testament, which makes it such an invaluable source for the study of all aspects of social, economic and legal aspects of the periods of history it depicts.[40]

Against Lehmann's suggestion, it is noteworthy that Genesis 23 never mentions the Hittite king to whom feudal services are supposedly due.

Adopting a different stance Gene M. Tucker proposes that the Genesis account of Abraham's purchase of the land resembles closely a Neo-Babylonian dialogue document.[41] Such documents were used around 700–500 BC to transfer property from one owner to another. Tucker writes, "The similarities between this type of contract and Genesis 23 are striking, though the Old Testament narrative preserves a much fuller account of the negotiations. The dialogue document's pattern is reflected in Ephron's quoted 'offer' (vs. 15), Abraham's acceptance described in the third person (vs. 16aα), the payment clause (vs. 16aβb), and the transfer clause (vss. 17–18) which includes a description of the property."[42] Tucker's proposal is interesting, but

---

[39] Manfred R. Lehmann, "Abraham's Purchase of Machpelah and Hittite Law," *BASOR* 129 (1953): 15–18.

[40] Lehmann, "Abraham's Purchase of Machpelah and Hittite Law," 18.

[41] Gene M. Tucker, "The Legal Background to Genesis 23," *JBL* 85 (1966): 77–84.

[42] Tucker, "Legal Background to Genesis 23," 82. Tucker's approach is supported by Thompson, *Historicity of the Patriarchal Narratives*, 295–96, and Van Seters, *Abraham in History and Tradition*, 98–100.

there are several weaknesses. First, his suggestion is based on a very selective reading of Genesis 23. He takes into account only verses 15–18, ignoring the rest of the chapter. Second, contrary to what Tucker claims, there is no evidence pointing to the existence of "dialogue documents" in the early second millennium BC.[43]

Offering an alternative approach to the legal features in Genesis 23, Raymond Westbrook suggests that the account describes "a legal fiction of double transfer."[44] According to Westbrook, some land transactions from the archives of the Royal Palace of Ugarit "take the curious form of a tripartite transaction whereby the king intervenes not merely as a witness but as an intermediary through whose hands the property passes from one party to the other."[45] Transactions of this nature are also recorded in Hittite and Elamite documents dated to about 1600 BC. Westbrook suggests that when Abraham purchases the burial cave the local Hittites are involved in a "double transfer." If Westbrook is correct, the events of Genesis 23 reflect a practice that is known to have existed in the second millennium BC.

These different attempts to locate Genesis 23 in its ANE environment illustrate well the challenge facing modern readers. Identifying accurately appropriate parallels is not straightforward.[46] Of these three possibilities, Westbrook's is perhaps the most compelling, yet even it may not be an exact parallel.[47] Fortunately, the events recorded in Genesis 23 are comprehensible without a knowledge of ANE practices.

Alongside the challenge of identifying accurately relevant ANE parallels to patriarchal practices, there is, second, the danger of what Samuel Sandmel called "parallelomania."[48] Sandmel defines parallelomania as "that extravagance among scholars which first overdoes the supposed similarity in passages and then proceeds to describe source

---

[43] Martin J. Selman, "The Social Environment of the Patriarchs," *TynBul* 27 (1976): 117–24.

[44] Raymond Westbrook, "Purchase of the Cave of Machpelah," *Israel Law Review* 6 (1971): 37.

[45] Westbrook, "Purchase of the Cave of Machpelah," 36. The Ugaritic evidence dates from the 2nd millennium BC.

[46] For a balanced assessment, see Martin J. Selman, "Comparative Customs and the Patriarchal Age," in Millard and Wiseman, *Essays on the Patriarchal Narratives*, 93–138.

[47] Stephen C. Russell, "Abraham's Purchase of Ephron's Land in Anthropological Perspective," *BibInt* 21 (2013): 153–70, highlights how various details of the narrative in Gen 23 are in keeping with a "generalized scheme for understanding land tenure" developed by Max Gluckman.

[48] Samuel Sandmel, "Parallelomania," *JBL* 81 (1962): 1–13.

and derivation as if implying literary connection flowing in an inevitable or predetermined direction."[49]

Given the limited ANE evidence, it is not surprising that scholars often exaggerate the links between biblical and non-biblical texts. This is especially evident in interpretations of the Genesis creation and flood narratives that draw heavily on other ANE documents that feature similar, but not identical, events (e.g., Enuma Elish; the Atrahasis Epic; the Epic of Gilgamesh).[50] The greatest caution needs to be exercised to avoid either reading into the Genesis account ideas that are derived from other ANE documents or supposing that the author/compiler of Genesis is unduly influenced by non-Israelite traditions that he may or may not embrace. Because we know so little about the process by which Genesis was composed, it is easy to speculate regarding all kinds of influences. Due to insufficient evidence, such speculations are impossible to prove or disprove. For this reason, priority should be given to interpreting passages in Genesis in the light of their own literary context.

In reading any part of Genesis we must not replace the present literary context with an ANE cultural context that superimposes upon the text a meaning that was never intended by the author/compiler of Genesis. Getting the balance right is an exacting task for all commentators. In an academic world that is constantly in pursuit of new knowledge, there is a temptation to exalt new hypothetical readings over older interpretations in order to gain scholarly recognition. However, new is not necessarily better.

V. Authorship and Date of Composition

Genesis itself contains no explicit statements regarding authorship and date of composition. The book says nothing about the author/compiler who selected, organized, and edited its contents. The text of Genesis, however, implies that he or she is a reliable and omniscient narrator. It is also apparent, as we have observed, that Genesis is

---

[49] Sandmel, "Parallelomania," 1.

[50] A good example of an exaggerated dependence of ancient Near Eastern literature to interpret the early chapters of Genesis is Joseph Blenkinsopp's study, *Creation, Un-Creation, Re-Creation: A Discursive Commentary on Genesis 1–11* (London: T&T Clark, 2011).

closely tied to the books of Exodus to Kings, introducing the metanarrative formed by these interconnected books. As the first volume in this metanarrative, Genesis sets the agenda for the subsequent story and anticipates future developments.

Given the absence of explicit information in the Old Testament regarding the formation of Genesis, it is no surprise that later generations created a tradition attributing its authorship and that of the rest of the Pentateuch to Moses. By New Testament times, the first five books of the Old Testament were commonly connected with Moses. This popular association, however, need not imply authorship but may simply be a recognition of the important role that Moses has within the Pentateuch; his birth and death frame the closely connected books of Exodus to Deuteronomy. Although the New Testament contains various references to Moses as a shorthand way of referencing the books of Genesis to Deuteronomy, there is no statement that unambiguously endorses the view that Moses penned everything in Genesis.[51]

Scholarly attempts to reconstruct the process by which the books of the Pentateuch were composed has generated a whole field of research in Old Testament studies.[52] Toward the end of the nineteenth century, the Documentary Hypothesis of Graf, Kuenen, and Wellhausen gained widespread support and for almost a century dominated academic discourse on the Pentateuch. All has changed in recent decades as more and more scholars have rejected this theory.[53] Due to insufficient evidence, the task of reconstructing how the Pentateuch was composed is daunting. It is no surprise that scholars have been unable to solve this problem. As Benjamin D. Sommer comments,

> For more than a century beginning in the mid-1800's, the Documentary Hypothesis represented a near-consensus among crit-

---

[51] See G. Ch. Aalders, *A Short Introduction to the Pentateuch* (London: Tyndale, 1949), 139–42.

[52] See the surveys in R. J. Thompson, *Moses and the Law in a Century of Criticism since Graf*, VTSup 19 (Leiden: Brill, 1970); Alexander, *From Paradise to the Promised Land*, 229–359.

[53] For a major critique of the Document Hypothesis, see R. Norman Whybray, *The Making of the Pentateuch: A Methodological Study*, JSOTSup 53 (Sheffield: JSOT Press, 1987). Whybray effectively demonstrates the shortcomings of the various criteria used to distinguish sources in the Pentateuch. Thomas L. Thompson, *The Literary Formation of Genesis and Exodus 1-23*, vol. 1 of *The Origin Tradition of Ancient Israel*, JSOTSup 55 (Sheffield: JSOT Press, 1987), 155, writes, "Differences in divine names, places names, references to individuals and groups, even differences in style and language, while often giving evidence for the lack of homogeneity in the tradition, do not justify the positing of distinct documents, separated by centuries."

> ical scholars who studied the composition of the Pentateuch. … The hypothesis in its broadest outlines commanded widespread respect, and it was assumed as the starting point for almost all discussions of the Pentateuch and the development of Israelite religion. In the last quarter of this century, however, this consensus has broken down. … The verities enshrined in older introductions have disappeared, and in their place scholars are confronted by competing theories which are discouragingly numerous, exceedingly complex, and often couched in an expository style that is … "not for the faint-hearted."[54]

Without a detailed knowledge of the sources used, scholarly efforts to explain how and by whom Genesis was composed are unlikely to be successful. What we can assume with a reasonable degree of certainty is that Genesis, along with the books of Exodus to Kings, was probably given its present shape not long after the final events recorded in 2 Kings 25, sometime around the year 560 BC.[55]

There is no compelling reason to believe that the materials recorded in Genesis did not exist for many centuries prior to this. Despite the claims of some scholars that elements of Genesis reflect a first millennium setting, there is nothing recorded in Genesis that could not have existed from the beginning of the second millennium BC, allowing for some obvious editorial remarks.[56] Due to the limited evidence available, we must be cautious in making claims regarding the dating of the traditions found in Genesis.[57] The suggestion that Genesis may have been given its present form in the sixth century BC does not mean that its account of events that date from the early second millennium BC and earlier is fabricated, as some scholars suggest.

---

[54] Benjamin D. Sommer, review of *The Pentateuch in the 20th Century: The Legacy of Julius Wellhausen*, by Ernest Nicholson, *Review of Biblical Literature* 2 (2000): 184.

[55] For a fuller discussion, see T. Desmond Alexander, "Authorship of the Pentateuch," in *Dictionary of the Old Testament: Pentateuch*, ed. T. Desmond Alexander and David W. Baker (Downers Grove: InterVarsity Press, 2003), 61–72.

[56] For example, the name Dan is used in 14:14, but this designation was given to the city only after the Israelite settlement in the land of Canaan (see Judg 18:29). The use of the name Rameses in 47:11 also appears to be anachronistic.

[57] See the sobering observations in Benjamin D. Sommer, "Dating Pentateuchal Texts and the Perils of Pseudo-Historicism," in *The Pentateuch: International Perspectives on Current Research*, ed. Thomas B. Dozeman, Konrad Schmid, and Baruch J. Schwartz, FAT 78 (Tübingen: Mohr Siebeck, 2011), 85–108.

VI. Outline

I. The creation of the heavens and the earth (1:1–2:3)

II. The offspring of the heavens and the earth (2:4–4:26)
  A. The man and woman in the garden of Eden (2:4–25)
  B. The couple betrays God (3:1–24)
  C. Adam and Eve's descendants (4:1–26)

III. The offspring of Adam (5:1–6:8)
  A. The line of Adam's descendants to Noah (5:1–32)
  B. The increasing wickedness of humanity (6:1–8)

IV. The offspring of Noah (6:9–9:29)
  A. Noah and the flood (6:9–9:19)
  B. The cursing of Canaan (9:20–29)

V. The offspring of Noah's sons (10:1–11:9)
  A. The family lines of Noah's sons (10:1–32)
  B. The city of Babylon (11:1–9)

VI. The offspring of Shem (11:10–26)

VII. The offspring of Terah (11:27–25:11)
  A. A brief introduction to Terah's family (11:27–32)
  B. God summons Abram (12:1–9)
  C. Abram in Egypt (12:10–20)
  D. Abram and Lot separate (13:1–18)
  E. Abram rescues Lot (14:1–24)
  F. God's covenant with Abram (15:1–21)
  G. The birth of Ishmael (16:1–16)
  H. The covenant of circumcision (17:1–27)
  I. The rescue of Lot from Sodom (18:1–19:29)
  J. Lot and his daughters (19:30–38)
  K. Abimelech takes Sarah to be his wife (20:1–18)
  L. Isaac becomes Abraham's heir (21:1–21)
  M. Abraham and Abimelech make a covenant (21:22–34)
  N. The testing of Abraham (22:1–19)
  O. Nahor's children (22:20–24)
  P. The death and burial of Sarah (23:1–20)
  Q. A wife for Isaac (24:1–67)
  R. The death of Abraham (25:1–11)

VIII. The offspring of Ishmael (25:12–18)

- IX. The offspring of Isaac (25:19–35:29)
    - A. The birth of Esau and Jacob (25:19–26)
    - B. Esau sells his firstborn-birthright (25:27–34)
    - C. Isaac in Gerar (26:1–33)
    - D. Isaac blesses Jacob (26:34–27:45)
    - E. Jacob flees from Esau (27:46–28:9)
    - F. Jacob at Bethel (28:10–22)
    - G. Jacob meets Rachel (29:1–12)
    - H. Jacob deceived by Laban (29:13–30)
    - I. Jacob's children (29:31–30:24)
    - J. Jacob prospers (30:25–43)
    - K. Jacob separates from Laban (31:1–55)
    - L. Jacob prepares to meet Esau again (32:1–23)
    - M. Jacob encounters God at Peniel (32:24–32)
    - N. Jacob meets Esau (33:1–20)
    - O. Dinah and Shechem (34:1–31)
    - P. Jacob at Bethel (35:1–15)
    - Q. The deaths of Rachel and Isaac (35:16–29)
- X. The offspring of Esau (36:1–37:1)
- XI. The offspring of Jacob (37:2–50:26)
    - A. Joseph is sold into slavery (37:2–36)
    - B. Judah and Tamar (38:1–30)
    - C. Joseph in Egypt (39:1–23)
    - D. Joseph and the king's prisoners (40:1–23)
    - E. Joseph interprets Pharaoh's dreams (41:1–57)
    - F. Joseph's brothers' first journey to Egypt (42:1–38)
    - G. Joseph's brothers return to Egypt (43:1–34)
    - H. Benjamin is accused of stealing (44:1–34)
    - I. Joseph reveals his identity (45:1–28)
    - J. Jacob's family relocates to Egypt (46:1–27)
    - K. Jacob's family settles in Egypt (46:28–47:12)
    - L. Joseph oversees the famine in Egypt (47:13–27)
    - M. Jacob requests to be buried in Canaan (47:28–31)
    - N. Jacob's blessing of Joseph and his sons (48:1–22)
    - O. Jacob blesses his twelve sons (49:1–28)
    - P. The death and burial of Jacob (49:29–50:14)
    - Q. Joseph's brothers bow before him (50:15–21)
    - R. The death of Joseph (50:22–26)

VII. Biblical and Theological Themes

A rich variety of biblical and theological themes may be mined from Genesis. The primary purpose of this section of the commentary is to identify those themes that are given prominence by the Genesis narrator as he tells this unique story that begins with the creation of the heavens and the earth and ends with the death of Joseph.

The narrative nature of Genesis means that biblical and theological themes are communicated through a developing storyline. For this reason, to appreciate these themes it is essential to consider the entire narrative. Readings that engage only with fragments of Genesis are more likely to misinterpret what the text communicates, for the whole is more than the sum of the parts. Unfortunately, many studies on Genesis atomize the text, resulting in theological readings that are not supported by a holistic interpretation of Genesis.

From a literary perspective, the opening episodes of Genesis set the scene for all that follows. The content of these episodes draws attention to the themes that will be developed in the rest of Genesis (and beyond). Consequently, it is important to appreciate how 1:1–4:26 sets the scene, introducing a series of complications that will shape the plot of Genesis. An awareness of these complications provides a helpful way of recognizing the main biblical and theological themes that run throughout Genesis.

The *tôlĕdôt* structure of Genesis cannot be ignored when reading Genesis as a coherent whole. The heading in 2:4 separates the initial creation account, with its seven-day structure, from the subsequent report of Adam and Eve's experience in the garden of Eden. Whereas 1:1–2:3 gives a cosmic perspective, focusing on the creation of the heavens and the earth, 2:4–4:26 concentrates attention on the place of humans within God's creation. Whereas 1:1–2:3 conveys a strong sense of order and structure, 2:4–4:26 recounts a changing situation that moves from order to chaos. In differing ways, both sections inform all that follows.

The creation account in Genesis 1 is developed around the concepts of forming and filling (see Comments on 1:2). The initial three days of creation describe the formation of time and places. These places—sky, land and seas—are then filled in days 4–6.[58] Finally, having completed the heavens and earth, God rests, blessing the seventh day and sanctifying it (2:1–3).

[58] Day 4, which focuses on the sky, describes how the sky is filled with lights that govern the organization of time, paralleling the creation of time in day 1.

Recent studies on the opening chapters of Genesis have drawn attention to how the account of God's creative activity displays features that suggest that the earth was formed to be his dwelling place. Commenting on how God is portrayed in Genesis 1, Middleton observes:

> The world is both a kingdom over which God rules and a cosmic building where a variety of creatures may live fruitfully together and flourish. ... But is it possible to specify further the metaphor of the world as a cosmic structure? Suppose we press the question, *what sort of building* is God making in Genesis 1? Although not immediately obvious, the unequivocal answer given from the perspective of the rest of the Old Testament is this: God is building a *temple*.[59]

In support of this idea, Middleton recalls the cultural context within which the book of Genesis was composed.

> The notion of the cosmos as temple has its roots in the ancient Near Eastern worldview, in which temples were commonly understood as the royal palaces of the gods, in which they dwelled and from which they reigned. Furthermore, creation, followed by temple building and then divine rest, is a central theme in Mesopotamian, and perhaps Ugaritic, mythology.[60]

Independently of Middleton, Walton arrives at a similar conclusion. Focusing on the opening statements of Genesis 2, Walton writes,

> On the seventh day we finally discover that God has been working to achieve a rest. This seventh day is not a theological appendix to the creation account, just to bring closure now that the main event of creating people has been reported. Rather, it intimates the purpose of creation and of the cosmos. God does not set up the cosmos so that only people will have a place. He also sets up the cosmos to serve as his temple in which he will find rest in the order and equilibrium that he has established.[61]

---

[59] J. Richard Middleton, *The Liberating Image: The Imago Dei in Genesis 1* (Grand Rapids: Brazos, 2005), 81 (italics original).

[60] Middleton, *The Liberating Image*, 81.

[61] John H. Walton, "Creation," in Alexander and Baker, *Dictionary of the Old Testament: Pentateuch*, 161; cf. John H. Walton, *The Lost World of Genesis One: Ancient Cosmology and the Origins Debate* (Downers Grove: InterVarsity Press Academic, 2009); Mark S. Smith, *The Priestly Vision of Genesis 1* (Minneapolis: Fortress, 2010), 108.

While the text of Genesis 1:1–2:3 does not explicitly state that the earth is created to become God's dwelling place, the indirect evidence points in this direction. Further support for the proposal that the earth is to function as God's residence also comes in the account associated with the garden of Eden. According to Wenham, the garden is presented as an "archetypal sanctuary:"

> The garden of Eden is not viewed by the author of Genesis simply as a piece of Mesopotamian farmland, but as an archetypal sanctuary, that is a place where God dwells and where man should worship him. Many of the features of the garden may also be found in later sanctuaries particularly the tabernacle or Jerusalem temple. These parallels suggest that the garden itself is understood as a sort of sanctuary.[62]

Among various parallels between the garden of Eden and the tabernacle and/or Jerusalem temple, Wenham list the following:[63]

- The garden of Eden, like later sanctuaries, is guarded by cherubim (Gen 3:24; Exod 25:18–22; 26:31; 36:35; 1 Kgs 6:23–29; 2 Chr 3:14).
- The tabernacle menorah (or lampstand) is designed to resemble a tree, possibly symbolizing the tree of life (Gen 2:9; 3:22; cf. Exod 25:31–35).[64] The association of Eden with the Jerusalem temple is suggested by the arboreal decorations that adorned the temple.[65]
- The Genesis account about the garden of Eden mentions gold and onyx (2:11–12). These materials are used in the manufacture of the high priest's garments (e.g., Exod 25:7, 11, 17, 31) and to decorate the tabernacle (e.g., Exod 25:7, 11–13; 28:9) and the temple (e.g., 1 Kgs 6:20; 1 Chr 29:2).

---

[62] Gordon J. Wenham, "Sanctuary Symbolism in the Garden of Eden Story," in *"I Studied Inscriptions before the Flood": Ancient Near Eastern, Literary, and Linguistic Approaches to Genesis 1-11*, ed. Richard S. Hess and David Toshio Tsumura (Winona Lake: Eisenbrauns, 1994), 399.

[63] Wenham, "Sanctuary Symbolism in the Garden of Eden Story," 399–404.

[64] Carol L. Meyers, *The Tabernacle Menorah: A Synthetic Study of a Symbol from the Biblical Cult*, ASOR Dissertation Series (Missoula: Scholars, 1976), 169–72.

[65] Margaret Barker, *The Gate of Heaven: The History and Symbolism of the Temple in Jerusalem* (London: SPCK, 1991), 57, writes, "Solomon built the temple as a garden sanctuary; the walls of the *hekal* were decorated with golden palm trees and flowers, set with precious stones; the bronze pillars were decorated with pomegranate patterns and the great lamp was a stylized almond tree."

- The LORD God walks in the garden of Eden as he later does in conjunction with the tabernacle (Gen 3:8; cf. Lev 26:12; Deut 23:14 [Heb 23:15]; 2 Sam 7:6–7).
- The combination of the Hebrew verbs עָבַד (*ʿābad,* "to serve, till") and שָׁמַר (*šāmar,* "to keep/guard/watch over,") which comes in God's instruction to the man "to work it [the garden] and watch over it"(Gen 2:15), is found elsewhere only in the Pentateuch in passages that refer to the duties of the Levities in the sanctuary (cf. Num 3:7–8; 8:26; 18:5–6). This suggests that God appoints Adam not simply to be a gardener, but rather a guardian of the garden sanctuary, just as the Levites were guardians of the tabernacle and the temple. God later stations cherubim to guard the garden (Gen 3:24).

Wenham's case for seeing the garden of Eden as an "archetypal-sanctuary" has much to commend it.[66] The parallels between the garden and later sanctuaries are also noted by Block, but he argues that these similarities do not necessarily prove that the garden is a sanctuary.[67] Rather, he suggests that later sanctuaries were viewed as resembling the garden of Eden. This is worthy of consideration, for the ongoing story in Genesis does not assume that God resides in or near the garden of Eden after Adam and Eve are expelled from it. God's residence is heaven, not earth.[68] Nevertheless, the overall movement within Scripture, beyond Genesis, is of God coming to dwell on the earth, a process that is facilitated by the construction of sanctuaries that resemble the garden of Eden.

---

[66] A largely overlapping list of parallels is provided by Gregory K. Beale, "The Final Vision of the Apocalypse and Its Implications for a Biblical Theology of the Temple," in *Heaven on Earth: The Temple in Biblical Theology*, ed. T. Desmond Alexander and Simon Gathercole (Carlisle: Paternoster, 2004), 197–99; cf. Gregory K. Beale, *The Temple and the Church's Mission: A Biblical Theology of the Dwelling Place of God*, NSBT 17 (Leicester: Apollos, 2004), 66–80; Gregory K. Beale, "Eden, the Temple, and the Church's Mission in the New Creation," *JETS* 48 (2005): 7–10; Richard M. Davidson, "Earth's First Sanctuary: Genesis 1–3 and Parallel Creation Accounts," *AUSS* 53 (2015): 65–89.

[67] Daniel I. Block, "Eden: A Temple? A Reassessment of the Biblical Evidence," in *From Creation to New Creation: Biblical Theology and Exegesis*, ed. Daniel M. Gurtner and Benjamin L. Gladd (Peabody: Hendrickson, 2013), 3–29.

[68] This is illustrated in Gen 18 when God comes to Abraham and speaks of having come down to investigate the wickedness of Sodom (Gen 18:20–21). Similarly, Jacob's vision at Bethel also points to God's residence being in heaven (Gen 28:12).

The first readers of Genesis 1–2 would quickly have concluded that these chapters are concerned with the construction of God's earthly residence. Belonging to a cultural world quite different from that of modern readers, it was commonplace for the creation of the world to be associated with the construction of a temple on the earth for a deity. Moreover, the establishment of God's sanctuary on the earth would entail the creation of a city, populated by those who serve in the temple.[69] Within this city, God and humans would live together in perfect harmony.[70] Since God commands people to fill the earth, this creates the expectation that the whole earth will become an arboreal temple-city, centered on the garden of Eden.

This expectation coalesces with the idea of God's kingdom being established on the earth, for kingship is closely linked to the concept of sanctuary/temple. Throughout the ANE the temples of deities were considered divine palaces. In Hebrew the noun הֵיכָל (*hêkāl*) denotes both "temple" and "palace."

In the light of these connections between temple and kingship, it is noteworthy that the opening chapters of Genesis associate kingship with the status and role that God delegates to humanity. Two features of Genesis 1 combine strongly to emphasize that humans are to be God's vicegerents, with the expectation that they will extend his kingdom throughout the earth as his representatives.[71]

First, God instructs humanity both to subdue (כבשׁ, *kbš*) the earth and to rule (רדה, *rdh*) over all the animals of the earth (1:28). People are given special authority over other creatures, and this sets them apart as different. The significance of this instruction to govern other creatures becomes clearer in Genesis 3. With tragic consequences, the human couple heed the promptings of the serpent and eat from the tree of the

---

[69] The link between temple and city is evident in the Mesopotamian creation story, Enuma Elish, which concludes with the building of Marduk's temple in the city of Babylon.

[70] Beale, "Final Vision of the Apocalypse," 201, remarks, "As Adam and Eve were to begin to rule over and subdue the earth, it is plausible to suggest that they were to extend the geographical boundaries of the Garden until Eden extended throughout and covered the whole earth." Cf. Beale, "Eden, the Temple, and the Church's Mission," 10–11.

[71] Gen 1 stands in marked contrast to other ancient Near Eastern accounts when it describes the status of human beings. Whereas the main Babylonian story of creation, Enuma Elish, presents the function of humans in terms of providing food for the gods, Genesis ascribes to people a divinely-given authority to rule over the earth. See Ian Hart, "Genesis 1:1–2:3 as a Prologue to the Book of Genesis," *TynBul* 46 (1995): 322.

knowledge of good and evil. By failing to rule over the serpent, Adam and Eve show disdain for their appointment as God's vicegerents.

Second, humans are created in the "image of God" (1:26–27). Within its original ANE setting, the expression "image of God" undoubtedly conveys royal connotations. As Wenham notes,

> The image makes man God's representative on earth. That man is made in the image and is thus God's representative on earth was a common oriental view of the king. Both Egyptian and Assyrian texts describe the king as the image of God.[72]

Building on the concept of humans as regal images, God instructs them to be fruitful, multiply, and fill the earth (1:28). This instruction implies that God's authority over the earth will be extended as people spread throughout it. This idea resembles a distinctive ANE practice. Rulers often set up images of themselves in distant parts of their kingdoms to remind subjects that their authority extended there.[73] As images of God, humans were to perform a similar function.

Genesis 1 conveys the idea that God's primary role for humans is to represent him, "exercising royal dominion over the earth."[74] As Middleton rightly claims,

> the writer of Genesis 1 portrays God as king presiding over "heaven and earth," an ordered and harmonious realm in which each creature manifests the will of the creator and is thus declared "good." Humanity is created *like* this God, with the special role of representing or imaging God's rule in the world.[75]

As God's representatives, the offspring of the human couple are to fill the earth, ruling on God's behalf. Uniquely, Genesis 1–2 emphasizes that all humans are to enjoy royal authority over other creatures, as well as guarding the sanctity of the place where God will dwell. Taken together these ideas imply that humans are to exercise roles normally associated

---

[72] Gordon J. Wenham, *Genesis 1–15*, WBC 1 (Waco: Word, 1987), 30.

[73] Gerhard von Rad, *The Theology of Israel's Historical Traditions*, vol. 1 of *Old Testament Theology* (Edinburgh: Oliver and Boyd, 1962), 146–47. See, for example, A. R. Millard and P. Bordreuil, "A Statue from Syria with Assyrian and Aramaic Inscriptions," *BA* 45 (1982): 124–43.

[74] Hart, "Genesis 1:1–2:3 as a Prologue," 322.

[75] Middleton, *The Liberating Image*, 26

with both kings and priests.[76] Strikingly, both genders are included in the fulfilment of these duties.

Genesis 1–2 highlights the divine appointment of humans as God's vicegerents on the earth. Against this background Genesis 3 recounts how Adam and Eve disastrously betray the trust that God places in them. Genesis 3 is exceptionally important, but the brevity of the narrative leaves many questions unanswered. A new and unexpected character is introduced into the narrative: a talking serpent. This mysterious creature, who is described as "the most cunning of all the wild animals that the Lord God had made" (3:1), is clearly no ordinary animal. While no explanation is given as to its origin, its words reveals that it opposes God's sovereign rule over the earth.[77]

By heeding the serpent's subtle promptings, the human couple fail as God's vicegerents. Instead of exercising authority over the crafty creature, they disregard God's instruction not to eat from "the tree of the knowledge of good and evil" (2:17), choosing to accept the truthfulness of the serpent's words. By betraying God, Adam and Eve overturn the divine ordering of creation. Misled by the serpent, Adam and Eve forfeit their role as God's vicegerents. Disastrously, their authority to rule over the earth passes to the serpent, for by their actions the human couple become enslaved to it.[78] The irony of their disobedience is that they reject their status as "images" of God in the mistaken hope of becoming "like God, knowing good and evil" (3:5).

The consequences of Adam and Eve's actions are immediate and far-reaching, introducing complications into the narrative that set the agenda for the rest of Genesis and beyond. These complications draw attention to certain important biblical and theological themes that are closely linked to one another. Although separating them runs the risk

---

[76] William J. Dumbrell, "Genesis 2:1–17: A Foreshadowing of the New Creation," in *Biblical Theology: Retrospect and Prospect*, ed. Scott J. Hafemann (Downers Grove: InterVarsity Press, 2002), 53–65, develops the idea that Adam is a king-priest with the role of expanding Eden into a world-wide sanctuary. The role of ancient Near Eastern kings as temple-builders is noted by Arvid S. Kapelrud, "Temple Building: A Task for Gods and Kings," *Orientalia* 32 (1963): 56–62.

[77] While later biblical texts claim that the "ancient serpent" is "the devil and Satan" (cf. Rev 12:9; 20:2), this is not explicitly stated in Genesis 3.

[78] The devil's status as "ruler of this world" is reflected in its ability to tempt Jesus by offering him "all the kingdoms of the world" (Matt 4:8–9; Luke 4:5–7). Elsewhere, referring to Satan, Jesus speaks of "ruler of this world" being judged (John 12:31; 16:11).

of distorting how they should be viewed, we shall consider them under the following headings: a future vicegerent; the blessing of the nations; everlasting covenants; the city of God.

§1 A Future Vicegerent

With poetic justice, God announces in the Garden of Eden that the woman's offspring will defeat the serpent (see Comments on 3:15). While it has become popular to assume that the Hebrew term זֶרַע (*zera*ᶜ, "offspring") refers to humanity in general, it denotes a single person, a fact supported by the syntax of 3:15 and confirmed by the ongoing story.[79] Confirming the importance of the woman's offspring in God's redemptive plan, the rest of Genesis highlights a unique patriline, suggesting that this lineage will eventually lead to an individual who will overcome the serpent.[80] Appropriately, the promised serpent-slayer will rule over the earth on God's behalf. He will fulfill the role of vicegerent, which Adam and Eve forfeited by obeying the serpent.

Those listed in the patriline that leads to the future vicegerent stand apart as special. The importance of Seth is underlined by the narrative structure of chapter 4. Initially, a contrast is drawn between Abel and Cain, the former finding favor with God because of the sacrifices he offers (4:4). Hope that Abel might be the offspring through whom the serpent is defeated is shattered when Cain brutally murders him. God's punishment of Cain is tempered with mercy, but the genealogical information concerning his offspring ends with Lamech, who is, like Cain, a murderer (4:23–24).[81] After tracing the patriline of Cain, the narrator jumps back seven generations to note that Adam and Eve had another son, "appointed" by God to replace Abel (4:25). The introduction of Seth undoubtedly links back to the promise in 3:15, for he is described as a

---

[79] See Jonathan M. Cheek, "Recent Developments in the Interpretation of the Seed of the Woman in Genesis 3:15," *JETS* 64 (2021): 215–36.

[80] See Alexander, "From Adam to Judah," 5–19; Alexander, "Genealogies, Seed and the Compositional Unity of Genesis," 255–70; T. Desmond Alexander, "Royal Expectations in Genesis to Kings: Their Importance for Biblical Theology," *TynBul* 49 (1998): 191–212; T. Desmond Alexander, "The Regal Dimension of the תלדות־יעקב: Recovering the Literary Context of Genesis 37–50," in *Reading the Law: Studies in Honour of Gordon J. Wenham*, ed. J. G. McConville and Karl Möller, LHBOTS 461 (Edinburgh: T&T Clark, 2007), 196–212; Jared M. August, "The Messianic Hope of Genesis: The Protoevangelium and Patriarchal Promises," *Themelios* 42 (2017): 46–62; Patterson, *Plot-Structure of Genesis*.

[81] He is also a polygamist (4:19).

replacement offspring (זֶרַע, *zera*ʿ) for Abel (see Comments on 4:25). The subsequent remarks in 4:26 that Seth had a son and that people started to call on the name of YHWH contrast sharply with the portrayal of Cain and his offspring.

The importance of Seth's family line is highlighted by the linear genealogy in Genesis 5. Not only does this genealogy contrast the offspring of Seth with those of Cain (see Comments on 5:6–32), but brief comments about Enoch and Noah offer grounds for believing that this particular line of offspring will lead to the serpent-slayer.[82] Building on the preceding narrative, the references to the sons of God and the daughters of men in Genesis 6 are best understood as pointing to the contrasting offspring of the godly and the ungodly (see Comments on 6:1–4).

Genesis 6 emphasizes how humanity fills the earth with violence, in sharp contrast to God's creation mandate that people should fill the earth as his benevolent vicegerents. Although God determines to destroy aggressive humanity, his gracious deliverance of Noah and his family from the flood offers hope of a new beginning.[83] To convey a sense of re-creation, the account of the flood echoes the initial creation account, with the dry land emerging from the waters.[84] The idea of a new start is further underlined by God's instructions to Noah in 9:1, 7, which echo his blessing of humanity in 1:28.

Hope of the serpent's defeat is associated with Noah, but the Genesis narrative reveals that human nature remains corrupt after the flood. Of Noah's three sons, Shem becomes the one through whom the patriline is continued (see Comments on 8:21). Another linear genealogy in Genesis 11, covering ten generations, leads to the introduction of Abram/Abraham into the story. The expectation is created that through Abraham God's blessing will be mediated to all the families of the ground, underlining the significance of the unique patriline traced from Adam to Abraham (see Comments on 12:1–3).

Within the Genesis narrative, the figure of Abraham occupies a prominent position. He is the recipient of various divine promises that

---

[82] Enoch enjoys a special relationship with God and does not die (5:22–24). The hope associated with Noah when Lamech names him (5:29) hints at a restoration of harmony between humans and the ground.

[83] See Dustin G. Burlet, *Judgment and Salvation: A Rhetorical-Critical Reading of Noah's Flood in Genesis* (Eugene: Pickwick, 2022).

[84] See Gary V. Smith, "Structure and Purpose in Genesis 1–11," *JETS* 20 (1977): 307–19.

culminate in a divine oath, promising that through Abraham's offspring all the nations of the earth will be blessed (22:18). This oath ratifies the covenant of circumcision through which God promises to make Abraham the father of many nations (see Comments on 17:4–5 and 22:16–18). Moreover, this covenant, which is described as everlasting (17:7, 13, 19), will pass from Abraham to his son Isaac (17:19–21). This links the outworking of the covenant of circumcision to the patriline that runs throughout Genesis. This covenant anticipates the coming of royal offspring (17:6, 16), recollecting the idea that humans were created to be God's vicegerents.[85] Importantly, the divine oath in 22:17 speaks of one of Abraham's offspring being victorious over his enemies, a remark that recalls God's promise that one of Eve's offspring will defeat the serpent (3:15; see Comments on 22:16–18).

The patriline moves from Abraham to Isaac, bypassing his older brother Ishmael. This introduces a motif that recurs in Genesis: a younger brother is favored over an older sibling. This motif is especially prominent in the *tôlĕdôt* section involving Esau and Jacob (25:19–35:29). After observing how Esau inappropriately sells his firstborn birthright to his younger twin brother for a bowl of lentil stew (25:27–34), the narrative traces the gradual transformation of Jacob as he becomes the recipient of the divine promises given to Abraham. Remarkably, in giving the blessing of the firstborn to Jacob, presuming him to be Esau, Isaac anticipates that his son will exercise universal dominion, a theme that echoes the idea of Abraham being the father of many nations (see Comments on 27:27–29). Subsequently, Jacob is blessed by God and becomes a source of blessing to others, especially his uncle Laban.

In the final *tôlĕdôt* section of Genesis, involving Jacob's children (37:2–50:26), the opening episode points toward Joseph being the one through whom the patriline will continue. His dreams associate him with royalty, and his father favors him as the one who will receive the blessing of the firstborn (cf. 1 Chr 5:1–2). Later, when Jacob blesses Joseph's two boys, he creates the expectation that the patriline will continue through Joseph's younger son Ephraim (see Comments on 48:17–20).

---

[85] Daniel S. Diffey, "The Royal Promise in Genesis: The Often Underestimated Importance of Genesis 17:6, 17:16 and 35:11," *TynBul* 62 (2011): 313–16, notes how the promise of kings is later repeated to Jacob in Gen 35:11.

This expectation, however, is complicated by what is narrated concerning Joseph's older brother Judah. The account of Joseph becoming a slave in Egypt is interrupted by an intriguing report that focuses on the continuation of Judah's firstborn lineage (38:1–30). This signals the possibility that the unique patriline may possibly be traced in the future through Judah's son Perez, who unexpectedly usurps at birth the firstborn status of his twin brother Zerah (38:27–30). Later, in chapter 49, Jacob's blessing of Judah hints at royalty arising from his descendants (see Comments on 49:10). This eventually comes to fulfilment when David is appointed king over Israel. Ruth 4:18–22 continues the patriline of Genesis from Perez to David (Ruth 4:18–22).

Viewed in its entirety, Genesis is undoubtedly interested in tracing a unique line of descendants that moves from Adam and Eve down to Jacob's sons, Joseph and Judah.[86] The use of *tôlĕdôt* headings that zoom in on certain individuals enables the author of Genesis to focus the reader's attention on this patriline. While there is a general expectation that this lineage should proceed through the eldest son, the principle of primogeniture is often overturned to the benefit of a younger brother, who receives the firstborn birthright. When this happens, the narrative provides grounds for rejecting older siblings (e.g., Esau despises his birthright [25:34]; Reuben sleeps with his father's concubine [35:22]).

A further way in which Genesis draws attention to the importance of the patriline is through the barrenness of the matriarchs. Sarah, Rebekah and Rachel are all unable to have children (11:30; 25:21; 29:31). Only through God's intervention are they empowered to bear sons, who form the next generation of the chosen patriline (21:1; 25:21; 30:22–24). God's direct involvement in providing sons for these women underscores the significance of the patriline for the fulfilment of his redemptive plans.

§2 The Blessing of the Nations

As the Genesis narrative progresses, more and more positive expectations are linked to the unique patriline. What begins as a pronouncement concerning the defeat of the serpent in 3:15 is expanded as additional elements are introduced. This is especially so in the Abraham narrative, where emphasis is given to the blessing of the nations. This motif

---

[86] See Paul Twiss, "A Tale of Two Brothers: The Messiah in Genesis 49," *MSJ* 33 (2022): 255–67.

not only stands in marked contrast to the curses that dominate human existence in chapters 3–11, but it is the climax of God's brief commission of Abraham in 12:1–3. Importantly, the initial promise of international blessing is subsequently confirmed by the everlasting covenant of circumcision, which God establishes with Abraham, affirming that he will become the father of many nations (17:4–6).[87] The future of this covenant is linked specifically to Abraham's son, Isaac, and not to his older brother Ishmael (17:19–21; 22:18).

From Abraham onward, the concept of blessing is closely associated with those who belong to the unique patriline. Not only do they receive God's blessing, but they also mediate it to others. God's blessing is evidenced through material prosperity. Reflecting this, Abraham's servant tells Laban, "The Lord has greatly blessed my master, and he has become rich. He has given him flocks and herds, silver and gold, male and female slaves, and camels and donkeys" (24:35). Isaac also enjoys prosperity because of divine blessing (26:12). A similar picture is evident for Jacob and Joseph, despite both men being exiled from Canaan with no possessions. Jacob eventually returns with many possessions. Joseph is transformed from being a prisoner in an Egyptian jail to becoming Pharaoh's deputy, receiving all the material benefits associated with such an exalted position of authority.

Blessed by God, the members of the patriline mediate God's blessing to others. This is most apparent in the accounts concerning Jacob and Joseph. With good reason, Laban says to Jacob, "The Lord has blessed me because of you" (30:27). In Egypt, God blesses the household of Potiphar "because of Joseph" (39:5), a prelude to the blessing that comes through Joseph to Egypt and the surrounding nations during years of famine. These blessings underscore the importance of the patriline, creating an expectation of something more wonderful in the future. Eventually, this comes to fulfilment in Jesus Christ.

To those features that point to the significance of the patriline in Genesis may be added the paternal blessing of the firstborn son. This

---

[87] Jason S. DeRouchie, "Counting Stars with Abraham and the Prophets," *JETS* 58 (2015): 459, comments, "It seems plausible, then, to understand Abraham's fatherhood over the nations primarily as a royal designation by which he and his wife Sarah, the 'princess' (Gen 17:15), are regarded as the founders of a new dynasty that will climax in a specific, royal descendant who will rule Israelites (both native-born and alien residents) and those from vassal nations."

custom is prominent in the *tôlědôt* section of Isaac (25:19–35:29), which focuses on the turbulent relationship between the twins, Esau and Jacob. Although Esau is the first to be born and automatically heir to the divine promises, he views his firstborn birthright as inconsequential. In marked contrast, his younger brother Jacob appreciates the significance of being the firstborn and seizes an opportunity to buy the firstborn birthright from his older brother (25:29–34). Subsequently, at the instigation of his mother Rebekah, Jacob pretends to be Esau to receive his father's blessing. This benediction is significant, for its contents reflect the divine promises given to Abraham, especially the blessing of the nations (see Comments on 27:27–29). Despite Esau's impassioned protests, Isaac affirms the benediction that he has bestowed on Jacob, causing Esau to plot the death of his brother (27:32–41). Throughout the *tôlědôt* section of Isaac (25:19–35:29), birthright and blessing are intimately linked.

The custom of an elderly father blessing his sons is repeated when Jacob assembles his son around his deathbed (49:1–33). On this occasion, every son is addressed by Jacob, but the patriarch's benedictions vary considerably, with some sons receiving exceptionally positive announcements but others receiving negative comments. In terms of both their length and content, the blessings associated with Judah and Joseph stand apart from all the others (49:8–12, 22–26).

By connecting the future of the patriline with both Joseph and Judah, the author of Genesis introduces an element of ambiguity into the narrative. This uncertainty is reflected in the arrangement of the episodes in the final *tôlědôt* section (37:2–50:26). Although priority is given to Joseph in Genesis 37, with the expectation that he will rule over his brothers, Genesis 38 unexpectedly introduces complications that center on the continuation of Judah's family line. Importantly, chapter 38 begins by focusing on the motifs of firstborn and offspring. The introduction of this material after the report of Joseph's departure to Egypt is noteworthy, given the interest that Genesis has in identifying the one who will defeat the serpent. Additionally, Genesis 38 concludes by recording a birth incident that highlights an unusual development involving the twin sons of Judah and Tamar. Although the midwife identifies Zerah as the firstborn and puts a scarlet thread on his wrist, Perez breaks out ahead of his twin brother. To a reader attuned to the overall message of Genesis, chapter 38 prompts the expectation that the future line of offspring may well descend from Judah through Perez. The subsequent transformation of Judah's character, highlighted by his willingness to take the place of Benjamin as a slave in Egypt (44:18–34), lends weight to this possibility. Previously, Judah had persuaded his brothers to sell Joseph into slavery in Egypt (37:26–27). Finally, the content of the blessing that Judah receives from his father Jacob strongly suggests that one of Judah's descendants will overcome the serpent (49:8–12).

While there are strong indications in Genesis that future royalty will come from the line of Judah, there is also reason to expect that Joseph's lineage will produce a king. From his initial dreams to his remarkable rise to power in Egypt, Joseph displays the integrity and wisdom that might be associated with a future vicegerent. This expectation is supported by the announcement that he receives from his father in 49:22–26. The emphasis in vv. 25–26 upon divine blessing recalls how those who belong to the unique patriline are blessed by God and are expected to be a source of blessing to others. Similarly, fruitfulness and victory in conflict are motifs that sit comfortably with what has been already revealed in Genesis about the special line of offspring. Finally, Joseph is designated "the prince of his brothers" (see Comments on 49:26). All of these factors offer grounds for believing that the unique patriline traced in Genesis will continue through Joseph's descendants.

The importance of Joseph's lineage is further emphasized by the events that take place immediately prior to Jacob's blessing of his twelve sons. Before Jacob addresses all of his own sons, he bestows special benedictions on Joseph's two sons, Manasseh and Ephraim. Strikingly, when doing this, Jacob intentionally gives the blessing of the firstborn to Ephraim, the younger of the two boys (48:13–20). Once again in Genesis the principle of primogeniture is reversed, creating the expectation that the patriline will continue through Ephraim.

In the light of how Genesis associates the patriline with both Joseph and Judah, it is noteworthy that the tribes of Ephraim and Judah play important roles within the Primary History (Genesis–Kings), often standing apart from the other tribes. When the Israelites send representatives to spy out the land of Canaan, only Caleb from the tribe of Judah and Joshua from the tribe of Ephraim bring back positive reports (Num 13:30; 14:6–9). In due course, as Moses' successor, Joshua leads the Israelites into the promised land. When the land of Canaan is allocated among the tribes who have crossed the River Jordan, Judah and Ephraim (and half of the tribe of Manasseh) are among the first to settle permanently in the land (Josh 15:1–63; 16:1–10). The other tribes are initially assigned land by lots, for much of their territory has yet to be possessed by the Israelites (Josh 18:1–19:48).

The important role played by Joshua in leading the Israelites into the land of Canaan fits comfortably with the expectation that a future vicegerent will come from the tribe of Ephraim. However, Joshua's descendants do not follow in his footsteps. The book of Judges portrays the moral and spiritual decline of the Ephraimites. While their failure is not necessarily responsible for Israel's idolatry, their behavior is usually contrasted unfavorably with that of others. When this happens, it conveys the impression that the Ephraimites perceive themselves as the tribe designated by God to provide leadership for the nation. After defeating the Midianites, Gideon must pacify the Ephraimites, who complain unnecessarily that he did not call them to fight against Midian (Judg 8:1–3). A similar pattern occurs when Jephthah overcomes the Ammonites. Once again, the Ephraimites complain that they were not called out to fight the Ammonites (Judg 12:1–6). On this occasion, their threats against Jephthah lead to the death of 42,000 Ephraimites. A further insight into the moral status of the Ephraimites comes in Judges 17, when Micah "from the hill country of Ephraim" sets up an idol in a shrine (Judg 17:1–13). This is followed by an episode that involves a Levite from Ephraim, who treats his wife with contempt. While the story highlights the despicable behavior of the men of Gibeah, who are Benjamites, the Levite from Ephraim is portrayed negatively for his heartless behavior toward his wife.[88]

In Judges, little is said to commend the Ephraimites for their leadership of the nation. Building on this, the ongoing Primary History records how the tribe of Ephraim is rejected by God, with kingship eventually being established with David, the youngest of Jesse's sons, from the tribe of Judah. This transfer of leadership from Ephraim to Judah coincides with the relocation of the ark of the covenant from Shiloh, in the region of Ephraim (1 Sam 4:4–11) to Jerusalem, the city

---

[88] The episodes involving Micah and the unnamed Levite both bring into play people from Bethlehem in Judah. In the light of subsequent developments this is noteworthy. It creates an interest link with the book of Ruth, which is set mainly in Bethlehem and anticipates the rise of David as king over Israel. See Eugene H. Merrill, "The Book of Ruth: Narration and Shared Themes," *BSac* 142 (1986): 132–33; Johnston, "Setting the Book of Ruth," 156–62.

of David (2 Sam 6:1–23). The presence in Jerusalem of the ark of the covenant, the footstool of the divine throne, confirms God's choice of David as his vicegerent over Israel.

Although Ephraim appears to be eclipsed by the tribe of Judah at this stage, the hope for a king descended from Ephraim does not disappear completely. Following the division of Solomon's kingdom, the northern kingdom comes under the rule of Jeroboam, an Ephraimite (1 Kgs 11:26–40). While Jeroboam failed to establish an ongoing dynasty, the tradition of a future king descended from Joseph continued to circulate, as reflected in the later Jewish expectation of a "Messiah ben Joseph."[89]

God's rejection of Ephraim and his choice of David is summarized in Psalm 78:67–72.[90] This development explains the ambiguity reflected in the book of Genesis regarding the patrilines of Joseph and Judah. The hope expressed in Genesis involving the defeat of the serpent through a future offspring of Adam and Eve becomes focused on the Davidic dynasty. This includes the expectation that all the nations of the earth will be blessed through a future king.[91]

Genesis has an important role to play in anticipating the centrality of the Davidic dynasty in Old Testament thought. This feeds into the New Testament understanding of Jesus Christ, as the son of David. The patriline introduced in Genesis finds fulfilment in Jesus Christ, the perfect vicegerent.[92] Viewed from the perspective of the Bible as

---

[89] Also known as "Messiah ben/bar Ephraim." See David C. Mitchell, *Messiah ben Joseph* (Newton Mearns: Campbell, 2016).

[90] See Alexander, "The Regal Dimension of the תלדות־יעקב,"207–10; Sarah Dalrymple, "Ephraim or Judah: Divine Sovereignty and the Potential for Kingship in Joshua-Judges," in Williamson and Cefalu, *The Seed of Promise*, 50–73.

[91] For a fuller discussion of these royal or messianic expectations in the Old Testament, see Philip E. Satterthwaite, Richard S. Hess, and Gordon J. Wenham, eds., *The Lord's Anointed: Interpretation of Old Testament Messianic Texts* (Grand Rapids: Baker, 1995); T. Desmond Alexander, *The Servant King: The Bible's Portrait of the Messiah* (Vancouver: Regent College Publishing, 2003); Daniel I. Block, "My Servant David: Ancient Israel's Vision of the Messiah," in *Israel's Messiah in the Bible and the Dead Sea Scrolls*, ed. Richard S. Hess and M. Daniel Carroll (Grand Rapids: Baker, 2003), 17–56; Herbert W. Bateman IV, Darrell L. Bock, and Gordon H. Johnston, *Jesus the Messiah: Tracing the Promises, Expectations, and Coming of Israel's King* (Grand Rapids: Kregel, 2010); Michael A. Rydelnik, *The Messianic Hope: Is the Hebrew Bible Really Messianic?*, NAC Studies in Bible and Theology 9 (Nashville: B&H, 2010); Torleif Elgvin, *Warrior, King, Servant, Savior: Messianism in the Hebrew Bible and Early Jewish Texts* (Grand Rapids: Eerdmans, 2022).

[92] See Dan G. McCartney, "*Ecce Homo*: The Coming of the Kingdom as the Restoration of Human Vicegerency," *WTJ* 56 (1994): 1–21.

a whole, Genesis not only provides the beginning of the genealogy of Jesus Christ, but notably it sheds significant light on the purpose of his life, introducing concepts that will be developed in other biblical books, but especially in the New Testament. Drawing on the motif of the blessing of the nations in Genesis, the apostle Paul underscores the significance of the promises given to Abraham and his singular "offspring" for understanding how Gentiles may be right with God through faith in Jesus Christ (Rom 4:1–25; Gal 3:7–9, 15–18).[93]

§3 Everlasting Covenants

The importance of the unique patriline for the divine plan of redemption is underscored by the special relationship that exists between its members and God. This is most visible in the cases of Noah and Abraham, with whom God establishes everlasting covenants. These divine covenants not only expand upon the hope associated with the defeat of the serpent, filling out the picture of what will be achieved through the woman's offspring, but they also give vital reassurance that God will be faithful to his promises.

The covenant involving Noah is first mentioned prior to the flood (6:18), when God promises to establish it with Noah. After the deluge destroys "everything on dry land" (7:22), Noah emerges from the ark with his family. He then sacrifices ascension offerings (8:20), gaining God's favor and the promise that God will never again "strike down every living thing" (8:21). To confirm this promise, God establishes his covenant with Noah, his sons and all the living creatures with them, guaranteeing that he will never again wipe out every creature with "the waters of the flood" (9:11). God places his "bow" in the clouds as an appropriate sign for this everlasting covenant (9:12–17).

---

[93] See C. John Collins, "Galatians 3:16: What Kind of an Exegete Was Paul?" *TynBul* 54 (2003): 75–86; Jason S. DeRouchie and Jason C. Meyer, "Christ or Family as the 'Seed' of Promise? An Evaluation of N. T. Wright on Galatians 3:16," *SBJT* 14 (2010): 36–48; Michael Riccardi, "The Seed of Abraham: A Theological Analysis of Galatians 3 and Its Implications for Israel," *MSJ* 25 (2014): 56–57; Kark Deenick, *Righteous by Promise: A Biblical Theology of Circumcision*, NSBT 45 (London: Apollos, 2018), 44–48. DeRouchie, "Counting Stars with Abraham and the Prophets," 460, remarks, "Within Genesis, the hope of blessing reaching the nations (Gen 12:3) is dependent on a single, male, royal offspring (Gen 22:17b–18; 49:8–10), the fulfillment of which only comes in the person of Jesus (see Acts 3:25–26; Gal 3:8, 14, 16)."

Some scholars argue that this covenant links back to an earlier covenant between God and Adam,[94] but this is most unlikely. The covenant with Noah guarantees specifically that God will not send another deluge of water "to destroy every creature" (9:15). If such a covenant promise preexisted the time of Noah, it would have prevented the flood from occurring. As it is, the covenant in Genesis 9 offers reassurance that God will exercise restraint in punishing humanity despite the prevalence of human wickedness on the earth.

The granting of the everlasting covenant in chapter 9 is set in the context of a renewing of creation. The flood story describes a fresh beginning for the earth, echoing the initial account of creation.[95] The disappearance and reappearance of dry land recalls the separation of land and water in Genesis 1. Moreover, the flood waters cleanse the earth from the defilement caused by human violence up to the time of Noah.[96] This cleansing results in renewed fertility, as evidenced by Noah's fruitful horticulture (9:20; see comments on 5:29).

Despite this new beginning after the flood, human nature remains corrupt. God himself affirms this when he states that man's inclination is evil from his youth (8:21). This assessment is reinforced by divine instructions that are intended to reduce the negative impact caused by the shedding of the lifeblood of every animal and every man (9:4–6). The subsequent report of Canaan's abuse of Noah (9:20–23) is a further indicator that human nature is far from perfect. Yet, in spite of the persistence of human corruption, God graciously establishes a covenant, guaranteeing that humanity will not be wiped out.

The covenant with Noah is paralleled by an everlasting covenant that God establishes with Abraham and his patriline. The details of this covenant are recorded in Genesis 17, but there are grounds for believing that the covenant is linked to the oath that God swears in 22:16–18. In Genesis 17 God's opening remarks to Abraham suggest that the establishment of the covenant of circumcision is conditional upon

---

[94] E.g., William J. Dumbrell, *Covenant and Creation: An Old Testament Covenantal Theology* (Exeter: Paternoster, 1984), 15–26; Peter J. Gentry and Stephen J. Wellum, *Kingdom through Covenant: A Biblical-Theological Understanding of the Covenants* (Wheaton: Crossway, 2012), 161–64.

[95] Smith, "Structure and Purpose in Genesis 1–11," 307–19.

[96] Tikva S. Frymer-Kensky, "Atrahasis Epic and Its Significance for Our Understanding of Genesis 1–9," *BA* 40 (1977): 147–55.

Abraham's obedience. Abraham is required to "walk before"[97] God and be blameless so that God may establish his covenant with him (see Comments on 17:1–2).[98] These conditions are later tested when God commands Abraham to sacrifice his much-loved son Isaac as an ascension offering on Mount Moriah. Since God had previously stated that the everlasting covenant of circumcision would be established with Isaac (17:19–21), it is noteworthy that the divine oath in chapter 22 comes in the context of his life being spared. The contents of the oath speak of the nations of the earth being blessed through an offspring of Abraham; in 12:3 the blessing of the families of the ground is linked to Abraham himself. Additionally, God's assurance to Isaac in 26:2–5 that he and his descendants will possess "these lands" alludes back directly to the oath in 22:16–18 and emphasizes the importance of Abraham's obedience. These factors suggest that the divine oath in Genesis 22 is linked to the covenant introduced in Genesis 17.[99]

The primary goal and purpose of the covenant that God offers to establish with Abraham in Genesis 17 is described in terms of God's multiplying Abraham greatly (17:2) so that Abraham becomes the "father of many nations" (17:4–5).[100] Set against the background of God's initial call of Abraham (12:1–3), God's covenant confirms that "many nations" will be blessed through Abraham, their spiritual father (see Comments on 17:4–5). The emphasis upon "nations" underscores that the covenant is not primarily about Abraham becoming a great nation, although this is included. Genesis 17:8 picks up on the gift of land (Canaan) to Abraham's offspring after him, echoing the covenant recorded in Genesis 15, where God guarantees unconditionally that Abraham will

---

[97] The CSB translation of "walk before me" is "live in my presence" (17:1). Similar expressions, in the form "walk with God," come in 5:22 and 6:9.

[98] Noah is also described as being "blameless" and walking with God (6:9).

[99] For a fuller discussion, see T. Desmond Alexander, "Genesis 22 and the Covenant of Circumcision," *JSOT* 25 (1983): 17–22; Paul R. Williamson, *Abraham, Israel and the Nations: The Patriarchal Promise and Its Covenantal Development in Genesis*, JSOTSup 315 (Sheffield: Sheffield Academic, 2000), 234–53.

[100] It is noteworthy that this distinctive aspect of the covenant in ch. 17 often gets overlooked completely. David Andrew Dean, "Covenant, Conditionality, and Consequence: New Terminology and a Case Study in the Abrahamic Covenant," *JETS* 57 (2014): 300, includes no discussion of this significant difference between the covenant episodes in chs. 15 and 17. Dean views the covenant of ch. 17 as building upon the covenant of ch. 15, being "a reaffirmation and more precise specification of earlier-made divine covenant obligations, with the addition of covenant regulations on the vassal group" (302).

have numerous descendants who will possess territory located between Egypt and Syria. The covenant in chapter 17, however, is much broader in scope than the covenant in chapter 15, for its primary focus is upon Abraham becoming the father of many nations, whereas chapter 15 speaks only of one nation.[101]

Apart from its emphasis on "nations," the covenant in chapter 17 is classified as "everlasting" (17:7, 13) and has its own distinctive sign, circumcision (17:10–14, 23–27). The choice of circumcision as the sign for the covenant is noteworthy, for it draws attention to male offspring, a reminder of the importance of the patriline that will lead to a vicegerent who will defeat the serpent.[102] This emphasis is reinforced by the way in which God insists that the covenant will be established with Isaac, who is yet to be born, and not with Ishmael (17:18). God's announcement, which is initially challenged by Abraham (17:19–21), has important ramifications for how the covenant should be understood. The covenant will be established with the members of the patriline and only with them. This introduces an important distinction between those who mediate the blessing of the covenant and those who are recipients of the blessing.[103] After Abraham, the covenant will be established with Isaac, yet Ishmael and all the other male members of Abraham's household are circumcised. All of the latter will benefit from the blessing that God bestows on those who view Abraham as their "father." In this context, the concept of "father" is not limited to a direct biological relationship, for some of the males in Abraham's household were bought from foreigners (17:12–13, 27). Later in Genesis, as Abraham's heir to the covenant of circumcision, Joseph speaks of how God has made him "father to Pharaoh, lord of his entire

[101] The covenant in Gen 17 differs in many respects from that described in Gen 15, suggesting that it should be viewed as a distinctive entity. For a fuller discussion of the relationship between chs. 15 and 17, see Williamson, *Abraham, Israel and the Nations*, 212–14; Paul R. Williamson, "Covenant," in *New Dictionary of Biblical Theology*, ed. T. Desmond Alexander and Brian S. Rosner (Leicester: Inter-Varsity Press, 2000), 422–24; Paul R. Williamson, *Sealed with an Oath: Covenant in God's Unfolding Purpose*, NSBT 23 (Downers Grove: InterVarsity Press, 2007), 84–91; Alexander, "The Regal Dimension of the תלדות־יעקב,"196–212. While some scholars conflate the covenants in chs. 15 and 17 (e.g., Gentry and Wellum, *Kingdom through Covenant*, 263–80; Andrew Chinpeng Ho, "A Paragon of Faith? Doubting Abraham," *Themelios* 42 [2017]: 459–60), it is best to see the covenant of ch. 15 as being subsumed into the more extensive covenant of circumcision.

[102] See Deenick, *Righteous by Promise*, 49.

[103] Cf. Jason S. DeRouchie, "Circumcision in the Hebrew Bible and Targums: Theology, Rhetoric, and the Handling of Metaphor," *BBR* 14 (2004): 182n11.

household, and ruler over all the land of Egypt" (45:8). Within Genesis, the covenant of circumcision is established with first Abraham, then Isaac, then Jacob, and finally Joseph. The establishment of the covenant is linked to the patriline, whereas the benefits of the covenant extend to others. Beyond Genesis, the covenant is associated initially with individuals from the tribe of Ephraim, before being linked in the time of Samuel to David from the tribe of Judah (Ps 78:67–72).

While the covenants in chapters 15 and 17 have unique features that distinguish them, they share the idea that Abraham will have numerous offspring. As regards these offspring, Genesis 17 introduces several important distinctions. First, there is the single offspring, with whom the covenant of circumcision will be established.[104] This offspring belongs to the patriline that will eventually produce the serpent slayer. Second, Abraham's offspring will multiply to form a great nation that will take possession of the land of Canaan. Here the emphasis is on Abraham's biological descendants, that is, his "offspring after him" (17:8). This relates back to the divine guarantee of nationhood, involving many descendants (15:1–6) and land (15:7–21), given to Abraham in Genesis 15. Third, Abraham will be the father of many nations, an expectation that extends his fatherhood beyond the nation of Israel to include all those who look to Abraham and his patriline for divine blessing. Importantly, the scope of the covenant in Genesis 17 goes well beyond the divine guarantee of nationhood that has already been given in Genesis 15. By extending Abraham's fatherhood to the nations, the covenant of circumcision subsumes within it the covenant of chapter 15. Yet in doing so, chapter 17 maintains a subtle distinction between Abraham's offspring "after him" and the other nations who benefit from his "fatherhood."[105]

---

[104] See Deenick, *Righteous by Promise*, 39–44.

[105] This analysis of Abraham's offspring differs in important ways from that of Gentry and Wellum, *Kingdom through Covenant*, 632–33, who distinguish four categories: (1) "*natural* (physical) seed," that is "every person who was in any way physically descended from Abraham, such as Ishmael, Isaac, the sons of Keturah, and by extension Esau, Jacob, etc."; (2) "*natural (physical), yet special* seed tied to God's elective purposes, namely Isaac, and by extension Jacob and the entire nation of Israel"; (3) "the *true/unique* seed, namely Christ (Gal. 3:16), in a typological way"; (4) the "*spiritual*" seed of Abraham, which includes "all believers." Gentry and Wellum fail to recognize that the "*natural (physical), yet special* seed" is not the "entire nation of Israel" but rather the unique patriline that will lead via the Davidic dynasty to Jesus Christ. Blessing comes to the nations not through the nation of Israel, but through a future royal descendant of Abraham. See also T. Desmond Alexander, "The Hope for the Blessing of the Nations in the Book of Genesis," in *Hope for the World from*

Although priority is given to a single nation in chapter 15, in chapter 17 the emphasis falls on nations, especially given the twofold mention of "father of many nations" (vv. 4–5), the rationale given for changing Abraham's name (v. 5) and the remark in v. 6 that God will make nations of Abraham (lit. "I will give you for nations"). In the light of the distinction that is developed in chapters 15 and 17 between the nation consisting of Abraham's "offspring after him" and other nations, DeRouchie argues that the covenant in chapter 17 anticipates "two distinct covenant eras," each linked to the fatherhood of Abraham.[106] The first period is national, relating to Israel and associated with the Mosaic covenant. The second is international, relating to the new covenant established through Jesus Christ. While this distinction between two covenantal eras has much to commend it from a wider biblical perspective, a chronological progression from one era to another is not especially clear in chapter 17. Indeed, in the remainder of Genesis, blessing is mediated by members of the patriline to others, many of whom are not circumcised. Abraham's role as the father of many nations may not be exclusively a New Testament development, although it undoubtedly takes on greater significance with the coming of Jesus Christ.

Since the covenant of circumcision is bound to the concept of Abraham being the "father of many nations," this strongly implies that circumcision is not viewed by the author/compiler of Genesis as simply a marker of ethnic or racial identity. The covenant of Genesis 17 looks outward to the nations, while building on the promise of nationhood associated with Abraham's offspring "after him." The international aspect to the covenant is evident at its inception, for the men who are circumcised in Genesis 17 include both those born within Abraham's household and those bought as slaves from foreigners (17:12–13, 27). Genesis 17 assumes that everyone

---

the Old Testament: Essays in Honour of J. Gordon McConville on his70th Birthday, eds. David G. Firth, Jamie A. Grant and Alison Lo (2025), 7-17.

[106] DeRouchie, "Counting Stars with Abraham and the Prophets," 459–61. He writes, "Genesis 17 envisions a day when Abraham's 'fatherhood' will expand beyond ethnic Israelites to include the nations" (460). DeRouchie suggests that this two-stage development is introduced in 12:1–3; Abraham must become a great nation before the families of the ground are blessed through him. See also Gentry and Wellum, *Kingdom through Covenant*, 632–33, 96; Jason S. DeRouchie, "Father of a Multitude of Nations: New Covenant Ecclesiology in OT Perspective," in *Progressive Covenantalism: Charting a Course between Dispensational and Covenant Theologies*, ed. Stephen J. Wellum and Brent E. Parker (Nashville: B&H Academic, 2016), 7–38; Riccardi, "Seed of Abraham," 51–64.

within Abraham's household, of whom there may have been many (cf. 14:14, which mentions "318 trained men, born in his household"), would have considered Abraham to be their "father." However, only Ishmael and later Isaac and the sons of Keturah (25:1-6) could claim this biologically.

The link made between the covenant of circumcision and the blessing of the nations through an offspring of Abraham has an important bearing on our understanding of Genesis 34. When Simeon and Levi encourage the men of Shechem to be circumcised, they do so on the pretext that this will bring them into a closer relationship with Abraham's descendants. This is a ruse, creating an opportunity for Simeon and Levi to murder the male inhabitants of Shechem (34:25–26). Although they attempt to justify their action, their father Jacob regrets what they have done (49:5–7). The covenant of circumcision is intended to bring blessing to the nations, not death.

In the New Testament, the apostle Paul focuses on the covenant of circumcision to undermine the claims of those who argue that Gentiles are expected to keep the Sinai covenant. After emphasizing that the promises were spoken to Abraham and his seed (who is Christ), Paul says: "My point is this: The law, which came 430 years later, does not invalidate a covenant previously established by God and thus cancel the promise. For if the inheritance is based on the law, it is no longer based on the promise; but God has graciously given it to Abraham through the promise" (Gal 3:17–18).[107] According to Paul, the eternal covenant that God establishes with Abraham and his singular offspring finds its fulfilment not through the creation of Israel as a nation but through the blessing of those from the nations who are counted as Abraham's spiritual offspring.

§4 The City of God

Within Genesis various motifs come together to suggest that behind the divine creation of the cosmos lies the expectation that God will dwell with humanity in a holy temple-city on the earth. In the light of this, the opening two chapters of Genesis record how God creates humans with the intention that they should be involved in transforming the earth into

[107] The covenant of circumcision guarantees divine promises relating to the blessing of the nations; the covenant at Mount Sinai establishes a special relationship between God and the Israelites. The two covenants are very different in nature and ought to be clearly distinguished from each other. To this end, the author of Hebrews distinguishes between God's promise and oath to Abraham and the "first covenant" that was given at Mount Sinai (Heb 6:13–18; 8:6-7).

a divine residence. To this end, they are initially given a holy status that enables them to be in God's presence. God also authorizes people to rule over the earth as his vicegerents, establishing his kingdom throughout the world. To fulfil this task, they are instructed to be fruitful and multiply and fill the earth (1:28). Behind these latter instructions is the expectation that the ever-growing human population will form a temple-city.

When we place the book of Genesis in its original cultural context, it should not surprise us that the opening chapters of Genesis prepare the way for the creation of an extraordinary city where God will dwell in harmony with humanity. In the ANE, individual gods were often associated with particular cities, with the inhabitants of the city revering the deity whose temple stood at the heart of their metropolis (e.g., the city of Babylon is linked to the god Marduk). In their cultural setting, the earliest readers of Genesis would have automatically associated the creation of God's sanctuary on the earth with a city, realizing that the garden of Eden was to be at its heart. However, they may not have envisaged this as involving the creation of a physical temple within the city.

Tragically, however, the actions of Adam and Eve put in jeopardy the fulfilment of God's creation project. Tempted by the serpent, the human couple betray God and are consequently expelled from the garden of Eden. Nevertheless, the concept of city-building continues to be an important motif in the ongoing narrative. It features in the account of Cain's life: "Cain became the builder of a city, and he named the city Enoch after his son" (4:17). Cain associates the city with his descendants, a somewhat ominous development in the light of what follows, with the list of Cain's offspring leading to Lamech, a polygamist and murderer (4:23–24).

The motif of city-building reappears most prominently in 11:1–9, in the last episode before the introduction of Abraham into the narrative. In the light of God's plan to live with humanity on the earth, the short account of the building of Babel/Babylon[108] is highly significant. Babel/Babylon is the archetypal godless city, casting a long shadow over the whole Bible.

---

[108] While this city has for centuries been designated "Babel" in English translations, readers of the CSB may be slightly disconcerted to discover that "Babel" has become "Babylon." The Hebrew term בָּבֶל (*bābel*) appears over 200 times in the Old Testament and is normally rendered "Babylon" in English translations. In modern English versions there are usually only two exceptions to this rule, Gen 10:10 and 11:9, but a few translations replace "Babel" in Gen 10:10 with "Babylon" (e.g., NIV; JPS). The designation "Babylon" in Gen 11:9 is both

At Babel/Babylon the world's population unites to make a name for itself. People aspire to displace God, not just on earth but also in heaven.[109] Arrogantly they attempt to build an edifice that will give them access to heaven itself.[110] Following in the footsteps of Adam and Eve, who were tempted to become like God (3:5), the builders of Babel/Babylon desire to establish themselves as supreme in heaven as well as on earth.

The construction of Babel/Babylon illustrates two contrasting sides of human nature: innovation and hubris. Babel/Babylon is "an ambivalent image."[111]

> On one side we can see the human longings for community, achievement, civilization, culture, technology, safety, security, permanence and fame. But countering these aspirations we sense the moral judgment against idolatry, pride, self-reliance, the urge of material power and the human illusion of infinite achievement.[112]

The building of Babel/Babylon typifies every human enterprise that exalts the creature over the Creator. People use their divinely given abilities to build the city, but they disregard the one who has gifted them as city-builders. The construction of Babel/Babylon is a perverse mockery of what God intended when he commissioned humans to be his vicegerents, establishing his kingdom on the earth.

Babel/Babylon is undoubtedly presented in Genesis as the antithesis of the holy city that God desires to build on the earth. It also becomes its great rival and opponent. This is a significant theme, appearing in both Testaments. Beyond Genesis, the quest to create God's temple-city on the earth eventually results in King David's capture of Jerusalem (2 Sam 5:6–12). Subsequently, David brings to Jerusalem the footstool of God's throne, the ark of the covenant. With this a special relationship is established between God and Jerusalem, as the city becomes the capital of God's kingdom on

---

justified and highly appropriate, but to preserve a sense of continuity with past readings of 11:1–9, we shall refer to this city as Babel/Babylon in this section. See Comments on 11:1–9.

109 The narrator mocks their attempt to reach heaven by observing that God needs to come down to see the city and its tower (11:5).

110 CSB speaks of "a tower with its top in the sky" (11:4). The Hebrew term שָׁמַיִם (*šāmayim*) translated "sky" in CSB can denote "heaven" or "heavens" (cf. 1:1).

111 "Babel, Tower of," in *Dictionary of Biblical Imagery*, ed. Leland Ryken, James C. Wilhoit, and Tremper Longman III (Downers Grove/Leicester: Inter-Varsity Press, 1998), 67.

112 "Babel, Tower of," 67.

earth. In due course Jerusalem's status as God's city is enhanced when Solomon builds there a magnificent temple/palace (1 Kgs 5–7).

Several centuries after Solomon's construction of a temple for YHWH, Jerusalem is captured in 586 BC by the Babylonians. After a long siege, the Babylonians sack Jerusalem and demolish its walls and its temple, taking into captivity some of the population, including the Davidic king (2 Kings 25:1–21). In the light of God's creation project to establish his temple-city on the earth, the Babylonian destruction of Jerusalem is highly ironic. It looks as if Babel/Babylon has won the day. Jerusalem and all that it stands for is reduced to ashes. God's plan to establish his kingdom on the earth, which seemed to be gradually unfolding, receives a major setback. While a variety of Old Testament texts indicate strongly that the Babylonian destruction of Jerusalem is due to the waywardness of the people of Judah and the Davidic kings, this in no way lessens the idea that Babylon signifies human opposition to the creation of God's temple-city on the earth.[113] Yet, while the establishment of ancient Jerusalem as God's temple-city is clearly linked to his creation plan, it is not perceived as fulfilling all that God intended. As many of the Old Testament prophets affirm, ancient Jerusalem merely anticipates something greater in the future; it prefigures the existence of an extraordinary new Jerusalem.[114]

Babel/Babylon's opposition to God takes on added significance in Genesis because the city is associated with aggressive human leadership or kingship. The first reference in Genesis to Babel/Babylon comes in Genesis 10, when the city is linked to a kingdom associated with a powerful hunter called Nimrod.

> [8] Cush fathered Nimrod, who began to be powerful in the land.
> [9] He was a powerful hunter in the sight of the Lord. That is why

---

[113] Babylon's significance is highlighted in Nebuchadnezzar's vision of a statue made of different materials. The head of gold represents Nebuchadnezzar, the king of Babylon (Dan 2:1–49).

[114] For a fuller discussion, see T. Desmond Alexander, *The City of God and the Goal of Creation*, Short Studies in Biblical Theology (Wheaton: Crossway, 2018). See also Ben C. Ollenburger, *Zion, City of the Great King: A Theological Symbol of the Jerusalem Cult*, JSOTSup 41 (Sheffield: JSOT Press, 1987); Barry G. Webb, "Zion in Transformation: A Literary Approach to Isaiah," in *The Bible in Three Dimensions*, ed. David J. A. Clines, Stephen E. Fowl, and Stanley E. Porter, JSOTSup (Sheffield: JSOT Press, 1990), 65–84; J. Gordon McConville, "Jerusalem in the Old Testament," in *Jerusalem Past and Present in the Purposes of God*, ed. P. W. L. Walker (Croydon: Deo Gloria Trust, 1992), 21–51; Lois K. Fuller Dow, *Images of Zion: Biblical Antecedents for the New Jerusalem*, New Testament Monographs 26 (Sheffield: Sheffield Phoenix Press, 2010).

> it is said, "Like Nimrod, a powerful hunter in the sight of the LORD." [10] His kingdom started with Babylon, Erech, Accad, and Calneh, in the land of Shinar. [11] From that land he went to Assyria and built Nineveh, Rehoboth-ir, Calah, [12] and Resen, between Nineveh and the great city Calah (10:8–12).

This brief description of Nimrod sets him apart from others in Genesis 10; no other individual is highlighted in this way. Nimrod is a city-builder and the first city linked to him is Babel/Babylon. However, his kingdom extends beyond Babel/Babylon to include other cities in southern Mesopotamia, and, depending on how vv. 11–12 are interpreted, Nimrod either builds cities in Assyria or, perhaps more likely, is the inspiration for Asshur, who constructs cities to the north of Babel/Babylon.[115] This results in the creation of "the great city."[116]

Nimrod's role as a city builder is linked to his designation as "a powerful hunter in the sight of the LORD." While this description could be interpreted in a positive manner (cf. NJPS),[117] the expression "in the sight of" could mean "facing" or "opposite." This latter sense is more in keeping with the context of Genesis 1–11, which denounces the spread of violence on the earth (cf. 6:11; unfortunately, CSB translates חָמָס [*ḥāmās*] as "wickedness"; most English translations have "violence"). Nimrod's designation as a hunter/warrior stands at odds with what God intended when he commissioned people to govern the earth as his vicegerents.[118]

---

[115] An alternative translation of v. 11 is possible, making Asshur the subject of the sentence. This reading is reflected in the KJV: "Out of that land went forth Asshur, and builded Nineveh, and the city Rehoboth, and Calah ..." (10:11; cf. NJB, NJPS). See Comments on 10:8–12. With either reading of v. 11, this passage brings together the cities and peoples later associated with the downfalls of the northern kingdom of Israel (i.e., the Assyrians) and the southern kingdom of Judah (i.e., the Babylonians).

[116] English versions differ in their understanding of the "great city." The Hebrew text places the words "the great city" after the name Calah, not before Calah, as implied by the CSB translation. While "the great city" could refer to Calah alone, more likely the expression "the great city" refers to the cities of Nineveh, Rehoboth-Ir, Resen, and Calah collectively. In the book of Jonah, the designation "great city" is linked to Nineveh (Jonah 1:2; 3:2–3; 4:11). Jonah 3:2–3 states that it took three days to cross the "great city of Nineveh," which implies a region greater than the walled city of Nineveh. See T. Desmond Alexander, "Jonah," in David W. Baker, T. Desmond Alexander, and Bruce K. Waltke, *Obadiah, Jonah, Micah*, TOTC 26 (Downers Grove: InterVarsity Press, 2009), 61–63.

[117] The NJPS rendering "a mighty hunter by the grace of the LORD" seems most unlikely, given the characterization of Babel/Babylon in 11:1–9.

[118] See Mary Katherine Y. H. Hom, "'...A Mighty Hunter before YHWH': Genesis 10:9 and the Moral-Theological Evaluation of Nimrod," *VT* 60 (2010): 63–68.

This negative appraisal of Nimrod is confirmed by the ambition of the builders of Babel/Babylon, who stand in opposition to God. God expects people to govern the world peacefully, but 10:8–12 implies that Nimrod uses power to establish a kingdom that is a perversion of the kingdom that God desires to create on the earth. Later, in the biblical story, the kingdoms of Assyria and Babylon, both associated with Nimrod, will assail militarily the kingdoms of Israel and Judah, with tragic consequences.

By connecting Nimrod with Babel/Babylon, the author of Genesis introduces the concept of contrasting cities and kingdoms. Rather than establishing God's kingdom on the earth through the building of a holy temple-city, people construct alternative cities and kingdoms. Against this background God summons Abraham to fulfil a central role in bringing God's kingdom to the earth.

The Terah *tôlĕdôt* (11:27–25:11) highlights in some detail the significance of Abraham. Whereas the builders of Babel/Babylon seek to make a name for themselves (11:4), God promises to make Abraham's name great (12:2). Like Noah, Abraham comes in the unique patriline that will eventually produce the serpent-slayer. But the Abraham narrative contributes much more to the biblical story than merely identifying another member of the patriline and indicating its future direction through Isaac and not Ishmael. Two major elements within the Abraham narrative may be linked to the concept of the temple-city: land and descendants.

Within the Abraham narrative divine promises concerning land and descendants occur frequently, sometimes as separate promises and sometimes combined in the concept of nation.[119] At the outset, Abraham is instructed by God to leave his homeland and migrate to a new land (12:1–2). Although Sarah, his wife, is childless, God promises Abraham that he will become a "great nation" (12:2). After Abraham arrives in Canaan, God promises the land to him on several occasions (12:7; 13:14–17). The promise of numerous descendants is given specifically in Genesis 13:16 when God states that he will make Abraham's offspring "like the dust of the earth." However, because he remains childless, Abraham eventually asks God for confirmation that he will have an heir (15:2–3). In response, God tells him that his descendants will be as numerous as the stars of

[119] The term גּוֹי (*gôy*, "nation") implies people possessing territory. See E. A. Speiser, "'People' and 'Nation' of Israel," *JBL* 79 (1960): 157–63; Aelred Cody, "When Is a Chosen People Called a Gôy?", *VT* 14 (1964): 1–6; Ronald E. Clements, "*goy*," *TDOT*, 2:426–33.

the sky (15:5). Abraham then seeks confirmation that he will possess the land (15:8). God provides another sign, involving various sacrificial animals and "a smoking fire pot and a flaming torch" (15:17). The initial promise of nationhood, given in 12:2, is guaranteed by an unconditional covenant that God makes with Abraham (15:18–21). This covenant is later integrated into a more significant everlasting covenant, in which God promises Abraham that he will multiply him greatly (17:2) and he will become the "father of many nations" (17:4–5).[120]

God's promises to Abraham concerning land and descendants are echoed in a divine oath that is given to Abraham in Isaac's presence on Mount Moriah (22:16–18). The context for the oath is significant, for Abraham's obedience to God has been severely tested; God has instructed him to sacrifice Isaac, the one through whom the covenant of circumcision will be established. After the angel of YHWH intervenes, God swears by himself that he will bless Abraham with "offspring as numerous as the stars of the sky and the sand on the seashore" (22:17). The oath then speaks of Abraham's offspring taking possession of the gate of his enemies.[121] Switching from numerous offspring to one offspring, the oath focuses on an individual, who will not only be victorious over his opponents, but will also mediate blessing to "all the nations of the earth" (22:18). As in Genesis 17, God's oath draws a distinction between the many offspring of Abraham and the unique line of offspring. To add to the significance of this occasion, the divine oath given to guarantee these promises is made on a mountain in the land of Moriah (22:2), possibly the location where years later YHWH will appear to David and where Solomon will construct the Jerusalem temple (2 Chr 3:1).

Beyond the Abraham narrative, the promises associated with the covenant of circumcision are linked to Isaac and then Jacob. Not only does God confirm these promises personally to Isaac (26:2–5, 24) and Jacob (35:11–12; cf. 28:13–15), but also both patriarchs refer to them when

---

[120] The covenant of circumcision, which introduces an international dimension to Abraham's role in God's purposes, confirms the earlier divine promise that "all the families of the ground" will be blessed through Abraham (12:3). In 12:1–3 the promise of international blessing is the climax of God's call of Abraham. See Comments on 12:1–3.

[121] Although CSB reads "their enemies," there are good grammatical grounds for seeing the offspring mentioned in v. 17b as denoting an individual (cf. KJV; JPS; ESV). See T. Desmond Alexander, "Further Observations of the Term 'Seed' in Genesis," *TynBul* 48 (1997): 363–67.

blessing offspring (28:3–4; 48:4). While there is a strong tendency on the part of commentators to focus on the promise of nationhood linked to Abraham's offspring "after him," all of the allusions back to the covenant of circumcision in the second half of Genesis mention features that look beyond the existence of a single nation (26:4 mentions "lands"; 28:3 refers to "an assembly of peoples"; 35:11 mentions "an assembly of nations"; 48:4 refers to "many nations").[122] Although the promise of a nation descended biologically from Abraham is exceptionally important in Genesis, it stands alongside the expectation that Abraham's fatherhood will impact the nations. Through Abraham and his offspring, who belong to the unique patriline, God will bless the nations.

As we have already noted in Biblical and Theological Themes §3, the covenant of circumcision encapsulates all that God plans to do through Abraham and his offspring. Importantly, at the heart of this covenant is God's assurance that Abraham will become numerous (17:2) and extremely fruitful (17:6). These specific promises recall the creation mandate given to humanity to multiply and be fruitful (1:28), a mandate that is subsequently repeated to Noah and his sons (9:1, 7).

Alongside the expectation of numerous descendants (both biologically and metaphorically), the covenant of circumcision also highlights the acquisition of "land," in particular the land of Canaan for Abraham's offspring "after him" (17:8). This aspect of the covenant recalls the divine mandate that humans are to "fill the earth" (1:28). While Abraham's offspring "after him" will occupy the territory allocated to them, by inference other nations that have Abraham as their spiritual father will fill the rest of the earth. Consequently, the fulfilment of the covenant of circumcision will play a significant role in accomplishing God's creation project. And if, as we have argued above, this involves the formation of a temple-city, it is noteworthy that in Genesis the divine promises to the patriarchs are often given at "temporary sanctuaries" in anticipation of their fulfilment through the establishment of a permanent sanctuary.[123]

---

[122] Recalling the international dimension of the covenant of circumcision, 27:29 refers to "peoples" and "nations" and 49:10 to "peoples." Beyond the *tôlědôt* section of Terah (11:27–25:11), only one divine speech (46:3) does not mention or allude to nations.

[123] Beale, "Eden, the Temple, and the Church's Mission," 14, observes that in Genesis various sacrificial sites appear to function as "impermanent, miniature forms of sanctuaries." Strikingly, these altars are often linked to theophanies, when God recalls the

Beyond Genesis, the books of Exodus to Kings describe how Abraham's biological descendants establish Jerusalem as the city of God, climaxing in the building of a resplendent temple during the reign of Solomon (1 Kgs 6–7). However, due to the sinfulness of the city's population, and especially its leadership, various Old Testament prophets predict the fall of Jerusalem to the Babylonians. At the same time, these prophets anticipate the creation of a new Jerusalem, where God will dwell with his people.[124] Importantly, the prophet Isaiah associates this new Jerusalem with the divine creation of new heavens and a new earth (Isaiah 65:17–18), an idea that is developed in the New Testament by various writers. Paul, for his part, contrasts the "present Jerusalem" with the "Jerusalem above" (Gal 4:25–26). The author of Hebrews exhorts his readers to look forward to the city that is yet to come (Heb 13:14; cf. 11:8–10, 13–16), the "heavenly Jerusalem" (Heb 12:22). The apostle John records in the book of Revelation his vision of a heavenly Jerusalem descending to earth as part of a new heavens and new earth (Rev 21:1–2). These events bring to completion God's creation project that is introduced in the opening chapters of Genesis.

---

creation mandate that people are to be fruitful, fill the earth and rule over it (1:28). See 9:1, 7; 22:17–18; 26:24; 35:11–12.

[124] For a fuller discussion, see Donald E. Gowan, *Eschatology in the Old Testament* (Philadelphia: Fortress, 1986), 85–114; Alexander, *The City of God*.

EXPOSITION

I. The Creation of the Heavens and the Earth (1:1–2:3)

1 In the beginning God created the heavens and the earth.

2 Now the earth was formless and empty, darkness covered the surface
of the watery depths, and the Spirit of God was hovering over the sur-
face of the waters. 3 Then God said, "Let there be light," and there was
light. 4 God saw that the light was good, and God separated the light
from the darkness. 5 God called the light "day," and the darkness he
called "night." There was an evening, and there was a morning: one day.

6 Then God said, "Let there be an expanse between the waters, separat-
ing water from water." 7 So God made the expanse and separated the
water under the expanse from the water above the expanse. And it was
so. 8 God called the expanse "sky." Evening came and then morning:
the second day.

9 Then God said, "Let the water under the sky be gathered into one place,
and let the dry land appear." And it was so. 10 God called the dry land
"earth," and the gathering of the water he called "seas." And God saw
that it was good. 11 Then God said, "Let the earth produce vegetation:
seed-bearing plants and fruit trees on the earth bearing fruit with seed
in it according to their kinds." And it was so. 12 The earth produced veg-
etation: seed-bearing plants according to their kinds and trees bearing
fruit with seed in it according to their kinds. And God saw that it was
good. 13 Evening came and then morning: the third day.

14 Then God said, "Let there be lights in the expanse of the sky to sep-
arate the day from the night. They will serve as signs for seasons and
for days and years. 15 They will be lights in the expanse of the sky to
provide light on the earth." And it was so. 16 God made the two great
lights—the greater light to rule over the day and the lesser light to rule

over the night—as well as the stars. [17] God placed them in the expanse
of the sky to provide light on the earth, [18] to rule the day and the night,
and to separate light from darkness. And God saw that it was good. [19]
Evening came and then morning: the fourth day.

[20] Then God said, "Let the water swarm with living creatures, and let
birds fly above the earth across the expanse of the sky." [21] So God cre-
ated the large sea-creatures and every living creature that moves and
swarms in the water, according to their kinds. He also created every
winged creature according to its kind. And God saw that it was good.
[22] God blessed them: "Be fruitful, multiply, and fill the waters of the
seas, and let the birds multiply on the earth." [23] Evening came and then
morning: the fifth day.

[24] Then God said, "Let the earth produce living creatures according to
their kinds: livestock, creatures that crawl, and the wildlife of the earth
according to their kinds." And it was so. [25] So God made the wildlife of
the earth according to their kinds, the livestock according to their kinds,
and all the creatures that crawl on the ground according to their kinds.
And God saw that it was good.

[26] Then God said, "Let us make man in our image, according to our
likeness. They will rule the fish of the sea, the birds of the sky, the
livestock, the whole earth, and the creatures that crawl on the earth."

[27] So God created man in his own image; he created him in the image
of God; he created them male and female.

[28] God blessed them, and God said to them, "Be fruitful, multiply, fill the
earth, and subdue it. Rule the fish of the sea, the birds of the sky, and
every creature that crawls on the earth." [29] God also said, "Look, I have
given you every seed-bearing plant on the surface of the entire earth
and every tree whose fruit contains seed. This will be food for you, [30]
for all the wildlife of the earth, for every bird of the sky, and for every
creature that crawls on the earth—everything having the breath of life
in it—I have given every green plant for food." And it was so. [31] God saw
all that he had made, and it was very good indeed. Evening came and
then morning: the sixth day.

[1] So the heavens and the earth and everything in them were completed.
[2] On the seventh day God had completed his work that he had done, and
he rested on the seventh day from all his work that he had done. [3] God
blessed the seventh day and declared it holy, for on it he rested from
all his work of creation.

Context

As the introductory section to Genesis, 1:1–2:3 provides a distinctive and selective description of what God did to establish the earth as we know it. There is a sophistication to what is narrated in Genesis 1 that belies its apparent simplicity.[1] Waltke and Fredricks describe it as "an artistic, literary representation of creation."[2] Given the era in which Genesis was composed, the author's intention in recounting the creation of the world was not motivated by a desire to explain what occurred from a scientific perspective. As Longman rightly notes, the emphasis is upon a theological understanding of creation, appreciating God's relationship to the world and the unique status of human beings as those who are appointed by God to establish his kingdom throughout the earth.[3]

Understanding the purpose of 1:1–2:3 provides an important guide as to the form and nature of what is said. At the outset, God is introduced as preexisting everything that he creates. Importantly, this opening section of Genesis sets the scene for the narrative that follows by informing the reader about the hierarchical relationships involving God, humans, and other earthly creatures. Particular attention is given to the fact that humans alone are mandated by God to rule over all other earthly creatures.

When reading 1:1–2:3, we need to be sensitive to what the author desires to communicate. The description is highly selective, focusing on what is essential for the reader to understand the author's message. Much is left unsaid. Details of what God does are kept to a minimum; a panoramic picture is sketched using broad brush strokes. Different areas of habitation are distinguished (land, sea, sky/heavens) and the process of filling them begins as God creates living creatures to inhabit the sky, sea and land.

The seven-day structure used in 1:1–2:3 distinguishes this passage from the rest of Genesis, a distinction confirmed by the *tôlĕdôt* heading in 2:4, which marks the start of a new section. Days 1 to 6 are marked by the concluding formula, "Evening came and then morning: the ... day." After the first occurrence of this formula in verse 5, Days 2–5 all begin with the expression, "Then God said ..." Neither of these recurring expressions comes in the description of Day 7 in 2:1–3, setting it apart from what is

---

[1] For a discussion of these issues, see J. Daryl Charles, ed., *Reading Genesis 1-2: An Evangelical Conversation* (Peabody: Hendrickson, 2013); Vern S. Poythress, *Christian Interpretations of Genesis 1*, Christian Answers to Hard Questions (Phillipsburg: P&R, 2013).

[2] Bruce K. Waltke and Cathi J. Fredricks, *Genesis: A Commentary* (Grand Rapids: Zondervan, 2001), 78. In arriving at this assessment, they draw on Henri Blocher, *In the Beginning: The Opening Chapters of Genesis* (Leicester: Inter-Varsity Press, 1984), 50–59.

[3] Tremper Longman III, "What Genesis 1–2 Teaches (and What It Doesn't)," in *Reading Genesis 1-2: An Evangelical Conversation*, ed. J. Daryl Charles (Peabody: Hendrickson, 2013), 103–28.

recorded for Days 1–6. Day 7 focuses on God's resting from all his work, confirming that he has finished this initial creative activity. The absence of any comment regarding the end of Day 7 leaves open the possibility that this day is to be understood as not having come to an end.

Based on how each of Days 2–6 is introduced, it seems likely that the reader is to assume that the report of Day 1 begins in verse 3, which starts with the words, "Then God said ..." Taken together verses 3–5 initiate a pattern that is repeated in Days 2–6, although subsequent days expand upon this pattern. Since the opening words of verse 3 resembles the start of other days, this raises the question, what is the relationship of verses 1–2 to the rest of the passage? The answer is not straightforward and has been much debated. Undoubtedly, verse 2 sets the scene for what follows with its references to "darkness" and "waters," the former being specifically mentioned again in Day 1 and the latter in Days 2 and 3. Verse 2 provides essential background information for understanding God's actions in Days 1–3. Additionally, there is good reason to view God's creative activity in Days 1–6 as corresponding to the expression "formless and empty" in verse 2. In Days 1–3 God gives shape to what is "formless" and in Days 4–6 he fills what is "empty."

Whereas verse 2 sets the scene by anticipating what is to follow, verse 1 primarily introduces God, who is the subject of the creative activity described in verses 3–31. While verse 1 could possibly refer to an initial creative act on God's part, it is more likely a summary statement that introduces all that is about to be narrated (see Comments on 1:1–2).

By structuring the opening section of Genesis around seven days, the author highlights the design and order of all that occurs. He also gives to the account a majestic tone; everything goes according to plan. As Fishbane comments,

> The text thus provides a reflection of an orderly, harmonious creation. The alternation of the narrator's voice with divine speech, of description with prescription, serves to present "the creation" as a dispassionate recitation recurrently punctuated with vital divine energy. The text shifts rhythmically between actions and results which utilize the same words ("separate" ... "call" ... "see" ... "make") and sequences. Its economy of vocabulary and technique produces a dictum of controlled energy and force.[4]

[4] Fishbane, *Text and Texture*, 8.

The literary style of 1:1–2:3 presents God as a majestic, powerful, cosmic organizer who is transcendent over all of creation. Habel remarks:

> He issues his command and the results are automatic. God appears as a being who stands outside of his cosmos and controls it with his mighty word. Hence the possible "anthropomorphic" expressions of Genesis 1 ("God said," "God saw," and "God rested") are reserved in character and tend to preserve the transcendence of God. They do not suggest the close proximity of a God who acts and looks like man.[5]

Throughout 1:1–2:3 emphasis is placed upon the structuring and ordering of what God summons into being. Everything has its place, and an important hierarchy is established with humanity being commissioned as God's vicegerents on the earth. Even the conclusion of the account (2:1–3) emphasizes this sense of completion by describing how God rests from his labors.

The picture of creation in 1:1–2:3 stands in contrast to subsequent developments in the book of Genesis, as the order and harmony of creation descends into chaos and conflict. As the events of Genesis 3 reveal, this outcome is due to the failure of the human couple to fulfill their duty as God's vicegerents. No blame can be placed at God's feet, for the repeated refrain in chapter 1 emphasizes that everything he creates is "good" (1:4, 10, 12, 18, 21, 25) or "very good" (1:31).

While the account in Genesis 1 describes in large measure the creation of material objects, the emphasis is not on how God manufactures them. Rather Genesis 1 describes the structuring of "time" into different periods and the ordering of "space" into different habitats, land, sea, and sky/heavens, each with their own distinctive inhabitants. Days 1 and 4 stand apart, because the emphasis is not so much on the creation of materials, but on how time is ordered. Walton helpfully highlights this distinction by noting that God names the light "day." He writes, "It was

---

[5] Norman C. Habel, *Literary Criticism of the Old Testament* (Philadelphia: Fortress, 1971), 24. A similar point is made by Fishbane, *Text and Texture*, 8: "The formality of its sequences, the repetition of its key words, and the serialization of its contents combine to produce several theological meanings: that Elohim, alone, 'at the beginning,' created a good, ordered world; that He 'separated' and hierarchically ordered the primordial mass into a 'good' pattern; that the created world of nature is, as a result, a harmony; and that Elohim is Omnipotent and without rival."

not the element of light itself that God called *yôm* ('day') but the period of light."[6] Building on this he concludes that "day one does not concern itself with the creation of the physicist's light, that is, light as a physical element with physical properties. Day one concerns something much more significant, something much more elemental to the functioning of the cosmos and to our experience of the cosmos. On day one, God created time."[7] Support for Walton's reading of 1:3–5 comes in the corresponding Day 4, which notes how there are "two great lights—the greater light to rule over the day and the lesser light to rule over the night" (1:16). Additionally, the lights "in the expanse of the sky" are to serve "as signs for seasons and for days and years" (1:15). With the creation of "light," God establishes a recurring sequence that alternates between light and darkness, with the references to "evening" and "morning" marking the beginning and ending of the darkness.

These observations regarding Days 1 and 4 suggest that the author of Genesis 1 is not primarily interested in describing how God brought into being the physical materials that compose our universe, which he undoubtedly does. Rather, the author's interest is in how this world is organized, first, as regards time, and second, as we shall see, as regards a hierarchy among animated life, with humans receiving authority from God to govern "the fish of the sea, the birds of the sky, the livestock, the whole earth, and the creatures that crawl on the earth" (1:26).

If we grant that the author's primary intention is to explain how the world is organized, rather than how materials are manufactured, it may be easier to understand why the description is presented in two panels of three days, with Days 4–6 corresponding in large measure with Days 1–3. The two panels describe first "habitats" and then "inhabitants."[8] Importantly, if the focus is on organization, rather than manufacture, we should be cautious in drawing conclusions regarding how Genesis 1 informs our understanding of the creation of the world from a scientific perspective. In the light of this distinction, it might be helpful to compare Genesis 1 to an account of how someone might create a "home," rather

[6] Walton, "Creation," 163–64.

[7] Walton, "Creation," 163–64.

[8] Tremper Longman III, *How to Read Genesis* (Downers Grove: InterVarsity Press, 2005), 105; cf. Middleton, *The Liberating Image*, 75, who speaks of "static regions and mobile occupants." According to Blocher, *In the Beginning*, 51n45, this theory is traced back to M. J. Lagrange, "Hexameron (Gènese 1 à, 2,4)," *RB*, 5 (1896), 382.

than an account of how a "house" is constructed. The former focuses more on how items are organized, the latter on how items are manufactured.

The way we choose to approach Genesis 1 has a major bearing on discussions about the relationship between science and the Bible. Science has the potential to enable us to know the process of creation, but it cannot shed light on the purpose of creation. This is where the Genesis account comes into its own. It reveals truth that cannot be ascertained by other means. There is good reason to think that the author of Genesis addresses the "Why?" question of creation, rather than the "How?" question. As Waltke and Fredricks remark:

> Genesis is prescriptive, answering the questions of who and why and what ought to be, whereas the purpose of science is to be descriptive, answering the questions of what and how. The narrator of the creation account is not particularly concerned with the questions a scientist asks; rather, he wants to provide answers to the questions science cannot answer—who has created this world and for what purpose?[9]

Those who read 1:1–2:3 in the hope that it will shed light on the science of how the universe came into existence run the risk of missing the substance of what the author of Genesis wishes to communicate. With good reason, Wenham observes,

> The Bible-versus-science debate has, most regrettably, sidetracked readers of Gen 1. Instead of reading the chapter as a triumphant affirmation of the power and wisdom of God and the wonder of his creation, we have too often bogged down in attempting to squeeze Scripture into the mold of the latest scientific hypothesis or distorting scientific facts to fit a particular interpretation. When allowed to speak for itself, Gen 1 looks beyond such minutiae. Its proclamation of the God of grace and power who undergirds the world and gives it purpose justifies the scientific approach to nature. Gen 1, by further affirming the unique status of man, his place in the divine program, and God's care for him, gives a hope to mankind that atheistic philosophies can never legitimately supply.[10]

---

[9] Waltke and Fredricks, *Genesis*, 75.

[10] Wenham, *Genesis 1–15*, 40.

Appreciating the danger of misreading Genesis 1, Gordon remarks,

> It is particularly important that those who claim to identify with "the biblical position" on beginnings do justice to what the text is seeking to communicate and do not express their commitment by imposing their own schemes upon it. Otherwise, it becomes necessary for Genesis to be defended against its defenders.[11]

Genesis 1 describes a deity who is unique in the ancient world. Against the prevailing culture of surrounding nations, 1:1–2:3 provides a distinctive monotheistic description of creation. Other ANE creation accounts are strongly polytheistic in nature, involving a variety of gods, not all of equal standing. In the Babylonian account of origins, Enuma Elish, the creation of the earth comes after a duel between two deities, when the victor, Marduk, splits in half the body of the defeated goddess, Tiamat, to form the earth and the sky. Genesis 1 stands well apart from such creation accounts.[12]

While Genesis 1 stands apart from other ANE accounts, some have argued that it was composed as a polemic against alternative creation stories.[13] However, Arnold rightly notes that there is little in Genesis to suggest that it was deliberately composed with other ANE accounts in view. He writes,

> If we consider [Genesis 1:1–2:3] an ideological polemic, we must admit it is not specifically so and only indirectly. It contains no theomachy, or cosmic conflict among the gods, or victory enthronement motif. ... Israel's God has no rivals. There can be no struggle with forces opposed to his actions or corresponding

---

[11] Robert P. Gordon, "The Week That Made the World: Reflections on the First Pages of the Bible," in McConville and Möller, *Reading the Law*, 228–29.

[12] On Gen 1 and ANE materials, see C. John Collins, "Reading Genesis 1–11 with the Grain: Analogical Days," in Charles, *Reading Genesis 1-2*, 75–77. Differences in style and content make it highly unlikely that the author of Genesis was influenced by other ANE accounts. Underlining the distinctiveness of Gen 1 in the ancient world, John H. Stek, "What Says the Scriptures?" in *Portraits of Creation: Biblical and Scientific Perspectives on the World's Formation*, ed. Howard J. Van Till (Grand Rapids: Eerdmans, 1990), 231–32, writes, "But an attentive reading of the whole against the background of the several myths of the ancient Near East discloses a view of God, humanity, and world that, whatever its more or less incidental affinities with conceptions abroad in Israel's environment, stands in striking opposition to almost all that those religions had in common." Cf. Nahum M. Sarna, *Understanding Genesis*, The Heritage of Biblical Israel 1 (New York: Jewish Theological Seminary of America, 1966), 9, 11.

[13] E.g., Gerhard F. Hasel, "The Polemic Nature of the Genesis Cosmology," *EvQ* 46 (1974): 81–102.

> to his power. There can be no victory enthronement motif because God's victory was never in doubt; rather, God has never *not* been enthroned. There can be no enthronement portrait here because God has not *become* sovereign; he has simply never been *less than* sovereign.[14]

In support of this position, Tsumura demonstrates, despite claims to the contrary, that "the background of the Genesis creation story has nothing to do with the so-called *Chaoskampf* myth of the Mesopotamian type, as preserved in the Babylonian 'creation' myth Enuma Elish. In Gen 1, there is no hint of struggle or battle between God and this *tehom*—water."[15] Adopting a similar stance, Wenham remarks, "Gen 1 is more than a repudiation of contemporary oriental creation myths; it is a triumphant invocation of the God who has created all men and an invitation to all humanity to adore him who has made them in his own image."[16]

Comments

1:1–2. For all their apparent simplicity, the opening two verses of Genesis have prompted much discussion and disagreement. In large measure, this is the result of scholars believing that these verses are packed with theological insights that can be teased out by a careful exegesis of the text. Yet, this assumption runs the risk of reading into the text more than what the original author ever intended to say. A more cautious approach might recognize that any author, no matter how skilled, can communicate only a limited message in a small number of words. The opening two verses of Genesis, consisting of twenty-one words in Hebrew, leave many questions unanswered. To assume otherwise promotes eisegesis rather than

---

[14] Arnold, *Genesis*, 32 (italics in original). Walton refers to the conflict among the gods as "theomachy." John H. Walton, "Creation in Genesis 1:1–2:3 and the Ancient Near East: Order out of Disorder after *Chaoskampf*," *Calvin Theological Journal* 43 (2008): 49.

[15] David Toshio Tsumura, *Creation and Destruction: A Reappraisal of the Chaoskampf Theory in the Old Testament* (Winona Lake: Eisenbrauns, 2005), 143. Cf. Rebecca S. Watson, *Chaos Uncreated: A Reassessment of the Theme of "Chaos" in the Hebrew Bible*, BZAW 341 (Berlin: Walter de Gruyter, 2005); Walton, "Creation in Genesis 1:1–2:3," 48–63. Karl Möller writes, "The passage does not talk about primordial combat, and it emphasizes the complete and unchallenged mastery of Israel's God in creation." Karl Möller, "Images of God and Creation in Genesis 1–2," in *A God of Faithfulness: Essays in Honour of J. Gordon McConville on His 60th Birthday*, ed. Jamie A. Grant, Allison Lo, and Gordon Wenham, LHBOTS 538 (New York: T&T Clark, 2011), 17.

[16] Wenham, *Genesis 1–15*, 10.

exegesis, especially when some scholars are determined to demonstrate that these verses support a particular theological belief.

The opening word in Genesis, בְּרֵאשִׁית (*bĕrēʾšît*), is most often translated "In the beginning" (e.g., ESV; KJV; NIV; RSV). This reading is favored by many commentators, especially because it supports the theological concept of *creatio ex nihilo* ("creation from nothing"), affirming that God exists prior to the creation of the universe. However, the MT has no definite article and a comparison with other uses of בְּרֵאשִׁית (*bĕrēʾšît*) in Jeremiah 26:1; 27:1; 28:1; 49:34 suggests that the noun could be used here as a construct with the sense "beginning of."[17] Viewed in this way, verse 1 does not describe a completed action, but merely introduces what God is about to do. The verse could be translated, "When God began to create the heavens and the earth ..." If we adopt this approach, verse 1 offers a summary of what is about to be narrated in the rest of the chapter.

The choice between these two ways of reading verse 1 is finely balanced.[18] Verse 1 is either an independent, main clause, marking the first stage of what God does, or a summary/title, anticipating all that will be described in verses 2–31. Each reading has implications for how subsequent verses are interpreted. However, contrary to what is sometimes claimed, neither approach undermines the idea that God alone is responsible for all that exists within the universe. As Mathews remarks, "Regardless of how one reads 1:1–3, there is no room in our author's cosmology for co-eternal matter with God when we consider the theology of the creation account in its totality."[19]

Verse 1 introduces God as the creator. In contrast to other ANE creation accounts, Genesis 1 is firmly monotheistic in outlook. The term אֱלֹהִים (*ʾĕlōhîm*), which is used throughout chapter 1 to denote God, is a generic noun meaning deity; the personal name יהוה ("YHWH") first appears in 2:4. The designation אֱלֹהִים (*ʾĕlōhîm*) distinguishes God from all

---

[17] Joüon, 443, offers the translation, "At the beginning of God's creation of the heaven and the earth." Cf. H. M. Orlinsky, "The Plain Meaning of Genesis 1:1–3," *BA* 46 (1983): 207–9.

[18] For a fuller discussion, coming down on the side of the traditional reading of v. 1 as a first act of creation, see Wenham, *Genesis 1–15*, 11–15; Jiri Moskala, "Interpretation of *bere'šît* in the Context of Genesis 1:1–3," *AUSS* 49 (2011): 117–52; Richard M. Davidson, "The Genesis Account of Origins," in *The Genesis Creation Account and Its Reverberations in the Old Testament*, ed. Gerald A. Klingbeil, Creation in the Bible Series (Berrien Springs: Andrews University Press, 2015), 61–69. Richard E. Averbeck, "A Literary Day: Inter-Textual, and Contextual Reading of Genesis 1–2," in Charles, *Reading Genesis 1–2*, 9–10, contends that v. 1 is a title.

[19] Kenneth A. Mathews, *Genesis 1–11:26*, NAC 1A (Nashville: Broadman & Holman, 1995), 139.

that is created. Although plural in form, אֱלֹהִים (ʾĕlōhîm) is almost always used with singular verbs throughout the Old Testament when referring to Israel's God, YHWH. The use of the singular verb בָּרָא (bārāʾ) emphasizes God's role in creation, for he alone is almost always the subject of this verb in the Old Testament.[20] Observing that the verb בָּרָא (bārāʾ) can be used interchangeably with other verbs of making,[21] Fretheim concludes, "The use of the verb *bārāʾ* may witness to an understanding that no analogy drawn from the human sphere can *exhaust* the meaning of God's creative activity."[22]

Most English versions render הַשָּׁמַיִם (*haššāmayim)* as "the heavens" (e.g., ESV; CSB; NIV; NRSV), but a few opt for "the heaven" or "heaven" (e.g., JPS; KJV; NJB; NJPS). The same word, without the definite article, is used later in verse 8 by God to name "the expanse 'sky.' " In a similar fashion אֶרֶץ (*ʾereṣ* "earth,") without the definite article, is the name given by God in verse 10 to "the dry land."

The expression "heaven and earth" normally denotes "the entire universe, the totality of God's creation (Gen 1:1; Deut 4:26; Ps 121:2; 146:6; Mark 13:31; Acts 17:24)."[23] For this reason, the CSB footnote offers the alternative translation "created the universe." However, if verse 1 is read as an initial creative act and not as a summary/title relating to what follows, then the reference to "the heavens and the earth" must denote something other than the items subsequently named "heaven/sky" and "earth" in Days 2 and 3 (see Comments on vv. 8 and 10). Recognizing this issue, Mathews writes:

> Although the phrase "heavens and earth" surely points to a finished universe where it is found elsewhere in the Old Testament, we cannot disregard the fundamental difference between those passages and the context presented in Genesis 1 before us, namely, that the expression may be used uniquely here since it concerns the exceptional event of creation itself.

---

[20] Bill T. Arnold, *Genesis* (Cambridge: Cambridge University Press, 2009), 36, notes that the root ברא (*br*ʾ) has God as subject only in the *qal* and *niphal*; in the *piel* it is used of humans (e.g., Josh 17:15, 18; Ezek 21:24; 23:47). Cf. Raymond C. Van Leeuwen, "ברא," *NIDOTTE*, 1:731–32, who cautions against overloading the verb with "semantic freight."

[21] In Gen 1:27, the verb בָּרָא (*bārāʾ*) is used in parallel to the verb עָשָׂה (*ʿāśâ*) "to make."

[22] Terence E. Fretheim, *God and World in the Old Testament: A Relational Theology of Creation* (Nashville: Abingdon, 2005), 37 (italics in original).

[23] Mitchell G. Reddish, "Heaven," *ABD*, 3:90.

> To insist on its meaning as a finished universe is to enslave the expression to its uses elsewhere and ignore the contextual requirements of Genesis 1.[24]

This issue disappears if verse 1 is viewed as a summary/title for what follows.

It is difficult to determine the precise meaning of הָאָרֶץ (*hāʾāreṣ*, "the earth") in verse 2. The "earth" mentioned here must denote something other than the "dry land" that is called אֶרֶץ (*ʾereṣ*, "earth") in verse 10.[25] By placing the noun הָאָרֶץ (*hāʾāreṣ*, "the earth") at the start of verse 2 before the verb הָיְתָה (*hāytâ*), the author creates a circumstantial sentence that introduces several items, setting the scene for what follows. If verse 2 is intended to describe events that followed chronologically the creation of the "heavens and the earth" mentioned in verse 1, it would have been more natural to use a *wayyiqtol* verb at the start of verse 2.[26] From a grammatical perspective there is no reason to presuppose that the circumstances described in verse 2 came into being after God's creating "the heavens and the earth." We should not suppose that something has occurred to make the earth, mentioned in verse 1, become תֹהוּ וָבֹהוּ (*tōhû wābōhû*, "formless and empty"). The syntax of verses 1–2 does not point toward a "gap" theory, which would also importantly entail believing that verses 3–31 describe a *second* divine creation of the earth. The rest of Scripture offers no evidence to suggest that the opening chapter of Genesis recounts a remaking or renewing of the earth.

Regardless of how verse 1 is interpreted, as a circumstantial sentence verse 2 sets the scene for what follows in verses 3–31. While some scholars assume that the expression תֹהוּ וָבֹהוּ (*tōhû wābōhû*) describes a chaotic state, Tsumura demonstrates that it "simply means 'emptiness' and refers to the earth, which was a desolate and empty place, 'an unproductive and uninhabited place.' "[27] Tsumura adds that "both the biblical context and extra-biblical parallels suggest that the phrase *tōhû wābōhû* in Gen 1:2 has nothing to do with 'chaos.' "[28] In the light of the expression תֹהוּ וָבֹהוּ (*tōhû wābōhû*, "formless and empty"), it is worth recalling

---

[24] Mathews, *Genesis 1–11:26*, 142.

[25] To underline the complexity of what is being discussed here, Wenham, *Genesis 1–15*, 15, suggests that the meaning of הָאָרֶץ (*hāʾāreṣ*, "the earth") in v. 2 may be different from that in v. 1. He suggests that "compounded with 'heaven' " in v. 1 it "designates the whole cosmos."

[26] See Orlinsky, "Plain Meaning of Genesis 1:1–3," 208.

[27] Tsumura, *Creation and Destruction*, 35.

[28] Tsumura, *Creation and Destruction*, 43.

that in a general way Days 1–3 focus on giving form or structure to what is formless, and Days 4–6 focus on filling what is empty. As Goldingay remarks, "The sovereign creativity of God consisted in turning empty void into meaningful whole."[29]

Verse 2 anticipates what God will do in Days 1–2. The parallelism of the second and third clauses introduces a correspondence between "the watery depths" (תְּהוֹם, *tĕhôm*) and "the waters" (הַמָּיִם, *hammāyim*); both terms refer to the same object.[30] At the same time a contrast is drawn between "the darkness" and "the Spirit of God," which are said to be over "the surface of" the watery depths and the waters respectively. In the Hebrew text no verb is associated with the darkness; it is static over the watery depths. In marked contrast, the reference to the "Spirit of God" hovering over the waters gives a sense of expectation that something is about to happen. With a minimum of detail, verse 2 sets the scene for what will be described in Days 1 and 2 respectively, when first God separates the darkness by creating periods of light, forming day and night (vv. 3–5), and then, second, separates the waters by creating the "sky" (vv. 6–8). Since verse 2 prepares for what God will do in Days 1–2, involving the "darkness" and the "waters," there is no reason to assume that the circumstances described in verse 2 were not created by God (cf. Ps 148:4–5; Isa 45:7).

Opinion is divided over how the expression רוּחַ אֱלֹהִים (*rûaḥ ʾĕlōhîm*) should be understood. The word רוּחַ (*rûaḥ*) can mean "wind" or "spirit." While most English versions opt for the translation "Spirit of God" (e.g., CSB; ESV; KJV; NET; NIV; RSV; cf. JPS, which has "spirit of God"), several render it "a wind from God" (NRSV; NJPS; cf. NJB, which has "a divine wind" and NAB, which has "a mighty wind," understanding the term אֱלֹהִים [*ĕlōhîm*] as denoting a superlative). Wenham favors the translation "Wind of God" "as a concrete and vivid image of the Spirit of God."[31] Elsewhere in the Old Testament, the expression רוּחַ אֱלֹהִים (*rûaḥ ʾĕlōhîm*)

---

[29] John Goldingay, *Old Testament Theology: Israel's Gospel* (Downers Grove: InterVarsity Press Academic, 2003), 81.

[30] It is frequently claimed that by employing the term תְּהוֹם (*tĕhôm*), the author of Genesis is deliberately alluding to the Babylonian goddess Tiamat, who was slain by Marduk. This seems highly unlikely. The use of תְּהוֹם (*tĕhôm*) in Gen 49:25 suggests that the word was not always viewed negatively (cf. Prov 8:27–28) and there is no reason to assume a negative connotation in the present context, especially when it is used in parallel with "the waters" (הַמָּיִם, *hammāyim*).

[31] Wenham, *Genesis 1–15*, 17.

does not usually refer to a wind. More common is the idea that the Spirit of God empowers people to perform certain tasks (e.g., equipping Bezalel to supervise the construction of the portable sanctuary, Exod 31:3; 35:31; cf. Gen 41:38; Num 24:2; 1 Sam 10:10).

1:3–5. These verses, which record the first day of divine activity, establish a pattern that will be repeated throughout the remaining days. Each day begins with God speaking (vv. 3, 6, 9, 14, 20, 24; cf. vv. 11, 26, 28, 29) and ends with the refrain: "Evening came and then morning: ... day" (vv. 5, 8, 13, 19, 23, 31). Between these elements, there is regularly a movement from command, "Let ... be" (vv. 3, 6, 9, 14; cf. vv. 11, 20, 22, 24, 26), to fulfilment, "And it was so" (vv. 7, 9, 11, 15, 24, 30; cf. v. 3), to approval, "saw ... good" (vv. 4, 10, 12, 18, 21, 25, 31). Variations occur in order and wording, especially as the days progress. Day 1 provides the simplest sequence.

Throughout chapter 1, all that is created comes into existence through divine words of command. God merely speaks to form or fill. God's use of commands emphasizes his majestic power, highlighting the ease with which he undertakes the whole process. His word alone is sufficient to create all that exists in the cosmos. Yet, it would be a mistake to assume that God's creative activity never involves any actions on his part or always entails *creatio ex nihilo*. The picture is more complex, especially when the description of God's making of the man and the woman in Genesis 2 is brought into consideration. In addition, because elements within creation are assigned roles that will involve ongoing activity, the expectation is created that this is merely the beginning of what God has planned, not a completed account. While God's part in the initial process is viewed as "very good" (1:31) and he consequently rests (2:1–3), the focus of attention shifts to see how humans will fulfil the role that has been delegated to them.

Within Days 1–3 the creative process is marked by separations: light from darkness; water from water; dry land from water. The separation between light and darkness is understood not in terms of the physical qualities of light and darkness as electromagnetic radiation but in terms of the difference between "day" and "night" (v. 5). As Walton rightly observes the emphasis on Day 1 is about the ordering of time.[32] Day 1 describes the creation of alternating periods of light and darkness; it is

---

[32] Walton, "Creation," 163–64.

not simply about the creation of light after darkness. God establishes a rhythm of day followed by night, a pattern that will be repeated throughout the rest of chapter 1. The importance of this ordering is reinforced by the seven-day structure which gives shape to all that is recorded in 1:1–2:3. The separation of light from darkness will be mentioned later in Day 4, in connection with the creation of the "two great lights" (vv. 16–18). The introduction of the terms "day" and "night" in v. 5, followed by references to "evening" and "morning," all set within the context of a seven-day structure, suggests that the framework for this account of creation reflects the weekly experience of the Israelites, in which the seventh day was considered a day of rest. God's creative activity is set out here by analogy. As Gordon remarks, "It appears that the human experience of the working week has provided the construct within which the divine acts of creation and cessation from work are presented."[33]

The creation of "day" and "night" in Day 1 presents an unusual problem if this account of creation is understood as a logical, scientific account that is reported in chronological order. Only in Day 4 is reference made to the creation of "lights in the expanse of the sky to separate the day from the night" (v. 14). The correspondence between Days 1 and 4 is noteworthy, with light and darkness, day and night being mentioned in connection with both days. The simple distinction between day and night in Day 1 is expanded upon in Day 4 with mention of "signs for seasons and for days and years" (v. 14). Alongside this process of distinguishing, God names different items (vv. 5, 8, 10). Naming happens only on Days 1–3.

God's approval of what has occurred is conveyed through the common term טוֹב (*ṭôb*, "good"), which recurs throughout the chapter (vv. 4, 10, 12, 18, 21, 25, 31). While we might be inclined to imagine that the repeated use of טוֹב *ṭôb* "good" points to the perfection of all that is created, this is an unwarranted assumption. At one level, God's instructions for creatures to be fruitful and fill the earth implies that what God initiates is not the finished product. At another level, God's delegation of authority to humans to rule over the earth possibly hints that all is not perfect (see Comments on 1:26–31). This will become more apparent as the Genesis narrative unfolds. In the light of later developments, it would

---

[33] Gordon, "The Week That Made the World," 237. Collins, "Reading Genesis 1–11 with the Grain," 73–92, understands the days of Gen 1 to be analogical. Similarly, Averbeck, "Literary Day," 27, adopts an "analogical or, if you wish, anthropomorphic" approach.

seem somewhat naïve on the part of the author of Genesis 1 to claim that everything is perfect. If Genesis 1 describes a creation that is flawless in every way, it becomes difficult to account for the presence of evil in this world. Nevertheless, the specific actions that God undertakes in Genesis 1 as regards the creation of the earth and its creatures may be viewed as " very good" (1:31).

Unlike most English versions, in CSB verse 5 concludes with the statement: "There was an evening, and there was a morning: one day." Since this is the very first day to be created, and the reader has yet to be made aware of the existence of other days, the use of the cardinal "one" at the end of verse 5 is appropriate. Subsequently, ordinal numbers (e.g., second, third) are used to number the days. The term "day" at the end of verse 5 denotes something different from what is meant when God calls the light "day" in the same verse. The "one day" includes a period of darkness, whereas the previous mention of "day" in verse 5 excludes darkness. Everything that has been described from the start of verse 3 to the end of verse 5 composes "one day." Evening and morning alone do not form "one day," but merely mark the start and end of darkness/night. On this basis, and as is common elsewhere in the Pentateuch, the day is perceived as starting with sunrise.[34]

1:6–8. If Day 1 is God's response to the "darkness" mentioned in verse 2, Day 2 focuses on the "waters" introduced in the same verse. As darkness is separated by a period of light to form day and night, the waters are separated by an "expanse" (רָקִיעַ, *rāqîaᶜ*). How ancient Israelites perceived this expanse/firmament is difficult to know; outside of the present chapter the term is used infrequently in the Old Testament (Ps 19:2; 150:1; Ezek 1:22–23, 25–26; 10:1; Dan 12:3). God names the "expanse" שָׁמַיִם (*šāmayim*). Like the majority of modern English versions, CSB adopts the translation "sky" (cf. NAB; NET; NIV; NLT; NRSV; NJPS). Some English versions prefer the rendering "heaven/Heaven" (ESV; JPS; NAS; KJV; NJB; RSV). Later in chapter 1, the expression רְקִיעַ הַשָּׁמַיִם (*rĕqîaᶜ haššāmayim*) is the location associated with the sun, moon, and stars (vv. 14–15, 17) and flying birds

[34] See David Miano, *Shadow on the Steps: Time Measurement in Ancient Israel*, Resources for Biblical Study 64 (Atlanta: SBL, 2010), 8–13. The idea of the day starting with sunset reflects Babylonian influence after the fall of Jerusalem in 586 BC. Before the exile, Israelites viewed the day as starting with sunrise.

(v. 20).[35] The sky/heaven is the first region to be given a name. We must wait for Day 3 for names to be assigned to "the gathering of the waters" under the sky and the "dry land" (v. 10). The end of the second day is marked by the refrain that mentions evening and morning (v. 8).

1:9–13. Day 3 builds on Day 2 by focusing on the water under the sky. By gathering these to one place, God causes dry land to appear (v. 9). In what is the final act of naming in the chapter, God designates the waters "seas" and the dry land "earth" (v. 10). With this, three distinctive regions are established, and in due course each will be filled with its own kind of mobile inhabitants. The creation of these three regions is an important feature of the account. This is underlined by the fact that the only names given by God in chapter 1, apart from "day" and "night" are "sky," "earth" (denoting dry land, not the entire planet), and "seas."

Day 3 introduces a variation to the pattern found in Days 1–2. There is a second command involving the production of vegetation (v. 11). This development is closely tied to the creation of the dry land, for the "earth" is to produce vegetation. Strikingly, God's instructions in verse 11 are echoed by an almost word-for-word description of their fulfilment in verse 12. Through this repetition attention is drawn to the concept of plants producing seeds "according to their kinds." The introduction of the concept of "seed" is noteworthy, for the entire book of Genesis will trace a particular line of human "seed." Since Day 3 involves two creative activities, the expression "And God saw that it was good" occurs twice (vv. 10, 12).

1:14–19. With Day 4, we begin to witness the filling of the various regions that have been formed in Days 1–3. God places "lights" in "the expanse of the sky" (v. 14). By not using the nouns "sun" and "moon" to denote the two great lights, God's command highlights the link that exists between the "lights" (מְאֹרֹת, *mĕʾōrōt*; plural of מָאוֹר, *māʾôr*) and "light" (אוֹר, *ʾôr*). This establishes a strong correspondence between Days 1 and 4; the greater and lesser lights rule over the day and night respectively "to separate light from darkness." In addition, to distinguishing day from night, the great lights also have a bearing on the timing of "seasons"[36]

---

[35] Like other terms used in this chapter, שָׁמַיִם (*šāmayim*) may denote different things at different points in the narrative. The use of the expression "expanse of the sky" may be intended to distinguish this region from heaven where God is present.

[36] Robert P. Gordon, "Evensong in Eden: As It Probably Was Not in the Beginning," in *Leshon Limmudim: Essays on the Language and Literature of the Hebrew Bible in Honour of A. A.*

and "years." As in Day 1, the ordering of time is the primary concern as regards what is being created by God. The motif of ruling will reappear in Day 6, when God delegates responsibility to humans to govern the earth.

1:20–23. Regarding Day 5 the focus of attention is on the creatures that will fill the "waters" and the "expanse of the sky" (v. 20), the two regions that are distinguished on Day 2 prior to the creation of the dry land on Day 3. For the first time, animated creatures are mentioned, with each type being associated with a particular region. Something of the variety of the creatures in the water is conveyed through the mention of the "large sea-creatures and every living creature that moves and swarms in the water, according to their kinds" (v. 21). After seeing that everything is "good" (v. 21), God blesses them. The emphasis on multiplying, which is linked to both water creatures and birds, implies that the process of filling these two regions will require time. It is noteworthy that in addressing the sea creatures, God uses expressions that will later be applied to humans; they are to "be fruitful, multiply, and fill" (v. 22; cf. v. 28). Repetition in Genesis 1 conveys a sense of order to all that God does.

1:24–31. As might be expected given what has already been said, Day 6 is about the filling of the dry land/earth. The importance of this stage is underlined by the details provided; the report of this day exceeds in length what is said about any other day. As with Days 1–2 and 4–5, some correspondence is created between Day 3 and Day 6. Not only do Days 3 and 6 have a particular interest in the dry land, named "earth" in verse 10, but both days mention the vegetation that grows on the earth (vv. 11–12, 29–30). In addition, on both days God speaks twice (1:9, 11, 24, 26) and observes twice that the outcome is "good" (1:10, 12, 25, 31).

On Day 6, God commands that the earth should bring forth "living creatures" (v. 24). His words underline that he is initiating a program of activity that involves the participation of creation itself. As Ollenburger notes:

> While God alone acts as creator in this artistic and liturgical account, the objects of God's creation themselves become subjects, actively participating in the emergence of a well-ordered world. For example, rather than simply speaking an-

---

Macintosh, ed. David A. Baer and Robert P. Gordon (London: T&T Clark, 2013), 25, helpfully observes that the term מוֹעֲדִים (*môʿădîm*, "seasons") is best rendered "festivals" (cf. NJB; NIV 2011 has "sacred times"). These are times set according to the lunar calendar.

> imals into existence, God assigns this function to the earth: "Let the earth bring forth" (*tôṣēʾ hāʾāreṣ*, v. 24). This assignment does not compromise God's singular status as the creator. As first to the earth, so God also speaks to the waters: "Let the waters swarm with swarms of living creatures" (v. 20)—but God then creates (*bārāʾ*) those very creatures (v. 21). The earth and the waters do not cocreate with God but, rather, respond to God's initiative.[37]

By involving creation, God indicates that his commands begin a process that will require time to be completed. While God himself will finish all that is necessary for his plans for the earth to be completed (see 2:1–3), Genesis 1 records the first stage. There is an expectation of more to come.[38] This is only the prelude to a longer story.

The description of the process by which the earth will be filled begins by focusing on three main categories of land animals: "livestock, creatures that crawl, and the wildlife of the earth" (v. 24). Some commentators assume that the distinction between creatures that crawl and the wildlife of the earth is one of size, the former being small and the latter large. Provan, however, argues that "wildlife of the earth" refers to predators, but "creatures that crawl" (רֶמֶשׂ, *remeś*) refers to non-predatory animals.[39] The categories are repeated in verse 25 with minor variations in wording and in a different order, possibly implying that there is no hierarchy intended by the sequence in which they are mentioned. Once more God approves of the outcome (v. 25).

As with Day 3, a second divine command is given on Day 6. Importantly, this addresses the creation of humans, bringing God's creative activity to

---

[37] Ben C. Ollenburger, "Creation and Peace: Creator and Creature in Genesis 1–11," in *The Old Testament in the Life of God's People: Essays in Honor of Elmer A. Martens*, ed. Jon M. Isaak (Winona Lake: Eisenbrauns, 2009), 145.

[38] Zoltan Dörnyei, *Progressive Creation and the Struggles of Humanity in the Bible: A Canonical Narrative Interpretation* (Eugene: Pickwick, 2018), contends that the primal creation is followed by a long process of transformation.

[39] Iain W. Provan, *Discovering Genesis: Content, Interpretation, Reception*, Discovering Biblical Texts (London: SPCK, 2015), 123–24. Picking up on the issue of predation, Waltke and Fredricks, *Genesis*, 64, comment, "The contrast between domesticated and wild animals distinguishes cattle from carnivores." Averbeck, "Literary Day," 24, draws on Ps 104:20–21 to argue that the text of Genesis 1 "is neither saying directly nor intending to suggest that there were no carnivorous animals in the original creation." See also Ronald E. Osborn, *Death before the Fall : Biblical Literalism and the Problem of Animal Suffering* (Downers Grove: InterVarsity Press Academic, 2014).

a climax. Not surprisingly, the statement "Let us make man in our image, according to our likeness" has prompted much discussion. Scholars have debated at length the significance of God's use of the plural "us" and "our." In a narrative that is strongly monotheistic in outlook, the use of the plural is exceptionally unusual.[40] Clines helpfully categorizes proposed interpretations under six headings: (1) "an unassimilated fragment of myth" (an older polytheistic tradition is preserved in the present text); (2) "address to creation" ("us" includes what God has already made); (3) "plural of majesty" (the royal "we"); (4) "address to the heavenly court" (God includes the heavenly beings that surround his throne); (5) "self-deliberation or self-summons" (God addresses himself); and (6) "duality within the Godhead" (this is evidence of a plurality within the deity).[41] Of these possibilities, a majority of commentators lean toward either (4) or (5), but almost everyone recognizes that there are drawbacks to these proposals.[42] Supporting the tentative suggestion of Clines, Keiser offers a compelling case in favor of a plurality in God's being.[43] In doing so, he draws attention to the way in which the narrator in verse 27 qualifies the statement, "So God created the human in his own image," by paralleling the singular object "him (in the image of God)" with the plural object "them (male and female)." Keiser contends that the references to God and humankind as both singular and plural establishes a correspondence between them. He suggests that "the text's presentation of the plurality of humanity in terms of sexual diversity in some manner reflects something of the unity in the plurality of God."[44] Coming to a similar conclusion, Mathews states that "a plurality within the unity of the Godhead may be derived from the

---

[40] A further example of God's use of the plural "us" comes in Gen 3:22: "the man has become like one of us, knowing good and evil." God's words recall what the serpent says in Gen 3:5: "you will be like God, knowing good and evil."

[41] David J. A. Clines, "The Image of God in Man," *TynBul* (1968): 63–69; cf. Gerhard F. Hasel, "Meaning of 'Let Us' in Gn 1:26," *AUSS* 13 (1975): 58–66.

[42] In favor of (4) are, among others, Gerhard von Rad, *Genesis: A Commentary*, 2nd ed., OTL (London: SCM, 1972), 58–59; Wenham, *Genesis 1–15*, 27–28. View (5) is supported by, among others, U. Cassuto, *A Commentary on the Book of Genesis: Part I: From Adam to Noah* (Jerusalem: Magnes, 1961), 55; Claus Westermann, *Genesis 1–11: A Commentary*, trans. John J. Scullion (Minneapolis: Augsburg, 1984), 144–45; C. John Collins, *Genesis 1–4: A Linguistic, Literary, and Theological Commentary* (Phillipsburg: P&R, 2006), 59–61.

[43] Thomas A. Keiser, "The Divine Plural: A Literary-Contextual Argument of Plurality in the Godhead," *JSOT* 34 (2009): 131–46. See also Hasel, "Meaning of 'Let Us' in Gn 1:26," 58–66.

[44] Keiser, "The Divine Plural," 137.

passage,"[45] although he correctly notes that the use of the plural is insufficient to establish the Christian doctrine of the Trinity. God's remarks are consistent with the concept of the Trinity, but there is insufficient evidence in Genesis 1 to determine the nature of the unity and plurality that is associated with God. Importantly, the author of Genesis implies that something of God's nature is reflected in the way in which a man and a woman complement one another, a theme that is developed at length in 2:4–25. In the human relationship there is both unity and plurality with the two becoming "one flesh" (2:24).[46] This sense of unity involving male and female suggests that there is a relational dimension to God's nature.

Less controversial is the scholarly discussion concerning the word אָדָם (*ʾādām*), translated "man."[47] The term is introduced here, not as a proper name "Adam," but as a generic term denoting humankind. As the final clause of verse 27 makes clear, the word אָדָם (*ʾādām*) is not gender specific.[48] For this reason, Alter makes a good case for translating הָאָדָם (*hāʾādām*) in verse 27 as "the human."[49]

In a significant statement, God speaks of creating humans "in our image, according to our likeness" (v. 26). The first of these terms, צֶלֶם (*ṣelem*, "image") is repeated twice in verse 27. From a survey of the occurrences of צֶלֶם (*ṣelem*) in the Old Testament it is evident that the term normally denotes a physical object that resembles another.[50] As for the term דְּמוּת (*dĕmût*), it conveys a sense of resemblance.[51] These two

---

[45] Mathews, *Genesis 1-11:26*, 163.

[46] The man says of the woman, "This one, at last, is bone of my bone and flesh of my flesh" (2:23).

[47] On the complex issue of how to understand best the use of the word אָדָם (*ʾādām*), see R. S. Hess, "Splitting the Adam: The Usage of *ʾādām* in Genesis i-v," in *Studies in the Pentateuch*, ed. J. A. Emerton, VTSup 41 (Leiden: Brill, 1990), 1–15; Richard S. Hess, "Adam, Father, He: Gender Issues in Hebrew Translation," *BT* 56 (2005): 146–47.

[48] Grammatically it is masculine, but it is worth noting that the feminine form אֲדָמָה (*ʾădāmâ*) means "ground/earth" and not "woman." The term אָדָם (*ʾādām*) draws attention to the close relationship that exists between humans and the ground. This is highlighted in 2:7, which speaks of God forming הָאָדָם (*hāʾādām*) from the dust of the ground (cf. 3:19).

[49] Robert Alter, *Genesis* (New York: Norton, 1996), 5; cf. Richard M. Davidson, *Flame of Yahweh: Sexuality in the Old Testament* (Peabody: Hendrickson, 2007), 22–24.

[50] Gen 1:26–27; 5:3; 9:6; Num 33:52; 1 Sam 6:5, 11; 2 Kgs 11:18; 2 Chr 23:17; Pss 39:6 [Heb. 7]; 73:20; Ezek 7:20; 16:17; 23:14; Amos 5:26.

[51] Gen 1:26; 5:1, 3; 2 Kgs 16:10; 2 Chr 4:3; Ps 58:5; Isa 13:4; 40:18; Ezek 1:5, 10, 13, 16, 22, 26, 28; 8:2; 10:1, 10, 21–22; 23:15; Dan 10:16.

nouns appear to be synonyms.[52] Most interesting is the use of the terms צֶלֶם (*ṣelem*, "image"), and דְּמוּת (*dĕmût*, "likeness") in Genesis 5:3: "Adam was 130 years old when he fathered a son in his likeness, according to his image, and named him Seth" (5:3). Echoing what is said in 1:26, but reversing the order of the words, Seth is viewed as resembling his father, although viewed as a unique person in his own right.

Over the centuries, the concept of people being made in the *imago Dei* has provoked considerable discussion.[53] From the text of Genesis itself, the best clue to understand its significance comes in the statement, "They will rule the fish of the sea, the birds of the sky, the livestock, the whole earth, and the creatures that crawl on the earth" (v. 26). Unfortunately, many English versions fail to appreciate the significance of the simple or weak *waw* "and" that is attached to the *yiqtol* verb יִרְדּוּ (*yirdû*, "they will rule"). In this context the conjunction has the sense "so that" (cf. NET; NIV).[54] God's purpose behind making people in his image and likeness is tied to their role in ruling over the earth. According to Ollenburger, "Humanity's creation in (or as) the image of God and on the model of God's likeness has as its purpose the designated responsibility for human beings to rule or to exercise governance over or among the other creatures."[55] This connection

---

[52] The same Greek term εἰκών (*eikōn*) is used in 1:27 and 5:1 to translate צֶלֶם (*ṣelem*) and דְּמוּת (*dĕmût*) respectively. Further evidence pointing to the terms being synonyms come in a ninth-century BC statue that has a bilingual text in Assyrian and Aramaic. Millard and Bordreuil, "Statue from Syria," 140, write: "The statue is referred to by two Aramaic words, both with Hebrew cognates. The initial word of the inscription introduces it as *dmwt'*, "the image." At the start the second part the word used in the Aramaic is *ṣlm*, "statue," in the Assyrian its cognate *ṣalmu*. This is not a means of distinguishing the two parts of the inscription, for *dmwt'* reappears three lines later. These two words in their Hebrew dress are the famous "image" and "likeness" in God's creation of man in Gen 1:26; cf. 5:3. Their clear application to this stone statue, the only ancient occurrence of the words as a pair outside the OT, provides fuel for the debate over the meaning of the clause in Genesis 1."

[53] See Anthony A. Hoekema, *Created in God's Image* (Grand Rapids: Eerdmans, 1986), 33–65; Gunnlaugur A. Jónsson, *The Image of God: Genesis 1:26–28 in a Century of Old Testament Research*, ConBOT 26 (Stockholm: Almqvist & Wiksell, 1988).

[54] The cohortative ("let us make") is followed by וְיִרְדּוּ (*wĕyirdû*). When the sequence cohortative + *wĕ* + *yiqtol* is used, the *yiqtol* may indicate purpose or result; cf. S. R. Driver, *A Treatise on the Use of the Tenses in Hebrew and Some Other Syntactical Questions*, 10th ed. (Oxford: Clarendon, 1892), 64–65; *GKC* §109f; Thomas O. Lambdin, *Introduction to Biblical Hebrew* (London: Darton, Longman and Todd, 1973), 119. According to Middleton, *The Liberating Image*, 53, "The syntax ... points to 'rule' as the *purpose*, not simply the consequence or result, of the *imago Dei*."

[55] Ollenburger, "Creation and Peace," 146.

between "image" and "ruling" is reinforced by the emphasis that is given in verse 28 to humans exercising authority over the creatures that occupy the three regions (sky, land, and sea) created by God. As Hart remarks, "Exercising royal dominion over the earth as God's representative is the basic purpose for which God created man."[56] For humans to be made in the "image of God" is to be given regal status relative to other earthly creatures.

God commissions humans to govern all land animals, birds, and fish. By repeating this point twice within three verses, the author of Genesis 1 emphasizes God's delegation of authority to humankind to rule over the earth on his behalf. This underscores the special status of humans: "One receives the impression that this resemblance to Elohim is a concession to human nature beyond its due, a gratuitous elevation of man to a higher level: else, why the solemn deliberation preceding the act of creation, and why the exultant hymn which follows it, stressing not so much man's creation as his creation in the image of God?"[57]

In the light of how Genesis 1 associates the "image of God" with humans ruling over the earth, it is noteworthy that in the ANE, in both Egypt and Mesopotamia, the phrase "image of God" was commonly linked to kings. The king was viewed as a living image of a god. By way of illustration, Ramesses II (1290–1224 BC) describes his divine image status with these words:

> Utterance of the divine king, Lord of the Two Lands, lord of the form of Khepri, in whose limbs is Re, who came forth from Re, whom Ptah-Tatenen begat, King Ramses II, given life; to his father, from whom he came forth, Tatenen, father of the gods: "I am thy son whom thou hast placed upon thy throne. Thou hast assigned to me thy kingdom, thou hast fashioned me in thy likeness and thy form, which thou hast assigned to me and hast created."[58]

As this quotation reveals, by associating kingship with being made in the image of Re, Ramesses claims divine authority to rule over his nation.[59]

---

[56] Hart, "Genesis 1:1–2:3 as a Prologue," 322.

[57] David Tobin Asselin, "Notion of Dominion in Genesis 1–3," CBQ 16 (1954): 283.

[58] James Henry Breasted, *Ancient Records of Egypt: The Nineteenth Dynasty*, 4 vols. (Chicago: University of Chicago Press, 1906), 3:181. For further examples, see Middleton, *The Liberating Image*, 108–22.

[59] The name Ramesses means "son of Ra."

While in the ANE the concept of being made in the image of a deity was linked to individual kings, setting them apart from others, Genesis 1 undermines the idea that royalty is for only a selected few. There is a democratization of royalty in Genesis 1.[60] However, as we shall observe in the rest of Genesis, humans tragically fail to exercise dominion as God's vicegerents. Although they are created with the capacity to rule, they abuse this ability, filling the earth with violence (6:11–13).

God delegates authority to humans to rule over the earth and all its creatures. In verses 26 and 28 the verb רדה (*rdh,* "to rule") is used. While רדה (*rdh*) is not always used to denote royal dominion, the verb comes in Psalm 72:8 to describe the reign of a righteous king over the earth. Importantly, Hart writes, "The command to 'have dominion' (רְדוּ, vv. 26, 28) is not merely a declaration that man will enjoy kingly rank; it is the apportioning of a task, an ongoing task which would be well translated by the more modern word 'manage.' "[61] Although these verses are often interpreted as being anti-environmental,[62] nothing in verse 26 implies that humans are to exploit the natural world for their own benefit. As Middleton remarks,

> the writer of Genesis 1 portrays God as king presiding over "heaven and earth," an ordered and harmonious realm in which each creature manifests the will of the creator and is thus declared "good." Humanity is created *like* this God, with the special role of representing or imaging God's rule in the world.[63]

---

[60] Hart, "Genesis 1:1–2:3 as a Prologue," 319; Middleton, *The Liberating Image*, 121, 204.

[61] Hart, "Genesis 1:1–2:3 as a Prologue," 323.

[62] James Limburg, "The Responsibility of Royalty: Genesis 1–11 and the Care of the Earth," *Word & World* 11 (1991): 125, observes, "The Judeo-Christian tradition continues to be understood as anti-environmental, and the *locus classicus* for those making this charge continues to be the text about dominion in Gen 1." Alluding to this passage, Lynn White, "The Historical Roots of Our Ecological Crisis," *Science* 155 (1967): 1207, comments, "Hence we shall continue to have a worsening ecologic crisis until we reject the Christian axiom that nature has no reason for existence save to serve man." In the light of this comment, it is worth recalling the comment of Christ, the perfect vicegerent, that he came to serve and not to be served (Mark 10:45).

[63] Middleton, *The Liberating Image*, 26. Provan, *Discovering Genesis*, 57, writes, "The dominion given to human beings in Genesis 1–2, then, is not to be thought of in terms of *lording it over* the rest of creation, but in terms of just governance on behalf of the creator" (italics in original). Craig G. Bartholomew, "The Theology of Place in Genesis 1–3," in McConville and Möller, *Reading the Law*, 181, comments, "Dominion is best understood as a royal stewardship in which humankind's role is to serve, develop and indwell the creation such that it is enhanced and God is honoured."

While there is every expectation that humanity's oversight of the world should mirror God's rule over the whole of creation, the introduction of the verb כבשׁ (*kbš*, "make subservient") in verse 28 gives cause for further reflection. Whereas the verb רדה (*rdh*, "to rule") conveys a sense of authority being exercised for the benefit of all parties, the verb כבשׁ (*kbš*) carries connotations of force being used to ensure compliance. Although Ollenburger contends that כבשׁ (*kbš*) applies here to agricultural activity that "requires some governance of animals,"[64] Möller suggests that "the human task envisaged here may involve some kind of struggle."[65] While it is important not to misinterpret what is said here, a forward glance to Genesis 3 reveals that Adam and Eve fail to exercise authority over the serpent. By rejecting God's instructions and heeding the serpent, they neglect to fulfil their mandate to rule over the earth and its creatures. By their actions, they reject the hierarchy instituted by God in 1:26–28. Possibly the use of כבשׁ (*kbš*) in verse 28 anticipates the challenge the human couple will face from the serpent. While no clarification is provided in the opening chapters of Genesis to explain the existence of a creature that openly challenges God's authority, the presence of the serpent reveals that everything on earth is not perfect prior to Adam and Eve's rejection of God's instructions.

As well as ruling over other creatures, the first human couple, as God's representatives, are instructed to be fruitful and fill the earth (v. 28). The wording of verse 28 recalls verse 22, which focuses on the creatures associated with the sea and air. Implicit in verse 28 is the idea that God's authority will be extended throughout the earth as people increase in number and disperse outwards. According to Welker:

> The biological couple that is supposed to multiply and spread is destined to have dominion over the earth and the animals. We must not let Gen. 1:26 split apart nor let Gen. 1:27 and 1:28 go their separate ways. Both being fruitful and multiplying, on the one hand, and subduing the earth and having dominion over it, on the other hand, stand in close connection to each other.[66]

---

[64] Ollenburger, "Creation and Peace," 147.

[65] Möller, "Images of God and Creation in Genesis 1–2," 23. Provan, *Discovering Genesis*, 64, comments that "there are already forces in God's good world that *require* being ruled and subdued" (italics in original).

[66] Michael Welker, "Creation and the Image of God: Their Understanding in Christian Tradition and the Biblical Grounds," *Journal of Ecumenical Studies* 34 (1997): 446.

Verses 26–27 suggest that a correlation should be drawn between humans filling the earth and their mandate to rule over it. In the light of this, some scholars suggest that a knowledge of the ANE background sheds valuable light on this instruction to fill the earth. In the ANE a ruler's image was set up in distant parts of his kingdom to indicate that his authority reached there.[67] Von Rad writes:

> The close relation of the term for God's image with that for the commission to exercise dominion emerges quite clearly when we have understood *ṣelem* as a plastic image. Just as powerful earthly kings, to indicate their claim to dominion, erect an image of themselves in the provinces of their empire where they do not personally appear, so man is placed upon earth in God's image as God's sovereign emblem. He is really only God's representative, summoned to maintain and enforce God's claim to dominion over the earth. The decisive thing about man's similarity to God, therefore, is his function in the non-human world.[68]

Adopting a similar view, Averbeck comments, "Like the statue of a king, we are the 'statue' of a king too, the divine king, and we have been set up in the midst of God's creation to represent him and his interests."[69] As images of God, humans are to rule over the earth as his vicegerents, and the ever-increasing human population is expected to extend God's kingdom throughout the earth.

By emphasizing that humans are to rule over all other creatures on earth, Genesis 1 anticipates the events recorded in Genesis 3. By failing as God's vicegerents to exercise authority over the serpent, the human couple betray God. Genesis 1 also prepares for the events in Genesis 3 by highlighting God's provision of food for humans derived from the fruit of trees (v. 29). As Genesis 3:6 states, the woman was attracted to eat from the fruit of the tree of the knowledge of good and evil because she saw that "the fruit was good for food and pleasing to the eye." Verse 30, however, implies that other creatures will eat "green plants." Later, this distinction has a bearing on the punishment that God imposes upon the man (3:18).

---

[67] von Rad, *Theology of Israel's Historical Traditions*, 146–47.

[68] von Rad, *Genesis*, 59–60.

[69] Averbeck, "Literary Day," 25.

After creating humans in his image, God pronounces a final evaluation of all that has been done. It is "very good" (v. 31). Cassuto writes, "An analogy might be found in an artist who, having completed his masterpiece, steps back a little and surveys his handiwork with delight, for both in detail and in its entirety it had emerged perfect from his hand."[70] In a similar vein, Childs comments, "God pronounced his workmanship good and blessed it. The creation rested in its perfection; no further work was needed."[71] However, contrary to what Cassuto and Childs claim, Genesis 1 implies that the earth is not complete; it has yet to be filled. In the light of this, it is premature to claim that creation is "perfect." More helpful is Westermann's suggestion that "the meaning [of טוֹב] is rather functional: 'good for ...' The world which God created and devised as good is the world in which history can begin and reach its goal and so fulfill the purpose of creation."[72] Recalling the use of the term "subdue" in verse 28, Fretheim notes, "The word *subdue* makes it clear that the divine evaluation 'good' does not mean that the creation is 'perfect' in the sense of needing no further development or attention or, for that matter, being unable to fail."[73]

While we must be cautious not to assume that creation is perfect due to God's remark that all is "very good" (v. 31), the repeated use of the term "good" throughout Genesis 1 strongly conveys the idea that God himself is both good and the one who determines what is good. This has a bearing on how we perceive the subsequent story, which involves the human couple desiring to "be like God, knowing good and evil" (3:5). Dörnyei contends that "the newly created material world was pronounced 'very good' at the end of the sixth day not because it was complete and perfected but rather because it contained all that was needed to set into motion a progression that will eventually culminate in the realization of the kingdom of God on earth."[74]

2:1–3. Day 7 displays a significant break from the pattern that has been repeated throughout Days 1–6. There is no record of God adding to

---

[70] Cassuto, *From Adam to Noah*, 59.

[71] Brevard S. Childs, *Biblical Theology of the Old and New Testaments: Theological Reflection on the Christian Bible* (London: SCM, 1992), 385.

[72] Westermann, *Genesis 1–11*, 166.

[73] Fretheim, *God and World in the Old Testament*, 52 (italics in original). Later, he writes, "That the divine command, 'subdue the earth,' is needed at all means that the evaluative word *good* does not mean perfect; the creation is not a static reality, forever fixed just as God initially created it" (276). Provan, *Discovering Genesis*, 63–64, makes a similar point.

[74] Dörnyei, *Progressive Creation*, 40.

what he has already formed and filled. He has completed "the heavens and the earth and everything in them" (v. 1). To emphasize the completion of God's work, the verb כלה (*klh*, "to complete/finish") is repeated at the start of verse 2.[75] With the completion of all that he intended to do, God "rests on the seventh day" (v. 2). There is no reason to assume that this rest is due to tiredness on the part of God. The divine activity described in chapter 1 appears to be undertaken with the greatest of ease. The verb וַיִּשְׁבֹּת (*wayyišbōt*), translated "and he rested" in CSB, might be better rendered "and he ceased" (cf. NET; NJPS).[76] Having stopped work, God blesses the seventh day and makes it holy.

Interestingly, verses 2–3 use the term מְלַאכְתּוֹ (*mĕlaʾktô*, "his work") three times with reference to what God has done. Almost always in the Old Testament, this noun denotes human activity (e.g., Gen 39:11; Exod 12:16; 20:9–10). Drawing on this observation, Hart remarks, "The use of this word is surprising, since one of the author's emphases throughout the chapter is on the uniqueness of the work of creation; the most probable reason for its use is that it was intended to emphasize the correspondence between God's work and man's."[77] The pattern of six days of work provides a model for humans to follow, but this, as Wenham notes, "does not necessarily imply that the six days of creation are the same as human days."[78] In line with this, in discussing Exodus 20:11, Shead notes that Genesis 2:3a speaks of God blessing "the seventh day," whereas the Decalogue speaks of YHWH blessing "the Sabbath day." He comments, "The altered quotation compares the Israelite Sabbath to the Seventh Day, not in order to equate those two days in every respect, but rather to show that God's action of blessing and sanctifying applies equally to both. Verse 11b is a shorthand way of saying, 'which is why Yahweh blessed not only the seventh day, but also the Sabbath.'"[79] Given the differences in wording between the two verses, it is erroneous to view Exodus 20:11b as quoting Genesis 2:3a. Strikingly, there is no mention in Genesis 2 of the ending of Day

---

75 The passive form (*pual*) of the verb is used in v. 1, but the active form (*piel*) comes in v. 2, with God as the subject.

76 Exod 23:12 brings together the verbs שׁבת (*šbt*, "to stop working") and נוח (*nwḥ*, "to rest"). In this context the first action provides the conditions for the second to take place.

77 Hart, "Genesis 1:1–2:3 as a Prologue," 316.

78 Wenham, *Genesis 1–15*, 40.

79 Andrew G. Shead, "Sabbath," in Alexander and Rosner, *New Dictionary of Biblical Theology*, 746,

7, unlike Days 1–6. In keeping with the comments about God having finished his work of creation, there is no suggestion that this "week" of special divine activity will be followed by another. The idea of humans enjoying the same experience of rest is picked up by later biblical writers (e.g., Ps 95:11; Heb 3:11; 4:3, 5).

Bridge

As the opening section of Genesis, 1:1–2:3 sets the scene for all that follows. Emphasizing God's creative activity in making the world, this passage proclaims that there is only one God, who exists without rivals.[80] In contrast to the polytheistic outlook of other ANE cultures, Genesis 1 presents God as an omnipotent creator. As Waltke and Fredricks remark, "His creation reveals his immeasurable power and might, his bewildering imagination and wisdom, his immortality and transcendence, ultimately leaving the finite mortal in mystery."[81] By seeing God as the ultimate creator of everything that exists, Genesis 1 presents a doctrine of creation that

> is preeminently an affirmation about the sovereignty of God and the absolute dependence of all creatures. To say that Yahweh made the earth is to confess that it belongs to its Maker; Yahweh is its Owner (Pss. 24:1–2; 89:11[12]; 95:5). Nothing in the realm of creation should be glorified, for the creation points beyond itself to the God who is high and lifted up and is therefore worthy of the praise of human beings and all other creatures.[82]

In addition to proclaiming the absolute sovereignty of God over all that he alone has created, Genesis 1 introduces the idea of a personal God who establishes relationships with others. While the relational aspect of God's nature is revealed more fully in subsequent chapters of Genesis,

---

[80] Gordon J. Wenham, *Rethinking Genesis 1–11: Gateway to the Bible: The Didsbury Lectures 2013*, Didsbury Lecture Series (Eugene: Cascade, 2015), 14, comments, "The God of Genesis is unique and without rivals."

[81] Waltke and Fredricks, Genesis, 59. Fretheim, *God and World in the Old Testament*, 270–71, writes, "Genesis 1 stresses the divine initiative, imagination, transcendence, and power. ... The placement of Genesis 1 suggests that these divine characteristics should stand at the beginning and in the foreground in any discussion of creation."

[82] Bernhard W. Anderson, *From Creation to New Creation: Old Testament Perspectives* (Minneapolis: Fortress, 1994), 28. Wenham, *Genesis 1–15*, 10, writes, "Gen 1 is more than a repudiation of contemporary oriental creation myths; it is a triumphant invocation of the God who has created all men and an invitation to all humanity to adore him who has made them in his own image."

it is already evident in his decision to create humans in his own image. Importantly, the biblical portrayal of a personal creator stands in sharp contrast to the concept of an impersonal creation that is a result of mass, energy, or matter, or all three in combination, plus time and chance.

By commanding humans to exercise authority over all other earthly creatures, God establishes a hierarchical order, which he declares to be "very good." Implicit in God's instructions is the expectation that humans will rule over other earthly creatures as God would govern them. Delegated to be God's vicegerents, humans enjoy a uniquely privileged position. Yet, as we shall see, they disastrously fail to fulfill their divine appointment when confronted by the mysterious serpent, which successfully tempts them to disregard God's instructions. The serpent's actions need to be understood against the background of humans having been commissioned to be God's vicegerents on earth with the expectation that they shall rule over all the animals.

II. The Offspring of the Heavens and the Earth (2:4–4:26)

A. The Man and Woman in the Garden of Eden (2:4–25)

> 4 These are the records of the heavens and the earth, concerning their
> creation. At the time that the LORD God made the earth and the heavens,
> 5 no shrub of the field had yet grown on the land, and no plant of the
> field had yet sprouted, for the LORD God had not made it rain on the land,
> and there was no man to work the ground. 6 But mist would come up
> from the earth and water all the ground. 7 Then the LORD God formed
> the man out of the dust from the ground and breathed the breath of
> life into his nostrils, and the man became a living being.
>
> 8 The LORD God planted a garden in Eden, in the east, and there he placed
> the man he had formed. 9 The LORD God caused to grow out of the ground
> every tree pleasing in appearance and good for food, including the tree
> of life in the middle of the garden, as well as the tree of the knowledge
> of good and evil.
>
> 10 A river went out from Eden to water the garden. From there it divided
> and became the source of four rivers. 11 The name of the first is Pishon,
> which flows through the entire land of Havilah, where there is gold. 12
> Gold from that land is pure; bdellium and onyx are also there. 13 The
> name of the second river is Gihon, which flows through the entire
> land of Cush. 14 The name of the third river is Tigris, which runs east of
> Assyria. And the fourth river is the Euphrates.

[15] The LORD God took the man and placed him in the garden of Eden to
work it and watch over it. [16] And the LORD God commanded the man,
"You are free to eat from any tree of the garden, [17] but you must not eat
from the tree of the knowledge of good and evil, for on the day you eat
from it, you will certainly die." [18] Then the LORD God said, "It is not good
for the man to be alone. I will make a helper corresponding to him." [19]
The LORD God formed out of the ground every wild animal and every
bird of the sky, and brought each to the man to see what he would call
it. And whatever the man called a living creature, that was its name. [20]
The man gave names to all the livestock, to the birds of the sky, and to
every wild animal; but for the man no helper was found corresponding
to him. [21] So the LORD God caused a deep sleep to come over the man,
and he slept. God took one of his ribs and closed the flesh at that place.
[22] Then the LORD God made the rib he had taken from the man into a
woman and brought her to the man. [23] And the man said:

> This one, at last, is bone of my bone and flesh of my flesh;
> this one will be called "woman," for she was taken from man.

[24] This is why a man leaves his father and mother and bonds with his
wife, and they become one flesh. [25] Both the man and his wife were
naked, yet felt no shame.

Context

The opening section of Genesis provides a very distinctive, panoramic overview of God's creative activity. Importantly, it sets the scene for the events that are about to unfold in 2:4–3:24. Having introduced the three regions for animated life—land, sea and air—and their respective inhabitants, the next section of Genesis offers a close-up description of events that take place on land, centering on the creation of the human couple and their presence within a garden in Eden. This shift from a panoramic view to close-up fittingly reveals a more intimate picture of God's relationship to humans.[83] This is reflected in the fact that God is

[83] Möller, "Images of God and Creation in Genesis 1–2," 7, helpfully notes the importance of reading Gen 1–2 as a sequential narrative, with Gen 2 complementing what is said in Gen 1.

> Different interpretative possibilities suggest themselves simply by the given sequentiality of the two chapters. Fish once described literature as a 'kinetic art,' noting that during the reading process the book does not remain stationary but is moving (pages are turning and lines are receding into the past as we read), and we are moving with it. ... Accordingly, Fish speaks of the 'temporal flow of the reading experience' and 'the developing responses of the reader in relation to the words as they succeed one another in time.'
>
> For Genesis 1–2 this means that the text's initial focus on the creation of an ordered world by a transcendent God eventually gives way to a more picturesque account that portrays God as immanent, intimate and involved. Human beings also now truly come to the fore, as they

no longer simply designated אֱלֹהִים (*ʾĕlōhîm*, "God"). He is referred to as יְהוָה אֱלֹהִים (*yhwh ʾĕlōhîm*, "YHWH God"), the term "YHWH" being God's personal name. With this shift in focus from the broad canvas of the whole earth to a more detailed description of how humans are placed in the garden in Eden, we witness another dimension to God's nature. As Habel observes regarding the portrayal of God in chapters 2–4,

> Here his immanence, personal nearness, and local involvement on the human scene are basic features. Yahweh is not a detached sovereign overlord but a God at hand as an intimate master. He is a God with whom man has ready contact and immediate responsibility. Accordingly the anthropomorphisms of Genesis 2–4 are so bold that they almost seem to depict Yahweh in terms of human limitations. He moulds with his hands as a potter, he breathes into the mouth of a clay model, he plants a garden, he searches for a man, he has private conversations with man, woman, and beast, and he places a mark on yet another man.[84]

In keeping with this portrayal of YHWH's close contact with humans, Fretheim rightly emphasizes the relational character of creation.[85] Importantly, Genesis 2 does not simply draw attention to the divine-human relationship. It also highlights the existence of close relationships between the human and the ground and between the man and the woman. As we shall see, the ongoing story of Genesis will reveal how these different relationships are disrupted when Adam and Eve are punished by YHWH for eating from the tree of the knowledge of good and evil.

It is often stated that the early chapters of Genesis contain two accounts of creation that originated from different authors. However, the narrative does not record parallel accounts of creation, but complementary descriptions of events that in the main do not overlap. We move from a panoramic overview to a more focused account that contains details that have not been included in the initial portrayal of creation. "Since the second narrative more or less starts where the first leaves off, with the creation of the man/Adam and his placing in the garden

---

are allowed to participate in the completion of creation and are freed from the confines of grammatical objectivity. The temporal process of reading leads readers to revise their first impressions of God and humankind; and, far from trumping J's account, P's version now receives a corrective, as the reader finds out more about God, human beings and creation.

[84] Habel, *Literary Criticism of the Old Testament*, 25.

[85] Fretheim, *God and World in the Old Testament*.

prepared for him, the two narratives dovetail to a considerable degree even while they exhibit their own special features and emphases."[86] By setting these accounts side by side the opening chapters of Genesis give complementary portrayals of God. He is both transcendent and immanent, distant and close, beyond knowing and knowable.

In recent years a trend has developed toward viewing Eden as a sanctuary where God dwells. Gordon helpfully lists the most salient features, although he acknowledges that these are of "variable quality":

> the garden is planted in the east (2:8), which is the cardinal point associated with temple access (Ezek 40:6; 43 :4); the description of Adam's responsibility in terms of "working" and "keeping" uses terms with liturgical possibilities (2:15; cf. Num 3:7–8; 8:26; 18:5–6); the tree of life in the middle of the garden (2:9) mirrors the stylized tree in the outer compartment of the tabernacle (Exod 25:31–40; Lev 24: 1–4); the onyx stone of 2:12 recalls the high priest's ephod and breastpiece (Exod 25:7; 28:9; 35:27; 39:6, 13); the "good" gold of 2:12 points to the extensive use of gold in the furnishing of the tabernacle and temple; God "walks about" in the garden (3:8) just as, through his presence in the tabernacle, he "walks among" his people (Lev 26: 11–12); God clothes Adam and Eve when their nakedness is exposed (3:21), just as his priests are specially "clothed" in order to carry out their duties in the tabernacle (e.g., Exod 28:41; 29: 8–9); and, finally, there is a small cluster of tabernacle features in 3:24, describing the expulsion and its sequel, when God "stations" (škn) cherubim (cf. Exod 25:18–22; 26:31; I Kgs 6:23–29) on the east side of Eden in order to guard the way to the tree of life.[87]

The evidence for linking the garden of Eden with later Israelite sanctuaries is compelling, but, as Block observes, these parallels do not necessarily require the garden to be a sanctuary.[88] It is equally possible that later sanctuaries were thought to resemble the garden of Eden, recalling the time when humans enjoyed intimate access to God.

---

[86] Gordon, "The Week That Made the World," 240.

[87] Gordon, "Evensong in Eden," 18–19. Cf. Wenham, "Sanctuary Symbolism," 399–404; Beale, "Final Vision of the Apocalypse," 197–99; cf., e.g., Beale, *The Temple and the Church's Mission*, 66–80; Beale, "Eden, the Temple, and the Church's Mission," 7–10; Davidson, "Earth's First Sanctuary," 65–89; J. Daniel Hays, *The Temple and the Tabernacle: A Study of God's Dwelling Places from Genesis to Revelation* (Grand Rapids: Baker, 2016), 20–27.

[88] Block, "Eden: A Temple?," 3–29.

The evidence for God dwelling in the garden of Eden, or close to it, is weak.[89] Although the garden is clearly associated with God's presence, the text of Genesis 2–3 says nothing that points conclusively to God dwelling there permanently. The reason for Adam and Eve's expulsion is not primarily to send them away from God's presence, but to prevent them taking and eating from the tree of life (Gen 3:22). Beyond Genesis 3, God's presence is associated principally with heaven,[90] until he chooses to dwell within the portable sanctuary constructed at Mount Sinai (see Exod 40:34–38).

Comments

2:4–7. The start of a new section within the book of Genesis is marked by the heading "These are the records of the heavens and the earth." CSB translates the Hebrew noun תּוֹלְדוֹת (*tôlĕdôt*) as "records." While this is not entirely inappropriate, it fails to convey the idea that the noun is derived from the verb "to give birth." The term תּוֹלְדוֹת (*tôlĕdôt*) describes what comes forth from what is named immediately after it, in this instance "the heavens and the earth."[91] Having described in 1:1–2:3 the creation of the heavens and the earth, the Genesis narrative now proceeds to describe what occurs next. The panoramic view of creation is followed by a close-up description of what happens when God creates the human couple. According to Bartholomew, "this shift in focus to the earth" is signaled by the "inversion of 'heavens and earth' to 'earth and heavens' " in 2:4b.[92]

The second half of v. 4 begins with בְּיוֹם (*bĕyôm*, "in the day of") (cf. KJV; NRSV; ESV). As an idiom, it is not to be taken literally as denoting a period of 24 hours. It should not be interpreted as contradicting how God's creative activity has been described as occurring over six days in

---

[89] In support of the idea that the garden is attached to a sanctuary where God dwells, Walton suggests that "Eden proper would be the Holy of Holies, and the garden adjoins it as the antechamber." John H. Walton, "Eden, Garden of," in Alexander and Baker, *Dictionary of the Old Testament: The Pentateuch*, 205.

[90] Genesis 18:20–21 speaks of God's coming down to investigate the wickedness of Sodom. Similarly, Jacob's vision at Bethel also points to God's residence being in heaven (Gen 28:12).

[91] In Genesis other occurrences of אֵלֶּה תּוֹלְדוֹת (*ʾēlle tôlĕdôt*) (with minor variations in spelling) come in 6:9; 10:1; 11:10, 27; 25:12, 19; 36:1, 9; 37:2 (cf. 5:1). For more on how this formula is used to structure the book of Genesis, see Introduction. II. Structure of Genesis.

[92] Bartholomew, "Theology of Place in Genesis 1–3," 183. It is noteworthy that with the inversion of "earth" and "heavens," the definite article is dropped before both nouns. If the expression "the heavens and the earth" denotes the totality of creation (see 1:1), it seems likely that the phrase "earth and heavens" denotes merely the dry land (see 1:10) and the expanse between the waters above and below (see 1: 8).

Genesis 1. For this reason, CSB renders it "at the time that"; some translations simply use "when" (NIV; NET; NJPS).

The close-up description of how YHWH God forms the human couple, locating them in the garden in Eden, is introduced in verses 4–6 by general observations that set the scene for what follows. For the first time, verse 4 introduces the divine designation יְהוָה אֱלֹהִים (*yhwh ʾĕlōhîm*, "YHWH God)." The use of God's personal name, YHWH, is most appropriate for the narrative in 2:4–3:24, which focuses on the special relationship that exists between God and the human couple. There is no need to assume that the change in divine names from 1:1–2:3 to 2:4–3:24 is due to different authors being responsible for these sections. As the words of the serpent in chapter 3 illustrate, the use of יְהוָה (*yhwh*, "Lord") is determined by thematic considerations; the serpent, which is presented as God's opponent, deliberately avoids using God's personal name.

Verse 5 begins by referring to two types of vegetation. "The phrase, *siah-hassadeh,* refers to the wild vegetation that grows spontaneously after the onset of the rainy season, and *ʿeseb-hassadeh* refers to cultivated grains."[93] In the light of this distinction between the uncultivated "shrub of the field" and the cultivated "plant of the field," verse 5 states that "there was no wild vegetation because there was no rain, and there was no cultivated grain because there was no cultivator."[94] The final words of verse 5 introduce the close connection that exists between "man" (אָדָם, *ʾādām*) and the ground (הָאֲדָמָה, *hāʾădāmâ*),[95] the former being tasked to work the latter in order that it might produce plants (cf. 2:15; 3:23).

Verses 6–7 describe God's response to the situation recorded in verse 5. Countering the lack of uncultivated plants, God provides an אֵד (*ʾēd*) to water repeatedly the "entire surface of the land." The meaning of the rare term אֵד (*ʾēd*) is open to debate. While "stream" (NAB; NRSV) or "streams"

---

[93] Mark D. Futato, "Because It Had Rained: A Study of Gen 2:5–7 with Implications for Gen 2:4–25 and Gen 1:1–2:3," *WTJ* 60 (1998): 3. Futato assumes that this account is told from the perspective of someone "living in the Syro-Palestinian Levant" (3n8). Terje Stordalen, "Man, Soil, Garden: Basic Plot in Genesis 2–3 Reconsidered," *JSOT* 53 (1992): 10–11, also contends for a distinction between wild and cultivated plants.

[94] Futato, "Because It Had Rained," 5.

[95] To convey the wordplay of the Hebrew text, some scholars adopt the translations "earthling" and "earth" or "groundling" and "ground" for אָדָם (*ʾādām*) and אֲדָמָה (*ʾădāmâ*). While this draws out the wordplay in the Hebrew text, it fails to preserve the strong connection that exists between this first human and the name Adam that is later given to him (5:1). See Hess, "Splitting the Adam," 1–15; Hess, "Adam, Father, He," 146–47.

(NIV) is favored by some translations, others adopt "mist" (KJV; ESV: RSV; JPS; NAS) or "springs" (NET; NLT).[96] Futato argues for "rain cloud," given that verse 5 refers to a lack of rain on the earth.[97]

While the regular provision of water supports the growth of the "shrub of the field," verse 7 describes the provision of a human to "work the ground" in order to grow the cultivated plants of the field (v. 5). Taking dust from the ground (הָאֲדָמָה, *hāʾădāmâ*), YHWH God forms the human (הָאָדָם, *hāʾādām*). The close bond between the human and the ground is reflected in their names; הָאֲדָמָה (*hāʾădāmâ*) has the appearance of being the feminine form of הָאָדָם (*hāʾādām*).[98]

Like a potter, God shapes the dust of the ground into a human (cf. Isa 64:8 [Heb 64:7]). The human-shaped "dust" is animated by God's breath. Although the expression נֶפֶשׁ חַיָּה (*nepeš ḥayyâ*) is rendered "a living soul" in KJV (cf. JPS), the translation "living being" or "living creature" is more appropriate. The same expression is used to denote animals in 1:20, 21, 24. Importantly, for the author of Genesis, the human does not possess a נֶפֶשׁ (*nepeš*, "soul") but is a נֶפֶשׁ חַיָּה (*nepeš ḥayyâ*, "a living being").

The image of YHWH God breathing life into the nostrils of the human conveys vividly the special status that humans enjoy in God's creation. "*Formed* expresses the relation of craftsman to material ...; while *breathed* is warmly personal, with the face-to-face intimacy of a kiss and the significance that this was an act of giving as well as making; and self-giving at that."[99] God is personally involved in giving life to the human whom he has formed. This perspective on the creation of humans conveys the closeness of the bond that exists between Creator and creature, complementing what is said in Genesis 1 concerning humans being appointed as God's vicegerents.

2:8–9. Verses 8–9 identify the location where the events described in 2:15–3:24 occur. Importantly, this location is designated a "garden" (גַּן, *gan*). This implies that it was an enclosed area with an entrance

---

[96] Mathews, *Genesis 1-11:26*, 195–96, favors the concept of "underground streams."

[97] Futato, "Because It Had Rained," 7–9. Max Rogland, "Interpreting אד in Genesis 2.5–6: Neglected Rabbinic and Intertextual Evidence," *JSOT* 34 (2010): 379–93, also argues that אֵד (*ʾēd*) refers to a cloud of some kind.

[98] Although the two words are very similar, Wenham, *Genesis 1-15*, 59, suggests that there may not be any etymological link between them.

[99] Derek Kidner, *Genesis: An Introduction and Commentary*, TOTC (Leicester: Inter-Varsity Press, 1967), 60; italics in original.

that could be guarded to stop others entering the garden (cf. 3:24). Bartholomew suggests that the designation "garden" conveys royal connotations.[100]

> Rather than Gen 2 presenting an image of primitivism, it would appear to portray an area bounded, probably by walls, which is carefully landscaped and intensively cultivated with orchards and the like. It may well have included buildings—its urban connotations in the ancient Near East are particularly interesting in the light of the tendency to portray Eden as a form of primitivism. Thus God, as King, a central image of God in Gen 1, plants a garden, and as the under-kings, Adam and Eve dwell in the garden, which is a royal residence.[101]

This image of the garden may be helpfully contrasted with the image of "the field" (הַשָּׂדֶה, *haśśādeh*) that is mentioned twice in verse 5 and will appear again in connection with wild animals (2:20; 3:1, 14) and the cultivated plants that the humans will eat after being expelled from the garden (3:18). Whereas the concept of "field" conveys a sense of open country that lacks protection, the concept of a garden signals security and safety (cf. Isa 5:1–6). Moreover, the statement that YHWH God causes to grow "every tree pleasing in appearance and good for food" (v. 9) implies that there is an abundant provision within this aesthetically delightful location. This is a place to be enjoyed, a true paradise.[102] And yet, as we

---

[100] Bartholomew, "Theology of Place in Genesis 1–3," 187, writes:

Gardens were an important part of the irrigation economies of Mesopotamia and Egypt; in the case of wealthy and influential persons, the garden could be expansive and generally adjoined the residence. The ancient Egyptians also cultivated gardens, orchards and parks, and wealthy families often maintained country estates where the owners could relax amidst flowers, fruit trees and ponds. Within the Old Testament, Yahweh Elohim's planting of a garden may be comparable with Qoheleth's planting of vineyards, founding of gardens and parks, and creation of pools from which to water the forest of growing trees. This would fit with the royal fiction in Ecclesiastes, since such projects cohere with the description of the projects of kings in the ancient Near East. That it was generally the wealthier who owned gardens affirms the monarchical dimension, albeit democratized of the imago dei as presented in Gen 1.

[101] Bartholomew, "Theology of Place in Genesis 1–3," 187. See also M. Hutter, "Adam als Gärtner und König (Gen 2:8,15)," *Biblische Zeitschrift* 30 (1986): 258–62.

[102] The LXX uses παράδεισος (*paradeisos*), a Persian loan word, to translate גַּן (*gan*). In line with this, the garden is associated with the concept of "paradise" in Western culture, as reflected in John Milton's *Paradise Lost*.

shall discover in verse 18, this ideal environment lacks a vital ingredient for the well-being of the human whom God has just made.

The garden is located "in Eden" (v. 8). The name Eden probably refers to a region that is much larger than the garden. Speiser suggests that Eden is derived from the Sumerian *edin*, meaning "steppe."[103] In the light of the distinction that the narrative draws between "garden" and "field," Speiser's proposal seems unlikely. Millard and Bordreuil contend, based on a similar Aramaic word, that it means "a place of luxuriance."[104] The CSB translation states that Eden is "in the east" (v. 8). However, the Hebrew term translated "in the east" could equally mean "eastward" (cf. 13:11), possibly implying that the garden was oriented toward the east.

While the enclosed garden is filled with an abundance of trees of different varieties, two are picked out for special mention. In the middle of the garden is the "tree of life" (v. 9). Later, God prevents the disobedient human couple from eating from this tree lest they live forever (3:22). This tree reappears in the apostle John's vision of new Jerusalem, where the tree bears "twelve kinds of fruit, producing its fruit every month" and its leaves "are for healing the nations" (Rev 22:2; cf. 2:7; 22:14, 19).[105]

Apart from the tree of life, special mention is made of the "tree of the knowledge of good and evil" (v. 9). This tree will figure prominently in the ensuing narrative when the human couple eats from its fruit, disregarding God's prohibition that to do so will bring death (v. 17). Whereas one tree is associated with life, the other is linked to death. Given its association with death, it seems unlikely that the expression "knowledge of good and evil" is simply a merism, as suggested by Sarna, denoting knowledge of "everything."[106] Sarna goes on to suggest, drawing on passages like 2 Samuel 14:17, 20 and Deuteronomy 1:39, that "it is best to understand 'knowledge of good and bad' as the capacity to make independent judgments concerning human welfare."[107] While the concept of "good" has been repeatedly introduced in chapter 1 as regards God's creative activity, this is the first reference to "evil." From what develops

---

[103] E. A. Speiser, *Genesis*, 2nd ed., AB 1 (Garden City: Doubleday, 1964), 16.

[104] Millard and Bordreuil, "Statue from Syria," 140; cf. A. R. Millard, "The Etymology of Eden," *VT* 34 (1984): 103–6.

[105] While the book of Proverbs has various references to a "tree of life" (3:18; 11:30; 13:12; 15:4), there is no reason to assume that these refer to the tree in the garden of Eden.

[106] Nahum M. Sarna, *Genesis: The Traditional Hebrew Text with the New JPS Translation*, JPS Torah Commentary (New York: Jewish Publication Society, 1989), 19.

[107] Sarna, *Genesis*, 19.

in chapter 3, "knowing good and evil" is clearly an attribute that at this stage distinguishes God from humans (cf. 3:5, 22). From the context, it would appear to denote God's ability to determine what is good and what is evil. If Adam and Eve are to be Godlike, they too would also need to be able to determine what is good and what is evil. By aspiring to have this level of knowledge, the human couple seek to become autonomous in determining good from evil.[108] The irony of their action is their failure to recognize the evil that underlies the serpent's insinuations. Their failure to trust God by obeying his instructions has profound implications for the whole of creation. This becomes evident to the human couple after they eat from the tree. According to the book of Proverbs, the fear of the Lord is the beginning of true knowledge (Prov 1:7; cf. Job 28:28; Ps 111:10; Prov 9:10). The way to true wisdom is through obedience, not by grasping fruit from the tree of the knowledge of good and evil.

2:10–14. The chronological sequence is broken at the start of verse 10 as the narrator provides additional information about a river that goes out from Eden to water the garden.[109] It seems likely that the river irrigates the garden before dividing to become four rivers. The presence of a river that feeds four other rivers points to an abundance of water in Eden to sustain the trees growing within the garden. By linking the river that flows through the garden to four rivers associated with different regions, the narrator places Eden in an elevated and central location. Some, but not all, of the place and river names resonate with later entities, but some of these names may be used here of entirely different locations or features. The name Pishon occurs only here in the Old Testament. The name Havilah has a definite article in the Hebrew text, distinguishing it from later uses of the name in Genesis 10:7, 29; 25:18; 1 Samuel 15:7. Outside of Genesis the name Gihon is used of a water source to the east of Jerusalem in 2 Chronicles 32:30; 33:14 and, with a variation in spelling, in 1 Kings 1:33, 38, 45. However, in the present context Gihon is associated with the land of Cush, a title that elsewhere in the Old Testament is linked to the land

[108] W. Malcolm Clark, "A Legal Background to the Yahwist's Use of 'Good and Evil' in Genesis 2–3," *JBL* 88 (1969): 277, writes, "Man takes upon himself the responsibility of trying apart from God to determine whether something is good for himself or not. It is not that man has no knowledge before and gains knowledge, or that to know good and evil means to experience evil in addition to good. Rather, man himself declares what is good. He does what is good in his own eyes rather than what is good in the eyes of God."

[109] The Hebrew syntax of v. 10 breaks the *wayyiqtol* verb sequence that runs throughout vv. 7–9.

of Ethiopia and possibly also the hills of western Iran. The names Tigris and Euphrates are commonly associated with the two great rivers that merge before flowing into the Persian Gulf. Ancient cartographers gave the name Mesopotamia, which in Greek means "between rivers," to the region encompassed by these two rivers. Since the Tigris flows through Assyria and not to the east of it, as verse14 states, the name אַשּׁוּר (*ʾaššûr*) may denote here the city of Asshur and not the country of Assyria. While the abundance of names in verses 10–14 gives the impression that Eden was a specific region, the location remains a mystery. In the light of the humans' expulsion from Eden, the author of Genesis is unlikely to have expected his readers to travel to Eden in search of the garden. However, he may have included some of the distinctive features mentioned in these verses to highlight connections between the garden and later Israelite sanctuaries (e.g., the reference to gold and precious stones; the river flowing out of the garden). A similar river appears in John's vision of new Jerusalem (Rev 22:1–2; cf. Ezek 47:1–12).

2:15–17. These verses pick up the storyline from verse 8–9. YHWH God settles the man in the garden, implying that this is the location where he is to remain.[110] The final part of verse 15 has prompted much discussion. First, the pronoun "it," which is attached to both verbs, is feminine in Hebrew. However, the antecedent noun גַּן (*gan*, "garden") is masculine. While the expression "garden of Eden" may be conceived as being feminine,[111] it is also possible that the pronoun alludes back to the feminine noun אֲדָמָה (*ʾădāmâ*, "ground"), recalling the final words of verse 5: "there was no human to work the ground."[112] This link would underline the close and significant relationship that exists between the human and the ground. In the ensuing narrative this relationship becomes severely disrupted (e.g., 3:17; 4:11; 5:29).

Second, both verbs in the phrase לְעָבְדָהּ וּלְשָׁמְרָהּ (*lĕʿobdāh ûlĕšomrāh*,"to work it and watch over it") have a broad semantic range. NJPS adopts the translation "to till it and tend it"; ESV has "to work it and keep it"; NET offers "to care for it and to maintain it." Later, in 3:24, the verb שָׁמַר (*šāmar*) is used with the sense "to guard" with reference to the way to

---

[110] Although CSB uses the English verb "placed" in vv. 8 and 15, two different Hebrew verbs are used. The verb in v. 15 is used later of the ark coming to rest on the mountains of Ararat (8:4).

[111] See Stordalen, "Man, Soil, Garden," 16n1.

[112] This proposal is supported by Gordon, "Evensong in Eden," 20.

the tree of life. Wenham observes that the verbs עָבַד (ʿābad) and שָׁמַר (šāmar) are used in proximity elsewhere in the Pentateuch with reference to the duties of the Levites at the portable sanctuary (Num 3:7–8; 8:26; 18:5–6). While it is possible that a subtle connection is being made here between the human's duties in the garden of Eden and those of the Levites at the sanctuary, the correspondence is not particularly obvious. The duties assigned to the human do not resemble closely those of the Levites. Nevertheless, the introduction of the verb שָׁמַר (*šāmar*) possibly implies that the human's duty extends beyond being a gardener to being a guardian.[113]

Immediately after placing the human in the garden, YHWH God warns him against eating from the "tree of the knowledge of good and evil," which has been mentioned briefly in verse 9. Importantly, this prohibition is preceded by God's statement that the human is permitted to eat from every tree in the garden. The restriction introduced by God is clearly not intended to prevent the human from finding enjoyment and satisfaction in the garden. God's generosity in providing abundantly for the human makes his subsequent eating from the tree of the knowledge of good and evil even more reprehensible. There is no shortage of food in the garden.

The prohibition against eating from the tree of the knowledge of good and evil reveals that God has created the human with sufficient freedom that he can either obey or disobey his Creator. The human is no puppet, programmed to conform automatically to the will of the one who has made him. For God to grant such freedom to a creature is highly significant, for it introduces into the creative process an important dynamic. For the human to have absolute freedom to choose, the possibility is created that he may decide to disobey God and go his own way. If God was not to grant this possibility and accept the consequences, then the human would be merely a puppet. The capacity to reject God's instructions is a clear indicator that humans have been specially privileged by God. However, all this comes with a great risk. It opens the door for evil to exist in the world.[114] In the light of this possibility, we should not be surprised that the divine prohibition against eating from the tree of the knowledge of good and evil comes with the serious warning that to do so will result in death.

---

[113] Dumbrell, "Genesis 2:1–17," 53–65, suggests that Adam as a king-priest will expand Eden into a worldwide sanctuary.

[114] For a recent discussion of these issues, see Pierre Gilbert, *God Never Meant for Us to Die: The Emergence of Evil in the Light of the Genesis Creation Account* (Eugene: Wipf and Stock, 2020).

For God's words to be meaningful, it seems likely that death must already be a concept with which the human is familiar. Importantly, this threat of death is later contradicted by the serpent, which looks to tempt the woman by focusing on the benefits that may be gained by eating fruit from the tree of the knowledge of good and evil (3:4–5). The human's actions involving the tree will take on great significance. While the phrase "on the day you eat from it" could imply that death will occur shortly after the eating, it is possible that "day" is used here in a more general way.[115]

2:18–20. After mentioning God's warning against eating from the fruit of the tree of the knowledge of good and evil, the narrative highlights YHWH God's concern for the well-being of the human: "It is not good for the human to be alone." The divine assessment that the human's loneliness is "not good" stands in sharp contrast to the repeated assessments of "good" (1:4, 9, 12, 18, 21, 24) and "very good" (1:31) in Genesis 1. In response YHWH God speaks of creating "a helper corresponding to him" (v. 18).

The use of the term עֵזֶר (*ʿēzer*, "helper") has led some to suggest that this denotes someone who is inferior to the man.[116] Yet, of the nineteen occurrences of the common noun עֵזֶר (*ʿēzer*) outside of Genesis 2, all but three refer to God as Israel's helper (Exod 18:4; Deut 33:7, 26, 29; Pss 20:2 [Heb. 3]; 33:20; 70:5 [Heb. 6]; 89:19 [Heb. 20]; 115:9–11; 121:1–2; 124:8; 146:5; Hos 13:9; the other three uses of ʿēzer refer to military allies: Isa 30:5; Ezek 12:14; Dan 11:34). In the light of this evidence there is no reason to assume that "helper" denotes someone of inferior status.[117]

A positive understanding of "helper" is reinforced by the prepositional phrase כְּנֶגְדּוֹ *kĕnegdô* "corresponding to him," which has the sense of being an equal partner, what we might consider a "soulmate."[118] Importantly, the initiative for the creation of the "helper" rests with God. The human's role is merely to identify the one that corresponds to him. God's assessment that the human is incomplete without a corresponding helper is striking. As subsequent events will reveal, the man and the woman,[119] as

---

[115] For a fuller discussion, see Comments on 3:17–19.

[116] E.g., David J. A. Clines, "What Does Eve Do to Help? And Other Irredeemably Androcentric Orientations in Genesis 1–3," in *What Does Eve Do to Help? And Other Readerly Questions to the Old Testament*, JSOTSup (Sheffield: JSOT Press, 1990), 30–32.

[117] See Davidson, *Flame of Yahweh*, 29, who contends that עֵזֶר (*ʿēzer*, "helper") is a relational term with no sense of rank attached to it. Alter, *Genesis*, 9, prefers the translation "sustainer" over "helper" because it avoids the implication that the helper is in some way inferior.

[118] Davidson, *Flame of Yahweh*, 30.

[119] Verse 23 introduces the term אִישׁ (*ʾîš* "man/husband") into the narrative, drawing attention to how this term is related to אִשָּׁה (*ʾiššāh* "woman/wife").

husband and wife, complement each other in a significant way, becoming "one flesh" (2:24). This recalls the intriguing link that is made in 1:27 between humans being created in the divine image as male and female.

According to verse 19, the process by which YHWH God creates "every wild animal and every bird of the sky" is similar to how the human was created (cf. v. 7), and, like the human, each becomes a נֶפֶשׁ חַיָּה (*nepeš ḥayyâ*, "a living creature") (cf. v. 7). Nevertheless, despite these similarities, "no helper was found as his complement." Whereas verse 20 mentions three categories of creatures that are named by the human, only two of these are listed in verse 19 in connection with YHWH God bringing the creatures to the human. This may imply that domesticated "livestock" are present in the garden of Eden, but the wild animals (lit., animals of the field) and birds live outside the garden. This observation may have a bearing on how we should perceive the presence in the garden of the serpent, one of the wild animals. As a חַיַּת הַשָּׂדֶה (*ḥayyat haśśādeh*) (3:1), its normal habitat is outside the garden. Just as God names different aspects of creation (cf. 1:5, 8, 10), the human names the living creatures. By doing so, the human exercises the authority that God has bestowed on him as vicegerent (cf. 1:26–28).

2:21–25. In response to the human's failure to find a suitable companion from among all the other creatures, YHWH God creates a woman. The man's reaction emphasizes her suitability: "This one ... is bone of my bone and flesh of my flesh" (v. 23). To highlight the complementary nature of their relationship, the man draws attention to how they are designated אִישׁ (*ʾîš*, "man/husband") and אִשָּׁה (*ʾiššāh*, "woman/wife") (v. 23). The introduction of both terms into the narrative for the first time in Genesis emphasizes the harmonious relationship that God creates between the man and the woman. In the same way that the terms אָדָם (*ʾādām*, "human") and אֲדָמָה (*ʾadāmah*, "ground") reflect humanity's relationship with the ground, the terms אִישׁ (*ʾîš*, "man/husband") and אִשָּׁה (*ʾiššāh*, "woman/wife") convey the close correspondence that exists between the man and woman. Observing how the male nouns אָדָם (*ʾādām*) and אִישׁ (*ʾîš*, "man/husband") are used in conjunction with the female nouns אֲדָמָה (*ʾadāmah*, "ground") and אִשָּׁה (*ʾiššāh*, "woman"), Hess writes:

> the primary concern of the use of the term *ʾādām* is not its male gender, but its relation to *ʾadāmah* "ground." The primary concern of the term *ʾîš* "man" is its relation to *ʾiššāh* "woman." In both cases, the masculine/feminine gender correspondence establishes and enhances the relationship between the two. In

> neither case is the purpose of the gender to establish male orientation or dominance any more than it is to establish female orientation. Rather, the purposes of the gender correspondences are to define harmonious relationships as created by God. The man takes care of the earth, as his species have been given charge over it. The woman, created from the side of the man, is a helper to work and live together with the man. It is this harmony of relationships that is the point of Genesis ch. 2, and the breakdown of that harmony as a consequence of willful sin that forms the key theme of ch. 3 (including the judgements).[120]

In creating the woman, it would have been possible for YHWH God to repeat the process by which the human was shaped from the dust of the ground, but God deliberately creates her from the body of the man.[121] This process sets the woman apart from all other creatures, for they, like the man, are created from the ground (v. 19). To make the woman, YHWH God takes a rib from the man. The term צֵלָע (*ṣēlāʿ*), translated "rib" in this context, often denotes "side." Matthew Henry conveys well the symbolic meaning of the woman being created from the man's side. He writes, "That the woman was *made of a rib out of the side of Adam*; not made out of his head to rule over him, nor out of his feet to be trampled upon by him, but out of his side to be equal with him, under his arm to be protected, and near his heart to be beloved."[122] By observing that YHWH God "caused a deep sleep to come over the man," the narrator underscores that the man has no active role in the creation of the woman; she is entirely the result of divine creativity.

Genesis 2 graphically describes the creation of both male and female, with verse 23 introducing the designations אִישׁ (*ʾîš*, "man/husband") and אִשָּׁה (*ʾiššāh*, "woman/wife). Building on this verse 24 presents the heterosexual nature of the marital relationship as a paradigm, stating that when a man and a woman come together in intimacy, they become

---

[120] Hess, "Adam, Father, He," 147.

[121] The CSB translation "made" in v. 22 renders the Hebrew verb בָּנָה (*bānâ*), which has the sense of "build." This is the first use of this verb in the opening chapters of Genesis and indicates that the process of making the woman differs from that used for other creatures, including the man.

[122] Matthew Henry, *An Exposition of the Old Testament: Wherein Each Chapter is Summed up in Its Contents: The Sacred Text Inserted at Large, in Distinct Paragraphs, Each Paragraph Reduced to Its Proper Heads: The Sense Given, and Largely Illuminated: With Practical Remarks and Observations. Old Testament*, vol. 1 (London: James Nisbet, 1857). Henry's sentiments reflect a commonly repeated assessment by Christian exegetes.

"one flesh." Verse 24 strongly implies that the marriage relationship is intended by God to be monogamous. And the process of leaving parents and clinging to one's spouse conveys a sense of permanence.[123] The paradigm established by the events of Genesis 2 points toward a husband-wife relationship that is exclusive, intimate, and permanent. However, while Genesis 1–2 underlines the importance and harmony of the heterosexual marital relationship, Genesis 3 describes how the harmony intended by God is jeopardized by the catastrophic events that occur in the garden of Eden when the human couple disregard God's instructions.

Much discussion of human sexuality in the opening chapters of Genesis has been dominated by the issue of hierarchy. Although by no means unanimous, there is a long-standing tradition within the Christian church that these chapters establish a hierarchy, with the man either being superior to the woman or exercising leadership in relation to the woman. Modern discussions of the biblical teaching on gender acknowledge this long-standing tradition, with some affirming it but others rejecting it. Some contemporary feminist scholars readily accept that the opening chapters of Genesis proclaim male superiority, but in doing so they see the biblical text as reflecting an outdated and unacceptable patriarchal worldview.

An analysis of the main arguments for a hierarchical interpretation of the marital relationship in Genesis 1–2 suggests that we should be cautious about embracing this long-standing tradition. A patriarchal reading of Genesis 1–2 existed comfortably in ancient cultures where women were already viewed as inferior to men. In such cultures there was little impetus to challenge this social norm. Yet, the creation account in Genesis 1 encourages an approach to gender that sees both male and female being made in the image of God (1:27).

For some scholars, male superiority is implied by the woman being created from the man's rib. This rests, however, on the mistaken assumption that the concept of derivation implies subordination. Although the man is derived from the ground (2:7), there is no reason to conclude that he is inferior to it. The logic of the argument of derivation is also questionable from another perspective; all subsequent generations of men are derived from women. This does not, however, justify female superiority over men.

---

[123] This is the thrust of what Jesus states when quoting v. 24 in Matt.19:4–6 and Mark 10:6–9.

It is also inappropriate to infer that the woman is subordinate to the man simply because she is created afterwards. If the argument of priority of creation was applied in Genesis 1, human beings would be inferior to all other creatures. Nor can the man's superiority be proposed on the basis that he names the woman. We should not assume that the one giving the name has authority over the one named. Even within the book of Genesis, this thesis cannot be sustained, for the Egyptian slave-woman Hagar names God (16:13). Furthermore, it is not certain that the man is responsible for naming the woman; the passive verb יִקָּרֵא (*yiqqārēʾ*, "be called") in 2:23 leaves open the possibility that she is already known as אִשָּׁה (*ʾiššāh*, woman/wife) before the man speaks (cf. 2:22).

Some scholars have argued for male superiority based on the observation that God speaks first to the man, prohibiting him from eating from the tree of the knowledge of good and evil (vv. 16–17). However, priority is given to this, not because the man is superior to the woman, but because the man's presence in the garden before the creation of the woman requires him to be aware of this danger. God's warning emphasizes the danger posed by the fruit of the tree; it is not intended to highlight man's superiority vis-à-vis the woman.

The movement within 2:4–25 is not from superior to inferior, but from incomplete to complete. The chapter emphasizes the harmony and oneness that exists when the man and woman come together. The man does not feel complete either in himself or with the companionship of creatures that are subordinate to him. Only in the divinely fashioned woman, who is "flesh of his flesh and bone of his bone" (2:23), does the man encounter a soulmate, an appropriate counterpart. The making of the woman marks the climax of the narrative as a suitable companion is created by YHWH God for the man. This climax does not coincide with the formation of the man, but with the coming together of the man and the woman. In agreement with many other scholars, Davidson states, "Gen 2, like Gen 1, contains no statement of dominance, subordination, or leadership submission in the relationship of the sexes."[124]

The expectation that the man should leave his father and mother (v. 24) points toward the exclusive nature of the husband-wife relationship.[125]

---

[124] Davidson, "The Genesis Account of Origins," 34.

[125] Robert B. Lawton, "Genesis 2:24: Trite or Tragic?," *JBL* 105 (1986): 98, argues that v. 24 is best translated: "Therefore a man should/was to leave his father and mother and cling to his wife, and they should/were to become one flesh."

While the Old Testament emphasizes the importance of children caring for their parents, the newly formed husband-wife relationship takes precedence over commitments to parents. As a new relationship is established, the woman does not merely become an addition to the man's existing family. Together the couple become "one flesh," a reference to sexual intimacy, recalling the divine commission that people are to be fruitful and multiply and fill the earth with the intention of establishing God's authority over other creatures (1:28). According to Wenham, becoming "one flesh"

> does not denote merely the sexual union that follows marriage, or the children conceived in marriage, or even the spiritual and emotional relationship that it involves, though all are involved in becoming one flesh. Rather it affirms that just as blood relations are one's flesh and bone ..., so marriage creates a similar kinship relation between man and wife. They become related to each other as brother and sister are.[126]

The final words of this passage reveal that the human couple are naked but have no sense of embarrassment about this. This will change after they eat from the tree of the knowledge of good and evil (3:7). The use of the term עֲרוּמִּים (*ʿărûmmîm*, "naked") in verse 25 creates a link with the adjective עָרוּם (*ʿārûm*, "cunning") that describes the serpent in 3:1.

Bridge

A Christian understanding of human gender must take as its starting point the affirmation in the opening chapter of Genesis that God created humanity as male and female (1:27). The significance of this statement is developed in Genesis 2, where the subject of human sexuality occupies center stage. The account of the formation of the man and the woman comes to a noteworthy climax with the declaration: "This is why a man leaves his father and mother and bonds with his wife, and they become one flesh" (2:24). Undoubtedly, the opening chapters of Genesis are intended, in part at least, to inform the reader of God's design for marriage.

In a world where the relationship between sex and gender is much debated, who determines which sexual relations are acceptable and suitable for the flourishing and well-being of human society? According to the

[126] Wenham, *Genesis 1–15*, 71.

opening chapters of Genesis, God's ideal for intimate human relationships is fulfilled through heterosexual marriage that is exclusive and permanent.

The narrative in 2:4–25 describes how the man is provided with a partner who will be like him, but not necessarily identical to him, a female equivalent. However, as Davidson helpfully observes:

> Although the text of Gen 1–2 implies complementarity between the sexes, it presents no stereotypical roles that constitute the "essence" of manhood and womanhood respectively. Both sexes are made in the image of God; both are given the command to be fruitful and multiply; both are commanded to fill the earth and subdue it; both are commanded to have dominion over all the other creatures (1:27–28). They are equal partners corresponding to each other, with full reciprocity and mutuality and without hierarchy (2:18). Any attempt to distill the essence of the "roles" of man and woman respectively from the opening chapters of Genesis is going beyond the revelation of the text. Complementary wholeness without hierarchy is the portrait of sexuality in Gen 1–2.[127]

The woman complements the man, with both coming together in a way that bonds them together to make "one flesh" (2:24). "[I]t is God who united the man and the woman, creating the 'one flesh,' and it is his will that this new relationship not be destroyed."[128] The emphasis within the passage is clearly on the harmony that exists in this relationship, which will lead to the creation of other harmonious relationships involving men and women.

Genesis 2 is a reminder that individualism is not a good thing. God's solution was not to create another man, identical in every respect, to the first man, but to create a woman who is a suitable counterpart to the man. If we extrapolate from this, it suggests that a wholesome society should value equally both men and women. The early chapters of Genesis have much to say to societies where women are treated as inferior members.

---

[127] Davidson, "The Genesis Account of Origins," 39. He later says, "Gen 1–2 presents God's divine ideal for men and women at creation to be one of equality in both nature and function, with no superiority or leadership of the male and no inferiority of submission of the female" (79).

[128] Wayne J. H. Stuhlmiller, "One Flesh: In the Old and New Testaments," *Consensus* 5 (1979): 6.

While God's ideal is for heterosexual monogamy, in which people find sexual fulfilment and reproductive fruitfulness, the rest of Genesis reveals that the outworking of this ideal is disrupted by the events described in Genesis 3. Men and women may aspire to establish faithful monogamous relationships, but this is far from easy. Remarkably, running throughout the rest of Genesis we witness various relationships that depart from the ideal intended by God. Even the great patriarchs Abraham and Jacob/Israel fall short of maintaining this monogamous ideal.[129] Yet, God graciously includes them within the patriline that will lead to Jesus Christ. Later, as Jesus observes (Matt 19:8; Mark 10:5), due to the corruptness of the human heart, God permitted divorce (Deut 24:1–4). However, this falls short of the ideal that God desired from the beginning.

The prominence given to the subject of human gender in the opening chapters of Genesis centers not on male-female relationships in general, but on the male-female relationship in the context of marriage. This observation needs to be underlined because there is an ever-present danger of mistakenly applying what the present text of Genesis has to say regarding marriage to all male-female relationships. Genesis 1–2 addresses the topic of gender in the context of marriage and marriage alone.

Although it is not stated explicitly, the early chapters of Genesis imply that as human beings are fruitful and increase in number the boundaries of the garden will be extended to fill the whole earth. Beale writes, "As Adam and Eve were to begin to rule over and subdue the earth, it is plausible to suggest that they were to extend the geographical boundaries of the Garden until Eden extended throughout and covered the whole earth."[130] Understood in the light of its ANE expectations, an increasing population would result in the creation of a city. Genesis 1–2 anticipates that through time the whole earth will become a holy city, where God and humanity will live together in perfect harmony.[131]

---

[129] James McKeown, *Genesis*, Two Horizons Old Testament Commentary 1 (Grand Rapids: Eerdmans, 2008), 34, comments, "Although polygamy is practiced throughout the OT and many prominent characters have several wives, the ideal of one man and one woman is presented unequivocally in this passage."

[130] Beale, "Final Vision of the Apocalypse," 201. See also Beale, "Eden, the Temple, and the Church's Mission," 10–11.

[131] This is developed more fully in Alexander, *The City of God*.

B. The Couple Betrays God (3:1–24)

1 Now the serpent was the most cunning of all the wild animals that
the Lord God had made. He said to the woman, "Did God really say, 'You
can't eat from any tree in the garden?'"

2 The woman said to the serpent, "We may eat the fruit from the trees in
the garden. 3 But about the fruit of the tree in the middle of the garden,
God said, 'You must not eat it or touch it, or you will die.'"

4 "No! You will not die," the serpent said to the woman. 5 "In fact, God
knows that when you eat it your eyes will be opened and you will be like
God, knowing good and evil." 6 The woman saw that the tree was good
for food and delightful to look at, and that it was desirable for obtaining
wisdom. So she took some of its fruit and ate it; she also gave some to
her husband, who was with her, and he ate it. 7 Then the eyes of both
of them were opened, and they knew they were naked; so they sewed
fig leaves together and made coverings for themselves.

8 Then the man and his wife heard the sound of the Lord God walking
in the garden at the time of the evening breeze, and they hid from the
Lord God among the trees of the garden. 9 So the Lord God called out to
the man and said to him, "Where are you?"

10 And he said, "I heard you in the garden, and I was afraid because I
was naked, so I hid."

11 Then he asked, "Who told you that you were naked? Did you eat from
the tree that I commanded you not to eat from?"

12 The man replied, "The woman you gave to be with me—she gave me
some fruit from the tree, and I ate."

13 So the Lord God asked the woman, "What is this you have done?"

And the woman said, "The serpent deceived me, and I ate."

14 So the Lord God said to the serpent:
Because you have done this,
you are cursed more than any livestock
and more than any wild animal.
You will move on your belly
and eat dust all the days of your life.
15 I will put hostility between you and the woman,
and between your offspring and her offspring.
He will strike your head,
and you will strike his heel.

16 He said to the woman:
I will intensify your labor pains;
you will bear children with painful effort.

Your desire will be for your husband,
yet he will rule over you.

[17] And he said to the man, "Because you listened to your wife and ate
from the tree about which I commanded you, 'Do not eat from it':
The ground is cursed because of you.
You will eat from it by means of painful labor all the days of your life.
[18] It will produce thorns and thistles for you, and you will eat the
plants of the field.
[19] You will eat bread by the sweat of your brow
until you return to the ground,
since you were taken from it.
For you are dust,
and you will return to dust."

[20] The man named his wife Eve because she was the mother of all the
living. [21] The LORD God made clothing from skins for the man and his
wife, and he clothed them.

[22] The LORD God said, "Since the man has become like one of us, knowing
good and evil, he must not reach out, take from the tree of life, eat, and
live forever." [23] So the LORD God sent him away from the garden of Eden
to work the ground from which he was taken.[24] He drove the man out
and stationed the cherubim and the flaming, whirling sword east of the
garden of Eden to guard the way to the tree of life.

Context

The introduction of a new character into the narrative signals the beginning of a series of events that will profoundly disrupt the harmonious picture that has been painted in 2:4–25. Having set the scene by introducing God's warning to the human couple that they must not eat from the tree of the knowledge of good and evil (2:16–17), Genesis now tells us how the humans disregard God's command, listening instead to the insinuations of a malevolent snake that is somewhat ominously described as being "the most cunning of all the wild creatures that the LORD God had made" (3:1).

Genesis 3 narrates events that reveal how the divine ordering of creation is overturned with catastrophic outcomes. Genesis 2:4–25 brings to the fore God's relationship to the human, the human's relationship to the ground, and the relationship between the man and the woman. All of these are in harmony, but this will all change. The presence of a mysterious serpent who challenges God's authority discloses that evil already exists before Adam and Eve betray God. As to the history of this malevolent creature, the early chapters of Genesis are silent. There are gaps in the narrative that cannot be easily filled. Given the serpent's existence, the human couple should possibly be viewed as guardians of sacred space in an imperfect world and not merely gardeners set in the middle of a perfect world.[132] However we view affairs prior to Adam and Eve's betrayal of God, their actions transform their human nature and disrupt their relationships with God, one another, and the rest of creation.

For disregarding God's instructions, the human couple are expelled from the garden. The seriousness of what occurs is underlined by the fact that God stations cherubim and a flaming, whirling sword to prevent humans from reentering the garden to eat from the tree of life (3:24).

The description of what took place is highly significant, especially when viewed against all that is said in 2:4–25 concerning the matrix of positive relationships that are established by God. As a result of the serpent's actions, God's plans for humanity and the world are turned upside down. God's ongoing response to what happens will be revealed in the rest of Genesis and beyond.

The laconic nature of the Genesis narrative leaves many questions unanswered. This is especially true of chapter 3. The unexpected appearance of a serpent that is hostile to YHWH God takes the reader by surprise. What is the serpent's history? Why does it deceive the human couple? Why do the human couple listen to the serpent rather than God? Such questions are not addressed by the narrator. Importantly, we must not allow speculative answers to distract us from what the text is saying. Restraining our curiosity, we should focus solely on what the author has chosen to reveal. While human inquisitiveness urges us to fill the gaps, these details are not needed to comprehend the ongoing narrative. Unnecessary speculation may inappropriately influence our reading of the rest of Genesis.

Comments

3:1–5. A new scene is marked in verse 1 by the introduction of the serpent as a new character. Attention is drawn to the serpent by placing the noun נָחָשׁ (*nāḥāš*, "serpent") before the verb in verse 1; the more usual sequence in Hebrew narrative is verb followed by noun. The appearance of a serpent is unexpected, especially given that it is a "wild animal"

---

[132] Compare the use of the verb שָׁמַר (*šāmar*) in 2:15 and 3:24. In the latter verse it is used with the sense "to guard" with reference to accessing the tree of life.

(lit. "an animal of the field"; cf. KJV, JPS, ESV). This is not a creature that we would normally expect to find in the garden. The description of the serpent as a "wild animal" recalls God's instructions in 1:28 that the human couple are to rule over "every creature that crawls on the earth." Unfortunately, the subsequent actions of the human couple reveal that they fail to exercise authority over the serpent. By heeding the serpent's words, they submit to its authority and come under its control.

Adding a sense of suspense, the serpent is described as "the most cunning of all the wild animals." While the Hebrew adjective עָרוּם (*ʿārûm*) can be rendered "prudent" (Prov 12:16 ESV) or "sensible" (Prov 13:16 CSB), it also conveys on occasions a negative nuance (e.g., Job 5:12). If there is ambiguity regarding the meaning of עָרוּם (*ʿārûm*), the serpent's initial words immediately confirm that its intentions are focused on undermining God's authority. By describing the serpent as עָרוּם (*ʿārûm*), the narrator creates an interesting wordplay with the term עֲרוּמִּים (*ʿărûmmîm*, "naked") that is used in 2:25 to describe the human couple. This play on words connects the protagonists in the story.

The serpent's initial words have the appearance of being an innocent question. Yet, they are cleverly designed to engage the woman in a conversation that will have life-changing consequences for everyone involved. Strikingly, the serpent always speaks of "God" and not "YHWH God." Its refusal to use God's personal name is a subtle indication of its disdain for the Creator. Echoing God's instructions in 2:16, the serpent subtly alters what God says by introducing a "not" and making the verb less emphatic. Whereas God's words emphasize his generosity in providing food, the serpent implies the exact opposite. The serpent sows a seed of doubt that God may not be as generous as the woman supposes.

The woman attempts to correct the serpent's misunderstanding, but her words in verses 2–3 do not match what God said previously. She fails to describe the tree in the middle of the garden as "the tree of the knowledge of good and evil" and she introduces the idea that God prohibited the man and the woman from touching it. While on the surface the woman's paraphrase of God's instructions appears accurate, and even more restrictive, the small changes that she makes may indicate that she, or possibly the man, who may have repeated the instructions to her, did not take to heart all that God said. As Hess observes, "The woman reports the warning in the lightest possible terms, omitting both the sense of the consequence occurring on the same day and the emphatic form of the verb, 'lest you die.' "[133] The woman's response to the serpent possibly signals that she is amenable to rejecting God's command, as her subsequent actions confirm.[134] Although God's instruction not to eat from the tree of the knowledge of good and evil was given to the man prior to the creation of the woman, both the serpent and the woman assume that the prohibition was applicable to all humans. From all that is said, there is no reason to assume that the woman is more easily deceived than the man simply because the serpent addressed her first.

The serpent's emphatic announcement, "No! You will certainly not die" (v. 4) contrasts sharply with God's strict warning (2:17). The serpent challenges God's authority by contradicting what he has said. Adding to this, the serpent proceeds to suggest that God has intentionally restricted the human couple's access to the tree to prevent them becoming like God, "knowing good and evil" (v. 5). At this point, the human couple, as God's vicegerents, should have responded by exerting authority over the serpent, as God had commissioned them (1:26, 28). Unfortunately, they neglect to do this, betraying the one who appointed them to rule on his behalf. Ironically, although God has made them in his image and likeness (1:26), the human couple desire personal autonomy. Being God's vicegerents is insufficient for them. By heeding the serpent, they disregard YHWH God, the one who has given them authority to rule over the whole earth.

God is the one who declares what is "good" (or "not good"). The serpent challenges the humans to reject God's ordering. They are to decide for themselves, taking on God's role. Implicitly, by accepting what the serpent says, they exalt the serpent over God. The serpent's words carry more authority that those of God. By their response the human couple elevate a creature above the Creator. In doing so, they come under the control of the serpent, who becomes the *de facto* ruler of this world (cf. Matt 4:8–9; Luke 4:5–7; John 12:31; 14:30; 16:11).

---

[133] Richard S. Hess, "The Roles of the Woman and the Man in Genesis 3," *Themelios* 18 (1993): 16.

[134] Jeffrey J. Niehaus, *When Did Eve Sin? The Fall and Biblical Historiography* (Bellingham: Lexham, 2020), contends that Eve's firsthand report of what God said should not be interpreted as adding to or altering what God said to Adam in 2:17. Rather, it is a fuller, accurate account of what YHWH God said. Niehaus adopts this view to align with the idea that, according to his reading of the apostle Paul's words in 1 Tim 2:14, Eve only sinned after the serpent deceived her. However, Paul may have viewed the deception as beginning with the serpent's first words to the woman.

The serpent is the master of half-truths. Even some modern commentators are persuaded that it, unlike God, tells the truth.[135] From one perspective, it could be argued that the serpent is correct when it claims that the eyes of the human couple will be opened and they will not die. And God's words in verse 22 confirm, as the serpent claimed, that the man "has now become like one of us, knowing good and evil." Yet, even if we grant that the serpent is possibly correct regarding these items, other claims by the serpent are false. Contrary to what the serpent says, subsequent events do not portray the couple as becoming equal to God. Eve's remark that the serpent deceived her (v. 13) strongly implies that the serpent did not speak the whole truth. If its words were true, there would be no deception. While the human couple do not immediately die physically, they die spiritually, being alienated from the One who is the source of life.

The image of a talking serpent, boldly opposing God, is strange, suggesting that this is no ordinary creature. The present episode does not expand upon the identity of the serpent, but later traditions associate "the ancient serpent" with "the Devil and Satan, the one who deceives the whole world" (Rev 12:9; cf. John 8:44; 1 John 3:8; Rev 20:2).[136] As McKeown observes, "Its devious arguments and malicious intention are enough to make it clear that this snake symbolizes evil—not the belligerent, aggressive kind of evil, but the subtle and seductive kind."[137]

Given the serpent's actions, we should observe that evil is already present in the world before Adam and Eve disobey God. There is another story to be told regarding the history of the serpent.

3:6–7. Encouraged by the serpent, the woman surveys the tree of the knowledge of good and evil. Like every tree in the garden, according to 2:9, this tree is aesthetically "pleasing in appearance" and bears fruit that is "good for food" (v. 6). However, the woman believes that it is also desirable for obtaining insight, as reflected in its designation as "the tree of the knowledge of good and evil." Despite God's prohibition

---

[135] Robert P. Gordon, "The Ethics of Eden: Truth-Telling in Genesis 2–3," in *Ethical and Unethical in the Old Testament: God and Humans in Dialogue*, ed. Katharine J. Dell, LHBOTS 528 (London; New York: T&T Clark International, 2010), 11–33, provides a helpful discussion of the debate surrounding this issue.

[136] For a fuller discussion, see Paul R. Williamson, "Snakes and Dragons: A Neglected Theological Trajectory of Genesis 3:15 in Scripture?," in Williamson and Cefalu, *The Seed of Promise*, 332–52; cf. Dörnyei, *Progressive Creation*, 158.

[137] McKeown, *Genesis*, 34–35.

against eating its fruit, the woman takes and eats. She also gives to her husband and he eats. The expression "with her" (v. 6) indicates that the man is present when the woman takes from the tree. Fully aware of what she does, he does not intervene to stop her. The man and the woman both yearn after personal autonomy. Misguided in their quest to attain knowledge of good and evil, the couple associate themselves with evil by listening to the serpent.

As soon as they eat, the man and the woman become aware that they are naked. Their lack of clothing becomes an immediate source of embarrassment. Consequently, they attempt to cover themselves by using fig leaves. Their reaction signals that something in their nature has changed due to eating the fruit from the tree of the knowledge of good and evil. Moreover, their reaction to their nakedness conveys a sense of alarm. This becomes even more apparent when their nakedness causes them to hide from God (vv. 8–10). They have acquired "knowledge," but this "knowledge" does not enhance their experience of life. It alienates them from their Creator. Subsequent chapters of Genesis highlight the tragic consequences of Adam and Eve's actions as their descendants engage in fratricide and fill the earth with violence.

3:8–13. Although the CSB translation reads "at the time of the evening breeze," the Hebrew text is less specific as regards the time of day, speaking simply of the "breezy time of day" (NJPS).[138] The brief description of YHWH God "walking in the garden" conveys a sense of calm. However, because of their nakedness, the man and woman are fearful of God and hide among the trees of the garden.[139] Fear causes them to hide. There is no escaping the consequences of their disobedience. Rather than listening to the voice of God, the man has listened to the voice of his wife. When questioned by God, the man and the woman separately shift the blame to

---

[138] Daniel C. Timmer, *Creation, Tabernacle, and Sabbath: The Sabbath Frame of Exodus 31:12–17; 35:1–3 in Exegetical and Theological Perspective*, Forschungen zur Religion und Literatur des Alten und Neuen Testaments 227 (Göttingen: Vandenhoeck & Ruprecht, 2009), 81n71, rejects the view of Jeffrey J. Niehaus, "In the Wind of the Storm: Another Look at Genesis iii 8," *VT* 44 (1994): 263–67; Jeffrey J. Niehaus, *God at Sinai* (Grand Rapids: Zondervan, 1995), 155–59, that God's appearance in the garden is a 'storm-theophany.'

[139] Clark, "Legal Background," 277, highlights the irony of the man's comment about hearing God and being afraid: "Man has not 'heard the voice of Yahweh,' with all that phrase means in terms of obedience."

another. While both humans hide, the Hebrew text places the emphasis on the man and his interaction with God in verses 9–11.[140]

3:14–15. After questioning the man and the woman, God addresses the serpent, whom the woman has just blamed for deceiving her (v. 13). Underlining the seriousness of what has occurred, God pronounces judgement, placing the serpent under the severest curse. Whereas in Genesis 1, God's blessing is linked to the prospering of living creatures (1:22, 28), cursing is the antithesis of blessing, signaling God's displeasure.

While the CSB translation, like others (e.g., NLT) takes the preposition מִן (*min*), which comes after the verb "cursed," as indicating a comparative ("more than"), it is more likely that it indicates here separation from other creatures.[141] There is no reason to assume that other creatures were cursed to a lesser degree due to the actions of the serpent. As punishment the serpent will be forced to go around on its belly and eat dust (v. 14), signs of disgrace and humiliation.

As a further punishment, God announces that there will be hostility between the serpent and the woman, and between their respective "offspring." While the initial reference to "offspring" could denote descendants in the plural—on its own the Hebrew noun זֶרַע (*zera*ʿ) may denote either one descendant or many descendants—the final part of God's speech favors a singular interpretation of "offspring."[142] YHWH God indicates that one of Eve's descendants will strike the head of the serpent. The woman's offspring will punish the serpent, but this will not be achieved without hurt to the human victor. Both parties to the conflict will suffer injury, but the image of the woman's offspring bruising the head of the serpent suggests that the latter will be wounded fatally. By way of contrast, the serpent only bruises the heel of the woman's descendant. Since the serpent targeted the woman in the garden of Eden, there is an element of poetic justice when God speaks of the woman's offspring punishing the serpent. As Cefalu helpfully remarks, "God will not allow

---

[140] In v. 8b, the use of a singular verb וַיִּתְחַבֵּא (*wayyitḥabbē*ʾ, "and he hid") with a compound subject ("the man and his wife") draws attention to "the man"; see E. J. Revell, "Concord with Compound Subjects and Related Uses of Pronouns," *VT* 43 (1993): 69–87.

[141] Compare the similar expression in 4:11, where the curse on Cain involves separation from the ground (see JPS, NJB, NRSV).

[142] The case for this is developed by C. John Collins, "A Syntactical Note (Genesis 3:15): Is the Woman's Seed Singular or Plural?," *TynBul* 48 (1997): 139–48; Collins, *Genesis 1–4*, 155–59. See Cheek, "Recent Developments," 215–36.

the entire race to go the way of the serpent. A seed shall come from the woman who shall ultimately crush the serpent's head (Gen 3:15)."[143]

A long tradition favors a reading of verse 15 that views it as the first biblical reference to a messiah-like figure. Early evidence for a singular interpretation of "offspring" comes in the pre-Christian Septuagint translation of Genesis. This Greek translation uses the masculine singular pronoun αὐτός (*autos*) to denote the one who will strike the head of the serpent.[144] Had the translator desired, other options were available in Greek to indicate a plural reading of the Hebrew text. In Christian tradition, verse 15 became known as the *Protevangelium*, the first announcement of the Gospel.

Unfortunately, over the centuries Christian interpreters have frequently read into this verse more than the text of Genesis says. Viewed in isolation from the rest of Genesis, verse 15 provides limited evidence to suggest that it refers directly to Jesus Christ and his defeat of Satan. However, when read in the context of the whole of Genesis, taking into account how the ongoing narrative traces the offspring of Eve through a unique line of descendants, there is good reason to see God's pronouncement regarding the defeat of the serpent as promising an individual who will succeed where Adam and Eve failed.[145] The subsequent narrative develops the programmatic agenda introduced in 3:15. We see this initially when, following Cain's murder of Abel, the promised offspring of the woman is associated with the descendants of Seth (see 4:25).

If a plural interpretation of the woman's offspring is adopted in verse 15, as many commentators favor,[146] this must surely imply that all of Eve's descendants will be responsible for the defeat of the serpent. This is the conclusion of Abernethy and Goswell, who write, "Victory in Gen. 3:15,

---

[143] Rita F. Cefalu, "Royal Priestly Heirs to the Restoration Promise of Genesis 3:15: A Biblical Theological Perspective on the Sons of God in Genesis 6," *WTJ* 76 (2014): 367.

[144] R. A. Martin, "The Earliest Messianic Interpretation of Genesis 3:15," *JBL* 84 (1965): 425–27.

[145] For a fuller discussion, see Alexander, "From Adam to Judah," 5–19; Alexander, "Genealogies, Seed and the Compositional Unity of Genesis," 255–70; T. Desmond Alexander, "Messianic Ideology in the Book of Genesis," in Satterthwaite, Hess, and Wenham, *The Lord's Anointed*, 19–39.

[146] E.g., Hermann Gunkel, *Genesis*, trans. Mark E. Biddle, Mercer Library of Biblical Studies (Macon: Mercer University Press, 1997), 20–21; John Skinner, *Genesis*, 2nd ed., ICC (Edinburgh: T&T Clark, 1930), 80–81; Speiser, *Genesis*, 24; von Rad, *Genesis*, 93; Bruce Vawter, *On Genesis: A New Reading* (Garden City: Doubleday, 1977), 83–84; Westermann, *Genesis 1-11*, 260–61.

then, anticipates the victory of humanity over evil through obedience to God resulting in restored relationships with one another, God, and creation."[147] Such a reading, however, sits uncomfortably with the evidence provided in the rest of Genesis, especially the account of the flood in chapters 6–9 where only Noah is viewed as being righteous.[148]

3:16. After addressing the serpent, God speaks to the woman, announcing her punishment for disregarding his instructions. The expression עִצְּבוֹנֵךְ וְהֵרֹנֵךְ (*ʿiṣṣĕbônēk wĕhērōnēk*) is rendered by most English versions as "pains in childbearing" or something very similar. This translation rests on the assumption that the Hebrew expression is an example of hendiadys.[149] An alternative rendering would be "your painful toil and your pregnancy." According to Meyers, the noun הֵרוֹן (*hērôn*) does not refer to childbirth, but rather pregnancy in general.[150] She also observes that עִצָּבוֹן (*ʿiṣṣābôn*, "toil") is not linked to childbirth elsewhere in the Old Testament. For these reasons, she rejects the idea that the two nouns form a hendiadys referring to birth pains. She suggests that they refer to the woman's "productive work" and her "procreative role," observing that עִצָּבוֹן (*ʿiṣṣābôn*) comes in verse 17b, referring to the "painful toil" that the man must undertake in order to eat.[151] Consequently, she translates God's initial words to the woman as: "I will greatly increase your work and your pregnancies; (along) with toil you shall give birth to children."[152] While

---

[147] Andrew T. Abernethy and Gregory Goswell, *God's Messiah in the Old Testament: Expectations of a Coming King* (Grand Rapids: Baker Academic, 2020), 13.

[148] See T. Desmond Alexander, "The Hope for the Blessing of the Nations in the Book of Genesis," in *Hope for the World from the Old Testament: Essays in Honour of J. Gordon McConville on his 70th Birthday*, eds. David G. Firth, Jamie A. Grant and Alison Lo (2025), 7–17.

[149] E.g., Speiser, *Genesis*, 24. A slightly different explanation is offered by Collins, *Genesis 1-4*, 153n18, who takes "the 'and' to be a *waw*-explicative, and 'your pregnancy' as an accusative of specification."

[150] Carol L. Meyers, "Gender Roles and Genesis 3:16 Revisited," in *The Word of the Lord Shall Go Forth: Essays in Honor of David Noel Freedman*, eds. Carol L. Meyers and M. O'Connor (Winona Lake: Eisenbrauns, 1983), 337–54; cf. Cassuto, *From Adam to Noah*, 165

[151] Meyers, "Gender Roles," 345. Provan, *Discovering Genesis*, 87, contends that עִצָּבוֹן (*ʿiṣṣābôn*) refers to "generalized pain" and is not restricted to childbearing.

[152] Meyers, "Gender Roles," 344. Although Meyers assumes that God will increase the number of pregnancies, it is possible that his comment refers to the length of the pregnancy. The Hebrew term הֵרֹנֵךְ (*hērōnēk*, "your pregnancy") is singular. See Hess, "Roles of the Woman and the Man," 17.

Meyer's approach has much to commend it, some scholars continue to favor retaining the concept of hendiadys.[153]

The wording of the second half of verse 16 has given rise to a variety of interpretations. The noun תְּשׁוּקָה (*tĕšûqâ*, "craving/desire/turning") occurs in the Old Testament elsewhere only in Genesis 4:7 and Song of Songs 7:11. There is no reason to assume that it refers to sexual desire, despite its presence in Song of Songs.[154] Its use in verse 16 corresponds to how it is used in 4:7, especially given the presence in both verses of the verb מָשַׁל (*māšal*, "to rule"). The parallels between 3:16 and 4:7 suggest that they should be interpreted in similar ways. In 4:7, sin's desire is to possess/control Cain, but he is encouraged by God to resist it.[155] If 3:16 is read in a similar way, the woman's desire is to control her husband, but he is encouraged by God to resist her.[156]

Scholars differ in their interpretation of verse 16b, depending upon how the husband-wife relationship is understood in Genesis 1–2. Some come to verse 16 with the premise that Genesis 1–2 affirms male hierarchy or leadership. Starting from this position, several differing interpretations have been suggested for verse 16b. (a) Describing the future, verse 16b affirms that the woman will oppose male dominance. In the light of the man's failure to restrain the woman's actions, God commands the man to exercise leadership in the future. (b) In verse 16b God commands the woman to find blessing in the future by submitting to her husband, having failed to do so prior to this. Others come to verse 16 with the understanding that chapters 1–2 present an egalitarian view of the marital relationship. Starting with this premise, different interpretations of verse 16b are possible. (a) Verse 16b describes female subordination to men as a future

---

153 See Davidson, *Flame of Yahweh*, 59–60. Favoring hendiadys, he understands עִצָּבוֹן (*ʿiṣṣābôn*) as "toil" not "pain."

154 Joel N. Lohr, "Sexual Desire? Eve, Genesis 3:16 and תשוקה," *JBL* 130 (2011): 227–46 demonstrates that the earliest translations of v. 16 do not support adopting a sexual connotation for the noun תְּשׁוּקָה (*tĕšûqâ*), which he takes to mean "return/turning."

155 See Comments on 4:7.

156 Susan T. Foh, "What Is the Woman's Desire," *WTJ* 37 (1975): 376–83; cf. Mathews, *Genesis 1–11:26*, 250–51; Collins, *Genesis 1–4*, 159–60; Provan, *Discovering Genesis*, 86. Foh, Mathews, and Collins all assume that Gen 1–2 supports man's headship/leadership over the woman, but their interpretation of v. 16b does not rest on this assumption. Foh's approach is challenged by Janson C. Condren, "Toward a Purge of the Battle of the Sexes and 'Return' for the Original Meaning of Genesis 3:16b," *JETS* 60 (2017): 227–45, who favors the meaning "return" for תְּשׁוּקָה (*tĕšûqâ*). However, Condren fails to address adequately the correspondence between 3:16 and 4:7 and how this might inform the interpretation of 3:16.

reality, but this is to be understood as an evil consequence of sin. God never intended a wife to be subject to her husband, but this becomes a fact of life due to the fallen nature of humanity. (b) God's pronouncement in verse 16b is prescriptive, requiring a woman to be submissive to her husband. This requirement is not to be understood as God's ideal but is rather a concession to the inherent sinfulness of human beings.

In view of the enigmatic nature of God's pronouncement concerning the woman, we should be cautious in siding with a particular reading of this verse. Without reading too much into what is said in verse 16b, we may conclude that from this time onward the relationship between husband and wife will not reflect fully the harmonious unity that God intended. As Foh remarks, "These words mark the beginning of the battle of the sexes. ... The rule of love founded in paradise is replaced by struggle, tyranny and domination."[157] Because they have eaten from the tree of the knowledge of good and evil, the human couple will not experience the harmony and oneness that God intended when he formed the woman to be a soulmate for the man.

3:17–19. After addressing the serpent and the woman, God turns his attention to the man. YHWH God rebukes the man for attributing greater authority to his wife's words than to God's command. By disobeying God's unambiguous instruction not to eat from the tree of the knowledge of good and evil, the man comes under judgment. Since the man's disobedience involved eating, it is appropriate that his punishment should also focus on eating.

As a result of the man's actions, God curses the ground. From what is said by Lamech regarding the naming of Noah in 5:29, God's curse upon the ground has a lasting impact. Whereas 2:5 highlights the expectation that the human (אָדָם, *ʾādām*) will work the ground (הָאֲדָמָה, *hāʾădāmâ*) and 2:7 underlines that God created the human (הָאָדָם, *hāʾādām*) from the dust of the ground (הָאֲדָמָה, *hāʾădāmâ*), this activity will now require עִצָּבוֹן (*ʿiṣṣābôn*, "painful toil"), the same toil that is mentioned in connection with the woman in verse 16. To compound Adam's hardship in cultivating food, the ground will produce "thorns and thistles" (v. 18).

Whereas God had generously provided an abundance of food for the human couple in the garden of Eden (2:9), the man's punishment will involve expulsion from the garden (cf. v. 23), and he will be forced to

---

[157] Foh, "What Is the Woman's Desire," 382.

eat "the plants of the field" (v. 18). In chapter 2 the "garden" (גַּן, *gan*) is associated with trees that bear fruit, whereas "the field" (הַשָּׂדֶה, *haśśādeh*) denotes the region outside the garden, where עֵשֶׂב (*ʿēśeb*, "plants") grow.

According to 1:29–30, humans were expected to enjoy the seeds of plants and the fruit of trees, whereas other creatures were to eat "every green plant." In stating that the man will eat "the plants of the field," God anticipates the couple's expulsion from the garden. The man will be forced to toil strenuously—"by the sweat of your brow"—to produce food throughout his entire life.

Lastly, God indicates that the creative process by which the man was made will be reversed. Formed out of "the dust from the ground" (2:7), the man on dying will return to "dust." God had warned the man that death would be a consequence of eating from the tree of the knowledge of good and evil (2:17). By way of underlining this outcome, God actively prevents the human couple from eating from the tree of life (2:22).

God's remarks concerning the punishment of the man clearly imply that he will continue to live for a time before returning to the dust from which he was formed. How does this fit with God prior statement in 2:17 that the man will certainly die "on the day" that he eats from the tree of the knowledge of good and evil? Several observations may help explain this apparent inconsistency. First, the expression "on the day" (בְּיוֹם, *bĕyôm*) may simply be an idiom meaning "when" (cf. NIV translation of 2:17). The same expression comes in 2:4 to denote the time when "the Lord God made the earth and the heavens." In 2:4 בְּיוֹם (*bĕyôm*) does not refer to one specific day; chapter 1 speaks of God's creative activity being spread over six days. A similar example occurs in 1 Kings 2:37 regarding the warning issued by Solomon to Shimei. Solomon threatens to have Shimei put to death "on the day" that he leaves Jerusalem. The punishment, however, is not enforced on the very day that Shimei leaves Jerusalem (cf. 1 Kgs 2:40–46). Second, it is possible that the divine pronouncement involving death in 2:17 does not refer to physical death (i.e., a return to the dust) but denotes spiritual death (i.e., alienation from God, the source of life).

3:20–21. Having recorded the judgments that God pronounces on the serpent, woman and man in verse 14–19, the narrator mentions several other details to bring closure to this episode. The man names the woman Eve, חַוָּה (*ḥavvâ*), which means "life."[158] This involves a wordplay on the adjective חַי (*ḥay*, "living"). Against the background of God's remark regarding human mortality (v. 19), this naming of Eve underlines the importance of the woman's procreative role. Without offspring, the divine promise regarding the defeat of the serpent cannot be fulfilled. The book of Genesis is especially interested in human offspring, underlining the importance of women in the outworking of God's plans for the earth. The inability of women to bear children will surface in the ongoing narrative as an obstacle to the fulfilment of God's purposes.

The brief reference to YHWH God's clothing of the human couple with animal skins is sometimes interpreted as involving a sacrifice. Waltke and Fredricks comment, "The killing of an animal necessary to make garments of skin may suggest/imply the image of a sacrifice for sin."[159] Building on this, they state, "Through (God's) sacrifice, he restores the alienated couple to fellowship with him and one another."[160] In a similar vein, Davidson argues that the clothing of Adam and Eve with animal skins marks their priestly status.[161]

However, there is no evidence to suggest that the making of the garments involves a sacrifice. Contrary to the claim of Waltke and Fredricks, the human couple are not restored to fellowship with God but expelled from the garden of Eden. As for the garments being priestly clothing, this seems highly unlikely in the light of how priests are clothed elsewhere in the Old Testament (see especially Exod 28). Linen is normally used to make priestly clothing, avoiding the use of any material that involves the death of an animal, including leather sandals. Rather than being a positive statement, the clothing of the human couple with skins is more likely to convey the idea that they now resemble other earthly creatures, having lost their special status as God's vicegerents. Their future diet (v. 18) and their eviction from the garden (vv. 23–24) also signal that they have forfeited through disobedience their divine commission to rule over the earth on God's behalf.

3:22–24. The final verses of chapter 3 focus on the expulsion of the human couple from the garden of Eden and the measures that God puts in place to prevent them accessing the tree of life. Acknowledging that

---

158 The LXX translates the Hebrew name as Ζωή *Zōē*, the Greek term for "life."

159 Waltke and Fredricks, *Genesis*, 95n56.

160 Waltke and Fredricks, *Genesis*, 95.

161 Davidson, *Flame of Yahweh*, 58.

the human couple have been changed through eating from the tree of the knowledge of good and evil, YHWH God expresses his concern that they might now eat from the tree of life, which is first mentioned briefly in 2:9, and live forever. The expression "become like one of us" possibly indicates that there is a plurality associated with God's nature (see Comments on 1:26).

Previously God placed the man in the garden "to work (עָבַד, *ʿābad*) ... and take care of (שָׁמַר, *šāmar*)" the ground (2:15). The same Hebrew verbs reappear in verses 23–24. However, on this occasion, the tasks are separated. Whereas God instructs the humans "to work (עָבַד, *ʿābad*) the ground" outside the garden, he places cherubim and a flaming sword at the eastern entrance of the garden "to guard (שָׁמַר, *šāmar*) the way to the tree of life."

Elsewhere in the Old Testament, cherubim are mentioned primarily in connection with the tabernacle/temple (e.g., Exod 25:18–20, 22; 1 Kgs 6:23, 25, 27–29, 32, 35) and God's presence (e.g., Ezek 10:1–4, 6–9, 15–20). They appear to be two-winged, or possibly four-winged,[162] creatures, unlike seraphim, which have six wings (Isa 6:2, 6). The images of cherubim associated with the tabernacle and temple suggest that they are commonly viewed as controlling access to God.

As an additional measure to prevent the humans from approaching the tree of life, God places at the entrance to the garden a sword of fire that constantly whirls preventing anyone from safely passing it. Only in the future new Jerusalem is human access to the tree of life restored (Rev 22:2, 14). Observing the consequences of being expelled from Eden, Morales writes,

> The path of exile through Eden's gates was, therefore, a path from life to death, from light to darkness, from harmony to dysfunction and strife, from health to sickness, from security to violence, from compassion to inhumanity, from wholeness to brokenness, from peace with God to enmity—from a life of friendship with God to alienation.[163]

[162] If the winged creatures described in Ezek 1 are cherubim, they have four wings. While the term "cherubim" is not used in Ezek 1 to denote the creatures linked to the throne-chariot on which God is present, it appears in Ezek 10:2–22. See Daniel I. Block, *The Book of Ezekiel: Chapters 1–24*, NICOT (Grand Rapids: Eerdmans, 1997), 314–27.

[163] L. Michael Morales, *Exodus Old and New: A Biblical Theology of Redemption*, Essential Studies in Biblical Theology (Downers Grove: InterVarsity Press Academic, 2020), 9.

Bridge

Assessments of the significance of Genesis 3 differ enormously. Brueggemann describes the narrative as "an exceedingly marginal text,"[164] because there are few direct references to it in the rest of the Old Testament. Yet, it has a profound impact upon the plot of the narrative that runs from Genesis to Kings, influencing the storyline that follows. With good reason, all that happens in the garden of Eden is extremely important for comprehending the human condition. As F. F. Bruce observes:

> Not surprisingly, later reflexion found in the Genesis 3 narrative more than meets the eye—not simply a primitive act of disobedience which resulted in a variety of disasters but the motif of a counterfeit likeness to God which involved an attempt to establish moral autonomy. This attempt so completely constitutes the essence of sin that the fall narrative, whether interpreted historically or symbolically, has rightly come to occupy a central place in this department of traditional Christian theology.[165]

Adam and Eve's disobedience endangers the fulfilment of God's creation plan to make the earth his dwelling-place. With good reason, Cefalu observes,

> The privileges of divine presence, blessing, and mission so intricately bound up with obedience to God and reverence toward his garden sanctuary have now been forfeited. Adam's failure to guard the garden's sanctity by succumbing to the serpent's temptation has resulted in devastating consequences for the entire creation and the human race.[166]

The human couple's intimate relationship with God is shattered, as they are driven from the garden. As Walton notes, "in the aftermath of the fall, the greatest loss was not paradise; it was God's presence." Furthermore, as God warned (2:17), Adam and Eve come under the power of death. In this context, "death" is not necessarily the end of physical life, but isolation from the one who gives life. This is symbolized by the fact that they are denied access to the "tree of life" (3:22–24).

---

[164] Walter Brueggemann, *Genesis*, Interpretation (Atlanta: John Knox, 1982), 41.

[165] F. F. Bruce, "Sin, Redemption, and Sacrifice: A Biblical and Patristic Study," *Biblica* 54 (1973): 116.

[166] Cefalu, "Royal Priestly Heirs," 361–62.

As soon as they eat from the "tree of the knowledge of good and evil," Adam and Eve experience a profound inner transformation; they become ashamed of their nakedness and seek to cover themselves by using the leaves of plants. However, before he expels them from the garden, God clothes them with garments made from animal skin (Gen 3:21). Since they now resemble the animals, over whom God intended them to rule, their clothing possibly signals that they no longer have God's authority to oversee other creatures as his representative.

Despite having forfeited their authority as God's vicegerents, Adam and Eve retain an ability to govern, and this passes to their descendants. Tragically, humans misuse their inherent gift to rule and fill the earth with violence. From Cain's murder of Abel onward, Genesis records humanity's failure to conform to God's expectations. People are so violent that their actions defile the earth with bloodshed. God's regret at the wickedness of humanity prompts him to destroy them utterly through a terrible flood. Only Noah finds favor in God's eyes, and on his account a small remnant is saved from the flood.

The impact of death on humanity due to Adam and Eve's actions is highlighted by the apostle Paul in 1 Corinthians 15. Contrasting Adam and Jesus Christ, he writes, "For since death came through a man, the resurrection of the dead also comes through a man. For just as in Adam all die, so also in Christ all will be made alive" (1 Cor 15:21–22). Emphasizing the significance of Christ's resurrection, Paul later remarks, "For he must reign until he puts all his enemies under his feet. The last enemy to be abolished is death" (1 Cor 15:25–26). As God's perfect vicegerent, Christ reverses the consequences of Adam and Eve's betrayal of God. In the process of doing this, as Paul notes elsewhere, the whole of creation "will also be set free from the bondage to decay" (Rom 8:21).

The theme of sin and death in Genesis 2–3 is also discussed by the apostle Paul in Romans 5:12–21.[167] Highlighting Christ's role in delivering humans from death, the author of Hebrews writes, "Now since the children have flesh and blood in common, Jesus also shared in these, so that through his death he might destroy the one holding the power of death—that is, the devil—and free those who were held in slavery all their lives by the fear of death" (Heb 2:14–15).

---

[167] See Dörnyei, *Progressive Creation*, 70–73.

C. Adam and Eve's Descendants (4:1–26)

1 The man was intimate with his wife Eve, and she conceived and gave
birth to Cain. She said, "I have had a male child with the LORD's help." 2
She also gave birth to his brother Abel. Now Abel became a shepherd
of flocks, but Cain worked the ground. 3 In the course of time Cain
presented some of the land's produce as an offering to the LORD. 4 And
Abel also presented an offering—some of the firstborn of his flock and
their fat portions. The LORD had regard for Abel and his offering, 5 but
he did not have regard for Cain and his offering. Cain was furious, and
he looked despondent.

6 Then the LORD said to Cain, "Why are you furious? And why do you
look despondent? 7 If you do what is right, won't you be accepted? But
if you do not do what is right, sin is crouching at the door. Its desire is
for you, but you must rule over it."

8 Cain said to his brother Abel, "Let's go out to the field." And while
they were in the field, Cain attacked his brother Abel and killed him.

9 Then the LORD said to Cain, "Where is your brother Abel?"

"I don't know," he replied. "Am I my brother's guardian?"

10 Then he said, "What have you done? Your brother's blood cries out
to me from the ground! 11 So now you are cursed, alienated from the
ground that opened its mouth to receive your brother's blood you have
shed. 12 If you work the ground, it will never again give you its yield.
You will be a restless wanderer on the earth."

13 But Cain answered the LORD, "My punishment is too great to bear! 14
Since you are banishing me today from the face of the earth, and I must
hide from your presence and become a restless wanderer on the earth,
whoever finds me will kill me."

15 Then the LORD replied to him, "In that case, whoever kills Cain will
suffer vengeance seven times over." And he placed a mark on Cain so
that whoever found him would not kill him. 16 Then Cain went out from
the LORD's presence and lived in the land of Nod, east of Eden.

17 Cain was intimate with his wife, and she conceived and gave birth to
Enoch. Then Cain became the builder of a city, and he named the city
Enoch after his son. 18 Irad was born to Enoch, Irad fathered Mehujael,
Mehujael fathered Methushael, and Methushael fathered Lamech. 19
Lamech took two wives for himself, one named Adah and the other
named Zillah. 20 Adah bore Jabal; he was the father of the nomadic
herdsmen. 21 His brother was named Jubal; he was the father of all who
play the lyre and the flute. 22 Zillah bore Tubal-cain, who made all kinds
of bronze and iron tools. Tubal-cain's sister was Naamah.

> [23] Lamech said to his wives:
> Adah and Zillah, hear my voice;
> wives of Lamech, pay attention to my words.
> For I killed a man for wounding me,
> a young man for striking me.
> [24] If Cain is to be avenged seven times over,
> then for Lamech it will be seventy-seven times!

> [25] Adam was intimate with his wife again, and she gave birth to a son
> and named him Seth, for she said, "God has given me another child in
> place of Abel, since Cain killed him." [26] A son was born to Seth also, and
> he named him Enosh. At that time people began to call on the name
> of the LORD.

Context

The opening chapter of Genesis introduces the expectation that the human population will increase to fill the earth (1:28). In a similar vein, God's remarks to the serpent and the woman contain references to offspring (3:15) and children (3:16) respectively. And the naming of Eve highlights her role in procreation. Against this background, chapter 4 begins by briefly describing the birth of two sons to Eve: Cain and Abel. God's positive attitude toward Abel suggests that he may contribute in some way to the defeat of the serpent that God announces in 3:15. However, Abel's untimely death at the hands of Cain undermines any hope that might be associated with these brothers. Although Cain is Eve's firstborn son, his line of offspring leads to Lamech (4:18–24), who, as both a bigamist and murderer, is an unlikely candidate to defeat the serpent. Importantly, the patriline of Cain ends with Lamech, who sees himself as resembling his ancestor. At this point, the author of Genesis jumps back in time to observe that Eve gave birth to a third son, Seth. In marked contrast to Cain's lineage, the account of the patriline of Seth is marked by positive statements in 4:25–26 and continues to be traced throughout the rest of Genesis. The quest for the one who will overcome the serpent is linked to Seth's descendants.[168]

[168] See the fuller discussion in Patterson, *Plot-Structure of Genesis, 59-71.*

Comments

4:1–2. The Hebrew text of Genesis marks the start of a new episode by placing the subject, הָאָדָם (*hāʾādām*, "the human")[169] prior to the verb; usually in biblical Hebrew narrative the subject comes after the verb. With a minimum of detail, the narrative records how Eve conceives and gives birth to Cain. While the narrator emphasizes that Eve is the man's wife, she is the one who speaks following the birth of Cain. Cain's name (קַיִן *qayin*) is linked to the verb קָנִיתִי *qānîtî* "I have acquired" that comes in the short statement made by Eve.

While many English versions render the final part of Eve's comment as "with the Lord's help" (CSB, NLT; cf. ESV, NIV, NRSV), the Hebrew text simply says אֶת־יְהוָה (*ʾet-yhwh*), which could be rendered "with YHWH."[170] Eve recognizes YHWH's part in enabling her to bear Cain. This emphasis on the woman's role in giving birth is possibly intended to pick up on God's remark that the offspring of the woman shall overcome the serpent (3:15).

A second son is born to Eve. His name in Hebrew is הֶבֶל (*hebel*), which, due to the pausal form used at the end of the first clause in verse 2, has come into English as Abel.[171] The noun הֶבֶל (*hebel*), which can mean "a breath" (cf. Isa 57:13), occurs frequently in the book of Ecclesiastes, where it is often used to describe the "futility/meaninglessness/absurdity" of life (e.g., Eccl 1:2). It seems unlikely that Abel was named הֶבֶל (*hebel*) due to these negative connotations. However, his name conveys well the nature of his life, which is brought to a swift end at the hands of his brother Cain.

To set the scene for the next part of the narrative, verse 2b provides a short description of Abel and Cain, contrasting their differing responsibilities. According to Fishbane, "The Cain-Abel narrative picks up the inner dynamic of Genesis 3 through repetition of key words and images."[172]

4:3–7. Verses 3–5 contrast God's response to the different gifts presented by Cain and Abel. God's attitude toward the brothers is not determined by the type of gift (פְּרִי הָאֲדָמָה [*pĕrî hāʾădāmâ*, "fruit of the ground"] versus בְּכֹרוֹת צֹאנוֹ [*bĕkōrôt ṣōʾnô*, "firstborn of his flock"]), but by quality, a point brought out by the mention of "firstborn" and the inclusion of

---

[169] Some English versions translate הָאָדָם (*hāʾādām*) using "Adam." Hess, "Splitting the Adam," 4, locates the first use of אָדָם (*ʾādām*) as a proper noun in 4:25. Cf. Hess, "Adam, Father, He," 147.

[170] The LXX translates the Hebrew expression as διὰ τοῦ θεοῦ *dia tou theou* "through God."

[171] The LXX refers to him consistently as Αβελ *Abel*.

[172] Fishbane, *Text and Texture*, 26.

the expression וּמֵחֶלְבֵהֶן (*ûmēḥelbēhen*, "and their fat portions"). The use of the term מִנְחָה (*minḥâ*, "offering") for both types of gift suggests that Abel's flock offering is not presented here as an atoning sacrifice; there is nothing in the text to suggest that any offering made by the two brothers was placed on an altar to be consumed by fire.[173] In contrast to Abel, Cain merely brings "some of the land's produce," not necessarily the best or the firstfruits. As Waltke and Fredricks comment, "Cain's sin is tokenism. He looks religious, but in his heart he is not totally dependent on God, childlike, or grateful."[174] As the author of Hebrew notes, "By faith Abel offered to God a better sacrifice than Cain did. By faith he was approved as a righteous man, because God approved his gifts, and even though he is dead, he still speaks through his faith" (Heb 11:4).

YHWH responds in different ways to Cain and Abel. He "had regard for Abel and his offering," but not for Cain and his offering. The verb שָׁעָה (*šāʿâ*), which occurs only twelve times in the Old Testament, conveys a sense of looking toward someone or something. In essence, God sees Abel and his offering, but he does not see Cain and his offering. Consequently, Cain becomes very angry and looks despondent. Most likely Cain is jealous because his younger brother has usurped him by gaining God's favor.

Echoing the narrator's comments at the end of verse 5, YHWH questions Cain regarding his feelings of anger and despondency (v. 6). He then proceeds to set two options before Cain. On the one hand, if he does what is right, he will gain acceptance. His current inability to gain God's favor is not beyond reversal. God offers Cain hope.

On the other hand, God warns Cain that without restorative action on his part, he is likely to become prey to sin. The noun חַטָּאת (*ḥaṭṭāʾt*, "sin") is normally understood to be feminine, but in this clause the associated verb רֹבֵץ (*rōbēṣ*, "crouching") is masculine. Possibly, "sin" is being personified here and refers to something other than merely acting inappropriately.[175] "Sin" appears to be a force that is stalking Cain with the intention of controlling his actions.

---

173 The first reference to sacrifices that are offered on an altar comes in 8:20–21.

174 Waltke and Fredricks, *Genesis*, 97.

175 Joaquim Azevedo, "At the Door of Paradise: A Contextual Interpretation of Gen 4:7," *Biblische Notizen* 100 (1999): 45–59, suggests that חַטָּאת (*ḥaṭṭāʾt*) denotes here a "purification offering" (cf. Lev 4:21, 24; 5:9, 11–12). However, purification offerings are closely tied to the cleansing of defilement from the tabernacle/temple. There is little reason to assume that in this context חַטָּאת (*ḥaṭṭāʾt*) refers to a "purification offering"

God's warning is expressed in language that echoes what was said to Eve in 3:16. According to Mann, "Yhwh's speeches to Cain push back against the assumption that sin must have dominion in the world. From Yhwh's perspective, sin can be overcome."[176] Some scholars suggest that the image of sin crouching at the door alludes to a Babylonian demon that threatens people inside a building. This suggestion is speculative, and the allusion seems unlikely.

4:8–16. Rather than making amends by offering a better gift to God, Cain directs his anger toward his brother. Ignoring YHWH's words of encouragement and warning in verse 7, Cain's initial failure is compounded by what he does subsequently. He speaks to his brother, but the Hebrew text does not record what he says. The CSB rendering, "Let's go out to the field," is derived from the ancient LXX and SamP translations. Either an early Hebrew scribe omitted the phrase or the earliest translations added it, sensing that something was missing. The evidence is finely balanced between these alternatives. With or without the phrase, the text is readable.

Although the reader is already aware of this fact, the narrator states twice in verse 8 that Abel is Cain's brother. This repetition underscores the hideousness of Cain's murderous action. Cain's attitude is so debased that he is prepared to kill his own brother. He does so with premeditation. The wickedness of Cain stands in sharp contrast to the righteousness of Abel (cf. Matt 23:35; Heb 11:4).

Aware of what has happened, God confronts Cain by asking about Abel. When questioned by God, Cain denies responsibility, adding to the shamefulness of his actions. Displaying callous indifference, he expresses a mindset that has become ubiquitous throughout the history of humanity: "Am I my brother's guardian?" (v. 9). Through the repetition of the verb שָׁמַר (*šāmar*, "to keep/guard") Cain's failure to guard Abel recalls Adam's failure to guard the garden (cf. 2:15; 3:24).

Whereas ESV renders the expression קוֹל דְּמֵי אָחִיךָ צֹעֲקִים (*qôl dĕmê ʾāḥîkā ṣōʿăqîm*) as "The voice of your brother's blood is crying out," NIV takes the initial קוֹל (*qôl*, "voice") to be an exclamation: "Listen! Your brother's blood cries out."[177] In support of the NIV translation, the verb צֹעֲקִים

[176] Steven T. Mann, "Let There Be Cain: A Clash of Imaginations in Genesis 4," *JSOT* (2021): 17.

[177] GKC §146b offers the translation, "Hark! thy brother's blood is crying."

(*ṣōʿăqîm*, "crying out") is plural, agreeing with the plural construct noun דְּמֵי (*dĕmê*, "blood") whereas קוֹל (*qôl*, "voice") is singular (cf. NLT; NRSV; NJPS).

Abel's blood cries out from the ground. Throughout Genesis 2–4, the ground (אֲדָמָה, *ʾădāmâ)* features often. Formed from the ground, humans were meant to enjoy a harmonious relationship with it. However, this special relationship has already been altered by Adam and Eve's betrayal of God in the garden. The ground is cursed because of the human couple (3:17). Cain's actions introduce a further degree of alienation from the ground, especially given that he is presented in verse 2 as one who "worked the ground." Elsewhere in the Pentateuch, attention is drawn to the idea that bloodshed defiles the land (e.g., Num 35:33–34; Deut 21:1–9). The impact of humanity's alienation from the ground is reflected later in Lamech's comments regarding his son Noah (5:29).

God's judgment of Cain begins with a curse (v. 11), with words that recall how the serpent was cursed by God (3:14). YHWH's statement vividly portrays the ground opening its mouth to drink Abel's blood. At the end of verse 11, the CSB translation "blood you have shed" does not quite capture the personal nature of the Hebrew text which reads "blood from your hand" (cf. ESV, NIV). Underlining Cain's alienation from the ground, God states that when Cain works the ground it will no longer give of its best to him.

Implicit in Cain's punishment is the idea that humans are meant to enjoy a sense of belonging to a particular location that provides for their needs. Exile runs counter to God's plan for people. Underlining the impact of Cain's punishment, God uses the expression נָע וָנָד (*nāʿ wānād*, "a fugitive and a wanderer"), which CSB renders "restless wanderer," to describe Cain's future (v. 12); Cain repeats this phrase in verse 14. The name נוֹד (*nôd*, "Nod") in verse 16 forms a wordplay with נָד (*nād*, "wanderer"), which may explain why Cain can be viewed as settling in this region, known as "wandering." The location of Nod is unknown, but it is positioned east of Eden. Just as God drove out Adam and Eve from the garden of Eden (3:24), so God drives Cain further eastward (v. 14).

Cain responds to God's speech by stating that his punishment "is too great to bear" (v. 13). The LXX translation interprets this as meaning: "My punishment is too great for me to be forgiven" (NETS). However, it is perhaps more likely that Cain is responding to the weight of the punishment, which, according to his words in verse 14, will lead to him being killed by others. Remarkably, given Cain's lack of concern for the life of his brother, God graciously promises protection to Cain (v. 15). Yet, despite all that has happened, Cain shows no sign of remorse.

4:17–24. Since the untimely death of Abel means that he is unable to establish a patriline, the narrator focuses on the descendants of Cain. These are traced through five generations of presumably firstborn sons, concluding with Lamech. A father-son linkage produces an orderly patriline in verses 17–18. However, this scheme is interrupted in verses 19–22 with the introduction of Lamech's wives, Adah and Zillah. As Chapman observes, "At the generation of Lamech, when the language of paternal begetting gives way to maternal bearing, the line splits laterally into two maternal groupings."[178] By focusing on Lamech's wives, the patriline recorded in verses 17–18 is ended. While Lamech's remarks in verse 24 highlight his connection to Cain, the narrator offers no record of how Cain's patriline continues after Lamech. Underlining this disruption to the patriline, Jubal and Naamah are both introduced through sibling connections, without direct reference to either father or mother.

Before tracing Cain's patriline to Lamech, the narrator briefly mentions one final detail regarding Cain's life. Cain begins the process of building a city,[179] which he names after his son. His actions reflect, on the one hand, a God-given desire to form a community, and, on the other hand, a godless desire to center this community around humans. As Morales comments, "Within its literary and theological context, this city can only be understood as an effort to replace Eden's framework for humanity's life together with God. As such Cain's city-building marks corrupt humanity's transition to a new goal of fulfillment, a fabricated purpose, the quest for self-realization apart from God's own agenda for creation and human history. Cain has set in motion the city-of-man project."[180] What Cain sets in motion will later surface in 11:1–9 with the building of Babel/Babylon.

---

[178] Cynthia R. Chapman, *The House of the Mother: The Social Roles of Maternal Kin in Biblical Hebrew Narrative and Poetry*, AYBRL (New Haven: Yale University Press, 2016), 1. Chapman's study throws interesting light on how the book of Genesis traces a special patriline while also recording the creation of new households.

[179] The phrase וַיְהִי בֹּנֶה עִיר (*wayhî bōne ʿîr*) conveys the sense "he was building a city"; see Joüon, 382.

[180] Morales, *Exodus Old and New*, 10.

Apart from their names, no details are given regarding the members of Cain's patriline in verses 17–18. Their names, however, are not without significance. As Satterthwaite observes,

> The names in Cain's line (4:17–24), for example, seem to be related to words that suggest urban culture (Irad), religion (Mehujael, Methusael), art and music (Adah, Zillah, Naamah), and religious processions (Jabal, Jubal, Tubal-Cain). But none of this culture and religion can prevent the murderous passion of Cain recurring in a yet more lethal form in Lamech, seven generations later (4:23–24).[181]

The description of Lamech in verses 19–24 begins by noting that he has two wives. He disregards the concept of monogamous marriage that has been presented as God's ideal in 2:23–24. He boasts to his wives of killing a man for striking him, an action that is unjustified in the light of the principle of *lex talionis* set out in Exodus 21:23–25; no punishment should exceed the crime. Lamech's boast in verse 24 picks up on God's promise to avenge Cain sevenfold (v. 15), but Lamech speaks of being avenged seventy-seven times. He views himself as "a new Cain,"[182] but as superior to his ancestor. Despite Lamech's boasting, however, the author of Genesis takes no interest in tracing the patriline of Lamech. Attention is now focused on a very different patriline that begins with another son born to Adam and Eve.

4:25–26. After tracing Cain's patriline for five generations to Lamech, the narrative unexpectedly jumps back in time to record the birth of a third son to Adam and Eve. His conception and birth are described in verse 25, which, with some minor variations and some differences associated with the naming of the son, resembles 4:1. The birth of Seth sets the scene for the introduction of a new patriline that will be traced through ten generations in Genesis 5. As we shall see, Seth's patriline is very different in character from that of Cain. Significantly, it leads us toward the offspring of Eve who will overcome the serpent.

Whereas 4:1 does not identify the person who names Cain, v. 25 states that Eve names this third son. She calls him Seth (שֵׁת, *šēt*), which means "appointed," creating a wordplay with the verb שָׁת (*šāt*, "appoint/give").

[181] Philip E. Satterthwaite, "Genealogy in the Old Testament," *NIDOTTE*, 4:660–61. He draws on Richard S. Hess, *Studies in the Personal Names of Genesis 1-1*, Alter Orient und Altes Testament 234 (Kevelaer: Butzon & Bercker, 1993), 111–62.

[182] Richard S. Hess, "Lamech in the Genealogies of Genesis," *BBR* 1 (1991): 22.

Seth's name underlines God's part in providing him as a replacement for Abel. By speaking of him as another "offspring" (זֶרַע, *zera*ᶜ), Eve's words recall God's remarks to the serpent in 3:15 that the woman's offspring (זֶרַע, *zera*ᶜ) will overcome the serpent.[183] According to Collins, Eve's statement "looks back to the rest of the pericope and forward to what follows in Genesis with its reference to the seed/offspring theme; also, by acknowledging that neither Abel nor Cain was the promised 'offspring' of 3:15, it invites us to look beyond the immediate descendants of Adam and Eve."[184]

The introduction of Seth as a replacement for Abel is immediately followed by a reference to Seth's son, Enosh (v. 26). While nothing specific is said about Enosh, the final half of verse 26 offers a glimmer of hope regarding humanity's relationship with God. Most English versions state that "people began to call on the name of the Lord," but the Hebrew text does not contain the term "people." A more literal rendering would be: "Then it was begun to call upon the name of the Lord."[185] The lack of a specific subject suggests that worship of YHWH was not universal among the increasing human population.

Bridge

Chapter 4 plays an exceptionally important role within the book of Genesis, identifying the son through whom the patriline of Adam and Eve will be established. Although Abel finds favor with God, his untimely death at the hands of Cain creates a dilemma. Can the one who will overcome the serpent come from the descendants of Cain, a murderer? This possibility is eventually ruled out after Cain's patriline is traced to Lamech. Perceiving himself to be greater than Cain, Lamech murders a young man. Although Lamech has children, the author of Genesis subtly concludes Cain's patriline by deliberately listing Lamech's children under the names of his wives.

After exhausting the patriline of Cain, the Genesis narrator jumps back in time to record that Eve bore a third son, Seth. His unexpected appearance offers hope that there may yet be a patriline descended from Adam

---

183 By way of comparison, in 4:1 Eve speaks of having brought forth a "man" (אִישׁ, ʾîš).

184 Collins, *Genesis 1–4*, 209.

185 See Robert P. Gordon, "Who 'Began to Call on the Name of the Lord' in Genesis 4:26b? The MT and the Versions," in *Let Us Go up to Zion: Essays in Honour of H. G. M. Williamson on the Occasion of His Sixty-Fifth Birthday*, ed. Iain W. Provan and Mark J. Boda (Leiden: Brill, 2012), 57–68.

and Eve that will produce an offspring who will defeat the serpent, as God announced in 3:15. Seth's birth sets the scene for the linear genealogy in chapter 5 that traces Adam's patriline to Noah.

Cain's depravity in killing his own brother is noted by later biblical writers (see 1 John 3:12; Jude 11). By way of contrast, Abel's righteousness is mentioned in several places (Matt 23:35; Luke 11:51; Heb 11:4; 12:24).

III. The Offspring of Adam (5:1–6:8)

A. The Line of Adam's Descendants to Noah (5:1–32)

> [1] This is the document containing the family records of Adam. On the day that God created man, he made him in the likeness of God; [2] he created them male and female. When they were created, he blessed them and called them mankind.
>
> [3] Adam was 130 years old when he fathered a son in his likeness, according to his image, and named him Seth. [4] Adam lived 800 years after he fathered Seth, and he fathered other sons and daughters. [5] So Adam's life lasted 930 years; then he died.
>
> [6] Seth was 105 years old when he fathered Enosh. [7] Seth lived 807 years after he fathered Enosh, and he fathered other sons and daughters. [8] So Seth's life lasted 912 years; then he died.
>
> [9] Enosh was 90 years old when he fathered Kenan. [10] Enosh lived 815 years after he fathered Kenan, and he fathered other sons and daughters. [11] So Enosh's life lasted 905 years; then he died.
>
> [12] Kenan was 70 years old when he fathered Mahalalel. [13] Kenan lived 840 years after he fathered Mahalalel, and he fathered other sons and daughters. [14] So Kenan's life lasted 910 years; then he died.
>
> [15] Mahalalel was 65 years old when he fathered Jared. [16] Mahalalel lived 830 years after he fathered Jared, and he fathered other sons and daughters. [17] So Mahalalel's life lasted 895 years; then he died.
>
> [18] Jared was 162 years old when he fathered Enoch. [19] Jared lived 800 years after he fathered Enoch, and he fathered other sons and daughters. [20] So Jared's life lasted 962 years; then he died.
>
> [21] Enoch was 65 years old when he fathered Methuselah. [22] And after he fathered Methuselah, Enoch walked with God 300 years and fathered other sons and daughters. [23] So Enoch's life lasted 365 years. [24] Enoch walked with God; then he was not there because God took him.

[25] Methuselah was 187 years old when he fathered Lamech. [26] Methu-
selah lived 782 years after he fathered Lamech, and he fathered
other sons and daughters. [27] So Methuselah's life lasted 969 years;
then he died.

[28] Lamech was 182 years old when he fathered a son. [29] And he named
him Noah, saying, "This one will bring us relief from the agonizing la-
bor of our hands, caused by the ground the LORD has cursed." [30] Lamech
lived 595 years after he fathered Noah, and he fathered other sons and
daughters. [31] So Lamech's life lasted 777 years; then he died.

[32] Noah was 500 years old, and he fathered Shem, Ham, and Japheth.

Context

After tracing the patriline of Cain for seven generations to the birth of Lamech's three sons and one daughter (4:17–24), the Genesis narrative jumps back in time to record the birth of another son to Adam and Eve. Whereas the record of Cain's line concludes by focusing on Lamech's killing of a young man, the initial picture of Seth's patriline offers a contrasting picture. Seth's son, Enosh, is associated with people calling upon the name of YHWH (4:26).

This sets the scene for the linear genealogy recorded in chapter 5.[186] In the light of God's announcement that an offspring of the woman will overcome the serpent (3:15), the expectation is created in chapters 4–5 that this offspring will be a descendant of Seth. The linear genealogy in chapter 5 is the first of two in Genesis that trace the unique lineage that will lead to the serpent-slayer (cf. 11:10–26). The introduction of Noah at the end of the genealogy (vv. 28–32) prepares the way for the longer narrative section that will focus on Noah's remarkable rescue from the great flood.

Two of the names found in Cain's patriline are also given to two of Seth's descendants. Cain's Enoch is associated with a city (4:17), whereas Seth's Enoch has a special relationship with God and is taken up (5:24). Cain's Lamech is associated, first, with bigamy, resulting in sons who develop differing skills (4:19–22), and, second, with violence that manifests itself in the killing of a young man (4:23–24). In marked contrast,

---

[186] The distinction between "linear" and "segmented" genealogies is discussed by Robert R. Wilson, *Genealogy and History in the Biblical World* (New Haven: Yale University Press, 1977), 9. A linear genealogy takes the basic form: A gives birth to B, B gives birth to C, C gives birth to D. A segmented genealogy takes the basic form: A gives birth to B, C, D. B gives birth to E, F, G. C gives birth to I, J, K. D gives birth to L, M, N.

Seth's Lamech is associated with a son, Noah, who will bring relief to those affected by God's curse upon the ground (5:29). Both comparisons reflect the different orientations of the patrilines.[187] Whereas Cain's family is focused on earth-centered enterprises (city building, cultural activities, technology), Seth's family is oriented toward pleasing God. This distinction between the descendants of Cain and Seth continues in 6:1–4 in connection with the "sons of God" and the "daughters of mankind," and in 6:5–8 with regard to the contrast between Noah and the rest of humanity (cf. 6:8–13).

Comments

5:1–5. The opening words of this section describe what follows as the "document" or "record" of the תּוֹלְדֹת אָדָם (*tôlědōt ʾādām*), which CSB translates as "family records of Adam." As noted in the Comments on 2:4, the term *tôlědôt* occurs at various points in Genesis in expressions that mark the beginning of new sections within the book (6:9; 10:1, 32; 11:10, 27; 25:12–13, 19; 36:1, 9; 37:2). The word *tôlědôt* refers to what will come forth from the person named, in this case Adam. The present heading is distinctive, introducing a genealogy that lists a patriline that begins with Adam and ends with Noah. A similar linear genealogy occurs in 11:10–26.

The use of the Hebrew term אָדָם (*ʾādām*) in verses 1–2 presents a challenge for translators. The second half of verse 1 states, "On the day that God created אָדָם (*ʾādām*), he made him in the likeness of God." Most English versions translate this occurrence of אָדָם (*ʾādām*) as "man" (ESV, CSB, NJPS), "mankind" (NIV), or "humankind" (NET; NRSV). Adopting a different approach, NJB renders אָדָם (*ʾādām*) in verse 1b as "Adam." However, in verse 2, where it is stated that God named them אָדָם (*ʾādām*), NJB uses "humankind" to translate אָדָם (*ʾādām*) . This third occurrence of אָדָם (*ʾādām*) in verses 1–2 is rendered "mankind" by CSB (cf. NIV). From what is said in verse 2, אָדָם (*ʾādām*) cannot be translated using the proper name "Adam"; in this verse it denotes not a specific individual, but humanity in a more general way.[188] The use of אָדָם (*ʾādām*) in verses1–2 to denote both a specific individual and humanity draws

---

[187] See Cefalu, "Royal Priestly Heirs," 365.

[188] A more literal rendering of the Hebrew of the final part of 5:2 is: "and he called their name *ʾādām* in the day of their being created."

on what has been recorded previously in chapters 1–3.[189] The wording of 5:1b–2 echoes 1:26–27, emphasizing that humans, both male and female, were made in the image of God. The use of אָדָם (*ʾādām*) in 5:1a to denote an individual reflects what is said in 3:17, 21.[190]

The opening verses of chapter 5 remind the reader of God's purpose in creating humanity. Despite all the negative events that are recorded in chapters 3–4, hope for the future will come through the line of Seth. However, before introducing Seth by name, the reader learns that this son resembles Adam. By using the terms "likeness" (דְּמוּת, *dĕmût*) and "image" (צֶלֶם, *ṣelem*), verse 3 echoes 1:26, which refers to humanity being made to resemble God. By stating that Seth resembles Adam, rather than God, the narrator possibly signals that humanity's relationship to God has been changed due to the events of chapter 3. If being made in the image of God is linked to the concept of being God's vicegerent, humanity no longer fulfils this role after their expulsion from the garden of Eden. However, the hope exists that an offspring of the woman will defeat the serpent. By implication this victory will involve a restoration of the divine image in humanity. The mention of other sons and daughters in verse 4 underlines that this genealogy, unlike many others in the Old Testament, is concerned to identify only the next important member in the patriline. This has an important bearing on the nature and purpose of the genealogy. It traces a unique lineage that will ultimately lead to an offspring who will reverse the tragic consequences of Adam and Eve's betrayal of God in the garden of Eden.

The reference to Adam living a total of 930 years is remarkable in the light of both modern lifespans and those recorded throughout much of the rest of the Old Testament. However, Adam is not alone within the chapter 5 genealogy in living more than 900 years. Only Enoch and Lamech are exceptions. And in the case of Enoch the explanation introduces a further surprise; he does not die but is taken away by God (v. 24). The lifetimes of those listed are exceptionally long, compared to most ancient and modern expectations, but there are other ANE texts that associate longevity with the earliest generations of humanity. The Sumerian

---

[189] See Hess, "Splitting the Adam," 1–15. Cf. David J. A. Clines, "אדם, the Hebrew for 'Human, Humanity': A Response to James Barr," *VT* 53 (2003): 297–310.

[190] Throughout most of chs. 2–3 and even in 4:1, הָאָדָם (*hāʾādām*) is used to denote "the man." See Comments on 2:7.

King List, which provides a list of kings who reigned in southern Iraq in the third millennium BC, opens with these words:

> After kingship had descended from heaven, Eridu became (the seat) of kingship. In Eridu Alulim reigned 28,800 years as king; Alalgar reigned 36,000 years—two kings reigned 64,800 years. Eridu was abandoned, (and) its kingship was carried off to Badtibira. In Badtibira, Enmenluanna reigned 43,200 years; Enmengalanna reigned 28,800 years; Dumuzi, the shepherd, reigned 36,000 years—three kings reigned 108,000 years.[191]

Compared to the Sumerian King List, the Genesis figures are small.

In contrast to Cain's lineage, which records no periods of time, Seth's line is marked by the longevity of its members. In the light of humanity's exclusion from the "tree of life," these long lifespans possibly signal that those concerned enjoyed God's favor. Scholarly attempts to uncover a symbolic explanation for the large numbers have not proved successful.[192]

5:6–27. This section of the linear genealogy follows a recurring pattern that is broken only in verses 21–24 in connection with Enoch.[193] The pattern is:

> Person A was X years old when he fathered Person B. Person A lived X years after he fathered Person B, and he fathered other sons and daughters. So Person A's life lasted X years; then he died.

---

[191] Samuel Noah Kramer, *The Sumerians: Their History, Culture, and Character* (Chicago: University of Chicago Press, 1963), 328. One of the earliest surviving copies of this list is the Weld-Blundell Prism, which is dated to around 2170 BC. Toward the end of the Sumerian King List, the reigns of kings become much shorter. We read: "In Isin, Ishbi-Erra reigned 33 years as king; Shuilishu, the son of Ishbi-Erra, reigned 10 years; Idin-Dagan, the son of Shuilishu, reigned 21 years; Ishme-Dagan, the son of Idin-Dagan, reigned 20 years; Lipit-Ishtar, the son of Ishme-Dagan, reigned 11 years; Ur-Ninurta reigned 28 years; Bur-Sin, the son of Ur-Ninurta, reigned 21 years; Lipit-Enlil, the son of Bur-Sin, reigned 5 years; Erraimitti reigned 8 years; Enlilbani reigned 24 years; Zambia reigned 3 years; Iterpisha reigned 4 years; Urdukuga reigned 4 years; Sinmagir reigned 11 years. (Total) fourteen kings reigned 203 years" (p. 331).

[192] The numbers listed in the MT, LXX, and SamP do not always correspond, but are internally consistent in each textual tradition. Gerhard Larsson, "Septuagint Versus Massoretic Chronology," *ZAW* 114 (2002): 511–21, contends that the MT preserves the earliest figures, which were subsequently emended to produce those found in the other textual traditions.

[193] The pattern begins in v. 3, but with additional remarks about Adam's son, and ends in v. 32, with some variation in vv. 28–32 concerning Noah.

As is typical of linear genealogies, only one person is named in each generation. By this means the genealogy remains focused on a single line of offspring that runs from Adam to Noah. By including three references to periods of time in connection with each person, the genealogy gives the impression of recording historical information.[194] By totaling the first two time periods to give a final total of years lived, the genealogy underscores that every member of the line had a long lifespan. Exclusion from the tree of life, however, means that no one lives forever. Yet, remarkably, Enoch stands apart from everyone else in chapter 5 because he does not die but is taken by God (v. 24).[195] The concept of being taken by God is associated elsewhere with Elijah (2 Kgs 2:10) and refers to his ascension from earth to heaven. Presumably something similar happened to Enoch. Several psalms also speak of being taken by God in the context of deliverance from death (cf. Pss 49:15; 73:24).

Enoch's experience of being taken by God is linked to the fact that he "walked with God." When applied to humans, the *hithpael* (reflexive) form of the verb הָלַךְ (*hālak*) is most often used in Genesis to indicate a close and continuous relationship with God (cf. 6:9; 17:1; 24:40; 48:15). The same verb is used of God walking in the garden of Eden (3:8). Subsequent references to individuals walking with God recall how Adam and Eve may have once experienced God's presence. Whereas everyone else in the genealogy of chapter 5 is said to have "lived" so many years after fathering other sons and daughters, Enoch is said to have walked with God. A striking distinction is made between simply living and walking constantly with God. With good reason, Enoch's faith is commended in Hebrews 11:5. Remarkably, unlike the other members of this patriline, Enoch does not die, but is taken by God (v. 24; cf. Ps 49:15).

Surviving for 969 years, Methuselah is the longest living person mentioned in the Bible. According to the figures concerning lifespans in 5:25–28 and 7:6, Methuselah died in the year of the flood.

---

[194] Linear genealogies on their own cannot to be used to construct absolute chronologies. It is possible that some generations are passed over. See Andrew E. Steinmann, "Gaps in the Genealogies in Genesis 5 and 11?," *BSac* 174 (2017): 141–58. Wilson, *Genealogy and History*, 133–34, observes that there was a tendency in the ANE to limit the maximum length of a written genealogy to ten generations. He notes that ANE genealogies are sometimes modified by the addition or omission of names. Examples of names being omitted are found in biblical texts (e.g., compare 1 Chr 6:3–14 and Ezra 7:1–5; cf. William Henry Green, "Primeval Chronology," *BSac* 47 [1890]: 285–303).

[195] Verse 24 departs from the patten found in vv. 5, 8, 11, 14, 17, 20, 27, 31.

5:28–32. The birth of Noah moves the genealogy toward a conclusion. A play on words is created in verse 29 by the similar sounding Hebrew words נֹחַ (*nōaḥ*, "Noah") and יְנַחֲמֵנוּ (*yĕnaḥămēnû*, "he will comfort us/bring us relief"). The name Noah is not derived from the verb נִחָם (*niḥām*, "to comfort/bring relief"), but is based on the Hebrew verb נוח (*nwḥ*), meaning "to rest."[196] According to Provan, "Lamech is not merely anticipating *comfort* amid painful toil ... but looking for *relief* from the curse of the ground mentioned in Genesis 3.17. The fulfilment of this hope is found after the flood when Noah becomes the first person to plant a vineyard."[197] The brief description of Noah being "a man of the soil" (אֲדָמָה, *ʾădāmâ*, 9:20) points toward the fulfilment of Lamech's words. In the postdiluvian era he enjoys a degree of harmony with the ground.

When Lamech refers to the עִצָּבוֹן (*ʿiṣṣĕbôn*, "agonizing labor") "caused by the ground the Lord has cursed" (v. 29), his words recall what God said in 3:17: "The ground is cursed because of you. You will eat from it by means of painful labor (עִצָּבוֹן, *ʿiṣṣābôn*) all the days of your life." The noun עִצָּבוֹן, (*ʿiṣṣābôn*) comes elsewhere in the Old Testament only in connection with the judgment that God announces upon Eve in 3:16. Importantly, Lamech looks to Noah for help regarding the pain associated with humanity's broken relationship with God.

While Lamech's optimistic comments about Noah (v. 29) anticipate the vital role that he will play in fulfilling God's plan for the earth, the brief observation in verse 32 that Noah had three sons suggests that the unique patriline will not end with Noah but will be continued through one of his sons. We should not expect Noah to be the serpent-slayer (cf. 6:9–10).

Bridge

The patriline that descends through Seth stands apart from that associated with Cain. Whereas the line of Cain is associated with "urban culture (Irad), religion (Mehujael, Methusael), art and music (Adah, Zillah, Naamah), and religious processions (Jabal, Jubal, Tubal-Cain)," according to Satterthwaite, "the line of Adam through Seth (Gen 5:1–32) contains names that suggest the thoughts of substitution (Seth; cf. 4:25), the renewal

---

[196] The Hebrew root נוח (*nwḥ*) will reappear in the story of the flood in connection with the ark resting (8:4), the dove finding no resting place (8:9) and God smelling a pleasing or restful aroma (8:21).

[197] Provan, *Discovering Genesis*, 110 (italics in original).

and reestablishment of humankind (Enosh, Kenan), praise (Mahalalel), prayer for God to come down and aid (Jared), and rest from labor (Noah).[198]

Heightening this contrast between the patrilines of Cain and Seth, Lamech's remarks concerning Noah in 5:29 raise expectations that he will have an important role to play in the ongoing story. This hope is reinforced by the broader picture of humanity that is recorded in 6:1–8. Against the background of humanity's malevolent behavior, Noah is once again identified as standing apart from the rest of society (6:8). Those who are true to God do not always go with the flow of popular opinion.

B. The Increasing Wickedness of Humanity (6:1–8)

> [1] When mankind began to multiply on the earth and daughters were
> born to them, [2] the sons of God saw that the daughters of mankind were
> beautiful, and they took any they chose as wives for themselves. [3] And
> the Lord said, "My Spirit will not remain with mankind forever, because
> they are corrupt. Their days will be 120 years." [4] The Nephilim were
> on the earth both in those days and afterward, when the sons of God came to the daughters of mankind, who bore children to them. They were the powerful men of old, the famous men.
>
> [5] When the Lord saw that human wickedness was widespread on the earth and that every inclination of the human mind was nothing but
> evil all the time, [6] the Lord regretted that he had made man on the earth,
> and he was deeply grieved. [7] Then the Lord said, "I will wipe mankind, whom I created, off the face of the earth, together with the animals, creatures that crawl, and birds of the sky—for I regret that I made them."
> [8] Noah, however, found favor with the Lord.

Context

The genealogy of chapter 5 focuses on named individuals in each generation, who form part of the patriline that is carefully traced throughout the book of Genesis. In marked contrast, 6:1–8 offers a broad perspective on events that have occurred over the time span of the genealogy in chapter 5, in what is sometimes called the antediluvian age. Strong links exist between the chapter 5 genealogy and 6:1–8, with the conclusions to both passages focusing on Noah.[199] Whereas chapter 5 offers a narrow view of Adam's descendants, 6:1–8 provides a panoramic perspective.

---

[198] Satterthwaite, "Genealogy in the Old Testament," 660–61.

[199] See Mathews, *Genesis 1-11:26*, 320–22; Carol M. Kaminski, *Was Noah Good? Finding Favour in the Flood Narrative*, LHBOTS 563 (London: Bloomsbury T&T Clark, 2014), 24–63,

Although the family information regarding the descendants of Cain and Seth in chapters 4–5 has contrasted their behavior, suggesting that Seth's lineage is more godly than that of Cain, according to 6:1–2, these patrilines did not remain segregated, but intermingled through marriage.[200] After further brief observations about humanity in the antediluvian period (6:3–4), the panoramic overview in 6:1–8 concludes by contrasting God's differing attitudes toward Noah and the rest of humanity (6:5–8), setting the scene for the next main section in Genesis, the *tôlĕdôt* of Noah (6:9–9:29).

Comments

6:1–3. The opening description of humanity's increase on the earth recalls both God's mandate to multiply in 1:28 and the close connection between "mankind" הָאָדָם (*hāʾādām*) and the "earth" הָאֲדָמָה (*hāʾădāmâ*) in 2:5, 7; 3:17.[201] Against this background, verse 2 records how "the sons of God"[202] are attracted by the beauty of the "daughters of mankind" and take them as wives. In many English versions the plural adjective טֹבֹת (*ṭōbōt*) is translated "beautiful." The singular form טֹב (*ṭōb*) is translated "good" in 1:4, 10, 12, 18, 21, 25, 31; 2:9, 12, 18; 3:6, where it is often used in conjunction with the verb "to see." In chapter 1 God sees that various items are "good"; in chapter 3 the woman sees that "the tree of the knowledge of good and evil" (2:9, 17) is "good" for food. In the light of how טֹב (*ṭōb*) has been used in the opening chapters of Genesis, the translation of טֹבֹת (*ṭōbōt*) as "beautiful" is too restrictive. It may have been more than their appearance that attracted the sons of God to the daughters of mankind.

While there has been much discussion about the precise identity of these sons and daughters, to which we shall return shortly, their coming together appears innocent. Some commentators suggest that the actions of the "sons of God" are in some way evil, but Cassuto rightly notes that

---

demonstrates that 6:5–8 is the conclusion to the *tôlĕdōt* of Adam and not the beginning of the *tôlĕdōt* of Noah.

[200] The topic of endogamous marriage becomes an important motif later in Genesis. Abraham claims to have married his half-sister (20:12); Isaac marries his cousin Rebekah (24:24); Jacob marries his cousins Leah and Rachel (29:12). Esau, who is criticized for marrying Hittite women (26:34–35), subsequently marries Ishmael's daughters (28:6–9).

[201] CSB translates הָאֲדָמָה (*hāʾădāmâ*) as "ground" in 2:7, but "earth" in 6:1.

[202] This expression could also be understood as meaning "the sons of the gods." Given the prior use of אֱלֹהִים (*ʾĕlōhîm*) in chs. 1–4, the singular "God" is the more likely reading.

there is "not a single word" in verses 2–3 "alluding to rape or adultery or to any act against the Lord's will."[203]

The assumption that verb 2 records inappropriate activity influences the CSB translation of verb 3, where God declares: "My Spirit will not remain with mankind forever, because they are corrupt. Their days will be 120 years." A survey of English versions reveals that the first part of God's remark has been interpreted in other ways. NIV has "My Spirit will not contend with humans forever, for they are mortal." NJPS reads: "My breath shall not abide in man forever, since he too is flesh."[204]

God's statement is difficult to interpret for several reasons. First, complications arise regarding the meaning of רוּחִי (*rûḥî*, "my spirit/Spirit"). In Genesis alone, the noun רוּחַ (*rûaḥ*) denotes a variety of things: e.g., "breath" (e.g., 6:17; 7:15, 22), "wind" (e.g., 8:1), "spirit" (e.g., 41:38). Various prophetic passages record how God speaks of pouring out or putting "my Spirit" on people (Isa 44:3; 59:21; Ezek 36:27; 37:14; 39:29; Joel 2:28, 29 [Heb. 3:2]).

Second, the meaning of verse 3a is difficult to determine because the term יָדוֹן (*yādôn*) occurs only here in the whole of the Old Testament. Although some translations render יָדוֹן (*yādôn*) as "strive" (KJV, NAS) or "contend" (NIV), most opt to follow the earliest Greek version, the LXX, and adopt the translation "abide" (ESV) or "remain" (CSB, NET, NRSV, NJPS).[205] As an alternative, NJB suggests that יָדוֹן (*yādôn*) means "be responsible."

Third, in verse 3 the Hebrew noun בָּשָׂר (*bāśār*) is usually rendered "flesh" (ESV, KJV, NAS, NJB, NJPS) or "mortal" (NIV, NET). CSB opts for the rendering "corrupt," but this goes beyond the normal semantic range of בָּשָׂר (*bāśār*). The noun has already appeared in 2:21, 23, 24, in conjunction with the creation of the woman, who resembles the man in bone and "flesh." These verses conclude with the noteworthy remark that when "a man leaves his father and mother and bonds with his wife, and they become one flesh (בָּשָׂר, *bāśār*)" (2:24). The term בָּשָׂר (*bāśār*) also appears frequently in the story of the flood, where the expression כָּל־בָּשָׂר (*kol-bāśār*) is used to denote all living creatures, both human and animal (6:12,

---

[203] Cassuto, *From Adam to Noah*, 294. Cf. Wenham, *Genesis 1–15*, 141, who dismisses previous suggestions by commentators that v. 2 involves rape or polygamy. The expression וַיִּקְחוּ לָהֶם נָשִׁים (*wayyiqḥû lāhem nāšîm*, "they took ... as wives for themselves") is the normal expression for marriage (e.g., 12:19; 24:4, 67; 26:34).

[204] Cf. Alter, *Genesis*, 26.

[205] See Westermann, *Genesis 1–11*, 375, for additional arguments based on cognate languages.

13, 17, 19; 7:15, 16, 21; 8:17; 9:11, 15–17). Most likely, in verse 3a בָּשָׂר (*bāśār*) denotes the idea that humans are creatures of flesh and blood.

Taking all these factors into consideration, any proposed interpretation of God's words in verse 3a must be tentative. Before proposing a solution, we must address a further issue that involves verse 3b.

At one level the meaning of verse 3b is straightforward. It states that his/their (with reference back to "mankind" in v. 3a) days will be 120 years. Unfortunately, it is not entirely clear how this should be understood. The most likely interpretation is that God determines here to limit the lifespan of everyone to 120 years. This makes reasonable sense read against the background of the lifespans recorded in chapters 5, where most of those named live over 900 years. However, against this proposal is the fact that some characters in the rest of Genesis enjoy lifespans that go beyond 120 years (e.g., Abraham lives 175 years, Isaac 180 years, Jacob 147 years). However, these examples may be exceptions, for most later figures do not exceed 120 years (e.g., Joseph lives 110 years, Moses 120 years, Joshua 110 years; Aaron is a minor exception, living 123 years).[206] It may be that the longer lives of Abraham, Isaac, and Jacob reflect their special relationship with God. Alternatively, it has been suggested that God's statement concerning 120 years ought to be read in conjunction with the coming of the great flood that will bring all human life to an end, apart from Noah and his immediate family. Keil writes, "This sentence, as we may gather from the context, was made known to Noah in his 480th year, to be published by him as 'preacher of righteousness' (2 Pet. ii. 5) to the degenerate race."[207] While Keil's proposal is possible, no hint has yet been given to suggest that God intends to destroy the whole of humanity; this is first introduced in 6:5–7. Taking into consideration the context in which verse 3 is set, it seems likely that God's announcement concerns the general lifespan that humans may expect to experience. Because they are creatures of flesh, like other animals, they shall be animated by God's spirit/breath for no more than 120 years.

With this interpretation of verse 3 in view, let us consider the identity of the "sons of God" and the "daughters of mankind." The former group has prompted the most discussion, with three proposals enjoying substantial

---

[206] See Gen 50:26; Deut 34:7; Josh 24:29; Num 33:39.

[207] C. F. Keil and F. Delitzsch, *The Pentateuch*, Biblical Commentary on the Old Testament (Edinburgh: T&T Clark, 1869), 136; cf. Kidner, *Genesis*, 85. Noah is 600 years old at the start of the flood (7:6).

support: angelic beings; rulers; sons of Seth.[208] While there is a long history of Jewish and Christian commentators adopting the view that the "sons of God" are heavenly creatures,[209] the sudden introduction of such non-human beings into the Genesis narrative is most unexpected. Although there is some evidence that the expression "sons of God" might possibly denote heavenly creatures,[210] the idea of angels marrying humans seems unlikely.[211]

Alternative explanations involving only humans are possible. As a reaction against speculations about angels, Jewish scholars from the second century AD onward proposed that the "sons of God" were kings or rulers.[212] This idea is developed by Kline, who argues that in the ANE kings were often viewed as being sons of gods.[213] Adopting this approach, he suggests that the "sons of God" are human kings descended from the line of Cain. However, in the light of how the patrilines of Cain and Seth are contrasted in chapters 3–4, it seems unlikely that those in Cain's line would be identified as being "sons of God."

A more likely scenario is that the expression "sons of God" refers to Seth's descendants. This interpretation has enjoyed considerable support

---

[208] Other options have also been suggested. For example, McKeown, *Genesis*, 49, includes as a possibility "the 'dramatis personae' who featured in the mythical stories of Israel's neighbors," some of whom were viewed as semi-divine (e.g., Gilgamesh). Lyle M. Eslinger, "A Contextual Identification of the *bene ha'elohim* and *benoth ha'adam* in Genesis 6:1–4," *JSOT* 4 (1979): 65–73, contends that the "daughters of men" are Sethite women and the "sons of God" are Cainites.

[209] See Wenham, *Genesis 1-15*, 139, for fuller details. For a recent defense of this position, see Willem A. VanGemeren, "The Sons of God in Genesis 6:1–4 (an Example of Evangelical Demythologization)," *WTJ* 43 (1981): 320–48. One of the earliest known expositions of this passage comes in the third century BC book of Enoch, where the brief description in Genesis becomes the pretext for a much fuller description of events that involve 200 angels taking human wives who bear great giants that practice human cannibalism.

[210] References to the "sons of God" in Job 1:6; 2:1; 38:7 are usually taken to refer to heavenly beings, but their precise identity is not clear; they are never called angels in these passages. The same is true of Pss 29:1 and 89:6 [Heb. 7], where the expression בְּנֵי אֵלִים (*bĕnê ʾēlîm*, "sons of God") is used. Although appeal is often made to 1 Pet 3:19–20; 2 Pet 2:4; Jude 6, 14–15 in support of the "sons of God" being angels, these passages may be alluding to events other that those mentioned in Gen 6:1–3; see Mathews, *Genesis 1-11:26*, 327–28. Jude, for example, alludes to several other events that are not recorded in the Old Testament (e.g., the archangel Michael contending with the devil over the body of Moses; words spoken by Enoch).

[211] Keil and Delitzsch, *The Pentateuch*, 131, note that "Christ Himself distinctly states that the angels cannot marry (Matt. xxii. 30; Mark xii. 25; cf. Luke xx. 34 sqq.)."

[212] P. S. Alexander, "The Targumim and Early Comments on 'Sons of God' in Genesis 6," *JJS* 23 (1972): 60–71.

[213] Meredith G. Kline, "Divine Kingship and Genesis 6:1–4," *WTJ* 24 (1962): 187–204.

over the centuries, being the preferred position of Augustine, Aquinas, Luther, and Calvin.[214] In line with this, it is worth recalling that Luke's genealogy of Jesus concludes by identifying Adam as the "son of God" (Luke 3:38). Against this proposal is the observation that the expression "daughters of mankind" appears to denote women in general, with no distinction being made between those descended from Cain and those from Seth. A resolution to this problem may rest in the fact that not all Seth's descendants are necessarily viewed as "sons of God." The two expressions, "sons of God" and "daughters of mankind," may best be understood as denoting respectively those who are godly, displaying Godlike characteristics, and those who reflect humanity's post-Eden nature, displaying ungodly characteristics.[215] Such a contrast has already been highlighted in chapters 4–5 with reference to certain members of the lines of Cain and Seth. While a distinction exists between these two groups of people, 6:1–2 indicates that they do not remain segregated, but intermarry. It comes as no surprise, therefore, that only Noah, of all Seth's descendants, is described as being "a righteous man, blameless among his contemporaries" (6:9).

6:4. Verse 4 adds to the enigmatic nature of this section of Genesis. No conjunction links verse 4 to the immediately preceding verses, suggesting that the introduction of הַנְּפִלִים (*hanněpilîm*, "the Nephilim") is not directly connected to the "daughters of mankind" bearing children to the "sons of God." In verse 4 the phrase אֲשֶׁר יָבֹאוּ בְּנֵי הָאֱלֹהִים אֶל־בְּנוֹת הָאָדָם וְיָלְדוּ לָהֶם (*ăšer yābōʾû běnê hoʾĕlōhîm ʾel-běnôt hāʾādām wěyāldû lāhem*, "when the sons of God came to the daughters of mankind, who bore children to them") defines the period during which the Nephilim existed. There is no reason to assume that the "sons of God" were the fathers of the Nephilim. By noting that the Nephilim existed in the antediluvian period and afterwards, verse 4 implies that they are a class of people rather than a clan or tribe descended from one individual.[216] This understanding is supported

---

[214] For a recent defense of this position, see Cefalu, "Royal Priestly Heirs," 351–70; cf. Mathews, *Genesis 1-11:26*, 323–32.

[215] In support of this understanding, the use of הָאֱלֹהִים (*hāʾĕlōhîm*, "God") and הָאָדָם (*hāʾādām*, "mankind)" in construct chains in v. 2 is intended to convey quality or condition. See GKC §128s-v.

[216] The designation הַנְּפִלִים (*hanněpilîm*, "the Nephilim") also supports the idea that they are a class of men. The English word "Nephilim" is a transliteration of the Hebrew term, which the LXX translates as γίγαντες (*gigantes*), meaning "giants" (cf. KJV). Elsewhere in the Old Testament, הַנְּפִלִים (*hanněpilîm*, "the Nephilim") appears only in Num 13:33, where the translation "giants" is adopted by KJV and NJB. While "giants" fits well in Num 13:33,

by the concluding words of verse 4, which speak of them being הַגִּבֹּרִים (*haggibbōrîm*, "the powerful men") who were אַנְשֵׁי הַשֵּׁם (*anšê haššēm*, "the famous men").[217] This description draws attention to their reputation as warriors, a significant detail, given that God's condemnation of humanity in 6:11–13 focuses on how they have filled the earth with violence. As Mathews rightly observes, the term גִּבֹּר (*gibbōr*) "is often used of fierce warriors (e.g., Josh 10:2; 2 Sam 17:2; 23:8; Amos 2:16)."[218] Apart from the present verse, גִּבֹּר (*gibbōr*) occurs elsewhere only in Genesis in 10:8–9 with reference to Nimrod, who makes a name for himself (10:9; cf. 11:4) and is responsible for founding the city of Babel/Babylon.[219] While some English versions convey a positive assessment of the Nephilim by describing them as "the heroes of old, men of renown" (NIV; cf. NET, NJB, NRSV, NJPS), a negative appraisal would be more appropriate. It is best to see them as infamous warriors rather than famous heroes.

6:5–8. Verses 1–4 lay the foundation for what is recorded in verses 5–8. After the text has noted the integration of the "sons of God" and the "daughters of mankind" (v. 2), the restriction to be placed upon the lifespan of humans (v. 3), and the existence of infamous warriors (v. 4), verses 5–8 summarize God's assessment of humanity. The ubiquity of human wrongdoing is captured in verse 5 through reference to its extent ("widespread on the earth"), intensity ("every inclination of the human mind was nothing but evil"), and duration ("all the time"). The bleakness of this assessment is overwhelming. Although brief, it is a damming indictment. There is no suggestion here that humankind is intrinsically good. On the contrary, human nature is portrayed as being inherently evil, a consequence of Adam and Eve's betrayal of God in the Garden of Eden.

In the light of verse 5, it is no surprise that verses 6–7 describe God's reaction regarding the creation of humankind in terms of regret and

---

we cannot be fully certain that this is the meaning of the Hebrew term. Based on etymology, the term הַנְּפִלִים (*hannĕpilîm*, "the Nephilim) may be related to the verb נָפַל (*nāpal*, "to fall"), but it is unlikely that it means "the fallen ones," for which the correct form would be הַנֹּפְלִים (*hannōpĕlîm*) (cf. Josh 8:25).

[217] The expression אַנְשֵׁי הַשֵּׁם (*anšê haššēm*) literally means "men of the name." It is noteworthy that Noah calls one of his sons שֵׁם (*šēm*, "Shem"), which means "name" (5:32) and he is the son through whom the unique patriline is traced (11:10–26). Later, God promises to make Abram's name great (12:2).

[218] Mathews, *Genesis 1-11:26*, 338n138.

[219] On the name of the city, see Comments on 10:8–12. It will be argued later that Nimrod is viewed as a man of violence.

grief. Due to the ubiquitous evil of humanity God is deeply troubled. The description of YHWH's response is noteworthy because it does not major on divine anger or resentment, but rather on disappointment and sorrow. God's feelings of regret are compounded by the fact that he has created humanity.

Whereas in Genesis 1 God saw that all was טֹב (*ṭōb*, "good") (1:4, 10, 12, 18, 21, 25, 31), in 6:5 he sees that the רָעָה (*rāʿâ*, "evil") of humankind abounds on the earth and that the thoughts of human hearts are רַע (*raʿ*, "evil") all the time. Since the antonym of טֹב (*ṭōb*, "good") is רַע (*raʿ*, "evil"), v. 5 underlines that the earth is no longer as God intended. In the light of this, God decides to wipe out humanity from the earth, as well as land animals, creatures that crawl and birds.[220] This decision, however, pains God's heart.

The verb נחם (*nḥm*) comes at the start of verse 6 and the end of verse 7 with God as the subject in both instances. The KJV speaks of God repenting, whereas most modern English versions render the verb "to regret." Parunak argues that the *niphal* form of the verb means "to suffer emotional pain."[221] This understanding of נחם (*nḥm*) is often associated with a change of heart involving disappointment concerning a prior action. Most English versions opt for the translation "the Lord regretted" in 6:6 (e.g., ESV, CSB, NIV, NET, NJB, NJPS), with some reading "I am sorry" in 6:7 (e.g., ESV, NAS, NRSV).

God's decision to wipe הָאָדָם (*hāʾādām*, "mankind") from the face of the הָאֲדָמָה (*hāʾădāmâ*, "earth") (v. 7) marks the reversal of what he did in forming הָאָדָם (*hāʾādām*, "the man") from the dust of the הָאֲדָמָה (*hāʾădāmâ*,"ground") (2:7). While verses 5–7 indict humanity, God's judgment will result in the destruction of land animals, creatures that crawl and birds, distinctive categories that are mentioned in 1:24–26, 28, 30. The lack of reference in verse 7 to the "fish of the sea" (cf. 1:26, 28) anticipates the nature of the punishment that will befall all the other creatures.

Against the somber background of God's assessment of humanity and the pronouncement that they will be destroyed, verse 8 introduces an

---

[220] The inclusion of other creatures is later modified by God's command to Noah to preserve two of all living creatures (6:19–20). The survival of all living creatures is tied to the deliverance of Noah, a reminder of the important role that the offspring of the woman will play in saving the whole of creation from the control of the "serpent."

[221] H. Van Dyke Parunak, "A Semantic Survey of NḤM," *Biblica* 56 (1975): 512–32.

important glimmer of light: Noah finds favor with YHWH. The syntax of verse 8 deliberately highlights the contrast between Noah and the rest of humanity.[222] The name Noah is placed before the verb, breaking the *wayyiqtol* verb sequence. As reflected in most English versions, the initial conjunction in verse 8 is best translated "but" (EVS, KJV, NET, NIV, NJB, NRSV, NJPS; cf. the use of "however" in CSB). God's attitude toward Noah recalls the hope that Lamech expresses in 5:28. The linear genealogy of chapter 5 and the panoramic narrative of 6:1–8 both come to an optimistic climax in the person of Noah. Drawing on the verbal connections between 5:29 and 6:6–8, Mathews notes that "God's grief over the sinfulness of humanity will find a reprieve in the godly Noah (8:21)."[223] With good reason, the next major narrative section of Genesis details Noah's special relationship with God (6:9–9:28).

The Hebrew term translated "favor" is חֵן (*ḥēn*), a word that coincidentally consists of the same consonants used in the name נֹחַ (*nōaḥ*, "Noah"). Although the expression "to find favor in the eyes of someone" occurs frequently in Genesis (e.g., 18:3; 19:19; 30:27; 32:5 [Heb. 6]; 33:8, 10, 15; 34:11; 39:4; 47:25, 29; 50:4), almost always it comes in the context of human relationships, with one party hoping to secure or enjoy the approval of another. In verse 8, God views Noah positively in contrast to the rest of humanity (vv. 5–7). While an individual may sometimes hope by his or her actions to gain the favor of another, חֵן (*ḥēn*) is not something that one is under an obligation to show; it is an act of grace. However, an individual may seek to gain the favor of another by acting in a particular way. The grounds for this will be disclosed in the next verse, which marks the start of the *tôlĕdôt* of Noah (6:9–9:29).[224]

---

[222] Bill T. Arnold and J. H. Choi, *A Guide to Biblical Hebrew Syntax*, 2nd ed. (Cambridge: Cambridge University Press, 2018), 182, notes the in 6:9 the subject Noah comes before the verb "to place *emphasis on the subject*" (italics in original).

[223] Mathews, *Genesis 1–11:26*, 347. The Hebrew text of 6:6 contains noteworthy links with Lamech's remarks in 5:27, involving the roots נחם (*nḥm*), עשׂה (*ʿśh*), and עצב (*ʿṣb*). Noah is the one who will bring relief to the pain of both humanity and God.

[224] Kaminski, *Was Noah Good?*, contends (a) that Noah is not excluded from the divine condemnation of humanity in 6:5, and (b) that חֵן *ḥēn* denotes "favor" that is not merited but given graciously. She concludes that God's favor toward Noah is underserved. While these observations are important, she fails to address adequately the narrator's positive assessment of Noah in 6:9, which she takes to be a "proleptic statement that anticipates the divine verdict in 7:1" (198). However, it is difficult to avoid the conclusion that Noah's relationship with God, reflected in his walking with God, has some bearing on why he and

Bridge

The linear genealogy of 5:1–32 and the panoramic overview of 6:1–8 each conclude with expectations that Noah will play a central role against the background of humanity's wickedness that has impacted all of creation. God's promise in 3:15 that an offspring of the woman will overcome the serpent has still to be fulfilled. All now centers on Noah, as God intervenes to restrain humanity's prolific wickedness. The situation calls for unprecedented action on the part of God as he makes a fresh beginning by sending a great flood that will destroy all living creatures apart from those preserved by Noah and his family in a specially constructed ark.

The state of the world in the antediluvian period is a stark reminder of humanity's proclivity for evil. Little has changed. Violence toward others, at all levels, continues to impact the lives of countless people. From domestic abuse to ethnic cleansing, the human tendency to treat others as objects to abuse is endemic.[225] And human violence is not limited to the abusive treatment of other people. It includes the natural environment. In the light of Scripture and experience, one of the greatest heresies of modern times is the claim that people are intrinsically good.[226] Against the background of human evil, the book of Genesis points to the hope that comes through the promised offspring of the woman. At this stage of the story, this hope centers on Noah, whom God will rescue from the judgment that is about to descend on defiant humanity.

---

his family, in contrast to others, are spared from the flood. As the subsequent narrative highlights, Noah obeys God's commands faithfully (6:22; 7:5, 9). The positive nature of Noah's character is an important component in the story. This need not mean, however, that his survival is not due to the graciousness of God. By claiming that Noah found favor in God's eyes (6:8) prior to any mention of his integrity (6:9), the narrator possibly signals that Noah's deliverance from the flood relies on God's unmerited favor as much as on Noah's righteousness. The fact that Noah offers sacrifices immediately after exiting the ark indicates a recognition on his part that he needs to atone for his failings as a person.

[225] This is illustrated with particular reference to women by Elaine Storkey, *Scars Across Humanity: Understanding and Overcoming Violence Against Women* (London: SPCK, 2015). Her book catalogues the wide variety of ways in which women today are the targets of violence. These include selective abortion and infanticide, female genital mutilation, early and enforced marriage, honor killings, domestic violence, trafficking and prostitution, rape, and sexual violence during war.

[226] For a helpful study of how sin impacts humanity, see Cornelius Plantinga, *Not the Way It's Supposed to Be: A Breviary of Sin* (Grand Rapids: Eerdmans, 1995).

IV. The Offspring of Noah (6:9–9:29)

A. Noah and the Flood (6:9–8:12)

9 These are the family records of Noah. Noah was a righteous man,
blameless among his contemporaries; Noah walked with God. 10 And
Noah fathered three sons: Shem, Ham, and Japheth.

11 Now the earth was corrupt in God's sight, and the earth was filled with
wickedness. 12 God saw how corrupt the earth was, for every creature
had corrupted its way on the earth. 13 Then God said to Noah, "I have
decided to put an end to every creature, for the earth is filled with
wickedness because of them; therefore I am going to destroy them
along with the earth.

14 "Make yourself an ark of gopher wood. Make rooms in the ark, and
cover it with pitch inside and outside. 15 This is how you are to make it:
The ark will be 450 feet long, 75 feet wide, and 45 feet high. 16 You are
to make a roof, finishing the sides of the ark to within eighteen inches
of the roof. You are to put a door in the side of the ark. Make it with
lower, middle, and upper decks.

17 "Understand that I am bringing a flood—floodwaters on the earth
to destroy every creature under heaven with the breath of life in it.
Everything on earth will perish. 18 But I will establish my covenant
with you, and you will enter the ark with your sons, your wife, and
your sons' wives. 19 You are also to bring into the ark two of all the
living creatures, male and female, to keep them alive with you. 20 Two
of everything—from the birds according to their kinds, from the live-
stock according to their kinds, and from the animals that crawl on the
ground according to their kinds—will come to you so that you can keep
them alive. 21 Take with you every kind of food that is eaten; gather it
as food for you and for them." 22 And Noah did this. He did everything
that God had commanded him.

7:1 Then the LORD said to Noah, "Enter the ark, you and all your household,
for I have seen that you alone are righteous before me in this generation.
2 You are to take with you seven pairs, a male and its female, of all the
clean animals, and two of the animals that are not clean, a male and its
female, 3 and seven pairs, male and female, of the birds of the sky—in
order to keep offspring alive throughout the earth. 4 Seven days from
now I will make it rain on the earth forty days and forty nights, and
every living thing I have made I will wipe off the face of the earth." 5
And Noah did everything that the LORD commanded him.

6 Noah was six hundred years old when the flood came and water cov-
ered the earth. 7 So Noah, his sons, his wife, and his sons' wives entered

the ark because of the floodwaters. [8] From the clean animals, unclean
animals, birds, and every creature that crawls on the ground, [9] two of
each, male and female, came to Noah and entered the ark, just as God had
commanded him. [10] Seven days later the floodwaters came on the earth.

[11] In the six hundredth year of Noah's life, in the second month, on the
seventeenth day of the month, on that day all the sources of the vast
watery depths burst open, the floodgates of the sky were opened, [12] and
the rain fell on the earth forty days and forty nights. [13] On that same
day Noah along with his sons Shem, Ham, and Japheth, Noah's wife,
and his three sons' wives entered the ark with him. [14] They entered it
with all the wildlife according to their kinds, all livestock according to
their kinds, all the creatures that crawl on the earth according to their
kinds, every flying creature—all the birds and every winged creature—
according to their kinds. [15] Two of every creature that has the breath of
life in it came to Noah and entered the ark. [16] Those that entered, male
and female of every creature, entered just as God had commanded him.
Then the LORD shut him in.

[17] The flood continued for forty days on the earth; the water increased
and lifted the ark so that it rose above the earth. [18] The water surged and
increased greatly on the earth, and the ark floated on the surface of the
water. [19] Then the water surged even higher on the earth, and all the high
mountains under the whole sky were covered. [20] The mountains were
covered as the water surged above them more than twenty feet. [21] Every
creature perished—those that crawl on the earth, birds, livestock, wildlife,
and those that swarm on the earth, as well as all mankind. [22] Everything
with the breath of the spirit of life in its nostrils—everything on dry land
died. [23] He wiped out every living thing that was on the face of the earth,
from mankind to livestock, to creatures that crawl, to the birds of the sky,
and they were wiped off the earth. Only Noah was left, and those that
were with him in the ark. [24] And the water surged on the earth 150 days.

[8:1] God remembered Noah, as well as all the wildlife and all the livestock
that were with him in the ark. God caused a wind to pass over the earth,
and the water began to subside. [2] The sources of the watery depths
and the floodgates of the sky were closed, and the rain from the sky
stopped. [3] The water steadily receded from the earth, and by the end
of 150 days the water had decreased significantly. [4] The ark came to
rest in the seventh month, on the seventeenth day of the month, on
the mountains of Ararat.

[5] The water continued to recede until the tenth month; in the tenth
month, on the first day of the month, the tops of the mountains were

visible. 6 After forty days Noah opened the window of the ark that he had
made, 7 and he sent out a raven. It went back and forth until the water
had dried up from the earth. 8 Then he sent out a dove to see whether
the water on the earth's surface had gone down, 9 but the dove found
no resting place for its foot. It returned to him in the ark because water
covered the surface of the whole earth. He reached out and brought it
into the ark to himself. 10 So Noah waited seven more days and sent out
the dove from the ark again. 11 When the dove came to him at evening,
there was a plucked olive leaf in its beak. So Noah knew that the water
on the earth's surface had gone down. 12 After he had waited another
seven days, he sent out the dove, but it did not return to him again.

Context

The preceding narrative in 5:1–6:8 has drawn attention to the importance of Noah by recording Lamech's optimistic remarks about him (5:29) and by noting how he finds favor in God's sight (6:8). Noah stands apart from all others in his generation, and the expectation is created that he will play a significant role in the patriline that has descended from Adam and Eve through Seth. In the light of these expectations, a new *tôlĕdôt* heading in 6:9 focuses on what will come forth from Noah.

The *tôlĕdôt* section associated with Noah is dominated by the coming of a great flood, which God sends due to the violence of humanity on the earth. The initial phase of human existence of the earth is brought to a tragic end by this flood, but Noah and his family survive. By following God's instructions to construct a massive ark, Noah and his family are protected from the floodwaters. Only this small group of humans survives from the antediluvian world. Noah's actions after coming out of the ark cause God to establish an eternal covenant that guarantees protection to future generations. There will be no second catastrophic flood.

Various scholars have observed that the flood narrative exhibits a symmetrical design with the second half of the narrative being a mirror image of the first half. Cassuto sets out the concentric nature of the flood story in the following way:[227]

---

[227] U. Cassuto, *A Commentary on the Book of Genesis: Part II: From Noah to Abraham* (Jerusalem: Magnes, 1964), 30–33.

A 6:9–12
  B 6:13–22
    C 7:1–5
      D 7:6–9
        E 7:10–16
          F 7:17–24
          F' 8:1–14
        E' 8:15–17
      D' 8:18–22
    C' 9:1–7
  B' 9:8–11
A' 9:12–17

Anderson proposes a similar, but not identical, structure:[228]

Transitional introduction (6:9–10)
  1. Violence in God's creation (6:11–12)
    2. First divine address: resolution to destroy (6:13–22)
      3. Second divine address: command to enter the ark (7:1–10)
        4. Beginning of the flood (7:11–16)
          5. The rising flood waters (7:17–24)
            GOD'S REMEMBRANCE OF NOAH
          6. The receding flood waters (8:1–5)
        7. The drying of the earth (8:6–14)
      8. Third divine address: command to leave the ark (8:15–19)
    9. God's resolution to preserve order (8:20–22)
  10. Fourth divine address: covenant blessing and peace (9:1–17)
Transitional conclusion (9:18–19)

Anderson's scheme highlights how the reference to God's remembering Noah in 8:1 functions as the turning point in the story. The same observation is made by Wenham,[229] who illustrates the literary structure of the narrative as follows:

[228] Bernhard W. Anderson, "From Analysis to Synthesis: The Interpretation of Genesis 1–11," *JBL* 97 (1978): 23–39, esp. 38.

[229] Gordon J. Wenham, "The Coherence of the Flood Narrative," *VT* 28 (1978): 336–48, esp. 338. Wenham elsewhere offers a further palistrophe based on a consideration of the different scenes which compose the narrative. See Wenham, *Genesis 1-15*, 157–58.

A Noah (vi 10a)
B Shem, Ham and Japheth (10b)
C Ark to be built (14–16)
D Flood announced (17)
E Covenant with Noah (18–20)
F Food in the ark (21)
G Command to enter ark (vii 1–3)
H 7 days waiting for flood (4–5)
I 7 days waiting for flood (7–10)
J Entry to ark (11–15)
K Yahweh shuts Noah in (16)
L 40 days flood (17a)
M Waters increase (17b–18)
N Mountains covered (19–20)
O 150 days waters prevail (21–24)
P GOD REMEMBERS NOAH (viii 1)
O' 150 days waters abate (3)
N' Mountain tops visible (4–5)
M' Waters abate (5)
L' 40 days (end of) (6a)
K' Noah opens window of ark (6b)
J' Raven and dove leave ark (7–9)
I' 7 days waiting for waters to subside (10–11)
H' 7 days waiting for waters to subside (12–13)
G' Command to leave ark (15–17(22))
F' Food outside ark (ix 1–4)
E' Covenant with all flesh (8–10)
D' No flood in future (11–17)
C' Ark (18a)
B' Shem, Ham and Japheth (18b)
A' Noah (19)

Adding to these concentric structures, Radday offers an alternative arrangement that captures something of the movement into and out of the ark, as well as the waters rising and abating:[230]

---

[230] Yehuda T. Radday, "Chiasmus in Hebrew Biblical Narrative," in *Chiasmus in Antiquity: Structures, Analyses, Exegesis*, ed. John W. Welch (Hildesheim: Gerstenberg, 1981), 50–115, esp. 99.

A Divine monologue (6:3, 7)
  B it grieved Him to His heart (6:6)
    C "I will establish My covenant" (6:18)
      D Four stages of entering the ark "as commanded" (6:22, 7:5, 9, 16)
        E "Go into the Ark" (7:1)
          F the foundations of the deep burst forth (7:11)
            G Seven verbs of "ascent": increase, bore, rose (7:17), prevailed, increased greatly (7:18), prevailed mightily, mountains were covered (7:19)
            G' Seven verbs of "descent": subsided (8:1), were restrained (8:2), receded, abated (8:3), came to rest (8:4), continued to abate, mountains were seen (8:5)
          F' the fountains of the deep were closed (8:2)
        E' "Go forth from the ark" (8:11)
      D' Four stages of leaving the ark (once a raven, thrice a dove) (8:7, 8, 10, 12)
  B' the Lord said in His heart (8:20 [sic.])
    C' "I establish My covenant" (9:9)
A' A Divine monologue (9:12–16)

To the variety of mirror images already noted, it could be argued that the references to the clean animals in 7:1–9 and 8:20–22 balance each other.

A Introduction (6:9–12)
  B First Divine Speech: promise of the covenant (6:13–22)
    C Preparation for sacrifice involving clean animals (7:1–10)
      D The rising of the waters (7:11–24)
        E GOD REMEMBERED NOAH (8:1)
      D' The retreat of the waters (8:2–19)
    C' Sacrifice involving clean animals (8:20–22)
  B' Final Divine Speech: ratification of the covenant (9:1–16)
A' Conclusion (9:17–19)

These palistrophes appear impressive at first sight, but Emerton highlights various shortcomings.[231] Furthermore, a comparison of these

[231] J. A. Emerton, "An Examination of Some Attempts to Defend the Unity of the Flood Narrative in Genesis: Part I," *VT* 37 (1987): 401–20; J. A. Emerton, "An Examination of Some Attempts to Defend the Unity of the Flood Narrative in Genesis: Part II," *VT* 38 (1988): 1–21.

proposed structures reveals the existence of many differences, some significant, between them.[232] Due to these disparities, the palistrophes cannot be superimposed on top of each other to form one single mirror structure. In the light of this, we should recognize that the plot of the flood story creates natural correspondences that center around the waters rising and abating. This accounts for many of the features noted in the concentric structures. Despite the limitations of the different palistrophes, the two halves of the flood narrative correspond on many points. In the light of these correspondences, there are good grounds for believing that the story has been carefully composed.

With the discovery and decipherment of ANE texts in the nineteenth century and afterwards, scholars have become aware of other documents that describe how certain people survived a great flood by constructing an ark-like vessel. The Gilgamesh and Atrahasis epics from Mesopotamia are the best-known examples. While some features of these stories bear a close resemblance to the biblical account, there is insufficient evidence to suggest that the biblical author was dependent upon these other accounts, or vice versa.[233]

Comments

6:9–10. Verse 9 begins with a *tôlĕdôt* heading that marks the start of a new section within the book of Genesis (6:9–9:29). The subsequent narrative focuses mainly on Noah, before revealing in 9:18–29 something about the differing natures of his three sons. Considering the expectations created by 5:29 and 6:8, Noah's introduction as a major figure in Genesis begins by highlighting his positive attributes. He is "a righteous man, blameless among his contemporaries" (v. 9). The narrator's assessment of Noah as צַדִּיק (*ṣaddîq*, "righteous") is confirmed later when God says to Noah, "I have seen that you alone are righteous before me in this generation" (7:1). The adjective תָּמִים (*tāmîm*), translated "blameless," conveys the idea of being whole or complete, without blemish. In Genesis, the term occurs elsewhere only in 17:1, where God instructs Abraham to walk before him and be blameless. Abraham is to be a second Noah. God expects Abraham to resemble Noah as regards moral rectitude. In the Pentateuch תָּמִים

[232] For example, items HI and H'I' in Wenham's palistrophe belong to the non-corresponding sections 3 and 7 in Anderson's structure.

[233] For a helpful survey and summary, see Wenham, *Genesis 1–15*, 159–66.

(*tāmîm*) is frequently used in connection with sacrificial animals; in most instances offerings to God must be free from any defect (cf., e.g., Lev 1:3, 10; 3:1, 6, 4:3, 23). Due to his moral integrity, Noah differs sharply from the rest of society, which has been judged by God to be "evil" (6:5). In addition, Noah enjoys a close relationship with God. The final words of verse 9 record that he walks with God, a concept that is used twice in connection with Enoch (5:22, 24) and implies an ongoing relationship of faithful obedience to God.[234] While the initial description of Noah in verse 9 is exceptionally positive, indicating that he will play a significant role in God's plans for creation, the mention of his three sons in verse 10 signals that the quest for the offspring of the woman, who will overcome the serpent, will not end with Noah.

6:11–22. Attention turns from Noah and his sons to the state of the earth/land. While the Hebrew noun אֶרֶץ (*ʾereṣ*) is often translated "earth," it may also denote an area or region of land (e.g., 12:1, 7; 23:7, 12, 13; 24:5). Since אֶרֶץ (*ʾereṣ*) can denote either all dry land (as in 1:10) or a smaller region, we must be cautious when assessing the extent of the corruption mentioned in verses 11–13. At this stage in Genesis, there is no reason to assume that the human population was dispersed throughout the whole earth; the first indication of this happening comes in 11:1–9. This has important implications as regards the nature of the flood. For this reason, some scholars contend that the flood described in chapters 6–9 should be viewed as localized, not covering the entire world.[235] This is a possible interpretation that can be reconciled with what is said elsewhere in Scripture.[236] Whatever position is adopted, the important point is that the whole of humanity comes under God's judgment and is punished, apart from Noah and his immediate family.

One concept dominates verses 11–12: the corruption of the earth/land. The threefold repetition of the verb שׁחת (*šḥt*) underlines that the earth/land has become corrupted by the actions of "all flesh." Relatively little is said about the precise nature of this corruption. The same verb occurs

---

[234] The word order of the Hebrew text in v. 9 gives prominence to God; a literal rendering would read: "With God walked Noah."

[235] James Gracey Murphy, *A Critical and Exegetical Commentary on the Book of Genesis with a New Translation* (Edinburgh: T&T Clark, 1863), 193, argues that, because the human population was still relatively small, a worldwide flood was not necessary to punish all humans.

[236] For example, the reference to the "world" in 2 Pet 3:6 may denote "all human beings" and not necessarily the physical earth.

with earth/land as subject in Exodus 8:24 [Heb. 20], describing how the land of Egypt is devastated by a swarm of insects, probably mosquitoes.[237] By way of clarifying how the earth/land has become corrupted, verses 11 and 13 speak of it being filled with חָמָס (*ḥāmās*), a term that denotes "wickedness" (CSB; cf. NJB, NJPS) or "violence" (e.g., ESV, NET, NIV, NRSV). Responsibility for the earth/land's corruption is attributed to כָּל־בָּשָׂר (*kol-bāśār*), an expression that possibly denotes here both humans and other creatures.[238] Although it seems strange that God's judgment should include other creatures, the Pentateuch provides evidence to suggest that animals are held accountable for the deaths of humans.[239] The destruction of the animals and birds in the great flood suggests that they are complicit in filling the earth/land with violence.[240] Their fate may well be linked to the failure of humans to exercise dominion on God's behalf over all the creatures of the earth/land. While the punishment of other creatures is tied closely to the fate of humanity, it is noteworthy that the subsequent preservation of other creatures is due to Noah's obedience to God.

In the light of the earth/land's corruption, God pronounces his judgment upon "all flesh" (v. 13). The decreed punishment mirrors the actions of "all flesh." As they have destroyed creation, so they will be destroyed;[241] their violence will be matched by the violence of the flood that will come upon them. The verb שׁחת (*šḥt*), which appears in verses 11–12 with

---

[237] See T. Desmond Alexander, *Exodus*, Apollos OT Commentary 2 (London: Apollos, 2017), 182–83.

[238] All occurrence of the expression כָּל־בָּשָׂר (*kol-bāśār*) in chs. 6–9 appear to denote both humans and animals (6:12, 13, 17, 19; 7:16, 21; 8:17; 9:11, 15–17). The second century BC Book of Jubilees provides an ancient retelling of this passage. Jubilees 5:2 states: "And lawlessness increased on the earth and all flesh corrupted its way, alike men and cattle and beasts and birds and everything that walks on the earth—all of them corrupted their ways and their orders, and they began to devour each other, and lawlessness increased on the earth and every imagination of the thoughts of all men (was) thus evil continually" (R. H. Charles, *The Apocrypha and Pseudepigrapha of the Old Testament*, vol. 2, *Pseudepigrapha* [Oxford: Clarendon, 1913], 20).

[239] This is evident in 9:5. The case of the goring ox is noteworthy (Exod 21:28–32). The animal forfeits its life for killing a person. By requiring the death of the animal, the biblical legislation differs from that of surrounding cultures. See J. J. Finkelstein, "The Ox That Gored," *Transactions of the American Philosophical Society* 71 (1981): 5–47.

[240] Samuel L. Boyd, "The Flood and the Problem of Being an Omnivore," *JSOT* 43 (2018): 168, writes, "This violence pertains to massive bloodshed with animals killing people, people killing animals, and people killing people, in other words 'all flesh.' "

[241] To capture the link between the different uses of שׁחת (*šḥt*), Wenham, *Genesis 1-15*, 171, translates the verb consistently as "to ruin."

reference to how the earth has been corrupted by violence/wickedness, is used in verses 13, 17 to describe the divine destruction of "all flesh." The repeated use of the verb may be intended to underline the principle of *lex talionis*: the level of punishment should correspond to the seriousness of the crime.

After announcing to Noah his decision to destroy every creature due to the earth/land being filled with their violence/wickedness, God instructs Noah to build a massive wooden ark with rooms[242] (vv. 14–16). God's directions give an idea of the basic structure, outlining its dimensions and main features (e.g., roof, door, decks).[243] God then speaks of the ark's purpose (vv. 17–20). By way of explanation, God informs Noah that he is going to send a massive flood that will destroy every living creature (v. 17).[244] This is the first mention of the flood. Noah, however, will be safe; he will take refuge in the ark with his family and two of every living creature (vv. 18–20). The three types of creatures mentioned in verse 20, which echo those mentioned in 6:7, recall the distinctive categories of land creatures listed in 1:24–26, 28, 30. Much about the flood narrative recalls the Genesis 1 account of creation; it is a story of de-creation and re-creation.

Observing how human violence in the Pentateuch is viewed as defiling or polluting the earth/land, Frymer-Kensky writes:

> It is the filling of the earth with *hāmās* and its resultant pollution that prompts God to bring a flood to physically erase everything from the earth and start anew. The flood is not primarily

---

[242] This is the only occurrence in the Old Testament of the plural noun קִנִּים (*qinnîm*, "rooms)"; in the singular it normally denotes a "nest" (e.g., Deut 22:6; 32:11). Given the variety of creatures that will inhabit the ark, "nests" would seem an appropriate term to designate what Noah is to prepare. Due to the influence of Edward Ullendorff, "Construction of Noah's Ark," *VT* 4 (1954): 95–96, NJB amends the MT to read קָנִים (*qānîm*), which is then translated "reeds." However, in the Old Testament קָנִים (*qānîm*) is never associated with reeds used in the construction of boats; it denotes rather a rod or branch (cf. Exod 25:32, 37:18) that may sometimes be used for measuring lengths (Ezek 42:16–19). Boyd, "The Flood and the Problem of Being an Omnivore," 165–67, mistakenly assumes that the supposed reference to "reeds" in 6:14 provides evidence that the biblical account is closely related to Mesopotamian traditions regarding the construction of an ark.

[243] The mention of a roof is important for it ensures that the ark is not swamped by the rain that falls.

[244] CSB renders יִגְוָע (*yigwāʿ*) at the end of v. 17 with the words "will perish" (cf. NIV, NJB, NJPS); other translations adopt the reading "will die" (KJV; ESV; NRSV). However, in the light of 25:8, 17; 35:29, the verb גוע (*gwʿ*) appears to denote an action that precedes the act of dying. It may refer to breathing one's last.

> an agency of punishment (although to be drowned is hardly a pleasant reward), but a means of getting rid of a thoroughly polluted world and starting again with a clean, well-washed one.[245]

Although Frymer-Kensky mistakenly plays down the punitive nature of the flood, she is correct in noting how the flood cleanses the earth/land from the defilement caused by the violence/wickedness of all flesh.

God's words of reassurance in verses 18–20 are linked to a brief remark at the start of verse 18 that God will establish his covenant with Noah. Nothing more is said about this covenant prior to the coming of the flood. However, after everyone emerges safely from the ark, God establishes a covenant with Noah and his sons, their offspring, and every living creature with them (9:8–9). It seems likely that the covenant mentioned briefly in 6:18 anticipates the covenant described in 9:8–17.[246]

God's speech ends with another instruction; he commands Noah to gather food for every creature that will enter the ark (v. 21). In addressing Noah God issues two directives: Noah is to construct an ark and stockpile food. Although God lists those who will enter the ark (vv. 19–20), the command to embark will be given later (7:1–4).[247] Finally, verse 22 states briefly that Noah did all that God commanded. By the end of chapter 6, the reader can assume that the ark is constructed and filled with provisions.

7:1–5. Having previously instructed Noah to build the ark and store food (6:14, 21), God now commands him to enter the vessel (v. 1). Additional details are given regarding the creatures that are to be brought into the ark (vv. 2–3). Seven pairs of each type of "clean" animals are to be preserved, but only one pair of animals considered "unclean." As regards birds, verse 3 is slightly ambiguous; the seven pairs probably refer only to birds designated "clean" (cf. 8:20). No explanation is given to account for the distinction between clean and unclean

---

245 Frymer-Kensky, "Atrahasis Epic," 153.

246 Dumbrell, *Covenant and Creation*, 15–26, contends that when God refers to "my covenant" in 6:18, he is alluding to an already existing covenant. See also Gentry and Wellum, *Kingdom through Covenant*, 161–64. The evidence for an earlier covenant is exceptionally weak, as highlighted by Williamson, *Abraham, Israel and the Nations*, 190–206; cf. Steven D. Mason, *"Eternal Covenant" in the Pentateuch: The Contours of an Elusive Phrase*, LHBOTS 494 (New York ; London: T&T Clark, 2008), 47–87.

247 On the basis that 7:1–3 supposedly parallels 6:18b–20, it is sometime stated by source critics that the command to enter the ark is duplicated (see, for example, Habel, *Literary Criticism of the Old Testament*, 32–33). However, a close reading of the text reveals that the instruction to enter the ark is given only in 7:1–3.

animals. Drawing on the regulations regarding clean and unclean foods in Leviticus 11:1–47, and to a lesser extent in Deuteronomy 14:3–20, the most significant distinction between clean and unclean animals is their diet. Most unclean animals appear to be carnivores, whereas clean animals are herbivores. The bias toward preserving more herbivores may be an intentional reaction against the violence/wickedness that causes God's judgment to descend upon the earth/land. The transformation of carnivores into herbivores is associated elsewhere in the Old Testament with the new creation (see Isa 65:25; cf. 11:7). The preservation of additional clean animals in the ark may have been necessary for food or sacrifices (cf. 8:20).[248]

Verse 4 introduces the first of various chronological notices regarding the duration of the flood. Some of these describe periods of time in terms of 7, 40 or 150 days (7:4, 10, 12, 17, 24; 8:3, 6, 10, 12). Other notices give specific dates in terms of day and month, and sometimes year (7:11; 8:4–5, 13–14). Together they reveal that the period from entering to leaving the ark is about 375 days.[249]

In directing him to enter the ark, God highlights Noah's righteousness (v. 1). Yet again the narrative emphasizes how Noah's integrity sets him apart from his contemporaries (cf. 6:9). The future well-being of all creation rest on Noah, underlining the importance of the unique patriline. Noah responds obediently to God's instructions (v. 5). With minor variations in wording verse 5 echoes 6:22. With similar comments coming in 7:9, 16, these references to Noah's obedience to God form a short, but important, refrain within the story, confirming his righteousness.

7:6–9. Verse 6 interrupts the flow of events to provide some circumstantial information regarding Noah's age at the time of the flood. Previously, 5:32 had stated that he was 500 years old when his first son was born. A hundred years have passed; all his sons are now married, but

[248] This may also have a bearing on God's instructions in 9:2–3 regarding animals that may be eaten (see Comments on 9:2–3).

[249] It is often claimed that the references to 40 days and 150 days in the account of the flood reflect two different sources, one of which held the duration of the flood to be 40 days and the other 150 days. Yet, the present account takes the total period of the flood, from entry into the ark to exit from the ark, to be about 375 days. Within such a longer period, it is no surprise that there should be shorter periods that refer to different stages in the rising and abating of the flood waters. If the present story is a combination of two different traditions, it is difficult to understand why the redactor would preserve contradictory figures for the length of the flood.

without children. Verses 7–9 confirm the identity of those who take refuge in the ark. The additional observation is made that all the creatures came to Noah and entered the ark (v. 8).[250] For a third time, the narrator notes that Noah does as God commands him (v. 9b; cf. 6:22; 7:5).

7:10–16. Verse 10 marks the start of the next phase in the story. Seven days pass from when God gives the command to enter the ark at the start of the flood (v. 10, cf. v. 4). To underline the significance of this occasion, verse 11 records the date on which the flood commences with reference to Noah's age. This is the first of five specific dates that are recorded in the story (cf. 8:4, 5, 13, 14). The last of these in 8:14, which mentions that the earth/land has dried out, reveals that the flood lasted for one year and 10 days from beginning to end, approximately 375 days.

God initiates the flood by sending rain that continues day and night for forty days (v. 12). The wording of verse 11 implies that the flood was created by two different sources of water. On the one hand, rain descended as "the floodgates of the sky were opened" and, on the other hand, water gushed out of springs that are associate with תְּהוֹם (*tĕhôm*, "watery depths"). The use of this term recalls 1:2. As the waters cover the dry ground, the events of chapter 7 represent a reversal of what occurs in Genesis 1.

After a general description of the source of the flood, verses 13–16 confirm the identity of those in the ark, noting that they are present because they obeyed God's command (v. 16). Their obedience plays a crucial part in ensuring their safety. Those who perish under the flood waters have disobeyed God, following in the footsteps of Adam and Eve. Verses 13–16 repeat and expand upon what is said in verses 7–9. The repeated details reinforce God's desire to preserve every type of creature so that the earth/land can be repopulated after the flood. Verse 13 records the names of Noah's three sons, who have previously been mentioned only in 5:32 and 6:10. Verse 14 introduces the expression "according to their kinds," echoing the creation account in 1:24–25 and God's words in 6:20. Verse 14 ends with וְכָל־הָעוֹף לְמִינֵהוּ כֹּל צִפּוֹר כָּל־כָּנָף (*wĕkol-hāʿôp lĕmînēhû kōl ṣippôr kol-kānāp*), which literally reads "and every the bird according to its kind, every fowl, every winged creature." The use of different terms to denote birds and flying insects underscores God's desire to preserve every type of creature.

---

[250] In the Hebrew text one verb is used to describe their coming and entering.

7:17–24. On the assumption that a month is thirty days, the period from the seventeenth day of the second month (7:11) to the seventeenth day of the seventh month (8:4) is 150 days. This would suggest that the two references to 150 days in 7:24 and 8:3 both refer to the period between these two dates. Within this period of five months, there is a period of forty days, denoting the time when rain descends on the earth/land (7:12, 17).[251] These chronological notices highlight the severity of the flood, making it unlikely that anyone or any creature, including birds, could have survived outside the ark. Even the mountains are fully covered with water (vv. 19–20).[252]

Verses 21–23 underline the destructive nature of the flood, which wipes out "every living thing that was on the surface of the ground, from mankind to livestock, to creatures that crawl, to the birds of the sky" (v. 23). Four times the verb גבר (*gbr*, "to rise/surge") is used with the "waters" as subject in verses 18–24. Its use recalls the reference to הַגִּבֹּרִים (*haggibbōrîm*, "the powerful men") in 6:4. The latter, however, are impotent before the flood waters; they are unable to save themselves. God's decision to punish "all flesh," apart from those in the ark, is fulfilled.

8:1–5. Verse 1 marks the turning point in the story, highlighting yet again the importance of Noah's relationship with God. Importantly, God is responsible for the rescue of every person and every creature in the ark. The image of God causing a רוּחַ (*rûaḥ*, "wind") to pass over the earth/land recalls the reference to the רוּחַ אֱלֹהִים (*rûaḥ ʾĕlōhîm*, "Spirit of God") "hovering over the surface of the waters" in 1:2. As in Genesis 1, the dry land emerges from the waters (1:9–10). The flood begins to recede, and the sources of the waters are turned off. The events described in verse 2 reverse the actions recorded in 7:11–12. The syntax of the Hebrew text in verse 3 points to the gradual decline of the waters. By the end of 150 days, the waters have abated from their peak enough for the ark to be grounded on one of the mountains of Ararat (v. 4).[253] The ark settles on a mountain

---

[251] The reference to forty days in v. 17 could possibly denote the time that the earth/land was entirely submerged by the flood, but it is more likely to be the period of forty days mentioned in v. 12. In the light of 8:4–5 the earth/land was probably covered with water for a period longer than forty days.

[252] The mountains are fifteen cubits (approximately twenty-two feet) underwater; the ark itself was thirty cubits (approximately forty-five feet) high (6:15).

[253] Mount Ararat is the name given to the highest peak in a range of mountains located in modern eastern Turkey. Verse 4 does not say that the ark settled on Mount Ararat, but

top, but the waters still cover the earth/land.[254] The chronological notices in verses 4 and 5 indicate that a period of about seventy-three days passes between the ark resting on the mountain and the tops of the mountains becoming visible. Everything points to the flood waters receding slowly.

8:6–12. As the flood waters continue to abate, Noah sends out two birds from the ark. The first, a raven, does not return but survives away from the ark as the waters slowly dry up from the earth. As an omnivore, the raven can scavenge for carrion, a solemn reminder that "all flesh" outside the ark has perished in the flood. Noah also sends out a dove.[255] However, unlike the raven, which feeds on the carcasses of dead creatures, the dove is not an omnivore and depends upon plants to survive. Because it is unable to find suitable food, it returns to the safety of the ark. A week later Noah releases the dove again. On this occasion it comes back later in the day with a "plucked olive leaf" (v. 11), a sign that some vegetation has started to grow again. After another week, Noah sends out the dove for a third time. This time it does not return, evidence that the earth has dried up and vegetation is growing again. The scene is set for everyone to disembark from the ark.

Bridge

The account of the flood is not quite complete at this stage. We have still to read in 8:13–9:19 of Noah's exit from the ark and the events that take place immediately after this. The first part of the flood story highlights the reality of God's punishment of humanity because of its violent behavior. Only Noah stands apart due to his righteousness. Having found favor in God's eyes, Noah enjoys a special relationship with God that benefits his immediate family. Alongside Noah, they are protected from the flood waters that cover the entire country (see 2 Pet 2:5, 9–10). By graciously saving Noah, his family and different kinds of creatures from the destructive floodwaters, God ensures the continuation of life

---

on the mountains of Ararat. The biblical text does not identify with any precision the place where the ark came to rest.

[254] The verb נוח (*nwḥ*) is used to describe the ark settling on the top of the mountains of Ararat. The same Hebrew root is later found in 8:9 in the noun מָנוֹחַ (*mānôaḥ*, "resting place"). It also underlies the name נֹחַ (*nōaḥ*, "Noah") (see Comments on 5:29).

[255] Some source critics argue that the use of two birds is due to two different accounts of the flood having been combined to form the present account. The birds, however, fulfil two contrasting, but complementary, roles in the telling of the story. There is no need to suppose that they reflect the prior existence of two separate flood stories.

on earth. With good reason, Noah is included among those named in Hebrews 11 who demonstrate their trust in God. Noah's commitment to building the ark requires faith.

B. The Aftermath of the Flood (8:13–9:17)

> 13 In the six hundred and first year, in the first month, on the first day of the month, the water that had covered the earth was dried up. Then Noah removed the ark's cover and saw that the surface of the ground was drying. 14 By the twenty-seventh day of the second month, the earth was dry.
>
> 15 Then God spoke to Noah, 16 "Come out of the ark, you, your wife, your sons, and your sons' wives with you. 17 Bring out all the living creatures that are with you—birds, livestock, those that crawl on the earth—and they will spread over the earth and be fruitful and multiply on the earth." 18 So Noah, along with his sons, his wife, and his sons' wives, came out. 19 All the animals, all the creatures that crawl, and all the flying creatures—everything that moves on the earth—came out of the ark by their families.
>
> 20 Then Noah built an altar to the Lord. He took some of every kind of clean animal and every kind of clean bird and offered burnt offerings on the altar. 21 When the Lord smelled the pleasing aroma, he said to himself, "I will never again curse the ground because of human beings, even though the inclination of the human heart is evil from youth onward. And I will never again strike down every living thing as I have done. 22 As long as the earth endures, seedtime and harvest, cold and heat, summer and winter, and day and night will not cease."
>
> 9:1 God blessed Noah and his sons and said to them, "Be fruitful and multiply and fill the earth. 2 The fear and terror of you will be in every living creature on the earth, every bird of the sky, every creature that crawls on the ground, and all the fish of the sea. They are placed under your authority. 3 Every creature that lives and moves will be food for you; as I gave the green plants, I have given you everything. 4 However, you must not eat meat with its lifeblood in it. 5 And I will require a penalty for your lifeblood; I will require it from any animal and from any human; if someone murders a fellow human, I will require that person's life. 6 Whoever sheds human blood, by humans his blood will be shed, for God made humans in his image. 7 But you, be fruitful and multiply; spread out over the earth and multiply on it."
>
> 8 Then God said to Noah and his sons with him, 9 "Understand that I am establishing my covenant with you and your descendants after you, 10 and with every living creature that is with you—birds, livestock, and all wildlife of the earth that are with you—all the animals of the earth

that came out of the ark. [11] I establish my covenant with you that never again will every creature be wiped out by floodwaters; there will never again be a flood to destroy the earth."

[12] And God said, "This is the sign of the covenant I am making between me and you and every living creature with you, a covenant for all future generations: [13] I have placed my bow in the clouds, and it will be a sign of the covenant between me and the earth. [14] Whenever I form clouds over the earth and the bow appears in the clouds, [15] I will remember my covenant between me and you and all the living creatures: water will never again become a flood to destroy every creature. [16] The bow will be in the clouds, and I will look at it and remember the permanent covenant between God and all the living creatures on earth." [17] God said to Noah, "This is the sign of the covenant that I have established between me and every creature on earth."

Context

The account of God's gracious rescue of Noah from the flood continues in this section. Two short chronological notices in 8:13–14 reveal that the surface of the ground dries up slowly. With this the process of cleansing the earth/land from the defilement of violence/wickedness is complete and all is set for a new beginning. At last, it is possible for everyone to leave the ark. By echoing the initial account of creation in Genesis 1, much of the language in 8:13–9:19 conveys a picture of re-creation. As the story moves into the postdiluvian era, attention focuses on God's solemn commitment to every living creature that there will never be another devastating flood to wipe out the whole of humanity.

God's use of a great flood to punish humanity is noteworthy. The flood cleanses the earth, which has been defiled due to human violence.[256] This marks a new beginning, which is signaled by how the account of the flood echoes the initial account of creation in 1:1–2:3. According to Smith, the following correspondences exist:

> (a) Since man could not live on the earth when it was covered with water in chaps. 1 and 8, a subsiding of the water and a separation of the land from the water took place, allowing the dry land to appear (1:9–10; 8:1–13); (b) "birds and animals and every creeping thing that creeps on the earth" are brought forth to "swarm upon the earth" in 1:20–21, 24–25 and 8:17–19; (c) God establishes the days and seasons in 1:14–18 and 8:22; (d) God's blessing rests upon

[256] Frymer-Kensky, "Atrahasis Epic," 147–55.

> the animals as he commands them to "be fruitful and multiply on the earth" in both 1:22 and 8:17; (e) man is brought forth and he receives the blessing of God: "Be fruitful and multiply and fill the earth" in 1:28 and 9:1, 7; (f) man is given dominion over the animal kingdom in 1:28 and 9:2; (g) God provides food for man in 1:29–30 and 9:3 (this latter regulation makes a direct reference back to the previous passage when it includes the statement, "As I have given the green plant"); and (h) in 9:6 the writer quotes from 1:26–27 concerning the image of God in man.[257]

With the subsidence of the floodwaters, Noah and his family emerge from the ark into a recreated earth. However, human nature has not changed. As 8:21 states, "The inclination of the human heart is evil from youth onward."

Comments

8:13–19. As the flood took a long time to engulf the earth/land, it takes an equally long period to subside completely. Verse 13 records the start of a new year; about ninety days have passed since the tops of the mountain had become visible (8:5). A further chronological notice in verse 14 reveals that it takes approximately another fifty-seven days before the ground has dried out sufficiently for the ark's residents to exit. Only at this stage are conditions suitable for everyone to disembark. Having entered the ark in response to God's command, Noah leaves only after being instructed by God (vv. 15–16). Echoing God's instructions in verses 16–17a, verses 18–19 recount their fulfilment. Once more Noah obeys God.

The end of the flood marks the start of a new phase in God's plans for the earth and its inhabitants. God expects all the creatures to "spread out" on the earth/land and "be fruitful and multiply" (v. 17). His desire recalls the initial creation account in which these same verbs are used to describe how the earth is to be filled (cf. 1:20–22, 28).

8:20–22. Noah's first recorded activity after disembarking from the ark is to build an altar and offer sacrifices (v. 20). These sacrifices are designated עֹלֹת (*ʿōlōt*), which most English versions translate as "burnt offerings." This is the first reference in the Old Testament to this type of offering. The designation "burnt offerings," however, fails to convey adequately the idea that this type of offering ascends toward God. It

---

[257] Smith, "Structure and Purpose in Genesis 1–11," 310–11.

would be better to refer to these sacrifices as "ascension offerings"; this designation is more in keeping with the meaning of the Hebrew root עלה (*ʿlh*), which has the sense "go up." The animals and birds are consumed in their entirety by fire on the altar, with the smoke of the offering ascending to God. This movement is conveyed in the expression וַיַּעַל עֹלֹת (*wayyaʿal ʿōlōt*), which could be translated "and he caused to ascend ascension offerings." The repetition of the Hebrew root עלה (*ʿlh*) is noteworthy, emphasizing that the offering goes upward.[258] When later the tabernacle is constructed, the burnt/ascension offering is viewed as the most important of all sacrifices.[259] As the offering ascends as smoke, God smells its pleasing aroma. The act of smelling is highlighted in the expression וַיָּרַח יְהוָה אֶת־רֵיחַ הַנִּיחֹחַ (*wayyāraḥ yhwh ʾet-rêaḥ han-nîḥōaḥ*), which could be rendered: "and YHWH smelled the pleasing/restful smell."[260] This is the only time in the Old Testament that God is said to smell a sacrifice,[261] but the concept is often associated with offerings that are consumed by fire on an altar. The noun נִיחוֹחַ (*nîḥôaḥ*, "pleasing/soothing substance)" only occurs in the Old Testament in conjunction with רֵיחַ (*rêaḥ*, "aroma/smell").[262] On the basis of his response in vv. 21–22, the smell from the sacrifice has a positive impact on God.[263] Noah's offering has a "restful... , soothing, pacifying effect on God."[264]

---

[258] See T. Desmond Alexander, *Face to Face with God: A Biblical Theology of Christ as Priest and Mediator* (Downers Grove, IL: InterVarsity Press, 2022), 70–75.

[259] Christian A. Eberhart, "A Neglected Feature of Sacrifice in the Hebrew Bible: Remarks on the Burning Rite on the Altar," *HTR* 97 (2004): 485–93, notes that the different types of offerings listed in the opening chapters of Leviticus require all or part of the offering to be transformed into smoke, which then ascends to God as a pleasing aroma. The prime example of this is the burnt/ascension offering.

[260] The expression רֵיחַ־נִיחוֹחַ לַיהוָה (*rêaḥ-nîḥôaḥ lyhwh*, "a pleasing/restful aroma to the Lord") is used of the burnt/ascension offering in Lev 1:9, 13, 17. The same expression occurs in connection with other types of offerings (see Lev 2:2, 9, 12; 3:5, 16; 4:31; 6:15, 21 [Heb. 8, 14]), implying that this is an essential component of all offerings made by fire.

[261] In Lev 26:31, God indicates in a list of curses that he will not smell the soothing aroma associated with offerings. Several passages highlight the inability of idols to smell (Deut 4:28; Ps 115:6), implying that they cannot be appeased by offerings burnt on altars.

[262] The Hebrew root נוח (*nwḥ*) underlies the name נֹחַ (*nōaḥ*, "Noah"), which is associated with rest (see Comments on 5:29).

[263] The concept of sacrifices giving off a soothing aroma is found in other ANE texts. When Utnapishtim in the Epic of Gilgamesh offered sacrifices after a great flood, we are told, "The gods smelled the savor, The gods smelled the sweet savor, The gods crowded like flies about the sacrificer" (James B. Pritchard, ed., *Ancient Near Eastern Texts*, 3rd ed. [Princeton: Princeton University Press, 1969], 95.)

[264] Wenham, *Genesis 1-15*, 189.

In the light of this, God determines never to "strike down every living thing" as he has just done (v. 21).

From the immediately surrounding context of verses 20–22 it is apparent that Noah's offerings are not simply intended to thank God for deliverance from the flood. Nor are they intended primarily to gain God's favor for Noah himself. God has already shown favor to Noah in saving him from the flood (cf. 6:8). Importantly, the offerings impact God's attitude toward humanity in general. As Skinner comments, "Noah's first act is to offer a sacrifice, not of thanksgiving but (as v. 21 shows) of propitiation: its effect is to move the Deity to gracious thoughts toward the new humanity."[265] This is evident from God's words to himself in verses 21–22. In what is a rare occurrence in Genesis, the omniscient narrator enables the reader to see into the mind of God. God's decision leads to the establishment of the covenant that is recorded in chapter 9.

God's remark that he "will never again curse the ground because of human beings" are sometimes interpreted as a reference back to the curse pronounced upon the ground in 3:17. However, various factors argue against this. In the Hebrew text different verbs are used to denote the act of cursing in these verses; the wording of verse 21 does not resemble 3:17 as closely in the Hebrew original as most English versions suggest. Additionally, in verse 21 the adverb עוֹד (*ʿôd*, "again") is positioned after the infinitive verb לְקַלֵּל (*lĕqallēl*, "to curse") and not after לֹא־אֹסִף (*lōʾ-ʾōsip*, "I will not add"). In the parallel expression "I will never again strike down every living thing as I have done" the adverb עוֹד (*ʿôd*, "again") is positioned immediately after the verb לֹא־אֹסִף (*lōʾ-ʾōsip*, "I will not add"). Commenting on the placement of עוֹד (*ʿôd*, "again") in v. 21, Cassuto writes, "The curse on the ground ... remained valid, except that the Lord promised not to add thereto, that is, not to aggravate further man's position on earth. I will not curse any more—more than it is already cursed. In the second instance, the meaning is that the Lord would not bring universal retribution upon humanity as He did in the days of Noah: I will never again destroy, that is, I shall not destroy a second time."[266] Noting the distinctive order of the words, Wenham helpfully comments, "God is not lifting the curse on the ground pronounced in 3:17 for man's disobedience but promising not to add to it. The flood was

---

[265] Skinner, *Genesis*, 157.

[266] Cassuto, *From Noah to Abraham*, 120.

a punishment over and above that decreed in 3:17. ... Furthermore, it is quite apparent that the curses pronounced in Gen 3—weeds, toil, pain, death, enmity with serpents—are part of man's present experience, so that 8:21 cannot be stating that they are lifted after the flood."[267]

Although God promises never to destroy humanity with another flood, he recognizes that "the inclination of the human heart is evil from youth onward" (v. 21). His words recall what is said in 6:5: "that every inclination of the human mind was nothing but evil all the time." While the language of verse 21 may be more muted, there is no indication that humanity's nature has change for the better in the postdiluvian era. Without God's willingness to tolerate humanity's constant tendency toward perversity, there can be no hope.

Acknowledging that human beings bear responsibility for the flood due to their violence/wickedness, God recognizes that they have an inherent propensity to be evil. This does not mean that everything they do is evil. Rather, the bias in human nature is toward evil. No one needs to be taught to do wrong; it comes naturally. This predisposition toward being evil does not disappear after the flood. God, however, will exercise restraint in punishing the misdeeds of humanity. This does not mean that God will never punish people. Even in the book of Genesis divine justice is exercised by way of punishment (e.g., the destruction of the cities of the plain in ch. 19). Elsewhere in the Old Testament, there is ample testimony that the people of Israel are punished severely by God for their sins.[268] Retaining the right to punish evildoers, God promises not to wipe out the whole of humanity.[269] The references to time periods in verse 22 recall 1:14–18.

9:1–7. In response to Noah's burnt offerings, God blesses Noah and his sons, instructing them to be fruitful and multiply and fill the earth (v. 1); God has already expressed a similar expectation regarding other creatures in 8:17. The wording of verse 1 recalls 1:28 (cf. 5:2), but as a comparison of the two passages reveals, God's remarks in chapter 9 omit any reference to subduing the earth or ruling over other creatures. This

---

[267] Wenham, *Genesis 1–15*, 190.

[268] The book of Lamentations provides a graphic testimony to divine justice being exercised against the inhabitants of Jerusalem.

[269] See Terence E. Fretheim, "Violence and the God of the Old Testament," in *Encountering Violence in the Bible*, ed. Markus Zehnder and Hallvard Hagelia, The Bible in the Modern World 55 (Sheffield: Sheffield Phoenix, 2013), 124–27.

omission is noteworthy, especially when God's speech ends in 9:7 by repeating the instruction to be "fruitful and multiply" and, with a minor change in wording, "spread out over the earth" (cf. 1:20–21; 7:21; 8:17).[270] Whereas God's blessing in 1:28 includes the idea of humanity exercising authority over the earth on God's behalf, this role is not mentioned after the flood. This reflects the reality that by heeding the serpent in the garden of Eden, Adam and Eve betrayed the trust that God had placed in them to be his vicegerents. As the story of Genesis reveals, from chapter 3 onward humanity misuses its God-given ability to manage other creatures, filling the earth/land with violence (6:11, 13). Because "the inclination of the human heart is evil from youth onward" (8:21), people cannot govern the world and its creatures as God's representatives. Tragically, history testifies to the grim reality that humanity has never exercised dominion over the world graciously and justly for the benefit of all creatures.

God's speech in verses 2–6 has an ominous tone, beginning with references to "fear and terror"[271] and ending with remarks about the punishment of those who shed human blood. God's comments are directed at restraining the malevolent actions of people in the postdiluvian world. Making allowance for the evil inclination of humanity, especially involving violence, God permits humans to kill other creatures for food (vv. 2–3). However, to acknowledge that God is the source of all life, humans are prohibited from eating blood. A similar prohibition comes in Leviticus 17:10–14, where the additional observation is made that blood has a special role to play in making atonement on the altar (cf. Lev 3:17; 7:26–27; 19:26; cf. 1 Sam 14:32–34). In the light of the ban on eating blood, Deuteronomy 12 speaks of blood being drained out of meat before it is eaten (vv. 16, 23–25). This ban on eating blood is reaffirmed in Acts 15:20.

There is a long tradition of interpretation in favor of the idea that God's words in verse 3 introduce an important transformation from an original creation in which all land creatures, including humans, were

---

[270] It should be noted that some scholars favor emending the text of v. 7, replacing the final וּרְבוּ־בָהּ (*ûrĕbû-bāh*, "and multiply on it") with וּרְדוּ־בָהּ (*ûrĕdû-bāh*, "and rule over it"). There is, however, no manuscript evidence to suggest that this emendation reflects the most original form of the text.

[271] Citing Deut 1:21; 11:25; 31:8, Wenham, *Genesis 1–15*, 192, notes the "distinctly military terminology" of the expression "fear and terror." Cf. Provan, *Discovering Genesis*, 121, who writes, "The animals (or at least some of them) now look upon their human counterparts not simply as subjects look upon their king (Gen. 1), but as residents of a land look upon a conquering army; that is what this language of 'fear and dread' implies (cf. Deut. 11.25)."

herbivores to a new world order in which humans are now permitted by God to be carnivorous.[272] While there has been much support for this reading of verse 3, there are arguments to the contrary.[273] God's comment in verse 3 specifies that humans may eat כָּל־רֶמֶשׂ (*kol-remeś*, "every crawling thing"). Importantly, in Genesis the term רֶמֶשׂ (*remeś*) does not normally denote all land creatures, a fact reflected in the LXX translation πᾶν ἑρπετόν (*pan herpeton*), which means "every crawling thing/reptile." Further evidence that רֶמֶשׂ (*remeś*) refers to a particular category of animal comes in 1:24–25, where three types of land animal are mentioned: "livestock, creatures that crawl, and the wildlife of the earth." Of these three categories, the latter two are mentioned in 9:2; no reference is made in verse 2 to "livestock" (i.e., domesticated cattle).[274] Possibly domesticated livestock are not mentioned because they already belong in human hands (that is, are under human control). It is also possible that people are already permitted to eat livestock. They may be the "clean" animals mentioned in 7:2. As for the distinction between "wildlife of the earth" and "creatures that crawl," Provan suggests that these categories refer to predatory and non-predatory wild animals respectively.[275] If this distinction holds, and we cannot be entirely certain, it comes close to reflecting the difference between clean and unclean animals in Leviticus 11: clean land animals have "divided hooves and ... chew the cud" (Lev 11:3); unclean animals have claws and are predators. By restricting humanity's diet to non-predatory animals, God may have hoped to reduce the violence/wickedness that defiled the earth prior to the flood.

---

[272] This viewpoint is defended by, among others, Victor P. Hamilton, *The Book of Genesis: Chapters 1–17*, NICOT (Grand Rapids: Eerdmans, 1990), 313–14; Andrew E. Steinmann, *Genesis: An Introduction and Commentary*, TOTC 1 (Downers Grove: InterVarsity Press, 2019), 105. Alter, *Genesis*, 38 writes, "Vegetarian man of the Garden is now allowed a carnivorous diet (this might conceivably be intended as an outlet for his violent impulses), and in consonance with that change, man does not merely rule over the animal kingdom but inspires it with fear." Some scholars suggest that although it was God's original intention for humans to eat plants and fruit, they became carnivores after being expelled from the garden of Eden. In the light of this, God's instructions in 9:3 give permission for what had become the post-fall practice of eating meat.

[273] The discussion that follows draws heavily on Provan, *Discovering Genesis*, 120–24.

[274] Verse 2 has a chiastic structure (ABBA). In the first half, fear and terror are linked to "every living creature on the earth" and "every bird of the sky." In the second half, "every creature that crawls on the ground, and all the fish of the sea" are placed under human authority ("given into your hands," NIV).

[275] Provan, *Discovering Genesis*, 123. Alternatively, some scholars suggest that the distinction is between large and small animals.

The statement in verse 6, "Whoever sheds human blood, by humans his blood will be shed," consists of a tight concentric pattern in the Hebrew text, where the Hebrew words are arranged in the pattern: shed, blood, human, human, blood, shed.[276] This arrangement underlines the principle of talion; the punishment should be no more or no less that the crime deserves.[277] An important distinction is made here between human and animal life. Whereas the blood of animals may be shed without fear of punishment (vv. 3–4), the same is not true for human lives. As the final part of verse 6 affirms, recalling 1:26–28, humans were originally made in the image of God. From the outset of creation people are distinguished from animals, and that distinction remains important, even given humanity's broken relationship with God. People continue to have a value in God's eyes that sets them apart from other creatures. This applies to all classes of people. Later, at Mount Sinai, God ensures that even the lives of slaves are protected; an owner cannot kill his slave and expect to go free (Exod 21:20).

The reference to shedding human blood in verse 6 probably implies murder and not manslaughter. This distinction is noted elsewhere in the Pentateuch (Exod 21:12–14, 20–21; Deut 19:1–13; Num 35:9–34). Given the focus in God's speech on preserving human life, Alter comments, "Perhaps the ban on bloodshed at this point suggests that murder was the endemic vice of the antediluvians."[278] According to Numbers 35, bloodshed defiles the land. Such defilement can only be removed "by the blood of the person who shed it" (Num 35:33). While the issue of people killing other people is addressed in this passage, it should not be overlooked that the prohibition against taking human life applies also to animals (v. 5). In the light of this, according to Exodus 21:28–32, a goring ox that kills a person must be put to death and its meat cannot be eaten. This requirement,

---

[276] Markus Zehnder, "Cause or Value: Problems in the Understanding of Gen 9,6a," *ZAW* 122 (2010): 81–89, contends that the word בָּאָדָם (*bāʾādām*) in the expression "by humans his blood will be shed" conveys the double meaning of "through man" and "for the value of man" (88).

[277] Cf. Exod 21:23. The concept of moral equivalence underlies biblical legislation; the punishment should be equivalent to the harm caused by the crime. Although this is often expressed in terms of "life for life, eye for eye," the application of the principle did not involve death or mutilation. Manslaughter did not necessarily require the death of the guilty party. The punishment is equivalent to the wrong done, but not necessarily identical in terms of physical harm. For a fuller discussion, see Alexander, *Exodus*, 483–89.

[278] Alter, *Genesis*, 38. Gen 4 gives two examples of humans killing other humans.

which underlines the importance of human life, sets the biblical legislation apart from other ANE law codes.[279]

9:8–11. After commissioning Noah and his sons to spread out over the earth/land, God intimates that he will establish his covenant with them and their descendants after them. God refers briefly to this covenant prior to the flood (6:18). The use of the present participle מֵקִים (*mēqîm*, "am establishing") in verse 9 implies that the covenant is being initiated at this specific time. This is confirmed by God's remarks in verse 12 regarding the sign of the covenant, where the use of the present participle נֹתֵן (*nōtēn*, "am giving/making") implies that the covenant is only now being made. There is no reason to assume that because God refers to the covenant as "my covenant" (v. 9) this recalls a previously existing covenant.[280] Rather it emphasizes that God is the author and guarantor of the covenant. Moreover, since the covenant is specifically intended to reassure future generations that there will never be another devastating flood (v. 11), it is difficult to see how a covenant with such a guarantee enshrined within it could have been in place before the first flood occurred. Importantly, the covenant is made with "every creature that is with you" (v. 10), that is, all the creatures that were in the ark. The assurance that God will never again cut off

---

[279] See Moshe Greenberg, "Some Postulates of Biblical Criminal Law," in *Yehezkel Kaufmann Jubilee Volume*, ed. Menahem Haran (Jerusalem: Magnes, 1960), 15–16; Alexander, *Exodus*, 489–91. Because the ox is guilty of bloodshed, after it has been put to death, its meat cannot be eaten; possibly, as with meat derived from predators (see Lev 11:1–47), it is viewed as unclean.

[280] This is suggested by Gentry and Wellum, *Kingdom through Covenant*, 155–61 (drawing on Dumbrell, *Covenant and Creation*, 25–26), who argue that the verb קום (*qwm*) is never used in connection with the launch of a new covenant; they contend that the verb כרת (*krt*) is used to mark the initiation of a covenant. However, this assessment of the use of the two verbs is questionable (see Williamson, *Abraham, Israel and the Nations*, 195–203). Rather, the verb קום (*qwm*) is used for covenants that are "everlasting" (v. 16; cf. 17:7, 13, 19); such covenants are established by God with each new generation. In this regard, the covenant of ch. 9 resembles closely the covenant of ch. 17: both are everlasting covenants (9:16; 17:7, 13, 19); both are accompanied by appropriate signs (9:12–14; 17:11); both use the expressions הֵקִים בְּרִית (*hēqîm bĕrît*) (9:9, 11, 17; 17:7, 19, 21) and נָתַן בְּרִית (*nātan bĕrît*) (9:12; 17:2); both are spoken of by God as "between me and you" (9:12, 15; 17:2, 7) but also include the descendants of Noah and Abraham (9:9, 12; 17:7, 9); both guarantee that the beneficiaries of the covenants will not be "cut off" (9:11; 17:14) (see Alexander, "Genesis 22 and the Covenant of Circumcision," 19–20). The covenant of Gen 15 is merely given as a guarantee to Abraham that his descendants will possess the land of Canaan. This latter covenant is subsumed into the covenant of Gen 17, which focuses on Abraham's spiritual fatherhood of many nations.

כָּל־בָּשָׂר (*kol-bāśār*, "every creature") (v. 11) underlines his concern for the whole of creation and not merely humans.

9:12–17. God's speech is briefly interrupted by the insertion at the start of verse 12, "And God said ..." This marks the start of a new segment in the divine speech, in which the emphasis will be upon the sign of the covenant. God describes the sign as a קֶשֶׁת (*qešet*, "bow"). The noun קֶשֶׁת (*qešet*) may denote a bow used by a hunter (27:3) or soldier (Isa 5:28), but in this context it refers to a rainbow. The triple reference to "clouds" in verses 13–16 confirms that a rainbow is meant. The use of a rainbow as the sign of the covenant is highly fitting since they are only visible when it rains; "rain" played a significant part in causing the flood (7:12).[281] The rainbow is both a reminder of what happened and a reassurance that the same will not occur again.[282] After addressing Noah and his sons (see v. 8), God speaks directly to Noah (v. 17), emphasizing that the covenant is with כָּל־בָּשָׂר (*kol-bāśār*, "every creature"), repeating what has already been said in verses 15 (x2), 16, and 17. This highlights God's ecological concern for the well-being of all creatures.

Bridge

Important developments occur after Noah and his family emerge from the ark. Prior to the flood God had spoken of establishing his covenant with Noah (6:18) and had instructed Noah to take into the ark additional pairs of clean animals (7:2–3). When Noah emerges from the ark, he offers up burnt/ascension offerings. This leads to the divine establishment of an eternal covenant between God and Noah and all creatures. Noah's role throughout the flood story is significant and points to the importance of the patriline that is traced throughout Genesis and beyond. Furthermore, his burnt/ascension offerings after exiting the ark are a reminder of the importance that similar offerings will play in reestablishing a harmonious relationship between God and humanity.

---

281 Other covenant signs (e.g., circumcision; Sabbath) are appropriate to the nature of the covenant being ratified (see Exegesis on 17:11–14).

282 Circumcision and the Sabbath are the signs of the Abrahamic and Sinai covenants respectively (see Gen 17:11; Exod 31:13, 17).

C. The Cursing of Canaan (9:18–29)

[18] Noah's sons who came out of the ark were Shem, Ham, and Japheth.
Ham was the father of Canaan. [19] These three were Noah's sons, and
from them the whole earth was populated.

[20] Noah, as a man of the soil, began by planting a vineyard. [21] He drank
some of the wine, became drunk, and uncovered himself inside his tent.
[22] Ham, the father of Canaan, saw his father naked and told his two
brothers outside. [23] Then Shem and Japheth took a cloak and placed it
over both their shoulders, and walking backward, they covered their
father's nakedness. Their faces were turned away, and they did not see
their father naked.

[24] When Noah awoke from his drinking and learned what his youngest
son had done to him, [25] he said:

> Canaan is cursed.
> He will be the lowest of slaves to his brothers.

[26] He also said:

> Blessed be the Lord, the God of Shem;
> Let Canaan be Shem's slave.
> [27] Let God extend Japheth;
> let Japheth dwell in the tents of Shem;
> let Canaan be Shem's slave.

[28] Now Noah lived 350 years after the flood. [29] So Noah's life lasted 950
years; then he died.

Context

The *tôlĕdôt* section that begins in 6:9 initially concentrates on Noah's role in preserving the lives of his immediate family and pairs of every creature from the flood that covers the land, but it also anticipates future developments involving his sons. While his three sons are named in 6:10 (cf. 5:32), little is said about them throughout the account of the flood in 6:9–9:17. Their exit from the ark in 9:18 set the scene for the events recorded in 9:20–28. The brief remark in 9:19 that "from them the whole earth was populated" anticipates the contents of chapter 10, a distinctive *tôlĕdôt* section that records the descendants of Shem, Ham and Japheth.

Comments

9:18–19. These verses create a bridge between the flood narrative and the next two sections of Genesis. Attention is focused on Noah's three sons, Shem, Ham, and Japheth. Without explanation, the reader is told that Ham is the father of Canaan. This information alerts the reader to expect that Canaan will play a part in the episode about to be told. As 10:6–20 reveals, Ham fathers other sons, and Canaan appears to be his youngest son (cf. 10:6, where Canaan is listed after Cush, Mizraim, and Put). Whereas the reference to Canaan prepares for the events recorded in verses 20–27, the brief comment in verse 19 about the whole earth being populated from Noah's sons anticipates the genealogical information recorded in chapter 10.

9:20–23. The opening words of verse 20 imply that after the flood Noah began to be a אִישׁ הָאֲדָמָה (*ʾîš hāʾădāmâ*, "man of the soil/ground"), an expression that recalls how the first man was formed of dust taken from "the ground" (2:7), how later "the ground" was cursed because of Adam and Eve's actions in the garden of Eden (3:17), and how Lamech, in naming Noah, expressed hope that Noah would bring relief from the hard labor caused by "the ground" YHWH had cursed (5:29). God's intention at creation was that people should live in harmony with "the ground" and enjoy its abundance, but this was clearly not the experience of people prior to the flood. The brief description of Noah as a "man of the soil" possibly holds out hope that in the postdiluvian era things may improve.

Initially, this appears to be happening given Noah's ability to plant a vineyard and enjoy its wine. However, an abundance of wine leads to Noah becoming drunk, which in turn causes him to uncover himself inside his tent (v. 21). With a minimum of detail, the narrator then describes how Ham, seeing his father's nakedness, goes outside to tell his brothers. While verses 21–22 provide an exceptionally brief report of what happened, the narrator mentions yet again that Ham is the father of Canaan (cf. v. 18).[283] The enigmatic nature of verses 21–23 has prompted much debate as to what happened to Noah. We can only speculate, but Noah's subsequent remarks in verses 24–27 appear to attribute full responsibility to Canaan, Ham's son.

---

[283] Recognizing that Canaan is the one cursed by Noah in v. 25, Herbert Edward Ryle, *The Book of Genesis: The Cambridge Bible for Schools and Colleges* (Cambridge: Cambridge University Press, 1914), 127, contends unnecessarily that the earliest form of this story had Canaan as Noah's third son. He speculates that the words "Ham, the father of" were added by a later compiler. A similar solution as to why Canaan is cursed is proposed by John Day, "Noah's Drunkenness, the Curse of Canaan, Ham's Crime, and the Blessing of Shem and Japheth (Genesis 9:18–27)," in Baer and Gordon, *Leshon Limmudim*, 33–35; cf. Vawter, *On Genesis*, 138–40.

Learning of their father's nakedness, Shem and Japheth with great discretion cover their father, taking care to avoid looking at his naked body (v. 23). Some English versions introduce a contrast between the actions of Shem and Japheth and those of Ham by translating the initial conjunction at the start of verse 23 as "But" (NAS, NIV, NJPS). However, had the narrator intended to contrast their actions this could have been signaled more clearly. The use of the *wayyiqtol* verb וַיִּקַּח (*wayyiqqaḥ*, "and he took") at the start of verse 23 does not imply contrasting action but rather the continuation of a sequence of events. There is no reason to assume that Ham's behavior in verse 22 is malevolent, contrary to what many commentators claim. On the contrary, by reporting his father's nakedness to his two brothers, Ham initiates the process of covering Noah's nakedness. Without sufficient warrant in the text, Ham is frequently criticized as responsible for whatever misdemeanor may have occurred within the tent.[284] Yet, as we shall see, the testimony of Noah points to Canaan as the perpetrator, not his father Ham.

Noah's nakedness recalls how Adam and Eve became conscious of their nakedness after eating in defiance of God from the tree of the knowledge of good and evil (3:7). On that occasion, God clothed them, a gracious act on his part, covering their nakedness (3:21). Shem and Japheth take steps to cover Noah's nakedness. Their action corresponds with God's action in clothing Adam and Eve.

9:24–27. After recovering from his drunkenness, Noah realizes what "his youngest son" has done to him (v. 24). The reference to "his youngest son" is noteworthy because Noah proceeds in verse 25 to pronounce a curse on Canaan, Ham's son. Strikingly, on every occasion when the sons of Noah are listed, the pattern is always "Shem, Ham, and Japheth" (5:32; 6:10; 7:13; 9:18; 10:1; 1 Chr 1:4). While the listing of names does not always reflect the chronological order of birth (see 25:9 where Isaac is listed before Ishmael), it is noteworthy that Ham is consistently listed before Japheth. This would imply that Ham is not the youngest of the brothers and, therefore, cannot be the "youngest son" mentioned by

[284] Day, "Noah's Drunkenness," 32–33, helpfully highlights the weaknesses of various proposals regarding the supposed sin of Ham. However, his own suggestion that there was "a serious failure of filial obligation on Ham's part" lacks clear textual support.

Noah in verse 24.[285] More likely is the possibility that the "youngest son" is Noah's grandson, Canaan.[286]

Although Canaan is not named directly by the narrator as the one responsible for Noah's nakedness, several factors point toward him as the guilty party. First, the introduction of Canaan as Ham's son in verses 18 and 22 is unusual. Apart from Shem, Ham, and Japheth, he is the only other descendant of Noah named in this passage. Why, we might ask, is Canaan specifically included? Second, the fact that Canaan alone is the object of Noah's curse in verse 25 and is mentioned twice by Noah in verses 26–27 is significant.[287] Commentators who assume that Ham is the guilty party struggle to justify Noah's cursing of Canaan. It runs counter to Old Testament moral standards for a child to be punished for the actions of a parent (cf. Deut 24:16; Ezek 18:1–32). Moreover, the description of Ham's actions in reporting Noah's nakedness to his two brothers in verse 23 provides inadequate grounds for finding him guilty of any misdemeanor. His actions may be interpreted as being entirely innocent. Third, Canaan comes last in the list of Ham's sons in 10:6 (cf. 1 Chr 1:8). This would possibly qualify him to be called Noah's "youngest son," since the designation "son" is

---

[285] Wenham, *Genesis 1–15*, 201, lists a variety of explanations that have been proposed to justify Ham being the youngest son. He favors Cassuto's suggestion that the order of names is "not chronological but euphonic" due to shorter names being placed first. See Cassuto, *From Noah to Abraham*, 165. However, if Ham was Noah's youngest son, we might have expected the narrator to signal this more clearly, especially given its importance for correctly understanding Noah's indictment in v. 24.

[286] Cassuto, *From Noah to Abraham*, 153–54, also notes that in traditional Jewish literature various sources claim that "Canaan himself was the transgressor, or at least was an accessory to his father's iniquity" (153). See, e.g., Pirke Rabbi Eliezer 23.

[287] Regrettably, some interpreters handle the present text with considerable disregard for what it says. For example, Jason A. Bembry, "Justifying Slavery via Genesis 9:20–27: The Vicious Legacy of Racist Interpretation of the Bible," *Stone-Campbell Journal* 23 (2020): 71, claims that "Ham was the original recipient of his father's curse and that the curse was subsequently transferred to Canaan" to reflect "Israel's enslavement of Canaanites in the days of the Judges." He writes, "Gen 9:25 became a justification of Canaan's enslavement as described in Israel's history. Later, however, this revision would be reversed. The curse of Canaan would be projected back upon Ham and ultimately used to justify a different kind of slavery far from the Israelite homeland" (71). Bembry rightly decries the use of Noah's curse to justify racial inequality against people of African descent, but his approach is deeply flawed for he perpetuates the myth that Ham was the one cursed by Noah, something that the biblical text does not say.

not restricted in Hebrew thought to the first generation of children.[288] Canaan fits this description much better that his father Ham. Fourth, if Ham is the guilty party, why is his punishment restricted to Canaan? Should not all his sons bear equal responsibility, if this is indeed what is happening as regards Canaan? Why does Noah target only Canaan? In the light of these factors, the simplest and most satisfactory explanation for Noah's cursing of Canaan is that Canaan, and he alone, is responsible for whatever took place in the tent when Noah was naked. As the victim of what occurred, Noah's testimony to the identity of the perpetrator is of primary importance.

In response to what has happened, Noah curses and blesses others. For the first time in Genesis, a human pronounces curses and blessing on others. This introduces a motif that recurs throughout Genesis. The members of the patriline become a source of blessing or cursing for others, although this is not always tied to the uttering of blessings or curses. Later, God will promise Abraham, "I will bless those who bless you, I will curse anyone who treats you with contempt, and all the peoples on earth will be blessed through you" (12:3) (see Biblical and Theological Themes §2). Noah's words recall the judgments that God has pronounced on the serpent (3:14) and on Cain (4:11).[289] Noah is not the one who is implementing the curse. He indicates that Canaan's actions have resulted in him being cursed by God.

Noah's short speech establishes a hierarchy of relationships within his family. Canaan, as the guilty party, will be, according to the CSB translation, "the lowest of slaves to his brothers" (v. 25; cf. NET, NIV, NRSV, NJPS). Alternatively, some English versions render the Hebrew phrase עֶבֶד עֲבָדִים (*ʿebed ʿăbādîm*) as "a servant of servants" (ESV, KJV, NAS). This highlights the challenge of interpreting accurately what is meant by the word עֶבֶד (*ʿebed*), a term that appears over 800 times in the Old Testament. As Schultz observes, since the term "can be used to describe relationships that involve no obligations, no social inferiority, and only temporary conditions ... it is best to understand the *ʿebed* as one who is dependent on another and accordingly carries out his will or acts for his

[288] In 31:28, Laban refers to his grandsons as בָּנַי (*bānay*, "my sons"). From a different, but complementary, perspective, 10:21 describes Shem as the "father of all the sons of Eber." The subsequent verses reveal that Shem fathers Arpachshad, who fathers Shelah, who fathers Eber.

[289] For a similar use of the verb אָרוּר (*ʾārûr*), see the list of curses in Deut 27:15–26.

benefit, rather than emphasising other commonalities such as the great difference in status ..., the exclusivity of the relationship ..., or belonging to another."[290] According to Noah's words, the curse on Canaan makes him subordinate to all of "his brothers" (v. 25), not merely Shem and Japheth, although Canaan's relationship to Shem is highlighted twice in verses 26–27. Importantly, there is no justification for using Noah's statement regarding Canaan to support the subjugation of one ethnic group as chattel-slaves by another.[291]

While Noah's curse upon Canaan emphasizes his subordination to his brothers, Noah's blessing of Shem and Japheth commends them for their action in covering his nakedness. At the outset, Noah blesses "the Lord, the God of Shem" (v. 26). This brief remark implies that Shem acted as he did because of his positive relationship with YHWH. Building on this, Noah proceeds to contrast Japheth's relationship to Shem with that of Canaan. Whereas Noah indicates that Canaan must be subordinate to Shem, a fact that is stated twice using the same words, he prays that God will increase Japheth's descendants and enable them to enjoy a harmonious relationship with Shem's descendants. Noah's use of the jussive verb יַפְתְּ (*yapĕt*, "may he extend") at the start of verse 27 is an intentional wordplay on the name יֶפֶת (*yepet*, "Japheth"). This image of Japheth's expansion is reflected in chapter 10, where his descendants become "the peoples of the coasts and islands" (10:5).

Noah's remarks about Shem suggest that he will exercise authority over his brothers for their benefit. In the case of Japheth, this is to offer

---

[290] R. Schultz, "Servant, Slave," *NIDOTTE*, 4:1184. He helpfully writes, "One must not allow the negative associations deriving from the modern practice of slavery, involving oppressive servitude and a demeaning chattel-like status, to color one's understanding either of the ancient institution or the biblical image" (1185).

[291] Although Noah's curse is limited to Canaan, it has wrongly been taken to apply to all the descendants of Ham. See Thomas V. Peterson, *Ham and Japheth: The Mythic World of Whites in the Antebellum South*, ATLA Monograph 12 (Metuchen: Scarecrow, 1978); Stephen R. Haynes, *Noah's Curse: The Biblical Justification of American Slavery* (New York: Oxford University Press, 2002); David M. Goldenberg, *The Curse of Ham: Race and Slavery in Early Judaism, Christianity, and Islam* (Princeton: Princeton University Press, 2003); Sylvester A. Johnson, *The Myth of Ham in Nineteenth-Century American Christianity: Race, Heathens, and the People of God*, Black Religion, Womanist Thought, Social Justice (New York: Palgrave Macmillan, 2004); David M. Whitford, *The Curse of Ham in the Early Modern Era: The Bible and the Justifications for Slavery*, St. Andrew's Studies in Reformation History (Farnham: Ashgate, 2009); David M. Goldenberg, *Black and Slave: The Origins and History of the Curse of Ham*, Studies of the Bible and Its Reception 10 (Berlin: de Gruyter, 2017).

support with an emphasis upon living together in harmony; in the case of Canaan, Shem may be expected to restrain his nephew's evil behavior. As Shem and Japheth acted together to cover Noah's nakedness, Noah's hope for them is that they should dwell in harmony.

9:28–29. The wording of these verses recalls the pattern found in the genealogy of chapter 5, where the total lifespan of each named individual is listed, prior to a reference to their death (e.g., 5:4–5, 7–8, 10–11). Whereas in the genealogy, the number of years "lived ... after" is given in relation to the birth of a first child, with Noah the most important chronological event during his lifetime is the flood. The brief reference to his death in verse 29 brings the account of Noah's life to a conclusion.

Bridge

Noah belongs to the patriline that will ultimately lead to the one who will overcome the serpent. In the light of his special standing with God, he ought to be treated with respect, even when drunk and naked. Canaan fails to do this. In the light of Noah's curse of his grandson Canaan and the description of the Canaanites in 10:15–19, it is noteworthy that there are a series of comments in the Terah *tôlĕdôt* that draw attention to the Canaanites, associating them with evil behavior (see 12:6; 13:7, 10, 13; 14:22–24; 18:20; 19:14, 24–25). The book of Genesis reveals that children often repeat the sins of their parents (e.g., Isaac, like Abraham, passes off his wife as his sister; Jacob, who deceives his father, has sons who deceive him).

Noah's lapse into drunkenness is a serious reminder of the pernicious nature of sin. Even those who are members of the patriline are not exempt from shortcomings due to humanity's corrupted nature. Yet, as McKeown helpfully observes, "The aim of the passage is not to condone or condemn wine but to emphasize that Shem, the ancestor of the Israelites, was blessed while Canaan, the ancestor of the Canaanites, was cursed."[292] While it may be tempting to assume that Noah's curse of Canaan and blessing of Shem impacts future generations, Noah's actual words make no reference to future generations. This incident, however, reveals that weal and woe may be determined by how people treat the key members of the divinely chosen patriline (cf. 12:3).

---

[292] McKeown, *Genesis*, 65.

V. The Offspring of Noah's Sons (10:1–11:9)

A. The Family Lines of Noah's Sons (10:1–32)

1 These are the family records of Noah's sons, Shem, Ham, and Japheth.
They also had sons after the flood.

2 Japheth's sons: Gomer, Magog, Madai, Javan, Tubal, Meshech, and Tiras.
3 Gomer's sons: Ashkenaz, Riphath, and Togarmah. 4 And Javan's sons:
Elishah, Tarshish, Kittim, and Dodanim. 5 From these descendants, the
peoples of the coasts and islands spread out into their lands according
to their clans in their nations, each with its own language.

6 Ham's sons: Cush, Mizraim, Put, and Canaan. 7 Cush's sons: Seba, Havilah,
Sabtah, Raamah, and Sabteca. And Raamah's sons: Sheba and Dedan.

8 Cush fathered Nimrod, who began to be powerful in the land. 9 He was
a powerful hunter in the sight of the Lord. That is why it is said, "Like
Nimrod, a powerful hunter in the sight of the Lord." 10 His kingdom
started with Babylon, Erech, Accad, and Calneh, in the land of Shinar.
11 From that land he went to Assyria and built Nineveh, Rehoboth-ir,
Calah, 12 and Resen, between Nineveh and the great city Calah.

13 Mizraim fathered the people of Lud, Anam, Lehab, Naphtuh, 14 Pathrus,
Casluh (the Philistines came from them), and Caphtor.

15 Canaan fathered Sidon his firstborn and Heth, 16 as well as the Jeb-
usites, the Amorites, the Girgashites, 17 the Hivites, the Arkites, the
Sinites, 18 the Arvadites, the Zemarites, and the Hamathites. Afterward
the Canaanite clans scattered. 19 The Canaanite border went from Sidon
going toward Gerar as far as Gaza, and going toward Sodom, Gomorrah,
Admah, and Zeboiim as far as Lasha.

20 These are Ham's sons by their clans, according to their languages, in
their lands and their nations.

21 And Shem, Japheth's older brother, also had sons. Shem was the father
of all the sons of Eber. 22 Shem's sons were Elam, Asshur, Arpachshad,
Lud, and Aram.

23 Aram's sons: Uz, Hul, Gether, and Mash.

24 Arpachshad fathered Shelah, and Shelah fathered Eber. 25 Eber had
two sons. One was named Peleg, for during his days the earth was di-
vided; his brother was named Joktan. 26 And Joktan fathered Almodad,
Sheleph, Hazarmaveth, Jerah, 27 Hadoram, Uzal, Diklah, 28 Obal, Abimael,
Sheba, 29 Ophir, Havilah, and Jobab. All these were Joktan's sons. 30 Their
settlements extended from Mesha to Sephar, the eastern hill country.

[31] These are Shem's sons by their clans, according to their languages, in their lands and their nations.

[32] These are the clans of Noah's sons, according to their family records, in their nations. The nations on earth spread out from these after the flood.

Context

With the death of Noah, a new *tôlĕdôt* heading marks the start of another section within Genesis. On this occasion, the heading involves all three of Noah's sons: Shem, Ham and Japheth. The contents of chapter 10 are structured around three headings that introduce respectively the sons of Japheth (v. 2), Ham (v. 6), and Shem (vv. 21–22). The sons are listed in reverse order of birth, beginning with Japheth, the youngest. Possibly Japheth is listed first because his descendants figure least in the story that has yet to unfold.[293] By placing Shem's descendants last, a link is formed with the linear genealogy that comes in 11:10–26.

Each section in chapter 10 ends with a colophon that refers to families, languages, lands, and nations (vv. 5, 20, 31).[294] Some variation exists regarding the contents of each section, suggesting that the chapter is not designed to be a comprehensive listing of all Noah's descendants but is intended to create a backdrop for understanding what follows in Genesis. Chapter 10 reminds the reader of how the earth is filled with different families and nations. Against this background the divine promises associated with Abraham speak of blessing for "all the families of the ground"[295] and "all the nations of the earth" (12:3; 22:18). In addition, the expanded comments about Nimrod in verses 8–12 introduce Babel/Babylon,[296] which will be the subject of 11:1–9. This episode helps to set the scene for the call of Abraham in chapter 12.

---

[293] In a similar fashion, the genealogies of Ishmael (25:12–18) and Esau (36:1–37:1) come before those of Isaac (25:19–35:29) and Jacob (37:2–50:26).

[294] Allen P. Ross, "Studies in the Book of Genesis, Part 2: The Table of Nations in Genesis 10—Its Structure," *BSac* 137 (1980): 347–48, observes that the colophon ending the listing of Japheth's sons, has the order "lands, languages, families, nations," whereas with Ham and Shem the order is "families, languages, lands, nations." The prominence given to "land" in connection with Japheth may be due to his descendants spreading out further than others, in fulfilment of Noah's pronouncement in 9:27.

[295] CSB opts for the translation "all the peoples on earth" (cf. NIV) in 12:3, but many English versions reflect more closely the Hebrew text which uses the term "families" (e.g., ESV, KJV, NET, NRSV, NJPS; cf. NJB which has "clans").

[296] On the name of the city, see Comments on 10:10.

Japheth's section is by far the shortest, containing only two expansions that list the sons of Gomer (v. 3) and Javan (v. 4). The sections concerning Ham and Shem are much fuller. In connection with Ham, special attention is given to Cush's son, Nimrod (vv. 8–12) and the sons of Canaan (vv. 15–19). With Shem's descendants, the family of Arpachshad receives special attention (vv. 24–30), anticipating its significance for the linear genealogy that is recorded in 11:10–26.

In all seventy-two names are listed, excluding Shem, Ham and Japheth.[297] Cassuto, who excludes Nimrod and Asshur, suggests that the number seventy is significant: "The family of the children of Noah is depicted as perfect in the number of its sons, and all mankind, which comprises the seventy nations that issued from these sons, is represented as an ideal creation in the number of its part."[298] Since Cassuto is mistaken in arriving at the figure seventy, his proposal that the table of nations is intentionally designed to reflect the perfection of God's creation is questionable.

In assessing the material in chapter 10, it is important to realize that the details given here may not necessarily reflect later circumstances due to the migration of people groups.[299]

Comments

10:1. A new *tôlĕdôt* heading introduces the material that runs from 10:1 to 10:32. Apart from the contents of chapter 10 being largely similar in nature, this section is framed by references to "after the flood" in verses 1 and 32. This *tôlĕdôt* section is unique in Genesis, listing the descendants of three brothers; other *tôlĕdôt* headings, apart from 2:4, name only one person.

10:2–5. The section devoted to Japheth's descendants is the most concise. After naming Japheth's seven sons (v. 2), only the sons of Gomer and Javan are listed in verses 3–4. According to verses 5, from these "the peoples of the coasts and islands spread out." In the light of this statement

---

[297] The number is reduced to seventy if Nimrod is omitted and the term אַשּׁוּר (*ʾaššûr*) in v. 11 denotes a person (Asshur) and not a place (Assyria). Provan, *Discovering Genesis*, 127, inappropriately states that "the total number of names in this list of peoples in Genesis 10 is 70, which appears to be a traditional way of summing up the totality of a people." If Shem, Ham, and Japheth are included the total number of names can be reckoned to be 75.

[298] Cassuto, *From Noah to Abraham*, 176–77.

[299] One of the most authoritative identification of these locations is provided in Anson F. Rainey and R. Steven Notley, *The Sacred Bridge: Carta's Atlas of the Biblical World* (Jerusalem: Carta, 2006).

and from an analysis of the names associated with Japheth's descendants, the impression is given that this side of Noah's family located over time to the north and west of Canaan, stretching possibly from the region surrounding the Black Sea westward along the northern coast of the Mediterranean Sea, including its islands.[300]

10:6–20. The section listing Ham's descendants initially follows the pattern adopted for Japheth (vv. 6–7). After this come three expansions concerning the descendants of Cush (vv. 8–12), Mizraim (vv. 13–14), and Canaan (vv. 15–19). In differing ways, these additional details have a bearing on the story that is told in the rest of Genesis; this accounts for the inclusion of this material. A final summary statement in verse 20, which resembles verse 5, brings this section to a close.

The statement that "Cush fathered Nimrod" (v. 8) probably implies that Nimrod is one of Cush's future descendants; Cush's sons have already been listed in verse 7 and Nimrod is not included. Throughout chapter 10 the verb יָלַד (*yālad*, "to become the father of") is used to introduce descendants that are not necessarily immediate sons but belong to future generations (cf. vv. 8, 13, 15, 21, 24–26). Nimrod's association with city building suggests that these events did not occur soon after the end of the flood.[301] The inclusion of detailed information about Nimrod is striking. He is a "mighty hunter," who establishes a kingdom that involves the cities of "Babylon, Erech, Accad, and Calneh, in the land of Shinar."[302] Like most English versions, the CSB rendering of verse 11 assumes that Nimrod went to Assyria and built further cities (e.g., ESV, NAS, NIV, NET, NRSV). However, a better translation of the Hebrew text is possible: "From that land Asshur went forth and built Nineveh ..." (e.g., KJV, NJB, NJPS). The Hebrew word אַשּׁוּר (*ʾaššûr*) can denote either a personal or place name. The absence of any preposition before אַשּׁוּר (*ʾaššûr*) suggests that the name refers to the one who comes forth from the land, rather than to the destiny of the one who comes forth (cf. Judg 14:14).[303] By focusing

---

[300] For a more details discussion of the names, see Wenham, *Genesis 1-15*, 216–19; Mathews, *Genesis 1-11:26*, 430–43.

[301] In later Jewish tradition, Nimrod is sometimes portrayed as a contemporary of Abraham.

[302] Nimrod's cities are located in southern Mesopotamia. Shinar is the ancient name for Babylonia. It is mentioned again in 14:1, 9.

[303] This latter interpretation is reflected in the earliest Greek translation (LXX) which reads: ἐκ τῆς γῆς ἐκείνης ἐξῆλθεν Ασσουρ (*ek tēs gēs ekeinēs exēlthen Assour*, "From that land came Assur").

on both Nimrod and Asshur as city builders responsible for establishing Babylon and Nineveh respectively, this short passage highlights the two cities most closely associated with God's judgement on the northern and southern kingdoms in the eighth and sixth centuries BC. Both cities are usually viewed as standing in opposition to Jerusalem, the city of God.

Verse 8 highlights how Nimrod began to be a גִּבֹּר (*gibbōr*, "powerful warrior") in the earth/land. Some English versions state that he was "the first on earth" to become such (cf. ESV, NJB, NRSV, NJPS). However, the term גִּבֹּר (*gibbōr*, "powerful warrior") is used in 6:4 of the Nephilim, the famous/infamous men who lived prior to the flood. Nimrod resembles them. This association is one of several reasons for believing that Nimrod is portrayed as the antithesis of what God desires people to be. The image of Nimrod as a גִּבֹּר (*gibbōr*, "powerful warrior") is reinforced in verse 9, where he is described twice as a גִּבֹּר־צַיִד לִפְנֵי יְהוָה (*gibbōr-ṣayid lipnê yhwh*, "powerful hunter before the Lord"). The inclusion of what is clearly a proverbial saying concerning Nimrod underlines the significance of this statement. What does it imply? Are we meant to interpret this remark positively or negatively?

The earliest known interpretations of this passage favor a negative assessment. This is helpfully summarized by Hom:

> Augustine, whose reading of 10:9 proved influential among early Christian writers, preferred understanding לִפְנֵי (*lipnê*) as "against" instead of the usual "before." Pseudo-Philo introduces Nimrod with "he began to be arrogant before the Lord." *Targum Neofiti* and the Fragment Targums understand לִפְנֵי (*lipnê*) as "before," but qualify Nimrod's prowess before the Lord as "in sin." Being that נִמְרֹד (*nimrōd*) could be understood as a Niphal form of מרד, (*mrd*) "to rebel," Philo reads the end of Gen 10:9 as "'a giant before God,' which clearly is opposition to the Deity." Elsewhere, Philo describes Nimrod as one who "began this desertion" by the "sons of earth," in relation to the fact that "his name means 'desertion [αὐτομόλησις (*automolēsis*)].' " Similarly, Talmudic interpretations describe Nimrod as one who "led all the world in rebellion against him [i.e., God]."[304]

[304] Hom, "'… A Mighty Hunter before YHWH': Genesis 10:9 and the Moral-Theological Evaluation of Nimrod," 64. The full quotation from Augustine reads:

This has been misunderstood by some through the ambiguity of the Greek word, and they have translated it, not "against the Lord," but "before the Lord"; for ἐναντίον (*enantion*)

Some ancient writers adopted a more positive assessment of Nimrod (e.g., Ephrem the Syrian, Chrysostom), but they reflect a minority position. The weight of evidence favors a negative appraisal of Nimrod. This view is supported by vocabulary in verses 8–10 that resonates with other passages having negative connotations. As we have already noted, the term גִּבֹּר (*gibbōr*, "powerful warrior") is associated with the Nephilim of 6:4.[305] References to Babel/Babylon,[306] Shinar, and the building of cities link Nimrod to the God-defiant city-builders of 11:1–9.[307] The observation that Nimrod's kingdom begins with Babel/Babylon carries negative connotations, especially for ancient readers who perceived Babel/Babylon as the archetypal human city that stood in opposition to God. As a warrior-king, Nimrod exemplifies the misuse of the abilities that God gave to humans in order that they might graciously rule over the earth as his vicegerents. Nimrod's kingdom is established and maintained by power, in marked contrast to the kingdom that God seeks to create on the earth. And what begins with Nimrod is replicated by Asshur,[308] leading to the creation of further cities, Nineveh being the first of these.[309]

---

means both "before" and "against." In the Psalm (95:6) this word is rendered, "Let us weep before the Lord our Maker." The same word occurs in the book of Job (15:13), where it is written, "Thou hast broken into fury against the Lord." And so this giant is to be recognized as a hunter "against the Lord." And what is meant by the term "hunter" but deceiver, oppressor, and destroyer of the animals of the earth? He and his people therefore, erected this tower against the Lord, and so gave expression to their impious pride; and justly was their wicked intention punished by God, even though it was unsuccessful (Augustine, *The City of God* [*NPNF* 1/2:313]).

For a fuller survey of how Nimrod is portrayed negatively in Jewish and Christian traditions, see K. van der Toorn and P. W. van der Horst, "Nimrod before and after the Bible," HTR 83 (1990): 16–29.

305 Later in Genesis, the noun צַיִד (*ṣayid*, "hunting") is linked to Esau (e.g., 25:27–28; 27:5), contrasting him negatively with Jacob.

306 Some English versions adopt the translation "Babel" for the name of the city, which is called בָּבֶל (*bābel*) in Hebrew (e.g., KJV, ESV, NET, NRSV). However, this same name comes over 200 times in the Hebrew Bible and is normally translated as "Babylon." For this reason, CSB adopts the translation "Babylon" (cf. NIV, NJPS). The same name comes in 11:9, but here CSB is one of very few translations to have "Babylon"; most English versions, including NIV and NJPS, have Babel.

307 See Mathews, *Genesis 1–11:26*, 450. In the light of the link with Babel/Babylon, it is noteworthy that the name Nimrod may be understood as meaning "we will rebel."

308 Asshur's father is not identified, although he is portrayed as being like Nimrod. One of the sons of Shem is also known as Asshur (v. 22).

309 Although the CSB translation of v. 12 implies that Calah is "the great city," it is more likely that the designation "great city" includes all the places named, beginning with Nineveh. In the book of Jonah, Nineveh is designated "the great city" (Jonah 1:2; 3:2–3; 4:11),

In verses 13–14 attention switches to the descendants of Ham's second son Mizraim, whose name elsewhere in the Old Testament denotes Egypt/Egyptians. The names of those descended from Mizraim, are all plural nouns, implying that these are the names of clans/tribes, and not of specific individuals. While some of Mizraim's descendants are associated with north Africa, others are usually linked to Asia Minor and Crete.

In the transition from Mizraim's descendants to those of Canaan, Ham's youngest son, nothing is said about the descendants of Ham's third son, Put. Apart from Sidon and Heth in verse 15, the Hebrew names used in verses 16–18 to denote Canaan's descendants have a distinctive ending,[310] signaling that they were the inhabitants of the location preserved in their name. The Jebusites, for example, are linked to the city of Jebus, later renamed Jerusalem. The brief remark that "afterwards the Canaanite clans scattered" (v. 17) suggests that these clans did not remain restricted to their original locations. This is reflected in their association with various cities, including "Sodom, Gomorrah, Admah, and Zeboiim" (v. 19), all of which are named together in the account of Lot's rescue by Abraham (14:2, 8). As verse 19 indicates, Canaan's descendants are in the region that runs from Sidon in the north to Gaza in the south and eastward to the Jordan River and Dead Sea. The locating of Canaan's descendants within the cities of the western Levant is noteworthy, especially in the light of the Terah *tôlĕdôt* (11:27–25:11), in which God promises to give this territory to Abraham's descendants (e.g., 15:18–21). By providing such a detailed list of Canaan's descendants in verses 15–19, a bridge is possibly created between Noah's remarks concerning Canaan in 9:25–27 and later developments involving Abraham, a descendant of Shem, and the inhabitants of the region designated the "land of Canaan" (12:5, 13:12; 17:8; 23:2, 19). Although the descendants of Ham tend to be located in southwestern Asia and northeastern Africa, there is no reason to assume (a) that they should all be viewed as having dark skin or (b) that people with dark skin are in any way inferior to those with pale skin. Unfortunately, interpreters of 9:20–27 and 10:6–20 have not always handled these texts judiciously but have used them to justify inappropriate racial and social attitudes.[311]

---

but this probably denotes a region which includes the cities of Calah and Rehoboth-ir; see Alexander, "Jonah," 61–63.

[310] The î ending indicates a *nomina gentilicia*; see Joüon, 467.

[311] For a more details discussion of the names associated with Ham, see Wenham, *Genesis 1-15*, 219–27; Mathews, *Genesis 1-11:26*, 443–58.

10:21–31. Although Shem is always named first in the listings of Noah's sons, he and his descendants come last in chapter 10. This cannot be due to the insignificance of Shem, for he will reappear at the head of the linear genealogy that makes up a new *tôlĕdôt* section in 11:10–26. As happens elsewhere, details regarding the patriline traced throughout Genesis are normally placed after those of other descendants.

While most English versions correctly state that Shem is older than Japheth (e.g., CSB, ESV, NET, NAS, NJB, NLT, RSV, NRSV, NJPS), the NIV says that Japheth is Shem's older brother.[312] The adjective הַגָּדוֹל (*haggādôl*), which literally means "the great," is best understood as qualifying the whole of the construct chain אֲחִי יֶפֶת (*ʾăḥî yepet*, "brother of Japheth") and not merely the name Japheth. The whole expression is best translated: "the elder brother of Japheth."

Besides highlighting Shem's relationship to Japheth, verse 21 gives prominence to Shem's relationship as "father" to "all the sons of Eber." The reference to Eber in verse 21 is significant for he is born several generations after Shem, as verse 24 reveals (cf. 11:10–15). Importantly, the name עֵבֶר (*ʿēber*, "Eber") is linked to the designation עִבְרִי (*ʿibrî*, "Hebrew"), used of Abraham in 14:13 and Joseph in 39:17. According to the linear genealogy in 11:10–26, Abraham is a descendant of Eber.

The listing of Shem's sons and their descendants is somewhat selective. Of Shem's five sons, only the descendants of Aram and Arpachshad are mentioned. Little is said about Aram's sons in verse 23, but verses 24–30 follow a particular line of Arpachshad's descendants before focusing on Peleg and Joktan, the sons of Eber.[313] Verse 25 explains why Eber calls his son Peleg, observing that "during his days the earth was divided." The name Peleg is derived from the Hebrew verb נִפְלְגָה (*niplĕgâ*), which means "it was divided." Peleg's name probably alludes to the events described in 11:8–9 when God scatters the inhabitants of Babel/Babylon throughout the earth. Since Peleg is listed again in the linear genealogy of Shem's descendants in 11:10–26, no details are given in chapter 10 about his sons. Attention turns to his brother Joktan, who fathers ten sons (vv. 26–29).[314]

---

312 Cassuto, *From Noah to Abraham*, 218, is probably mistaken in contending that Japheth is the eldest of the brothers.

313 In his genealogy of Jesus, Luke expands upon the lineage of Arpachshad by adding Cainan between Shelah and Arphaxad (i.e., Arpachshad) in Luke 3:35–36.

314 For a more details discussion of the names associated with Ham, see Wenham, *Genesis 1–15*, 227–32; Mathews, *Genesis 1–11:26*, 458–65.

Although there is a broad consensus that the descendants of Joktan, based on their names, should be located in the region of Arabia, no agreement exists as to the precise location of the places mentioned in verse 30.

10:32. A final colophon brings the *tôlĕdôt* of Noah's sons to a conclusion, although it is immediately followed by an episode that is closely tied to all that is described in chapter 10. The twofold repetition of the term גּוֹי (*gôy*, "nation") in verse 32 underlines that one purpose behind this genealogical information is to establish how all the nations of the earth are descended from the one family that survived the flood (cf. vv. 5, 20, 31). Additionally, the concluding words of this section prepare for 11:1–9 by mentioning the spreading out of the nations. The Tower of Babel/Babylon episode has already been anticipated by remarks concerning Nimrod (v. 10) and Peleg (v. 25).

Bridge

The genealogical information in Genesis 10 offers a broad perspective on the growth of human society, categorized by clans or families, languages, territories, and nations. The account is not exhaustive, but rather selective, emphasizing details that are specifically relevant to the unfolding narrative in Genesis. For this reason, special attention is given to Nimrod, the founder of Babel/Babylon (vv. 8–10). While he is not named specifically in 11:1–9, it is difficult to imagine that the narrator of Genesis did not intend the reader to link Nimrod to the events narrated in 11:1–9. His portrayal as a "powerful hunter," who opposes God and establishes a kingdom, suggests that he would be at one with the tower-builders of Babel/Babylon, who want to make a name for themselves. Whereas the city-builders of 11:1–9 initially speak the same language, God prevents them from undertaking a similar project by causing them to speak different languages (11:7–9). This outcome is reflected in various references to languages in 10:5, 20, 31. The picture of clans/families and nations spreading out over the earth sets the scene for the call of Abraham, through whom blessing will come to them (12:3; 18:18; cf. 22:18).

B. The City of Babylon (11:1–9)

> [1] The whole earth had the same language and vocabulary. [2] As people
> migrated from the east, they found a valley in the land of Shinar and
> settled there. [3] They said to each other, "Come, let us make oven-fired
> bricks." (They used brick for stone and asphalt for mortar.) [4] And they

said, "Come, let us build ourselves a city and a tower with its top in the
sky. Let us make a name for ourselves; otherwise, we will be scattered
throughout the earth."

5 Then the LORD came down to look over the city and the tower that the
humans were building. 6 The LORD said, "If they have begun to do this
as one people all having the same language, then nothing they plan to
do will be impossible for them. 7 Come, let's go down there and confuse
their language so that they will not understand one another's speech."
8 So from there the LORD scattered them throughout the earth, and they
stopped building the city. 9 Therefore it is called Babylon, for there the
LORD confused the language of the whole earth, and from there the LORD
scattered them throughout the earth.

Context

This short episode is included within the *tôlĕdôt* section of Genesis that introduces the descendants of Noah's sons, Shem, Ham and Japheth (10:1–11:9). Various details link the listing of these descendants in chapter 10 to the account of the building of the city of Babel/Babylon in 11:1–9. Chronologically, the construction of Babel/Babylon and its tower is probably contemporaneous with the references to the adulthood of Nimrod (10:10)[315] and the birth of Peleg (10:25).[316] The mention of "languages" (10:5, 20, 31) and the general picture of the descendants of Shem, Ham, and Japheth spreading out across the earth correspond with the divine judgment that comes upon the citizens of Babel/Babylon (11:9).

The account of Babel/Babylon's construction sheds light on the mindset of postdiluvian humanity, prior to the scattering of the people to form different nations, each with its own language. While the image of people working together in harmony with the common goal of constructing a city may seem quite innocent, even commendable,[317] their shared ambition reveals their strong antipathy toward God. Noting the dichotomy present in the episode, one writer states:

315 The mention of Shinar and Babel/Babylon in 10:10 creates a geographical link with 11:2 and 11:9 respectively.

316 The name Peleg is linked to the idea of the earth being divided; see Comments on 10:25.

317 Theodore Hiebert, "The Tower of Babel and the Origin of the World's Cultures," *JBL* 126 (2007): 29–58, contends that the story should be interpreted positively, explaining "the origin of the world's cultures" (53). The shortcomings of his interpretation of the story are highlighted by André Lacocque, "Whatever Happened in the Valley of Shinar? A Response to Theodore Hiebert," *JBL* 128 (2009): 29–41.

> What a wealth of human meanings converge in the single image of Babel! It is an ambivalent image, evoking powerful feelings of a wide range. On one side we can see the human longings for community, achievement, civilization, culture, technology, safety, security, permanence and fame. But countering these aspirations we sense the moral judgment against idolatry, pride, self-reliance, the urge of material power and the human illusion of infinite achievement.[318]

As Kidner observes, "The primeval history reaches its fruitless climax as man, conscious of new abilities, prepares to glorify and fortify himself by collective effort. The elements of the story are timelessly characteristic of the spirit of the world."[319] This spirit yearns for the autonomy and power that God alone possesses.

While the desire to build a city reflects an innate yearning that God has placed in humans (see Biblical and Theological Themes §4), those responsible view the city and the tower as a monument to their own ability. They confidently assert that they have the capacity to access heaven through the construction of a great tower. Their aspiration to connect with heaven, where God dwells, recalls how the serpent tempted Eve in the garden of Eden by suggesting that the human couple could be "like God" (3:5). The rebelliousness of the arrogant city builders highlights how the unified human population of the earth/land attempts to challenge the boundaries established by God. Their actions are far from innocent as they grasp after greater autonomy and power. They view God as irrelevant and unnecessary.

Verses 1–9 form a carefully composed episode that abounds in verbal assonance and wordplays.[320] Mathews highlights one aspect of the word play in this passage involving the repetition of the term הָבָה (*hābâ*, "come"):

---

[318] "Babel, Tower of," 67.

[319] Kidner, *Genesis*, 109.

[320] For a helpful brief summary, see Allen P. Ross, "Studies in the Book of Genesis, Part 4: The Dispersion of the Nations in Genesis 11:1–9," *BSac* 138 (1981): 120–22. J. P. Fokkelman, *Narrative Art in Genesis*, 2nd ed. (Eugene: Wipf and Stock, 2004), 11–45, discusses in detail how it is possible to find a concentric pattern underlying the description of all that occurs. Cf. Isaac Kikawada, "The Shape of Genesis 11:1–9," in *Rhetorical Criticism: Essays in Honor of James Muilenburg*, ed. Jared J. Jackson and Martin Kessler (Pittsburgh: Pickwick, 1974), 18–32.

> This expression of community collaboration occurs twice in parallel (vv. 3–4) and is imitated afterward, with sarcasm, by the deliberations of God, "Come, let us go down" (v. 7). The phonetic play among these successive speeches, with their preponderance of the sounds *l*, *b*, and *n*, show their interdependency: *hābâ nilbĕnâ lĕbēnîm* ... *hābâ nibneh lānû* ... *hābâ nērĕdâ wĕnābĕlâ* ("Come, let's make bricks ... Come, let us build ourselves ... "Come, let us go down and confuse").[321]

Such literary features are ironic in a short story that recounts a dramatic transition from people being able to communicate effectively with each other using only one language to people speaking multiple languages that undermine effective communication.

Comments

11:1–2. The opening reference to "the whole earth" having the "same language and vocabulary" sets the scene, highlighting the unity of the postdiluvian human population. As sometimes happens elsewhere in Genesis, the expression כָּל־הָאָרֶץ (*kol-hāʾāreṣ*) may denote here "the whole land," a strong possibility given that the events in this episode are placed a few generations after Noah's family exited the ark and the people inhabit one location. At this stage the descendants of Noah's sons have yet to spread out over the earth, forming nations with their own languages (10:5, 20, 31). Although this episode is placed after chapter 10, the events described within it are concurrent with events recorded in chapter 10; 11:1–9 is something of a flashback in time, explaining how numerous languages came into being despite the human population sharing a common ancestry. Verse 1 emphasizes that the population of the whole earth/land speaks one language. This is what we might expect in the immediate aftermath of the great flood, when only one family survived the deluge.

On the direction of travel in verse 2, English versions adopt contrasting interpretations of the Hebrew term מִקֶּדֶם (*miqqedem*). Some take it to mean "from the east" (e.g., CSB, ESV, KJV, NRSV, NJPS), whereas others favor "eastward" (e.g., NET, NIV, NJB). The use of the same term in 13:11 favors the reading "eastward," for Lot clearly moves in that direction when separating from Abraham. In Genesis movement toward

---

[321] Mathews, *Genesis 1–11:26*, 480.

the east is usually indicative of movement away from God. Regardless of their direction of travel, the people settle in the land of Shinar, a location in southern Mesopotamia, associated with the region of ancient Babylonia (modern Iraq, south of Baghdad). The mention of Shinar recalls what is said in 10:10 concerning the kingdom established by Nimrod. Confirmation of this link will come in 11:9 with the naming of Babel/Babylon, which is the first city listed in 10:10. Unlike the region where the ark came to rest (8:4), the "valley" or plain in Shinar lacks mountains that ascend upward toward the sky. The people will look to create an artificial mountain by building a tower. The brief remark that the people "settled there" underlines that this is to be their permanent residence. They have no intention of moving elsewhere, as their words in verse 4 confirm. Whereas God's intention was for humans to be fruitful and fill the earth (1:28; 9:1; cf. 9:9), Noah's descendants at this stage are content to remain in one place. If they aspire to move, it is upwards toward heaven (v. 4).

11:3–4. Due to the absence of stone in the extensive alluvial plain created by the Tigris and Euphrates rivers, the city builders are forced to develop a technology for creating bricks from which they can fashion the city and especially its tower. The use of "oven-fired bricks" and "asphalt" to build the tower corresponds with what archaeologists have discovered regarding the construction of ziggurats in Lower Mesopotamian. Excavations at Ur by Leonard Woolley reveal that the core of the ziggurat was made of sunbaked bricks, with fired bricks being used to cover the external facades. Interestingly, the outer layer of oven-baked mud bricks was held together by bitumen. While we cannot tell if the tower constructed by the people of Babel/Babylon functioned as a ziggurat, it is nevertheless noteworthy that towers were a common feature in the cities of ancient Babylonia.

The Hebrew syntax of verse 4 emphasizes that the people construct the city and tower so that they may "make a name" for themselves (see NIV). The goal of the building enterprise is to make the people famous. Two observations shed light on this ambition. First, their desire for fame may be linked to what is said in 6:4 regarding the Nephilim, who were "powerful" and "famous men." Nimrod, who is mentioned in connection with Babel/Babylon in 10:8–10, resembles the Nephilim and enjoyed fame. Importantly, the renown of these men is due to their exercise of power as גִּבֹּרִים (*gibbōrîm*, "mighty men"). The author of Genesis views the source of their fame negatively. "Sin is closely related to this urge to make a 'name' for oneself apart from God, but God demands that humans recognize their true nature and their need to be accountable to him."[322] Second, whereas the people of Babel/Babylon want to make a name for themselves by their own efforts, by way of contrast God speaks of making Abraham's name great (12:2). Unlike the city builders, who have no place for God in their planning, Abraham will receive fame through divine action. The people hope that creating a name for themselves will bind them together in a cohesive manner and prevent them from being "scattered throughout the earth" (v. 4). Their fear, however, becomes a reality when God disperses them (vv. 8–9).

In their desire to be famous, the people look to create a city with a great tower that extends upwards so that its top is in the sky/heavens. The Hebrew term שָׁמַיִם (*šāmayim*) may refer to the sky/heavens (e.g., CSB, ESV, NIV) or heaven (e.g., KJV, NAS, NJB) where God dwells. While their ambition may be limited to constructing a massive skyscraper, the godless nature of their enterprise suggests that their desire to have the top of the tower in שָׁמַיִם (*šāmayim*, "heaven/heavens/sky") is not simply about the height of the tower. Their actions challenge the restriction that God had placed upon them by limiting their habitation to the earth.

11:5–7. Although a few translations begin verse 5 with "But the Lord," the Hebrew text does not signal a contrast between the actions of the people and God; a normal *wayyiqtol* verb reports YHWH's descent to see the city and the tower. Despite the city builders' intention to create a tower with its top in the sky/heavens, of necessity God must come down to see what is happening. Their tower remains well short of reaching heaven, God's abode. As Mathews remarks, "Despite the monumental efforts of the Babelites to reach 'to the heavens' (v. 4), the Lord 'came down' from heaven to witness their puny efforts (v. 5)."[323]

YHWH's words reveal his assessment of the situation. His remarks underline the seriousness of the situation. There is no hint of God mocking the people for the failure of their enterprise. On the contrary, he concludes that "nothing they plan to do will be impossible for them," if they continue to have the same language (v. 6). In the light of this

---

[322] W. Osborne, "Babel," in Alexander and Baker *Dictionary of the Old Testament: Pentateuch*, 75.

[323] Mathews, *Genesis 1–11:26*, 468.

possibility, God decides to confuse their language. A further reference to going down in verse 7 underlines the distance that exists between earth and heaven, an obstacle that presents no problem to God, but one that is insurmountable to humans by their own efforts. By confusing their language, God will prevent the people from understanding each other. As Ringgren observes, God's action "is both punishment and a preventive measure; it prevents men from going too far in their pride."[324] God's use of the imperative "Come" followed by a first-person plural verb recalls the words of the city builders in verses 3–4. The use of the first-person plural verb also recalls 1:26, where God says, "Let us make man in our image, according to our likeness." The disruption of humanity's unity distances them further from reflecting God's nature.

11:8–9. What the builders feared—being scattered (v. 4)—becomes a reality, as YHWH "scatter[s] them throughout the earth" (v. 8). This correlates with the genealogical information recorded in chapter 10, which pictures the nations spreading out on the earth (10:32). God's intention at creation was that humans should fill the earth (1:28; cf. 9:1). While the scattering of the people throughout the earth is in line with this, the city builders have shown no desire to rule over the earth on God's behalf. Their dispersal merely prevents them from using all their resources for a common purpose.

Work on constructing the city ceases as the people are unable to communicate effectively with one another. Appropriately, the location is called בָּבֶל (*bābel*) in Hebrew; a phonetic wordplay links this name with the verb בָּלַל (*bālal*, "to confuse").[325] On the translation of the Hebrew name בָּבֶל (*bābel*) as "Babel/Babylon," see Comments on 10:10.[326]

Bridge

This episode is not a polemic against city building, for God's ultimate purpose is the creation on earth of a city where he will dwell with this holy people. However, Babel/Babylon is the antithesis of the city that

---

[324] Helmer Ringgren, "בָּבֶל *bābhel*," *TDOT*, 1:467.

[325] Mathews, *Genesis 1-11:26*, 482n189, perceptively observes:

> Babel would also be a fitting name for our "postmodern" world of pluralism, deconstructionism, and therefore "noncommunication," which declares the autonomy of text and reader and sets meaning afloat in a sea of uncertainty. Revolt against divine and absolute truth has fated lost humanity to wander aimlessly and alone in a silent, chaotic world.

[326] While the author of Genesis draws out a connection between the city's name and God's action, the Akkadian name for Babylon, *bāb-ili*/*bāb-ilāni*, means "gate of the god(s)."

God desires to create on the earth. Its builders have no place for God in their plans, believing that they themselves can overcome the distance that separates them from God's abode. With good reason, Babel/Babylon becomes the archetypal symbol of humans living in opposition to God.

In the aftermath of Babel/Babylon, God calls Abraham to begin a process that will lead to the creation of the city of God. Ultimately, this city will be inhabited by people from every tribe, nation, and language (Rev 7:9; cf. 21:24–27; 22:1–4). To this end, the coming of the Spirit upon the believers on the day of Pentecost results in a partial reversal of the disunity that arises out of the creation of different languages at Babel/Babylon. Comparing 11:1–9 with Acts 2, Spina writes:

> In the LXX version of the story, God decided to confound (Gk *sygcheōmen*) the people's language (Gk *glōssan*) so that they could not understand one another's speech (Gk *phōnēn*). Conversely, in Acts the disciples "began to speak in other tongues" (2:4; Gk *glōssais*). This in turn produced a "sound" (2:6; Gk *phōnēs*) at which the multitude was "bewildered" or "confused" (2:6; Gk *synechythē*). At Babel, God transformed a single language into many, creating confusion; at Jerusalem the Holy Spirit made it possible for many languages to be understood as one, creating unity. At Babel, language was used to promote a human agenda ("Let us make a name for ourselves"); at Jerusalem, the "new" language was used to announce the "mighty works of God" (Acts 2:11).[327]

Despite its brevity, the Genesis account of the building of Babel/Babylon casts a long shadow over the whole of the biblical story. Babel/Babylon, as a symbol of human endeavor stands in opposition to the city of God, not only in the period of the Old Testament but also in the period of the New Testament, as the final chapters of the book of Revelation reveal.[328]

VI. The Offspring of Shem (11:10–26)

> 10 These are the family records of Shem. Shem lived 100 years and
> fathered Arpachshad two years after the flood. 11 After he fathered
> Arpachshad, Shem lived 500 years and fathered other sons and daugh-
> ters. 12 Arpachshad lived 35 years and fathered Shelah. 13 After he

[327] Frank A. Spina, "Babel (Place)," *ABD*, 1:562.

[328] For a fuller discussion, see Alexander, *The City of God*.

> fathered Shelah, Arpachshad lived 403 years and fathered other sons
> and daughters. 14 Shelah lived 30 years and fathered Eber. 15 After he
> fathered Eber, Shelah lived 403 years and fathered other sons and
> daughters. 16 Eber lived 34 years and fathered Peleg. 17 After he fa-
> thered Peleg, Eber lived 430 years and fathered other sons and daugh-
> ters. 18 Peleg lived 30 years and fathered Reu. 19 After he fathered Reu,
> Peleg lived 209 years and fathered other sons and daughters. 20 Reu
> lived 32 years and fathered Serug. 21 After he fathered Serug, Reu
> lived 207 years and fathered other sons and daughters. 22 Serug lived
> 30 years and fathered Nahor. 23 After he fathered Nahor, Serug lived
> 200 years and fathered other sons and daughters. 24 Nahor lived 29
> years and fathered Terah. 25 After he fathered Terah, Nahor lived 119
> years and fathered other sons and daughters. 26 Terah lived 70 years
> and fathered Abram, Nahor, and Haran.

Context

Another *tôlĕdôt* heading marks the start of a new section within Genesis. The genealogy in 11:10–26 follows a distinctive pattern, which resembles but is not identical to the pattern used in 5:3–32. With only one male descendant being named in each generation, the linear genealogy highlights the patriline of Shem to Terah. By naming Terah's three sons, the pattern of the genealogy is broken in verse 26. The mention of Abram prior to Nahor and Haran suggests that the patriline will be continued through Abram. This is what occurs in the narrative section that runs from 11:27–25:11, but there are grounds for believing that Abram may not be the eldest of the three sons (see Comments on 11:26).

Comments

11:10–11. The patriline from Adam to Noah continues through Shem. The brief reference to "after the flood" (cf. 9:28; 10:1, 32) links the genealogy to the narrative that precedes it. The names of all Shem's sons are listed in 10:22, but strikingly Arpachshad is not placed first in the list, suggesting that he is not the firstborn son. Nevertheless, he is the one through whom the patriline is traced. The patriline in Genesis is often traced through someone other than the firstborn son. By placing Shem's patriline immediately after the Babel/Babylon episode an interesting contrast is created based on Shem's name, which means "name." As Satterthwaite observes, "After the account of the tower of Babel (11:1–9), whose builders attempt 'to make a name' for themselves (v. 4), the genealogy of Shem (= 'name') in vv. 10–26, part of the continuing line of promise, suggests an ironic commentary: Humans in their pride may oppose God, but only God can give their lives significance."[329]

11:12–25. While the genealogy gives the appearance of moving from father to son, later tradition, as reflected in Luke 3:35–36, implies that in one instance at least the genealogy moves from father to grandson. According to Luke 3:35–36, Arphaxad (Arpachshad) had a son, called Cainan, who was the father of Shelah. There are good grounds to be cautious about reconstructing a precise chronology of the early chapters of Genesis based on the linear genealogies in chapters 5 and 11.[330]

11:26. The pattern of the genealogy is broken at this point through the naming of Terah's three sons: Abram, Nahor, and Haran (cf. 5:32). This brings the *tôlĕdôt* section that starts in 11:10 to a conclusion. A new *tôlĕdôt* heading in 11:27 signals the start of the next section within Genesis. While it would be natural to suppose that Abram was born when Terah was seventy years old, the mention of Nahor and Haran creates a degree of confusion. It is unlikely that all three sons were born in the same year. Furthermore, the normal pattern of the genealogy in verses 10–25 is broken; there is no mention of how many years Terah lived after he fathered a named son. We must wait until 11:32 to learn that Terah lived a total of 205 years. No mention is made of Terah having other sons and daughters, yet according to Abraham in 20:12, Terah was the father of Sarah, having taken another wife.

With all three sons being named in verse 26, we should be open to the possibility that the arrangement of their names does not necessarily indicate their birth order. It is possible that Abram was not born in Terah's seventieth year, and that Haran is the eldest of Terah's sons (see Comments on 11:27–30), This has important consequences in the light of Stephen's claim in Acts 7:4 that Abram left the location called Haran[331] after Terah's death. According to Genesis 12:4, Abram was 75 years old when he separated from his family in Haran. If Abraham was born when

---

[329] Satterthwaite, "Genealogy in the Old Testament," 661.

[330] See Green, "Primeval Chronology," 285–303; Steinmann, "Gaps in the Genealogies," 141–58.

[331] The name of the town should not be confused with the name of Abraham's brother; the spelling of the two words in Hebrew is not the same, despite both names appearing identical in most English versions. In Hebrew the spelling of the name of Abram's brother, Haran הָרָן (*hārān*), is distinguished from the name of the location Haran חָרָן (*ḥārān*). In most English versions this distinction is not apparent. Perhaps for this reason, NIV adopts the spelling "Harran" for the location (cf. LXX), but Haran for the person.

Terah was 70, and left Haran when he was 75 years old, Terah would have been only 145 years old at the time of Abram's departure. Based on 11:32, he would have lived another 60 years after Abram when to Canaan. The Samaritan Pentateuch, an early translation of Genesis to Deuteronomy, records that Terah died when he was 145 years old, not 205. This would harmonize with Stephen's claim, if Abram was born when Terah was 70 years old. Alternatively, it is possibly that only Haran was born when Terah was 70, with Abram being born many years later, perhaps when Terah was 130 years old.[332] Abram is possibly listed first in verse 26 due to his prominence in the subsequent narrative, not because he is the firstborn.

Bridge

The genealogy in 11:10–26 resembles the linear genealogy in 5:1–32, both listing ten generations. Passing swiftly over many generations, the Genesis narrative jumps from Shem, Noah's son, to Terah. After this, a major narrative section is devoted to Terah's offspring, focusing especially on his son Abram/Abraham (11:27–25:11). Belonging to the patriline that descends from Adam and Eve, Abram/Abraham becomes a source of blessing for the nations of the earth. God's initial promises to Abram are subsequently confirmed through two covenants, the second of which centers on Abraham being the spiritual father of many nations. The divine promises given to Abraham subsequently pass to Abraham's son Isaac, his grandson Jacob and his great-grandson Joseph.

VII. The Offspring of Terah (11:27–25:11)

A. A Brief Introduction to Terah's Family (11:27–32)

> [27] These are the family records of Terah. Terah fathered Abram, Nahor, and Haran, and Haran fathered Lot. [28] Haran died in his native land, in Ur of the Chaldeans, during his father Terah's lifetime. [29] Abram and Nahor took wives: Abram's wife was named Sarai, and Nahor's wife was named Milcah. She was the daughter of Haran, the father of both Milcah and Iscah. [30] Sarai was unable to conceive; she did not have a child. [31] Terah took his son Abram, his grandson Lot (Haran's son), and his daughter-in-law Sarai, his son Abram's wife, and they set out together from Ur of the Chaldeans to go to the land of Canaan. But when they came to Haran, they settled there. [32] Terah lived 205 years and died in Haran.

---

[332] Steinmann, "Gaps in the Genealogies," 158, offers a similar analysis.

Context

The linear genealogy in 11:10–26 traces the patriline from Shem to Terah. Normally only one son is named as the lineage moves from one generation to the next. This pattern is broken with Terah in verse 26, when three sons are mentioned: "Abram, Nahor, and Haran." After this a new *tôlĕdôt* heading is introduced in verse 27, signaling the start of a new section in the book of Genesis. As is usual with the *tôlĕdôt* headings, the content of the subsequent material focuses on the offspring of the person named in the heading, in this instance Terah. What begins in 11:27 continues as a narrative until 25:11. Most of the content of the Terah *tôlĕdôt* centers on Abram, later renamed Abraham (17:5). Importantly, verses 27–32 set the scene for all that is to follow by briefly providing essential background information that enables the reader to understand the subsequent narrative. Attention is given to the location of Terah's family, the relationship of Lot to Abram, the identity of the wives of Abram and Nahor and the barrenness of Sarai, later renamed Sarah (17:15).[333]

Comments

11:27–30. A *tôlĕdôt* heading marks the start of a new section in Genesis. By focusing on Terah's offspring, in particular Abram, 11:27–25:11 forms the longest narrative section in Genesis. The account of God's interaction with Abram is exceptionally important, emphasizing how Abram will play a vital role in God's plan to redeem humanity from the terrible consequences of Adam and Eve's betrayal in the garden of Eden. In the light of the part played by Abram, it is noteworthy that, according to Sarna, his name probably means "he is exalted with respect to father," that is, he belongs to a distinguished lineage.[334] Alternatively, the name Abram could mean "exalted father" or "father is exalted."

Anticipating later developments in the narrative, we are told of Haran's death, "in his native land, in Ur of the Chaldeans." The expression "Ur of the Chaldeans" has prompted discussion regarding the location of

---

[333] See Nahum M. Sarna, "The Anticipatory Use of Information as a Literary Feature of the Genesis Narratives," in *The Creation of Sacred Literature: Composition and Redaction of the Biblical Text*, ed. Richard Elliot Friedman (Berkeley: University of California, 1981), 78–79, for fuller comments on how the carefully selected material in vv. 27–32 anticipates later developments in Genesis.

[334] Nahum M. Sarna, "Abraham," in *Encyclopaedia Judaica* (1972), 112.

Ur.[335] Excavations by Leonard Woolley from 1922 to 1934 at Tell el-Muqayyar in southern Babylonia revealed the existence of a substantial city known as Ur that existed toward the end of the third millennium and into the second millennium BC. Alternatively, there is evidence from the nineteenth century BC of a location called Ura'u, situated near Haran in northern Mesopotamia. Neither location is identified in ancient texts with reference to "Chaldeans," the name associated with the Kaldu people who settled in southern Babylonia about 900 BC and exercised influence there until about 500 BC. The association of Ur with the Chaldeans is probably anachronistic as regard the historical situation in the time of Abram; the two names may have been linked at a later stage to clarify the location of Ur for people living long after the time of Abram.[336]

The death of Haran leaves Lot fatherless. Consequently, he is at liberty to relocate with Abram to Canaan. Lot appears to have no brothers, but two sisters, Milcah and Iscah (v. 29). Although he is listed after Abram and Nahor in verses 26–27, Haran was possibly the eldest of the brothers. This would help explain why his brother Nahor marries Haran's daughter Milcah (v. 29). The practice of marrying a close relative, endogamy, recurs at other places in Genesis (20:12; 24:4; 28:2; 29:13–30), although this practice was later restricted under the Sinai covenant (cf. Lev 18:9; 20:17; Deut 27:22).

The narrator introduces Sarai, later renamed Sarah (17:15), and Milcah, the wives of Abram and Nahor. Sarai possibly means "princess"; Milcah may mean "queen." Both names could be related to Mesopotamian deities,[337] but the author of Genesis makes no mention of this. Sarai's barrenness is highlighted, anticipating God's promise to Abram that he will become a great nation (12:2). Sarai's inability to have children introduces a major tension into the Genesis narrative that will not be resolved until chapter 21. How will the unique line of offspring be continued through Abram? How will Abram father a great nation?

11:31–32. Terah relocates his family from southern Mesopotamia to Haran in northern Mesopotamia. Haran is mentioned in the late third

---

[335] See A. R. Millard, "Where Was Abraham's Ur? The Case for the Babylonian City," *Biblical Archaeology Review* 27 (2001): 52–53, 57.

[336] Something similar occurs in Gen 14, where older place names are updated for the benefit of the reader (e.g., Bela is Zoar; En-mishpat is Kadesh) and the name Dan is used anachronistically in place of Laish (see Exegesis on 14:14).

[337] See Steinmann, *Genesis*, 143.

millennium BC Ebla tablets, and the modern town of Harran in Turkey has archaeological remains that date back to the twentieth century BC. While Terah's ambition was to relocate his family to Canaan, they settle in Haran, where Terah dies.[338] According to Joshua 24:2, Terah worshiped other gods. This may be a factor in God's summons to Abram to leave his father's house.

Bridge

This short section provides information that is essential for understanding the ongoing story in Genesis. The reference to Sarai's barrenness creates a barrier to the fulfilment of God's promises to Abram concerning numerous descendants. The death of Lot's father explains why Lot journeys with Abram and why Abram is especially concerned for the well-being of his nephew. The reference to Terah's family settling in Haran and the naming of Nahor sets the scene for later events involving the acquisition of wives for Isaac and Jacob.

B. God Summons Abram (12:1–9)

1 The Lord said to Abram:
Go out from your land,
your relatives,
and your father's house
to the land that I will show you.
2 I will make you into a great nation,
I will bless you,
I will make your name great, and you will be a blessing.
3 I will bless those who bless you,
I will curse anyone who treats you with contempt,
and all the peoples on earth
will be blessed through you.

4 So Abram went, as the Lord had told him, and Lot went with him.
Abram was seventy-five years old when he left Haran. 5 He took his
wife Sarai, his nephew Lot, all the possessions they had accumulat-
ed, and the people they had acquired in Haran, and they set out for
the land of Canaan. When they came to the land of Canaan, 6 Abram
passed through the land to the site of Shechem, at the oak of Moreh.
(At that time the Canaanites were in the land.) 7 The Lord appeared
to Abram and said, "To your offspring I will give this land." So he
built an altar there to the Lord who had appeared to him. 8 From
there he moved on to the hill country east of Bethel and pitched his

338 On the age of Terah at death, see Comments on 11:26.

> tent, with Bethel on the west and Ai on the east. He built an altar to the LORD there, and he called on the name of the Lord. [9] Then Abram journeyed by stages to the Negev.

Context

After providing a brief introduction to Terah's family in 11:27–32, the narrator records a short speech that YHWH makes to Abram. In large measure this speech sets the agenda for almost everything that is recorded in the Abraham narrative and beyond. The significance of God's words to Abram cannot be overestimated. As McKeown observes:

> The programmatic passage in Genesis 12:1–3, in which the root *brk* occurs five times, is all the more salient and noteworthy because of the dark canvas of the primeval narratives against which the new divine-human relationship is portrayed (Gen 1–11). The blessing of Abraham is strategically positioned between the primeval narrative and the patriarchal narratives so that it marks a turning point in the book of Genesis, a turning point from an agenda dominated by cursing to one that is dominated by blessing. It represents a new phase in God's relationship with his world, since through Abraham all nations will be blessed.[339]

With its emphasis upon Abram's name being made great and nations being blessed, YHWH's invitation to Abram is presented as a response to the events recorded in 11:1–9. Like Noah, his ancestor, Abram offers hope to a world that is estranged from God. All depends, however, on his willingness to obey God's call, abandoning the security of family and homeland, for an unknown future in another country. According to Acts 7:2–4, God first summoned Abram while Terah's family was resident in Ur of the Chaldeans. We cannot know from the text of Genesis whether the divine speech recorded in 12:1–3 is the original invitation or a subsequent repetition of what God said.[340] After his father's death in Haran, Abram fulfils God's instructions to leave his family and homeland.

---

[339] James McKeown, "Blessings and Curses," in Alexander and Baker, *Dictionary of the Old Testament: Pentateuch*, 85.

[340] A few English translations render the opening words of 12:1 as "The Lord had said to Abram" (NIV, NLT, cf. KJV), placing this speech at some point prior to the death of Terah in Haran.

Comments

12:1–3. It is widely recognized that God's speech to Abram (or Abraham as he is will be known after his name is changed in 17:3) is exceptionally significant within the book of Genesis, marking the beginning of a new phase in God's redemptive activity.[341] His instructions and promises to Abram highlight the motifs that will shape the Terah *tôlĕdôt* (11:27–25:11) and set the agenda for all that follows in Genesis and beyond.[342] The command-promise structure of the speech suggests that the fulfilment of the promises is conditional upon Abram's response. God will in due course confirm these promises through two distinct covenants in chapters 15 and 17, the second of which is linked to an oath that God swears in 22:16–18. The call of Abram needs to be understood in the light of the rest of the Abram narrative; the ongoing story gives clarity to what at first may appear ambiguous. God's words to Abram emphasize the cost of obedience, for he must sacrifice the security associated with country, clan and father's household.[343]

While the overall sense of YHWH's words to Abram is clear, the speech presents several interpretive challenges. The syntax of verses 1–3 is complex due to the use of imperative and cohortative verbs linked together in a chain through the repeated use of the conjunction "and."[344] The second half of verse 2 can be translated, "I will make your name great; and be a blessing" (cf. JPS: "and be thou a blessing").[345] This highlights the presence of a second imperative verb in the speech, the first coming at the very

---

[341] E.g., James Muilenburg, "Abraham and the Nations: Blessing and World History," *Int* 19 (1965): 393; Hans Walter Wolff, "Kerygma of the Yahwist," *Int* 20 (1966): 137; Ronald E. Clements, *Abraham and David: Genesis XV and Its Meaning for Israelite Tradition*, Studies in Biblical Theology, Second Series 5 (London: SCM, 1967), 15; John Goldingay, "The Patriarchs in Scripture and Tradition," in Millard and Wiseman, *Essays on the Patriarchal Narratives*, 3; Claus Westermann, *The Promises to the Fathers: Studies on the Patriarchal Narratives*, trans. David E. Green (Philadelphia: Fortress, 1980), 156; Elmer A. Martens, *Plot and Purpose in the Old Testament* (Leicester: Inter-Varsity Press, 1981), 26, 32; Claus Westermann, *Genesis 12-36: A Commentary*, trans. John J. Scullion (Minneapolis: Augsburg, 1985), 146.

[342] E.g., John Bright, *Covenant and Promise: The Prophetic Understanding of the Future in Pre-Exilic Israel* (London: SCM, 1977), 24; Wenham, *Genesis 1-15*, 283; Charles H. H. Scobie, "Israel and the Nations: An Essay in Biblical Theology," *TynBul* 43 (1992): 285–86.

[343] Dan Rickett, "Rethinking the Place and Purpose of Genesis 13," *JSOT* 36 (2011): 35n10.

[344] Most English versions omit to replicate in translation all of the occurrences of the Hebrew conjunction "and."

[345] Cf., e.g., S. R. Driver, *The Book of Genesis* (London: Methuen & Co., 1905), 144; Laurence A. Turner, *Announcements of Plot in Genesis*, JSOTSup 96 (Sheffield: JSOT Press, 1990), 53–55.

start ("go out"). However, most English versions interpret the expression וֶהְיֵה בְּרָכָה (*wehyē běrākâ*) as a promise ("and you will be a blessing").[346]

The interpretation of וֶהְיֵה בְּרָכָה (*wehyē běrākâ*) is very much dependent upon whether (a) the imperative comes at the end of a series of phrases and is dependent upon the preceding cohortative וַאֲגַדְּלָה (*waʾăgaddělâ*, "I will make great") or (b) the phrase starts a new grammatical section within the speech, paralleling the initial imperative "go." Adopting the former view, Gesenius and Kautzsch state that frequently an imperative that is dependent on a jussive (cohortative) expresses "a consequence which is to be expected with certainty, and often a consequence which is intended, or in fact an intention."[347] Mathews favors this approach and so translates the final part of verse 2 "so that you will be a blessing."[348]

Alternatively, the sequence imperative + cohortative is often used to express the purpose or result of a command.[349] On the basis of their "volitional form," Waltke and O'Connor take the cohortative verbs in verse 2 to signify "purpose or result" because they come after an initial imperative. They translate 12:1–2: "Leave your country ... and I will make you a great nation and bless you and magnify your name."[350] Adopting this approach, it is possible that the imperative וֶהְיֵה בְּרָכָה (*wehyē běrākâ*) followed by the cohortative וַאֲבָרֲכָה (*waʾăbārăkâ*) marks the start of the second half of the divine speech, having the sense "and be a blessing so that I may bless ..." Since the second half of the speech is dominated by the motif of blessing, it seems more natural to view the second imperative וֶהְיֵה (*wehyē*, "be") as an instruction that introduces this part of God's address to Abram.[351]

---

[346] E.g., CSB, ESV, KJV, NIV, NASB, NLT, NRSV, RSV. William Yarchin, "Imperative and Promise in Genesis 12:1–3," *Studia Biblica and Theologica* 10 (1980): 164–78, favors reading the imperative in v. 2 as a promise.

[347] *GKC* §110i.

[348] Kenneth A. Mathews, *Genesis 11:27–50:26*, NAC 1B (Nashville: Broadman & Holman, 2005), 107n51; cf. McKeown, *Genesis*, 77.

[349] In such contexts the cohortative normally expresses purpose or result (cf. *GKC §108d*; Driver, *Treatise*, 64; Lambdin, *Introduction to Biblical Hebrew*, 119; Joüon *§116b*). To highlight this syntactic arrangement, the imperatives "go" and "be a blessing" are followed by "so that."

[350] *IBHS*, §34.6a.

[351] Cf. Hamilton, *Genesis: Chapters 1–17*, 369; Everett Fox, *The Five Books of Moses: Genesis, Exodus, Leviticus, Numbers, Deuteronomy; a New Translation with Introductions, Commentary, and Notes*, vol. 1, The Schocken Bible (New York: Schocken, 1995), 55; Goldingay, *Old Testament Theology: Israel's Gospel*, 213; J. Richard Middleton, "The Blessing of Abraham and the *Missio Dei*: Reframing the Purpose of Israel's Election in Genesis 12:1–3," in *Orthodoxy and*

Whether וֶהְיֵה בְּרָכָה (*wehyē bĕrākâ*) is taken to be a command or an intention/promise, the whole speech offers two significant but distinct outcomes. The first part of the speech highlights the idea that Abram will become a "great nation"; the second half emphasizes Abram's special role in restoring the broken relationship between God and humanity by mediating God's blessing to the "families of the earth." This implies an international dimension to what Abram will achieve, moving beyond the expectation that he will become a great nation. Against the background of Genesis 1–11, it is very fitting that the climax of God's call of Abram is the possibility of blessing for "all the peoples on earth."[352] Yet this is not a guarantee of divine blessing for everyone; as the first half of verse 3 makes clear, those who disdain Abram will exclude themselves from experiencing God's favor.

Scholars have debated extensively the precise meaning of the *niphal* verb וְנִבְרְכוּ (*wĕnibrĕkû*) in verse 3, rendered "will be blessed" in CSB (cf. ESV, NIV, NRSV).[353] The issue is complicated by the fact that the *niphal* form of the verb ברך (*brk*) is used in 12:3 and 18:18 with reference to Abram and in 28:14 with reference to Jacob, but the *hithpael* of ברך (*brk*) is used in 22:18 and 26:4 in conjunction with "your offspring." Some scholars argue that these similar expressions support a "reflexive" ("they will bless

---

Orthopraxis: Essays in Tribute to Paul Livermore, ed. Douglas R. Cullum and J. Richard Middleton (Eugene: Pickwick, 2020), 58–59.

[352] Commenting on the second half of v. 3, Wenham, *Genesis 1-15*, 278, remarks, "This clause brings the passage to a triumphant and universal conclusion." Cf. Mathews, *Genesis 11:27-50:26*, 108, who views the final promise as "the ultimate goal of the previously stated intentions toward Abram." Similarly, Dumbrell, *Covenant and Creation*, 65 observes that the final clause of v. 3 "is most probably to be taken as a result clause indicating what will be the consummation of the promises that the preceding verses have announced." Cf. Robert E. Longacre, "Weqatal Forms in Biblical Hebrew Prose: A Discourse-Modular Approach," in *Biblical Hebrew and Discourse Linguistics*, ed. Robert D. Bergen (Winona Lake: Eisenbrauns, 1994), 54.

[353] There are three possible readings of the *niphal* verb נִבְרְכוּ in v. 3: (a) a passive ("they will be blessed"); (b) a middle ("they will find blessing"); or (c) a reflexive ("they will bless themselves"). The passive sense is adopted in the earliest versions (LXX, Targum Onkelos, Vg; cf. Acts 3:25; Gal 3:8; see Oswald Thompson Allis, "The Blessing of Abraham," *Princeton Theological Review* 25 (1927): 263–98; Hamilton, *Genesis: Chapters 1-17*, 374–76). A strong case for the passive (or medio-passive) reading of the *niphal* is made by Benjamin J. Noonan, "Abraham, Blessing, and the Nations: A Reexamination of the Niphal and Hitpael of ברך in the Patriarchal Narratives," *HS* 51 (2010): 73–93. Cf. Yarchin, "Imperative and Promise in Genesis 12:1–3," 164–78; Williamson, *Abraham, Israel and the Nations*, 220–34; Williamson, *Sealed with an Oath*, 80–81; Chee-Chiew Lee, "Once Again: The Niphal and the Hithpael of ברך in the Abrahamic Blessing for the Nations," *JSOT* 36 (2012): 279–96.

themselves") understanding of both the *niphal* and *hithpael* forms,[354] but Williamson helpfully proposes that the *niphal* implies a less direct communication of blessing.[355] Abram and Jacob have a role to play in bringing God's blessing to others, but ultimately this blessing will come most fully through a future offspring (see Biblical and Theological Themes §1).

The interpretive ambiguities associated with וְנִבְרְכוּ (*wĕnibrĕkû*) in v. 3 are lessened somewhat by taking into consideration what is said in verse 3a and what is narrated subsequently in Genesis. Verse 3a makes clear that the source of blessing is YHWH, not Abram; God is the one who blesses. Nevertheless, Abram plays a part in the process of blessing, for those who honor Abram will be divinely favored.[356] What this entails is not disclosed at this stage. However, as the narrative continues, it becomes clearer that Abram will bring blessing to others by becoming the father of many nations (see Comments on Gen 17:4–6).

God makes remarkable promises to Abram, but their fulfilment is not immediately obvious. To become a great nation, Abram must relinquish the security of his own family and relocate elsewhere. However, the prospect of Abram becoming a great nation seems remote; his wife is childless (Gen 11:30). It requires considerable faith on the part of Abram to believe God's promises and respond appropriately. Abram's confidence in God is an important motif in the Terah *tôlĕdôt* (cf. Gen 15:6), a theme recognized by New Testament writers.[357]

The promise of nationhood is closely tied to the promise that God will make Abram's name great. This promise probably focuses on kingship, and not simply on Abram becoming famous. A similar promise is given to King David (2 Sam 7:9). Within the Abraham narrative itself, Abram

---

[354] Cf. RSV, NET, NJPS. This alternative reading lessens the part that Abraham will play in mediating God's blessing to others; it implies merely that others will want to be blessed like Abraham.

[355] Williamson, *Sealed with an Oath*, 81.

[356] This is not a promise of universal blessing, for the one who treats Abraham with contempt will be divinely cursed. A subtle distinction is drawn between the many who will be blessed and the one who will be cursed. God's desire is to bless, not curse. Alter, *Genesis*, 51, unfortunately fails to see this distinction and proposes that the text should be emended to give a plural reading, as found in the early versions. This is not required. The emphasis on blessing and not cursing is underscored by the fivefold repetition of the verb "to bless" in vv. 2–3. On the importance of the promise of blessing, see Victor P. Hamilton, "Genesis: Theology of," *NIDOTTE*, 4:667.

[357] See Rom 4:1–25; Gal 3:1–9; James 2:21–24; Heb 11:8–19.

is portrayed as having a status like that of local kings (cf. Gen 23:6).[358] Developing this, Hahn contents that the concept of "great name" may also point to international suzerainty.[359]

12:4–6. Verse 4 emphasizes that Abram obeyed YHWH without hesitation. The author of Hebrews views Abram's obedience as evidence of his faith (Heb 11:8); Abram is confident that what God promises will become a reality. Lot's father, Haran, had died in Ur (Gen 11:28), before the rest of the family moved to Haran. Like Abram, Lot had migrated to Haran. Unlike the rest of Abram's family, Lot decides to accompany his uncle to Canaan. Abram's household was extensive; at a later stage he had 318 "trained men, born in his household" (Gen 14:14). Lot may well have had similar quantities of possessions and herdsmen. The brief reference to all the possessions which Abram and Lot had acquired in Haran anticipates the conflict that will arise between their herdsmen (Gen 13:1–18). The repeated references to Canaan and Canaanites in verses 5–6 not only underline that the land is already inhabited but also recall Genesis 9:25–27, which enigmatically speaks of Canaan being subservient to his brothers.

12:7–9. By appearing to Abram at Shechem, God confirms that this is the land promised in verse 1. Abram relocates to east of Bethel, where he builds another altar. In Genesis, altars are often linked to temporary divine appearances (cf. Exod 20:24), possibly anticipating the creation of a more permanent sanctuary. Their existence confirms God's gift of the land to Abram and his descendants. Bethel will figure prominently in the story of Jacob's flight to Haran (Gen 28:10–22; cf. 35:1–8). On the brief remark about Abram calling "on the name of the Lord," see Comments on 4:26. Abram's trek then takes him further southward to the region of the Beersheba valley.[360]

Bridge

Genesis 12:1–3 is one of the great mission statements of the Old Testament, underscoring God's desire to bless, rather than curse, humanity.[361] As Wright observes,

---

[358] Alexander, "The Regal Dimension of the תלדות־יעקב,"200.

[359] Scott W. Hahn, *Kinship by Covenant: A Canonical Approach to the Fulfillment of God's Saving Promises*, AYBRL (New Haven: Yale University Press, 2009), 106–7.

[360] The Hebrew name Negev means "south" (cf. Gen 13:14).

[361] Patrick D. Miller Jr., "Syntax and Theology in Genesis xii 3a," *VT* 34 (1984): 475, observes, "The call of Abraham helps to make clear that the God of biblical faith ... is

> God's declared commitment is to bring blessing to the nations through Abraham: "All the families of the earth will be blessed through you" (12:3). Repeated six times in Genesis alone, this affirmation is the foundation of biblical mission, for it declares the mission of God. The creator God's mission is nothing less than to bless the nations of humanity. So fundamental is this divine agenda that Paul defines the Genesis declaration as "the gospel in advance" (Gal. 3:8). And the concluding vision of the whole Bible signifies the fulfillment of the Abrahamic promise, as people from every nation, tribe, language, and people are gathered among the redeemed in the new creation (Rev 7:9). Thus both the gospel and mission begin in Genesis, and both are located in the redemptive intention of the creator to bless the nations. Mission is God's address to the problem of fractured humanity and is universal in its ultimate goal and scope.[362]

Summarizing the promises in Genesis 12:1–3, many scholars speak of a "tripartite formula of land, descendants and blessing,"[363] but the promises are not formulated using these three categories. The primary emphases are upon nationhood and the blessing of the nations, and these expectations are subsequently confirmed by two covenants in chapters 15 and 17. Taken together, the two covenants focus on Abram becoming the father of a nation and of many nations, with the first covenant in chapter 15 being incorporated into the second and more extensive covenant of chapter 17 (see Biblical and Theological Themes §3). While some

---

clearly bent toward blessing and mercy toward the human creature. ... When Yahweh sent Abram out, it was to bring about blessing, not curse. That is the good report which the Bible transmits to each generation."

[362] Christopher J. H. Wright, "Reading the Old Testament Missionally," in *Reading the Bible Missionally*, ed. Michael W. Goheen, The Gospel and Our Culture (Grand Rapids: Eerdmans, 2016), 113; cf. Christopher J. H. Wright, *The Mission of God: Unlocking the Bible's Grand Narrative* (Nottingham: Inter-Varsity Press, 2006), 199–221. M. Daniel Carroll R, "Blessing the Nations: Toward a Biblical Theology of Mission from Genesis," *BBR* 10 (2000): 24, writes, "Gen 12:1–3 discloses that the mission of Abram and his descendants is to be a blessing. This blessing both for themselves and the world is to come from God's hand. The blessing to others will be realized directly through the people of God, but their lives can serve also as a paragon of a relationship with Yahweh." Carroll associates the blessing with Abraham's descendants, but the rest of Genesis reveals that the blessing will come through only one of his offspring.

[363] E.g., David J. A. Clines, *The Theme of the Pentateuch*, JSOTSup 10 (Sheffield: JSOT Press, 1978), applies this threefold structure to the whole of the Pentateuch.

scholars suggest that the Abrahamic covenant begins with the divine speech in 12:1–3, there is no covenant ratification ritual at this stage.[364]

God's promise to bless the nations is linked to a unique line of Abram's descendants. Consequently, in Genesis the promises of 12:1–3 are associated with Isaac and Jacob. Tellingly, Fishbane observes, "Abram is promised land, seed, and blessing in 12:1–3 and this is echoed for Isaac in 26:3f. and Jacob in 28:13f. What is of added interest is that these elements are also repeated for each father after the successful completion of his tasks at the end of each patriarchal unit (22:17f., 26:24, 35:12)."[365]

The blessing associated with the patriarchs is later linked to the Davidic dynasty, ultimately finding its fulfilment in Jesus Christ. The apostle Peter explicitly affirms that God's promise to Abraham to bless all the families of the earth is fulfilled through Jesus Christ (Acts 3:25–26). Similarly, the apostle Paul considers God's promise of blessing for the nations as "the gospel" proclaimed "ahead of time to Abraham" (Gal 3:8). Furthermore, Paul affirms that this blessing comes through Jesus Christ, who is the offspring of Abraham alluded to in Genesis.[366]

Adopting the lifestyle of a seminomadic herdsman, Abraham moves from location to location. Throughout his lifetime in Canaan, he resides in a tent. In the light of this, the author of Hebrews concludes that Abraham looked forward in faith "to the city that has foundations, whose architect and builder is God" (Heb 11:10). The divine promise of nationhood may well have encouraged Abraham to have this expectation. The author of Genesis undoubtedly contrasts the call of Abraham with the God-defiant activity of the city-builders of Babel/Babylon (Gen 11:1–9).

---

[364] In Heb 6:13–18 the author points to the fact that God's promise to Abraham (possibly Gen 12:1–3) was confirmed by an oath (a reference to Gen 22:16–18). The promise and the oath are viewed as "two unchangeable things." The oath in Gen 22 may well be linked to the covenant of Gen 17; cf. Alexander, "Genesis 22 and the Covenant of Circumcision," 17–22.

[365] Michael A. Fishbane, "Composition and Structure in the Jacob Cycle (Gen 25:19–35:22)," *JJS* 26 (1975): 36. John E. Anderson, "Jacob, Laban, and a Divine Trickster? The Covenantal Framework of God's Deception in the Theology of the Jacob Cycle," *PRSt* 36 (2009): 8–9, comments, "Scholars have not failed to recognize this important point of passing on the promise to Abraham, noting the pervasiveness of the promise theme in Gen 12–36 and identifying it as perhaps the central motif and organizing principle of the ancestral narratives." Cf. P. V. Premsagar, "Theology of Promise in the Patriarchal Narratives," *Indian Journal of Theology* 23 (1974): 112; Turner, *Announcements of Plot in Genesis*, 115–16; Claus Westermann, *Blessing: In the Bible and the Life of the Church* (Philadelphia: Fortress, 1978), 54; Goldingay, "Patriarchs in Scripture and Tradition," 22.

[366] Cf. Collins, "Galatians 3:16," 75–86; DeRouchie and Meyer, "Christ or Family," 36–48; Deenick, *Righteous by Promise*, 44–48.

C. Abram in Egypt (12:10–20)

> 10 There was a famine in the land, so Abram went down to Egypt to stay
> there for a while because the famine in the land was severe. 11 When
> he was about to enter Egypt, he said to his wife Sarai, "Look, I know
> what a beautiful woman you are. 12 When the Egyptians see you, they
> will say, 'This is his wife.' They will kill me but let you live. 13 Please
> say you're my sister so it will go well for me because of you, and my
> life will be spared on your account." 14 When Abram entered Egypt,
> the Egyptians saw that the woman was very beautiful. 15 Pharaoh's
> officials saw her and praised her to Pharaoh, so the woman was taken
> to Pharaoh's household. 16 He treated Abram well because of her, and
> Abram acquired flocks and herds, male and female donkeys, male and
> female slaves, and camels.
>
> 17 But the Lord struck Pharaoh and his household with severe plagues
> because of Abram's wife Sarai. 18 So Pharaoh sent for Abram and said,
> "What have you done to me? Why didn't you tell me she was your wife?
> 19 Why did you say, 'She's my sister,' so that I took her as my wife? Now,
> here is your wife. Take her and go!" 20 Then Pharaoh gave his men
> orders about him, and they sent him away with his wife and all he had.

Context

The threat of famine prompts Abram to seek refuge in Egypt, where the Nile River may have lessened the impact of drought. Abram's actions take him out of the promised land and lead to a situation that threatens the fulfilment of the divine promise of nationhood. The narrator does not explicitly state that Abram acts contrary to God's will, but his deceitful behavior in Egypt implies a lack of faith in God's ability to protect him and Sarai. Years later, when Isaac is tempted to go to Egypt in another period of famine, God restrains him from going there (Gen 26:1–6).

Comments

12:10–13. When a severe famine causes Abram to relocate from southern Palestine to Egypt, Abram fears that someone will kill him to have Sarai, his wife, due to her exceptional beauty.[367] The deliberate repetition of the phrase "in the land" in verse 10 possibly draws attention to the fact that

[367] The topic of Sarah's beauty has engendered discussion for at this stage she is at least 65 years old. Given that she is recorded as being 127 years old when she dies, we should not automatically assume that her appearance resembled a modern woman aged 65. See Hwagu Kang, *Reading the Wife/Sister Narratives in Genesis: A Textlinguistic and Type-Scene Analysis* (Eugene: Pickwick, 2018), 74–75.

Abram is leaving the land promised to him by God (cf. v. 7). Not only is Abram leaving the promised land, but his actions endanger his own life. To protect himself, Abram asks Sarai to pretend that she is his sister.[368] He will repeat this ruse later in Gerar (Gen 20:1–18). As Westermann rightly observes, "[Abraham] does not think of an intervention of God; he does not appear here as a man of faith. Faced with the threat of death, he surrenders what he ought not surrender."[369]

12:14–16. Abram's ruse backfires and Pharaoh takes Sarai to become part of his household. The narrator's record of what happened is exceptionally brief, but the manner of it possibly implies that Abram was unable to prevent the Egyptians from taking Sarai. Pharaoh will later be held responsible and punished for taking Sarai (v. 17). While Pharaoh is generous to Abram,[370] the loss of his wife is a barrier to the fulfilment of the divine promises. Among the items bestowed on Abram, possibly as a betrothal gift, are camels. Some scholars have claimed that camels were not domesticated in the period of the patriarchs and references to them in Genesis are anachronistic, but such claims are no longer justified.[371]

---

[368] This is a half-truth, for Abraham claims in Gen 20:12 that Sarah is indeed his sister, "the daughter of my father though not the daughter of my mother." E. A. Speiser, "The Wife-Sister Motif in the Patriarchal Narratives," in *Oriental and Biblical Studies: Collected Writings of E. A. Speiser*, ed. J. J. Finkelstein and Moshe Greenberg (Philadelphia: University of Pennsylvania Press, 1967), 62–88, draws on ANE material to find a deeper significance in the wife-sister status of Sarah. His proposal has been rightly rejected by others (e.g., Samuel Greengus, "Sisterhood Adoption at Nuzi and the "Wife-Sister" in Genesis," *Hebrew Union College Annual* 46 [1975]: 5–31; Daniel H. Gordis, "Lies, Wives and Sisters: The Wife-Sister Motif Revisited," *Judaism* 34 [1985]: 344–59).

[369] Westermann, *Genesis 12-36*, 164.

[370] The *waw*-consecutive sequence of verbs is broken in v. 16 by the introduction of a parenthetical clause, which names Abraham before the verb. This creates a contrast between what has happened to Sarah and to Abraham. Ironically Sarah's misfortune results in Abraham benefiting materially, an outcome that echoes through the repetition of the verb יטב (*yṭb*) Abraham's request to Sarah in v. 13: "so that it may go well for me because of you." There is no need to assume that all of Abraham's future wealth comes from Pharaoh (cf. 12:5; Cassuto, *From Noah to Abraham*, 354–55).

[371] Contrary to the impression given by the CSB translation (compare KJV, ESV, NRSV, NJPS), the list ends with female donkeys and then camels, possibly indicating that they were the fewest in number. Quoting William Foxwell Albright, *Archaeology and the Religion of Israel* (Baltimore: Johns Hopkins Press, 1942), 96, Martin Heide, "The Domestication of the Camel: Biological, Archaeological and Inscriptional Evidence from Mesopotamia, Egypt, Israel and Arabia, and Literary Evidence from the Hebrew Bible," *Ugarit Forschungen* 42 (2010): 368, writes, "Albright's dictum that 'any mention of camels in the period of Abraham is a blatant anachronism' (Albright, 1942, 96) is questionable. The archaeological and inscriptional

12:17–20. God's timely intervention rescues Sarai from the predicament created by Abram's flawed ruse. Ironically, Abram, who was to be a source of blessing for the nations, is partially responsible for the affliction that comes upon Pharaoh and his household.[372] The narrator does not reveal what happened between Sarai and Pharaoh, if anything.[373] The report of God striking Pharaoh with severe plagues is often used to suggest that this episode in Abram's life parallels typologically the later experience of the Israelites in Egypt. However, the similarities between Abram's experience and that of the Israelites are largely superficial and do not provide compelling evidence to support a typological connection. The plural noun נְגָעִים (*nĕgāʿîm*), translated "plagues," is never used in Exodus or elsewhere to denote the supernatural events that took place when Moses and Aaron confronted Pharaoh in Egypt.[374] The singular noun נֶגַע (*negaʿ*) is used in Exodus 11:1, but it is best understood as referring to a "blow" or "strike."[375] Pharaoh's expulsion of Abram and Sarai from Egypt preserves their marriage, keeping alive the possible fulfilment of God's promises to Abram involving descendants.

Bridge

Despite responding positively to God's call to go to a new land, Abram's subsequent actions in Egypt reveal a lack of trust in God. He appears to have forgotten God's promises that he will become a great nation and a source of blessing for the nations (12:1–3). Fear frequently creates doubt regarding God's power to fulfil his promises. While the crisis in Egypt is partially of Abram's making, with the Egyptians bearing

---

evidence allows at least the domesticated Bactrian camel to have existed at Abraham's time." Cf. Kitchen, *On the Reliability of the Old Testament*, 338–39.

[372] As Brueggemann, *Genesis*, 129, observes, "When Abraham acts faithlessly, as he has obviously done, curse is released in the world."

[373] Y. Peleg, "Was the Ancestress of Israel in Danger? Did Pharaoh Touch (נגע) Sarai?," *ZAW* 118 (2006): 197–208, speculates that Pharaoh "touched" Sarah on the basis that God's punishment of Pharaoh is described using the verb נָגַע ("to touch/strike"). However, this is hardly evidence sufficient to prove that Pharaoh slept with Sarah.

[374] See T. Desmond Alexander, "Translation or Tradition: A Brief Survey of Some Translational Issues in the Book of Exodus," *BT* 74 (2023), 179–91.

[375] Many modern English versions follow the KJV in rendering נְגָעִים (*nĕgāʿîm*) as "plagues" in v. 17. However, this is misleading, for in the early seventeenth century, when the KJV was first produced, the English word "plague," based on the Latin *plaga*, had the sense of a "blow" or "strike" (cf., e.g., 2 Sam 7:14; Ps 89:32 [Heb. 33]; Isa 53:8). The manner in which God struck Pharaoh and his household is not explicitly stated; the Hebrew text does not necessarily imply that God struck them with diseases (cf. NET, NIV).

some responsibility, nevertheless God graciously intervenes to save both Abram and Sarai.

D. Abram and Lot Separate (13:1–18)

> 1 Abram went up from Egypt to the Negev—he, his wife, and all he had,
> and Lot with him. 2 Abram was very rich in livestock, silver, and gold.
> 3 He went by stages from the Negev to Bethel, to the place between
> Bethel and Ai where his tent had formerly been, 4 to the site where he
> had built the altar. And Abram called on the name of the Lord there.
>
> 5 Now Lot, who was traveling with Abram, also had flocks, herds, and
> tents. 6 But the land was unable to support them as long as they stayed
> together, for they had so many possessions that they could not stay
> together, 7 and there was quarreling between the herdsmen of Abram's
> livestock and the herdsmen of Lot's livestock. (At that time the Canaan-
> ites and the Perizzites were living in the land.)
>
> 8 So Abram said to Lot, "Please, let's not have quarreling between you
> and me, or between your herdsmen and my herdsmen, since we are
> relatives. 9 Isn't the whole land before you? Separate from me: if you go
> to the left, I will go to the right; if you go to the right, I will go to the left."
>
> 10 Lot looked out and saw that the entire plain of the Jordan as far as
> Zoar was well watered everywhere like the Lord's garden and the land
> of Egypt. (This was before the Lord destroyed Sodom and Gomorrah.) 11
> So Lot chose the entire plain of the Jordan for himself. Then Lot jour-
> neyed eastward, and they separated from each other. 12 Abram lived
> in the land of Canaan, but Lot lived in the cities on the plain and set
> up his tent near Sodom. 13 (Now the men of Sodom were evil, sinning
> immensely against the Lord.)
>
> 14 After Lot had separated from him, the Lord said to Abram, "Look from
> the place where you are. Look north and south, east and west, 15 for I
> will give you and your offspring forever all the land that you see. 16 I
> will make your offspring like the dust of the earth, so that if anyone
> could count the dust of the earth, then your offspring could be counted.
> 17 Get up and walk around the land, through its length and width, for
> I will give it to you."
>
> 18 So Abram moved his tent and went to live near the oaks of Mamre at
> Hebron, where he built an altar to the Lord.

Context

Abram returns to Canaan from Egypt, retracing his steps to the place where he had built an altar near Bethel (cf. 12:8). The subsequent departure of Lot to the Jordan Valley sets the scene for God to confirm that this is the land where Abram's descendants will become a great nation. With Lot's departure Abram has separated fully from his father's household. As Rickett contends, "Abraham and Lot's separation is about Abraham coming into alignment with God's original command in Gen. 12.1."[376] When these conditions are met, God affirms in verses 14–17 that Abraham's numerous descendants will occupy all the territory surrounding him. Possession of the land is the central focus of this chapter. Other themes, such as Abram's generosity or Lot's removal as a potential heir, are of secondary concern. The events of chapter 13 are a first step toward the fulfilment of God's promises in Genesis 12:1–3.

Comments

13:1–4. These verses deliberately recall 12:8–10, naming the same locations, but in reverse order. Verse 1, in particular, brings to a conclusion the events narrated in 12:10–20 and, with its reference to Lot, prepares the way for the next episode. Abram and his household retrace their steps back to where he had previous built an altar to YHWH. The patriarch's return to this particular place confirms that this is the land to which God had called him in 12:1. However, verses 5–7 introduce factors that complicate Abram's claim to this territory.

13:5–7. Lot, who has accompanied Abram all the way to Egypt and back, has his own flocks and herds. The region to the east of Bethel, however, has insufficient pasture and water for all their livestock. Under pressure, the herdsmen of Abram and Lot quarrel. To complicate matters, others inhabit the land: Canaanites and Perizzites (cf. 12:6).

13:8–9. To avoid conflict between their herdsman, Abram proposes that he and Lot should part company. Generously, Abram offers his nephew first choice of the land.

13:10–13. Possibly influenced by the famine that had forced them to go to Egypt, Lot chooses the Jordan Valley. Not only does the entire valley have a water supply like "the land of Egypt," but also the abundance of water recalls "the LORD's garden," a reference to the garden of Eden, which was noted as a plentiful source of water, supplying four major rivers (Gen 2:10–14). But the valley's abundant water cannot disguise the evil of its inhabitants. What Lot fails to see, the narrator discloses to the reader: YHWH will destroy Sodom and Gomorrah (v. 10),[377] an event to be described

[376] Rickett, "Rethinking the Place and Purpose of Genesis 13," 51.

[377] Both cities are associated with Noah's grandson Canaan (Gen 10:15–19), who is cursed to be subservient to his brothers (9:25–27). The location of both cities is uncertain, although

more fully in Genesis 19. And after he reports the parting of the ways, with Lot setting up his tent near to Sodom,[378] the narrator adds the further observation that the men of Sodom were exceptionally wicked (v. 13).[379] As Rickett observes, "Sodom, Gomorrah and its inhabitants are spatially antithetical to Abraham, God and the land of Canaan."[380] Adding to the negative appraisal of Lot's choice, the narrator mentions that he "journeyed eastward" (v. 11), a remark that recalls the eastward journeys of Adam and Eve (Gen 3:23–24) and Cain (Gen 4:16) away from God's presence. As subsequent episodes will reveal, Lot's choice places his life in danger (chs. 14, 19).

13:14–18. With Lot's departure, God speaks reassuringly to Abram, affirming with "greater explicitness" the promise of land: "First, the land is more precisely defined: 'all ... which you see.' Second, it is given to Abram as well as to his descendants. And third, it is given in perpetuity, 'forever.' "[381] In promising the land to Abram, God also emphasizes that he will have numerous descendants. Both land and descendants are necessary for Abram to become a "great nation" as God promised in Genesis 12:2. Here Abram's countless descendants are compared to the dust of the earth; later they will be compared to the stars of the sky (15:5; 22:17) and the sand on the seashore (22:17). Obeying God's instruction to journey throughout the land, Abram settles near Hebron, where he constructs another altar to YHWH (cf. 12:7–8). These sacred sites anticipate God's permanent presence in the land.

Bridge

Through his experience in Egypt, Abram possibly learns to rely more fully on God. This may explain his willingness to give Lot first choice regarding the land. If God is for him, Abram has nothing to fear. Lot's decision to move toward Sodom appears to be motivated by the plain's abundant supply of water, which will ensure suitable pasture for Lot's flocks and herds. However, his selfish choice ignores the potential danger of living near the city of Sodom with its evil population. Lot's choice will have significant implications for his future security, placing him in danger on two separate occasions (see chs. 14 and 19).

---

they may have been situated toward the southern end of the Dead Sea.

[378] When we next hear of Lot, he is living inside the city of Sodom (14:12; cf. 19:3–11).

[379] Sarna, "Anticipatory Use," 80, sees these negative comments about Sodom and Gomorrah as part of a larger literary feature in Genesis that highlights the corruption of the Canaanites.

[380] Rickett, "Rethinking the Place and Purpose of Genesis 13," 41.

[381] Wenham, *Genesis 1-15*, 298.

Despite gifting the Jordan plain to Lot, Abram is reassured by God that he and his descendants will possess all of the land that is visible to him. God will later confirm this promise through a covenant (see 15:1–21).

E. Abram Rescues Lot (14:1–24)

[1] In those days King Amraphel of Shinar, King Arioch of Ellasar, King
Chedorlaomer of Elam, and King Tidal of Goiim [2] waged war against
King Bera of Sodom, King Birsha of Gomorrah, King Shinab of Admah,
and King Shemeber of Zeboiim, as well as the king of Bela (that is, Zoar).
[3] All of these came as allies to the Siddim Valley (that is, the Dead
Sea). [4] They were subject to Chedorlaomer for twelve years, but in the
thirteenth year they rebelled. [5] In the fourteenth year Chedorlaomer
and the kings who were with him came and defeated the Rephaim in
Ashteroth-karnaim, the Zuzim in Ham, the Emim in Shaveh-kiriathaim,
[6] and the Horites in the mountains of Seir, as far as El-paran by the wil-
derness. [7] Then they came back to invade En-mishpat (that is, Kadesh),
and they defeated the whole territory of the Amalekites, as well as the
Amorites who lived in Hazazon-tamar.

[8] Then the king of Sodom, the king of Gomorrah, the king of Admah,
the king of Zeboiim, and the king of Bela (that is, Zoar) went out and
lined up for battle in the Siddim Valley [9] against King Chedorlaomer of
Elam, King Tidal of Goiim, King Amraphel of Shinar, and King Arioch
of Ellasar—four kings against five. [10] Now the Siddim Valley contained
many asphalt pits, and as the kings of Sodom and Gomorrah fled, some
fell into them, but the rest fled to the mountains. [11] The four kings took
all the goods of Sodom and Gomorrah and all their food and went on.
[12] They also took Abram's nephew Lot and his possessions, for he was
living in Sodom, and they went on.

[13] One of the survivors came and told Abram the Hebrew, who lived near
the oaks belonging to Mamre the Amorite, the brother of Eshcol and
the brother of Aner. They were bound by a treaty with Abram. [14] When
Abram heard that his relative had been taken prisoner, he assembled
his 318 trained men, born in his household, and they went in pursuit
as far as Dan. [15] And he and his servants deployed against them by
night, defeated them, and pursued them as far as Hobah to the north
of Damascus. [16] He brought back all the goods and also his relative Lot
and his goods, as well as the women and the other people.

[17] After Abram returned from defeating Chedorlaomer and the kings
who were with him, the king of Sodom went out to meet him in the
Shaveh Valley (that is, the King's Valley). [18] Melchizedek, king of Salem,
brought out bread and wine; he was a priest to God Most High. [19] He
blessed him and said:

Abram is blessed by God Most High, Creator of heaven
and earth,
[20] and blessed be God Most High
who has handed over your enemies to you.

And Abram gave him a tenth of everything.

[21] Then the king of Sodom said to Abram, "Give me the people, but take the possessions for yourself."

[22] But Abram said to the king of Sodom, "I have raised my hand in an
oath to the Lord, God Most High, Creator of heaven and earth, [23] that I
will not take a thread or sandal strap or anything that belongs to you,
so you can never say, 'I made Abram rich.' [24] I will take nothing except
what the servants have eaten. But as for the share of the men who
came with me—Aner, Eshcol, and Mamre—they can take their share."

Context

The narrative of chapter 14 is set within the context of God's promise that Abram will become a great nation, taking control of the land of Canaan. The Jordan Valley, which proved attractive to Lot, was divided politically into small city states, each with its own king. Five of these kings form an alliance in the hope of freeing themselves from a confederation composed of four powerful kings from the region of Mesopotamia. When conflict breaks out, Lot is taken captive, prompting Abram to intervene militarily on behalf of his nephew. Abram's successful rescue of Lot and other captives from Sodom places him on a par with the kings of the region, a fitting status for one who is to become the father of many nations. Abram's subsequent interaction with the kings of Salem and Sodom sheds important light on his reliance on God for the fulfilment of the promises of nationhood and international blessing. Unlike the eastern kings, Abram is not prepared to use force to establish his control over the territory of Canaan.[382]

Comments

14:1–12. Verses 1–11 have the appearance of being an ancient record that has been updated by the author of Genesis so that his readers will

[382] For a brief critique of three different assessments of the dating of the material in ch. 14, see T. Desmond Alexander, *From Paradise to the Promised Land: An Introduction to the Pentateuch*, 4th ed. (Grand Rapids: Baker Academic, 2022), 267-70. This draws heavily on a fuller discussion in J. Gordon McConville, "Abraham and Melchizedek: Horizons in Genesis 14," in *He Swore an Oath: Biblical Themes from Genesis 20–50*, ed. R. S. Hess, P. E. Satterthwaite, and G. J. Wenham (Grand Rapids: Baker, 1994), 93–118.

identify correctly the places named.[383] To this report the narrator appends the story of Abram's rescue of Lot.[384] The names of the kings in this campaign report are in keeping with the geographical regions from which they come,[385] but none is mentioned in the relatively small number of surviving extra-biblical texts from the Early and Middle Bronze periods (c. 3500–1500 BC). The initial successful military campaign of the eastern kings takes them by the King's Highway in Transjordan toward the Gulf of Aqaba before they turn north toward Hazazon-tamar, later named En-Gedi (see 2 Chr 20:2). Perhaps taken by surprise, the kings of the Jordan Valley abandon their cities, leaving their citizens unprotected and vulnerable. Seizing the opportunity, the eastern kings abduct some of the people, including Lot, as plunder to become slaves.

14:13–16. Lot's abduction is reported to Abram, who is designated a "Hebrew" (v. 13) to distinguish him from his three allies, who are all Amorites. Elsewhere in the Old Testament, the term "Hebrew" is used, sometimes by foreigners, to designate the ethnic group to which Abram's descendants belong (cf., e.g., Gen 39:14, 17; 41:12; Exod 1:15–17, 19; 2:6, 11; 21:2; Deut 15:12). The designation is possibly derived from Abram's ancestor Eber (Gen 10:21; 11:14–16). The term resembles the verb to "cross over," suggesting that it may have been given to those who "cross over" the land. This would reflect well Abram's semi-nomadic lifestyle. The term is sometimes mistakenly linked to *habiru/hapiru*,[386] a term that comes in the fourteenth-century BC el-Amarna letters, referring to people who were on the margins of settled communities. Despite the successes of the eastern kings against others, Abram courageously acts to rescue Lot. Turner interprets Abram's willingness to rescue Lot as evidence that he considers Lot to be his heir and the one through whom the divine

---

383 Alternative names are provided for Bela (Zoar; see Gen 19:22), Siddim (Salt Sea, the Hebrew designation for the Dead Sea), En-mishpat (Kadesh). Additionally, in v. 14 the use of Dan (for Laish) is anachronistic (cf. Judg 18:29). Dan is the name given to one of Jacob's sons (Gen 30:6).

384 The two reports are joined by making the specific report of Lot's abduction in v. 12 parallel the general report in v. 11.

385 "Shinar" refers to southern Mesopotamia. "Ellasar" may denote northern Mesopotamia; the name "Arioch" occurs in ancient texts from Mari and Nuzi. "Elam" lies to the east of southern Mesopotamia. "Tidal" is possibly a Hittite name.

386 Wenham, *Genesis 1-15*, 313; McKeown, *Genesis*, 86. Waltke and Fredricks, *Genesis*, 231, dismisses the link with *habiru/hapiru*, preferring to see the term "Hebrew" as derived from the name of Abraham's ancestor, Eber.

promises will be fulfilled.[387] However, this assessment does not appear to be supported by Abram's remarks in 15:3, where he does not name Lot as his heir. The kings are routed by a surprise attack and escape northward toward their homelands. Dan is the name which the Israelites later give to Laish (see Judg 18:27–29).

14:17–24. Abram is welcomed back by two kings, who display very different attitudes to what has happened. Melchizedek acknowledges that God is the source of Abram's success; the king of Sodom attributes the victory to the patriarch's own ability. Abram deliberately sides with Melchizedek, rejecting the king of Sodom's "winner takes all" approach. He firmly dismisses the king of Sodom's attempt to forge an alliance with him, for he is aware of the wickedness of the inhabitants of Sodom (cf. Gen 13:13). Abram will not become king of Canaan by overthrowing others by force. He does not exploit his victory, but patiently waits for God to reward him (cf. 15:1).

The Valley of Shaveh lies to the east of Jerusalem; it was later named the King's Valley (2 Sam 18:18). Salem, a shorter form of Jerusalem (Ps 76:2 [Heb. 3]), sounds like the Hebrew word for "peace" (cf. Heb 7:2). Melchizedek appears unexpectedly on the scene, not having been mentioned previously as one of the kings involved in the Jordan Valley confederation. He also stands apart from the other kings by being a "priest" to *El Elyon* "God Most High" (v. 18). Elsewhere in Genesis, other attributes are attached to *El*, the common Semitic term for God (e.g., *El Roi*, "the God who sees" [16:13]; *El Shaddai*, "God Almighty" [17:1]; *El Olam*, "the Everlasting God" [21:33]). All of these designations are used of YHWH. In the context of a polytheistic culture, Abram subsequently equates "God Most High, Creator of heaven and earth" with YHWH, "the LORD" (v. 22). There is only one God, although different names may be used to highlight different aspects of his nature. Melchizedek's designation of God as creator, or possibly "possessor" (ESV),[388] of heaven and earth underlines that God is not merely a family or national deity. He is sovereign overall, as Genesis 1 affirms.

Melchizedek's name, which is typical of the second millennium BC Canaanite names, may be interpreted in various ways. If either Melek or Zedek is understood to refer to a deity, the name could mean "Melek is righteous" or "Zedek is my king" (cf. the name Malkiel in Genesis 46:17,

---

[387] Turner, *Announcements of Plot in Genesis*, 69.

[388] Alter, *Genesis*, 61, opts for the translation "possessor."

which means "El is my king"). Alternatively, as reflected in Hebrew 7:2, the name can mean "king of righteousness." As a priest-king, Melchizedek is associated with the motifs of peace and righteousness. Although very little is said in the Old Testament about Melchizedek, he becomes a figure of note. Building upon what is said in Psalm 110:4, the author of Hebrews designates Jesus Christ as a priest in the "pattern of Melchizedek" (Heb 5:6,10; 6:20; 7:11,17), contending that his priesthood is superior to that of the tribe of Levi, because Abram gives Melchizedek a tithe of the booty (see Heb 5:1–10; 6:20–7:22).

Melchizedek views Abram as blessed and blesses God for granting victory to Abram. The repetition of the motif of blessing recalls God's promises to Abram in Genesis 12:1–3. Acknowledging the veracity of what Melchizedek says, Abram gives him a tithe, or tenth, of the booty.[389] This is noteworthy because Melchizedek has played no part in the rescue of Lot. The gift illustrates how those who bless Abram will be blessed in return (Gen 12:3).

Abram's response to the king of Sodom bears no resemblance to his reaction to Melchizedek. The king of Sodom's apparent generosity masks his true intentions. He wants to put Abram in his debt, but what he offers is not truly his to give. Abram rightly distances himself from the godless words of the king of Sodom. He will not be won over by the offer of riches. His integrity, as one called to be a source of blessing to the nations, prevents him from siding with the king of Sodom. Abram will not become a great nation through reliance on his own military might. He will not act like the other kings, who dominate the first half of this episode.

Bridge

Throughout Genesis, violence toward others reflects a misuse of humanity's divinely given authority to rule over the earth. In this chapter, human kings, with the exception of Melchizedek, use power to control and exploit others. In the light of Lot's abduction, Abram cannot be a passive onlooker. He acts decisively to rescue the helpless captives. But he does not relish the use of military power to achieve God's purposes. Intentionally subduing others by force is a betrayal of how God wishes to establish his kingdom of peace on earth (compare Jesus' rejection of the

---

[389] A tenth appears to be the share that would be given to a king (cf. 1 Sam 8:15, 17).

use of the sword at his arrest; see Matt 26:51–53; Luke 22:49–51). In this context, Abram stands apart, for he will not use force to enrich himself from the misfortune of others, even if in the eyes of others this is the legitimate plunder of the victor in battle.

The unexpected appearance of Melchizedek in this passage provides an interesting example of a priest-king who is superior to Abram. Melchizedek is referenced in Psalm 110, as an example of a priest who is not from the tribe of Levi. Drawing on the oath that God makes in Psalm 110:4, the author of Hebrews argues that Jesus, like Melchizedek, does not belong to a priestly dynasty.[390] The positive picture of Melchizedek in this passage, who comes with "bread and wine" to Abram, contrasts sharply with that of the king of Sodom who comes empty-handed.

F. God's Covenant with Abram (15:1–21)

> [1] After these events, the word of the Lord came to Abram in a vision:
>
> Do not be afraid, Abram. I am your shield; your reward will be very great.
>
> [2] But Abram said, "Lord God, what can you give me, since I am childless
> and the heir of my house is Eliezer of Damascus?"3 Abram continued,
> "Look, you have given me no offspring, so a slave born in my house
> will be my heir."
>
> [4] Now the word of the Lord came to him: "This one will not be your
> heir; instead, one who comes from your own body will be your heir." [5]
> He took him outside and said, "Look at the sky and count the stars, if
> you are able to count them." Then he said to him, "Your offspring will
> be that numerous."
>
> [6] Abram believed the Lord, and he credited it to him as righteousness.
>
> [7] He also said to him, "I am the Lord who brought you from Ur of the Chaldeans to give you this land to possess."
>
> [8] But he said, "Lord God, how can I know that I will possess it?"
>
> [9] He said to him, "Bring me a three-year-old cow, a three-year-old female goat, a three-year-old ram, a turtledove, and a young pigeon."
>
> [10] So he brought all these to him, cut them in half, and laid the pieces
> opposite each other, but he did not cut the birds in half. [11] Birds of prey

---

[390] The NIV translation of Ps 110:4 is misleading for modern readers because it refers to "the order of Melchizedek." The CSB translation "according to the pattern of Melchizedek" is preferable; neither Melchizedek nor Jesus belongs to a priestly order. Their priesthood is unique to each of them. See Alexander, *Face to Face with God*, 92–106.

> came down on the carcasses, but Abram drove them away. [12] As the sun
> was setting, a deep sleep came over Abram, and suddenly great terror
> and darkness descended on him.
>
> [3] Then the Lord said to Abram, "Know this for certain: Your offspring
> will be resident aliens for four hundred years in a land that does not
> belong to them and will be enslaved and oppressed. [14] However, I will
> judge the nation they serve, and afterward they will go out with many
> possessions. [15] But you will go to your fathers in peace and be buried at
> a good old age. [16] In the fourth generation they will return here, for the
> iniquity of the Amorites has not yet reached its full measure."
>
> [17] When the sun had set and it was dark, a smoking fire pot and a flaming
> torch appeared and passed between the divided animals. [18] On that day
> the Lord made a covenant with Abram, saying, "I give this land to your
> offspring, from the brook of Egypt to the great river, the Euphrates
> River: [19] the land of the Kenites, Kenizzites, Kadmonites, [20] Hethites,
> Perizzites, Rephaim, [21] Amorites, Canaanites, Girgashites, and Jebusites."

Context

The opening words of this chapter presuppose an awareness of what has just happened. In the light of Abram's rescue of Lot and his response to the kings of Salem and Sodom, God speaks to Abram again, reassuring him of divine protection and success. Despite God's earlier statements that Abram's descendants will possess the land (12:7; 13:14–17), Abram remains childless. God's reference to a great reward in 15:1 provides an opportunity for Abram to ask concerning his heir. The events that follow conclude with an unconditional promise in the form of a covenant, guaranteeing Abram that his descendants will possess the land of Canaan.

According to Waltke and Fredricks, Genesis 15 displays a clear structure, with verses 7–21 paralleling verses 1–6:

- A The Lord makes a promise to Abraham, using the formula "I am" (15:1).
  - B Abraham apprehensively questions the Lord, addressing him with the rare title "Sovereign Lord" (15:2–3).
    - C The Lord reassures Abraham by symbolic acts: the display of stars with reference to the seed (15:4–6).
- A' The Lord makes a promise to Abraham, using the formula "I am" (15:7).
  - B' Abraham apprehensively questions the Lord, addressing him with the rare title "Sovereign Lord" (15:8).

C' The Lord reassures Abraham by symbolic acts: the burning torch and the smoking kiln through the carcasses with reference to the land (15:9–21).[391]

The first part of the structure focuses on descendants, whereas the second part focuses on land. Both elements are necessary to create a nation (see 12:2).

Comments

15:1. Abram has turned down the spoils presented to him by the king of Sodom. Subsequently, God, the divine king, reassures Abram that his reward will be very great.[392] In a vision, probably at night, God describes himself as a "shield." The Hebrew noun מָגֵן (*māgēn*), which denotes a "shield" used as protective armor (e.g., Judg 5:8; 2 Sam 1:21), is used metaphorically of God as one who protects (e.g., Deut 33:29; 2 Sam 22:3, 31). By using this term, a striking wordplay is created between God's words and those of Melchizedek. As Curtis observes,

> In Gen 14:20 Melchizedek praises God as the one who delivered (*miggen*) Abram from his enemies. In 15:1 Abram is afraid, and Yahweh says to him, "Do not fear; I am a deliverer (*magen*) to you." The repetition of the root *mgn* suggests that it was Yahweh's past activity on Abram's behalf that should provide the basis for present trust in Yahweh—a trust that would eliminate Abram's fear.[393]

Having deliberately dismissed warfare as the means of establishing control over the land of Canaan, Abram relies solely upon God to bring this about. Yet even Abram needs divine reassurance that all will be fulfilled as God promised.

15:2–5. God's affirmation that Abram's reward will be very great (v. 1) presents Abram with an opportunity to ask God regarding the way in which the divine promises will be fulfilled. How can a childless Abram become a great nation or a source of blessing to the nations? At this time Abram

---

[391] Waltke and Fredricks, *Genesis*, 239; cf. Wenham, *Genesis 1–15*, 325.

[392] The KJV and NIV translations of v. 1 imply that God himself is Abraham's reward. An alternative reading is possible and most modern English versions adopt the rendering: "your reward shall/will be very great" (cf. CSB, ESV, RSV, NJPS).

[393] Edward M. Curtis, "Structure, Style and Context as a Key to Interpreting Jacob's Encounter at Peniel," *JETS* 30 (1987): 129n4. The *piel* verb מִגֵּן with the sense "to hand over/deliver" is rarely used in the Old Testament (cf. Hos 11:8).

has no son to succeed him; a servant born in his household will be his heir.[394] Abram identifies this heir as "Dammesek Eliezer" (cf. LXX, NJPS), which most English versions interpret as "Eliezer of Damascus." The details regarding this individual are so scant that we cannot be sure of anything regarding his background and status within Abram's household. He could be the unnamed senior servant of Genesis 24:2, but we cannot be certain. He could have links with the city of Damascus,[395] mentioned in Gen 14:15, but this is speculation based solely on his name. Importantly, while Abram considers him to be his heir, he is not Abram's offspring (זֶרַע, *zeraʿ*). In response, God affirms that Abram's heir will not be "Dammesek Eliezer." Rather Abram himself will father an heir (v. 4). Then, by way of confirming this promise, God tells Abram that his offspring will be like the stars in number (v. 5; cf. Gen 22:17; 26:4; Exod 32:13; Heb 11:12). According to Deuteronomy 1:10, this promise is fulfilled when the Israelites leave Egypt (cf. Deut 10:22; 28:62).

15:6. The narrator does not describe Abram's immediate response to God's affirmations regarding an heir and many descendants. Rather, he breaks the sequence of *wayyiqtol* verbs by introducing an editorial comment about Abram. Since such assessments are rare in Old Testament narratives, their occurrences take on added significance. Writing concisely, the narrator associates Abram's trust in God with righteousness.

Christian and Jewish interpretations of Genesis 15:6 tend to diverge.[396] On the one hand, Christian interpreters in the main have concluded that Abram, due to his trust in God, comes into a right relationship with God. In other words, righteousness is imputed to Abram because of his belief that YHWH will be true to what he has promised. Faith, rather than actions, causes Abram to be viewed as righteous by God. This emphasis on righteousness coming through faith reflects the approach of the apostle Paul in Galatians 3 and Romans 4. On the other hand, Jewish commentators view verse 6 as affirming that, because of his faithfulness

---

394 Although CSB introduces the term "slave" in v. 3, the Hebrew text reads *ben-bêtî* which means "a son of his house/household." Gen 14:14 states that Abraham had 318 men "born in his household." It was not uncommon in the ANE for childless couples to appoint someone from their household as their heir.

395 The term "Damascus" appears in Gen 14:15. Verse 2 involves a word play וּבֶן־מֶשֶׁק בֵּיתִי הוּא דַּמֶּשֶׂק אֱלִיעֶזֶר (*ûben-mešeq bêtî hûʾ dammeśeq ʾĕlîʿezer*) (Gen 15:2). מֶשֶׁק (*mešeq*) is a *hapax legomenon* of uncertain meaning; BDB offers the suggestion "acquisition, possession."

396 See R. W. L. Moberly, "Abraham's Righteousness (Genesis xv 6)," in Emerton, *Studies in the Pentateuch*, 108–9.

to God, Abram is rewarded and in turn his merit brings blessing to Israel through the covenant that God makes with Abram. Reflecting his approach, Speiser translates verse 6: "He put his trust in Yahweh, who accounted it to his merit."[397] This latter interpretation relies heavily upon the assumption that verse 6 parallels closely what is said in Psalm 106:31 regarding Phinehas's righteousness. However, the two passages are sufficiently different to raise doubts about the appropriateness of using one to interpret the other.[398]

Read in its present context, Gen 15:6 clearly implies that YHWH credited צְדָקָה (*ṣĕdāqâ*, "righteousness") to Abram, because Abram trusted YHWH in an ongoing manner.[399] While the narrator does not explicitly state that Abram's righteousness paves the way for the covenant that God makes with him (see 15:18–20), and the covenant itself does not appear to be conditional upon Abram's future obedience, the patriarch's trust in God, leading to obedience, is an important underlying theme within the Abram narrative. "As the rest of the story makes plain, this faith leads to righteous action (e.g., 18:19), but only here in the Old Testament is it counted as righteousness."[400] Abram's faith in God's promises and his faithful obedience contribute to the important role that he plays in the outworking of God's redemptive plan. The apostle Paul draws on this verse, quoting it three times (Rom 4:3, 22; Gal 3:6), to support his argument that Gentile Christians can be considered righteous on the grounds of faith and do not need to be circumcised (Rom 4:1–25; Gal 3:1–9). This

---

[397] Speiser, *Genesis*, 110. Cf. NJPS: "And because he put his trust in the Lord, He reckoned it to his merit." Sarna, *Genesis*, 113, writes, "The idea is that Abram's act of faith made him worthy of God's reward, which is secured through a covenant."

[398] Moberly, "Abraham's Righteousness," 103–30, argues at length that Gen 15:6 should be read in the light of Ps 106:31, but he unfortunately dismisses too quickly (a) the differences between the passages, and (b) the possibility that Ps 106:31 means: "in every generation forever this action of Phinehas is reckoned to be a righteous deed." Importantly, by using the *niphal* (passive) form of the verb חשב (*ḥšb*, "reckon,") Ps 106:31 does not identify the subject of the verb. In Gen 15:6, which uses the *qal* form of חשב (*ḥšb*), God is clearly identified as the subject. See a fuller discussion in Stephen G. Dempster, "'He Believed the Lord': The Pedigree of Justification in the Pentateuch," in *The Doctrine on Which the Church Stands or Falls: Justification in Biblical, Theological, Historical, and Pastoral Perspectives*, ed. Matthew Barrett (Wheaton: Crossway, 2019), 37–62.

[399] The *waw*-consecutive sequence of verbs is broken at the start of v. 6. Wenham, *Genesis 1–15*, 329, observes, "The verbal form והאמן (*waw* + perfect) "he believed" probably indicates repeated or continuing action. Faith was Abram's normal response to the Lord's words." Cf. Mathews, *Genesis 11:27–50:26*, 166–67.

[400] Wenham, *Genesis 1–15*, 330.

verse is also quoted by the apostle James when he argues that faith results in good works (Jas 2:21–24).

15:7. After the narrator's observation in verse 6 regarding Abram's faith, this verse picks up the train of events from verse 5. In addition to reassuring Abram regarding numerous descendants, YHWH now repeats his promise to Abram concerning possession of the land of Canaan (cf. Gen 12:7; 13:14–17). For Abram to become a "great nation" (Gen 12:2), descendants and land are vital components. On "Ur of the Chaldeans," see Comments on 11:28–31.

15:8–12. After being shown the stars in the night sky, Abram possibly hopes for a similar kind of sign regarding possession of the land. His question "How can I know?" does not necessarily mean that Abram doubts God's promise, contradicting the narrator's assessment of Abram's trust in God in verse 6. Rather, he seeks some type of visual sign that the promise will be fulfilled.[401] This may reflect the fact that after being in Canaan for some years Abram remains both childless and landless.

Scholars continue to debate the nature of the ritual described in verses 9–17. All of the animals requested by God are considered suitable for sacrifice under the Levitical priesthood established centuries later, but they are not presented by Abram as offerings to be consumed by fire on an altar. Their use is quite different to that of the animals sacrificed at the sealing of the covenant at Mount Sinai (Exod 24:5). No ANE text has yet been discovered recording a ritual that resembles exactly what is described here. One of the closest parallels comes in Jeremiah 34:18–19, which speaks of people passing between the two halves of a slaughtered calf. The context in Jeremiah 34 suggests that this was a covenant ratification ceremony in which those present undertook a vow. Possibly the participants understood that if they broke this vow they would die like the calf, but it is not clear that the ritual was necessarily viewed as a self-malediction.[402] Drawing on this parallel, some scholars have concluded that Genesis 15 records a ritual in which God passes between the halves of the dead animals to undertake a self-curse.[403] However, this

---

[401] Dean, "Covenant, Conditionality, and Consequence," 297.

[402] On the complexity of interpreting the rituals in Gen 15 and Jer 34, see Åke Viberg, *Symbols of Law: A Contextual Analysis of Legal Symbolic Acts in the Old Testament*, ConBOT 34 (Stockholm: Almqvist & Wiksell, 1992), 52–69.

[403] Gentry and Wellum, *Kingdom through Covenant*, 250–56, favor interpreting the ritual in Gen 15 as a self-maledictory oath, similar to what happens in Jer 34. Cf. Thomas E.

proposal is rejected by others on the basis that such a self-curse is incompatible with God's eternal nature.[404] Drawing out the symbolism of what takes place, Wenham observes that the "smoking firepot" and "flaming torch" (v. 17) represent God, the sacrificial animals, Abram's descendants, and the birds of prey, their enemies.[405] The ritual plays out what will later happen when God comes to reside among Abram's descendants, delivering them from the Egyptians. The ritual symbolizes God's living among the Israelites after their deliverance from slavery in Egypt.

Only God passes between the animals and birds, indicating that he is the one making the covenant, guaranteeing what he has previously promised to Abram. After guarding the slaughtered animals, and as darkness descends, Abram falls into a deep sleep; the same Hebrew term תַּרְדֵּמָה (*tardēmâ*) is used to describe the "deep sleep" that comes upon Adam in 2:21. Elsewhere the term is associated with visions that come at night (Job 4:13; 33:15; cf. Isa 29:10–11). God speaks to him in a vision (cf. 15:1).

15:13–16. God's short speech to Abram provides reassurance that his descendants will possess the land, although not immediately. God has promised Abram that he will become a great nation (Gen 12:2), but he now tells Abram that his descendants will be enslaved in a foreign land before returning to take possession of the land of Canaan. This prediction anticipates Jacob's family migrating to Egypt (Gen 46:26–27). After the death of Joseph, the Israelites are enslaved by several Pharaohs, before being set free in the time of Moses (Exod 1–15). The reference to "four hundred years" is probably a round number[406] and indicates that considerable time will pass before Abram's descendants return to possess the

---

McComiskey, *The Covenants of Promise: A Theology of the Old Testament Covenants* (Grand Rapids: Baker Book House, 1985), 60–61.

[404] Mathews, *Genesis 11:27–50:26*, 171–72. Alternative ANE parallels to the Gen 15 ritual, rejecting the concept of a self-curse in favor of a covenant ratification rite, are offered by Gerhard F. Hasel, "The Meaning of the Animal Rite in Gen. 15," *JSOT* 19 (1981): 61–78; Richard S. Hess, "The Slaughter of the Animals in Genesis 15: Genesis 15:8–21 and Its Ancient Near Eastern Context," in Hess, Satterthwaite, and Wenham, *He Swore an Oath*, 55–65. Many scholars see the covenant ratification ceremony as involving a self-maledictory divine oath. As an argument against a self-curse, it should be noted that the birds are not divided in two.

[405] Gordon J. Wenham, "The Symbolism of the Animal Rite in Genesis 15: A Response to G. F. Hasel *JSOT* 19 (1981) 61–78," *JSOT* 22 (1982): 134–37.

[406] Exod 12:40 records that the Israelites spent 430 years in Egypt (cf. Gal 3:17). Since Joseph remained alive for about 70 years after the rest of his family migrated to Egypt, the maximum period of oppression could not have exceeded 360 years. The reference to

land of Canaan. Abram, however, will live to the age of 175 years (25:7–8), before being buried. The brief statement that Abram will go to his fathers in peace probably reflects a belief in life after death.[407]

God's final comment to Abram confirms that a long period of time ("four generations") will pass before Abram's descendants return to the land of Canaan.[408] Importantly, this homecoming coincides with "the iniquity of the Amorites" reaching "its full measure." The Amorites, descendants of Canaan, the son of Ham (Gen 10:15–16), are one of a number of people groups dwelling in the region (cf. 14:7; 15:19–21). They were found mainly in the hill country where the tribes of Judah, Ephraim and Manasseh first took possession of territory (cf. Num 13:29; Deut 1:7). According to Deuteronomy 18:9–12, all of the nations in Canaan practiced "detestable customs" that included child sacrifice, sorcery, and necromancy. God's comment in verse 16 implies that the return of Abram's descendants will coincide with the punishment of the Amorites. Although God is patient in not punishing immediately the sin of humans, there is a limit to the degree of wrongdoing that he will tolerate.[409]

15:17. The final part of the unique ritual involves a "smoking fire pot and a flaming torch" passing between the pieces. "Smoke" and "fire" are sometimes associated with a theophany (cf. Exod 3:2; 13:21–22; 14:24; 19:18). As Abram passively observes, God passes between the animals and birds that have been killed and laid out on the ground. While this may be an act of self-malediction, the symbolism of what takes place favors Wenham's proposal that this anticipates the Israelite exodus from

---

400 years is best understood as a round number, giving a general sense of the timeline expected by God.

[407] Cf. Philip S. Johnston, *Shades of Sheol: Death and Afterlife in the Old Testament* (Leicester: Apollos, 2002), 33–35; Paul R. Williamson, *Death and the Afterlife: Biblical Perspectives on Ultimate Questions*, NSBT 44 (London: Apollos, 2017), 39–40.

[408] The context would imply that a generation was viewed as spanning about 100 years. Abraham was 100 years old when Isaac was born (Gen 21:5).

[409] According to John H. Walton and J. Harvey Walton, *The Lost World of the Israelite Conquest: Covenant, Retribution, and the Fate of the Canaanites* (Downers Grove: InterVarsity Press, 2017), 256, "Genesis 15:16 does not say that the conquest was delayed so that the Canaanites could build up a balance of enough sin to warrant their destruction; it says that the conquest was delayed so that the violence and turmoil would not occur during the lifetime of either Abraham or his Amorite allies." This interpretation, however, does not explain why the return of Abraham's descendants should be delayed for centuries. Why would God ensure that Abraham and his allies will avoid violence, yet let his descendants be mistreated as slaves in another country?

Egypt when God comes to dwell in the midst of the people.[410] The pledge that God makes does not appear to be conditional upon anything that Abram will do in the future. It is his reward for going to the land that God shows him (cf. Gen 12:1).

15:18–20. After describing what has taken place, the narrator concludes this section by noting that God made or "cut," using the verb כָּרַת (*kārat*), a covenant with Abram.[411] This is the first reference in the Bible to "cutting a covenant," and the terminology seems appropriate in the light of the ritual that has taken place.[412] The idiom "to cut a covenant" is used elsewhere in Genesis only when two human parties enter into a binding agreement with each other (Gen 21:27, 32; 26:28; 31:44). In these instances, both parties are involved in the giving of guarantees, but no rituals are described involving the cutting of animals in half.

The covenant that God makes guarantees descendants and land. This relates back to God's initial promise to Abram that he will become a "great nation" (12:2). Building upon the sign involving stars in verse 5, God declares to Abram the extent of the territory that will be given to his descendants. The land extends from the border with Egypt in the southwest to the River Euphrates in the northeast. In Abram's time this land belongs to various people groups, reflecting the existence of numerous, small city states in the early second millennium BC (cf. Gen 14:2, 8; Josh 12:1–24). Ten ethnic groups are listed here. Similar, but shorter, lists come in Exodus 3:8, 17; 13:5; 23:23; 33:2; 34:11; Deuteronomy 7:1; 20:17; Joshua 3:10; 9:1; 11:3; 12:8; 24:11; Judges 3:5; 1 Kings 9:20; 2 Chronicles 8:7; and Nehemiah 9:8 (cf. Num 13:29; Ezra 9:1). Many of the people groups listed here are descendants of Canaan, according to Genesis 10:15–19 (cf. 1 Chr 1:13–16), recalling the prediction that they would be subservient to the descendants of Shem. The books of Joshua to 2 Samuel recount

---

[410] Wenham, "Symbolism of the Animal Rite," 134–37.

[411] Some scholars maintain that the covenant made by God with Abraham is best understood as resembling an ANE royal land-grant treaty. Moshe Weinfeld, "The Covenant of Grant in the Old Testament and in the Ancient Near East," *JAOS* 90 (1970): 184–203, supports the idea of "land grant," but this is rejected by Gary N. Knoppers, "Ancient Near Eastern Royal Grants and the Davidic Covenant: A Parallel?," *JAOS* 116 (1996): 670–97.

[412] Gen 6:18; 9:9, 11, 17 speaks of God "establishing" (using the *hiphil* form of the verb קום) a covenant. Similar language appears in Gen 17:7, 19, 21. In these contexts, God's covenant is not simply made with one person, as in Gen 15, but with an individual and his offspring after him (cf. Gen 9:9). In line with this, the covenants in Gen 9 and 17 are described as being "permanent" or "everlasting" (Gen 9:12, 16; 17:7, 13, 19).

the slow process by which the Israelites took possession of this territory. According to Sarna, "The fact that the Jebusites invariably appear in the final position may be an intimation of David's capture of Jebusite Jerusalem, which was the culmination of his conquests."[413] According to 1 Kings 4:20, Solomon exercised control over all of the territory, "from the Euphrates River ... as far as the border of Egypt." However, several verses later, 1 Kings 4:25 implies that the land occupied by "Judah and Israel" extended only from Dan to Beersheba.

Bridge

God's assurance to Abram that he will have numerous descendants, who will possess the land of Canaan, takes the form of a solemn covenant. This covenant is important, guaranteeing unconditionally that Abram will become a great nation (see 12:2). On the basis of what occurs in Genesis 15, God assures Abram that he will be the father of the nation of Israel. However, this promise of nationhood will be subsequently subsumed into a more substantial, eternal covenant that will center on Abram being the father of many nations (see 17:1–27). This later covenant is all-important because it focuses on how all the families of the ground will be blessed through Abram (see 12:3).[414]

Central to the making of the covenant in Genesis 15 is God's recognition of Abram as "righteous" because he trusts God's word (15:6). As Dempster notes, "The covenant is given because of righteousness, which is given because of faith."[415] The idea of righteousness being associated with faith is highly significant. With good reason, the apostle Paul quotes Genesis 15:6 in Romans 4:3, 22 and Galatians 3:6, when he contends that Gentile followers of Jesus do not need to be circumcised to be righteous. According to Paul, if Abraham could be declared righteous by God based on faith, prior to being circumcised, then the same may be true for Gentiles, who demonstrate faith in God's promises (see Rom 4:1–25; Gal 3:1–9). The apostle James likewise recognizes the importance of righteousness based on faith, quoting Genesis 15:6, but he emphasizes this in the context of arguing that genuine faith will express itself in good

---

413 Sarna, *Exodus*, 14.

414 See Williamson, *Abraham, Israel and the Nations*, for a fuller discussion of the relationship between Gen 15 and 17.

415 Dempster, "'He Believed the Lord,'" 48.

works (see Jas 2:21–24; compare what Paul says in Eph 2:8–10 regarding salvation by faith that afterward produces good works).

G. The Birth of Ishmael (16:1–16)

> [1] Abram's wife Sarai had not borne any children for him, but she owned an Egyptian slave named Hagar. [2] Sarai said to Abram, "Since the LORD has prevented me from bearing children, go to my slave; perhaps through her I can build a family." And Abram agreed to what Sarai said. [3] So Abram's wife Sarai took Hagar, her Egyptian slave, and gave her to her husband Abram as a wife for him. This happened after Abram had lived in the land of Canaan ten years. [4] He slept with Hagar, and she became pregnant. When she saw that she was pregnant, her mistress became contemptible to her. [5] Then Sarai said to Abram, "You are responsible for my suffering! I put my slave in your arms, and when she saw that she was pregnant, I became contemptible to her. May the LORD judge between me and you."
>
> [6] Abram replied to Sarai, "Here, your slave is in your hands; do whatever you want with her." Then Sarai mistreated her so much that she ran away from her.
>
> [7] The angel of the LORD found her by a spring in the wilderness, the spring on the way to Shur. [8] He said, "Hagar, slave of Sarai, where have you come from and where are you going?"
>
> She replied, "I'm running away from my mistress Sarai."
>
> [9] The angel of the LORD said to her, "Go back to your mistress and submit to her authority." [10] The angel of the LORD said to her, "I will greatly multiply your offspring, and they will be too many to count."
>
> [11] The angel of the LORD said to her, "You have conceived and will have a son. You will name him Ishmael, for the LORD has heard your cry of affliction. [12] This man will be like a wild donkey. His hand will be against everyone, and everyone's hand will be against him; he will settle near all his relatives."
>
> [13] So she named the LORD who spoke to her: "You are El-roi," for she said, "In this place, have I actually seen the one who sees me?" [14] That is why the well is called Beer-lahai-roi. It is between Kadesh and Bered.
>
> [15] So Hagar gave birth to Abram's son, and Abram named his son (whom Hagar bore) Ishmael. [16] Abram was eighty-six years old when Hagar bore Ishmael to him.

Context

Despite God's reassurance to Abram that he will have numerous offspring (15:4–5), Sarai's barrenness continues to be a barrier to the fulfilment of the divine promises. After ten years in the land of Canaan, they still have no children, prompting Sarai to offer a possible solution. Adopting a practice that was occasionally used in similar circumstances in the ANE, she encourages Abram to take her maidservant, Hagar, as a second wife. By offering her servant to Abram, Sarai looks to maintain her position of authority as matriarch within the household. Sarai's attitude suggests that she fears being usurped if another wife provides Abram with a male heir.[416] Events, however, do not turn out as Sarai had hoped.

Comments

16:1–3. This episode begins by highlighting Sarai's inability to bear a child for Abram (cf. 11:30). The narrator contrasts her lack of a child with the fact that she has an Egyptian maidservant, whose name is Hagar. Hagar may have become Sarai's maidservant as a consequence of the family's brief stay in Egypt (12:10–20). The opening sentence emphasizes the status of both women within Abram's household. Sarai is Abram's wife; Hagar is Sarai's servant.[417] This sets the scene for the events that are about to develop.

Sarai's instructions to Abram give the impression that she is offering a solution to a problem that has been created by YHWH. From her perspective, God has prevented her from having children. While her comments convey a negative attitude toward God, they also indicate that she believes God capable of influencing the birth of children. In due course, God will demonstrate this power by enabling her to conceive (21:1–2).

---

[416] As Philip Y. Yoo, "Hagar the Egyptian: Wife, Handmaid, and Concubine," *CBQ* 78 (2016): 225–26, illustrates, various laws existed in the ANE to address the complex family relationships that are created when a man takes a slave woman as a second wife. While parallels may be drawn between circumstances described in Genesis and those found in ancient Mesopotamian laws, we have no grounds for believing that Mesopotamian laws would have had any legal standing with Abraham and his family. The laws illustrate, however, that various outcomes were possible. We must be careful that Mesopotamian customs are not imposed upon our interpretation of the Genesis text.

[417] The CSB translation "but she owned an Egyptian slave" does not reflect particularly well the wording of the Hebrew text, which more literally says, "and to her a female servant." Hagar may have been one of those given to Abraham by the Egyptian Pharaoh when he took Sarah into his household (12:16). By giving her to Abraham, Sarah bestows on Hagar the status of a second wife to Abraham.

Her impatience with God is understandable for she is about 75 years old. By giving her maidservant to Abram, Sarai presents herself as the one who will build a family for her husband. Her actions draw attention to how people often attempt to solve problems without relying on God. Not surprisingly, perhaps, her solution creates further complications.

Abram acquiesces to Sarai's demand, suggesting that he too struggles to believe that God will enable his wife to bear him a son. From a human perspective the proposed solution has some merit. Consequently, Abram takes Hagar to be his second wife. While the narrator stops short of condemning directly Abram's actions, the outcome is viewed as less than appropriate. As subsequent episodes will demonstrate, God intends for Sarai to be the mother of Abram's son. The solution to Abram's childlessness does not rest with Hagar. There is no instance throughout the Bible where the taking of additional wives is viewed positively.

Strikingly, verse 3 abounds with words that emphasize the status of the different characters within Abram's household. Although Sarai is willing that Hagar should become Abram's wife, Sarai expects Hagar to remain her maidservant.[418] However, Hagar's subsequent actions suggest that she no longer views herself as subservient to Sarai.[419] Most English versions do not follow the order of the Hebrew text, which places the reference to Abram dwelling in the land of Canaan, between Sarai's actions

---

[418] Such an arrangement may be found in Old Babylonian marriage contracts (Yoo, "Hagar the Egyptian," 219). Raymond Westbrook, "The Female Slave," in *Gender and Law in the Hebrew Bible and the Ancient Near East*, ed. Bernard M. Levinson, Tikva Frymer-Kensky, and Victor H. Matthews, JSOTSup 262 (Sheffield: Sheffield Academic, 1998), 214–38, draws attention to the different ways in which a female slave in the ANE could be viewed from the perspectives of either property or family law.

[419] The Genesis narrative reflects something of the tension that develops regarding Hagar's status within Abraham's household. While Hagar is consistently viewed as a שִׁפְחָה (*šipḥâ*, "maidservant") in ch. 16, her status is defined as an אָמָה (*ʾāmâ*, "slave woman") in ch. 21. As Gen 20:17–18 reveals, the designation אָמָה (*ʾāmâ*) appears to be used to denote female slaves who bear children to their master. Cf. F. Charles Fensham, "Son of a Handmaid in Northwest Semitic," *VT* 19 (1969): 312–21; Alexander, *Exodus*, 475–79. By way of contrast a שִׁפְחָה (*šipḥâ*) is a female slave who is not expected to have sexual relations with her master (cf. 20:14; see Yoo, "Hagar the Egyptian," 228). Hagar's status changes from שִׁפְחָה (*šipḥâ*) to אָמָה (*ʾāmâ*) when she becomes Abraham's wife. In Gen 30:4, 9 שִׁפְחָה (*šipḥâ*) is used of Bilhah and Zilpah to define their relationship to Rachel and Leah respectively; in these instances it would be less appropriate to use אָמָה (*ʾāmâ*) (*pace* Bernard S. Jackson, *Wisdom-Laws: A Study of the Mishpatim of Exodus 21:1–22:16* [Oxford: Oxford University Press, 2006], 96n100). Rachel's use of אָמָה (*ʾāmâ*) in 30:3 indicates that she is offering Bilhah as a "second" wife to Jacob so that he can have sexual relations with her.

in taking and giving Hagar to Abram. Abram and Sarai are now 85 and 75 years old respectively.

16:4–6. Sarai's comments to Abram in verse 2 emphasize that she intends Hagar to be a surrogate mother on her behalf. As was possible in the ANE, Hagar can become Abram's wife, while simultaneously remaining Sarai's maidservant. However, because she is carrying Abram's child, Hagar's attitude toward her mistress changes. Hagar seizes the opportunity to enhance her status within Abram's household. As verse 4b states, "her mistress becomes less important in her eyes." The use of the verb קלל (*qll*) recalls Genesis 12:3, where it is use of those who disdain Abram, treating him with contempt. Hagar's actions imply that she no longer sees herself as Sarai's maidservant.

Hagar may well have hoped that Abram would promote her within his household, but this does not happen. Abram responds to Sarai's complaint by affirming that Hagar is still Sarai's maidservant, despite becoming Abram's wife. Consequently, when Sarai treats Hagar harshly, she decides to flee. The verb ענה (*ʿnh*), used here of Sarai's action, probably implies that Sarai humiliated Hagar. Sarai responds in kind to Hagar's contempt for her.

16:7–12. Egyptian by birth, Hagar journeys toward her homeland. Her flight brings her to a desert spring on the way to Shur, a location to the east of the Nile Delta (cf. 25:18; 1 Sam 15:7). Unexpectedly, "the angel of the Lord" finds Hagar and speaks to her. This is the first occurrence in the Old Testament of an expression that comes 48 times in all.[420] While the expression in English implies that the angel is a living being who belongs to YHWH, many references to the "angel of the Lord" give the strong impression that the "angel" is YHWH himself (in addition to the present passage, see Gen 22:11–18; Exod 3:2–6; Judg 6:11–24). According to Stuart, the expression מַלְאַךְ יְהוָה (*malʾak yhwh*) is best understood as a "genitive of association," meaning "the angel that is YHWH."[421] Based on what is said in various passages regarding the "angel of the Lord," Niehaus suggests that the angel is "a theophanic presence of God."[422] God

[420] The closely related expression "angel of God" comes in Gen 21:17; 31:11; Exod 14:19; Judg 6:20; 13:6, 9; 1 Sam 29:9; 2 Sam 14:17, 20; 19:27 [Heb. 28]. The Hebrew term מַלְאַךְ can refer to a messenger, who is not a heavenly being (cf. Gen 32:3 [Heb. 4], 6 [Heb. 7]).

[421] Douglas K. Stuart, *Exodus*, NAC 2 (Nashville: Broadman & Holman, 2006), 110–11; cf. *IBHS*, §9.5.3.h.

[422] Niehaus, *God at Sinai*, 191.

himself appears, but not in all his majestic glory. In this way, God may speak directly to an ordinary person without undermining the belief that sinful people cannot have a face-to-face encounter with God.[423] As Stuart remarks, "The Angel Yahweh was not all there was to God but was a true and real representation of him."[424] Consequently, Hagar can rightly claim that she has seen God (v. 13).

The "angel of the LORD" instructs Hagar to return and submit to Sarai, her mistress. The command is striking for the instruction to submit to Sarai uses the same Hebrew verb ענה (ʿ*nh*) as that used in verse 6 to describe Sarai's humiliation of Hagar.[425] The instruction to return requires Hagar to be subservient to Sarai, but Hagar is subsequently assured by God that he will make her offspring very numerous.

God then speaks about the child to be born, emphasizing that through him God will respond to the suffering that Hagar has endured. The name given to the child, Ishmael, meaning "God hears," suggests that God is sympathetic to Hagar's situation. Although Hagar is being asked to be submissive to Sarai, God's words probably imply that her son will not be subservient to others (vv. 11–12). As reflected in the variety of translations found in English versions, the precise meaning of verse 12 is uncertain. The final words of verse 12 have been interpreted in a variety of ways: living near his relatives (so CSB, KJV, NJPS); living to the east of his relatives (cf. NAS); living in opposition to his relatives (cf. ESV, NIV, NJB, NRSV). The context suggests that Hagar's son will enjoy freedom, like a wild donkey, maintaining his independence. A similar, but not identical, expression is found in 25:18.

16:13–14. These verses underline God's concern for Hagar. God both hears, as the name Ishmael emphasizes, and sees. Consequently, Hagar refers to God as *El-roi*, meaning "God Who Sees," and she names the well "Beer-lahai-roi," which means "well of the Living One who sees me." Both names reflect her remarkable experience, for she goes on to speak in verse 13 of seeing the one who has seen her. As evident in the variety of English translations for the final part of verse 13, the precise meaning of Hagar's words is open to discussion. Booij makes a strong case for translating her words: "Would I have gone here indeed looking for him that

---

[423] Cf. Carol A. Newsom, "Angels," *ABD*, 1:250.

[424] Stuart, *Exodus*, 113; cf. U. Cassuto, *Commentary on Exodus* (Jerusalem: Magnes, 1967), 31.

[425] Verse 6 uses the *piel* form, whereas v. 9 uses the *hithpael*.

looks after me?"[426] This captures something of the unexpected nature of YHWH's appearance to Hagar. Here is a God who is interested in a runaway slave girl. By way of adding credence to this incident, the narrator notes that the location of the well is still known (cf. Gen 24:62; 25:11).

16:15–16. Without describing Hagar's return to Abram's household, the narrator concludes this episode by focusing on the birth of Ishmael. By naming the newborn boy, Abram confirms that he is the child's father. This relationship is underlined through repetition of the term "son" in verse 15. In the light of God's intervention with Hagar and his sending her back, Abram no doubt saw Ishmael as the divinely promised heir. This belief underlies his response to God in 17:18, and God's reply (17:20–21). At the age of 86, Abram sees Ishmael, appropriate called "God hears," as the answer to his request for an heir (cf. Gen 15:2–3). Yet God has other plans.

Bridge

The birth of Ishmael must have appeared to Abram and Sarai as the solution to their childlessness. Sarai's plan results in the birth of a son to Abram, and God's intervention in sending Hagar back to Sarai suggests that the process has divine approval. Subsequent developments will signal otherwise. Ishmael will be passed over in favor of a son that Sarai herself will bear to Abram (Gen 21:1–21).

Centuries later, the apostle Paul draws on this episode from Genesis to illustrate the difference in outlook between those who trust in the Sinai covenant for salvation and those who trust in Jesus Christ as the one who brings God's blessing to the nations in fulfilment of the Abrahamic covenant. In Galatians 4:23, Paul describes Ishmael as Abraham's son "born as a result of the flesh." Paul uses this expression to criticize "Abraham for relying on his own resources, powers and exertions to achieve the fulfilment of God's promises; in other words, for having confidence in the flesh."[427] Paul uses the contrast between Ishmael and Isaac to illustrate the difference between those who are looking to the covenant at Mount Sinai for salvation through human merit and those who look to Jesus Christ for salvation by faith. For Paul, God's plan to bless the nations through Jesus Christ finds its origin in the promises associated with the Abraham

---

[426] Th. Booij, "Hagar's Words in Genesis xvi 13b," *VT* 30 (1980): 1–7.

[427] David W. Gooding, *The Riches of Divine Wisdom: The New Testament's Use of the Old Testament* (Coleraine: Myrtlefield House, 2013), 230.

covenant. Paul indicates that the Jewish leaders in the Jerusalem of his day look to the Sinai covenant as the basis for their salvation; this, he argues, is a situation comparable to Hagar's experience, for her son does not share the inheritance with Isaac. By way of contrast, Paul associates the Jerusalem that is above with Isaac, the promised son. As Genesis 17 will reveal, the Abrahamic covenant, which focuses on how Jews and Gentiles will be the spiritual children of Abraham, will be established through Isaac, and not Ishmael.[428]

H. The Covenant of Circumcision (17:1–27)

> 1 When Abram was ninety-nine years old, the Lord appeared to him, say-
> ing, "I am God Almighty. Live in my presence and be blameless. 2 I will
> set up my covenant between me and you, and I will multiply you greatly."
>
> 3 Then Abram fell facedown and God spoke with him: 4 "As for me, here
> is my covenant with you: You will become the father of many nations.
> 5 Your name will no longer be Abram; your name will be Abraham, for
> I will make you the father of many nations. 6 I will make you extremely
> fruitful and will make nations and kings come from you. 7 I will confirm
> my covenant that is between me and you and your future offspring
> throughout their generations. It is a permanent covenant to be your
> God and the God of your offspring after you. 8 And to you and your
> future offspring I will give the land where you are residing—all the
> land of Canaan—as a permanent possession, and I will be their God."
>
> 9 God also said to Abraham, "As for you, you and your offspring after
> you throughout their generations are to keep my covenant. 10 This
> is my covenant between me and you and your offspring after you,
> which you are to keep: Every one of your males must be circumcised.
> 11 You must circumcise the flesh of your foreskin to serve as a sign of
> the covenant between me and you. 12 Throughout your generations,
> every male among you is to be circumcised at eight days old—every
> male born in your household or purchased from any foreigner and
> not your offspring. 13 Whether born in your household or purchased,
> he must be circumcised. My covenant will be marked in your flesh
> as a permanent covenant. 14 If any male is not circumcised in the
> flesh of his foreskin, that man will be cut off from his people; he has
> broken my covenant."
>
> 15 God said to Abraham, "As for your wife Sarai, do not call her Sarai, for
> Sarah will be her name. 16 I will bless her; indeed, I will give you a son

---

428 For a fuller discussion of Paul's use of the Genesis materials, see Gooding, *Riches of Divine Wisdom*, 222–39.

by her. I will bless her, and she will produce nations; kings of peoples will come from her."

17 Abraham fell facedown. Then he laughed and said to himself, "Can a child be born to a hundred-year-old man? Can Sarah, a ninety-year-old woman, give birth?" 18 So Abraham said to God, "If only Ishmael were acceptable to you!"

19 But God said, "No. Your wife Sarah will bear you a son, and you will name him Isaac. I will confirm my covenant with him as a permanent covenant for his future offspring. 20 As for Ishmael, I have heard you. I will certainly bless him; I will make him fruitful and will multiply him greatly. He will father twelve tribal leaders, and I will make him into a great nation. 21 But I will confirm my covenant with Isaac, whom Sarah will bear to you at this time next year." 22 When he finished talking with him, God withdrew from Abraham.

23 So Abraham took his son Ishmael and those born in his household or purchased—every male among the members of Abraham's household—and he circumcised the flesh of their foreskin on that very day, just as God had said to him. 24 Abraham was ninety-nine years old when the flesh of his foreskin was circumcised, 25 and his son Ishmael was thirteen years old when the flesh of his foreskin was circumcised. 26 On that same day Abraham and his son Ishmael were circumcised. 27 And all the men of his household—whether born in his household or purchased from a foreigner—were circumcised with him.

Context

God had promised Abram that he would become a great nation (12:2) and confirmed this by making a covenant (15:18). The subsequent birth of Ishmael offered hope to the patriarch and his wife that this promise of nationhood might become a reality. God, however, intended that Sarai herself would have a son. Thirteen years after the birth of Ishmael, YHWH appears unexpectedly to Abram. In relating what happens, the narrator focuses on the conversation between YHWH and Abram, with the former taking the lead. Instructing Abram to maintain a close relationship with him, God speaks of establishing a covenant that centers on Abram's role as the father of many nations. By focusing on "many nations," this covenant goes far beyond what is divinely guaranteed by the covenant of chapter 15. Although "blessing" is not mentioned directly in chapter 17, the idea of Abram being the father of many nations recalls the previous divine promise that all the families of the ground will be blessed through Abram (12:3). Whereas the events of chapter 15 emphasize that Abram will be the father of one nation, chapter 17 expands upon this to stress that Abram will be the father of many nations. Consequently, the covenant of chapter15 is subsumed into the covenant of circumcision, which has a much broader focus and is different in nature. In line with this, chapter 17 draws a subtle distinction between those who are the biological offspring of Abram and those who see Abram as their adopted father (see Biblical and Theological Themes §3).[429]

Although there are links between the covenants described in chapters 15 and 17, they are very different types of covenants. This becomes even more apparent when the covenant in chapter 17 is compared to the covenant that God makes with Noah and his descendants in chapter 9.

> Six important similarities can be observed. First, both of these covenants are described as eternal or everlasting covenants, *bᵉrîṯ ʿôlām* (9:16; 17:7, 13, 19). Second, these covenants are accompanied by an appropriate sign. In the case of Noah it is the rainbow (9:12–14), and in the case of Abraham it is circumcision (17:11). The rainbow is related to rain which in turn would remind the people of the flood. Circumcision relates to the procreation of descendants which is a point of emphasis in the covenant of chapter 17. Third, in both cases, the expressions used of the formation of the covenant are *hēqîm bᵉrîṯ* (9:9, 11, 17; 17:7, 19, 21) and *nāṯan bᵉrîṯ* (9:12; 17:2). Fourth, the covenants in chapters 9 and 17 are spoken of by God as "between me and you" (9:12, 15; 17:2, 7). However, at the same time they also include the descendants of Noah and Abraham (9:9,12; 17:7,9). Fifth, the benefit which each covenant brings for those

[429] Many scholars see the covenant in ch. 17 as being essentially a reiteration of the ch. 15 covenant with some additional details being added. Dumbrell, *Covenant and Creation*, 74, sees Gen 17 "as a consolidation of the Abrahamic covenant and as an extension of its detail." Similarly, Dean, "Covenant, Conditionality, and Consequence," 302, views ch. 17 as "a reaffirmation and more precise specification of earlier-made divine covenant obligations, with the addition of covenant regulations on the vassal group." Dean suggests that there are only two elements that come in ch. 17 that are not present in ch. 15: "the eternal aspect of the covenant" and "the promise that Abraham will sire kings" (300). However, he ignores completely the reference to Abraham being the "father of many nations." John D. Currid, "Genesis," in *A Biblical-Theological Introduction to the Old Testament: The Gospel Promised*, ed. Miles V. Van Pelt (Wheaton: Crossway, 2016), 59, says, "Whereas Genesis 15 describes the inauguration of the Abrahamic covenant, Genesis 17 declares the institution of the covenant seal, one that Abraham and his posterity would wear on their very flesh." Other scholars, who see only minor distinctions between the covenants in chs. 15 and 17, include Hamilton, *Genesis: Chapters 1-17*, 458–66; McComiskey, *The Covenants of Promise*, 16; Gentry and Wellum, *Kingdom through Covenant*, 250–73.

> with whom it is established is that they shall not be cut off (9:11; 17:14). Sixth, the divine command in 17:1, "Walk before me and be blameless," resembles the description of Noah in 6:9, "Blameless in his generation; Noah walked with God." The word "blameless," *tâmim,* is found only on these two occasions in the whole of Genesis.[430]

These similarities are noteworthy, for both covenants concern God's relationship with all the inhabitants of the earth. The covenant with Noah focuses on God not cursing the ground again because of human wrongdoing (8:21; 9:11, 15). The covenant with Abram centers on God blessing all the nations of the earth through Abram and one of his future descendants. The two covenants complement each other, reflecting God's desire to redeem humanity from the consequences of their sinful nature.

Comments

17:1–2. The repetition of the age formula regarding Abram creates a bridge between the conclusion to chapter 16 and the start of chapter 17. The story jumps from the patriarch being 86 years old to being 99 years old. Unexpectedly, God appears to Abram and addresses him. The brevity of the introduction suggests that this intervention has not been prompted by any anxiety on the part of Abram regarding the fulfilment of the divine promises. As the subsequent conversation reveals, Abram assumes that his natural heir is Ishmael (17:18), the son born to Hagar (16:15). God, however, comes to announce the birth of a son to Sarai.

YHWH introduces himself to Abram using the designation אֵל שַׁדַּי (*ʾēl šadday*, "God Almighty"). Previously, Melchizedek had used the epithet אֵל עֶלְיוֹן (*ʾēl ʿelyôn*, "God Most High") (14:19–20); Abram will later refer to God as אֵל עוֹלָם (*ʾēl ʿôlām*, "Eternal God") (21:33). In each instance the noun אֵל (*ʾēl*, "God") is qualified by another term that highlights a specific divine characteristic. In the present context emphasis is given to God's omnipotence, a fitting emphasis since God is about to promise Abram that Sarai herself will bear him a son through whom the divine promises will advance toward their fulfilment.

YHWH's introduction of himself as "God Almighty" is immediately followed by two related instructions to Abram. God commands Abram: "Live in my presence and be blameless." A similar combination of expressions

430 Alexander, "Genesis 22 and the Covenant of Circumcision," 19–20.

is used of Noah in 6:9, stressing his righteousness.[431] Unfortunately, the CSB translation of 17:1 disguises the similarity in Hebrew between 6:9 and 17:1. "Live in my presence" might be rendered more literally "Walk before me" (cf. ESV, NIV, NRSV), conveying the sense that Abram is to serve God faithfully. Following on from these instructions, verse 2 states that God will make his covenant with Abram and multiply him greatly; the wording recalls the creation mandate in Genesis 1:28 that people were to be fruitful and multiply and fill the earth. The syntax of verses 1–2 in Hebrew suggests that the fulfilment of the promises in verse 2 is dependent upon Abram's obedience to the commands in verse 1 (cf. ESV, NET, NIV).[432]

17:3–8. In response to God's initial words, Abram shows deference by bowing to the ground. God then speaks again. His speech begins with the pronoun אֲנִי (ʾănî, "I"), indicating that the first part of what he says (vv. 4–8) relates to his responsibility concerning the covenant that is being initiated. In a similar way, God's words are introduced in verses 9–14 by וְאַתָּה (wĕʾattâ, "And you") with reference to Abram, and in verses 15–16 by שָׂרַי אִשְׁתְּךָ (śāray ʾištĕkā, "Sarai your wife"), with reference to Sarai. By speaking of "my covenant," God underlines that he is the one setting the terms of this agreement with Abram. For this reason, "my covenant" need not refer here to a preexisting covenant.[433] The focus of this covenant is clearly defined through the repetition of the expression "father of many nations" in verses 4–5. Compared to the covenant made in chapter 15, the present covenant expands upon the role that Abram will have. His

---

[431] Whereas Abraham is to walk *before* God, Noah walked *with* God (cf. 5:24, which speaks of Enoch walking *with* God).

[432] The two imperatives of v. 1 are followed at the start of v. 2 by וְאֶתְּנָה (wĕʾettĕnâ), a cohortative attached to a non-converting conjunction *wĕ*. When the sequence imperative + *wĕ* + cohortative is used, the cohortative may indicate purpose or result (cf. *GKC §108d;* Driver, *Treatise*, 64; Lambdin, *Introduction to Biblical Hebrew*, 119; Joüon *§116b*). To highlight this syntactic arrangement, the conjunction *wĕ* is best translated "so that." God's words could be rendered: "Walk before me and be blameless so that I may make my covenant between me and you and so that I may greatly increase your numbers" (cf. ESV, NET, NIV). In the light of this, it is reasonable to assume that God promises here to make this covenant in the future, conditional upon Abraham's behavior. If so, the sealing of the covenant comes when God tests Abraham's obedience in Gen 22, an event that ends with God swearing an oath that guarantees Abraham numerous descendants. See Alexander, "Genesis 22 and the Covenant of Circumcision," 17–22; Williamson, *Abraham, Israel and the Nations*, 234–59; Williamson, *Sealed with an Oath*, 84–91.

[433] *Pace* Gentry and Wellum, *Kingdom through Covenant*, 260.

fatherhood is not confined to one nation, but will embrace many nations, a fact underlined by changing his name from אַבְרָם (ʾabrām, "Abram") to אַבְרָהָם (ʾabrāhām, "Abraham"), the latter resembling the expression אַב־הֲמוֹן (ʾab-hămôn, "father of many nations").[434] This change of name underscores the importance of the everlasting covenant that is now being established with Abraham and his offspring "after him." This event marks a new stage in Abraham's life, suggesting that this covenant differs from that made in chapter 15.

While the idea that Abraham will become the father of a great nation envisages him having many descendants who are his biological children, the concept of "father" is not restricted to biological paternity. The term אָב (ʾāb, "father") is sometimes "used of a variety of social roles that carried authority or exercised a protective or caring function. It could be used of a prophet (2 Kgs 6:21), priest (Judg 18:19), king (1 Sam 24:11), or governor (Isa 22:20–21)."[435]

Since Abraham never becomes the biological father of many nations, his fatherhood must be understood metaphorically. Acknowledging that "a purely biological interpretation" of the promise that Abraham will become a "multitude of nations" is unlikely, Hahn suggests that a solution lies "in the use of 'father' as a term for 'suzerain' in international treaties."[436] He writes, "Numerous studies have demonstrated that international political alliances were described in kinship terms in the ANE. Specifically, vassals were 'sons' and suzerains 'fathers.' "[437] Adopting a similar approach, DeRouchie writes, "It seems plausible, then, to understand Abraham's fatherhood over the nations primarily as a royal

---

434 According to Sarna, "Abraham," 112, the name Abraham is "more likely ... a mere dialectic variant of Abram, representing the insertion of h in weak verbal stems, a phenomenon known from Aramaic and elsewhere."

435 Christopher J. H. Wright, "אב (ʾab)," *NIDOTTE*, 1:221. In a similar vein, J. B. Payne, "אבה (ʾbh)," *TWOT*, 1:5, observes, "ʾāb may designate any man who occupies a position or receives recognition similar to that of a father: the 'father' of a servant is his master (2Kings 2:12); 'a father to the poor' (Job 29:16) is their protector; 'a father to the inhabitants of Jerusalem' (Isa 22:21) is their governor; and 'a father to Pharaoh' (Gen 45:8) is his advisor. The title 'Father' is thus used for one in authority (2Kings 2:12), whether prophet (2Kings 6:21), priest (Jud 18:19), or king (1Sam 24:11 [H 12]), or even—as a personification—the grave, 'Thou art my father' (Job 17:14)."

436 Hahn, *Kinship by Covenant*, 106.

437 Hahn, *Kinship by Covenant*, 106. Hahn also suggests that the "great name" of Genesis 12:2 "corresponds to kingship, and not just to kingship but to international suzerainty (fatherhood)" (107).

designation by which he and his wife Sarah, the "princess" (17:15), are regarded as the founders of a new dynasty that will climax in a specific, royal descendant who will rule Israelites (both native-born and alien residents) and those from vassal nations."[438] This understanding of Abraham's fatherhood underlies Paul's conclusion in Galatians 3:29 that those who belong to Christ "are Abraham's seed." The subsequent circumcision of all males in Abraham's household, including those who are clearly not Abraham's natural offspring, underlines that the benefits of the covenant are not restricted to Abraham's biological children. These offspring of Abraham extend beyond those who are described in chapter 17 as coming "after him," that is his biological descendants.

The final part of verse 6 breaks the *wayyiqtol* verb sequence of the MT by placing the noun "kings" immediately after the conjunction "and." This suggests that the reference to kings coming from Abraham ought to be linked to verse 7, which speaks of Abraham's offspring "after him." The promise of kings from Abraham is linked to the establishment of an everlasting covenant with a unique line of Abraham's descendants. Genesis will eventually associate this lineage with the tribes of Joseph/Ephraim and Judah.[439] Later in chapter 17, God states emphatically that the covenant of circumcision will be established with Isaac, but not Ishmael (vv. 19–21), confirming that the family line, already traced from Adam to Terah, will continue through Abraham to Isaac. Eventually, it will connect to the Davidic dynasty. In line with this, God also reassures Abraham that his descendants "after him" will take possession of the land of Canaan, as already guaranteed by the covenant in chapter 15.

17:9–14. After outlining his own responsibilities regarding the covenant, God mentions in verses 9–14 the obligations that Abraham and those who follow him must fulfil. This switch in focus is introduced at the start of verse 9 by the words, "As for you ..." For his part, Abraham must circumcise all the males associated with him. By speaking repeatedly of the covenant as "my covenant" (vv. 9–10, 13–14), God emphasizes that he has instituted it.

The use of circumcision as the sign of the covenant (cf. the rainbow in 9:12–13, 17) is noteworthy, given that this sign is not normally visible and

---

[438] DeRouchie, "Counting Stars with Abraham and the Prophets," 459.

[439] Cf. Diffey, "Royal Promise in Genesis," 313–16. In the time of Samuel, the tribe of Ephraim is rejected in favor of David from the tribe of Judah (see Ps 78:67–68).

only applicable to males. In addition, the inclusion of males who are not Abraham's biological offspring indicates that circumcision is not understood as denoting consanguinity. Furthermore, to complicate the picture, Abraham will circumcise Ishmael despite God's declaring that the covenant will be established not with Ishmael, but with Isaac, who is yet to be born. These factors suggest that the choice of sign is probably intended to point toward the significance of the promised offspring, who will overcome the serpent and mediate blessing to the nations of the earth.[440] As Deenick suggests, "The fact that the covenant is extended through a 'seed' and the inescapable reality that circumcision is conducted on the very instrument of procreation suggests that circumcision is bound up with the recollection of God's promise to Abraham of a 'seed,' and more particularly his promise to bless the world through Abraham's 'seed.' "[441] While the covenant will be established only with those individuals who compose the patriline descended from Abraham, the benefits of the covenant will extend to those who are circumcised. In time, the covenant promises will be associated with King David and his royal line (cf. Ps 89:3–4, 19–37), eventually being fulfilled through Jesus Christ (Gal 3:16).

17:15–16. The next part of God's speech is marked by the introduction: "As for Sarai your wife … ." After outlining the obligations that Abraham must fulfil, God speaks about Sarai. To confirm the importance of this covenant and her role within it, Sarai's name is changed to Sarah, both forms meaning "princess." God promises to bless Sarah, enabling her to bear Abraham a son. Closely echoing what is said about Abraham in verse 6, God states that Sarah will become "nations" and produce "kings."

17:17–18. Given their advanced years, Abraham reacts with disbelief concerning the divine promise that Sarah will bear a son. He laughs at the

---

[440] According to Joseph Blenkinsopp, "The 'Covenant of Circumcision' (Gen 17) in the Context of the Abraham Cycle (Gen 11:27–25:11): Preliminary Considerations," in *The Post-Priestly Pentateuch: New Perspectives on Its Redactional Development and Theological Profiles*, ed. Federico Giuntoli and Konrad Schmid, FAT 101 (Tübingen: Mohr Siebeck, 2015), 151, "Circumcision was the common practice among north-west Semitic peoples …" For this reason, the "non-Semitic Philistines" were designated the "uncircumcised" (cf., e.g., Judg 14:3; 15:18; 1 Sam 14:6). Later, in Genesis, the Hivite men of Shechem are circumcised (33:14–17, 22, 24).

[441] Deenick, *Righteous by Promise*, 49. Less likely is the suggestion of Kline that the act of circumcision symbolizes the punishment of being cut off. See Meredith G. Kline, *By Oath Consigned: A Reinterpretation of the Covenant Signs of Circumcision and Baptism* (Grand Rapids,: Eerdmans, 1968), 43, 87.

apparent absurdity of what God promises. This introduces a motif that will reappear in connection with Isaac, whose name means "he laughs." Sarah will laugh when she later overhears God promising Abraham that his wife will bear a son in the next year (18:12–13, 15; cf. 21:6). Given the seeming impossibility of Abraham and Sarah having a son, the patriarch reminds God of Ishmael, the son that he already has through Hagar, Sarah's Egyptian maidservant. From Abraham's perspective, he has no need of another son. Undoubtedly influenced by the fact that God instructed Hagar to return to Abraham's household after she ran away (16:9–15), Abraham views Ishmael as God's provision of an heir and the one through whom the patriline will continue. God, however, has other plans. Sarah, and not Hagar, will be the mother of Abraham's heir.

17:19–22. God responds to Abraham's request concerning Ishmael by emphasizing that Sarah will bear him a son. By naming him Isaac, which means "he laughs," God recalls Abraham's immediate response to the idea that he and Sarah would produce a son in their old age (cf. v. 17). This son will be exceptionally important, because the covenant will be established through him and his descendants "after him" (cf. v. 7), a point emphasized by repetition in verses 19 and 21.[442] While Isaac is privileged more highly, God also promises Abraham that Ishmael will be blessed. The details of the blessing recall how God blessed humanity at creation to be fruitful and multiply (1:28; cf. 9:1, 7). Although Ishmael will father twelve tribal leaders, they will compose only one nation. Unlike Abraham and his descendants "after him," Ishmael will not be the father of many nations. Abraham and Sarah have waited many years for a son of their own; God promises that they will have one within a year. With this promise God goes up from speaking with Abraham.

17:23–27. Obeying God's instructions, Abraham circumcised all the males associated with him, including those who are not his biological children. The reference to Abraham's age creates a minor inclusio with the opening verse of the chapter. The repetition of various details regarding the circumcision of all the men in his household underscores the immediacy and comprehensiveness of Abraham's obedience. Ishmael is also circumcised, even though the everlasting covenant will be established

[442] The word order of the Hebrew text in v. 21 underlines the contrast that exists between Isaac and Ishmael. By placing the object אֶת־בְּרִיתִי (ʾ*et-bĕrîtî*, "my covenant") before the verb אָקִים (ʾ*āqîm*, "I will establish"), the conjunction וְ (*wĕ*, "and") at the start of v. 21 functions more like "but" in English.

through Isaac. The inclusion of males bought from foreigners is in keeping with the concept of Abraham being the father of many nations.

Bridge

God's relationship with Abraham comes to an important point at this stage in the narrative. The covenant in chapter 15 guaranteed Abraham that he would be the father of one nation. God expands upon that earlier covenant by guaranteeing that Abraham will be the father of many nations. Whereas the covenant in chapter 15 assured Abraham that his numerous descendants would take possession of the land of Canaan, the covenant made in chapter 17 affirms that Abraham will be the father of many nations. This covenant expands considerably upon what is divinely promised in chapter 15, but obviously incorporates the previous covenant. Moreover, the covenant of circumcision will be established in the next generation only with Isaac, although the benefits of the covenant will extend more widely, including those who are not biologically related to Abraham. Importantly, the covenant of circumcision is linked in a unique way to the members of the unique patriline that is traced in the book of Genesis. Subsequently, the expectation develops that Abraham's heir will exercise authority over the nations (cf. Gen 27:29; 49:10). As a result, the nations will no longer be under the control of the evil one. What begins with Abraham eventually leads to the establishment of the Davidic dynasty.[443] Ultimately, the promise of fatherhood over the nations finds its fulfilment in Jesus Christ (Gal 3:1–18).[444]

I. The Rescue of Lot from Sodom (18:1–19:29)

> 1 The Lord appeared to Abraham at the oaks of Mamre while he was
> sitting at the entrance of his tent during the heat of the day. 2 He looked
> up, and he saw three men standing near him. When he saw them, he
> ran from the entrance of the tent to meet them, bowed to the ground,
> 3 and said, "My lord, if I have found favor with you, please do not go on
> past your servant. 4 Let a little water be brought, that you may wash
> your feet and rest yourselves under the tree. 5 I will bring a bit of bread
> so that you may strengthen yourselves. This is why you have passed
> your servant's way. Later, you can continue on."

---

443 Deenick, *Righteous by Promise*, 34–39, observes that a strong connection exists between "walking before Yahweh" and Davidic kingship.

444 DeRouchie and Meyer, "Christ or Family," 36–48.

"Yes," they replied, "do as you have said."

6 So Abraham hurried into the tent and said to Sarah, "Quick! Knead three measures of fine flour and make bread." 7 Abraham ran to the herd and got a tender, choice calf. He gave it to a young man, who hurried to prepare it. 8 Then Abraham took curds and milk, as well as the calf that he had prepared, and set them before the men. He served them as they ate under the tree.

9 "Where is your wife Sarah?" they asked him.

"There, in the tent," he answered.

10 The LORD said, "I will certainly come back to you in about a year's time, and your wife Sarah will have a son!" Now Sarah was listening at the entrance of the tent behind him.

11 Abraham and Sarah were old and getting on in years. Sarah had passed the age of childbearing. 12 So she laughed to herself: "After I am worn out and my lord is old, will I have delight?"

13 But the LORD asked Abraham, "Why did Sarah laugh, saying, 'Can I really have a baby when I'm old?' 14 Is anything impossible for the LORD? At the appointed time I will come back to you, and in about a year she will have a son."

15 Sarah denied it. "I did not laugh," she said, because she was afraid. But he replied, "No, you did laugh."

16 The men got up from there and looked out over Sodom, and Abraham was walking with them to see them off. 17 Then the LORD said, "Should I hide what I am about to do from Abraham? 18 Abraham is to become a great and powerful nation, and all the nations of the earth will be blessed through him. 19 For I have chosen him so that he will command his children and his house after him to keep the way of the LORD by doing what is right and just. This is how the LORD will fulfill to Abraham what he promised him." 20 Then the LORD said, "The outcry against Sodom and Gomorrah is immense, and their sin is extremely serious. 21 I will go down to see if what they have done justifies the cry that has come up to me. If not, I will find out."

22 The men turned from there and went toward Sodom while Abraham remained standing before the LORD. 23 Abraham stepped forward and said, "Will you really sweep away the righteous with the wicked? 24 What if there are fifty righteous people in the city? Will you really sweep it away instead of sparing the place for the sake of the fifty righteous people who are in it? 25 You could not possibly do such a thing: to kill the righteous with the wicked, treating the righteous and the wicked alike. You could not possibly do that! Won't the Judge of the whole earth do what is just?"

26 The Lord said, "If I find fifty righteous people in the city of Sodom, I will spare the whole place for their sake."

27 Then Abraham answered, "Since I have ventured to speak to my lord—even though I am dust and ashes—28 suppose the fifty righteous lack five. Will you destroy the whole city for lack of five?"

He replied, "I will not destroy it if I find forty-five there."

29 Then he spoke to him again, "Suppose forty are found there?"

He answered, "I will not do it on account of forty."

30 Then he said, "Let my lord not be angry, and I will speak further. Suppose thirty are found there?"

He answered, "I will not do it if I find thirty there."

31 Then he said, "Since I have ventured to speak to my lord, suppose twenty are found there?"

He replied, "I will not destroy it on account of twenty."

32 Then he said, "Let my lord not be angry, and I will speak one more time. Suppose ten are found there?"

He answered, "I will not destroy it on account of ten." 33 When the Lord had finished speaking with Abraham, he departed, and Abraham returned to his place.

19:1 The two angels entered Sodom in the evening as Lot was sitting in Sodom's gateway. When Lot saw them, he got up to meet them. He bowed with his face to the ground 2 and said, "My lords, turn aside to your servant's house, wash your feet, and spend the night. Then you can get up early and go on your way."

"No," they said. "We would rather spend the night in the square." 3 But he urged them so strongly that they followed him and went into his house. He prepared a feast and baked unleavened bread for them, and they ate.

4 Before they went to bed, the men of the city of Sodom, both young and old, the whole population, surrounded the house. 5 They called out to Lot and said, "Where are the men who came to you tonight? Send them out to us so we can have sex with them!"

6 Lot went out to them at the entrance and shut the door behind him. 7 He said, "Don't do this evil, my brothers. 8 Look, I've got two daughters who haven't been intimate with a man. I'll bring them out to you, and you can do whatever you want to them. However, don't do anything to these men, because they have come under the protection of my roof."

9 "Get out of the way!" they said, adding, "This one came here as an alien, but he's acting like a judge! Now we'll do more harm to you than to

them." They put pressure on Lot and came up to break down the door.
10 But the angels reached out, brought Lot into the house with them,
and shut the door. 11 They struck the men who were at the entrance of
the house, both young and old, with blindness so that they were unable
to find the entrance.

12 Then the angels said to Lot, "Do you have anyone else here: a son-in-
law, your sons and daughters, or anyone else in the city who belongs
to you? Get them out of this place, 13 for we are about to destroy this
place because the outcry against its people is so great before the LORD,
that the LORD has sent us to destroy it."

14 So Lot went out and spoke to his sons-in-law, who were going to marry
his daughters. "Get up," he said. "Get out of this place, for the LORD is
about to destroy the city!" But his sons-in-law thought he was joking.

15 At daybreak the angels urged Lot on: "Get up! Take your wife and your
two daughters who are here, or you will be swept away in the punish-
ment of the city." 16 But he hesitated. Because of the LORD's compassion
for him, the men grabbed his hand, his wife's hand, and the hands of
his two daughters. They brought him out and left him outside the city.

17 As soon as the angels got them outside, one of them said, "Run for
your lives! Don't look back and don't stop anywhere on the plain! Run
to the mountains, or you will be swept away!"

18 But Lot said to them, "No, my lords—please. 19 Your servant has indeed
found favor with you, and you have shown me great kindness by saving my
life. But I can't run to the mountains; the disaster will overtake me, and I
will die. 20 Look, this town is close enough for me to flee to. It is a small place.
Please let me run to it—it's only a small place, isn't it?—so that I can survive."

21 And he said to him, "All right, I'll grant your request about this matter
too and will not demolish the town you mentioned. 22 Hurry up! Run to
it, for I cannot do anything until you get there." Therefore the name
of the city is Zoar.

The sun had risen over the land when Lot reached Zoar. 24 Then out of
the sky the LORD rained on Sodom and Gomorrah burning sulfur from
the LORD. 25 He demolished these cities, the entire plain, all the inhabi-
tants of the cities, and whatever grew on the ground. 26 But Lot's wife
looked back and became a pillar of salt.

27 Early in the morning Abraham went to the place where he had stood
before the LORD. 28 He looked down toward Sodom and Gomorrah and all
the land of the plain, and he saw that smoke was going up from the land
like the smoke of a furnace. 29 So it was, when God destroyed the cities of
the plain, he remembered Abraham and brought Lot out of the middle
of the upheaval when he demolished the cities where Lot had lived.

Context

The childlessness of Abraham and Sarah has been a dominant theme in the preceding episodes. With God's announcement in 17:19–21 that Sarah will bear a son within a year the reader anticipates this outcome. However, the report of Isaac's birth is delayed by the inclusion of additional episodes that focus on the rescue of Lot from the destruction of Sodom (18:1–19:29) and Sarah's abduction by the king of Gerar (20:1–18). The former event builds upon Abraham's relationship with his nephew Lot, which has already featured prominently in chapters 13–14. Once more, Abraham intervenes on behalf of his nephew to save him from disaster. Lot's rescue from Sodom leads to his descendants settling east of the Jordan River, outside the territory promised by God to Abraham. Building on the expectation that all the nations of the earth will be blessed through Abraham, chapters 18–19 illustrate his special standing in YHWH's eyes.

Comments

18:1–8. The opening words of this new episode in the life of Abraham presuppose the preceding account; a more literal translation of the Hebrew text of verse 1 would read: "and Yahweh appeared to him at the oaks of Mamre." Abraham's name is first mentioned in verse 6. Abraham has previously camped at this location (cf. 13:18).

Whereas the introduction to chapter 17 states merely that YHWH appeared to Abraham without giving any details of how this occurred (cf. 12:7), the present episode describes vividly the minutiae of their encounter. At first sight, these details appear superfluous, but their inclusion is deliberate, highlighting Abraham's generosity in graciously offering hospitality to strangers and treating them with the utmost respect. His servant-like actions are noteworthy, especially in the light of God's having designated him "the father of many nations" (17:4–5). Abraham's care for these strangers is exemplary. He ensures that they may wash their feet and then serves them a substantial meal. Everything is done with the utmost urgency.[445] This vivid portrait of Abraham will be used by the narrator when he subsequently describes

[445] The verbs רוץ (*rwṣ*, "to run") and מהר (*mhr*, "to hurry") come two and three times respectively in vv. 2, 6–7, emphasizing the haste with which everything is done. ANE readers would not expect an elderly man of Abraham's status to run when performing these tasks.

Lot's parallel behavior at the start of chapter 19. Like Abraham, Lot is hospitable to strangers. The author of Hebrews 13:2 may well have in mind these occasions.

The three strangers resemble ordinary people and Abraham treats them as such, offering them the opportunity to wash their feet and enjoy a freshly cooked meal. While the Masoretic vowel pointing of אֲדֹנָי (*ʾădōnāy*) (masculine plural construct with first person suffix) in verse 3 implies that Abraham identifies the stranger as divine (comparing 15:2, 8, where אֲדֹנָי [*ʾădōnāy*] is used in conjunction with the divine name YHWH and 20:4 where Abimelech uses it to address God), the original unpointed consonantal text could also be read as אֲדֹנִי (*ʾădōnî*) (masculine sing. construct with first person suffix) denoting a human (cf. 23:6, 11, 15; the plural form is used in 19:2 with reference to the two angels). The narrative is ambivalent as to when Abraham realizes that one of the three "men" is YHWH,[446] but the reader knows this from the start of verse 1. If Abraham did not immediately realize the special identity of those who have suddenly appeared, his generous actions are all the more praiseworthy.

18:9–16. While the "men" eat in the shade under a tree, Abraham stands nearby ready to serve them. Sarah, however, remains in the tent that is pitched close by, listening to the men's conversation. To her surprise, one of them states that within a year she will have a son (v. 10). As Abraham had done previously (17:17), Sarah laughs in disbelief. She does this inside the tent out of sight from the men, but YHWH knows how she has reacted. He challenges Abraham, possibly revealing his true identity, although this is not stated explicitly. The text remains ambivalent.[447] Although Sarah and Abraham are beyond the normal age of having a child, YHWH affirms that nothing is impossible for him. By focusing on the motif of laughter, the present episode calls to mind God's announcement that the promised son is to be named Isaac, which means "he laughs" (17:21; cf. 21:3–6). Refreshed by Abraham's

---

[446] Jean-Louis Ska, "Genesis 18:6—Intertextuality and Interpretation: 'It All Makes Flour in the Good Mill,'" in *The Exegesis of the Pentateuch: Exegetical Studies and Basic Questions*, ed. Jean-Louis Ska, FAT 66 (Tübingen: Mohr Siebeck, 2009), 89–96, helpfully highlights the "ambivalence" of vv. 1–15, which appears to be a deliberate narrative feature of the text and not the result of different sources being edited together. Cf. Ska, "The Tree and the Tent: The Function of the Scenery in Gen 18:1–15," in Ska, *Exegesis of the Pentateuch*, 82–88.

[447] As Ska, "Genesis 18:6," 93, observes, "Yahweh could have said, 'Is anything impossible for *me*?'"

hospitality, the "men" leave, going eastward in the direction of the Jordan Valley. Abraham accompanies them for a short distance.

18:17–21. The CSB translation, like most English versions, implies that YHWH's words in verses 17–19 were spoken after the men left the oaks at Mamre, but the Hebrew text at the start of verse 17 allows for the possibility that these remarks were uttered at an earlier time. Verse 17 breaks the sequence of *wayyiqtol* verbs by deliberately placing the subject YHWH prior to the *qatal* verb אָמַר (*ʾāmar*, "said"). The start of verse 17 might be better rendered: "Now the Lord had said…" (cf. NJPS).

Verses 17–21 disclose YHWH's motivation for informing Abraham about the forthcoming destruction of Sodom. First, God stresses his commitment to making Abraham into a great nation and to blessing all the nations of the earth through him, echoing not only the initial call of Abraham in 12:1–3, but also the covenants in chapters 15 and 17. Second, God emphasizes that for his purposes to be fulfilled, Abraham will need to instruct his descendants "to keep the way of the Lord by doing what is right and just" (v. 19). As Wright observes, "[I]n a remarkably tight syntax, [verse 19] binds together election, ethics, and mission as three interlocking aspects of God's purpose. His choice of Abraham is for the sake of his promise to bless the nations, but the accomplishment of God's mission demands the ethical obedience of God's community—the fulcrum in the middle of the verse."[448]

In the context of wicked people being punished for their immoral behavior, God reveals that Abraham's role is tied to the creation of a morally righteous and just world. All who share in God's purpose for Abraham will experience God's favor, a point illustrated by God's rescue of Lot from the threatened city. As the subsequent dialogue between God and Abraham demonstrates, Lot's dramatic rescue is clearly linked to his righteous behavior. God's intention to bless all the nations of the earth through Abraham takes on greater significance when viewed in the light of humanity's perverse inclination to disregard "the way of the Lord." All who look to Abraham as their spiritual father may be viewed as belonging to his "house," which includes those who are not his biological children (cf. 17:12–13, 23).

God's words emphasize that the decision to punish is not taken lightly. While the outcry against both cities is loud, due to the serious nature of their sin, God takes it upon himself to investigate. His coming down underscores the gravity of the situation and the meticulousness with

---

[448] Wright, "Reading the Old Testament Missionally," 119.

which he fulfils his role as judge. God's intention to punish Sodom comes as no surprise to the reader of Genesis, for Sodom's status as an immoral city has already been indicated in a variety of ways. Sodom and Gomorrah are named, somewhat ominously, in connection with Canaan in 10:15–19 (cf. 9:25–27). In chapter 13, the narrator records: "Now the men of Sodom were evil, sinning greatly against the LORD" (13:13). In chapter 14 the king of Sodom is compared unfavorably with Melchizedek, the king of Salem.

18:22–33. Verses 17–21 set the scene for the dialogue that comes in verse 23–32. The departure of YHWH's two companions creates an opportunity for Abraham to intercede on behalf of his nephew Lot, who resides in Sodom. Although Lot is never named in the conversation, Abraham's concern for the "righteous" within Sodom is undoubtedly motivated by his concern for Lot and his family. Later, in 19:29, Lot's rescue is linked specifically to Abraham's intercession.

Importantly, Abraham's intercession focuses on the issue of justice: will God act unjustly by punishing the righteous alongside the wicked? Mentioning the concepts of righteousness and justice, Abraham's words recall those of YHWH in verse 19. Abraham is concerned that God will act ethically. "Won't the Judge of all the earth do what is just?" asks Abraham (v. 25). His concern is striking, given that God expects Abraham to "command his children and his house after him to keep the way of the LORD by doing what is right and just" (v. 19).

Recognizing the inappropriateness of challenging God's actions as "judge of all the earth" (v. 27), Abraham presents with considerable boldness various scenarios, involving ever reducing numbers of righteous people, from fifty to ten. God's responses consistently reveal that in punishing the wicked, he is not prepared to take the lives of the righteous. If as few as ten righteous people are found in the city, Sodom will not be destroyed. However, the subsequent episode reveals that only three people respond positively to the warning given by the two angels: Lot and his two daughters. Others are encouraged to flee from the city before it is destroyed, but they disregard this advice.

19:1–3. YHWH's two companions arrive at Sodom in the evening, having left the oaks of Mamre some hours previously. For the first time in the narrative they are identified as "angels" (cf. v. 15).[449] Lot, who is

---

[449] The Hebrew term מַלְאָךְ (*malʾāk*) is often used to denote a divinely appointed messenger. The term is used of both human and heavenly messengers.

sitting at the entrance to the city, sees them and, like Abraham, offers them hospitality, even though the men express a preference to spending the night in an open space within the city. The details of the story deliberately echo the start of chapter 18, revealing that Lot's actions mirror those of Abraham.[450] Lot's hospitality is an important pointer to his righteousness.[451] While both men display remarkable generosity to strangers, subtle variations between the two accounts may be significant. Verse 3 states that Lot baked "unleavened bread," suggesting perhaps that this meal was not quite on a par with the one prepared by Abraham. And whereas Sarah assists Abraham in preparing a substantial meal, Lot's wife is not mentioned. Her absence at this stage possibly anticipates what will happen to her later in the chapter (cf. v. 26).

19:4–11. The crowd that surrounds Lot's house comprises all the men of Sodom, both young and old. Ominously, they demand that Lot should hand over to them his two guests so that they may abuse them sexually. The horrific nature of their request testifies to their wickedness. Here is a society that approves of and participates in male rape.

Their determination to abuse the two strangers becomes very evident when they reject Lot's attempt to dissuade them. Knowing that the men of Sodom will not be easily deterred, Lot offers his two virgin daughters in place of the visitors. Given the choices open to him when faced with a hostile crowd, Lot probably views this as the lesser of two evils. Perhaps he hopes that the men of Sodom will renege and not harm either his daughters or the men. While it would have been easy and understandable for Lot to acquiesce in the face of the hostile mob, he nevertheless puts strangers before family.

While there is good reason to be troubled by Lot's response to the moral dilemma confronting him (and Lot himself may have been greatly troubled), we should not lose sight of the much greater evil being perpetrated by the men of Sodom. It is their heinous behavior that places Lot in this invidious situation. Moreover, Lot's stance on behalf of the visitors endangers his own well-being; the men of Sodom threaten to harm him more than the men he is defending (v. 9). Labeling him a "resident

---

[450] See B. Uffenheimer, "Genesis 18–19, A New Approach," in *Mélanges André Neher*, ed. E. A. Levy-Valense (Paris: A. Maisonneuve, 1975), 145–53; Van Seters, *Abraham in History and Tradition*, 216.

[451] This is highlighted in 2 Pet 2:6–8; see T. Desmond Alexander, "Lot's Hospitality: A Clue to His Righteousness," *JBL* 104 (1985): 289–91.

foreigner," the men of Sodom denounce Lot for judging them. Lot is not one of them and he has no right to condemn their actions. As the crowd surges toward the entrance to Lot's house, the two visitors come to Lot's aid by striking blind the assailants.

19:12–14. The men reveal to Lot the purpose of their journey to the city. They confirm that God has condemned the city to destruction because of its wickedness. They encourage Lot to warn those related to him. However, when Lot tells his future sons-in-law, they dismiss his warning with laughter.

19:15–22. The next morning the angels urge Lot to flee from the city because of its imminent destruction. When Lot is reluctant to leave, as an act of divine mercy the men physically drag him and his immediate family out of the city. Once more, they encourage Lot to get away as quickly as possible from Sodom for the entire plain is about to be decimated by fire. When they instruct Lot to flee to the mountains that surround the plain (v. 17), Lot petitions them to let him take refuge in a smaller city near to Sodom. In making this request courteously, Lot acknowledges the kindness that the men have already shown him. He then expresses his fear that he will not be able to get to the mountains before the valley is destroyed. Lot refers to the town as being מִצְעָר (*miṣʿar*, "small"); it subsequently gets the name צֹעַר (*ṣōʿar*, "Zoar").

19:23–26. As Lot reaches the safety of Zoar, God's punishment in the form of burning sulfur descends upon Sodom and Gomorrah. The destruction is total; nothing survives. And Lot's wife, disregarding the angel's instruction (v. 17), looks back with disastrous consequences (cf. Luke 17:32).

19:27–29. After describing what has happened to Lot, verses 27–29 focus briefly on Abraham, who has returned to the location where he had discussed with YHWH the fate of the righteous in Sodom. Viewing the scene, Abraham sees smoke ascending from the valley. By way of confirmation, the narrator associates the rescue of Lot with Abraham's intercession before YHWH on behalf of the righteous (cf. 18:22–33).

Bridge

The account of Lot's rescue from the city of Sodom is a stark reminder that human wickedness will not go unpunished. The destruction of Sodom and the other cities of the Jordan plain is frequently mentioned in the rest of the Bible as a warning to others concerning the reality of divine judgment (see Isa 3:9; Jer 23:14; Lam 4:6; Zeph 2:9; Luke 17:28–32; 2 Pet 2:6;

Jude 7). The unrepentant wicked cannot expect to escape God's punishment. However, Abraham's intervention on behalf of Lot underlines his importance as the father of many nations.

Lot's concern for the well-being of the two men who arrive at Sodom sets him apart from the other inhabitants of the city. Strikingly, his reception of the strangers parallels Abraham's hospitality, if to a lesser degree. The hospitable nature of both men, marked by generosity to strangers, is a sign of their righteous character (see 2 Pet 2:7–8). The author of Hebrew possibly alludes to the events of 18:1–19:29 when he remarks: "Don't neglect to show hospitality, for by doing this some have welcomed angels as guests without knowing it" (Heb 13:2).

J. Lot and His Daughters (19:30–38)

> 30 Lot departed from Zoar and lived in the mountains along with his
> two daughters, because he was afraid to live in Zoar. Instead, he and
> his two daughters lived in a cave. 31 Then the firstborn said to the
> younger, "Our father is old, and there is no man in the land to sleep
> with us as is the custom of all the land. 32 Come, let's get our father to
> drink wine so that we can sleep with him and preserve our father's
> line." 33 So they got their father to drink wine that night, and the
> firstborn came and slept with her father; he did not know when she
> lay down or when she got up.
>
> 34 The next day the firstborn said to the younger, "Look, I slept with
> my father last night. Let's get him to drink wine again tonight so
> you can go sleep with him and we can preserve our father's line."
> 35 That night they again got their father to drink wine, and the
> younger went and slept with him; he did not know when she lay
> down or when she got up.
>
> 36 So both of Lot's daughters became pregnant by their father. 37 The
> firstborn gave birth to a son and named him Moab. He is the father
> of the Moabites of today. 38 The younger also gave birth to a son, and
> she named him Ben-ammi. He is the father of the Ammonites of today.

Context

Prior to the imminent destruction of Sodom, the two messengers/angels had instructed Lot to flee to the hills/mountains (19:17). Fearful, however, that he would perish before reaching safety, Lot asked to flee to the smaller settlement of Zoar (19:18–22). At some stage after arriving there, Lot decides to heed the messengers/angels' instructions and relocate to the hills/mountains. Perhaps he fears that Zoar will suffer a fate like that of Sodom and Gomorrah. Consequently, Lot and his two daughters take up residence in an isolated cave.

Their departure from Zoar has significant implications for the women, who now find themselves contemplating the possibility that they will never be married and bear children. Motivated by the desire to provide offspring in order to continue Lot's family line, the women deviously get their father drunk so that they may have intercourse with him.

Ironically, Lot's treatment at the hands of his daughters recalls his willingness to hand them over to the men of Sodom (19:8). While their motivation is understandable, their actions reflect something of the moral depravity that had prompted God to destroy the cities of the valley. In this instance, the end does not justify the means. Their method of providing offspring, involving drunkenness and incest, invites condemnation. In the light of how the book of Genesis is interested in a righteous "offspring of the woman," Lot's sons are unlikely to be suitable candidates.

Comments

19:30–35. Fearful that they will be left childless, Lot's older daughter plots with her younger sibling to seduce their father when he is intoxicated. The brief description of what happens suggests that the daughters are fully responsible for what happens; Lot himself is oblivious to the fact that his daughter slept with him.[452] According to the twice repeated comment of the older sister (vv. 32, 34), their actions are intended to provide their father with זֶרַע (*zeraʿ*,"offspring"). In the context of Genesis as a whole, these references to "offspring/seed" are noteworthy. However, while the continuation of the family line is important, the means by which Lot's offspring are conceived are most inappropriate. While his future descendants will be related to the Israelites, their unseemly origins will influence how they are viewed by later generations of Israelites.

19:36–38. The names given to the two boys possibly hint at the incestuous nature of what has occurred. "Moab" resembles the Hebrew expression מֵאָבִינוּ (*mēʾābînû*, "from our father") (see vv. 32, 34). The name בֶּן־עַמִּי (*ben-ʿammî*) means "son of my people." The biblical traditions associated with the Moabites and Ammonites, Lot's descendants, tend to portray

[452] The narrator's repeated remark that Lot "did not know" (vv. 33, 35) what had happened is somewhat ironic given that the Hebrew verb יָדַע (*yādaʿ*, "to know") sometimes denotes sexual relations (cf. especially 19:8, where Lot uses the verb with reference to his daughters being virgins).

both nations negatively (e.g., Num 23–25; Deut 23:3–5[4–6 Heb]; 2 Kgs 3).[453] This tradition about the origin of the Moabites may well have colored how the people of Bethlehem viewed Ruth, a Moabitess (Ruth 1:3–4; 2:10; 4:5–6).

Bridge

This brief episode concerning the birth of sons to Lot's daughters is the last mention of Lot in Genesis. Lot and his family are now located outside the land of Canaan, separated from Abraham's household. While Abraham has had a significant role to play to ensure the survival of his nephew, the Genesis narrator will now focus on the birth of a son and heir to Abraham and Sarah.

K. Abimelech Takes Sarah to Be His Wife (20:1–18)

> [1] From there Abraham traveled to the region of the Negev and settled
> between Kadesh and Shur. While he was staying in Gerar, [2] Abraham
> said about his wife Sarah, "She is my sister." So King Abimelech of Gerar
> had Sarah brought to him.
>
> [3] But God came to Abimelech in a dream by night and said to him, "You
> are about to die because of the woman you have taken, for she is a
> married woman."
>
> [4] Now Abimelech had not approached her, so he said, "Lord, would you
> destroy a nation even though it is innocent? [5] Didn't he himself say to
> me, 'She is my sister'? And she herself said, 'He is my brother.' I did this
> with a clear conscience and clean hands."
>
> [6] Then God said to him in the dream, "Yes, I know that you did this with
> a clear conscience. I have also kept you from sinning against me. Therefore I have not let you touch her. [7] Now return the man's wife, for he is
> a prophet, and he will pray for you and you will live. But if you do not
> return her, know that you will certainly die, you and all who are yours."
>
> [8] Early in the morning Abimelech got up, called all his servants together,
> and personally told them all these things, and the men were terrified.

[453] A noteworthy exception is Ruth. While a Moabitess by birth, she expresses the desire to be viewed as an Israelite, who is loyal to Yahweh (Ruth 1:16–17). For a fuller discussion of the Moabites and Ammonites, see Gerald L. Mattingly, "Moabites," in *Peoples of the Old Testament World*, ed. Alfred J. Hoerth, Gerald L. Mattingly, and Edwin M. Yamauchi (Cambridge: Lutterworth, 1996), 317–34; Randall W. Younker, "Ammonites," in Hoerth, Mattingly, and Yamauchi, eds., *Peoples of the Old Testament World*, 293–316; Joel S. Burnett, "Transjordan: The Ammonites, Moabites, and Edomites," in *The World around the Old Testament: The People and Places of the Ancient Near East*, ed. Bill T. Arnold and Brent A. Strawn (Grand Rapids: Baker Academic, 2016), 309–52.

[9] Then Abimelech called Abraham in and said to him, "What have you done
to us? How did I sin against you that you have brought such enormous guilt
on me and on my kingdom? You have done things to me that should never
be done." [10] Abimelech also asked Abraham, "What made you do this?"

[11] Abraham replied, "I thought, 'There is absolutely no fear of God in
this place. They will kill me because of my wife.' [12] Besides, she really
is my sister, the daughter of my father though not the daughter of my
mother, and she became my wife. [13] So when God had me wander from
my father's house, I said to her: Show your loyalty to me wherever we
go and say about me: 'He's my brother.' "

[14] Then Abimelech took flocks and herds and male and female slaves, gave
them to Abraham, and returned his wife Sarah to him. [15] Abimelech said,
"Look, my land is before you. Settle wherever you want." [16] And he said to
Sarah, "Look, I am giving your brother one thousand pieces of silver. It is a
verification of your honor to all who are with you. You are fully vindicated."

[17] Then Abraham prayed to God, and God healed Abimelech, his wife,
and his female slaves so that they could bear children, [18] for the LORD had
completely closed all the wombs in Abimelech's household on account
of Sarah, Abraham's wife.

Context

After recording the divine deliverance of Lot from the wicked city of Sodom, the narrative focuses again on Abraham and Sarah. At this stage in Genesis, the reader expects that God's promises regarding the birth of a son to Sarah in 17:16–21 and 18:10–14 will soon be fulfilled. However, a critical complication arises that threatens to prevent Sarah from bearing Abraham a child. For no obvious reason, Abraham relocates his household southward to the region of Gerar (20:1). This sets the scene for what follows. Appearing not to have learnt from this experience in Egypt, Abraham pretends in Gerar that Sarah is his sister.[454] Sarah is then taken by Abimelech, king of Gerar, to be his wife. Only God's swift intervention rescues the situation, ensuring that Abimelech does not have intimate relations with Sarah. This resolves the crisis created by Abraham's actions, ensuring that all is in place for God to fulfil his promise of a son to the elderly couple.

---

[454] Later, in circumstances that are somewhat similar, Isaac also pretends in Gerar that his wife is his sister (26:1–11). For a fuller discussion of the relationship between these wife-sister episodes in Genesis, see Alexander, "The Wife/Sister Incidents of Genesis," 2–22; Alexander, "Are the Wife/Sister Incidents of Genesis Literary Compositional Variants?," 145–53; Alexander, *Abraham in the Negev*, 32–51; Kang, *Reading the Wife/Sister Narratives.*

Comments

20:1–2. No reason is offered for Abraham's relocation southward to the Negev, although years earlier Abraham had traveled to this region before going into Egypt (12:9–10).[455] Presumably, "from there" refers to the oaks of Mamre (18:1; cf. 18:16, 33). The transition to Gerar means that Abraham and Sarah are unknown to the local population. Consequently, the king of Gerar is unaware that Sarah is Abraham's wife. The name "Abimelech" means "my father is king." Since it was a common West Semitic royal name (cf., e.g., Judg 8:31; Ps 34:title [Heb. 1]), the Abimelech of chapter 26 could be a son or grandson of the king who appears in this chapter. Possibly, Abimelech was the throne name adopted by the kings of Gerar.

On its own, verse 2 offers no explanation as to why Abraham should declare that Sarah is his sister, creating the opportunity for Abimelech to take her. Importantly, this very brief description of Sarah's abduction presupposes that the reader is already familiar with the earlier wife-sister deception in 12:10–20 and the fuller reason for its purpose recorded there (12:11–13). While the reader of Genesis requires no repeat explanation at the start of chapter 20 for Abraham's action, the patriarch will later explain to the unsuspecting Abimelech the reason for the deception (v. 11).

In the chronology of the narrative, Sarah is ninety-nine years old and beyond the age of bearing children (cf. 17:17; 18:11–13). Whereas in 12:11–13 Abraham emphasizes her beauty as a reason for her possible abduction, no mention is made of her appearance in the present context. Mathews speculates that Abimelech may have been motivated to take Sarah in order to forge "an economic relationship with the Abraham clan."[456] Perhaps Abimelech sought an additional concubine to enhance his prestige as a king.

20:3–7. The presence of a definite article before the noun לַיְלָה (*lāylâ*, "night") probably implies that God appeared to Abimelech on the very night that Sarah was taken. The timing of God's intervention is significant, for it supports the narrator's claim that Abimelech does not have intercourse with Sarah. This fact, which is mentioned several times in the passage, is especially important in the light of Sarah becoming pregnant and bearing Isaac (20:1–3). The narrative of chapter 20 rules out any possibility that Abimelech might be the father of Isaac. By way of

[455] The Hebrew term נֶגֶב (*negeb*) denotes "south."

[456] Mathews, *Genesis 11:27–50:26*, 251.

contrast, the earlier episode in chapter 12 lacks any clear statement that Pharaoh did not sleep with Sarah. Most of the noteworthy variations that exist between the similar accounts in 12:10–20 and 20:1–18 are due to the necessity of demonstrating clearly that Sarah did not have intercourse with the king of Gerar.

God intervenes in a very personal way with Abimelech by speaking to him in a dream.[457] The record of their brief conversation highlights the issue of Abimelech's innocence. Had he been aware of Sarah's marital status, he would have acted otherwise, for Abimelech acknowledges that adultery is a great sin (v. 9). In his defense, Abimelech claims that both Abraham and Sarah colluded in the deception (v. 5). In the light of this, he raises the issue of divine justice: would God destroy an innocent nation? Ironically, the form of his question recalls both Abraham's intercession on behalf of Lot (18:23–32), and God's comment that "all the nations of the earth will be blessed" through Abraham (18:18). Responding to Abimelech, God invites him to demonstrate his innocence by returning Sarah to Abraham.

While God prevents Abimelech from committing adultery, it seems likely that Abimelech has taken Sarah without putting in place any formal marriage arrangement. From what is recorded, we should probably assume that he took Sarah to be an additional concubine.[458]

Interestingly, in addressing Abimelech, God refers to Abraham as a "prophet" (v. 7),[459] whose prayers will be effective in bringing blessing to others. The Hebrew verb פלל (*pll*) translated "pray" (vv. 7, 17) is not used widely in the Hebrew Bible, but when it occurs it often has the sense of intercede on behalf of another (e.g., Num 11:2; 21:7; Deut 9:20, 26).[460] This idea recalls the part that Abraham plays when he intercedes with God concerning Lot in chapter 18. Abraham's role as a prophet is linked to the divine promise that through him all the nations of the earth will be blessed (18:18; cf. 12:3).

---

[457] The use of a dream implies that Abimelech did not experience the presence of God as intimately as Hagar did when the 'angel of the Lord' appeared to her (16:7–14).

[458] Verse 17 refers to Abimelech's wife and female slaves. Only one wife is mentioned. The Hebrew term אַמְהֹתָיו (*amhōtāyw*, "female slaves") probably denotes concubines.

[459] This is the first reference in the Bible to a prophet.

[460] Intercessory prayer is not limited to prophets. However, they may have been expected to pray on behalf of others. In Jer 7:16, 11:14 and 14:11, God prohibits the prophet Jeremiah from "praying" for others.

20:8–13. God's intervention prompts an immediate response from Abimelech. When he tells his closest officials, they are "very much afraid" (NIV, NJB, NRSV). Their fearful reaction is noteworthy in the light of Abraham's subsequent comment in verse 11, for Abraham believed that the people of Gerar did not fear God. The attitude of Abimelech and his officials suggests otherwise. This, however, does not mean that they are worshipers of YHWH, like Abraham.

Addressing Abraham, Abimelech challenges the patriarch for having brought on the king and his kingdom "a great sin" (v. 9), implying the sin of adultery.[461] As Alter observes, "Abimelech vehemently castigates Abraham (with good reason), and Abraham stands silent, not knowing what to say. And so Abimelech repeats his upbraiding, in shorter form (verse 10)."[462]

Abraham's explanation to Abimelech is constructed on three pillars. First, Abraham was fearful that he would be killed by someone desiring his wife. This expectation rests on the premise that those living in the region of Gerar have low moral standards. Second, Abraham looks to justify his actions by claiming that he did not lie to Abimelech. In saying that Sarah was his sister, Abraham claims that he spoke the truth. This rests on the assertion that Sarah is his half-sister.[463] Third, Abraham attempts to justify his behavior by claiming that what he did was not out of the ordinary; he adopted this tactic on a regular basis. While Abraham looks to justify himself to Abimelech, his explanation, like his action, lacks integrity. It is unfairly judgmental, for he assumes that the population of Gerar is morally corrupt. It is self-centered, for he is primarily interested in preserving his own life. He does not appear to be worried about endangering his marital relationship with Sarah and jeopardizing the possibility that she will bear him a son, as promised by God (17:16–21; 18:10–14). It is a half-truth, for in claiming that Sarah is his sister he omits to say that she is also his wife. In addition, Abraham's

---

461 The expression "great sin" is used in several ANE documents with reference to adultery. Cf. Jacob J. Rabinowitz, "The 'Great Sin' in Ancient Egyptian Marriage Contracts," *JNES* 18 (1959): 73; W. L. Moran, "The Scandal of the 'Great Sin' at Ugarit," *JNES* 18 (1959): 280–81.

462 Alter, *Genesis*, 94.

463 The veracity of this claim is difficult to judge, for Sarah's genealogical information is not recorded in Genesis. Victor P. Hamilton, *The Book of Genesis: Chapters 18–50*, NICOT (Grand Rapids: Eerdmans, 1995), 68, allows for the possibility that Abraham's assertion may be a "total fabrication." The Levitical legislation associated with the Sinai covenant prohibited intercourse with a half-sister (Lev 18:9, 11; cf. Deut 27:22; 2 Sam 13:12; Ezek 22:11), suggesting that this tradition concerning Abraham marrying his sister is ancient.

words reflect a lack of trust in God's power to safeguard him and his family in order that the divine promises may be fulfilled. If we compare Abraham's words (vv. 11–13) with those of Abimelech (vv. 4–5), the latter is portrayed more positively. This contrast is striking in the light of God's expectation that Abraham is to "command his children and his household after him to keep the way of the Lord by doing righteousness and justice" (18:19). Yet despite his apparent shortcomings, Abraham retains the status of "prophet" in God's eyes (v. 7).

While the author of Genesis does not directly condemn Abraham's actions, the wording of verse 13 may imply a criticism. Although it is not immediately apparent in most English translations, the Hebrew text contains an unusual anomaly in that the verb associated with the subject "God" is in the plural. Normally, throughout the Old Testament verbs used with reference to God are in the singular.[464] In the light of this, it might be more natural to interpret Abraham's words as saying "when gods caused me to wander from my father's house ..."[465] Having been found out, Abraham may have been fearful of Abimelech's reaction.

20:14–18. Abimelech's response to Abraham's explanation is surprising. Not only does he return Sarah to her husband, as might be expected, but also he gives Abraham "sheep and cattle and male and female slaves." Then, in contrast to the action of Pharaoh in Egypt (12:19–20), he offers Abraham the opportunity to settle wherever he wishes in the territory of Gerar. Finally, focusing on Sarah, he gives "1,000 pieces of silver," an exceptionally large sum, to Abraham, whom he calls "her brother" (v. 16), in order to vindicate Sarah in the eyes of everyone who knows her.[466] Abimelech's generosity is noteworthy, especially in the light of how Abraham and Sarah have deceived him. As Holmgren remarks:

---

[464] There are only two other examples in Genesis where a plural verb is used with the subject אֱלֹהִים (*ʾĕlōhîm*): 31:53 and 35:7. In the first of these instances, the context supports the meaning "gods" and not "God."

[465] See Andrew J. Schmutzer, "Did the Gods Cause Abraham's Wandering? An Examination of התעו אתי אלהים in Genesis 20.13," *JSOT* 35 (2010): 149–66. Recognizing the unusual use of a plural verb, Waltke and Fredricks, *Genesis*, 287, suggests that the root might be *ʿwh*, rather than *tʿh*. Perhaps Abraham's choice of the plural verb is influenced by his belief that Abimelech is a polytheist.

[466] The Hebrew text uses the idiom כְּסוּת עֵינַיִם (*kĕsût ʿênayim*, "a covering of the eyes") to describe the purpose of the money given by Abimelech to Abraham. The precise meaning of this idiom is unclear, but the context would imply that the gift is intended to assure others that Sarah has not had intercourse with Abimelech.

> The picture painted of Abimelech in this narrative speaks of one who is guided by high moral standards. Though he was deceived by both Abraham and Sarah when he took Sarah into his household, he knows that his action inflicted a serious wound upon Sarah and her marriage. *Something happened that should not have taken place.* There must be public recognition of this act and action taken to provide healing. ... The taking of a wife from someone was a serious crime in the ancient world, for ... she was a sexual partner who would bear children and give future to her husband. ... A part of the restoration of Sarah to Abraham included providing for her public vindication by paying Abraham, the "victimized" husband, a sum of money (v. 16). In addition, however, the king went far beyond what was necessary and demonstrated great generosity by allowing the Hebrew couple to settle wherever they pleased in his land and giving sheep, oxen, and slaves to Abraham.[467]

After describing Abimelech's vindication of Sarah, the narrator concludes the episode by focusing on the infertility of Abimelech's wife and female slaves (or concubines) (vv. 17–18). Divine punishment has come upon the king and his household as a result of taking Sarah, but this detail has been hidden from the reader until the end of the episode. "By delaying the information until verse 18, the author highlights Story B's (20:1–18) distinctive theme compared with Story A (12:10–13:1): fertility and infertility are in the hands of God."[468] The final verses of chapter 20 create an interesting bridge with the opening verses of chapter 21, which record how God enables Sarah to become pregnant.

Bridge

This episode in the life of Abraham and Sarah takes on added significance in the light of God's promise that Sarah will bear Abraham a son, Isaac, through whom will continue the patriline that begins with Adam and

---

[467] F. C. Holmgren, "Looking Back on Abraham's Encounter with a Canaanite King: A Reversal of Expectations (Genesis 20:1–18)," *Currents in Theology and Mission* 37 (2010): 371. As Waltke and Fredricks, *Genesis*, 287, comment, Abimelech "protects Sarah's honor." Like Holmgren, Waltke and Fredricks view Abimelech as a Canaanite; they describe him as a 'God-fearing Canaanite king' (*Genesis*, 289). Although Holmgren marshals support for his belief that Abimelech was a Canaanite, in 26:1, Abimelech is identified as a Philistine. According to 15:19–21, the Canaanites were only one of various ethnic groups resident in the region of Palestine. Abimelech should not be categorized as a righteous Canaanite. Holmgren fails to see how Genesis in the main portrays the Canaanites negatively, with only a few exceptions (e.g., Tamar in ch. 38).

[468] Kang, *Reading the Wife/Sister Narratives*, 115.

Eve. Sarah's abduction by the king of Gerar threatens the fulfilment of God's promise that she would bear a son to Abraham. Yet, this episode introduces an interesting twist in the storyline. The continuation of the family line is put in jeopardy by the inappropriate actions of Abraham and Sarah. Although Abimelech takes Sarah to be part of his household, he is ignorant of her marital status. Through all that is recorded, Abimelech appears more righteous than Abraham. Yet, ironically, Abraham will be the one through whom God will bring blessing to the nations. Despite Abraham's lack of trust in God, God does not abandon his commitment to Abraham. And in the resolution, we see Abraham, as a prophet, being a source of blessing to those who are not part of his household.

L. Isaac Becomes Abraham's Heir (21:1–21)

> 1 The Lord came to Sarah as he had said, and the Lord did for Sarah what
> he had promised. 2 Sarah became pregnant and bore a son to Abraham
> in his old age, at the appointed time God had told him. 3 Abraham
> named his son who was born to him—the one Sarah bore to him—Isaac.
> 4 When his son Isaac was eight days old, Abraham circumcised him, as
> God had commanded him. 5 Abraham was a hundred years old when
> his son Isaac was born to him.
>
> 6 Sarah said, "God has made me laugh, and everyone who hears will
> laugh with me." 7 She also said, "Who would have told Abraham that Sar-
> ah would nurse children? Yet I have borne a son for him in his old age."
>
> 8 The child grew and was weaned, and Abraham held a great feast on
> the day Isaac was weaned. 9 But Sarah saw the son mocking—the one
> Hagar the Egyptian had borne to Abraham. 10 So she said to Abraham,
> "Drive out this slave with her son, for the son of this slave will not be a
> coheir with my son Isaac!"
>
> 11 This was very distressing to Abraham because of his son. 12 But God
> said to Abraham, "Do not be distressed about the boy and about your
> slave. Whatever Sarah says to you, listen to her, because your offspring
> will be traced through Isaac, 13 and I will also make a nation of the slave's
> son because he is your offspring."
>
> 14 Early in the morning Abraham got up, took bread and a waterskin,
> put them on Hagar's shoulders, and sent her and the boy away. She
> left and wandered in the Wilderness of Beer-sheba. 15 When the water
> in the skin was gone, she left the boy under one of the bushes 16 and
> went and sat at a distance, about a bowshot away, for she said, "I can't
> bear to watch the boy die!" While she sat at a distance, she wept loudly.

[17] God heard the boy crying, and the angel of God called to Hagar from heaven and said to her, "What's wrong, Hagar? Don't be afraid, for God has heard the boy crying from the place where he is. [18] Get up, help the boy up, and grasp his hand, for I will make him a great nation." [19] Then God opened her eyes, and she saw a well. So she went and filled the waterskin and gave the boy a drink. [20] God was with the boy, and he grew; he settled in the wilderness and became an archer. [21] He settled in the Wilderness of Paran, and his mother got a wife for him from the land of Egypt.

Context

At the outset of the Terah *tôlĕdôt*, Sarah's barrenness has stood as a substantial barrier to the fulfilment of the divine promises given to Abraham (11:30). Sarah herself has attempted to overcome this problem by giving her Egyptian servant, Hagar, to Abraham to be a surrogate mother (16:1–2). As a result, Hagar gives birth to a son, whom Abraham names Ishmael (16:15; cf. 16:11). In Abraham's eyes, Ishmael is his son and heir. However, Ishmael is not the son intended by God. Subsequently, God promises Abraham on two separate occasions that Sarah will bear him a son (17:16–21; 18:10–14). When Sarah is taken from Abraham's household by Abimelech, God intervenes, ensuring that she remains Abraham's wife (20:1–18). Finally, as God promised, Sarah gives birth to Isaac (21:1–2). This is clearly an exceptionally important development in the Genesis narrative; the patriline will be traced through Isaac. Yet, his birth introduces a new tension into the story. Abraham already has a son through Hagar. In the light of this, Sarah seeks confirmation that her son, Isaac, will be Abraham's heir. This results in the expulsion of Hagar and Ishmael from Abraham's household. These developments are narrated in 21:1–21.

Comments

21:1–2. A new episode begins in 21:1 and the wording in Hebrew has a poetic ring as the second half of verse 1 parallels the first half of the verse, but with variation in wording. By putting the subject YHWH before the first verb, the Hebrew text emphasizes how YHWH does for Sarah what he had promised (17:16–21; 18:10–14). God is true to his word. Through YHWH's involvement, Sarah becomes pregnant and gives birth to a son. For a third time in these opening verses the narrator highlights in verse 2 that this occurs as God had said. God makes possible what to others seemed impossible. Brief reference is made to Abraham's age in verse 2; a fuller comment comes in verse 5 and it is mentioned again in verse 7. The term לַמּוֹעֵד (*lammôʿēd*, "at the appointed time") recalls the specific promises made by God in 17:21 and 18:14.

21:3–7. By a careful choice of words the narrator stresses that this son belongs to Abraham; he is "*his son*, the one born *to him*, whom Sarah bore *to him*" (v. 3).[469] The importance of Isaac as Abraham's son is underlined further with "his son" being repeated after the name Isaac in verses 4 and 5.[470] Everything points to Isaac being Abraham's heir: Abraham names him and circumcises him, as God had commanded (17:12, 19). To underline the unexpected nature of the birth from a human perspective, the narrator informs the reader that Abraham is a hundred years old (v. 5); he was 99 years old when God promised Isaac (17:1, 24). At this stage, Sarah is about 90 years old (cf. 17:17). Given her age, Sarah speaks of the laughter that God has given her and others through the birth of Isaac. In doing so, she deliberately creates two wordplays on the name Isaac, which means "he laughs."[471]

21:8–13. The narrative moves swiftly from the birth of Isaac to his weaning, which is marked by a family celebration (cf. 1 Sam 1:22–25). By this stage, Isaac is possibly about three years old.[472] However, the laughter associated with Isaac's birth into Abraham's household is not shared by everyone. Through a further wordplay on the name Isaac, the narrator reveals that Hagar's son mocks Isaac.[473]

While the nature of Ishmael's exact action is unclear, his behavior is sufficient to alarm Sarah, who asks Abraham to send away Hagar and her son. Coats writes, "The threat of Ishmael throughout the narrative is that he would replace Sarah's son ... as the heir of Abraham. Now the wordplay so crucial for the whole story sets out the weight of

---

[469] Gordon J. Wenham, *Genesis 16–50*, WBC 2 (Dallas: Word, 1994), 80, observes, in the light of 16:15, that "who was born to him" is unnecessary, but its inclusion "serves to drive home the miraculous nature of the birth of a son to Sarah."

[470] In vv. 4 and 5 it would have been possible for the narrator to omit "his son" without making the text incomprehensible.

[471] The name Isaac in Hebrew is יִצְחָק (*yiṣḥāq*). The Hebrew text of Sarah's words in 21:6 read: צְחֹק עָשָׂה לִי אֱלֹהִים כָּל־הַשֹּׁמֵעַ יִצְחַק־לִי (*ṣĕḥōq ʿāśâ lî ʾĕlōhîm kol-haššōmēaʿ yiṣḥaq-lî*). The motif of laughter is also linked to the name Isaac in 17:17; 18:12–15; 21:9.

[472] Wenham, *Genesis 16–50*, 81; Waltke and Fredricks, *Genesis*, 293.

[473] The *piel* form of the verb צחק (*ṣḥq*) is used in v. 9, but the *qal* form is used in v. 6. Other examples of the *piel* form of the verb צחק (*ṣḥq*) suggest that it may convey a sense of mocking or ridicule (cf., e.g., 19:14; 39:14, 17). Cf. Wenham, *Genesis 16–50*, 82; Mathews, *Genesis 11:27–50:26*, 268–69. The apostle Paul in Gal 4:29, referring to this event, claims that Ishmael "persecuted" (ἐδίωκεν, *ediōken*) Isaac.

the conflict. It does not imply that Ishmael has done something amiss with Isaac. It suggests on the contrary, that Sarah saw Ishmael *mĕṣaḥēq*, playing the role of Isaac."[474]

Strikingly, the name Ishmael is never used by the narrator in verses 8–21. He is referred to as the son of Hagar the Egyptian, Abraham's slave/servant.[475] This designation underlines that his status within the family is not the same as Isaac's. Unlike Isaac, he is not the son of Abraham's first wife Sarah. In the light of Ishmael's mocking of Isaac, Sarah wants to ensure that he will not inherit with her son Isaac.[476]

Abraham, however, is reluctant to heed Sarah's request (v. 11). Abraham is Ishmael's biological father and he had previously considered him a suitable heir (17:18). Moreover, when Hagar, during her pregnancy, had run away from Abraham's household, the angel of the Lord had commanded her to return despite Sarah's mistreatment of her (16:9). Abraham had grounds for believing that Ishmael should remain part of his household. Influenced by these factors, Abraham is very displeased by Sarah's request.

God, however, intervenes, instructing Abraham to obey Sarah. By way of reassuring Abraham, God offers two guarantees. First, he tells Abraham that his offspring (זֶרַע, *zeraʿ*) will be continued through Isaac. This statement is significance in the light of Genesis as a whole, as the narrator traces the unique line of offspring that will lead to the one who will overcome the serpent (3:15; see Biblical and Theological Themes §1).[477] Second, he promises Abraham that Ishmael will become a nation (v. 13; cf. 17:20). This guarantee is notable, because God had covenanted with Abraham that he would be the father of many nations (17:4–6). While the unique line of offspring will not continue through Ishmael, nevertheless

[474] George W. Coats, *Genesis with an Introduction to Narrative Literature*, FOTL 1 (Grand Rapids: Eerdmans, 1983), 153.

[475] Hagar is designated an אָמָה (*ʾāmâ*, "servant/concubine") in this episode. She is a second wife to Abraham, but of lower status compared to Sarah. A similar distinction is implied in 20:17 involving Abimelech's household.

[476] Yoo, "Hagar the Egyptian," 225–26, draws on the Laws of Hammurabi §§170–171 to illustrate how the children of a slave woman might, or might not, inherit "property of the paternal estate" alongside the children of a man's "first-ranking wife." As the firstborn son of Abraham, Ishmael might possibly have expected to receive a double portion of the inheritance.

[477] God's comments about Abraham's offspring being reckoned through Isaac are quoted in Hebrews 11:18 in the context of discussing Abraham's willingness to offer up Isaac as a sacrifice when tested by God.

God will make his descendants numerous. In a similar vein, the angel of YHWH had previously told Hagar that her descendants would be "too many to count" (16:10).

21:14–19. The opening words of verse 14 imply that Abraham responded to God's instructions as soon as possible. With the new morning, Abraham sends off Hagar and Ishmael. In doing this, he provides some sustenance in the form of food and water, which Hagar places on her shoulders.

Unfortunately, some commentators assume that Abraham also places Ishmael on her shoulders,[478] but the Hebrew text implies merely that Ishmael accompanied her. Taking into consideration the present literary context of this episode, Ishmael is about sixteen years old when Isaac is weaned.[479] In keeping with this, God refers to Ishmael as a נַעַר (*naʿar*) (vv. 12, 17–18).[480] In Genesis this Hebrew noun "usually refers to young men capable of taking care of themselves"[481] (e.g., Joseph in 37:2). The author/editor responsible for shaping the Terah *tôlĕdôt* in its final form was clearly not troubled by the fact that Ishmael is about sixteen years old in this episode.

Hagar wanders in the "Wilderness of Beer-sheba," probably not aimlessly, but "charting a course, as in Genesis 16, from watering place to watering place."[482] The waterskin is emptied before Hagar finds another source of water in the wilderness, although the mention of bushes in verse 15 suggests that the location is not entirely arid. Later, we learn

---

[478] Yoo, "Hagar the Egyptian," 234, remarks, with reference to v. 14, "Ishmael is likely too big for Hagar to carry on her shoulder." Speiser, *Genesis*, 154, recognizes correctly that the Hebrew text is best understood as saying: "Early next morning Abraham got some bread and a skin of water to give to Hagar. He placed them on her back and sent her away with the child." Alter, *Genesis*, 99, also rejects the idea that Ishmael was placed on Hagar's shoulder, noting that the "biblical syntax permits the use of a transitive verb ('gave [them] to Hagar') interrupted by a participial clause ('placing [them] on her shoulder'), which then controls a second object ('the child')." Some English versions support this understanding. CSB reads, "Early in the morning Abraham got up, took bread and a waterskin, put them on Hagar's shoulders, and sent her and the boy away" (cf. NET, NIV, NLT). Some scholars exploit the idea that Ishmael is presented in this episode as a very young boy, in order to justify understanding 21:8–21 as a doublet of Gen 16. For a fuller discussion, see T. Desmond Alexander, "The Hagar Traditions in Genesis xvi and xxi," in Emerton, *Studies in the Pentateuch*, 131–48; Alexander, *Abraham in the Negev*, 52–69.

[479] On the basis of 17:25 he would have been 14 years old at the time of Isaac's birth.

[480] In vv. 14–16, the noun יֶלֶד (*yeled*, "boy") is used; in this context the use of יֶלֶד (*yeled*) reflects the birth-relationship between Hagar and Ishmael. It does not necessarily imply that Ishmael is a young child.

[481] Wenham, *Genesis 16–50*, 83.

[482] J. Gerald Janzen and John T. Noble, "Did Hagar Give Ishmael up for Dead? Gen. 21.14–21 Re-Visited," *JSOT* 44 (2020): 526.

that Abraham digs a well in this region in order to obtain water (21:30; cf. 26:18, which states that various wells were dug in the Valley of Gerar in the time of Abraham).

When their water supply is exhausted, Hagar puts Ishmael under a bush for shelter. While some commentators view this action as implying that Ishmael is a very young boy,[483] it is not inconceivable that he is a teenager, exhausted and frustrated after wandering for hours but now without water. If Ishmael had been a small child, Hagar might have continued to search for water while carrying him on her shoulder.

Most commentators suggest that Hagar emotionally anticipates that her son will soon die of thirst. Unable to witness his death close-up, she sits at a distance. Alternatively, her word, "I can't bear to watch the boy die!" may be translated, "Do not let me look on the death of the child." Understood in this way, Hagar distances herself from the child to pray.[484] Perhaps her action in sitting at a distance from Ishmael underlines her inability to do anything more on his behalf; in doing this she abandons him to God's care.

The wording of verse 17 highlights concisely God's concern for both Hagar and Ishmael. The first half of the verse focuses on God hearing the boy's crying,[485] whereas the second half of the verse introduces the response of "the angel of God" to Hagar. Once more, "the angel of God" speaks to Hagar.[486] Reassuringly, God tells Hagar not to be afraid, promising that he will not abandon her son but will make him into a great nation. God's words recall the guarantee that he gave to Abraham (21:13; cf. 17:20). God then enables Hagar to see a well, from which she is able to draw water to revive her son.

---

[483] E.g., Skinner, *Genesis*, 322–23; Yoo, "Hagar the Egyptian," 234.

[484] See Janzen and Noble, "Did Hagar Give Ishmael up for Dead?," 517–31.

[485] This observation from the narrator is echoed in the words attributed to the angel of God at the end of v. 17. The two brief comments about God hearing the boy provide a subtle and appropriate allusion back to the naming of Ishmael in 16:11: 'You will name him Ishmael, for the Lord has heard your cry of affliction.' The name Ishmael means 'God hears.' As Alter, *Genesis*, 100, observes, "The ghost of its etymology—'God will hear'—hovers at the center of the story."

[486] Previously, "the angel of the Lord" spoke to Hagar (16:7–13). See Comments on 16:7–12 regarding the use of the term "angel." Although the remark "God has heard the boy crying" (v. 17), might suggest that the angel is someone other than God, the wording of v. 18 implies that the speaker is God himself. Support for the idea that the expression "the angel of God" designates God himself comes from the fact that he calls "from heaven" (v. 17). An angel/messenger who is not God might be expected to come to Hagar on earth (cf. 22:11, 15).

21:20–21. These verses provide a succinct summary of Ishmael's early life away from Abraham's household. He continues to live in the wilderness, between Egypt and Canaan, south of Gerar, surviving as a hunter. His mother gets him a wife from Egypt, creating the possibility for him to have descendants. Later in Genesis, a short *tôlĕdôt* section lists Ishmael's sons and where they settled (25:12–18).

Bridge

As God promised, Sarah gives birth to a son, Isaac. Against natural expectations, his birth is a source of exuberant joy for Sarah and Abraham. In the immediate context of God's dealings with the women in Abimelech's household (20:17–18), the brief report of the birth of Isaac strongly suggests that God is responsible for enabling Sarah to conceive and give birth (cf. Gal 4:29 where Paul speaks of Isaac as "one born as a result of the Spirit"). God's miraculous intervention to continue the unique patriline becomes a recurring feature in the patriarchal narratives (cf. 25:21; 29:31–30:24). This underlines the importance of the lineage in the outworking of YHWH's redemptive plan for the earth and its inhabitants.

Responding to Abraham's reluctance to send Hagar and Ishmael away, God confirms Isaac as Abraham's heir. Inclusion in the patriline that will be responsible for the overthrow of the serpent does not always fall to the son who is born first (see Biblical and Theological Themes §1). God's overriding desire is that the nations should be blessed through Abraham and the unique line of offspring descended from him. The exclusion of others from this line, however, does not signal their divine rejection in terms of blessing. God's favor is not restricted to the line of descendants linked to God's promise of blessing; the line itself exists for the blessing of others. While the covenant that God makes with Abraham will be established with Isaac (17:19, 21), Ishmael, as one of those circumcised (17:23–27), is included among its beneficiaries. Consequently, God hears and answers the cry of Ishmael (21:17). Later, Ishmael will be present alongside Isaac at the burial of Abraham (25:9).

In Romans 9:6–9, the apostle Paul draws on the divine appointment of Isaac as Abraham's sole heir to support his contention that not all who are the biological descendants of Abraham are God's children. Quoting God's words to Abraham in Genesis 21:11, Paul contends that those who secure salvation through Abraham's unique offspring are the "children of the promise." In setting out his arguments, Paul makes no reference to Ishmael. There is no reason to assume that Paul excludes him from being one of God's children. Paul subsequently uses the birth account of the twins Esau and Jacob in Genesis 25 to emphasize that God's choice of Jacob is not based on human merit, but is a reflection of God's sovereign freedom to choose the members of the patriline that will bring blessing to the nations.

In Galatians, Paul uses the relationship between Ishmael and Isaac to illustrate the distinction that exists between those who hold to the old covenant linked to Mount Sinai and the new covenant associated with Jesus Christ. In presenting his case Paul suggests that the Jewish inhabitants of Jerusalem correspond to Hagar, a slave who gives birth to a son that is "born as a result of the flesh" (Gal 4:23). Paul emphasizes that Ishmael's birth is due to the human efforts of Abraham and Sarah to fulfil God's purposes. By way of contrast, Paul observes that Sarah is a free woman, who gives birth to a son, Isaac, "as the result of a divine promise" (Gal 4:23 NIV). Sarah corresponds to the "Jerusalem above" (Gal 4:26). Drawing on Genesis 21, Paul observes that just as Ishmael "persecuted the one born as a result of the Spirit" (Gal 4:29), so now those who are committed to the Sinai covenant persecute those who are the children of Abraham by faith.[487] Paul's entire argument in Galatians 3–4 rests on the assumption that the Abrahamic covenant in Genesis 17 promises blessing to the nations through one of Abraham's descendants.

M. Abraham and Abimelech Make a Covenant (21:22–34)

> [22] At that time Abimelech, accompanied by Phicol the commander of his army, said to Abraham, "God is with you in everything you do. [23] Swear to me by God here and now, that you will not break an agreement with me or with my children and descendants. As I have been loyal to you, so you will be loyal to me and to the country where you are a resident alien."
>
> [24] And Abraham said, "I swear it." [25] But Abraham complained to Abimelech because of the well that Abimelech's servants had seized.
>
> [26] Abimelech replied, "I don't know who did this thing. You didn't report anything to me, so I hadn't heard about it until today."

---

[487] For a fuller discussion of Paul's discussion in Gal 4:21–31, see Gooding, *Riches of Divine Wisdom*, 222–39.

[27] Abraham took flocks and herds and gave them to Abimelech, and the two of them made a covenant.

[28] Abraham separated seven ewe lambs from the flock. [29] And Abimelech said to Abraham, "Why have you separated these seven ewe lambs?"

[30] He replied, "You are to accept the seven ewe lambs from me so that this act will serve as my witness that I dug this well." [31] Therefore that place was called Beer-sheba because it was there that the two of them swore an oath. [32] After they had made a covenant at Beer-sheba, Abimelech and Phicol, the commander of his army, left and returned to the land of the Philistines.

[33] Abraham planted a tamarisk tree in Beer-sheba, and there he called on the name of the Lord, the Everlasting God. [34] And Abraham lived as an alien in the land of the Philistines for many days.

Context

The birth of Isaac and subsequent expulsion of Ishmael marks an important development in God's plans for Abraham. Isaac is confirmed as Abraham's sole heir. This sets the scene for the events that will be narrated in Genesis 22, when God tests Abraham by instructing him to sacrifice Isaac. However, before introducing this climactic event, the narrator inserts a short episode involving Abraham's relationship with Abimelech, king of Gerar. By separating the accounts of the expulsion of Ishmael and the testing of Abraham, the narrator prevents the reader from assuming that these events occur in close proximity chronologically. Whereas Ishmael's departure from Abraham's household is associated with Isaac's weaning (21:8–21), Isaac is clearly much older in Genesis 22; he is able to carry all the wood required for a sacrifice (22:6). The inclusion of 21:22–34 also functions as a reminder that the purpose underlying the birth of Isaac is the blessing of the nations. Abimelech's interaction with Abraham confirms that others may appreciate how God has blessed Abraham and consequently seek to live in harmony with him. This episode is all the more significant in the light of Abimelech's earlier abduction of Sarah (20:1–18). As Kang observes, "Gen 21:22–34 is clearly connected to Story B (Gen 20:1–18). ... More importantly, geographical indications in 20:1 and 21:34 function as an envelope for the whole story of Gen 20–21."[488]

---

[488] Kang, *Reading the Wife/Sister Narratives*, 104–5.

Comments

21:22–24. The inclusion of this short episode about Abimelech coming to Abraham is unexpected, given his previous action in taking Sarah. However, Abimelech's initial words convey a sense of reassurance as he affirms that God is with Abraham. On account of taking Sarah, Abimelech has had firsthand experience of God's special bond with Abraham. Interestingly, Abimelech requests that the relationship between Abraham and him should be marked by חֶסֶד (*ḥesed*), a term that conveys a sense of loyalty, faithfulness, love, and mercy (cf. Exod 20:6, where similar language is used to describe God's faithful love toward those who love him and keep his commands). Having shown חֶסֶד (*ḥesed*) toward Abraham, Abimelech seeks from Abraham a similar generosity of spirit for himself and the land where the patriarch is living as a foreign resident. The presence of Phicol, the commander of the army, may be designed to reassure Abraham that Abimelech's desire to live in peace with the patriarch has the support of others. The king and his army commander are at one in this request. Without discussion, Abraham immediately grants Abimelech's request (v. 24).

21:25–31. Abimelech's request that there should be good relations between him and Abraham opens the way for Abraham to raises the contentious issue of the ownership of a well. When he describes the situation to Abimelech, the king declares that he is entirely unaware of what has occurred; he has no knowledge of those responsible and Abraham had not informed him about this.

Verse 27 then states that Abraham gave both sheep and cattle to Abimelech and the two men made a covenant. The reference to cattle suggests that this initial gift is not directly related to the issue of ownership of the well. The gift of sheep and cattle forms part of the process by which the friendship treaty between Abraham and Abimelech is sealed. This gift is then followed by a further gift of seven ewe lambs to Abimelech. This additional gift surprises Abimelech, and he looks for an explanation from Abraham, which the patriarch gives (v. 30). Abraham may have deliberately chosen to give seven animals because the Hebrew words for "seven" שֶׁבַע (*šebaʿ*) and "swear/take an oath" שָׁבַע (*šābaʿ*) are very similar. Abimelech's acceptance of these seven ewe lambs as a witness to Abraham's role in digging the well demonstrates his acknowledgement of Abraham's claim.[489] The subsequent

---

[489] Something similar may have been the case when Abraham accepted the payment of 1,000 pieces of silver from Abimelech (20:16).

naming of the well captures the significance of the occasion; Beer-sheba בְּאֵר שֶׁבַע (*bĕʾēr šebaʿ*) could mean either "well of oath" or "well of seven."

Commenting on Abimelech's character, Holmgren remarks: "We are not given any details about this dispute, but if Abimelech had been a typical tyrant, he could have simply taken ownership of this well by force. It says something significant about him that he entered into negotiation with Abraham, out of which came a treaty that brought this dispute peacefully to an end (w. 25–34)."[490]

The reference to "Philistines" living in this region in the time of Abraham is unexpected for the term is usually associated with people who migrate to the southwest of Palestine shortly after 1200 BC. Given the number of different ethnic groups resident in Palestine, as reflected in the various lists recorded in the Pentateuch (e.g., 15:19–21; Exod 3:8, 17; 13:5; 23:23; 33:2; 34:11), it is possible that the people of Gerar in the time of Abraham are not related to those who arrive later, but the name "Philistine" is transferred to them.[491]

21:32–34. The tree that Abraham plants conveys a sense of security and permanence, as does the name that Abraham gives to God.[492] "It is significant that at Beersheba Abraham worshiped YHWH and called on him as God Everlasting, an acknowledgement not only of God's eternal nature but also of the enduring character of his promises, which Abraham had now begun to experience first-hand."[493] Nevertheless, in spite of living at Beer-sheba for many years, v. 34 observes that Abraham remained a foreigner among the Philistines.[494]

---

[490] Holmgren, "Looking Back on Abraham's Encounter," 372.

[491] On the complex issue of Pentateuchal references to the Philistines, see David M. Howard, "Philistines," *NIDOTTE*, 4:1048– 52; Kitchen, *On the Reliability of the Old Testament*, 339–41. See also David M. Howard, "Philistines," in Hoerth, Mattingly, and Yamauchi, *Peoples of the Old Testament World*, 231–50; Carl S. Ehrlich, "Philistia and the Philistines," in Arnold and Strawn, *The World around the Old Testament*, 353–77. See also Gen 10:14 which associates the term "Philistine" with "Mizraim" (the Hebrew name for Egypt) the son of Ham.

[492] אֵל עוֹלָם (*ʾēl ʿôlām*, "Everlasting God") is the third divine epithet used in the Terah *tôlĕdôt* based on the general designation אֵל (*ʾēl*, "God") (cf. אֵל עֶלְיוֹן [*ʾēl ʿelyôn*, "God Most High"], 14:18; אֵל שַׁדַּי [*ʾēl šadday*, "God Almighty"], 17:1). Each name highlights a different aspect of God's nature.

[493] Steinmann, *Genesis*, 216. As Wenham, *Genesis 16–50*, 94, observes, "The use of the divine epithet El-Olam suggests that God's long-term faithfulness to Abraham has been revealed through Abimelek's words and actions."

[494] Some English versions (e.g., ESV, KJV, NIV, NJB) fail to convey adequately that the verb וַיָּגָר (*wayyāgār*) implies living in a location as an alien/foreigner (cf. CSB, NRSV).

Bridge

Abimelech's recognition of Abraham's special standing with God prompts him to seek a friendship pact. Abimelech's actions and Abraham's response recalls the divine promise that "all the families of the ground" (12:3) and "all the nations of the earth" (18:18; cf. 22:18) are to be blessed through Abraham. This divinely-given blessing, however, is conditional upon how others treat Abraham (12:3). By making a covenant, each party agrees to show חֶסֶד (*ḥesed*, "loving-kindness/grace") toward the other. This spirit of generosity leads to a peaceful resolution of a situation that could easily become a source of conflict. The observation in 21:34 that Abraham "lived as an alien in the land of the Philistines" is picked up by the author of Hebrews in 11:9, where he says that Abraham "lived as a foreigner in the land of promise" and argues that the divine promise of land was not fulfilled during the lifetimes of the patriarchs Abraham, Isaac, and Jacob. They all looked forward to a future time when they would dwell in a city "whose architect and builder is God" (Heb 11:10).[495]

N. The Testing of Abraham (22:1–19)

> [1] After these things God tested Abraham and said to him, "Abraham!"
> "Here I am," he answered.
>
> [2] "Take your son," he said, "your only son Isaac, whom you love, go to
> the land of Moriah, and offer him there as a burnt offering on one of
> the mountains I will tell you about."
>
> [3] So Abraham got up early in the morning, saddled his donkey, and
> took with him two of his young men and his son Isaac. He split wood
> for a burnt offering and set out to go to the place God had told him
> about. [4] On the third day Abraham looked up and saw the place in the
> distance. [5] Then Abraham said to his young men, "Stay here with the
> donkey. The boy and I will go over there to worship; then we'll come
> back to you." [6] Abraham took the wood for the burnt offering and laid
> it on his son Isaac. In his hand he took the fire and the knife, and the
> two of them walked on together.
>
> [7] Then Isaac spoke to his father Abraham and said, "My father."
>
> And he replied, "Here I am, my son."
>
> Isaac said, "The fire and the wood are here, but where is the lamb for
> the burnt offering?"

---

[495] For a fuller discussion of the importance of the city, see Biblical and Theological Themes §4. See also Alexander, *The City of God*.

8 Abraham answered, "God himself will provide the lamb for the burnt
offering, my son." Then the two of them walked on together.

9 When they arrived at the place that God had told him about, Abraham
built the altar there and arranged the wood. He bound his son Isaac and
placed him on the altar on top of the wood. 10 Then Abraham reached
out and took the knife to slaughter his son.

11 But the angel of the LORD called to him from heaven and said, "Abra-
ham, Abraham!" He replied, "Here I am."

12 Then he said, "Do not lay a hand on the boy or do anything to him.
For now I know that you fear God, since you have not withheld your
only son from me." 13 Abraham looked up and saw a ram caught in the
thicket by its horns. So Abraham went and took the ram and offered
it as a burnt offering in place of his son. 14 And Abraham named that
place The LORD Will Provide, so today it is said: "It will be provided on
the LORD's mountain."

15 Then the angel of the LORD called to Abraham a second time from heav-
en 16 and said, "By myself I have sworn," this is the LORD's declaration:
"Because you have done this thing and have not withheld your only son,
17 I will indeed bless you and make your offspring as numerous as the
stars of the sky and the sand on the seashore. Your offspring will possess
the city gates of their enemies. 18 And all the nations of the earth will
be blessed by your offspring because you have obeyed my command."

19 Abraham went back to his young men, and they got up and went
together to Beer-sheba. And Abraham settled in Beer-sheba.

Context

In Jewish tradition, this episode in the life of Abraham is known as the "Aqedah" or "Binding" of Isaac. For a variety of reasons, but especially the dramatic tension created by God asking a father to kill his own son, the passage is one of the better-known stories in Genesis. While there is a temptation to explore the story in isolation from its literary context, this episode builds on much of the preceding Terah *tôlĕdôt,* bringing to a climax the divine promises that were first introduced conditionally when God instructed Abraham to leave his father's house (12:1–3). In faith, Abraham obeyed God's initial command and, as the years have passed, he has witnessed God's provision of a son and heir, Isaac. Before Isaac's birth, God assured Abraham that his son would play a vital role in the process leading to the fulfilment of the divine promises. Yet, toward the end of Abraham's life, God tests the patriarch's faith and obedience by challenging him to sacrifice Isaac as an ascension offering. Apart from the emotional pressure of having to take the life of one's own child, Abraham is very aware that God's promises are bound up with Isaac. As Mathews observes, "all of the past promises hang on Moriah's test."[496]

The magnitude of the test imposed upon Abraham by God cannot be understated. Having waited for years for the birth of a son, Abraham is now asked by God to kill him. In addition, God has previously told Abraham that his descendants will be traced through Isaac (21:12) and that God's covenant with Abraham will be established with Isaac and his offspring after him (17:19). The death of Isaac would appear to undermine all that God has previously said.

Why does God test Abraham's obedience at this stage in his life? No explicit answer is given, although a strong clue comes in the oath that God swears to Abraham (vv. 16–18). The oath begins and ends with a reference to Abraham's obedience, suggesting that the oath is the reward given to Abraham for his willingness to sacrifice Isaac, his only son, whom he loves. Although brief, the oath encapsulates important elements of the divine promises that have been given previously to Abraham.[497] Moreover, later in Genesis God's oath is viewed as the basis upon which the divine promises are established for Abraham's descendants (26:3). Yet, how is the divine oath a reward for Abraham? How does it add to what has been promised to Abraham prior to this?

One possible answer is that the oath provides a divine guarantee that what was merely promised conditionally will be fulfilled. The oath confirms or ratifies the covenant that is promised in Genesis 17. According to God's words in 17:1–2, the giving of the covenant is conditional upon Abraham walking before God and being blameless.[498] A similar pattern may be observed in Genesis 6–9 regarding the covenant that God makes with Noah and his sons. The covenant is promised (6:18); Noah is obedient (6:22); Noah offers up an ascension offering (8:20); God confirms the covenant (9:9, 11).[499] This same pattern is evident if chapters 17 and 22 are read

---

[496] Mathews, *Genesis 11:27–50:26*, 283.

[497] See Comments on 22:16–18. Perhaps the most significant omission is the specific promise of the land of Canaan to Abraham's offspring.

[498] See Comments on 17:1–2. In 17:2 God says, וְאֶתְּנָה בְרִיתִי בֵּינִי וּבֵינֶךָ (*wĕʾettĕnâ bĕrîtî bênî ûbênekā*, "and [so that] I will make my covenant between me and you"), and not, וַאֲנִי הִנְנִי מֵקִים אֶת־בְּרִיתִי אִתְּכֶם (*waʾănî hinnî mēqîm ʾet-bĕrîtî ʾittĕkem*, "and I myself am establishing my covenant with you"), as he does in 9:9.

[499] Alexander, "Genesis 22 and the Covenant of Circumcision," 19–20.

together, and by linking the two chapters various features are easier to explain. The testing of Abraham connects back to the conditional nature of what God says in 17:1–2; by obeying God Abraham demonstrates that he walks before God and is blameless (22:12). If the sole purpose of the testing was to ascertain the level of Abraham's obedience, the provision of the ram as a substitute sacrifice is hardly necessary after Abraham has passed the test. However, it seems likely that the sacrifice prepares the way for the giving of the divine oath, paralleling what happens when Noah emerges from the ark (8:20–21). As God's final statement to Abraham regarding the promises previously given, the oath provides the ultimate assurance that the promises will be fulfilled.[500] As the strongest guarantee given by God, the divine oath in 22:16–18 forms a fitting climax to the main part of the Terah *tôlĕdôt*, echoing the call of Abraham in 12:1–3.[501]

Apart from bringing the story of God's promises to Abraham to a climax, some commentators have noted how the events of chapter 22 parallel what happens in chapter 21 regarding Abraham's other son, Ishmael. As Waltke and Fredricks observe, "Hagar and Ishmael's rugged trek has striking parallels to the challenge Abraham and Isaac will have to face: (1) journey into the unknown at the command of YHWH; (2) provision for the journey; (3) child at the point of death; (4) intervention of God's messenger; (5) parent's sighting of the way out; and (6) promise of future blessing."[502] While there are similarities between the two episodes, there are also significant differences that must not be overlooked. The

---

[500] This idea is developed in Heb 6:13–18, where the author argues that the oath given in Gen 22:17 guaranteed God's promise to Abraham. In this passage, the promise and the oath are viewed as separate entities, but both affirm the same thing. The oath is given "because God wanted to show His unchangeable purpose even more clearly to the heirs of the promise" (Heb 6:17). Cf. Thomas R. Schreiner, *Commentary on Hebrews* (Nashville: B&H Publishing, 2015), 197–205.

[501] Whereas in 12:1–3 God makes promises that are conditional on Abraham's response, God's oath in 22:16–18 recalls what Abraham has already done. In 12:1–3 God issues two imperatives to Abraham that demand obedience; in 22:16–18 God acknowledges Abraham's faithful obedience to a prior command. Cf. R. W. L. Moberly, *From Eden to Golgotha: Essays in Biblical Theology*, South Florida Studies in the History of Judaism (Atlanta: Scholars Press, 1992), 73.

[502] Waltke and Fredricks, *Genesis*, 292; cf. Il-Seung Chung, "Hagar and Ishmael in Light of Abraham and Isaac: Reading Gen. 21:8–21 and Gen. 22:1–19 as a Dialogue," *ExpTim* 128 (2017): 573–82. Sarna, *Genesis*, 146, writes: "The Akedah, as the story is popularly called—because of the Hebrew stem '-*k*-*d*, 'to bind,' in verse 9—is organically connected with the preceding chapter. Abraham has lost one son and now seems about to lose the other. In both narratives, the child is saved by divine intervention at the critical moment, the only

departure of Ishmael, however, sets the scene for the events of chapter 22, adding to the dilemma that Abraham must face in responding to God's command to sacrifice Isaac. The fulfilment of the divine promises cannot be achieved through Ishmael; they rely on Isaac alone.

Comments

22:1–2. The events of chapter 22 are placed chronologically after all that has been recorded in chapter 21. By this stage in Abraham's life, Isaac is sufficiently old to carry all the wood necessary for the burning of an animal sacrifice (v. 6). At the outset, the narrator informs the reader that God intends to test Abraham. But no explanation is given for this. The verb "test" conveys the idea of examining or evaluating. In this instance, God comes to see if Abraham will obey him. When Abraham shows his willingness to obey, God remarks, "Now I know that you fear God" (v. 12).

God addresses Abraham by name; the use of his personal name in verse 1 is possibly intended to recall the covenant of chapter 17, which involved the patriarch's name being changed from Abram to Abraham. Verse 11 will echo God's initial word to Abraham, but with the repetition of his personal name, perhaps to convey a sense of urgency.

God's instruction highlights the special relationship that exists between Abraham and Isaac, adding to the magnitude of what God demands.[503] A literal rendering of the Hebrew text at the start of verse 2 would be "Take your son, your only, whom you love, Isaac." God's reference to Isaac as "your only" presupposes the departure of Ishmael, which God sanctioned (cf. 21:8–21). "Isaac is the child of the promise. In him every saving thing that God has promised to do is invested and guaranteed."[504] According to Sarna, the presence of the participle נָא (*nāʾ*) after the imperative קַח (*qaḥ*) "softens the command to an entreaty, as noted in Sanhedrin 89b, Genesis Rabba 55:7, and Rashi's commentary. Abraham has absolute freedom of choice. Should he refuse, he would not incur any guilt."[505]

---

two biblical instances of an angel calling from heaven to human beings. In both cases there is a fortuitous discovery: a well of water in the earlier story, a ram in the thicket here."

[503] Mathews, *Genesis 11:27–50:26*, 284, observes, "Repetition of the family connection, 'son,' 'only son,' and 'father,' heightens the pathos of the story." The bond between Abraham and Isaac is underlined throughout vv. 2–14 by the frequency of the nouns "father" and "son."

[504] von Rad, *Genesis*, 244. In line with this, Mathews, *Genesis 11:27–50:26*, 290, observes that "no test could be any more probing of the patriarch's loyalty, for even the taking of his own life would not pass the trial since the future promise lay with the boy."

[505] Sarna, *Genesis*, 147.

Not surprisingly, considerable attention has been given to the ethical conundrum presented in the story: is it morally acceptable for God to command a father to kill his own son as a religious sacrifice? Several factors should color our moral evaluation of what God does. First, the command to offer up Isaac as a whole-burnt offering is introduced to the reader as a test of Abraham's obedience to God. No greater test could have been set for Abraham. Not only is Isaac his only son,[506] whom he loves, but also Isaac is the one through whom God's covenant with Abraham will be established (17:19–21; 21:12). As Amit observes, "We may conclude that the epithets preceding Isaac's name are designed not only to show that God is aware of the awful predicament into which he is plunging Abraham but also to persuade the reader that this is a supremely difficult test."[507] The fact that God asks Abraham to do something that appears to run counter to God's nature intensifies the test. The reader's sense of moral revulsion at the request adds to the magnitude of the challenge being imposed on Abraham by God; Abraham undoubtedly sensed this too. Abraham is required to trust that God has a purpose in making this terrifying demand. The focus is on Abraham's willingness to obey God, when everything would appear to require the opposite. Second, this incident is unique. It is not presented as a paradigm for others to follow. The story must be viewed in the context of other passages that affirm God's abhorrence of child sacrifice.[508] The outcome of the story underlines that God does not expect fathers to sacrifice their sons to him. The unexpected provision of the ram signals that animal sacrifices are an appropriate substitute. Third, in setting this test God is prepared to intervene at the appropriate time to stop Abraham from killing Isaac. It is never God's intention that Isaac should die.

The precise location where Abraham will build the altar to sacrifice Isaac is not given. Abraham is merely told, "Go to the land of Moriah."[509] The name "Moriah" is found elsewhere in the Old Testament only in

---

[506] By this stage in the Terah *tôlĕdôt*, Ishmael has been sent away from Abraham's household, making Isaac his sole heir.

[507] Yairah Amit, "Progression as a Rhetorical Device in Biblical Literature," *JSOT* 28 (2003): 8.

[508] References to child sacrifice elsewhere in the Old Testament are consistent in denouncing it as abhorrent to YHWH (Lev 18:21; 20:2–5; Deut 12:31; 18:10). When practiced by Judeans, it is denounced as a sin (2 Kgs 21:6; 2 Chr 33:6; Jer 7:31–32; Ezek 16:20–21).

[509] The wording of the command to "go" is very distinctive (וְלֶךְ־לְךָ, *wĕlek-lĕkā*) and recalls God's command to Abraham in 12:1. Sarna, *Genesis*, 146, notes that the phrase "does not

2 Chronicles 3:1, which states that Solomon built "the Lord's temple in Jerusalem on Mount Moriah." It would be a noteworthy coincidence if the temple was constructed at the very location where God asked Abraham to sacrifice Isaac. However, about 1,000 years separate the two events and the Genesis account lacks sufficient detail to confirm an indisputable connection. It remains a possibility, but no theological significance rests on the locations being identical, apart from the general idea of divine revelations and sanctuaries being associated with mountains.[510]

Some scholars argue that the reference to the "third day" in verse 4 implies a three-day journey. This would place "the land of Moriah" well beyond Jerusalem if measured from Beersheba. However, the text does not mention a three-day journey, but speaks only of the "third day." The "first day" could be the day when God initially speaks to Abraham. Abraham and his companions begin their journey on the morning of the second day (v. 3) and may have traveled only one full day and a partial day before arriving at the mountain on the third day.[511] This would make it possible for the "land of Moriah" to be located in the region of Jerusalem.[512]

22:3–8. The narrator describes with maximum concision Abraham's response to God's instructions. The short report of Abraham's preparations early in the morning imply that he wastes no time in obeying the divine command. The patriarch does not disclose to others all the details of God's instructions, but he clearly intends to offer a sacrifice. When Abraham eventually arrives close to the mountain chosen by God, he parts company from the two young men who have journeyed with him.[513] For the first time since the test was initiated, the narrator records

---

occur again in the Bible, a fact that underscores the deliberate and meaningful nature of its use in these two passages."

[510] Alexander, *The City of God*, 43–63.

[511] The case for this is made by Steinmann, *Genesis*, 219.

[512] John H. Walton, *Genesis*, NIV Application Commentary (Grand Rapids: Zondervan, 2001), 510, contends that the location is not Jerusalem because Abraham takes wood for the sacrifice. Abraham would have known that wood would be available in the Jerusalem area. His argument is flawed in that Abraham undoubtedly takes dried wood that will ignite easily. Depending on the time of year, dry wood might not have been available in the Jerusalem area.

[513] The Hebrew text uses the same noun נַעַר (*na*ʿ*ar*) to denote both Isaac and the two men who go with Abraham. Unfortunately, the CSB translation in v. 5, in common with some other English versions, uses "boy" for נַעַר (*na*ʿ*ar*) when it applies to Isaac, but "young men" when the same noun is used for those accompanying Abraham (v. 3). Isaac and the two young men may well have been close companions of the same age.

Abraham's words to others. His statement "then we'll come back to you" has engendered much discussion. Does Abraham tell a blatant lie, knowing that he is about to kill Isaac?[514] Does Abraham's comment imply that he does not intend to kill Isaac, disobeying God's command at the last minute? Or does it reflect a genuine belief on the part of Abraham that Isaac will somehow survive this ordeal so that the divine promises involving him will be fulfilled. Readers may speculate as to what Abraham meant, but the author of Hebrews affirms that Abraham "considered God to be able even to raise someone from the dead" (Heb 11:19).[515]

The brief description in verse 6 is very poignant. With a minimum of detail, the author conveys well the drama of the occasion. Isaac carries the wood upon which he will be laid; Abraham carries the tools with which he will sacrifice Isaac. To add to the tension, the narrator remarks that the two of them walked together (וַיֵּלְכוּ שְׁנֵיהֶם יַחְדָּו, *wayyēlĕkû šĕnêhem yaḥdāw*), an observation repeated at the end of verse 8.

Not surprisingly, as they ascend the mountain Isaac questions his father about the missing sacrificial animal. Yet again, the narrative highlights the familial relationship as Isaac says, "My father," and Abraham responds with "My son" (v. 7). Isaac's query regarding the "lamb for the burnt offering" receives an unexpected response from Abraham: "God himself will provide the lamb for the burnt offering, my son" (v. 8). As with Abraham's earlier instruction to the two young men (v. 5), his response to Isaac may be interpreted in different ways, from being a blatant lie to a confident assertion of trust that God will indeed provide an alternative sacrifice. Whatever interpretation is adopted, Abraham evades saying that Isaac is the sacrifice. Most English versions translate שֶׂה (*śeh*) as "lamb" in verses 7–8, but the Hebrew term denotes a sheep or goat. Leviticus 22:28 uses the noun שֶׂה (*śeh*) to denote an animal old enough to have given birth.

22:9–15. The narrator reveals nothing of the feelings of Abraham and Isaac when they arrive at the top of the mountain. The reader is merely told that Abraham built the altar, arranged the wood, bound his son, and placed him on top of the wood (v. 9). He then stretched out his hand and grabbed the knife. We are not told how Abraham and Isaac felt

---

[514] Cf. Skinner, *Genesis*, 329.

[515] See Mitchell L. Chase, "The Genesis of Resurrection Hope: Exploring Its Early Presence and Deep Roots," *JETS* 57 (2014): 478–79.

about what was happening. No conversation is recorded between father and son. The concise record of what Abraham did implies compliance by both parties to what was taking place. Abraham obeys willingly, as God requested, and Isaac accepts his fate without resisting. There is no suggestion of any struggle or delay. Had he wished, Isaac was old enough to put up a struggle.

At the last possible minute, the "angel of the Lord" intervenes, speaking to Abraham from heaven. The designation "angel of the Lord" refers to God himself and not to another creature, as becomes obvious in the speech recorded in verses 16–18 (see Comments on 16:7–12). God's words (v. 11) recall how he addressed Abraham when he first laid down the challenge to sacrifice Isaac (v. 1). At this critical juncture he repeats Abraham's name, perhaps to convey the urgency of his intervention. Commanding Abraham not to harm his son, God reveals that he knows now that Abraham fears him (v. 12). Abraham passes God's test.

The reader might possibly expect the episode to conclude at this point. However, Abraham sees, perhaps at a distance, a ram that has just caught its horns in a bush.[516] He then takes the trapped animal and offers it as a burnt offering on the altar. The sudden appearance of the ram is noteworthy. It was not visible when Abraham bound Isaac, otherwise they might have been tempted to view it as a God-intended substitute.

The offering of the ram as an עֹלָה (ʾōlâ, "ascension offering") is an important element in the story for this is only the second occasion in Genesis that the term עֹלָה (ʾōlâ) has been used to denote a sacrifice.[517] Previously, the term was used when Noah emerged from the ark and offered sacrifices to God (8:20). By specifying in ch. 22 that the sacrifice is a burnt offering, in which the whole animal is consumed upon the altar, the narrator draws attention to an interesting parallel between the stories of Noah and Abraham. After Noah presented burnt offerings to God, God ratified the covenant that he has previously promised to Noah.

---

[516] The MT reads אַחַר (ʾaḥar) which is usually translated "behind," but Wenham, *Genesis 16-50*, 99, following Marvin H. Pope, "Enigmatic Bible Passages: The Timing of the Snagging of the Ram, Genesis 22:13," *BA* 49 (1986): 114–17, opts for the translation "just caught," taking אַחַר (*aḥar*) to mean "after" from a temporal perspective. A literal translation might be: "and he looked and behold a ram after it was seized in a thicket by its horns and he went ..." Speiser, *Genesis*, 163, emends אַחַר (ʾ*aḥar*) to read אֶחָד (ʾ*eḥād*, "one"), in line with the Samaritan Pentateuch. No emendation, however, is necessary if a temporal interpretation of אַחַר (ʾ*aḥar*) is adopted.

[517] In Genesis, עֹלָה (ʾōlâ, "burnt offering") only appears in 8:20; 22:2, 3, 6–8, 13.

After Abraham sacrifices the ram, God swears an oath. If the making of the sacrifice paves the way for the giving of the oath, this would explain why God provides the ram for Abraham to offer.

Abraham views the provision of the ram as providential. Recalling his earlier remark to Isaac that God would provide—literally, "see for himself"—an animal for the burnt offering (v. 8), Abraham names the location, יְהוָה יִרְאֶה (*yhwh yirʾeh*, "The Lord will see"). Allowing for a change of divine epithet from "God" to "the Lord," the place name echoes the opening words of Abraham's reply to Isaac. The narrator then adds the observation that this event has become the basis for the subsequent expectation that בְּהַר יְהוָה יֵרָאֶה (*bĕhar yhwh yērāʾeh*, "on the mountain of the Lord he/it will appear/be seen").[518] The proverbial nature of the saying makes it difficult to interpret with precision. It is ambiguous and may be read in different ways. It could imply that God will appear on the mountain of the Lord, which would be true for both Mount Sinai and Mount Zion.[519] Alternatively, it might be understood as saying that on the mountain of the Lord it will be provided, the "it" being unspecified, but presumably understood as whatever is needed. Perhaps both interpretations are intended. The narrator's reference to "today" underlines that Abraham's unique experience on the "mountain of the Lord" was viewed as paradigmatic by later generations (cf. 19:37–38; 47:26).

22:16–18. Some commentators have argued that the earliest version of the "binding" story did not include verses 15–18, with verse 19 originally following on directly after verse 14.[520] However, the divine oath that comes in verses 16–18 is God's response to Abraham's obedience. We might expect that God would reward Abraham in some way for the substantial test that he has endured. It also seems likely that the sacrifice of a burnt offering played a part in prompting God to swear the oath.

As the last recorded divine communication to Abraham in Genesis, verses 16–18 recall God's initial words to Abraham in 12:1–3. The two

---

[518] Although the verbal root ראה (*rʾh*) is repeated in v. 14, the MT pointing makes the form of the first verb *qal*, with the meaning "to see" (cf. v. 8, where the *qal* form is also used), whereas the second occurrence is *niphal* with the sense "to be seen/appear."

[519] In various biblical books, the "mountain of the Lord" denotes Mount Zion in Jerusalem (Ps 24:3; Isa 2:3; 30:29; Mic 4:2; Zech 8:3). The same expression also refers to Mount Sinai in Num 10:33.

[520] E.g., Skinner, *Genesis*, 331; J. A. Emerton, "The Origin of the Promises to the Patriarchs in the Older Sources of the Book of Genesis," *VT* 32 (1982): 18; Westermann, *Genesis 12–36*, 363.

speeches are not quite identical, but they have enough in common to create a noteworthy frame or inclusio around the main part of the Terah *tôlĕdôt*.[521] Whereas 12:1–3 contains two imperatives that demand Abraham's obedience, God's solemn oath in 22:16–18 begins and ends by highlighting Abraham's obedience to God. Whereas 12:1–3 involves divine promises that require Abraham's future obedience, the divine oath in 22:16–18 responds to what Abraham has already done. What had previously been promised subject to Abraham obeying God is now guaranteed by divine oath in response to Abraham's obedience.

Rarely in the Old Testament does God swear by himself.[522] As a divine oath, God's words carry great weight, a point developed by the author of Hebrews, who views the oath as adding to the promise already given (Heb 6:15–18). Since God swears by himself that he will unconditionally fulfil promises previously made to Abraham, the divine oath in verses 16–18 brings to an important climax all that has been narrated from the start of the Terah *tôlĕdôt*. Importantly, the content of the oath anticipates developments that lie in the future. If God's words in 12:1–3 shaped Abraham's future life, God's words in 22:16–18 are intended to shape the future beyond Abraham's lifetime.

After noting Abraham's willingness to sacrifice his son (v. 16), God proceeds to say that he will "indeed bless" Abraham and make his offspring numerous. This part of the divine oath reflects previous promises in which God said he would give Abraham numerous descendants (12:2; 13:16; 15:5; 17:5–6, 16). The Hebrew syntax at the start of verse 17 emphasizes the verbs "bless" and "make numerous."[523] The extent of Abraham's offspring is conveyed through two similes; they will be like "the stars of the sky and the sand of the seashore." The first of these recalls how God showed Abraham the stars of the sky as a sign that he would have numerous descendants (15:5). The second simile occurs here for the first time, although elsewhere Abraham's descendants are compared to the

---

[521] Moberly, *From Eden to Golgotha*, 73.

[522] See Mathews, *Genesis 11:27-50:26*, 297–98. The use of an oath here may suggest that the events of ch. 22 are linked to the covenant introduced in ch. 17. See Alexander, "Genesis 22 and the Covenant of Circumcision," 11–22; Williamson, *Abraham, Israel and the Nations*, 234–59.

[523] Most English versions use words like "indeed" and "greatly" to convey this emphasis, although most fail to convey adequately the emphatic nature of what God swears. The KJV reflects more literally the form of the Hebrew text, which involves the use of infinitive absolutes that are placed before *yiqtol* verbs: "in blessing I will bless thee, and in multiplying I will multiply … ."

"dust of the earth" (13:16). As similes, both comparisons are not to be taken literally (cf. Josh 11:4; 1 Sam 13:5 where large armies are described as being numerous like the "sand of the seashore"; the same simile is used of Solomon's wisdom in 1 Kgs 4:29 [Heb. 5:9]). The use of two similes adds weight to God's assurance that he will make Abraham's offspring numerous. God's guarantee of blessing and numerical increase recalls the creation account when God blessed the human couple and instructed them to be fruitful and multiply (Gen 1:28; cf. 9:1).

After guaranteeing that Abraham will have numerous descendants, the focus of the divine oath moves from Abraham's many descendants to one descendant. A few English versions capture this transition (e.g., KJV, ESV, JPS), but most take the repetition of זַרְעֲךָ (*zarʿăkā*, "your offspring") to imply that the final part of verse 17 also refers to numerous descendants. The choice between these alternatives is complicated by the fact that the noun זֶרַע (*zeraʿ*) does not have distinctive singular and plural forms.[524] However, it is noteworthy that the verb וְיִרַשׁ (*wĕyiraš*, "and he will possess") is singular, as is the pronoun suffix on אֹיְבָיו (*ʾōyĕbāyw*, "his enemies").[525] The most natural reading of the final part of verse 17 is "your offspring will possess the gate of his enemies."[526] The promise of victory recalls God's earlier comment regarding the "offspring of the woman" encountering hostility in overcoming the serpent (3:15).

Interpreting זַרְעֲךָ (*zarʿăkā*, "your offspring") as singular in verse 17b has important implications for verse 18, which focuses on the blessing of all the nations of the earth. Building upon the final part of verse 17, God swears that others will be blessed through one of Abraham's descendants.[527] This emphasis on one descendant is very much in keeping with how the book of Genesis traces a unique line of descendants, focusing

---

[524] The noun זֶרַע (*zeraʿ*) functions like the English words "fish" and "sheep," which retain the same form for both singular and plural.

[525] The term אֹיְבָיו (*ʾōyĕbāyw*, "his enemies") recalls the term אֵיבָה (*ʾêbâ*, "enmity") in 3:15.

[526] See Alexander, "Further Observations," 363–67, which draws on Collins, "A Syntactical Note," 139–48; cf. Gentry and Wellum, *Kingdom through Covenant*, 288; Andrew E. Steinmann, "Jesus and Possessing the Enemies' Gate (Genesis 22:17–18; 24:60)," *BSac* 174 (2017): 13–21. Contrary to the CSB translation, "gate" is singular in v. 17.

[527] The best translation of וְהִתְבָּרֲכוּ (*wĕhitbārăkû*) is probably "will be blessed"; less probable are the translations "will bless themselves" or "will find blessing" (see CSB footnote). The *hithpael* form of ברך (*brk*) is used in 22:18 and 26:4 in conjunction with "*your offspring*." The *niphal* form of ברך (*brk*) is used in 12:3, 18:18 and 28:14 with reference to Abraham and Jacob respectively. Williamson, *Sealed with an Oath*, 81, helpfully proposes that the *niphal* form of ברך (*brk*) implies a less direct communication of blessing.

on one individual in each generation. The remaining *tôlĕdôt* sections in Genesis support the idea that divine blessing is mediated through one person, with special attention being given to how Jacob and Joseph bring blessing to others (e.g., 30:27, 30; 39:5; 47:10).[528]

Within the Terah *tôlĕdôt,* there is undoubtedly progression from the initial call of Abraham (12:1–3) to the giving of the divine oath on Mount Moriah (22:16–18). Whereas the fulfilment of the promises in God's first speech is conditional upon Abraham's response, God's final speech to Abraham is an oath given in response to how Abraham has already obeyed. This oath guarantees unconditionally the fulfilment of what was promised previously, marking the climax to the episodes involving Abraham. While scholars have rightly observed the importance of God's initial words to Abraham in 12:1–3, they have generally not given equal weight to God's final words. Yet these are actually more important in understanding the significance of Abraham's relationship with God. Genesis 22:18 recalls what was said by God to Abraham in 12:3, but subtle variations in wording occur, especially in 22:18, where blessing is linked to Abraham's offspring rather than Abraham himself.[529]

Between the speeches in 12:1–3 and 22:16–18 various incidents are recorded. The early episodes in the Terah *tôlĕdôt* focus on identifying the territory where Abraham's descendants will become a great nation. Genesis 12–15 concludes with God covenanting that after a period of subjugation elsewhere, Abraham's descendants will possess the land of Canaan (15:18–21; cf. 12:7; 13:14–17). Thereafter, the narrative concentrates on the provision of a son, through whom God will establish his eternal covenant concerning Abraham being the father of many nations. Although Abraham and Sarah had attempted to provide a suitable heir by using a surrogate mother, God eventually enables Sarah to conceive and have a son, Isaac. As the son of promise he will have a vital part to play in God's plan to bless all the nations of the earth. However, in an unexpected twist, God challenges Abraham to demonstrate his obedience by sacrificing Isaac as a burnt offering. When Abraham passes the test, God confirms with a

---

528 The closest parallel to 22:18 in the Old Testament comes in Ps 72:17, where it says וְיִתְבָּרְכוּ בוֹ כָּל־גּוֹיִם (*wĕyitbārkû bô kol-gôyim*, "and all nations will be blessed in him"). The whole of Ps 72 looks forward in anticipation to the coming of a king who will exercise universal authority, bringing justice to the oppressed. This king will be a source of blessing to others. In v. 17, the psalmist is probably alluding to the divine oath in Gen 22:16–18.

529 Williamson, *Abraham, Israel and the Nations*, 223–28, 250–51.

solemn oath the promises linked to chapter 17. Remarkably, the divine oath in chapter 22 that guarantees God's promises makes no mention of the land of Canaan. The scope of what God swears comes closest to the idea of Abraham being the father of many nations (17:4–6).[530]

22:19. To avoid distracting the reader's attention away from the divine oath with too many details, the narrator brings closure to this climactic episode by describing briefly how Abraham rejoined the young men and returned to Beer-sheba.

Bridge

With the testing of Abraham, the main section of the Terah *tôlĕdôt* comes to a climactic conclusion. Importantly, the divine oath ends by indicating that all the nations of the earth will be blessed through one of Abraham's offspring. When he first called Abraham, God commanded him to be a blessing. As a result of his faith-inspired obedience (22:16–18), God swears an oath, building on promises that he had already given to Abraham. After guaranteeing Abraham numerous descendants, the second half of the oath focuses on the role that one of Abraham's offspring will play in the future. The ongoing story in Genesis develops this further by tracing a unique line of descendants leading to a future king. In the light of the broader Old Testament story the divine oath in 22:16–18 underpins the expectation that the nations of the earth will be blessed through a future Davidic king.

According to Acts 3:25–26, the apostle Peter highlights this hope when addressing fellow Jews in Jerusalem: "You are the sons of the prophets and of the covenant that God made with your ancestors, saying to Abraham, **And all the families of the earth will be blessed through your offspring.** [26] God raised up his servant and sent him first to you to bless you by turning each of you from your evil ways." For Peter, Jesus Christ is the "seed" or "offspring" promised to Abraham through whom others will be blessed.

The apostle Paul adopts a similar argument in Galatians 3, contending that Jesus Christ fulfils the divine oath given to Abraham in Genesis

[530] Hahn, *Kinship by Covenant*, 111, is partially correct when he writes, "In Genesis 22:15–18, the last and climactic promise of Genesis 12:2–3—blessing for all nations—is finally given covenant form, and the previous covenants of chs. 15 and 17 are ratified and confirmed." However, the oath in Gen 22 makes no specific reference to Abraham's descendants possessing the land of Canaan. If Ps 72 offers an insight into how this oath was understood, it speaks of a future king exercising authority over the whole earth, bringing justice to the oppressed (Ps 72:8–11).

22:16–18. Paul emphasizes correctly that the promise of blessing for the nations is to be fulfilled through only one of Abraham's descendants, whom he identifies as Jesus Christ (Gal 3:16).[531] The divine oath given by God to Abraham is central to Paul's understanding of Jesus as the one who brings to fulfilment the messianic expectations associated with the Davidic dynasty.[532] A similar understanding probably explains why Matthew begins his "royal" genealogy of Jesus with Abraham and not David (Matt 1:1–17; see Biblical and Theological Themes §1).

For New Testament writers, the account of Abraham's remarkable obedience to God's instruction to sacrifice Isaac provides a noteworthy illustration of true faith in God. In the light of God's promise to Abraham, "Your offspring will be traced through Isaac," the author of Hebrews interprets Abraham's willingness to sacrifice Isaac as evidence that Abraham believed God could raise the dead (Heb 11:17–19). From a different perspective, James uses the events of Genesis 22 to argue that Abraham's obedience is evidence of the faith by which he was declared righteous in Genesis 15:6. James writes,

> Wasn't Abraham our father justified by works in offering Isaac his son on the altar? You see that faith was active together with his works, and by works, faith was made complete, and the Scripture was fulfilled that says, Abraham believed God, and it was credited to him as righteousness, and he was called God's friend. You see that a person is justified by works and not by faith alone (Jas 2:21–24).

For James, inner faith expresses itself though outward actions; true faith can never be divorced from works.

O. Nahor's Children (22:20–24)

> 20 Now after these things Abraham was told, "Milcah also has borne
> sons to your brother Nahor: 21 Uz his firstborn, his brother Buz, Kem-
> uel the father of Aram, 22 Chesed, Hazo, Pildash, Jidlaph, and Bethuel."

---

[531] Cf. Collins, "Galatians 3:16," 75–86; James. M. Hamilton, "The Seed of the Woman and the Blessing of Abraham," *TynBul* 58 (2007): 271–73; DeRouchie and Meyer, "Christ or Family," 36–48.

[532] In Galatians 3, Paul also draws on the chronological priority of the Genesis account of Abraham to argue that the divine promises given to Abraham take precedence over the covenant that was sealed at Mount Sinai between God and the Israelites (Exod 19–24).

> [23] And Bethuel fathered Rebekah. Milcah bore these eight to Nahor, Abraham's brother. [24] His concubine, whose name was Reumah, also bore Tebah, Gaham, Tahash, and Maacah.

Context

This short section, which has a genealogical appearance, fulfils a significant role within the Terah *tôlĕdôt,* separating the main section of the Terah *tôlĕdôt* from a concluding appendix. Although 22:20–24 is short and does not follow the pattern of the main genealogies in Genesis, its contents are genealogical in nature. In Genesis genealogies are frequently used to separate narrative sections. Whereas God's speech in 12:1–3 introduces a train of events involving Abraham, the divine oath in 22:16–18 brings to an important climax God's dealings with Abraham. Framed by two significant divine speeches, 11:27–22:19 forms the core of the Terah *tôlĕdôt.* Coming after this, 23:1–25:11 functions as an extended appendix that recounts the deaths of Sarah (23:1–20) and Abraham (25:1–11), separated by a long episode that describes how a wife is acquired for Isaac (24:1–67). These episodes bring the Terah *tôlĕdôt* to an appropriate closure. The appendix is separated from the main narrative by 22:20–24.[533]

Comments

22:20–24. While this short section may give the appearance of being disconnected from what precedes and follows it, it is carefully integrated into the Terah *tôlĕdôt,* forming a bridge between the main story of Abraham's life and an appendix that brings closure by recounting the deaths of Sarah and Abraham, and the provision of a wife for Isaac. The latter is a vital development in order to ensure the continuation of the family line. The references to Nahor and his wife Milcah recall 11:27–29, where they are mentioned briefly. The comment in verse 20 that "Micah also has borne sons" presupposes the birth of Isaac to Sarah. An earlier mention of Milcah in 11:29 is followed by a reference to Sarah being unable to conceive and have children. No details of Milcah's family are recorded in Genesis 11; they are included here because they anticipate the events of chapter 24 (see especially 24:24, 47).

Bridge

By reintroducing Nahor into the story and naming other members of his family, the scene is set for the events that will be narrated in chapter 24.

---

[533] Cf. Alexander, *Abraham in the Negev*, 102–3.

Sarna highlights clearly how this short section anticipates the account of Abraham's acquiring a wife for Isaac.

> The remarks relating to "Kemuel the father of Aram" and "Bethuel being the father of Rebekah" are clues to the function of the genealogy and point to the reason for its presence here. The previous pericope closed with divine blessings, and for these to be fulfilled Isaac must marry and found a family. The list therefore mentions Rebekah, Bethuel, Milcah, Nahor, and Aram as an intimation of Isaac's forthcoming marriage to Rebekah daughter of Bethuel son of Milcah of the city of Nahor in Aram-naharaim. In this way, its presence after the Akedah (Gen 22:1–19) is purposeful, anticipating the events of ch. 24.[534]

P. The Death and Burial of Sarah (23:1–20)

> [1] Now Sarah lived 127 years; these were all the years of her life. [2] Sarah died in Kiriath-arba (that is, Hebron) in the land of Canaan, and Abraham went to mourn for Sarah and to weep for her.
>
> [3] Then Abraham got up from beside his dead wife and spoke to the Hethites: [4] "I am an alien residing among you. Give me burial property among you so that I can bury my dead."
>
> [5] The Hethites replied to Abraham, [6] "Listen to us, my lord. You are a prince of God among us. Bury your dead in our finest burial place. None of us will withhold from you his burial place for burying your dead."
>
> [7] Then Abraham rose and bowed down to the Hethites, the people of the land. [8] He said to them, "If you are willing for me to bury my dead, listen to me and ask Ephron son of Zohar on my behalf [9] to give me the cave of Machpelah that belongs to him; it is at the end of his field. Let him give it to me in your presence, for the full price, as burial property."
>
> [10] Ephron was sitting among the Hethites. So in the hearing of all the Hethites who came to the gate of his city, Ephron the Hethite answered Abraham: [11] "No, my lord. Listen to me. I give you the field, and I give you the cave that is in it. I give it to you in the sight of my people. Bury your dead."
>
> [12] Abraham bowed down to the people of the land [13] and said to Ephron in the hearing of the people of the land, "Listen to me, if you please. Let me pay the price of the field. Accept it from me, and let me bury my dead there."

---

[534] Sarna, "Anticipatory Use," 80.

[14] Ephron answered Abraham and said to him, [15] "My lord, listen to me. Land worth four hundred shekels of silver—what is that between you and me? Bury your dead." [16] Abraham agreed with Ephron, and Abraham weighed out to Ephron the silver that he had agreed to in the hearing of the Hethites: four hundred standard shekels of silver. [17] So Ephron's field at Machpelah near Mamre—the field with its cave and all the trees anywhere within the boundaries of the field—became [18] Abraham's possession in the sight of all the Hethites who came to the gate of his city. [19] After this, Abraham buried his wife Sarah in the cave of the field at Machpelah near Mamre (that is, Hebron) in the land of Canaan. [20] The field with its cave passed from the Hethites to Abraham as burial property.

Context

After it has reached a climax with the divine oath in 22:16–18, the reader anticipates that the Genesis narrative will move to the next generation to consider what happens when Isaac succeeds Abraham. Before this occurs, however, several events are recorded to bring closure to the story of Abraham's life. The first of these concerns the death and burial of Sarah. This is immediately followed by a lengthy description of how Abraham acquires a wife for Isaac (24:1–67), which ends by noting that Isaac "was comforted after his mother's death." While both events are in some measure tangential to the main plot of Genesis, which centers on tracing the patriline through which God will bless all the families of the ground, each episode contributes something important to the ongoing story. In the case of Sarah's death, Abraham's acquisition of a burial plot is significant in light of God's promise to Abraham that the land of Canaan will be "an eternal possession to you and your descendants after you" (17:8 NIV). The importance of this burial cave is underlined by subsequent references to it, which reveal that Abraham, Isaac, Jacob, Rebekah, and Leah are all laid to rest in this cave, in addition to Sarah (see 25:9–10; 49:29–31; 50:13).

Comments

23:1–2. The reference to Sarah's age marks the start of a new episode. Previously Abraham alluded to Sarah being 90 years old when God promised that she would give birth to Isaac (17:17). Throughout Genesis, the lifespan of individuals is often considerably higher than that experienced today; Abraham lived 175 years (25:7) and Isaac lived 180 years (35:28) (see Comments on 6:3).

The narrator links Sarah's death to Kiriath-arba (that is, Hebron). Centuries after Abraham's time, Kiriath-arba was renamed Hebron (cf.

Josh 14:15; 15:54; 20:7; Judg 1:10), possibly when Caleb took possession of the location (Josh 14:13–15). The name Hebron is used anachronistically in Genesis. The older name means "town of Arba." According to Joshua 14:15, "Arba was the greatest man among the Anakim" (cf. Josh 21:11). Genesis 13:18 mentions that Abraham camped "near the oaks of Mamre at Hebron" and built there an altar to YHWH. This appears to have been a location where Abraham often resided (cf. 14:13; 18:1). The oaks are possibly named after an Amorite called Mamre, who was bound to Abraham by treaty (14:13). Abraham's association with Mamre probably explains why the local population looked favorably upon him; he was known to them over a long period of time. The brief reference to the "land of Canaan" in verse 2, repeated in verse 19, may be deliberately intended to recall God's promise to Abraham that this land would be his "permanent possession" (17:8; cf. 12:7; 13:14–17; 15:18–21). Having lived with Sarah for more than sixty years, Abraham grieves over the death of his wife.

23:3–9. Abraham approaches the inhabitants of Hebron to buy a plot of land where he can bury Sarah. CSB uses the designation "Hethites" to translate the expression בְּנֵי־חֵת (*bĕnê-ḥēt*, "sons of Het"); most English versions adopt the translation "Hittites." This latter term is used of different groups of people in the ANE. It seems unlikely that the people of Hebron were related to the Hittites who lived in Anatolia and Syria. The Hethites are more likely to be Canaanites; Heth is named as a son of Canaan in 10:15.

Although Abraham's request involves a field that belongs to Ephron, son of Zohar, he initially addresses the local Hethite community because the transaction involves the permanent acquisition of property. As Russell helpfully notes,

> Although Ephron has an estate of production in the land, the Bnei Heth hold an estate of administration in Ephron's land. Their involvement in the transaction thus guarantees the permanent transfer to Abraham of rights to use the land as a burial site, including the right to bequeath the land to his heirs. By using language and gestures of deference and respect within the narrative, the characters affirm the rights of the other characters to participate in the negotiations. Their performance of politeness thus confirms the validity of the transaction.[535]

[535] Russell, "Abraham's Purchase of Ephron's Land," 170. Russell helpfully draws on the work of Max Gluckman who distinguishes between "estates of production" and "estates of

The formal nature of the discussion is highlighted by the event taking place at the city gate, involving all those who belonged to the city (note the reference to "his city" in vv. 10, 18).

As a semi-nomadic herdsman in Canaan for sixty years, Abraham has never purchased any land prior to Sarah's death. His self-designation as a "foreign resident" reflects his lifestyle.[536] The Hebrew term גֵּר (*gēr*) denotes anyone who is not a native of the region; modern equivalents in English would be "alien" (CSB), "migrant," "resident foreigner." People in this category are often in a more vulnerable position within society because they do not belong to the local ethnic group. The Israelites belonged to the category of *gēr* during their stay in Egypt. Consequently, God instructed the Israelites not to harass or exploit anyone who was a גֵּר (*gēr*) (Exod 22:21; 23:9). As more vulnerable members of the community, resident foreigners are often listed in the Old Testament alongside widows and the fatherless, a grouping that is sometimes called the "trio of the marginalized" (e.g., Exod 22:21–22; Deut 10:18–19; 24:17–22; Ps 146:9; Jer 7:6; Zech 7:10).

While Abraham highlights his vulnerability as a resident foreigner, the local inhabitants address him with great respect, affirming that he is a "prince of God among us" (CSB, NJB). Some English versions translate the expression נְשִׂיא אֱלֹהִים (*nĕśîʾ ʾĕlōhîm*) as "mighty prince" (KJV, NET, NIV, NRSV), taking the term אֱלֹהִים (*ʾĕlōhîm*) to indicate the superlative. However, commenting on the use of אֱלֹהִים (*ʾĕlōhîm*) as a superlative, Thomas remarks,

> If, when we say that the divine names in Hebrew are used to express the superlative, we mean that they have no religious significance at all and are merely intensifying epithets, I do not find a single example which decisively supports such a view. If, on the other hand, we mean that the divine names have the effect of raising a person or thing to a pre-eminent degree, the person or thing being brought into relationship with God, we may hold that the divine names have in this sense a superlative force.[537]

As Thomas correctly notes, it is a person's relationship with God that gives superlative force to the expression. For this reason, it is preferable

---

administration" as regards land tenure.

[536] Abraham describes himself using the expression גֵּר־וְתוֹשָׁב (*gēr-wĕtôšāb*) which emphasizes that he is not merely a temporary foreign resident; although not a native of Canaan, he has been living in the region for many years (cf. Lev 25:35, 47).

[537] D. Winton Thomas, "Consideration of Some Unusual Ways of Expressing the Superlative in Hebrew," *VT* 3 (1953) 215.

to adopt the translation "prince of God," recognizing that the inhabitants of Hebron are aware of Abraham's special relationship with God. Their view of Abraham recalls the divine promise that in him all the families of the ground will be blessed (Gen 12:3). Abraham responds with respect for the Hethites, bowing down to them (vv. 7, 12); he does not view his special role in the fulfilment of God's redemptive plan as grounds for treating others as inferior.

23:10–16. Ephron responds with great generosity, offering Abraham the land containing the cave at no cost. When Abraham insists on paying for the field, Ephron values it at 400 shekels of silver. A shekel was a measurement of weight, but it could vary because there were no standardized measurements, hence the CSB reads "standard shekels" or, as the NIV renders it, "the weight current among the merchants."[538] In 24:22 a wrist-bracelet weighs five shekels (cf. 24:47). It is difficult to draw comparisons with the cost of property mentioned elsewhere in the Old Testament (e.g., 2 Sam 24:24; 1 Kings 16:24; Jer 32:9). We should not jump to the assumption that the people of Kiriath-arba are "sharp-dealing Hittites" with whom Abraham must deal "for a mere gravesite."[539]

23:17–20. With the agreement of the people of Kiriath-arba, Abraham buys Ephron's field, guaranteeing its use as a burial site for Abraham and his family in perpetuity. Tradition locates the cave of Machpelah beneath the present Ibrahimi Mosque in Hebron.

Bridge

By acquiring this plot of land, Abraham establishes future rights to it for his family and puts down a marker that his descendants are to be associated with the land of Canaan, as God had already promised (12:7; 13:14–17; 15:18–21). If, as the author of Hebrews states, Abraham believed in life after death, he may well have expected that God's promise of the land to him as a "permanent possession" (17:8) would be fulfilled through a future resurrection of the dead (see Heb 11:9–10).

Q. A Wife for Isaac (24:1–67)

> [1] Abraham was now old, getting on in years, and the Lord had blessed him in everything. [2] Abraham said to his servant, the elder of his household who managed all he owned, "Place your hand under my

[538] For a brief discussion of various proposals regarding the historical background to Abraham's purchase of Machpelah, see Alexander, *From Paradise to the Promised Land*, 337-339.

[539] Alter, *Genesis*, 112.

thigh, 3 and I will have you swear by the Lord, God of heaven and God
of earth, that you will not take a wife for my son from the daughters
of the Canaanites among whom I live, 4 but will go to my land and my
family to take a wife for my son Isaac."

5 The servant said to him, "Suppose the woman is unwilling to follow me
to this land? Should I have your son go back to the land you came from?"

6 Abraham answered him, "Make sure that you don't take my son back
there. 7 The Lord, the God of heaven, who took me from my father's
house and from my native land, who spoke to me and swore to me, 'I will
give this land to your offspring'—he will send his angel before you, and
you can take a wife for my son from there. 8 If the woman is unwilling
to follow you, then you are free from this oath to me, but don't let my
son go back there." 9 So the servant placed his hand under his master
Abraham's thigh and swore an oath to him concerning this matter.

10 The servant took ten of his master's camels, and with all kinds of his
master's goods in hand, he went to Aram-naharaim, to Nahor's town.
11 At evening, the time when women went out to draw water, he made
the camels kneel beside a well outside the town.

12 "Lord, God of my master Abraham," he prayed, "make this happen for
me today, and show kindness to my master Abraham. 13 I am standing
here at the spring where the daughters of the men of the town are coming
out to draw water. 14 Let the girl to whom I say, 'Please lower your water
jug so that I may drink,' and who responds, 'Drink, and I'll water your
camels also'—let her be the one you have appointed for your servant
Isaac. By this I will know that you have shown kindness to my master."

15 Before he had finished speaking, there was Rebekah—daughter of
Bethuel son of Milcah, the wife of Abraham's brother Nahor—coming
with a jug on her shoulder. 16 Now the girl was very beautiful, a vir-
gin—no man had been intimate with her. She went down to the spring,
filled her jug, and came up. 17 Then the servant ran to meet her and
said, "Please let me have a little water from your jug."

18 She replied, "Drink, my lord." She quickly lowered her jug to her hand
and gave him a drink. 19 When she had finished giving him a drink, she
said, "I'll also draw water for your camels until they have had enough
to drink." 20 She quickly emptied her jug into the trough and hurried
to the well again to draw water. She drew water for all his camels 21
while the man silently watched her to see whether or not the Lord had
made his journey a success.

22 As the camels finished drinking, the man took a gold ring weighing
half a shekel, and for her wrists two bracelets weighing ten shekels of
gold. 23 "Whose daughter are you?" he asked. "Please tell me, is there
room in your father's house for us to spend the night?"

[24] She answered him, "I am the daughter of Bethuel son of Milcah, whom
she bore to Nahor." [25] She also said to him, "We have plenty of straw
and feed and a place to spend the night."

[26] Then the man knelt low, worshiped the Lord, [27] and said, "Blessed
be the Lord, the God of my master Abraham, who has not withheld his
kindness and faithfulness from my master. As for me, the Lord has led
me on the journey to the house of my master's relatives."

The girl ran and told her mother's household about these things. [29] Now
Rebekah had a brother named Laban, and Laban ran out to the man at
the spring. [30] As soon as he had seen the ring and the bracelets on his
sister's wrists, and when he had heard his sister Rebekah's words—"The
man said this to me!"—he went to the man. He was standing there by
the camels at the spring.

Laban said, "Come, you who are blessed by the Lord. Why are you stand-
ing out here? I have prepared the house and a place for the camels." [32]
So the man came to the house, and the camels were unloaded. Straw
and feed were given to the camels, and water was brought to wash his
feet and the feet of the men with him.

[33] A meal was set before him, but he said, "I will not eat until I have
said what I have to say."

So Laban said, "Please speak."

[34] "I am Abraham's servant," he said. [35] "The Lord has greatly blessed
my master, and he has become rich. He has given him flocks and herds,
silver and gold, male and female slaves, and camels and donkeys. [36]
Sarah, my master's wife, bore a son to my master in her old age, and he
has given him everything he owns. [37] My master put me under this oath:
'You will not take a wife for my son from the daughters of the Canaanites
in whose land I live [38] but will go to my father's family and to my clan to
take a wife for my son.' [39] But I said to my master, 'Suppose the woman
will not come back with me?' 40 He said to me, 'The Lord before whom
I have walked will send his angel with you and make your journey a
success, and you will take a wife for my son from my clan and from my
father's family. [41] Then you will be free from my oath if you go to my
family and they do not give her to you—you will be free from my oath.'

[42] "Today when I came to the spring, I prayed: Lord, God of my master
Abraham, if only you will make my journey successful! [43] I am standing
here at a spring. Let the young woman who comes out to draw water,
and I say to her, 'Please let me drink a little water from your jug,' [44]
and who responds to me, 'Drink, and I'll draw water for your camels
also'—let her be the woman the Lord has appointed for my master's son.

[45] "Before I had finished praying silently, there was Rebekah coming with her jug on her shoulder, and she went down to the spring and drew water. So I said to her, 'Please let me have a drink.' [46] She quickly lowered her jug from her shoulder and said, 'Drink, and I'll water your camels also.' So I drank, and she also watered the camels. [47] Then I asked her, 'Whose daughter are you?' She responded, 'The daughter of Bethuel son of Nahor, whom Milcah bore to him.' So I put the ring on her nose and the bracelets on her wrists. [48] Then I knelt low, worshiped the LORD, and blessed the LORD, the God of my master Abraham, who guided me on the right way to take the granddaughter of my master's brother for his son. [49] Now, if you are going to show kindness and faithfulness to my master, tell me; if not, tell me, and I will go elsewhere."

[50] Laban and Bethuel answered, "This is from the LORD; we have no choice in the matter. [51] Rebekah is here in front of you. Take her and go, and let her be a wife for your master's son, just as the LORD has spoken."

[52] When Abraham's servant heard their words, he bowed to the ground before the LORD. [53] Then he brought out objects of silver and gold, and garments, and gave them to Rebekah. He also gave precious gifts to her brother and her mother. [54] Then he and the men with him ate and drank and spent the night.

When they got up in the morning, he said, "Send me to my master."

[55] But her brother and mother said, "Let the girl stay with us for about ten days. Then she can go."

[56] But he responded to them, "Do not delay me, since the LORD has made my journey a success. Send me away so that I may go to my master."

[57] So they said, "Let's call the girl and ask her opinion."

[58] They called Rebekah and said to her, "Will you go with this man?"

She replied, "I will go." [59] So they sent away their sister Rebekah with the one who had nursed and raised her, and Abraham's servant and his men.

[60] They blessed Rebekah, saying to her:

Our sister, may you become
thousands upon ten thousands.
May your offspring possess
the city gates of their enemies.

[61] Then Rebekah and her female servants got up, mounted the camels, and followed the man. So the servant took Rebekah and left.

Now Isaac was returning from Beer-lahai-roi, for he was living in the Negev region. [63] In the early evening Isaac went out to walk in the field,

and looking up he saw camels coming. [64] Rebekah looked up, and when
she saw Isaac, she got down from her camel [65] and asked the servant,
"Who is that man in the field coming to meet us?"

The servant answered, "It is my master." So she took her veil and covered herself. [66] Then the servant told Isaac everything he had done.

[67] And Isaac brought her into the tent of his mother Sarah and took Rebekah to be his wife. Isaac loved her, and he was comforted after his mother's death.

Context

Compared to other episodes within the Terah *tôlĕdôt,* the account of how Isaac acquires a wife is by far the longest. In telling how Rebekah becomes Isaac's wife, the narrative highlights how divine providence plays a key part in shaping the patriline that lies at the heart of Genesis. God's guidance of Abraham's servant to Rebekah strongly suggests that she is the one chosen by God to be Isaac's wife. Additionally, Rebekah is shown to be a most suitable companion for Isaac, displaying generous hospitality to a stranger and his camels. More importantly, influenced by the servant's account of how God has blessed Abraham, Rebekah is willing to undertake in faith the journey that Abraham made. Her willingness to leave her family and homeland, as Abraham did (12:1–5), to marry a man she has never met, who lives about 500 miles away, reveals that she is a woman of deep faith. The reader senses that she is a most appropriate bride for Isaac, a match made in heaven.

Comments

24:1–9. Following on from the account of Sarah's burial, a new episode is introduced by highlighting how YHWH has blessed Abraham "in everything." At first sight this observation appears to have little relevance to the issue of finding a wife for Isaac. However, as Sarna notes, God's blessing of Abraham will later play an important part in the process of persuading Rebekah to travel from Aram-naharaim to Canaan.[540] Like the narrator of chapter 24, the servant will begin his story to Rebekah's family by focusing on God's blessing of Abraham (see v. 35). Abraham's role in God's plans underlies all that is recorded in chapter 24 and beyond.

Aware of how the mantle will pass to Isaac, Abraham is concerned that his son will not find a suitable wife. Fearful that a Canaanite bride

[540] Sarna, "Anticipatory Use," 80–81.

may undermine Isaac's special relationship with God, Abraham instructs his most senior and trusted servant to find a wife for Isaac from among Abraham's relatives in northern Mesopotamia.[541] To underline the seriousness of this quest, Abraham asked the servant to swear an oath. The precise nature of this ritual, which involves the servant placing his hand under Abraham's thigh, is debated. The servant complies with Abraham's request but tempers his response by asking permission to take Isaac to northern Mesopotamia if the woman he finds declines to travel back to Canaan with him. However, Abraham refuses to let Isaac travel with the servant, adding to the challenge of finding a suitable wife. What family is likely to let their daughter travel over 500 miles to marry a man they have never met? Abraham's reluctance to let Isaac travel to northern Mesopotamia underlines his belief that his family's future is linked to the land of Canaan. Later, Isaac and Rebekah will demand that their son Jacob should also get a wife from Paddan-aram (27:46–28:5). Abraham's remarks in verse 7 suggest that he is confident that God will guide his servant to a suitable wife for Isaac.

24:10–14. With a minimum of detail, the scene switches from Hebron to Aram-naharaim. The latter name means "Aram of the two rivers," a designation that denotes the northwestern part of Mesopotamia.[542] In search of Abraham's relatives, the servant comes to Nahor's town, Nahor being the name of Abraham's grandfather (11:22–25) and brother (11:26–27; 22:20).[543] To reach this location, the servant travels over 500 miles (800 km), a journey of about twenty days duration. To transport everything that he took with him for the journey, the servant used ten camels. There is evidence for the domestication of Bactrian camels toward the end of the third millennium BC to support the authenticity of this account.[544]

Drawing on Abraham's special standing with God, the servant prays that God will guide him to an appropriate wife for Isaac. The servant's priority in looking for a wife for Isaac is to find a woman who will be kind and generous toward a total stranger, characteristics that will be

---

[541] From Gen 9 onwards, the Canaanites are often portrayed as wicked (9:24–27; 10:6–20; 13:11–12).

[542] The name "Mesopotamia," derived from Greek, means "between the rivers."

[543] This town is elsewhere in Genesis called Haran חָרָן (*ḥārān*) in 11:31–32; 12:4–5; 27:43; 28:10; 29:4. See Comments on 11:26.

[544] Heide, "The Domestication of the Camel," 368, writes, "The archaeological and instructional evidence allows at least the domesticated Bactrian camel to have existed at Abraham's time."

evident through her willingness to water ten camels, a time-consuming task. The servant's request to God implies that such characteristics are in keeping with the kind of bride that God would choose for Isaac. In asking for divine assistance, the servant recognizes that God has the power to influence events. He asks for help not primarily for his own benefit but for Abraham's. Twice he speaks of God showing חֶסֶד (*ḥesed*, "kindness") toward Abraham (vv. 12, 14; cf. 24:27). The reference to חֶסֶד (*ḥesed*, "kindness") resonates with what the servant looks for in Isaac's potential bride.

24:15–21. The servant's prayer appears to be answered almost as soon as he has finished speaking. The narrator's introductory remarks about Rebekah strongly imply that she will be the answer to his petition. The reader swiftly learns in verse 15–16 that she is a relative of Abraham; she is carrying a jug on her shoulder, an item essential to fulfilling the servant's predetermined sign; she is very beautiful; and most importantly of all, she is not married.

As Rebekah comes up from the spring, the servant hurries to her to ask for a drink of water. She responds positively and, after he has finished drinking, she proceeds voluntarily to water his camels. Her actions correspond exactly to those listed by the servant in his prayer to YHWH (v. 14). Watching her intently and silently, the servant is left to wonder if she might be the answer to his prayer.

24:22–28. Convinced that Rebekah is God's choice for Isaac, the servant proceeds to reward Rebekah for her willingness to water the camels, before firing out several questions to her. As Vermeulen helpfully observes regarding the questions, "They tell us about a nervous, excited character who is supposed to ask the common questions, although in his heart he is already convinced that he has found Isaac's wife. ... This unconscious feeling of the right match is expressed by sound similarity in his words, as if the match also happens in language."[545]

In response to the servant's questions, Rebekah gives details of her family, mentioning her grandfather Nahor (11:26–27, 29; 22:20–23) and his wife Milcah (11:29; 22:20–23). God's role in providentially leading the servant to Rebekah prompts a response of worship. Kneeling down, the servant blesses God for acting with "kindness and faithfulness" toward Abraham. He is convinced that his success in finding Rebekah is due to God's special relationship with Abraham (v. 27).

---

[545] Karolien Vermeulen, "The 'Song' of the Servant—Gen 24:23," *VT* 61 (2011): 503.

24:29–33. A new character is introduced into the story: Laban, Rebekah's brother. After Rebekah runs to her home to tell what has happened, Laban runs to the well outside the town to meet Abraham's servant (v. 29). Little is said about Laban's character, but the narrator hints at his desire for wealth by mentioning that he went to the servant "as soon as he had seen the ring and the bracelets on this sister's wrists" (v. 30). Laban's longing for riches becomes a significant element in the story of Jacob's stay in Paddan-aram (29:1–31:55).

On meeting Abraham's servant, Laban is possibly impressed by the extensive cargo on the ten camels (cf. v. 10). He speaks of the servant being blessed by YHWH (v. 31), a comment that recalls the opening verse of the chapter. Laban then invites Abraham's servant to the family home. The welcome appears genuine and generous, with the animals being fed and the men's feet being washed. However, before eating, Abraham's servant gives priority to explaining the reason for his presence in their town.

24:34–49. The servant's lengthy speech repeats much of what the narrator has already said in the first part of the chapter. Occasionally, he adds details that highlight his firsthand knowledge of what happened (e.g., the gold ring given to Rebekah was a nose ring; compare v. 47 with v. 22). Strikingly, whereas the narrator merely comments that YHWH had blessed Abraham "in everything" (v. 1), the servant emphasizes Abraham's wealth, listing "sheep and cattle, silver and gold, male and female slaves, and camels and donkeys" (v. 35; cf. 12:16; 13:2; 20:14, 16). Perhaps he has already sensed that Laban and his family will let Rebekah marry Isaac if they see themselves as benefiting financially. Other factors may explain minor variations between the narrator's account and that of the servant. For example, perhaps to avoid giving a sense of Abraham's superiority and offending his relatives, the servant substitutes the shorter expression, "The Lord before whom I have walked"[546] (v. 40) for the much longer statement, "The Lord, the God of heaven, who took me from my father's house and from my native land, who spoke to me and swore to me, 'I will give this land to your offspring' " (v. 7). Subtle variations in the servant's report may also reflect the use of the Aramaic language by those living in the region of Paddan-aram.[547] The length of the servant speech adds suspense

[546] On the theological significance of this expression, see Exegesis on 5:22; cf. 6:8–9; 17:1.

[547] In 25:20 Bethuel and Laban are both designated אֲרַמִּי (ʾărammî, "Aramean") (cf. 28:5). See Gary A. Rendsburg, "Some False Leads in the Identification of Late Biblical Hebrew Texts:

to the account. The reader is kept waiting to know how Rebekah and her family will respond. Having previously said that God has shown "kindness and faithfulness" to Abraham (v. 27), the servant asks Laban to show him "kindness and faithfulness" (v. 49).

24:50–51. The reference to Bethuel is somewhat unexpected. He has not been named up to this point in the narrative, a surprising omission given that he is Rebekah's father. The mention of Rebekah's "mother's household" in verse 28 leads some commentators to assume that her father is dead. However, it may simply be that Rebekah broke the news of what happened to her mother, perhaps fearful of how her father might react to such an unexpected event.[548] It is not unusual for a narrator to avoid mentioning characters until their presence is essential.[549] Up to this point, Bethuel has had no active part to play in the story. Possibly he is very old, making Laban the de facto head of the family. In light of the servant's story, Laban and Bethuel consent to Rebekah becoming Isaac's wife, persuaded by the evidence of YHWH's providential guidance of the servant to Rebekah. Strikingly, their brief remarks are framed by references to YHWH.

24:52–61. The positive response of Laban and Bethuel causes the servant to bow down to YHWH. He acknowledges publicly God's part in giving him success in his quest for a wife for Isaac. He then bestows on Rebekah and her family extravagant gifts, confirming that YHWH has blessed Abraham with great wealth.

The sequence of verbs in verses 54–61 implies that these events took place with a minimum of delay. This is noteworthy, given the desire of Laban and his mother to delay the departure of Rebekah (v. 55). The servant, however, is keen to return to Abraham. When Rebekah's opinion is sought, she favors going immediately. Her willingness is a clear indication that she believes the events of the previous twenty-four hours to be of

---

The Cases of Genesis 24 and 1 Samuel 2:27–36," *JBL* 121 (2002): 24–35; Brian A. Bompiani, "Is Genesis 24 a Problem for Source Criticism?," *BSac* 164 (2007): 403–15.

548 References to a "mother's household" are rare in the Old Testament. The only other example comes in Ruth 1:8, where Naomi suggests to her two daughters-in-law that they should each return to their "mother's home." It seems unlikely that the fathers of Ruth and Orpah were both dead.

549 For example, v. 32 contains the first reference to the men who traveled with Abraham's servant; their existence is merely hinted at in v. 23 with the reference to "us."

YHWH. With no hesitation she affirms that she will go. Given all that this entails, Rebekah's actions reveal her deep trust in God.

To mark her departure, her family pronounce a blessing upon her, the wording of which is noteworthy. By wishing her many descendants and an offspring who will possess the gate of those who hate him,[550] Rebekah's family echo, perhaps unknowingly, the oath that God swore to Abraham in 22:16–18.[551] Everything points to Rebekah being a suitable wife for Isaac, their future marriage securing the continuation of the unique lineage though which God's promises to Abraham will be fulfilled.

24:62–67. Having recorded Rebekah's departure from her hometown in Aram-naharaim, the narrative jumps to Isaac in southern Canaan. The reference to Beer-lahai-roi recalls how God appeared to Hagar at this location (16:7–14). Skillfully, the narrator describes how Isaac sees the approaching camels (v. 63), before presenting the encounter from Rebekah's perspective. When she discovers that the man is Isaac, she veils her face, as was the custom during the betrothal period. While the reference to "the tent of his mother Sarah" (v. 67) seems out of place in the light of the account of Sarah's death and burial in the preceding chapter, it functions here to emphasize how Rebekah's presence as Isaac's wife consoles him after the death of his mother.

Bridge

This lengthy account of how Abraham's servant finds a wife for Isaac is a rich testimony to God's providential activity at work in the lives of those who trust him. The servant is a man of deep faith, who looks to God to answer prayer. He is also perceptive, seeking a prospective bride who generously cares for the well-being of others.

---

[550] The CSB translation, "May your offspring possess the city gates of their enemies" (24:60) fails to convey accurately the Hebrew text, which implies that "your offspring" ought to be understood as referring to an individual. See Alexander, "Further Observations," 363–67. Also, in the Hebrew text "gate" is in the singular. The ESV reading is preferable: "may your offspring possess the gate of those who hate him!" The final Hebrew word of the blessing in v. 60 differs from that used at the end of 22:17, although semantically both terms are very similar; the CSB translations gives the impression that the same Hebrew words are used in both passages.

[551] Steinmann, "Jesus and Possessing the Enemies' Gate," 15n4, notes, "Unlike Genesis 22:17, the blessing at Genesis 24:60 is in the form of a wish using an imperative verb (הֲיִי) and a jussive verb (וְיִירַשׁ)."

Like Abraham, Rebekah is willing to abandon the security of her family and homeland to travel to the land of Canaan, trusting that her future is safe in God's hands. The resulting marriage of Isaac to Rebekah offers hope that the patriline of Abraham, linked back to Adam and Eve through their son Seth, will be continued. The divine promises associated with this unique patriline will eventually be fulfilled through one of Isaac's descendants.

R. The Death of Abraham (25:1–11)

> 1 Abraham had taken another wife, whose name was Keturah, 2 and she
> bore him Zimran, Jokshan, Medan, Midian, Ishbak, and Shuah. 3 Jokshan
> fathered Sheba and Dedan. Dedan's sons were the Asshurim, Letushim,
> and Leummim. 4 And Midian's sons were Ephah, Epher, Hanoch, Abida,
> and Eldaah. All these were sons of Keturah. 5 Abraham gave everything
> he owned to Isaac. 6 But Abraham gave gifts to the sons of his concu-
> bines, and while he was still alive he sent them eastward, away from
> his son Isaac, to the land of the East.
>
> 7 This is the length of Abraham's life: 175 years. 8 He took his last breath
> and died at a good old age, old and contented, and he was gathered
> to his people. 9 His sons Isaac and Ishmael buried him in the cave of
> Machpelah near Mamre, in the field of Ephron son of Zohar the Hethite.
> 10 This was the field that Abraham bought from the Hethites. Abraham
> was buried there with his wife Sarah. 11 After Abraham's death, God
> blessed his son Isaac, who lived near Beer-lahai-roi.

Context

The final episode in the Terah *tôlědôt* records some further family details regarding Abraham, concluding with a brief description of his death and burial in the cave of Machpelah. This brings the Genesis account of Abraham's life to a conclusion and prepares the way for the next major section of the Genesis narrative, which traces the progress of the patriline through Isaac to Jacob. Importantly, subtle comments in 25:1–11 distinguish Isaac from the other sons of Abraham who belong to the maternal houses of Hagar and Keturah.[552] In a variety of ways the narrative underlines that Isaac is the designated heir to the "material and immaterial wealth of Abraham's house."[553]

---

552 See the fuller discussion in Chapman, *The House of the Mother*, 39–43.

553 Chapman, *The House of the Mother*, 39.

Comments

25:1–6. It comes as something of a surprise to learn that Abraham took another wife, Keturah. Possibly this occurred in the thirty-eight years that he outlived Sarah, although it may have happened sooner. Keturah, along with Hagar, is designated a פִּילֶגֶשׁ (*pîlegeš*) concubine in verse 6 (cf. 1 Chr 1:32). The same term, פִּילֶגֶשׁ (*pîlegeš*), is used to describe Bilhah, Rachel's maidservant, in 35:22, possibly suggesting that Keturah was a maidservant, whom Sarah gave to Abraham, as she did with Hagar (16:1–3). The narrative sheds no light on how Keturah became Abraham's concubine (or second wife). It does, however, state that she bore Abraham six sons, whom he sent away, as he did with Ishmael (21:14), to prevent them being co-heirs with Isaac (cf. 21:10). Chapman observes that the way in which these sons are designated "sons of Keturah" rather than "sons of Abraham" sets the maternal house of Keturah apart from the maternal house of Sarah (and of Hagar).[554] Verse 6 underlines that Keturah's sons, as well as Ishmael, Hagar's son, do not share in the inheritance that is given to Isaac, but are relocated outside the land promised by God to Abraham. Their departure confirms that Isaac is Abraham's sole heir (v. 5). Despite Abraham's fathering of other sons, the ongoing Genesis narrative is only interested in Sarah's offspring. This highlights that the author of Genesis is primarily concerned to trace the unique line of descendants that will lead to an individual who will eventually overcome the serpent and through whom all the nations of the earth will be blessed.

25:7–11. After establishing Isaac's status as sole heir, the final verses of the Terah *tôlĕdôt* record the death and burial of Abraham. Noting Abraham's exceptional age at death, the narrator describes how he is buried in the cave of Machpelah, which he previously bought from Ephron the Hethite (23:1–20). In recording the death and burial of Abraham, the narrator remarks that "he was gathered to his people" (v. 8). This concept, which appears elsewhere in death notices in the Old Testament (e.g., 25:17; 35:29; 49:29, 33), may indicate continued existence beyond death.[555] Interestingly, Ishmael assists Isaac with the burial of Abraham, an indication that he maintained a link with his father despite being sent away (21:10–13). The final words of the Terah *tôlĕdôt* pick up on the

---

[554] Chapman, *The House of the Mother*, 39–43.

[555] Wenham, *Genesis 16-50*, 160, suggests that this may refer "to the soul of Abraham being reunited with his dead relatives in the afterlife." See Johnston, *Shades of Sheol*, 33–34.

theme of blessing, recalling the importance of this theme in God's initial words to Abraham in 12:1–3. As God had blessed Abraham "in everything" (24:1), his blessing now rests on Isaac (cf. 26:3, 12, 24, 29). The divine promises given to Abraham in the Terah *tôlĕdôt* pass to Isaac. He is the one through whom the patriline will take its next step. And as heir to the divine promises, the eternal covenant of circumcision will be established with him (cf. 17:19–21).

Bridge

With the death of Abraham, the Genesis narrative focuses next on Isaac and his offspring, Esau and Jacob (25:19–35:29). However, before transitioning to the *tôlĕdôt* of Isaac, a short *tôlĕdôt* section is inserted focusing on Ishmael. As is often the case in Genesis, family information about individuals who are not part of the main patriline is recorded first. Ishmael's *tôlĕdôt* (25:12–18) is placed before that of Isaac (25:19–35:29). A similar pattern will occur later involving the *tôlĕdôt* sections of Esau (36:1–37:1) and Jacob (37:2–50:26).

VIII. The Offspring of Ishmael (25:12–18)

> [12] These are the family records of Abraham's son Ishmael, whom Hagar
> the Egyptian, Sarah's slave, bore to Abraham. [13] These are the names
> of Ishmael's sons; their names according to the family records are
> Nebaioth, Ishmael's firstborn, then Kedar, Adbeel, Mibsam, [14] Mishma,
> Dumah, Massa, [15] Hadad, Tema, Jetur, Naphish, and Kedemah. [16] These
> are Ishmael's sons, and these are their names by their settlements and
> encampments: twelve leaders of their clans. [17] This is the length of
> Ishmael's life: 137 years. He took his last breath and died, and was gath-
> ered to his people. [18] And they settled from Havilah to Shur, which is
> opposite Egypt as you go toward Asshur. He stayed near all his relatives.

Context

While the author of Genesis is primarily interested in tracing the unique lineage that will lead to the offspring who will overcome the serpent and bring blessing to the nations of the earth, the family lines of other participants in the story are briefly noted, usually in the form of segmented genealogies. Since these descendants will play no long-term role in the fulfilment of God's redemptive plan, they are mentioned prior to the introduction of the more significant participants in the story (cf. Esau's *tôlĕdôt* section comes before Jacob's in chs. 36–37). 'The account of the "unchosen" son (in this case, Ishmael) is provided prior to the (more extensive) account of the chosen son (in this case, Isaac).'[556] A *tôlĕdôt* heading introduces the short section on Ishmael (25:12; see Comments on 2:4).

Comments

25:12–16. The *tôlĕdôt* heading of Ishmael is expanded by a brief description that recalls how Sarah gave her Egyptian maidservant Hagar to Abraham (16:1–16).[557] The mention of Hagar's status highlights that Ishmael does not belong to the maternal house of Sarah and in this regard is not on a par with Isaac.[558] Ishmael's twelve sons are listed, each establishing clans over which they ruled. The mention of "twelve leaders" recalls God's promise to Abraham regarding Ishmael's numerous descendants in 17:20, where the same expression is found (translated "twelve tribal leaders" in CSB). God promised to make Ishmael into a great nation (17:20; 21:18); these verses point toward the future fulfilment of this promise. Ancient readers of Genesis might well have been able to associate the names of Ishmael's sons with particular peoples.[559]

25:17–18. Ishmael's age at death is noted, a recurring feature of similar reports in Genesis. The brief report of his death resembles that of Abraham (v. 8; cf. 35:29; 49:29, 33). The final comment about Ishmael has prompted very different translations of the Hebrew expression עַל־פְּנֵי כָל־אֶחָיו נָפָל (*ʿal-pĕnê kol-ʾeḥāyw nāpāl*), which literally reads "on the face of all his brothers he fell." Whereas KJV reads, "he died in the presence of all his brethren," the NIV has "And they lived in hostility toward all the tribes related to them." ESV renders the expression "He settled over against all his kinsmen," and NET has "They settled away from all their relatives." The closest parallel to this expression in the whole of the Old Testament comes in 50:1, which speaks of how Joseph fell upon his father's face in affection. In the light of 50:1, the final comment in verse 18, which appears to be about Ishmael rather than his descendants, would imply that he lived in harmony, not hostility, with his brothers. This would be

556 Provan, *Discovering Genesis*, 143.

557 On the Hebrew expression שִׁפְחַת שָׂרָה (*šipḥat śārâ*), which CSB translates as "Sarah's slave," see Exegesis on 16:1–3.

558 Chapman, *The House of the Mother*, 40.

559 See Mathews, *Genesis 11:27–50:26*, 360–62.

in keeping with his presence alongside Isaac at the burial of Abraham (25:9) and the fact that Esau marries Ishmael's daughter, Mahalath (28:9).[560]

Bridge

This short *tôlĕdôt* section concludes the narrator's interest in the lineage of Ishmael. Although he was the first son born to Abraham, he was not the son promised by God, the one through whom the patriline traced in Genesis would continue. As God indicated to Abraham, the covenant of circumcision would be established with Isaac, but not Ishmael (17:19–21). With this expectation in view, the Genesis narrative turns to consider Isaac and his offspring.

IX. The Offspring of Isaac (25:19–35:29)

A. The Birth of Esau and Jacob (25:19–26)

> 19 These are the family records of Isaac son of Abraham. Abraham fa-
> thered Isaac. 20 Isaac was forty years old when he took as his wife Re-
> bekah daughter of Bethuel the Aramean from Paddan-aram and sister
> of Laban the Aramean. 21 Isaac prayed to the Lord on behalf of his wife
> because she was childless. The Lord was receptive to his prayer, and his
> wife Rebekah conceived. 22 But the children inside her struggled with
> each other, and she said, "Why is this happening to me?" So she went
> to inquire of the Lord. 23 And the Lord said to her:
>
> Two nations are in your womb;
> two peoples will come from you and be separated.
> One people will be stronger than the other,
> and the older will serve the younger.
>
> 24 When her time came to give birth, there were indeed twins in her
> womb. 25 The first one came out red-looking, covered with hair like a
> fur coat, and they named him Esau. 26 After this, his brother came out
> grasping Esau's heel with his hand. So he was named Jacob. Isaac was
> sixty years old when they were born.

Context

Another *tôlĕdôt* heading announces the start of the next main narrative section in Genesis (see Comments on 2:4); this section runs from 25:19 to 35:29. Throughout 25:19–35:29 the narrator continues to trace the family line that will lead to the "offspring of the woman" (see Biblical and Theological Themes §1). Various episodes explore the

---

560 Wenham, *Genesis 16–50*, 165, mistakenly takes the final phrase of v. 18 to be a "direct quote from 16:12." However, the verb in 16:12 is יִשְׁכֹּן (*yiškōn*, "he will dwell").

choice between Esau, the older twin, loved by his father, and Jacob the younger twin, loved by his mother. Once again in Genesis, the principle of primogeniture is overturned, a motif that will reappear in chapters 37–50. Esau is the older of the twin boys born to Rebekah, but his younger brother Jacob will ultimately gain precedence over him, fulfilling the divine oracle that is given to Rebekah before the twins are born (25:23). The twins, however, are far from identical and the relationship between them is marked by conflict. At the heart of their discord lies the fact that they have strongly differing attitudes toward the divine promises given first to Abraham and then to Isaac. Under normal conditions these promises should pass to the son who holds the firstborn-birthright. But Esau places little value on his privileged position, unlike Jacob who yearns to be firstborn. Jacob's ambition alienates him from his older brother, as he exploits Esau's shortcomings to the full.

Table 1

A	oracle sought; Rebekah struggles in childbirth; *bĕkōrâ* ("birthright"); birth; themes of strife, deception, and infertility	25:19–34
B	interlude; strife; deception; *bĕrākâ* ("blessing"); covenant with foreigner	26:1–35
C	deception; *bĕrākâ* stolen; fear of Esau; flight from the land	27:1–28:9
D	encounter (verb: *pāgaʿ*) with the divine at a sacred site; near border; *bĕrākâ*	28:10–22
E	internal cycle opens; arrival; Laban at border; deception; wages	29:1–35
F	Rachel barren; Leah fertile Rachel fertile; Jacob increases the herds	30:1–24 30:25–43
E'	internal cycle closes; departure; Laban at border; deception; wages	31:1–55
D'	encounters (verb: *pāgaʿ*) with divine beings at sacred sites; near border; *bĕrākâ*	32:1–32
C'	deception planned; fear of Esau; *bĕrākâ* gift returned; return to land	33:1–20
B'	interlude; strife, deception; covenant with foreigner	34:1–31
A'	oracle fulfilled; Rachel struggles in childbirth; *bĕrākâ*; death, resolutions	35:1–22

Despite the episodic nature of 25:19–35:29, the narrator skillfully fashions the narrative into a highly structured, unified composition. As Fishbane has ably demonstrated, 25:19–35:29 was carefully composed using a mirror-image pattern.[561]

A oracle sought; Rebekah struggles in childbirth; *bĕkōrâ* ("birthright"); birth; themes of strife, deception, infertility (Gen 25:19–34)
  B interlude; strife; deception; *bĕrākâ* ("blessing"); covenant with a foreigner (Gen 26:1–35)
    C deception; *bĕrākâ* stolen; fear of Esau; flight from the land (Gen 27:1–28:9)
      D encounter (verb: *pāgaʿ*) with the divine at a sacred site near border; *bĕrākâ* (Gen 28:10–22)
        E internal cycle opens; arrival; Laban at border; deception; wages (Gen 29:1–35)
          F (Gen 30:1–43) Rachel barren; Leah fertile (Gen 30:1–24)
            Rachel fertile; Jacob increases the herds (Gen 30:25–43)
        E' internal cycle closes; departure; Laban at border; deception; wages (Gen 31:1–55)
      D' encounters (verb: *pāgaʿ* with divine beings at sacred sites near border; *bĕrākâ* (Gen 32:1–32)
    C' deception planned; fear of Esau; *bĕrākâ* gift returned; return to land (Gen 33:1–20)
  B' interlude; strife, deception; covenant with a foreigner (Gen 34:1–31)
A' oracle fulfilled; Rachel struggles in childbirth; *bĕrākâ*; death, resolutions (Gen 35:1–22)

The symmetrical structure of the narrative is created in part by the movement of Jacob from Canaan to Paddan-Aram and then back to Canaan. On leaving and returning to the land of Canaan, Jacob encounters God in

---

[561] Fishbane, *Text and Texture*, 42, slightly modified. Cf. Waltke and Fredricks, *Genesis*, 352; Gary A. Rendsburg, *The Redaction of Genesis* (Winona Lake: Eisenbrauns, 1986), 53–54. See also Provan, *Discovering Genesis*, 153–54, for a similar structure, although Provan makes no reference to Fishbane. Blum, "The Jacob Tradition," 181–86, also recognizes the closely unified nature of the episodes in ch. 25–35, although he considers chs. 26 and 34–35 to be more loosely connected. Rather than seeing chs. 25–33 (without ch. 26) as merely a "cycle of tales," he views it as "a major integrated story with themes of its own" (p. 182).

special ways. There is also a movement within the story from growing conflict between Jacob and Esau, involving the concepts of firstborn-birthright and blessing to eventual reconciliation. Even chapters 26 and 34, which at first sight may appear less connected to the rest of the story, are carefully placed to enhance the mirror-image pattern of the story.[562] As Niditch remarks, "The pattern of trickery/trickster-duped/reverse-trickery and plays on older-younger rivalry are ways in which the author ties together the Jacob narrative into a beautifully balanced whole."[563]

Picture 1

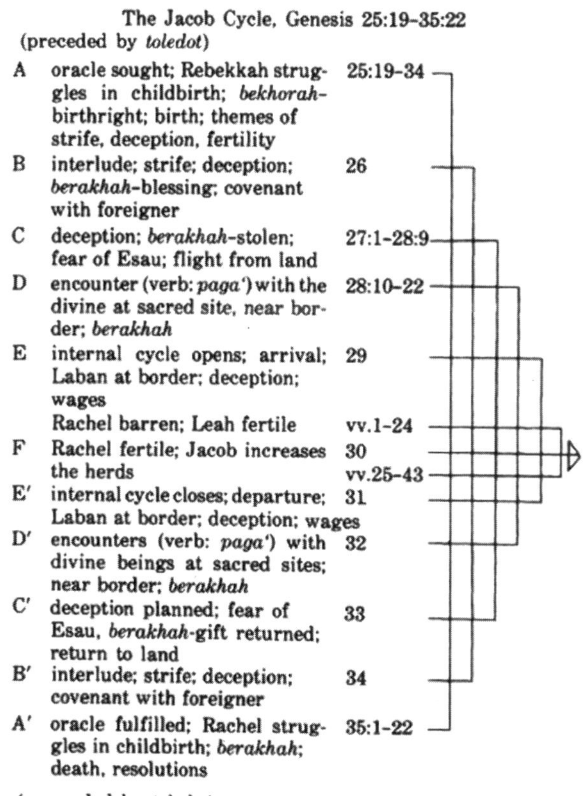

[562] Fishbane, "Composition and Structure," 32, writes, "The entire narrative is artfully woven together and paced."

[563] Susan Niditch, *Underdogs and Tricksters: A Prelude to Biblical Folklore*, New Voices in Biblical Studies (San Francisco: Harper & Row, 1987), 107–8.

Comments

25:19. The Hebrew term תּוֹלְדֹת *tôlĕdôt*, translated "family records" (see Comments on 2:4), refers to what is born. Consequently, the heading at the start of 25:19–35:29 focuses attention primarily on Isaac's sons, Esau and Jacob. Since there is no *tôlĕdôt* section devoted to what comes forth from Abraham himself, specific information about Isaac is incorporated into the Isaac *tôlĕdôt* (e.g., 26:1–33). This is signaled by the way in which the heading in verse 19 describes Isaac as "Abraham's son," before stating, "Abraham fathered Isaac." The twofold reference to Abraham being Isaac's father seems unnecessary. However, it sets this *tôlĕdôt* heading apart from all others, perhaps indicating that it incorporates what might be considered to be the *tôlĕdôt* of Abraham.[564]

25:20–21. Like Abraham and Sarah, Isaac and Rebekah are unable initially to have children.[565] Whereas many of the episodes associated with Abraham and Sarah center on their desire to have a child, almost nothing is said regarding the resolution of Rebekah's barrenness. With the briefest of details, we are told that "Isaac prayed to the Lord on behalf of his wife" and "the Lord was receptive to his prayer, and his wife Rebekah conceived" (v. 21).[566] Some twenty years, however, pass between Isaac marrying Rebekah and the birth of Esau and Jacob (25:20; 25:26). Isaac may have prayed for many years before his request was answered.

As reflected elsewhere in Genesis, the continuation of the patriline is due to divine intervention. Bethuel is named previously in 22:22–23 as a relative of Abraham and father of Rebekah; he also figures in chapter 24. The mention of "Laban the Aramean" recalls his presence in chapter 24 and anticipates the role that he will play in chapters 29–31, when Jacob flees to Paddan-aram to evade Esau's anger.[567]

---

[564] Schwartz, "Narrative Toledot Formulae in Genesis," 36, notes how the *tôlĕdôt* formula in 25:19 is distinctive, mentioning both Isaac and Abraham. We might have expected a section in Genesis headed "the *tôlĕdôt* of Abraham," followed by a section headed "the *tôlĕdôt* of Isaac." The author of Genesis has merged these together, possibly because there is relatively little to say about Isaac, who is presented in ch. 26 as resembling closely his father Abraham.

[565] Like Sarah (11:30), Rebekah is barren. The same will be true of Rachel (29:31).

[566] The Hebrew verb עתר (*ʿātar*), which comes in both *qal* and *niphal* forms in this verse, has the sense of "plead, entreat."

[567] Deut 26:5 records how the Israelites were to declare: "My father was a wandering Aramean. He went down to Egypt with a few people and resided there." The present verse underlines the Aramean roots of Isaac's family. Even the place name "Paddam-aram" underscores this connection, although the precise meaning of *paddam* is uncertain.

25:22–23. Prior to the birth of Esau and Jacob, Rebekah is conscious of a struggle between the children in her womb. This introduces a theme that will dominate the Isaac *tôlĕdôt*, as Esau and Jacob struggle with each other. The divine oracle given to Rebekah, however, anticipates that the concept of primogeniture will be reversed as the descendants of the older twin will serve those of the younger child. This prediction anticipates the strained relationship that will exist between the nations of Israel and Edom. As McKeown observes, "The lives and characteristics of these twins reflect in microcosm the nations that they foreshadow."[568] As is often the case in Genesis, progeny resembles its progenitor.

25:24–26. The names of the boys possibly reflect the circumstances of their birth, a common practice. However, the derivation of the name Esau is uncertain.[569] Jacob's name resembles the Hebrew word for heel (עָקֵב, *ʿaqeb*). And as Esau will intimate later (27:36), to grasp someone by the heel was understood as an idiom meaning "to cheat" or possibly "to supplant."[570] Until his name is later changed to Israel (32:28), Jacob will live with the connotation that he is a "cheater/supplanter," an idea that is appropriate in the light of how he treats others. The details recorded about the boys anticipate future developments in the narrative.[571]

The twins are born when Isaac is sixty years old. According to 25:7–8, Abraham died when Isaac was seventy-five years old (cf. 21:5). For thematic reasons, to complete the *tôlĕdôt* section of Terah, the death of Abraham is recorded prior to the start of the *tôlĕdôt* sections of Ishmael (25:12–18) and Isaac (25:19–35:29).

Bridge

This brief introductory section to the *tôlĕdôt* of Isaac is proleptic in nature, setting the scene for what is to follow. Attention is focused on Esau and

---

568 McKeown, *Genesis*, 127.

569 Various English versions (e.g., NET, NJB, NRSV, NJPS; cf. ESV) read "so they named him Esau" rather than "and they named him Esau." The Hebrew text does not imply a direct connection between the naming of Esau and his red and hairy appearance. Esau's appearance is more closely tied to his alternative name, Edom, but this "nickname" is given to him at a later stage (see Exegesis on 25:30). The color red probably applies to his complexion, rather than his hair (see Sarna, "Anticipatory Use," 81).

570 Waltke and Fredricks, *Genesis*, 381, notes that the Ugaritic verb *ʿqb* means "to deceive, impede." M. Malul, "*ʿāqēb* 'Heel' and *ʿāqab* 'To Supplant' and the Concept of Succession in the Jacob-Esau Narratives," *VT* 46 (1996): 190–212, sets forth the case for the meaning "to supplant."

571 See Sarna, "Anticipatory Use," 76–84.

Jacob, with the expectation that Jacob will gain precedence over his firstborn brother. The picture of the twins struggling within Rebekah's womb implies that there will be an ongoing struggle between them, fraternal conflict being a common theme within Genesis. Enough is said at this stage to suggest that the lineage of the woman's offspring will descend through Jacob and not Esau.

It is difficult to tell if the oracle given to Rebekah merely displays foreknowledge of what will happen or determines what will occur. The ensuing story gives grounds for believing that the characters involved bear some responsibility for the outcome. While Jacob can hardly be said to merit by his righteousness the birthright of the firstborn, there is good evidence that Esau lacks a positive attitude toward the benefits of being firstborn. Alluding to the Genesis story, the apostle Paul in Romans 9:10–13 emphasizes that God's choice of Jacob over Esau was not due to anything that Jacob did, but a consequence of God's sovereign choice. God is the one who determines membership of the unique patriline descended from Adam and Eve.

B. Esau Sells His Firstborn-Birthright (25:27–34)

> [27] When the boys grew up, Esau became an expert hunter, an outdoorsman, but Jacob was a quiet man who stayed at home. [28] Isaac loved Esau because he had a taste for wild game, but Rebekah loved Jacob.
>
> [29] Once when Jacob was cooking a stew, Esau came in from the field exhausted. [30] He said to Jacob, "Let me eat some of that red stuff, because I'm exhausted." That is why he was also named Edom.
>
> [31] Jacob replied, "First sell me your birthright."
>
> [32] "Look," said Esau, "I'm about to die, so what good is a birthright to me?"
>
> [33] Jacob said, "Swear to me first." So he swore to Jacob and sold his birthright to him. [34] Then Jacob gave bread and lentil stew to Esau; he ate, drank, got up, and went away. So Esau despised his birthright.

Context

In this section the narrative jumps forward in time; Esau and Jacob are now fully grown. Their differences in character are stated briefly (v. 27). Whereas Esau is drawn to the outdoor life and what might be perceived as the manly pursuit of hunting,[572] Jacob prefers a more domesticated

---

572 The Hebrew term צַיִד (*ṣayid*, "hunting, game"), which is frequently associated with Esau, has only been used before in Genesis in relation to Nimrod, who is described twice

environment. The radically different lifestyles of Esau and Jacob influence how their parents view them: Isaac loves Esau, but Rebekah loves Jacob. Within the context of Genesis as a whole, verses 27–34 are significant because they focus on the topic of the firstborn-birthright. Running through the *tôlĕdôt* section of Isaac is the question, Will the "offspring of the woman" be traced through the line of Esau or Jacob (see Biblical and Theological Themes §1)?

Comments

25:27–28. The dispositions of the twins could hardly be more opposite. Esau's outdoor lifestyle, which centers on hunting game, contrasts sharply with Jacob's preference to stay at home and engage in the domestic activity of cooking. Their different temperaments split their parents, with Isaac favoring Esau, but Rebekah favoring Jacob (cf. 27:5–6). While it may be dangerous to read too much into the brief observation that Isaac's love of Esau is motivated by his "taste for wild game,"[573] this remark may imply that Isaac's appetite inappropriately colors his assessment of Esau's character.

25:29–34. Returning home "from the field," Esau finds Jacob cooking. Tired and hungry, Esau rudely asks his twin brother for "some of that red stuff" to gulp down.[574] His disparaging description of Jacob's cuisine as "red stuff"[575] (the narrator in v. 34 more politely calls it "lentil stew") possibly reflects his haughty attitude toward his younger brother.[576] Yet

---

as a גִּבֹּר־צַיִד (*gibbōr ṣayid*, "powerful hunter") (10:9). In the context of Genesis 1–11 this designation has negative connotations (see Exegesis on 10:9). Esau's prowess as a hunter is probably not something that the narrator of Genesis views positively, although Provan, *Discovering Genesis*, 155, suggests that the Old Testament does not condemn hunting as such.

[573] Alter, *Genesis*, 128, observes that the Hebrew idiom, which literally says, "for the game in his mouth," points to the "absurdity of the material reason for Isaac's paternal favoritism."

[574] The Hebrew verb לעט (*lʿṭ*), which appears only here in the Old Testament, possibly means "swallow (greedily)" (BDB) or something similar. See Benno Jacob, *The First Book of the Bible: Genesis*, trans. Ernest I. Jacob and Walter Jacob (New York: Ktav, 1974), 168, but note the objection of Brian A. Bompiani, "Style Switching in the Speech of Transjordanians," *HS* 57 (2016): 55–57. In postbiblical Hebrew לעט (*lʿṭ*) is the verb used for animals' feeding. The CSB translation "Let me eat" does not convey well the coarse tone of Esau's request.

[575] The term "red" (הָאָדֹם, *ʾādōm*) is repeated twice for emphasis.

[576] The short aside at the end of v. 30 that Esau was named Edom (אֱדוֹם [*ʾĕdôm*], which resembles אָדֹם [*ʾādōm*, "red"]) may be Jacob's response to his brother's insulting description of his cooking. Jacob gets his own back on Esau by highlighting his red appearance (see v. 25). Alter, *Genesis*, 129, suggests that this incident "associates crude impatient appetite with Israel's perennial enemy (Edom)."

Esau is quite prepared to sell his birthright to Jacob for a bowl of vegetarian stew. Expressing no objection, Esau's action demonstrates that he views his firstborn status as of little value.[577] His contempt for his privileged status is captured by the narrator's description of what Esau did. Using five verbs in quick succession, the text says literally: "and he ate and drank and got up and went away and despised his birthright" (v. 34).[578] Recalling the divine oracle given to Rebekah in verse 23, Esau's indifference to, if not contempt for, his privileged position as firstborn is a strong indicator that he is an unsuitable heir for the divine promises given to Abraham and Isaac. And while Jacob's exploitation of his brother's hunger is scandalous, he rightly esteems the incomparable worth of the firstborn-birthright.[579] The contrasting attitudes of the brothers to the birthright set the tone for much that is to follow.

Bridge

Neither son merits the firstborn-birthright. Jacob selfishly exploits the situation for his own benefit. Esau, however, too readily sells his birthright for the cost of a bowl of stew. Looking to push the blame onto his brother, Esau later tells Isaac that he was deceived by Jacob into selling his birthright to him (27:36), but the present account provides limited evidence to support this claim. Tellingly, the author of Hebrews observes that Esau, whom he categorizes as "immoral" and "irreverent," forfeited the paternal blessing because he sold his firstborn-birthright (Heb 12:16–17).

For anyone nurtured within a Christian environment it is easy to despise the true worth of this inheritance. Equally, it is possible to strive after the grace of God for purely selfish motives, hurting others in the

---

[577] The birthright of the firstborn guaranteed a double portion of the family inheritance (cf. Deut 21:17). Waltke and Fredricks, *Genesis*, 363, following M. Tsevat, "*bek̲ôr*," *TDOT* 2: 126, state that when there are two sons the firstborn inherits everything. It is more likely that with two sons the firstborn inherits two-thirds of the father's estate. In the context of Genesis, possession of the birthright identifies those who belong to the patriline associated with the "offspring of the woman" (3:15).

[578] The Hebrew text places the act of despising after other everyday activities. By doing so, the narrator places Esau's action in despising his firstborn-birthright on a par with eating and drinking; it is of little consequence to Esau. Cf. Walton, *Genesis*, 558. English versions which begin the final part of the verse with "so" or "thus" add something that is not present in the Hebrew text.

[579] Waltke and Fredricks, *Genesis*, 363, writes of Jacob, "His value is right, but his method is wrong. Later God will transform his ambition into virtue (see 32:28)."

process. Jacob's spiritual journey will eventually result in him striving with God. Only then is he truly transformed from being a Jacob into an Israel.

C. Isaac in Gerar (26:1–33)

> 1 There was another famine in the land in addition to the one that had occurred in Abraham's time. And Isaac went to Abimelech, king of the Philistines, at Gerar. 2 The Lord appeared to him and said, "Do not go down to Egypt. Live in the land that I tell you about; 3 stay in this land as an alien, and I will be with you and bless you. For I will give all these lands to you and your offspring, and I will confirm the oath that I swore to your father Abraham. 4 I will make your offspring as numerous as the stars of the sky, I will give your offspring all these lands, and all the nations of the earth will be blessed by your offspring, 5 because Abraham listened to me and kept my mandate, my commands, my statutes, and my instructions." 6 So Isaac settled in Gerar.
>
> 7 When the men of the place asked about his wife, he said, "She is my sister," for he was afraid to say "my wife," thinking, "The men of the place will kill me on account of Rebekah, for she is a beautiful woman." 8 When Isaac had been there for some time, Abimelech king of the Philistines looked down from the window and was surprised to see Isaac caressing his wife Rebekah.
>
> 9 Abimelech sent for Isaac and said, "So she is really your wife! How could you say, 'She is my sister'?"
>
> Isaac answered him, "Because I thought I might die on account of her."
>
> 10 Then Abimelech said, "What is this you've done to us? One of the people could easily have slept with your wife, and you would have brought guilt on us." 11 So Abimelech warned all the people, "Whoever harms this man or his wife will certainly be put to death."
>
> 12 Isaac sowed seed in that land, and in that year he reaped a hundred times what was sown. The Lord blessed him, 13 and the man became rich and kept getting richer until he was very wealthy. 14 He had flocks of sheep, herds of cattle, and many slaves, and the Philistines were envious of him. 15 Philistines stopped up all the wells that his father's servants had dug in the days of his father Abraham, filling them with dirt. 16 And Abimelech said to Isaac, "Leave us, for you are much too powerful for us."
>
> 17 So Isaac left there, camped in the Gerar Valley, and lived there. 18 Isaac reopened the wells that had been dug in the days of his father Abraham and that the Philistines had stopped up after Abraham died. He gave them the same names his father had given them. 19 Then Isaac's servants dug in the valley and found a well of spring water there. 20 But the herdsmen of Gerar quarreled with Isaac's herdsmen and said, "The

water is ours!" So he named the well Esek because they argued with him.
[21] Then they dug another well and quarreled over that one also, so he
named it Sitnah. [22] He moved from there and dug another, and they did
not quarrel over it. He named it Rehoboth and said, "For now the LORD
has made space for us, and we will be fruitful in the land."

[23] From there he went up to Beer-sheba, [24] and the LORD appeared to him
that night and said, "I am the God of your father Abraham. Do not be
afraid, for I am with you. I will bless you and multiply your offspring
because of my servant Abraham."

[25] So he built an altar there, called on the name of the LORD, and pitched
his tent there. Isaac's servants also dug a well there.

[26] Now Abimelech came to him from Gerar with Ahuzzath his adviser
and Phicol the commander of his army. [27] Isaac said to them, "Why have
you come to me? You hated me and sent me away from you."

[28] They replied, "We have clearly seen how the LORD has been with you.
We think there should be an oath between two parties—between us
and you. Let us make a covenant with you: [29] You will not harm us, just
as we have not harmed you but have done only what was good to you,
sending you away in peace. You are now blessed by the LORD."

[30] So he prepared a banquet for them, and they ate and drank. [31] They
got up early in the morning and swore an oath to each other. Isaac
sent them on their way, and they left him in peace. [32] On that same day
Isaac's servants came to tell him about the well they had dug, saying to
him, "We have found water!" [33] He called it Sheba. Therefore the name
of the city is still Beer-sheba today.

Context

The account of Esau selling his firstborn-birthright to Jacob is followed by a series of short episodes that deliberately portray Isaac as resembling his father Abraham, conveying the sense that he is "a typological heir to Abraham."[580] Like Abraham, Isaac confronts famine in the land of Canaan; like Abraham, Isaac passes off his wife as his sister; like Abraham, Isaac is blessed by God and grows wealthy; like Abraham, he digs wells in the region of Gerar; like Abraham, he makes a covenant with Abimelech at Beer-sheba. These parallels convey well the idea that Isaac is truly Abraham's "seed" (see Biblical and Theological Themes §1).

---

[580] Alter, *Genesis*, 131. Provan, *Discovering Genesis*, 152, describes Isaac as a "pale reflection ... of his father." Observing the parallels between Abraham and Isaac, McKeown, *Genesis*, 129, uses "déjà vu" as the heading for 26:1–11, but this could be extended to cover almost all of ch. 26.

Importantly, the events of chapter 26 underline that the divine promises given to Abraham pass directly to Isaac, who is also blessed by God. This adds to the significance of Esau's rejection of his firstborn-birthright (25:29–34) and it sets the scene for the events of chapter 27, when Jacob receives from Isaac the paternal blessing normally given to the firstborn. Chapter 26 provides a necessary and relevant buffer between Jacob's buying the firstborn-birthright from Esau and Jacob's pretending to be Esau in order to be blessed by Isaac.[581]

Comments

26:1–6. Although Abraham lived in the region of Gerar for a period of time (20:1; 21:33–34), in his later years he appears to have settled further to the north, in the region of Hebron, where Sarah is buried (23:1–19). After the death of Abraham, Isaac is forced by famine to move south to Gerar. By this stage, Esau and Jacob are young adults.[582]

The narrator recalls in verse 1 that a famine had occurred in the time of Abraham. On that occasion, Abraham had journeyed into Egypt, where, for self-preservation, he had claimed that Sarah was his sister (12:10–20). In similar challenging circumstances, Isaac is instructed by God to remain at Gerar, where he encounters Abimelech, king of the Philistines.[583] Abraham also had dealings with a king of Gerar called Abimelech (20:2; 21:22). Since "Abimelech" means "My father is king," this name could have been a throne name given to successive kings. However, it is possible that this is the king with whom Abraham made a treaty (21:22–34).

God's speech emphasizes that the promises guaranteed to Abraham by divine oath in 22:16–18 will pass to Isaac, if he remains "in this land"

---

[581] *Pace* Blum, "The Jacob Tradition," 181–82, who views ch. 26 as only loosely connected to the Jacob-Esau story. Blum identifies "strife" and "blessing" as two of the main themes for the "major integrated story" involving Jacob and Esau. These themes are prominent in ch. 26, suggesting that this chapter is intentionally part of the "integrated story."

[582] Waltke and Fredricks, *Genesis*, 367, view this episode as "anachronous" on the assumption that the "wife-sister deception" presupposes that Isaac and Rebekah have no children. However, if by the time of the famine Abraham is dead, Esau and Jacob would have been in their late teens, if not older, and quite independent of their parents. See also Comments on 28:10.

[583] Holmgren, "Looking Back on Abraham's Encounter," 366–77, views Abimelech as a typical Canaanite. However, different ethnic groups, including Canaanites, coexisted in the territory promised to Abraham (cf. 15:19–21). On the use of the term "Philistine" in the Pentateuch, see Howard, "Philistines," 1048–52; Kitchen, *On the Reliability of the Old Testament*, 339–41.

(v. 3).[584] God underlines the importance of obedience, with verse 5 highlighting the role that Abraham's compliance played in securing the divine oath recorded in 22:16–18.[585] The reference to God's "mandate, commands, statutes, and instructions" in verse 5 implies a comprehensive obedience on the part of Abraham to everything that God said. "As the theology of our passage shows throughout, the divine purpose of the call assumes human responsibility and accountability in an obedient response."[586] God's promises to Abraham not only pass to Isaac but also they are linked to his descendants. Here, as in 12:1–3 and 22:16–18, the national and international dimensions of God's redemptive plan are emphasized (see exegesis of both passages for a fuller discussion).

26:7–11. As with Abraham and Sarah (12:11–13; 20:11), Isaac is fearful that he will be killed on account of Rebekah's beauty. Since they are unknown in the region of Gerar, Isaac asks Rebekah to pretend that she is his sister.[587] Isaac's ruse, however, is uncovered by Abimelech, who sees "Isaac caressing his wife."[588] With good reason, perhaps in the light of previous experience (cf. 20:1–18), Abimelech challenges Isaac regarding the deception. His words, "What is this you've done to us?" recall what he, or a prior king also called Abimelech, said to Isaac's father, Abraham (Gen 20:9). Abimelech's warning to his people (v. 11) is especially relevant in the light of God's reassurance to Abraham that those who bless him will be blessed, but those who disdain him will be cursed (12:3). This theme recurs throughout chapter 26.

26:12–16. Like Abraham (cf. 24:1, 35), Isaac is blessed by God, as promised in verse 3. However, the Philistines become jealous of Isaac's prosperity. To make life difficult for Isaac and his herdsmen, the Philistines

---

584 The imperative "stay" is followed by two *yiqtol* verbs that are not *wayyiqtol* in form. The sense is: "Stay so that I will be with you and bless you." While 26:2–5 does not echo everything that God says to Abraham in 22:16–18, some of what is said repeats exactly the wording of YHWH's oath to Abraham. See Comments on 22:16–18.

585 See Comments on 22:16–18.

586 Mathews, *Genesis 11:27–50:26*, 403.

587 The present account presupposes that the reader is already familiar with 12:10–20 and 20:1–18; see Alexander, "Are the Wife/Sister Incidents of Genesis Literary Compositional Variants?," 145–53; Kang, *Reading the Wife/Sister Narratives*, 140–69.

588 The MT reads, וְהִנֵּה יִצְחָק מְצַחֵק אֵת רִבְקָה אִשְׁתּוֹ, creating a word play involving the name Isaac (יִצְחָק, *yiṣḥāq*), which means "he laughs" (cf. 17:17; 18:12–15; 21:6, 9) and the masculine singular *piel* participle *měṣaḥēq*, which is variously translated "laughing" (ESV), "caressing" (CSB, NIV, NLT), "fondling" (RSV, NJB, NJPS). The wordplay implies that Isaac is being true to who he is by name.

destroy the wells that Abraham's servants had dug in the past (cf. 21:25–31). Eventually, Abimelech, fearful of Isaac's growing power, asks him to move away from the city of Gerar.

26:17–22. Isaac relocates but continues to live in the Valley of Gerar, settling in territory where Abraham had previously lived. Deliberately, the narrator portrays Isaac as following in his father's footsteps. Disputes over wells continue to dog Isaac, forcing him to move further and further away from Gerar. Eventually, he comes to a location where he is able to settle in peace. The movement from a hostile environment to one of harmony is signaled by the names of the locations. The narrator emphasizes that YHWH is the one who gives rest to Isaac.

26:23–33. Like Abraham (21:22–34), Isaac makes a covenant with Abimelech at Beer-sheba. While there are similarities in the descriptions of the two events, many details differ. On this occasion Abimelech is accompanied by both Ahuzzath and Phicol; only Phicol is mentioned in 21:22. Given how the Philistines had treated him, Isaac is surprised by their arrival. Abimelech, however, has observed that YHWH is with Isaac (v. 28) and has blessed him (v. 29). His remarks confirm that YHWH has fulfilled the promise given to Isaac in verse 3, and they echo what God has said to Isaac more recently at Beer-sheba (v. 24). The friendship treaty recalls how Abraham and his patriline are to be a source of blessing to the nations. Abimelech's request rests on this expectation.

Abimelech's desire to establish a friendship treaty with Isaac, as he (or his father) did previously with Abraham, conveys strongly the idea that Isaac resembles Abraham and as such is the legitimate and worthy heir to all the promises given to Abraham by God. The point is subtly emphasized by the way in which God identifies himself to Isaac as "the God of your father Abraham" (v. 24). Appropriately, like Abraham (cf. 12:7–8; 13:18), Isaac builds an altar and calls on the name of YHWH (v. 25). The Hebrew name for the well, שִׁבְעָה (*šibʿâ*), is linked to the name בְּאֵר שֶׁבַע (*bĕʾēr šebaʿ*) (see Comments on 21:31).

Bridge

In Genesis 17 God promised Abraham that the covenant of circumcision would be established with Isaac and not Ishmael (17:18–21). The events of chapter 26 confirm this by portraying Isaac as imaging his father Abraham. While the account of Isaac's life is much shorter than that of Abraham and of his son Jacob, he is clearly identified as Abraham's successor and the next member of the patriline that lies at the heart of Genesis. Having established Isaac's status as Abraham's heir,[589] attention returns in chapter 27 to his sons Esau and Jacob. Which of Isaac's sons will inherit the divine hope associated first with the offspring of the woman (3:15) and then later expanded upon in God's eternal covenant with Abraham (17:1–27)?

D. Isaac Blesses Jacob (26:34–27:45)

> [34] When Esau was forty years old, he took as his wives Judith daughter of Beeri the Hethite, and Basemath daughter of Elon the Hethite. [35] They made life bitter for Isaac and Rebekah.
>
> [27:1] When Isaac was old and his eyes were so weak that he could not see, he called his older son Esau and said to him, "My son."
>
> And he answered, "Here I am."
>
> [2] He said, "Look, I am old and do not know the day of my death. [3] So now take your hunting gear, your quiver and bow, and go out in the field to hunt some game for me. [4] Then make me a delicious meal that I love and bring it to me to eat, so that I can bless you before I die."
>
> [5] Now Rebekah was listening to what Isaac said to his son Esau. So while Esau went to the field to hunt some game to bring in, [6] Rebekah said to her son Jacob, "Listen! I heard your father talking with your brother Esau. He said, [7] 'Bring me game and make a delicious meal for me to eat so that I can bless you in the Lord's presence before I die.' [8] Now, my son, listen to me and do what I tell you. [9] Go to the flock and bring me two choice young goats, and I will make them into a delicious meal for your father—the kind he loves. [10] Then take it to your father to eat so that he may bless you before he dies."
>
> [11] Jacob answered Rebekah his mother, "Look, my brother Esau is a hairy man, but I am a man with smooth skin. [12] Suppose my father touches me. Then I will be revealed to him as a deceiver and bring a curse rather than a blessing on myself."
>
> [13] His mother said to him, "Your curse be on me, my son. Just obey me and go get them for me."
>
> [14] So he went and got the goats and brought them to his mother, and his mother made the delicious food his father loved. [15] Then Rebekah took the best clothes of her older son Esau, which were in the house, and had her younger son Jacob wear them. [16] She put the skins of the

[589] According to Waltke and Fredricks, *Genesis*, 367, the theme of the chapter is "Isaac inherits his father's divine blessing."

young goats on his hands and the smooth part of his neck. [17] Then she
handed the delicious food and the bread she had made to her son Jacob.

[18] When he came to his father, he said, "My father." And he answered,
"Here I am. Who are you, my son?"

[19] Jacob replied to his father, "I am Esau, your firstborn. I have done as
you told me. Please sit up and eat some of my game so that you may
bless me."

[20] But Isaac said to his son, "How did you ever find it so quickly, my
son?" He replied, "Because the LORD your God made it happen for me."

[21] Then Isaac said to Jacob, "Please come closer so I can touch you, my
son. Are you really my son Esau or not?"

[22] So Jacob came closer to his father Isaac. When he touched him, he
said, "The voice is the voice of Jacob, but the hands are the hands of
Esau." [23] He did not recognize him, because his hands were hairy like
those of his brother Esau; so he blessed him. [24] Again he asked, "Are
you really my son Esau?"

And he replied, "I am."

[25] Then he said, "Bring it closer to me, and let me eat some of my son's
game so that I can bless you." Jacob brought it closer to him, and he
ate; he brought him wine, and he drank.

[26] Then his father Isaac said to him, "Please come closer and kiss me,
my son." [27] So he came closer and kissed him. When Isaac smelled his
clothes, he blessed him and said:

> Ah, the smell of my son is like the smell of a field that the
> LORD has blessed.
> [28] May God give to you from the dew of the sky
> and from the richness of the land an abundance of grain
> and new wine.
> [29] May peoples serve you
> and nations bow in worship to you.
> Be master over your relatives;
> may your mother's sons bow in worship to you.
> Those who curse you will be cursed,
> and those who bless you will be blessed.

[30] As soon as Isaac had finished blessing Jacob and Jacob had left the
presence of his father Isaac, his brother Esau arrived from his hunting.
[31] He had also made some delicious food and brought it to his father.
He said to his father, "Let my father get up and eat some of his son's
game, so that you may bless me."

[32] But his father Isaac said to him, "Who are you?"

He answered, "I am Esau your firstborn son."

33 Isaac began to tremble uncontrollably. "Who was it then," he said, "who hunted game and brought it to me? I ate it all before you came in, and I blessed him. Indeed, he will be blessed!"

34 When Esau heard his father's words, he cried out with a loud and bitter cry and said to his father, "Bless me too, my father!"

35 But he replied, "Your brother came deceitfully and took your blessing."

36 So he said, "Isn't he rightly named Jacob? For he has cheated me twice now. He took my birthright, and look, now he has taken my blessing." Then he asked, "Haven't you saved a blessing for me?"

37 But Isaac answered Esau, "Look, I have made him a master over you, have given him all of his relatives as his servants, and have sustained him with grain and new wine. What then can I do for you, my son?"

38 Esau said to his father, "Do you have only one blessing, my father? Bless me too, my father!" And Esau wept loudly.

39 His father Isaac answered him,

> Look, your dwelling place will be away from the richness
> of the land, away from the dew of the sky above.
> 40 You will live by your sword,
> and you will serve your brother.
> But when you rebel,
> you will break his yoke from your neck.

41 Esau held a grudge against Jacob because of the blessing his father had given him. And Esau determined in his heart: "The days of mourning for my father are approaching; then I will kill my brother Jacob."

42 When the words of her older son Esau were reported to Rebekah,
she summoned her younger son Jacob and said to him, "Listen, your
brother Esau is consoling himself by planning to kill you. 43 So now, my
son, listen to me. Flee at once to my brother Laban in Haran, 44 and stay
with him for a few days until your brother's anger subsides—45 until
your brother's rage turns away from you and he forgets what you have
done to him. Then I will send for you and bring you back from there.
Why should I lose you both in one day?"

Context

After focusing on Isaac in 26:1–33, the narrative returns to consider how the struggle between Esau and Jacob will develop. To set the scene for what follows, the narrator mentions briefly that Esau takes two foreign wives, who are a source of bitterness for Isaac and Rebekah

(26:34–35). This brief observation reinforces an already negative portrayal of Esau (cf. 25:29–34).

At the heart of the events describes in chapter 27 is the pronouncement of a special paternal blessing upon the "firstborn" son. Old and blind, Isaac decides that the time has come to bless Esau, although strangely he plans to do this privately. Rebekah, however, intervenes surreptitiously to ensure that the blessing is given to Jacob. Consequently, Jacob deprives his older brother not only of the firstborn-birthright (25:29–34) but also of the paternal blessing associated with it. When Esau confronts his father, Isaac refuses to revoke the blessing of the firstborn given to Jacob. As might be expected, Esau seeks revenge, setting in motion a train of events that will result in Jacob fleeing from Canaan to Paddan-aram. The events of chapter 27 recall the divine prediction in 25:23 that the older will serve the younger, but Jacob's departure suggests that Esau may have gained the upper hand in spite of Isaac having blessed Jacob. Subsequent developments will prove that this is not the case.

Comments

26:34–35. The brief description of Esau's Hethite[590] wives forms a separate pericope, bringing the reader's focus back to Isaac's sons.[591] By taking two wives, both of Hethite origin, Esau adds to the growing sense that the divine promises associated with Abraham and Isaac are not destined to be his.[592] Later, Rebekah expresses to Isaac her strong antipathy toward Esau's wives (27:46). Consequently, he encourages Jacob to take a wife from his own relatives in Paddan-aram (28:1–5). When Esau discovers this, he looks to make amends by marrying a daughter of Ishmael (28:8–9). (For more on Esau's wives, see Comments on 36:2–3).

27:1–4. To set the scene for the events narrated in chapter 27, Isaac is introduced as very old and blind.[593] Isaac's old age accounts for his decision to bless Esau at this stage; his blindness explains why Jacob is able

---

[590] Most English versions prefer to translate הַחִתִּי (*haḥittî*) as "Hittite"; see Comments on 23:3–9, where CSB uses Hethites to denote the population of Hebron.

[591] Sarna, "Anticipatory Use," 81, helpfully observes, "This extraordinary addendum, totally unrelated to what precedes, must either be a clumsy interpolation or else, on the contrary, its very discontinuity and irregularity belong to the rhetorical strategies of a gifted writer and constitute an important element of the creative process."

[592] Alter, *Genesis*, 136.

[593] Isaac is 137 years old, and Jacob and Esau are 77 years old. Although the impression is given at the start of ch. 27 that Isaac is about to die, he lives to be 180 years old.

to disguise himself successfully as his brother. The paternal blessing is meant to confirm Esau as heir to the divine promises given to Abraham and Isaac, but the narrator has already given indications that Esau does not appreciate the privilege and responsibility associated with these promises.

In the light of this, several factors suggest that Isaac's desire to bless Esau is inappropriate. First, this will be done in secret; only Esau is informed of Isaac's intention to bless him. To make such an important occasion a private affair is unusual (cf. 48:1–49:28),[594] suggesting that Isaac intentionally wishes to exclude both Rebekah and Jacob.[595] Second, Isaac deliberately ignores or is unaware of the fact that Esau had previously sold his firstborn-birthright to Jacob. This factor may explain the secretive nature of the arrangement that Isaac makes with Esau, for Jacob would have had grounds to object to the legitimacy of what Isaac was doing. Third, Isaac's desire to bless Esau seems to be motivated by a craving for gourmet food, a factor that recalls what was said previously about Isaac's preference for Esau over Jacob (cf. 25:28).[596] These observations raise questions about the appropriateness of Isaac's decision to bless Esau. Isaac appears to be more than just physically blind. Ironically, the narrator describes Esau as בְּנוֹ הַגָּדֹל (*bĕnô haggādōl*, "his big son") (27:1; cf. 27:15, 42), whereas he later calls Jacob בְּנָהּ הַקָּטָן (*bĕnāh haqqāṭān*, "her little son") (27:15, 42). These designations give the impression that Esau is more important than Jacob. Yet, the reader has been made to expect that "the older will serve the younger" (25:23).

27:5–17. Aware of Isaac's intention to bless Esau, Rebekah intervenes on behalf of Jacob, her favorite son (25:28), instructing a reluctant Jacob to pretend that he is Esau. Jacob is clearly not the instigator of the deception, a point underlined by his fear of being cursed by his father should the ruse be discovered (v. 12).[597] Rebekah's willingness to bear any curse that Isaac might pronounce on Jacob indicates that she takes full responsibility for the deception. While she may be motivated simply out of love for Jacob,

---

[594] Wenham, *Genesis 16–50*, 205.

[595] Jin H. Han, "The Role of 'an Audience' in Isaac's Blessing in Genesis 27," *PRSt* 42 (2015): 6.

[596] Han, "The Role of 'an Audience,' " 8, writes, "The prominence given to the meal in Gen 27 threatens to degenerate the occasion into a farce financed by good food." Wenham, *Genesis 16–50*, 206, remarks that "Isaac's sensuality is more powerful than his theology."

[597] Although CSB translates כִּמְתַעְתֵּעַ (*kimtaʿtēaʿ*) in v. 12 using the term "deceiver," this is a rarely used word in the Old Testament; it possibly has more the sense of "making fun of someone" or "mocking someone" (cf. RSV, ESV, NET).

Rebekah possibly appreciates the significance of the paternal blessing in terms of God's redemptive plan. When Rebekah repeats almost verbatim what Isaac says to Esau (vv. 2–4), her version contains the additional words "in the Lord's presence" (v. 7). Rebekah is conscious of the divine dimension of the blessing. Since Jacob and Esau are physically very different (v. 11; cf. 25:28), Rebekah uses the skins of young goats to make Jacob appear hairy like Esau. By making Rebekah the subject of the verbs in vv. 15–17, the narrator underlines her central role in the deception.

27:18–25. In spite of Isaac's persistent questioning, Jacob succeeds in convincing his father that he is Esau. When Jacob says to Isaac that he is Esau "your firstborn" (v. 19), the term בְּכֹר (*bĕkōr*, "firstborn") is used for the first time in chapters 25–35. However, בְּכוֹרָה (*bĕkōrâ*) has figured prominently in 25:31–34 to denote the birthright of the firstborn. The use of בְּכֹר (*bĕkōr*) introduces into the narrative an important link between the concepts of בְּכוֹרָה (*bĕkōrâ*, "firstborn-birthright") and בְּרָכָה (*bĕrākâ*, "blessing").[598] The two concepts are intimately linked in Genesis. Not only does the firstborn receive the paternal blessing but also the firstborn is empowered to mediate blessing to others (see Biblical and Theological Themes §2).

27:26–29. Having satisfied his appetite, the stage is set for Isaac to bless his firstborn. However, Isaac uses one further test to identify his son; he smells him.[599] Having anticipated this possibility, Rebekah has clothed Jacob with Esau's garments (v. 15). Influenced by the scent from Esau's clothing, Isaac's opening words are highly ironic with their mention of a "field that the Lord has blessed." At no point has Esau been associated with God's blessing. Isaac then proceeds to bless his son, focusing on agricultural prosperity, dominion over others and the mediation of blessing or cursing.[600]

---

[598] Sarna, *Genesis*, 181, notes that in 27:1–28:9 the noun בְּרָכָה (*bĕrākâ*) appears "seven times and its verbal form exactly twenty-one times." This underlines the importance of the concept of blessing in this passage and recalls its importance in 12:1–3. See also Fokkelman, *Narrative Art in Genesis*, 98–99.

[599] Sarah Schwartz, "Isaac's Dual Test in the Blessings Narrative: A New Reading of Gen 27:18–29," *JSOT* 43 (2019): 693–711, helpfully observes that the narrator draws attention to the hairy arms (vv. 21–23) and the smell of a field (v. 27) in order to underline that Isaac's decision to bless Esau is influenced by his belief that Esau is a natural leader and, therefore, the more suitable son to inherit the divine promises given to Abraham and Isaac.

[600] Sarna, *Genesis*, 183, mistakenly concludes that Isaac's remarks relate "to national destiny rather than to the fate of an individual." This is not immediately apparent from what Isaac says.

While Isaac's vocabulary is distinctive, his comments regarding the obedience of the nations recalls the covenant of chapter 17 and Abraham's status as father of many nations. Viewed in the light of the eternal covenant established with Abraham and Isaac, the reference to peoples serving and nations bowing down is consistent with the story that unfolds in Genesis as a whole. Without this background, Isaac's expectations appear wildly grandiose and unrealistic. The idea of Jacob (or even Esau) exercising dominion over peoples and nations is quite amazing. Yet, it is in keeping with the belief that the patriline in Genesis will lead eventually to a special king (cf. 17:6; 22:17). In addition, Isaac's concluding comments about cursing and blessing recall God's words to Abraham in 12:3,[601] reinforcing the idea that the members of the unique lineage will mediate God's blessing to the nations. God's curse, however, will rest on those who disdain those chosen by God to form this line.

27:30–37. Oblivious to what has happened, Esau comes to Isaac, expecting to be blessed. Respectfully, he addresses his father,[602] who becomes very agitated, believing that he has already blessed his older son. As Isaac and Esau grasp the reality of what has happened, Isaac confirms that the blessing is "irrevocable"[603] (v. 31). Becoming exceptionally distraught, Esau pleads with his father to be blessed. Isaac, however, is powerless to change the situation, even though Jacob has acted "deceitfully."[604] Esau then proceeds to condemn his younger brother, claiming that Jacob, true to his name,[605] has cheated or supplanted him twice (v. 36).[606] Esau's assessment of how Jacob got the firstborn-birthright is at odds, however, with what the narrator has recorded in 25:29–34.

---

[601] The wording in Hebrew is similar, but not exactly the same.

[602] Esau's formal approach is reflected in how he addresses his father in v. 31; he moves from third person address to second person, a typical transition when speaking to someone in authority, according to Alter, *Genesis*, 141.

[603] Provan, *Discovering Genesis*, 157. This understanding of the blessing undermines the suggestion of Walton, *Genesis*, 554, that "there is no intrinsic authority vested in the blessing." On the contrary, such blessings have divine authority because of the special status of those making them; they are members of the unique lineage associated with the "offspring of the woman."

[604] In v. 35 "deceitfully" translates בְּמִרְמָה (*bĕmirmâ*) which has the sense of acting treacherously.

[605] Isaac avoids using Jacob's name in his conversation with Esau. Jacob is first named in v. 36, when Esau associates his name with "cheating" or "supplanting." See 25:26.

[606] According to Sarna, *Genesis*, 184, "There is no doubt where the author's sympathy lies. Esau is the innocent victim of a cruel ruse." This assessment is open to dispute. The author

Esau's remarks in verse 36 underline the importance of the link between firstborn-birthright and blessing, a link that is reflected in the wordplay involving בְּכֹרָתִי (*bĕkōrātî*, "my birthright") and בִּרְכָתִי (*birkātî*, "my blessing"). The unfolding story of Esau and Jacob centers on how the younger twin, who acquires both the firstborn-birthright and related paternal blessing, is established as the next in succession for the patriline traced in Genesis and consequently heir to the divine promises given to Abraham. When Isaac elucidates to Esau the content of the blessing that he has pronounced on Jacob (v. 37), his remarks recall the divine prediction that "the older will serve the younger" (25:23).[607]

27:38–40. Isaac responds to Esau's passionate request for a blessing with words that partially echo the blessing given to Jacob.[608] Isaac's blessing of Esau, however, is "strangely enigmatic and ambiguous"[609] for it is possible to interpret verse 39 as saying either that Esau will share in the abundance of the earth[610] or that he will be deprived of the earth's abundance.[611] Perhaps Isaac is deliberately ambiguous, for the future fortunes of Esau's descendants will be mixed. Recognizing that Jacob will rule over his brother, Isaac also states that Esau, who will live by the sword, will break free from his brother's control.[612] Isaac's words reveal that the struggle between Jacob

---

of Genesis has previously said that Esau despised his firstborn-birthright (25:34). It could be argued that Esau is now reaping the consequences of selling his firstborn-birthright for a bowl of stew. The narrator has also highlighted how Esau's choice of two wives distressed his parents (26:34–35). While the narrator conveys well Esau's distress at losing the blessing, the narrator's sympathy is not with Esau.

[607] The repetition of the noun גְּבִיר (*gĕbîr*, "master") in vv. 29 and 37, used only here in the whole of the Old Testament, underlines the fact that Jacob now has authority over Esau.

[608] The distinctive expressions "the dew of the sky" and "the richness of the land" are used in both blessings.

[609] Sarna, *Genesis*, 184. Cf. Laurence A. Turner, *Genesis*, Readings: A New Biblical Commentary (Sheffield: Sheffield Academic, 2000), 120–21.

[610] Positive readings of the blessing are found in KJV and NJPS. Alter, *Genesis*, 143, argues that both sons are to enjoy "the bounty of heaven and earth." He also rejects the suggestion that the reversal in the order of the expressions "the dew of the sky" and "the richness of the land" points to a reversal of fortune for Esau.

[611] Most modern English versions adopt this negative interpretation (e.g., CSB, ESV, NIV, NJB, NLT). Waltke and Fredricks, *Genesis*, 381, designates Isaac's blessing of Esau as "an antiblessing." Cf. Walton, *Genesis*, 556.

[612] Robert S. Kawashima, "Literary Analysis," in Evans, Lohr, and Petersen, *The Book of Genesis*, 96, writes, "He will eventually break free from his younger brother's dominion, but in the meantime he has been metaphorically reduced to a beast of burden."

and Esau will continue into future generations, a fact reflected in the often violent relationship between the nations of Israel and Edom.[613]

27:41–45. Angered by Jacob's actions, Esau plots to slay his brother once Isaac dies. As Waltke observes, Esau's desire to kill Jacob makes him resemble Cain and Lamech and associates him with "the seed of the Serpent" (3:15, 4:8, 23; cf. John 8:44).[614] Learning of Esau's intention, Rebekah instructs Jacob to take refuge with her relatives in the northwest of Mesopotamia. Believing that Esau's anger will subside quickly, she speaks of Jacob being a refugee for "a few days" (v. 44). The reality is otherwise, and she possibly never sees Jacob again.[615] Although Sarna allows for the possibility that "you both" (v. 45) could refer to Isaac and Jacob,[616] the verb אֶשְׁכַּל (*ʾeškal*), translated "lose" in CSB, has connotations of being left childless. Rebekah probably assumes that Esau will be put to death if he murders Jacob.

Bridge

As Genesis focuses on the patriline of the "offspring of the woman" it regularly introduces new aspects. With Abraham, the divine promises, confirmed by covenants, add a new dimension, creating the expectation that all the nations of the earth will be blessed through one of Abraham's descendants. As predicted, the eternal covenant of chapter 17 is established with Isaac, before passing to Jacob. The Jacob-Esau story adds a further dimension by highlighting the important connection that exists between the firstborn-birthright and the paternal blessing, both of which are associated with the one through whom the family line continues (see Biblical and Theological Themes §1).

Moral assessments of the behavior of the different characters in chapter 27 have ranged considerably over the centuries.[617] A variety of factors need to be considered and the evidence is finely balanced. Mitigating factors may lessen the guilt attached to Rebekah and Jacob for deceiving Isaac. Isaac's

---

[613] Various Old Testament texts shed light on this relationship and how Edom's violent actions bring them under divine judgment: Num 20:18; 1 Kgs 11:14–16; 2 Kgs 8:20–22; 14:7–10; Lam 4:21–22; Ezek 36:5; Joel 3:19; Amos 1:11; Obad 1:1–21; Mal 1:2–5.

[614] Waltke and Fredricks, *Genesis*, 381.

[615] Genesis provides no report of Rebekah's death and burial, apart from saying that she was interred with others at Hebron (49:31).

[616] Sarna, *Genesis*, 185.

[617] An interesting summary is provided by Provan, *Discovering Genesis*, 157–60.

decision to bless Esau privately appears to be motivated by appetite, rather than by an evaluation of Esau's worthiness of the blessing. Esau ignores or hides the fact that he has sold his firstborn-birthright to Jacob for a bowl of stew (25:29–34), although he readily refers to this after the deception (v. 36). Isaac's reaction after the deception is remarkable for not condemning Jacob or Rebekah (cf. v. 33),[618] and his subsequent blessing of Jacob in 28:1–4 reinforces the earlier blessing that Jacob received through deception.

In the light of these observations, the narrator may not be interested in pointing the finger of blame at any one person, for faults appear on all sides. He may be more concerned to highlight the outcome of what happens, for Isaac's blessing of Jacob establishes him as the heir to the divine promises given to Abraham. But the events of chapter 27 also place the fulfilment of these promises in jeopardy, for Esau threatens to kill Jacob. Consequently, the struggle between Jacob and Esau deepens and the family becomes more divided with Jacob having to leave the land of Canaan.[619] Can there possibly be any reconciliation for those involved as the divisions deepen?

Our actions have consequences, and it may not always be possible to undo what is done. The author of Hebrews, who criticizes Esau severely for selling his birthright, observes that when Esau looked to inherit the blessing, "he was rejected because he didn't find any opportunity for repentance, though he sought it with tears" (Heb 12:17).

While the Genesis narrator is primarily interested in how Jacob inherits the divine promises given to Abraham, he is also conscious that the attitudes and actions of subsequent generations may be influenced by the character of their ancestors.[620] Esau's descendants, the Edomites, will be condemned for their lack of brotherly compassion for the people of Israel.

---

[618] David J. Zucker, "The Deceiver Deceived: Rereading Genesis 27," *JBQ* 39 (2011): 46–58, speculates that Isaac was party to the deception, which was designed deliberately to help Jacob "go through a painful rite of passage in order to make his way in the world" (56). The evidence for this is not compelling.

[619] As Han, "The Role of 'an Audience,'" 10, observes, "The father trembles terribly. One brother threatens to kill the other. The mother scrambles to salvage both sons. One who is supposedly blessed gets uprooted."

[620] Alter, *Genesis*, 143, writes, "The elements that adumbrate future political configurations in no way diminish the complexity of these figures as individual characters. To the extent that there is a kind of political allegory in all these tales, it remains a secondary feature."

E. Jacob Flees from Esau (27:46–28:9)

> 46 So Rebekah said to Isaac, "I'm sick of my life because of these Hethite
> girls. If Jacob marries someone from around here, like these Hethite
> girls, what good is my life?"
>
> 28:1 So Isaac summoned Jacob, blessed him, and commanded him, "Do
> not marry a Canaanite girl. 2 Go at once to Paddan-aram, to the house
> of Bethuel, your mother's father. Marry one of the daughters of Laban,
> your mother's brother. 3 May God Almighty bless you and make you
> fruitful and multiply you so that you become an assembly of peoples. 4
> May God give you and your offspring the blessing of Abraham so that you
> may possess the land where you live as a foreigner, the land God gave to
> Abraham." 5 So Isaac sent Jacob to Paddan-aram, to Laban son of Bethuel
> the Aramean, the brother of Rebekah, the mother of Jacob and Esau.
>
> 6 Esau noticed that Isaac blessed Jacob and sent him to Paddan-aram to
> get a wife there. When he blessed him, Isaac commanded Jacob, "Do not
> marry a Canaanite girl." 7 And Jacob listened to his father and mother
> and went to Paddan-aram. 8 Esau realized that his father Isaac disap-
> proved of the Canaanite women, 9 so Esau went to Ishmael and married,
> in addition to his other wives, Mahalath daughter of Ishmael, Abraham's
> son. She was the sister of Nebaioth.

Context

The account of Jacob's deception of Isaac appears to be intentionally framed by brief references to the Hethite wives of Esau (26:34–35 and 27:46). This binds 28:1–9 to chapter 27 and builds upon Rebekah's instruction to Jacob to flee to Haran to escape the ire of Esau (27:43). By focusing on Esau's inappropriate choice of wives, Rebekah raises with Isaac the issue of finding a suitable spouse for Jacob. This results in Isaac sending Jacob to Paddan-aram to find a wife from among Rebekah's relatives, just as Abraham had sent there to get Rebekah for Isaac (24:1–67). The survival and continuation of the patriline requires that Jacob, as heir to the patriarchal covenant, should marry and have children.

Comments

27:46. Rebekah's evaluation of Hethite women is colored by her experience of Esau's wives (see 26:34–35). She fears that Jacob will follow Esau's example and marry a Hethite. On the term "Hethite," see Comments on 23:3–9.

28:1–5. Responding positively to Rebekah's anxiety, Isaac forbids Jacob from taking a Canaanite spouse;[621] he instructs him to find a wife from Laban's family in Paddan-aram. Although Abraham did not want Isaac to go to Paddan-aram (24:1–8), he nonetheless sent there his most-trusted servant to find a suitable wife for Isaac from his relatives in northwest Mesopotamia (24:1–67; cf. 25:20).

In verses 1 and 3–4 (cf. v. 6) the concept of blessing figures prominently, a significant feature given the motive for Jacob's deception of Isaac in chapter 27. Despite what has happened, Isaac affirms unambiguously that "the blessing of Abraham" (v. 4) now passes to Jacob, confirming the blessing of 27:28–29. Isaac's blessing of Jacob encapsulates the most important aspects of the divine promises granted to Abraham. His words in verse 3 echo chapter 17, recalling how God Almighty (*El Shaddai*; 17:1) promised to multiply Abraham greatly (17:2) and to make him extremely fruitful (17:6; cf. 17:20).[622] While priority is given in verse 3 to the covenant of chapter 17, with its emphasis upon Abraham becoming the spiritual father of many nations,[623] Isaac also states in verse 4 that Jacob will inherit the land of Canaan, recalling both 17:8 and the covenant ratified with Abraham in chapter 15.[624] In spite of sending Jacob as a single man to Haran, Isaac expects him to return to Canaan with a wife to inherit the land covenanted by God to Abraham. With good reason Jacob recalls the blessing of verses 3–4 decades later (see 48:4).

28:6–9. Verse 6 refers twice to Isaac's blessing of Jacob that is recorded in verses 1–4. Verse 7 presupposes Rebekah's instructions (27:43–45), as well as those of Isaac (28:1–4; cf. 28:6). Sensing belatedly his father's disapproval of "Canaanite women" (cf. 26:34–35), Esau takes a third wife, a daughter of

---

[621] In this context, the expression מִבְּנוֹת כְּנָעַן (*mibbĕnôt kĕnāʿan*, "from the daughters of Canaan)" (CSB "from the Canaanite women") is probably used as a broad term covering all the people groups resident in the land of Canaan; this would include the Hethites. See 10:15–19.

[622] The related concepts of multiplying and being fruitful may be traced back to 1:24–31 (cf. 9:1, 7).

[623] The expression "an assembly of peoples" (v. 3) is closely tied to the motif of Abraham being the father of many nations (see 17:4–6). The expression is repeated in 35:11, alongside instructions to be fruitful and multiply (cf. 17:2, 6).

[624] Isaac's reference to Jacob's possessing the land (v. 4) recalls the use of the verb יָרַשׁ (*yāraš*, "to possess/inherit") in 15:3, 4, 7, 8 (cf. 21:10; 22:17; 24:60), where it is used in connection with Abraham's offspring taking possession of the land of Canaan. The expression אֶרֶץ מְגֻרֶיךָ (*ʾereṣ mĕgurêkā*, "land where you live as a foreigner") (v. 4) is also used in 17:8, translated "the land where you are residing" in CSB.

Ishmael and granddaughter of Abraham, in the hope that her relationship to Abraham might gain Isaac's approval. For more on Esau's wives, see 36:2–3.

Bridge

Jacob's status as heir to the patriarchal promises is confirmed by the blessing that Isaac pronounces when he instructs Jacob to find a wife in Paddan-aram (28:1–4). Any lingering doubts regarding the legitimacy of the blessing acquired through Jacob's deception of Isaac are laid to rest. Through Isaac's blessing in verses 1–4, Jacob is identified as the next member of the patriline that goes back to Adam and Eve. However, the hopes associated with the family lineage will come to an end if Jacob remains unmarried and childless. Consequently, the focus moves in chapters 28–29 to Jacob's journey to Paddan-aram and his quest for a suitable wife.

F. Jacob at Bethel (28:10–22)

> [10] Jacob left Beer-sheba and went toward Haran. [11] He reached a certain place and spent the night there because the sun had set. He took one of the stones from the place, put it there at his head, and lay down in that place. [12] And he dreamed: A stairway was set on the ground with its top reaching the sky, and God's angels were going up and down on it. [13] The LORD was standing there beside him, saying, "I am the LORD, the God of your father Abraham and the God of Isaac. I will give you and your offspring the land on which you are lying. [14] Your offspring will be like the dust of the earth, and you will spread out toward the west, the east, the north, and the south. All the peoples on earth will be blessed through you and your offspring. [15] Look, I am with you and will watch over you wherever you go. I will bring you back to this land, for I will not leave you until I have done what I have promised you."
>
> [16] When Jacob awoke from his sleep, he said, "Surely the LORD is in this place, and I did not know it." [17] He was afraid and said, "What an awesome place this is! This is none other than the house of God. This is the gate of heaven."
>
> [18] Early in the morning Jacob took the stone that was near his head and set it up as a marker. He poured oil on top of it [19] and named the place Bethel, though previously the city was named Luz. [20] Then Jacob made a vow: "If God will be with me and watch over me during this journey I'm making, if he provides me with food to eat and clothing to wear, [21] and if I return safely to my father's family, then the LORD will be my God. [22] This stone that I have set up as a marker will be God's house, and I will give to you a tenth of all that you give me."

Context

The story of Jacob's journey to Paddan-aram is interrupted by an incident that occurs when he sleeps outdoors near the town of Luz. For the first time, God addresses Jacob directly, making this a highly significant occasion. Echoing the various blessings that Isaac had pronounced over Jacob, YHWH emphatically promises to bring Jacob back safely to Canaan so that the divine promises given to Abraham, and then Isaac, may be channeled through Jacob to his descendants. With its emphasis upon the divine promises, this episode recalls what has already transpired in the preceding narrative and anticipates Jacob's future return from Paddan-aram to Canaan. YHWH's words also indicate that Jacob, although presently single, will find a wife and have children of his own. This sets the scene for what will take place in Haran.

Comments

28:10–15. The mention of Beer-sheba in verse 10 implies that everything recorded in 27:1–28:9 took place chronologically after Isaac's servants dug a well there (26:32–33). Encouraged by his parents, Jacob travels from Beer-sheba toward Haran, in northwest Mesopotamia. From Beer-sheba to Haran is about 600 miles (965 km); from Beer-sheba to Bethel is about 60 miles (97 km).[625] After two or three days, Jacob comes to Luz (Bethel) around sunset. When asleep, Jacob has a vivid dream in which three things stand out:[626] a ladder/stairway;[627] angels; YHWH.

Jacob's vision begins with a ladder/stairway linking heaven to earth. This structure enables communication to take place between heaven

[625] The location of ancient Bethel is assumed to be modern Beitin. This identification was proposed by Edward Robinson and Eli Smith, *Biblical Researches in Palestine, Mount Sinai, and Arabia Petræa. A Journal of Travels in the Year 1838*, vol. 2 (Boston: Crocker & Brewster, 1841), 127–28, and supported by E. H. Palmer, *The Survey of Western Palestine. Arabic and English Name-Lists Collected by Lieutenants Conder and Kitchener, R. E. Transliterated and Explained by E. H. Palmer* (London: The Committee of the Palestine Exploration Fund, 1881), 226. The identification of Beitin as ancient Bethel has been questioned by David P. Livingston, "Location of Biblical Bethel and Ai Reconsidered," *WTJ* 33 (1970): 20–44; David P. Livingston, "Traditional Site of Bethel Questioned," *WTJ* 34 (1971): 39–50.

[626] Each of the three items is introduced by וְהִנֵּה (*wĕhinnē*). This repetition conveys a sense of surprise on the part of Jacob (cf. Fokkelman, *Narrative Art in Genesis*, 50–52).

[627] The term סֻלָּם (*sullām*) occurs only here in the Old Testament. Traditionally it has been translated "ladder" (e.g., ESV; KJV; NAS; NJB; NRSV; RSV), but many modern translations opt for "stairway" (CSB; NIV; NLT; NJPS). The precise nature of the structure that links heaven to earth is not important; what matters is its function. See C. Houtman, "What Did Jacob See in His Dream at Bethel? Some Remarks on Genesis xxviii 10–22," *VT* 27 (1977): 337–51.

and earth.[628] Jacob sees YHWH, possibly standing beside him. The CSB translation assumes that עָלָיו (*ʿālāyw*) in the expression וְהִנֵּה יְהוָה נִצָּב עָלָיו (*wĕhinnē yhwh niṣṣāb ʿālāyw*) means "beside him" (cf. NJB, NRSV, NJPS). Alternatively, it could mean "above it" or "beside it," referring to the ladder/stairway (cf. ESV, KJV, NAS, NIV, RSV). Either way, Jacob understands God to be present "in this place" (v. 16), which can be viewed as both "the house of God" and "gate of heaven" (v. 17).

Taking the initiative, YHWH speaks to Jacob, introducing himself as the God of Abraham and of Isaac (v. 13). The contents of the divine speech add to the growing sense that Jacob is the one who will follow in the footsteps of his father and grandfather. As Anderson observes, "What emerges to the fore in 28:13–15 is a recognition of Jacob as the sole recipient and bearer of the ancestral promise."[629] YHWH promises Jacob that his numerous descendants, like the dust of the earth,[630] will possess the land where Jacob is sleeping and spread out from it in every direction.[631] Additionally, God states that "all the peoples of earth" will be blessed through Jacob and his offspring.[632] YHWH's words recall what he swore on oath to Abraham in 22:16–18 and confirm the expectation given in Isaac's blessings of Jacob that the divine promises first given to Abraham now pass to Jacob.[633] While God reiterates the promises given to Abraham, he also recognizes that Jacob is about to leave the land of Canaan. YHWH reassures Jacob that he will go with him and bring him safely back to this land. The motif of God being with Jacob, mentioned in verse 15, which is picked up by Jacob in verse 20, reappears later in 31:3, 5.

28:16–17. The dream experience leaves Jacob with a deep sense of God's presence. Describing the place as "awesome" (v. 17), he concludes that the location is בֵּית אֱלֹהִים (*bêt ʾĕlōhîm*, "the house of God,") שַׁעַר הַשָּׁמָיִם

---

[628] The term מַלְאָךְ (*malʾāk*), often translated "angel," conveys the idea of a messenger or representative.

[629] Anderson, "Jacob, Laban, and a Divine Trickster?," 9.

[630] YHWH's comment in v. 14 that Jacob's numerous descendants will be like the dust of the earth echoes a similar promise made to Abraham in 13:16 (cf. 22:17).

[631] The mention of north, south, east, and west in v. 14 recalls God's promise to Abraham in 13:14.

[632] The *niphal* form of the verb בָּרַךְ (*bārak*, "to bless"), which is used here, is also used in 12:3 and 18:18; the *hithpael* form of בָּרַךְ (*bārak*) occurs in 22:18 and 26:4. See Comments on 22:18.

[633] Cf. George G. Nicol, "Story-Patterning in Genesis," in *Text as Pretext: Essays in Honour of Robert Davidson*, ed. Robert P. Carroll, JSOTSup 138 (Sheffield: JSOT Press, 1992), 219–22.

(*šaʿar haššāmāyim*, "the gate of heaven"). He subsequently names the place בֵּית־אֵל (*bêt-ʾēl*, "Bethel"), meaning "house of God" (v. 19).

28:18–22. Although Jacob is profoundly impacted by his encounter with YHWH and sensitive to the significance of the location, several factors suggest that he remains ambivalent about having YHWH as his God. First, he does not construct an altar, but only sets up a מַצֵּבָה (*maṣṣēbâ*, "marker" or "memorial stone").[634] This response may be contrasted with that of Abraham, who builds an altar after God appears to him near Bethel (12:7–8; cf. 13:3). Only much later, following Jacob's life-transforming encounter with God at Penuel (32:24–32), does Jacob fulfils God's instructions to build an altar at Bethel (35:1–7). Second, Jacob's vow to have YHWH as his God (vv. 20–21) is conditional upon God's protection and provision during the whole period of his exile from his father's house. As Alter observes, Jacob "wants to be sure God will fulfill His side of the bargain before he commits himself to God's service."[635] Only after his nighttime struggle with God at Penuel does Jacob (renamed Israel) speak of God as the "God of Israel" (33:20). Prior to this he speaks of YHWH as the God of other people (27:20; 31:5, 42; 32:9). These factors suggest that Jacob has still some way to go before he truly resembles Abraham and Isaac in his commitment to YHWH.

Through his vow (vv. 20–21), Jacob selfishly seeks to manipulate God to gain his protection and provision.[636] If God provides for Jacob, Jacob will in turn, as a reward for God's help, build a sanctuary at Bethel and pay tithes (cf. 14:20). Jacob has yet to learn that God's favor cannot be bought in so crude a way. While Jacob's theology is less than perfect, his desire to build a sanctuary and pay tithes is not entirely misplaced. By looking to construct a sanctuary, Jacob anticipates that God will live among his descendants. This expectation is an important part of the ongoing story, resulting in the construction of the temple in Jerusalem by King Solomon (see Biblical and Theological Themes §4). The gift of a tithe (a tenth) acknowledges YHWH's

---

[634] Although Jacob's actions appear to break a prohibition that Moses will later give the Israelites, prohibiting the setting up a מַצֵּבָה (*maṣṣēbâ*, "sacred pillar") (Deut 16:22), the immediate context in Deuteronomy suggests that it only applies when an altar is constructed at the same location (cf. Deut 16:21). Jacob, however, builds no altar.

[635] Alter, *Genesis*, 150.

[636] Walton, *Genesis*, 573, remarks that the vow "looks suspiciously like another bargain." Provan, *Discovering Genesis*, 162, writes, "[H]is vow appears to be as much a bargain as a commitment." Waltke and Fredricks, *Genesis*, 394, adopt a more positive reading of Jacob's vow.

special status (cf. 14:19); in the future Jacob's descendants will be expected to give a tithe to God (see Lev 27:30–33; cf. Num 18:21–32; Deut 14:22–29). The location, designated Bethel by Jacob, is close to the town of Luz (cf. Josh 16:2). Joshua 18:13 may imply that Bethel was on the southern slope of Luz. The town's name changes to Bethel only after the Israelites settle in Canaan (Judg 1:23, 26; cf. Gen 35:6; 48:3).

Bridge

God's revelation of himself to Jacob is an act of grace for Jacob does nothing to merit YHWH's presence. He builds no altar and offers no sacrifices. Houtman notes that the ladder/stairway descends toward the earth and "so the impression is made that the narrator wishes to express that the communication between heaven and earth is established by an initiative from on high, on part of God. The contact between heaven and earth exists by the grace of God."[637] God comes to Jacob to encourage him at a time when he might easily be filled with despair, but Jacob's response, while positive, is less than a whole-hearted commitment to serving YHWH. Jacob is a "work in process."[638] When many years later Jacob returns to Canaan from Paddan-aram, he experiences another dramatic encounter with God (32:24–32). After a period at Shechem Jacob returns to Bethel and builds there an altar (35:6–15). At Bethel God confirms that the promises given to Abraham and Isaac now pass to Jacob/Israel (35:10–12).

G. Jacob Meets Rachel (29:1–12)

> [1] Jacob resumed his journey and went to the eastern country. [2] He looked
> and saw a well in a field. Three flocks of sheep were lying there beside
> it because the sheep were watered from this well. But a large stone
> covered the opening of the well. [3] The shepherds would roll the stone
> from the opening of the well and water the sheep when all the flocks
> were gathered there. Then they would return the stone to its place
> over the well's opening.
>
> [4] Jacob asked the men at the well, "My brothers! Where are you from?"
>
> "We're from Haran," they answered.
>
> [5] "Do you know Laban grandson of Nahor?" Jacob asked them.

[637] Houtman, "What Did Jacob See," 351.

[638] Walton, *Genesis*, 574.

They answered, "We know him."

6 "Is he well?" Jacob asked.

"Yes," they said, "and here is his daughter Rachel, coming with his sheep."

7 Then Jacob said, "Look, it is still broad daylight. It's not time for the animals to be gathered. Water the flock, then go out and let them graze."

8 But they replied, "We can't until all the flocks have been gathered and the stone is rolled from the well's opening. Then we will water the sheep."

9 While he was still speaking with them, Rachel came with her father's
sheep, for she was a shepherdess. 10 As soon as Jacob saw his uncle La-
ban's daughter Rachel with his sheep, he went up and rolled the stone
from the opening and watered his uncle Laban's sheep. 11 Then Jacob
kissed Rachel and wept loudly. 12 He told Rachel that he was her father's
relative, Rebekah's son. She ran and told her father.

Context

After Jacob's dream-theophany at Bethel, the narrative jumps swiftly to Jacob's arrival at Haran. This marks the start of a series of episodes that are closely bound together, involving Jacob's relationship with his uncle Laban and his daughters (29:1–31:55). Waltke and Fredricks find here a mirror-image pattern, that centers on the birth of Joseph (30:22–24), a striking feature given the importance of Joseph in chs. 37–50.

A Introduction: meeting of brothers in peace (29:1–14a)
  B Laban's deception regarding Rachel (29:14b–30)
    C God's blessing on Jacob's seed in spite of conflict (29:31–30:21)
      X Birth of Joseph: turning point to leave (30:22–24)
    C' God's blessing on Jacob's property in spite of conflict (30:25–31:30)
  B' Rachel's deceptions regarding Laban's gods (31:31–42)
A' Conclusion: parting of brothers in peace pact (31:43–55)[639]

Jacob's arrival at Haran and his encounter with Rachel recalls the story of Abraham's servant's first meeting with Rebekah (24:11–27). While the well scenes have some things in common, there are striking differences. The servant prayed for God's guidance in finding a wife for Isaac, but Jacob at no point consults God in his quest for a wife. Rebekah waters the servant's camels, but Jacob waters Rachel's sheep. The servant comes with expensive

---

[639] Waltke and Fredricks, *Genesis*, 353. Cf. Fishbane, "Composition and Structure," 30–32.

gifts, but Jacob comes empty-handed. Despite these obvious differences, the impression is given that God providentially brings Jacob and Rachel together.

Comments

29:1–6. Jacob's long journey from Bethel to Haran is summarized in verse 1, in two phrases that translated literally read: "And Jacob lifted his feet and went toward the land of the sons of the east." The first idiom is understood by some English versions to mean that Jacob resumed his journey (cf. CSB, NIV, NJB, NJPS). NLT takes it to imply that he journeyed quickly. Other English versions simply read "Jacob went on his journey" (e.g., KJV, ESV, NAS, RSV, NRSV) without giving any special nuance to the idea of raising one's feet. As for the second phrase, the reference to the "sons of the east" is probably best taken as a general designation of the people who lived in the entire region of Mesopotamia, from Carchemish in the west to the Persian Gulf in the east.[640]

Verses 2–3 set the scene and provide details about the unusual arrangements that exist at this well for the watering of the animals.[641] When Jacob learns that the shepherds are from Haran, he asks regarding "Laban grandson of Nahor."[642] In response the shepherds point to Rachel, Laban's daughter. Rachel, whose name means "ewe," is bringing a flock of sheep and goats to be watered at the well (v. 6).

29:7–12. When Jacob sees Rachel with Laban's sheep, he takes the initiative, rolling the stone from the well and watering the animals. His actions must have startled Rachel, for Jacob flouts the local custom of waiting for all the flocks to arrive at the well. The text does not specify exactly the size of the stone that needs to be rolled away; it is described as large. Custom rather than size appears to be the reason for the stone not being moved by the shepherds. A chiasmus is created by the order of the activities in

---

[640] First Kgs 4:30 uses the expression "sons of the east" alongside "Egypt" to denote the regions surrounding Israel (e.g., to the southwest and to the north and east). Since Haran is to the northeast of Israel, the CSB translation "to the eastern country" may appear misleading to some readers, given the location of Haran.

[641] In the Pentateuch the Hebrew term עֵדֶר (*ʿēder*), used to denote a flock or herd, occurs only in passages involving Jacob (i.e., Gen 29:2–3, 8; 30:40; 32:16, 19 [Heb. 17, 20]). Gen 32:17 uses the term twice in conjunction with separate groups of goats, sheep, camels, cattle, and donkeys (32:15–16), which Jacob brought back from Paddan-aram.

[642] The Hebrew text speaks of Laban as בֶּן־נָחוֹר (*ben-nāḥôr*, "son of Nahor"), a good illustration of how in Israelite culture "son" is not restricted to denoting only children of the next generation. Cf. Matt 1:1 where Jesus is designated "the Son of David, the Son of Abraham."

verses 10–11: Jacob sees Rachel ("the ewe") and then the sheep;[643] he waters the sheep and then kisses Rachel. To add interest to the telling of the story, the narrator introduces a wordplay involving the similar sounding verbs וַיַּשְׁקְ (*wayyašq*, "and he watered") and וַיִּשַּׁק (*wayyiššaq*, "and he kissed").[644]

Bridge

This opening episode in the Jacob-Laban cycle sets the scene for what follows, introducing both Laban's daughter Rachel and his flocks. The story of Jacob's time in Haran revolves around his acquisition of both a wife and herds. Three times in verse 10 the narrator uses the expression לָבָן אֲחִי אִמּוֹ (*lābān ʾăḥî ʾimmô*, "Laban the brother of his mother") (which CSB renders "his uncle Laban") to denote the one who possesses Rachel ("the ewe") and the flock. By the time Jacob leaves Paddan-aram, Rachel and the flock will no longer belong to Laban. What Laban possesses at the start of the story will be Jacob's by the end. But Jacob's path to acquiring both Rachel and a flock will not be straightforward, for Laban is devious by nature. Jacob's willingness to break with local custom to water his uncle's sheep speaks of his independent spirit and signals that he is prepared to flout convention (as he has already done in depriving Esau of the firstborn-birthright and paternal blessing).

H. Jacob Deceived by Laban (29:13–30)

> [13] When Laban heard the news about his sister's son Jacob, he ran to meet him, hugged him, and kissed him. Then he took him to his house, and Jacob told him all that had happened.
>
> [14] Laban said to him, "Yes, you are my own flesh and blood."
>
> After Jacob had stayed with him a month, [15] Laban said to him, "Just because you're my relative, should you work for me for nothing? Tell me what your wages should be."
>
> [16] Now Laban had two daughters: the older was named Leah, and the younger was named Rachel. [17] Leah had tender eyes, but Rachel was shapely and beautiful. [18] Jacob loved Rachel, so he answered Laban, "I'll work for you seven years for your younger daughter Rachel."

---

[643] The narrator speaks of "Rachel the daughter of Laban, the brother of his mother" and the "sheep of Laban, the brother of his mother."

[644] Cf. Sarna, *Genesis*, 191.

[19] Laban replied, "Better that I give her to you than to some other man. Stay with me." [20] So Jacob worked seven years for Rachel, and they seemed like only a few days to him because of his love for her.

[21] Then Jacob said to Laban, "Since my time is complete, give me my wife, so I can sleep with her." [22] So Laban invited all the men of the place and sponsored a feast. [23] That evening, Laban took his daughter Leah and gave her to Jacob, and he slept with her. [24] And Laban gave his slave Zilpah to his daughter Leah as her slave.

[25] When morning came, there was Leah! So he said to Laban, "What is this you have done to me? Wasn't it for Rachel that I worked for you? Why have you deceived me?"

[26] Laban answered, "It is not the custom in this place to give the younger daughter in marriage before the firstborn. [27] Complete this week of wedding celebration, and we will also give you this younger one in return for working yet another seven years for me."

[28] And Jacob did just that. He finished the week of celebration, and Laban gave him his daughter Rachel as his wife. [29] And Laban gave his slave Bilhah to his daughter Rachel as her slave. [30] Jacob slept with Rachel also, and indeed, he loved Rachel more than Leah. And he worked for Laban another seven years.

Context

This passage continues the report of Jacob's arrival at Haran. After hearing from Rachel about Jacob, Laban warmly embraces his nephew, welcoming him into his household. So begins a long relationship that will result in Jacob being with Laban for about twenty years (31:38). In the light of previous statements about Jacob being served by other people (e.g., 25:23; 27:29; cf. 27:37, 40), the present passage underscores the opposite motif of Jacob serving Laban.[645] This plays out in subsequent episodes, for Jacob is forced to free himself and his future family from Laban's control in order to return to Canaan. Jacob's experience in Paddan-aram is part of a gradual process that will lead to his life being transformed by God.

Comments

29:13–14. Laban eagerly welcomes his nephew Jacob, who proceeds to explain why he has come to Haran. The narrator does not disclose the details of what Jacob told Laban, but the expression כָּל־הַדְּבָרִים הָאֵלֶּה (*kol-hadděbārîm hāʾēlle* "all these words"), which CSB renders, "all that

[645] Sarna, *Genesis*, 192, notes that "serve" is a key word in this pericope.

had happened," possibly implies that Jacob recounted to Laban the full story of the events recorded in 25:19–28:22. If so, Laban's response, "you are my own flesh and blood," may signal that he views Jacob as more than a relative;[646] Laban possibly believes that he and Jacob are one by nature, a point confirmed by Laban's deceptive behavior.[647]

29:15–20. Laban's offer to pay Jacob for his labor creates an opportunity for Jacob to propose marrying Rachel. ANE marriage customs required a would-be husband to give a betrothal present (often misleadingly called a bride-price) to the bride's father. In return the father would give a dowry to his daughter. These financial transactions offered some protection to the woman, should her marriage relationship break down; the dowry belonged to her and the betrothal present remained with her father. Having come to Haran with no wealth, Jacob is unable to provide a betrothal present. Consequently, he agrees to work for Laban for seven years to pay the betrothal present for Rachel. Laban's positive reply (v. 19) to an impoverished Jacob may be influenced by the fact that a Jacob-Rachel marriage would give Laban control of all the financial transactions of the marriage. For this reason, years later Laban is distraught when Jacob decides to return to Canaan, taking wives and property that, as *paterfamilias* (head of the family), Laban might have viewed as his.

In anticipation of what will happen later, the narrator offers a brief comment on the relative beauty of Leah and Rachel (v. 17),[648] before stating that Jacob loved Rachel. To underline the strength of Jacob's love for Rachel, the reader learns that the seven years seemed like a few days to Jacob "because of his love for her" (v. 20)

29:21–24. At the end of seven years, Jacob asks Laban to arrange the wedding. This will involve a public feast that will last a week (cf. Judg 14:10–18). However, on the first night, when the marriage is to be consummated, Laban

---

[646] The CSB translation of אַךְ עַצְמִי וּבְשָׂרִי אָתָּה (*ʾak ʿaṣmî ûbĕśārî ʾāttâ*, "Yes, you are my own flesh and blood") fails to capture the strong link that exists between this comment and the statement of Adam in 2:23. A more literal rendering of Laban's comment would be, "Surely you are my bone and my flesh."

[647] Turner, *Genesis*, 126, with reference to 24:28–67, suggests that Laban sees Jacob "as someone after his own heart." Provan, *Discovering Genesis*, 164, remarks, "Jacob, the cheat, has just met someone who can out-cheat him—a character noted in his own younger days for his greed (Gen. 24.22, 29–31)."

[648] The English versions offer a range of translations regarding the condition of Leah's eyes. Most favor the idea that they were "weak" (e.g., ESV, NAS, NIV, RSV, NJPS). Other terms used are "tender" (e.g., AV, CSB, NET) or "lovely" (NJB, NRSV). See McKeown, *Genesis*, 143.

gives Leah and not Rachel to Jacob. While modern readers may find the ruse difficult to imagine, ancient readers must have considered the account plausible. Various related factors may explain why Jacob did not realize until morning that he was with Leah. She may have been wearing a veil to hide her face (cf. 24:65), with possibly only her eyes being visible. In the darkness or semi-darkness of night Jacob may not have been able to distinguish Leah's eyes from those of Rachel. Jacob may also have been somewhat intoxicated due to the "feast" organized by Laban.[649] Jacob, who had deceived his father into believing that he was his brother, now suffers a similar deception involving sisters. As an aside, anticipating future developments (see 30:9–13), we are told that Laban assigns Zilpah to Leah as her personal servant.[650]

29:25–30. When Jacob discovers that he has been given Leah, he confronts Laban, accusing him of deception. Jacob's reproach of Laban recalls Isaac's description of what Jacob did when he disguised himself as Esau; the verb רמה (*rmh*, "to deceive") in verse 25 is cognate to the noun מִרְמָה (*mirmâ*, "deceit/fraud") (27:35). Laban, however, answers Jacob with an observation that must have cut deep. Highlighting the custom of giving priority to the eldest, Laban indirectly condemns what Jacob did when he deprived his older brother of the firstborn's blessing.

Laban then exploits Jacob's desire to marry Rachel, offering her as a second wife on two conditions. First, Jacob must complete the wedding celebrations with Leah, and, second, he must continue to serve Laban for a further seven years to meet the cost of Rachel's betrothal present. From the wording of verse 28 it is difficult to tell what time elapsed between Jacob's marrying Leah and Laban's giving Rachel to him. We should not automatically presume that Jacob "slept" with Rachel (v. 30) immediately after his seven days with Leah. In anticipation of later events, the reader learns that Laban gives Bilhah to Rachel as a maidservant; she will later provide Jacob children on behalf of Rachel (30:3–8). By ensuring that both daughters remain within his household, Laban retains practical control of their finances, an issue that will surface later (see 31:14–16; 31:43).

---

[649] The Hebrew term translated "feast" could also be rendered "drinking." Cf. J. A. Diamond, "The Deception of Jacob: A New Perspective on an Ancient Solution to the Problem," *VT* 34 (1984): 211–13, who draws a parallel with how a drunken Lot was unknowingly deceived by his daughters into having intercourse with them (19:32–33).

[650] It may also be possible that the gift of Zilpah to Leah represents part of the dowry. Since Jacob does not buy the maidservants, Laban may have considered their children as belonging to him (cf. Exod 21:4).

Bridge

In Haran, Laban enjoys the status of *paterfamilias* and he sees his avuncular relationship with Jacob as placing his impoverished nephew under his control.[651] This kinship bond is reinforced by cross-cousin marriage.[652] By becoming part of Laban's household, Jacob is not only accountable to his uncle but he also places in danger his own status as the one who should become *paterfamilias* in succession to Abraham and Isaac. Laban's warm embrace of Jacob may have initially pleased his nephew, but it threatens to undermine the continuation of the patriline traced in Genesis.

After seven years serving Laban, we discover that Jacob has met his match. "The deceiver is now deceived."[653] As commentators have long noted, Laban's ruse metes out poetic justice to Jacob. Cheated by Laban, Jacob has little choice but to marry both sisters, creating a situation that is far from perfect. Throughout Genesis, polygamy is always presented as less than ideal.[654] In addition, the fact that Jacob loves Rachel more than Leah will lead to considerable tension within the family.

I. Jacob's Children (29:31–30:24)

> [31] When the Lord saw that Leah was unloved, he opened her womb; but
> Rachel was unable to conceive.
>
> [32] Leah conceived, gave birth to a son, and named him Reuben, for she said,
> "The Lord has seen my affliction; surely my husband will love me now."
>
> She conceived again, gave birth to a son, and said, "The Lord heard that I
> am unloved and has given me this son also." So she named him Simeon.
>
> [34] She conceived again, gave birth to a son, and said, "At last, my hus-
> band will become attached to me because I have borne three sons for
> him." Therefore he was named Levi.

---

[651] Robert A. Oden, "Jacob as Father, Husband, and Nephew: Kinship Studies and the Patriarchal Narratives," *JBL* 102 (1983): 189–205.

[652] According to Oden, "Jacob as Father, Husband, and Nephew," 199, such an arrangement avoids "too much endogamy" and "too much exogamy."

[653] McKeown, *Genesis*, 144.

[654] It is associated first with Lamech (4:23) and then resurfaces with Abraham, when Sarah persuades him to take Hagar as a second wife (16:1–3). This relationship introduces complications regarding the identity of the heir to the divine promises. Centuries later, at Mount Sinai, God gives through Moses instructions prohibiting a man from marrying two sisters who are both alive (Lev 18:18).

35 And she conceived again, gave birth to a son, and said, "This time I will praise the LORD." Therefore she named him Judah. Then Leah stopped having children.

30:1 When Rachel saw that she was not bearing Jacob any children, she envied her sister. "Give me sons, or I will die!" she said to Jacob.

2 Jacob became angry with Rachel and said, "Am I in God's place, who has withheld offspring from you?"

3 Then she said, "Here is my maid Bilhah. Go sleep with her, and she'll bear children for me so that through her I too can build a family." 4 So Rachel gave her slave Bilhah to Jacob as a wife, and he slept with her. 5 Bilhah conceived and bore Jacob a son. 6 Rachel said, "God has vindicated me; yes, he has heard me and given me a son," so she named him Dan.

7 Rachel's slave Bilhah conceived again and bore Jacob a second son. 8 Rachel said, "In my wrestlings with God, I have wrestled with my sister and won," and she named him Naphtali.

9 When Leah saw that she had stopped having children, she took her slave Zilpah and gave her to Jacob as a wife. 10 Leah's slave Zilpah bore Jacob a son. 11 Then Leah said, "What good fortune!" and she named him Gad.

12 When Leah's slave Zilpah bore Jacob a second son, 13 Leah said, "I am happy that the women call me happy," so she named him Asher.

14 Reuben went out during the wheat harvest and found some mandrakes in the field. When he brought them to his mother Leah, Rachel asked, "Please give me some of your son's mandrakes."

15 But Leah replied to her, "Isn't it enough that you have taken my husband? Now you also want to take my son's mandrakes?"

"Well then," Rachel said, "he can sleep with you tonight in exchange for your son's mandrakes."

16 When Jacob came in from the field that evening, Leah went out to meet him and said, "You must come with me, for I have hired you with my son's mandrakes." So Jacob slept with her that night.

17 God listened to Leah, and she conceived and bore Jacob a fifth son. 18 Leah said, "God has rewarded me for giving my slave to my husband," and she named him Issachar.

19 Then Leah conceived again and bore Jacob a sixth son. 20 "God has given me a good gift," Leah said. "This time my husband will honor me because I have borne six sons for him," and she named him Zebulun. 21 Later, Leah bore a daughter and named her Dinah.

[22] Then God remembered Rachel. He listened to her and opened her womb. [23] She conceived and bore a son, and she said, "God has taken away my disgrace." [24] She named him Joseph and said, "May the Lord add another son to me."

Context

The account of Jacob's marriage to Leah and Rachel is immediately followed by a description of the sons born to Jacob. Through a series of brief reports, each son is introduced by name, each name reflecting something of the circumstances surrounding the son's birth. The births of eleven sons and one daughter are recorded. To add to the complexity of relationships within Jacob's family, Rachel and Leah both experience periods of barrenness and are unable to have children. To overcome this situation Rachel and then Leah resort to using Bilhah and Zilpah respectively as surrogate mothers. Consequently, Jacob ends up having eleven sons born to four different mothers.

Comments

29:31–35. Jacob's disparaging attitude toward Leah has unexpected consequences. Despite Jacob's love for the younger sister, it is through the "firstborn" sister that God provides Jacob with sons. The passive participle שְׂנוּאָה (*śĕnûʾâ*, "was unloved") is translated "was hated" in some English versions (e.g., ESV, KJV, RSV). This is too harsh a translation, especially since Jacob has sexual relations with Leah. The verb שׂנא (*śnʾ*) probably has the sense of "slight/despise"[655] or "love less." By enabling Leah to have children, YHWH demonstrates his concern for those who are mistreated by others.

The name of each son is linked by wordplay to Leah's comments: רְאוּבֵן (*rĕûbēn*, "Reuben") (meaning "look, a son") resembles רָאָה (*rāʾâ*, "has seen") (v. 32); שִׁמְעוֹן (*šimʿôn*, "Simeon") resembles שָׁמַע (*šāmaʿ*, "heard") (v. 33); לֵוִי (*lēwî*, "Levi") resembles יִלָּוֶה (*yillāwe*, "become attached") (v. 34), and יְהוּדָה (*yĕhûdâ*, "Judah") (meaning "may he [God] be praised"[656]) resembles אוֹדֶה (*ʾôde*, "I will praise") (v. 35). The names "Reuben" and "Simeon" pick up respectively on God's seeing and hearing Leah's plight. By the time Leah gives birth to Levi, she is hopeful that a third son will gain Jacob's favor. The birth of a fourth son causes Leah to praise YHWH. Leah's God-centered comments in verses 32, 33, and 35 indicate that she

---

655 Alter, *Genesis*, 155, suggests that it is "a technical, legal term for the unfavored co-wife."

656 A. R. Millard, "The Meaning of the Name Judah," *ZAW* 86 (1974): 216–18.

recognizes YHWH's role in providing her with sons. Significantly, she is the mother of both Levi and Judah, from whom are descended the Aaronic priests and the Davidic kings respectively.

30:1–8. Rachel's continuing childlessness makes her jealous of Leah. She vents her frustration on Jacob, implying that he is to blame. Rachel's demand of Jacob is striking in the light of later developments. She pleads for "sons"; otherwise she will die. Later, Rachel dies when giving birth to Benjamin, her second son (35:16–19). Alter tentatively suggests that Rachel's first words "foreshadow her premature death."[657] Jacob responds angrily to Rachel, shifting the blame to God. Whereas Isaac prayed for his barren wife Rebekah (25:21–22), there is no indication that Jacob prays for Rachel. Jacob may well believe that YHWH exists and has promised to care for him, but he appears to lack a personal commitment to YHWH as his God.

Like Sarah, who offered her maidservant Hagar to Abraham to be a surrogate mother (16:1–4), Rachel gives Bilhah to Jacob (v. 3). Subsequently, Bilhah bears two sons to Jacob. As was the custom in such situations, Rachel views them as her own, naming them Dan and Naphtali.[658] Both names are deliberately chosen by Rachel to express a sense of victory in her struggle with her older sister. The name דָּן (*dān*, "Dan") (meaning "vindication") is linked to the verb דָּנַנִּי (*dānannî*, "has vindicated me"); the name נַפְתָּלִי (*naptālî*, "Naphtali") (meaning "my wrestling") is linked to the terms נַפְתּוּלֵי (*naptûlê*, "wrestlings") and נִפְתַּלְתִּי (*niptaltî*, "I have wrestled").[659] The image of Rachel wrestling with God and her sister (v. 8) recalls Jacob's struggle with Esau in Rebekah's womb (25:22) and anticipates Jacob's struggle with God at Penuel (32:24–32).[660] Conflict is a recurring theme in Genesis. Jacob's struggle with Esau regarding the

---

657 Alter, *Genesis*, 158.

658 In v. 3 Rachel uses the expression עַל־בִּרְכַּי (*ʿal-birkay*, "on my knees") to emphasize that Bilhah's children will form a family for Rachel.

659 Unlike most other English versions, CSB translates the expression נַפְתּוּלֵי אֱלֹהִים (*naptûlê ʾĕlōhîm*, "my wrestling with God"). Other versions tend to favor the translation "mighty wrestlings" (e.g., ESV, NRSV, RSV; cf. KJV which reads "great wrestlings"; NIV has "great struggle"). It is not necessary to assume that the divine name in this context signifies an intensive with no reference to God himself (Wenham, *Genesis 16–50*, 245–46; cf. similar use of אֱלֹהִים in 23:6). See Skinner, *Genesis*, 387.

660 While different Hebrew words are used to denote the wrestling/struggling in these passages, Rachel's shout of victory גַּם־יָכֹלְתִּי (*gam-yākōlĕttî*, "I have won") (30:8) resembles וַתּוּכָל (*wattûkāl*, "have prevailed") (32:28; cf. 32:25).

birthright of the firstborn is now paralleled ironically in the struggle between Rachel and Leah.

30:9–13. Following Rachel's lead, Leah gives her maidservant Zilpah to Jacob to be another wife and surrogate mother. Two more sons are born, both of whom are named by Leah. Both names convey Leah's joy at having added further sons to her family. The name גָּד (*gād*, "Gad") (meaning "good fortune") reflects the term בְּגָד (*bĕgād*, "What good fortune") (v. 11); the name אָשֵׁר (*ʾāšēr*, "Asher") (meaning "happy one") reflects the terms בְּאָשְׁרִי (*bĕʾāšrî*, "I am happy") and אִשְּׁרוּנִי (*ʾiššĕrûnî*, "call me happy") (v. 13).

30:14–21. Reuben is probably about five years old when he finds the wild mandrakes and brings them to Leah. Leah's response to Rachel's request for some mandrakes reflects the ongoing hostility between the two sisters. Rachel may have enjoyed the flavor of the plant, or she may have believed that the fruit both increased female fertility and was an aphrodisiac.[661] If Rachel bought the mandrakes with the intention that they might help her become pregnant, it is highly ironic that the price Leah demands results in Leah, but not Rachel, becoming pregnant. Strikingly, Jacob is portrayed as a commodity to be traded by his wives. In this struggle between the sisters Jacob is powerless, becoming himself an object to be bought and sold for the price of some mandrakes.[662]

Perhaps the most notable element in the episode is the reference to God's listening to Leah, a point underlined by Leah's statement, "God has rewarded me for giving my slave to my husband" (v. 18).[663] Leah had ceased from having children (29:35). This is then reflected in the name יִשָּׂשכָר (*yiśśāśkār*, "Issachar") (possibly meaning "there is reward"), which is linked to the noun שְׂכָרִי (*śĕkārî*, "my reward") (with the sense "my wages"). The naming of Issachar also picks up on the expression שָׂכֹר שְׂכַרְתִּיךָ (*śākōr śĕkartîkā*, "I have surely hired you"), which relates to the circumstances of Issachar's conception (v. 16). When naming all her sons, apart from Levi, Leah acknowledges YHWH God.

---

[661] Mathews, *Genesis 11:27–50:26*, 486–87.

[662] The picture of the sisters bargaining recalls the episode of Jacob buying the birthright from Esau for a bowl of stew (25:27–34).

[663] The term שִׁפְחָה (*šipḥâ*) is used by free women as an expression of respect. CSB translation uses "slave" in v. 18, but "maidservant" might be a better option. Ruth uses this term of herself in Ruth 2:13, as does Hannah when speaking to Eli in 1 Sam 1:18.

Leah gives birth to a further son (v. 19). In naming him, Leah emphasizes that God has given her a good gift.[664] The name זְבֻלוּן (*zĕbulûn*, "Zebulun") (meaning "honor") is linked to the verb יִזְבְּלֵנִי (*yizbĕlēnî*, "will honor me"). "Leah probably reasoned that since God has shown her honor by the gift of a sixth son, then surely Jacob must give her the same consideration."[665] The birth of Dinah is also mentioned briefly (v. 21) in anticipation of later events (see 34:1–31).

30:22–24. Rachel eventually gives birth to a son. Notably, the brief report of Joseph's birth is introduced with the comment, "God remembered Rachel and God listened to her." The Hebrew text repeats "God," emphasizing that he is the subject of both verbs. On "God remembered Rachel," see Comments on 8:1. As God had listened to Leah (30:17), he now listens to Rachel (v. 22). The name יוֹסֵף (*yôsēp*, "Joseph") (meaning "may he add") is derived from the verb יסף (*ysp*, "add") (v. 24) and resembles the verb אסף (*ʾsp*, "taken away") (v. 23). With Joseph's birth Rachel senses that the shame of her childlessness is removed. As we shall see later, Rachel's request for another son has tragic consequences for her (see 35:16–20).

Bridge

In a book that is focused on tracing a unique patriline that descends from Adam and Eve through their son Seth, it is no surprise that attention should be given to the birth of Jacob's sons, one of whom will succeed Jacob as *paterfamilias* and become the next link in the lineage that will lead to the promised vicegerent. However, the picture is complicated by the fact that Jacob marries two sisters, one of whom is initially unable to have children. The rivalry between Rachel and Leah is not helped by the fact that Jacob favors Rachel over Leah, but Rachel cannot bear Jacob children, unlike her older sister. To exacerbate matters further, both sisters resort to using their maidservants, Zilpah and Bilhah, as surrogate mothers. In all eleven sons are born to Jacob during his time in Paddan-aram. While the order of birth clearly places Reuben as firstborn, the birth of Joseph to Rachel is an important landmark, for with his birth Jacob looks to return to the land of Canaan.

---

[664] The noun זֵבֶד (*zēbed*, "gift") and the related verb יִזְבְּלֵנִי (*yizbĕlēnî*, "has given me") occur only here in the Old Testament. These rare words look somewhat similar to the name זְבֻלוּן (*zĕbulûn*, "Zebulun").

[665] Mathews, *Genesis 11:27–50:26*, 489.

As long as Jacob remains in Paddan-aram, within Laban's household, he is not at liberty to establish his own household and be independent of Laban. Jacob's lack of authority over his own family is possibly reflected in the fact that Leah and Rachel name the sons born to them and their maidservants. Jacob plays no part in the naming of his sons, an unusual situation (contrast 16:15; 21:3; 25: 25–26 speaks of "they named" and "he named"). This suggests that considerable authority rests with his wives. Jacob even appears to be under their control, as reflected especially in 30:16, when Leah trades him to Rachel for some mandrakes. This portrayal of Jacob runs counter to the idea that he is part of a patriline that will lead to a king. This changes, however, when Jacob leaves Paddan-aram to return to Canaan.

J. Jacob Prospers (30:25–43)

> 25 After Rachel gave birth to Joseph, Jacob said to Laban, "Send me on my way so that I can return to my homeland. 26 Give me my wives and my children that I have worked for, and let me go. You know how hard I have worked for you."
>
> 27 But Laban said to him, "If I have found favor with you, stay. I have learned by divination that the Lord has blessed me because of you." 28 Then Laban said, "Name your wages, and I will pay them."
>
> 29 So Jacob said to him, "You know how I have served you and how your herds have fared with me. 30 For you had very little before I came, but now your wealth has increased. The Lord has blessed you because of me. And now, when will I also do something for my own family?"
>
> 31 Laban asked, "What should I give you?"
>
> And Jacob said, "You don't need to give me anything. If you do this one thing for me, I will continue to shepherd and keep your flock. 32 Let me go through all your sheep today and remove every sheep that is speckled or spotted, every dark-colored sheep among the lambs, and the spotted and speckled among the female goats. Such will be my wages. 33 In the future when you come to check on my wages, my honesty will testify for me. If I have any female goats that are not speckled or spotted, or any lambs that are not black, they will be considered stolen."
>
> 34 "Good," said Laban. "Let it be as you have said."
>
> 35 That day Laban removed the streaked and spotted male goats and all the speckled and spotted female goats—every one that had any white on it—and every dark-colored one among the lambs, and he placed his

sons in charge of them. [36] He put a three-day journey between himself and Jacob. Jacob, meanwhile, was shepherding the rest of Laban's flock.

[37] Jacob then took branches of fresh poplar, almond, and plane wood, and peeled the bark, exposing white stripes on the branches. [38] He set the peeled branches in the troughs in front of the sheep—in the water channels where the sheep came to drink. And the sheep bred when they came to drink. [39] The flocks bred in front of the branches and bore streaked, speckled, and spotted young. [40] Jacob separated the lambs and made the flocks face the streaked sheep and the completely dark sheep in Laban's flocks. Then he set his own stock apart and didn't put them with Laban's sheep.

[41] Whenever the stronger of the flock were breeding, Jacob placed the branches in the troughs, in full view of the flocks, and they would breed in front of the branches. [42] As for the weaklings of the flocks, he did not put out the branches. So it turned out that the weak sheep belonged to Laban and the stronger ones to Jacob. [43] And the man became very rich. He had many flocks, female and male slaves, and camels and donkeys.

Context

Jacob's relationship to Laban comes under the spotlight in this episode and the next. For fourteen years Jacob has served Laban faithfully and his presence has benefited his uncle's household significantly. With good reason Laban is keen to ensure that this arrangement will not change. However, the larger story demands that Jacob should return to Canaan. Jacob's continuing presence in Paddan-aram threatens to undermine the fulfilment of the divine promises given to Abraham and Isaac (cf. 28:13–15), the prediction given to Rebekah (25:23) and Isaac's blessing of Jacob (27:28–29; cf. 27:37, 40).

Wanting to retain control over Jacob, Laban looks to thwart Jacob's departure from Haran. But God has other plans. The peculiar happenings in this passage underline God's role in separating Jacob from his uncle/father-in-law. God prepares the way for Jacob's return to Canaan by taking animals that belong to Laban (and "resemble" him) and producing from them animals that will belong to Jacob (and "resemble" him).

Comments

30:25–34. Although Jacob has spent many years in Paddan-aram, he does not consider it his home. Having faithfully served Laban, he asks his permission to return to Canaan along with his wives and children. Jacob sees himself as accountable to Laban, a point underlined by Jacob's language in verse 26, when he speaks twice of having worked for (or served) him.[666] Laban is reluctant to see Jacob depart, having realized that YHWH has blessed him because of Jacob, a point emphasized through repetition in verses 27 and 30. Laban's remark is significant for he sees the "blessing as coming *only* from the personal God of Jacob."[667] As a polytheist, Laban recognizes the existence of various gods, but attributes the blessing to Jacob's God. When Laban says, "I have learned by divination ..." he may have resorted to inappropriate means, later prohibited by God (Lev 19:26; Deut 18:10). Alternatively, he may have drawn this inference by linking Jacob's presence with blessing.[668] Laban's remarks about Jacob being a source of blessing are significant, for the motif of blessing is important in Genesis (see Biblical and Theological Themes §2). The events narrated in this section illustrate how God's blessing is mediated through Jacob, recalling the divine promise of blessing (e.g., 12:3; 18:18; 22:18). This motif reappears in the Joseph story (39:5).

Greed influences Laban's response to his son-in-law. Laban's offer of "wages" seems generous, but he looks to buy Jacob's continued presence for his own benefit. Once more in the story of Jacob's life we have a situation involving bargaining. Will Jacob be persuaded by money to stay with Laban or will he return to Canaan? Perhaps surprisingly, Jacob does not ask for specific wages from Laban (v. 31). Possibly Jacob recognizes that God has the power to bless him materially, as he has already done with children. If so, Jacob trusts God to enrich him, not Laban.

Laban's flock consists of both sheep and goats. As payment, Jacob asks that he should be allocated all dark colored sheep and mottled[669] goats, with Laban retaining all the rest. As Park notes, "The sheep and the goats ... belong to the man whose name phonetically and semantically matches

[666] The Hebrew root עבד (*ʿbd*, "to serve") comes three times in v. 26 (cf. 29:15, 18, 20, 25, 27, 30). In the light of this, it is worth recalling how it is also used previously in statements that focus on the important motif of Jacob being served by others (e.g., 25:23; 27:29, 40).

[667] Anderson, "Jacob, Laban, and a Divine Trickster?," 14 (italics in original).

[668] An alternative interpretation of v. 26 is offered by Alter, who renders נִחַשְׁתִּי (*niḥaštî*, "I have prospered").

[669] Three different Hebrew words are used to denote the mottled animals: נָקֹד (*nāqōd*, "speckled"); עָקֹד (*ʿāqōd*, "streaked"); טָלוּא (*ṭālûʾ*, "spotted"). The final term possibly forms hendiadyses with נָקֹד (*nāqōd*) and עָקֹד (*ʿāqōd*) (cf. 31:8, where Jacob mentions only two patterns of markings). In 31:10, 12 the term בָּרֹד (*bārōd*, "speckled") is introduced.

the animal's appearance."[670] Laban, whose name means "white," is allocated the white sheep. The animals allocated to Jacob are either נָקֹד (*nāqōd*, "speckled") or עָקֹד (*ʿāqōd* "streaked"), terms that sound somewhat like Jacob's name יַעֲקֹב (*yaʿăqōb*).

30:35–36. Laban does all in his power to ensure that Jacob will not prosper and become rich. As soon as the agreement is concluded, Laban removes from his flock all the animals that could potentially produce offspring that would be allocated to Jacob. Laban gives the selected animals to his own sons, thereby denying Jacob possession of them.[671] As if to confirm that these animals are Laban's, the narrator observes that Laban (לָבָן, *lābān*) takes "every one that had any white (לָבָן, *lābān*) on it" (v. 35). Laban then separates from Jacob, living about fifty miles away.

30:37–43. Although Laban attempts to prevent his white sheep and single-colored goats from producing dark and mottled offspring respectively, Jacob uses multi-colored sticks to influence the breeding outcome of these animals. The outward form of the sticks corresponds with the appearance of the animals that will be conceived. No explanation is offered to account for the impact of the sticks. Might it be that this symbolic act is a kind of prayer? Or might it depend on a particular kind of breeding practice?[672] In addition, verses 41–42 indicate that Jacob employed selective breeding to ensure that the mottled and dark offspring were produced by the best animals in Laban's flock. Over a period of a few years, Jacob becomes very wealthy; the list of his possessions recalls similar summaries associated with Abraham (12:16; 24:35; cf. 26:12–13).

Bridge

Despite everything that Laban does to prevent Jacob's prospering, God ensures that Jacob becomes rich (v. 43). Though Jacob came to Paddan-aram with only a staff (see 32:10), God gives him both children and many possessions. This prepares the way for him to return to Canaan. Importantly, as Jacob later tells Rachel and Leah, God is the one who

---

[670] Song-Mi Suzie Park, "Transformation and Demarcation of Jacob's 'Flocks' in Genesis 30:25–43: Identity, Election, and the Role of the Divine," *CBQ* 72 (2010): 669.

[671] Speiser, *Genesis*, 238, comments, "Laban is delighted with the terms, and promptly proceeds to violate the spirit of the bargain by removing to a safe distance all the grown animals that would be likely to produce the specified sports."

[672] See the proposal in Scott B. Noegel, "Sex, Sticks, and the Trickster in Gen 30:31–43," *Journal of the Ancient Near Eastern Society* 25 (1997): 7–17.

extricates the animals from Laban's flock (31:9). As Park notes, "The flock is transformed from white (לבן, *lbn*) to black (חום, *ḥwm*), from white (לבן, *lbn*) to speckled (נקד, *nqd* and עקד, *ʿqd*), and from Laban's (לבן, *lbn*) to Jacob's (יעקב, *yʿqb*). The message conveyed with these puns is that Jacob is not stealing Laban's flocks but that Laban's flocks are being *transformed* into Jacob's."[673] Remarkably, the best animals in Laban's flock reproduce offspring that become Jacob's property. Given the process by which this happens, Laban has no grounds for claiming that Jacob has stolen what belongs to him. The natural markings of the animals determine ownership.[674]

The differences between the flocks underlines an important contrast between Jacob and Laban. They may be "brothers" as relatives, but they are not now "brothers" by character. The Jacob who returns to Canaan is not the Jacob who arrived in Paddan-aram twenty years previously. Jacob may have served Laban, but through that process, as we shall see in chapter 32, he is gradually transformed to become less like Laban and more like Abraham and Isaac. "The separation of the flock in 30:25–42, therefore, serves as an important symbol for the separation and demarcation of Jacob (Israel) as a separate entity from Laban (Aram)—a demarcation that, we will see, must happen in order for Jacob to get on his way to the land promised to his forebears and thus truly to become the nation of Israel."[675]

K. Jacob Separates from Laban (31:1–55)

> 1 Now Jacob heard what Laban's sons were saying: "Jacob has taken all that was our father's and has built this wealth from what belonged to our father." 2 And Jacob saw from Laban's face that his attitude toward him was not the same as before.
>
> 3 The Lord said to him, "Go back to the land of your fathers and to your family, and I will be with you."

---

673 Park, "Transformation and Demarcation," 671 (italics in original).

674 Anderson, "Jacob, Laban, and a Divine Trickster?," 3–23, contends that Jacob, with God's support, deceives Laban. But there is no deception in what happens here. Rather, the outcome recalls how God promised Abraham in 12:3 that those who bless Abraham will be blessed and those who treat him with contempt will be cursed (cf. 27:29). Laban is "rewarded" by God for his mistreatment of Jacob.

675 Park, "Transformation and Demarcation," 673.

4 Jacob had Rachel and Leah called to the field where his flocks were. 5 He said to them, “I can see from your father’s face that his attitude toward me is not the same as before, but the God of my father has been with me. 6 You know that with all my strength I have served your father 7 and that he has cheated me and changed my wages ten times. But God has not let him harm me. 8 If he said, ‘The spotted sheep will be your wages,’ then all the sheep were born spotted. If he said, ‘The streaked sheep will be your wages,’ then all the sheep were born streaked. 9 God has taken away your father’s herds and given them to me.

10 “When the flocks were breeding, I saw in a dream that the streaked, spotted, and speckled males were mating with the females. 11 In that dream the angel of God said to me, ‘Jacob!‘ and I said, ‘Here I am.’ 12 And he said, ‘Look up and see: all the males that are mating with the flocks are streaked, spotted, and speckled, for I have seen all that Laban has been doing to you. 13 I am the God of Bethel, where you poured oil on the stone marker and made a solemn vow to me. Get up, leave this land, and return to your native land.’ “

14 Then Rachel and Leah answered him, “Do we have any portion or inheritance in our father’s family? 15 Are we not regarded by him as outsiders? For he has sold us and has certainly spent our purchase price. 16 In fact, all the wealth that God has taken away from our father belongs to us and to our children. So do whatever God has said to you.”

17 So Jacob got up and put his children and wives on the camels. 18 He took all the livestock and possessions he had acquired in Paddan-aram, and he drove his herds to go to the land of Canaan, to his father Isaac. 19 When Laban had gone to shear his sheep, Rachel stole her father’s household idols. 20 And Jacob deceived Laban the Aramean, not telling him that he was fleeing. 21 He fled with all his possessions, crossed the Euphrates, and headed for the hill country of Gilead.

22 On the third day Laban was told that Jacob had fled. 23 So he took his relatives with him, pursued Jacob for seven days, and overtook him in the hill country of Gilead. 24 But God came to Laban the Aramean in a dream at night. “Watch yourself!” God warned him. “Don’t say anything to Jacob, either good or bad.”

25 When Laban overtook Jacob, Jacob had pitched his tent in the hill country, and Laban and his relatives also pitched their tents in the hill country of Gilead. 26 Laban said to Jacob, “What have you done? You have deceived me and taken my daughters away like prisoners of war! 27 Why did you secretly flee from me, deceive me, and not tell me? I would have sent you away with joy and singing, with tambourines and lyres, 28 but you didn’t even let me kiss my grandchildren and my daughters. You have acted foolishly. 29 I could do you great harm, but last night the God of your father said to me: ‘Watch yourself! Don’t say anything to Jacob, either good or bad.’

[30] Now you have gone off because you long for your father's fami-
ly—but why have you stolen my gods?"

[31] Jacob answered, "I was afraid, for I thought you would take your
daughters from me by force. [32] If you find your gods with anyone here,
he will not live! Before our relatives, point out anything that is yours
and take it." Jacob did not know that Rachel had stolen the idols.

[33] So Laban went into Jacob's tent, Leah's tent, and the tents of the two
concubines, but he found nothing. When he left Leah's tent, he went
into Rachel's tent. [34] Now Rachel had taken Laban's household idols, put
them in the saddlebag of the camel, and sat on them. Laban searched
the whole tent but found nothing.

[35] She said to her father, "Don't be angry, my lord, that I cannot stand
up in your presence; I am having my period." So Laban searched, but
could not find the household idols.

[36] Then Jacob became incensed and brought charges against Laban.
"What is my crime?" he said to Laban. "What is my sin, that you have
pursued me? [37] You've searched all my possessions! Have you found
anything of yours? Put it here before my relatives and yours, and let
them decide between the two of us. [38] I've been with you these twenty
years. Your ewes and female goats have not miscarried, and I have not
eaten the rams from your flock. [39] I did not bring you any of the flock
torn by wild beasts; I myself bore the loss. You demanded payment
from me for what was stolen by day or by night. [40] There I was—the
heat consumed me by day and the frost by night, and sleep fled from
my eyes. [41] For twenty years in your household I served you—fourteen
years for your two daughters and six years for your flocks—and you
have changed my wages ten times! [42] If the God of my father, the God
of Abraham, the Fear of Isaac, had not been with me, certainly now you
would have sent me off empty-handed. But God has seen my affliction
and my hard work, and he issued his verdict last night."

[43] Then Laban answered Jacob, "The daughters are my daughters; the
sons, my sons; and the flocks, my flocks! Everything you see is mine!
But what can I do today for these daughters of mine or for the children
they have borne? [44] Come now, let's make a covenant, you and I. Let it
be a witness between the two of us."

[45] So Jacob picked out a stone and set it up as a marker. [46] Then Jacob
said to his relatives, "Gather stones." And they took stones and made
a mound, then ate there by the mound. [47] Laban named the mound
Jegar-sahadutha, but Jacob named it Galeed.

[48] Then Laban said, "This mound is a witness between you and me
today." Therefore the place was called Galeed [49] and also Mizpah, for
he said, "May the Lord watch between you and me when we are out
of each other's sight. [50] If you mistreat my daughters or take other
wives, though no one is with us, understand that God will be a wit-

ness between you and me." [51] Laban also said to Jacob, "Look at this mound and the marker I have set up between you and me. [52] This mound is a witness and the marker is a witness that I will not pass beyond this mound to you, and you will not pass beyond this mound and this marker to do me harm. [53] The God of Abraham, and the gods of Nahor—the gods of their father—will judge between us." And Jacob swore by the Fear of his father Isaac. [54] Then Jacob offered a sacrifice on the mountain and invited his relatives to eat a meal. So they ate a meal and spent the night on the mountain. [55] Laban got up early in the morning, kissed his grandchildren and daughters, and blessed them. Then Laban left to return home.

Context

In chapter 31 the narrator focuses on events that take place in the twentieth year of Jacob's stay in Paddan-aram. The time has come for him to return to Canaan. However, fearful that his father-in-law will prevent him from leaving, Jacob sets out with all that he possesses without informing Laban. Outraged that Jacob has treated him with little respect, Laban pursues his son-in-law for several days. After a tense reunion, Laban and Jacob make a friendship treaty and part company, with Laban returning home and Jacob proceeding on his journey to Canaan.

Comments

31:1–3. As noted at the end of chapter 30, Jacob has grown wealthy by acquiring animals that "resemble" him. Motivated by jealousy Laban's sons accuse Jacob of prospering by taking what belongs to their father. Even Laban's attitude toward Jacob changes (v. 2). Into this context, YHWH speaks, instructing Jacob to return to the land of his fathers. YHWH's promise to be with Jacob (v. 3) recalls what he said previously at Bethel (28:15). The theme of God being with Jacob is picked up in 31:5 (cf. 31:7). Although he shares a common ancestry with Laban, Jacob's "fathers" and "family" are in Canaan, not Paddan-aram.

31:4–16. Speaking to Rachel and Leah, Jacob describes how God has protected him, despite Laban's machinations to prevent Jacob from prospering (vv. 5–9). He then tells them about a dream, in which "the angel of God" speaks to him,[676] explaining that God has influenced the breeding pattern of Laban's flock in response to Laban's unjust

[676] On the identity of the "angel of God," see Exegesis 16:7.

treatment of Jacob (vv. 10–12).[677] The "angel of God" identifies himself as the "God of Bethel" and briefly recalls the events narrated in 28:11–22, when God promised in a dream to protect and provide for Jacob. Twenty years later the God of Bethel summons Jacob to return to the land of his birth. Importantly, Jacob's speech underlines God's presence with him during his stay in Haran.

Rachel and Leah encourage Jacob to obey God, recognizing that they too have been exploited by their father. Laban's greed has deprived them and their children of assets that by right belong to them.[678] In the light of this, they affirm that everything that God has taken from Laban and given to Jacob belongs to them and their children (v. 16). As far as Rachel and Leach are concerned, God's actions have rectified an unjust situation.[679]

31:17–21. With the support of Rachel and Leah, Jacob takes advantage of Laban's absence and sets off for Canaan with all that he possesses. Without explanation,[680] and unknown to Jacob (v. 32), the narrator records tersely that "Rachel stole her father's household idols" (v. 19). The term תְּרָפִים (*tĕrāpîm*) in this instance probably refers to small figurines that Laban viewed as being his "gods" (v. 30). Jacob possibly refers to these same objects when he instructs his family to get rid of "foreign gods" (35:2). Jacob then "hides" them, probably by burial, "under the oak near Shechem" (35:4).

The narrator plays on the reference to Rachel stealing the household idols by stating in verse 20 that "Jacob stole the heart of Laban the Aramean" (cf. v. 26).[681] Most English versions understand the idiom of

---

[677] The animals are described as being עֲקֻדִּים נְקֻדִּים וּבְרֻדִּים (*ʿăquddîm nĕquddîm ûbĕruddîm*, "streaked, spotted, and speckled"). The last of these terms appears only here and in v. 12 in the Old Testament. All three words sound somewhat similar to the term for males הָעַתֻּדִים (*hāʿattudîm*).

[678] This may be an allusion to the betrothal present and/or dowry.

[679] Anderson, "Jacob, Laban, and a Divine Trickster?," 6–7, contends unnecessarily that God is complicit in "Jacob's deception of Laban." It is more appropriate, however, to view God's actions as thwarting Laban's exploitation of Jacob.

[680] Various reasons have been suggested to explain why Rachel steals her father's gods. Regardless of what her motive was, her action draws attention to the fact that Jacob does not share the polytheistic outlook of his father-in-law. Furthermore, a significant contrast is created: God speaks to Laban (v. 24), but his own household gods are silent and impotent (vv. 34–35).

[681] By describing Laban as "the Aramean" (cf. v. 24), the narrator deliberately emphasizes how he differs from Jacob.

stealing someone's heart to imply an act of deception (e.g., CSB, NET, NIV), trickery (e.g., ESV) or outwitting (e.g., RSV, NLT). The references to Rachel and Jacob stealing in verses 19–20 draw attention to one of the important motifs of this chapter. Underlying all that, Laban later says to his son-in-law the accusation that Jacob has stolen what rightfully belongs to Laban (see especially vv. 26, 27, 30, 31, 43).

Although most English versions translate הַר הַגִּלְעָד (*har haggilʿād*) as "hill country of Gilead" (v. 14), it is possible that in this context the expression denotes a specific mountain (cf. vv. 54–55; cf. Judg 7:3 where CSB reads "Mount Gilead"), which is named after the heap of stones that functions as a witness to the covenant made between Laban and Jacob (vv. 46–48).

31:22–24. Ten days after Jacob leaves Paddan-aram, Laban catches up with him. This places "Mount Gilead" about 300 miles to the south, some distance north of the region later known as Gilead, which is located east of the Jordan River. Contrary to what most commentators assume, the two locations should probably be viewed as unrelated (see Comments on 31:48–49 and the comment there on the name "Galeed-and-Mizpah").[682]

31:25–35. When Laban overtakes Jacob and his household, all parties camp for the night on Mount Gilead. Seeing himself as the head of the family, the *paterfamilias*,[683] Laban challenges Jacob for his secretive departure. In doing so, Laban speaks of Jacob having deceived him (v. 26). The phrase "You have deceived me ..." translates a Hebrew idiom that more literally states, "You have stolen my heart" (cf. v. 20). The motif of theft is continued by Laban's insinuating that Jacob has taken away his daughters "like prisoners of war." This latter accusation rests on the assumption that Laban's daughters belong to him and not Jacob, a claim that Laban will repeat in verse 43. Yet, Rachel and Leah have willingly agreed to go with Jacob (v. 16). To the list of items "stolen" by Jacob, Laban adds his gods (v. 30). The issue of ownership runs deep in this passage, building

---

[682] Judges 11:29 refers to Mizpah of Gilead, but this is probably another location.

[683] Charles Mabee, "Jacob and Laban: The Structure of Judicial Proceedings (Genesis xxxi 25–42)," *VT* 30 (1980): 192–207, interprets the events recorded in vv. 25–42 as establishing Jacob as a new *paterfamilias*, free from Laban's authority. Rachel's theft of the household gods may also have been viewed as undermining Laban's status as the head of the family. See Cyrus H. Gordon, "Biblical Customs and the Nuzu Tablets," *BA* 3 (1940): 5–6; Moshe Greenberg, "Another Look at Rachel's Theft of the Teraphim," *JBL* 81 (1962): 242.

on the previous section, where Jacob had gained flocks despite Laban's devious attempts to prevent this happening.

Although it is not immediately obvious in English versions, Laban switches from addressing only Jacob in verses 26–28 and 30, to addressing Jacob and his household in verse 29; "you" and "your" are plural in the Hebrew text of verse 29. The threat of verse 29 is to everyone, including Jacob. By referring to the "God of your father," Laban distinguishes this deity from his own "gods" (v. 30). Jacob's separation from Laban has significant religious implications.

Oblivious to Rachel's theft of the household gods, Jacob vehemently denies Laban's accusation, pronouncing the death penalty for anyone who might have them. This adds to the drama of the narrative, especially when Laban proceeds to search the tents, coming eventually to Rachel's tent. Her concealment of the "gods" in the saddlebag emphasizes their powerlessness and inability to communicate; this contrasts sharply with how God speaks to Laban (v. 24).

31:36–42. Responding to Laban's futile search for his gods, Jacob asserts his ownership of all that he has taken from Paddan-aram. While Laban has sought to take advantage of Jacob whenever possible, Jacob has never responded in kind. Ultimately, Jacob's wealth has come from "the God of Abraham, the Fear of Isaac" (v. 42). From the context, פַּחַד יִצְחָק (*paḥad yiṣḥāq*, "Fear of Isaac") denotes God (cf. v. 53, which has the expression פַּחַד אָבִיו יִצְחָק (*paḥad ʾābîw yiṣḥāq*, "Fear of his father Isaac"). This designation of God, which is unique to this passage in the Old Testament, underscores that God is one to be respected and honored, an idea that is in keeping with the warning given to Laban by God in verse 24 (cf. v. 29; cf. 20:11).

31:43–55. Laban responds to Jacob's speech (vv. 36–42) with an outburst in verse 43 that reflects his unwillingness to acknowledge Jacob's status as husband, father, and owner of everything that he has brought with him from Paddan-aram. Yet, despite Laban's claim that Jacob has stolen from him, he realizes that to move against Jacob will provoke God's anger. Consequently, he looks to establish a friendship treaty with Jacob. Although Laban initially states that the covenant is to protect his daughters (v. 50), he is possibly more concerned to ensure that Jacob will not attempt to replace him as *paterfamilias* in Paddan-aram (see v. 52).

The making of the covenant entails the use of stones as "witnesses." Jacob takes one stone "as a marker," as he did at Bethel (28:18, 22). Laban and his relatives, however, build a separate cairn with many stones (v. 46). Since in the ANE gods were usually invoked as witnesses to treaties, the design of the "witnesses" probably underlines Jacob's monotheistic belief in contrast to Laban's polytheism (see v. 32). Jacob's separation from Laban and his return to Canaan is also reflected in the names given to the cairn. The Aramaic-speaking Laban designates it Jegar-sahadutha, but Jacob calls it Galeed in keeping with Western Semitic terminology.[684] Although CSB, like most English versions, takes the name Mizpah (v. 49) to be an alternative name for Galeed, it is possible that the location was known by the expression "Galeed-and-Mizpah,"[685] perhaps to distinguish this location from others with a similar name (cf. the name Massah-and-Meribah in Exod 17:7; Num 20:13, 24 refers to another location known as the "waters of Meribah").[686]

Unlike most other English versions, which read "and the God of Nahor," CSB translates the expression וֵאלֹהֵי נָחוֹר (*wĕʾlōhê nāḥôr*, "and the gods of Nahor") (v. 53). Either translation is possible, but the weight of evidence possibly favors "gods of Nahor," given Laban's polytheistic beliefs.[687] In the MT the verb "judge" is plural, indicating that more than one god is involved.[688] Interestingly, while Laban invokes a number of gods to judge between them, Jacob swears only by one deity, whom he identifies as "the Fear of his father Isaac" (v. 53; see v. 42).

Bridge

This passage records the first stage in Jacob's return to the land of Canaan and his father's household. Jacob knows that separating from Laban will not be easy, given his father-in-law's character. In Paddan-aram, Laban is *paterfamilias*, exercising authority over his whole household, including Jacob, his wives, and their children. In keeping with the

---

[684] Galeed (גַּלְעֵד, *galʿēd*) is constructed from גַּל (*gal*, "heap of stones")and עֵד (*ʿēd*, "witness"). In v. 24 the mountain is called הַר הַגִּלְעָד *har haggilʿād*, a designation linked to the naming of the cairn. For comments on the presence of Aramaic words in this passages, see Brian A. Bompiani, "Style Switching in the Jacob and Laban Narratives," *HS* 55 (2014): 44–47.

[685] Ignoring the verse division, which was not in the earliest manuscripts, the Hebrew text reads גַּלְעֵד וְהַמִּצְפָּה (*galʿēd wĕhammiṣpâ*).

[686] The name Mizpah, which means "watchtower," is given to different locations. Among those mentioned are Jephthah's hometown, east of the River Jordan (see Judg 11:11, 29, 34); the valley of Mizpah in the north near Mount Hermon (Josh 11:3); a town in the Shephelah region (Josh 15:38); a town situated to the northwest of Jerusalem (Judg 20:1).

[687] Nahor is Laban's grandfather (see 22:20–23; 24:24, 29).

[688] In the LXX and SamP the verb "judge" is in the singular. The MT is more likely to be the original reading. See Schmutzer, "Did the Gods Cause Abraham's Wandering?," 157.

larger plot of Genesis, Jacob must return to Canaan to become *paterfamilias* in succession to Abraham and Isaac. As Abraham, in obedience to the call of God, separated from his family to migrate to Canaan, so Jacob must now follow in his footsteps. In doing so, Jacob must also separate from the religious and moral stance adopted by his relatives in Paddan-aram. As Park observes, "Israel is a kinship group that is descended from and related to other groups of people, yet at the same time it is a group separated by God whose very existence depends on its contradistinction from other peoples."[689]

L. Jacob Prepares to Meet Esau Again (32:1–23)

> 1 Jacob went on his way, and God's angels met him. 2 When he saw them,
> Jacob said, "This is God's camp." So he called that place Mahanaim.
>
> 3 Jacob sent messengers ahead of him to his brother Esau in the land of
> Seir, the territory of Edom. 4 He commanded them, "You are to say to
> my lord Esau, 'This is what your servant Jacob says. I have been staying
> with Laban and have been delayed until now. 5 I have oxen, donkeys,
> flocks, and male and female slaves. I have sent this message to inform
> my lord, in order to seek your favor.' "
>
> 6 When the messengers returned to Jacob, they said, "We went to your
> brother Esau; he is coming to meet you—and he has four hundred men
> with him." 7 Jacob was greatly afraid and distressed; he divided the
> people with him into two camps, along with the flocks, herds, and
> camels. 8 He thought, "If Esau comes to one camp and attacks it, the
> remaining one can escape."
>
> 9 Then Jacob said, "God of my father Abraham and God of my father
> Isaac, the Lord who said to me, 'Go back to your land and to your family,
> and I will cause you to prosper,' 10 I am unworthy of all the kindness
> and faithfulness you have shown your servant. Indeed, I crossed over
> the Jordan with my staff, and now I have become two camps. 11 Please
> rescue me from my brother Esau, for I am afraid of him; otherwise, he
> may come and attack me, the mothers, and their children. 12 You have
> said, 'I will cause you to prosper, and I will make your offspring like
> the sand of the sea, too numerous to be counted.' "
>
> 13 He spent the night there and took part of what he had brought with
> him as a gift for his brother Esau: 14 two hundred female goats, twenty
> male goats, two hundred ewes, twenty rams, 15 thirty milk camels with
> their young, forty cows, ten bulls, twenty female donkeys, and ten male

---

689 Park, "Transformation and Demarcation," 672.

donkeys. [16] He entrusted them to his slaves as separate herds and said to them, "Go on ahead of me, and leave some distance between the herds."

[17] And he told the first one: "When my brother Esau meets you and asks, 'Who do you belong to? Where are you going? And whose animals are these ahead of you?' 18 then tell him, 'They belong to your servant Jacob. They are a gift sent to my lord Esau. And look, he is behind us.' "

[19] He also told the second one, the third, and everyone who was walking behind the animals, "Say the same thing to Esau when you find him. [20] You are also to say, 'Look, your servant Jacob is right behind us.' " For he thought, "I want to appease Esau with the gift that is going ahead of me. After that, I can face him, and perhaps he will forgive me."

[21] So the gift was sent on ahead of him while he remained in the camp that night. [22] During the night Jacob got up and took his two wives, his two slave women, and his eleven sons, and crossed the ford of Jabbok. [23] He took them and sent them across the stream, along with all his possessions.

Context

After describing Laban's departure for Paddan-aram, the narrator proceeds to report Jacob's onward journey to Canaan and his reconciliation with Esau. However, before the estranged brothers meet each other after twenty years apart, Jacob experiences a life-transforming encounter with God (32:24–32). This significant event prepares the way for Jacob's reunion with Esau, enabling the hostility of the past to be set aside. Before this takes place, however, Jacob makes his own preparations for the reunion, at the heart of which is his petition for God's protection (32:9–12). The present passage sets the scene for Jacob's encounters with first God and then Esau.

Comments

32:1–2. With Laban's departure home, the narrative focuses on Jacob.[690] With a minimum of detail and explanation, the narrator reports that "God's angels" meet Jacob. Adding to this, Jacob remarks, "This is God's camp," and consequently he names the location Mahanaim, which means "two camps."[691]

---

[690] In the Hebrew text, 32:2 [Eng. 32:1] begins with a break in the waw-consecutive sequence, with the subject Jacob being placed before a *qatal* verb: וְיַעֲקֹב הָלַךְ (*wĕyaʿăqōb hālak*, "and Jacob went"). This marks the start of a new episode.

[691] "Two camps" probably denotes Jacob's camp and that of the angels. The motif of "two camps" reappears in vv. 7, 10.

This enigmatic passage is striking for various reasons. First, the impression is given that Laban's camp is now replaced by that of God's angels. While Laban's presence represented a threat to Jacob, God's angels possibly guarantee protection.[692] The angels will accompany Jacob on the rest of his journey. Second, the brief description in verses 1–2 recalls Jacob's overnight stay at Bethel (28:10–22), when Jacob also saw God's angels (28:12) and named the location Bethel, meaning "house of God" (28:17, 19, 22).[693]

32:3–5. Jacob might have returned quietly to Canaan, hoping to avoid Esau, who has moved to the mountainous region of Seir, which lies to the east of the valley running from the Dead Sea to the Gulf of Aqaba. However, taking the initiative, Jacob intentionally sends envoys to Esau with the hope of being reconciled to his brother.

Jacob's instructions to the messengers are deferential in tone. Not only does he refer twice to Esau as "my lord," but he refers to himself as Esau's "servant" (v. 4).[694] Jacob seeks Esau's favor (v. 5; cf. 33:8, 10, 15), a request normally made by someone of inferior standing to someone in a superior position. Jacob's deference to Esau is especially striking in the light of how Jacob had previously deprived Esau of the blessing of the firstborn. At that time, their father Isaac clearly indicated that Esau would serve Jacob (27:37; cf. 27:29, 40). In the present context, however, with submissive language, Jacob portrays himself as Esau's servant. Jacob will later adopt a similar attitude when he meets Esau (33:1–15). Jacob's stance toward his brother also runs counter to the divine oracle given to their mother Rebekah prior to their birth; this predicted that the older would serve the younger (25:23).

In a striking way, Jacob's actions in verses 3–7 are linked to verses 1–2. First, in the Hebrew text of this section, the noun מַלְאָכִים (*malʾākîm*) is repeated. However, with good reason, the English versions translate the same noun as "angels" in verse 1 and as "messengers" in verses 3 and

---

692 On the basis of the verb פָּגַע (*pāgaʿ*), which is usually translated "met" in v. 1, Waltke and Fredricks, *Genesis*, 440–41, interpret the angels' presence as menacing for Jacob; the verb occasionally means "to assail" (e.g., Exod 5:3; Ruth 2:22). However, too little is said in vv. 1–2 to be confident that Jacob's perceives the angels as hostile.

693 In the whole of the Old Testament, the expression מַלְאֲכֵי אֱלֹהִים (*malʾăkê ʾĕlōhîm*, "angels of God") occurs only on these two occasions (i.e., 28:12; 32:1[Heb. 2]).

694 It is possible to translate Jacob's instructions in v. 4 as saying: "Thus you shall say: 'To my lord, to Esau, thus says your servant Jacob: With Laban I have lived until now' " (cf. NJPS; Speiser, *Genesis*, 252).

6. Second, fearing an attack by Esau, Jacob splits his household into two camps (v. 7), an action that recalls the name Mahanaim, which means "two camps" (v. 2). The narrative possibly implies that Jacob's actions have been prompted in part by his vision of God's angels.

32:6–8. Jacob naturally assumes that Esau, accompanied by 400 men, will attack him; Abraham went successfully to war with only 318 men (14:14). Fearful for the safety of those with him, Jacob splits those accompanying him into two camps, in the hope that one might escape if the other is attacked.

32:9–12. Fearful of what may happen, Jacob petitions God for protection. The content and tone of his prayer, one of the longest in Genesis, is noteworthy, on three accounts. First, Jacob's prayer is marked by a humble acknowledgment that he is unworthy of the love and faithfulness that God has both shown him and promised him for the future (v. 9). This marks a new attitude on the part of Jacob. As Long rightly observes, "A careful reader sees a different Jacob when he prays at the Jabbok. At Bethel, Jacob bargained with God (28:20–22)."[695] In marked contrast, at Jabbok, he expresses humility, saying, קָטֹנְתִּי (*qāṭōnĕttî*, "I am too small to ...") (rendered "I am unworthy" in CSB) and describing himself as God's servant (v. 10 [Heb. 11]). Whereas in his earlier life, Jacob grasped after the status of firstborn to gain prominence, he now recognizes before God his own insignificance. He does not merit all that God has done for him.

Second, Jacob underlines God's love and loyalty. Over a period of twenty years, YHWH has cared for and prospered Jacob, despite Laban's efforts to thwart Jacob's progress. Using the divine name YHWH for the first time to address God (v. 9; translated "Lord" in CSB), Jacob highlights the divine characteristics of חֶסֶד (*ḥesed*, "love/grace/loyalty") and אֱמֶת (*ʾĕmet*, "truth/fidelity/faithfulness"), both of which are later emphasized by God himself when he reveals his nature to Moses on Mount Sinai, declaring that he, YHWH, is "abounding in faithful love and truth" (Exod 34:6). Jacob's petition is based on his belief that God will be true to the promises that he had previously given to Jacob.

Third, by referring to God as "God of my father Abraham and God of my father Isaac" (v. 9), Jacob associates himself with them and their special relationship with YHWH. He recognizes that he is privileged as heir to the divine covenant established with his fathers. In the light of

---

[695] Jesse Long, "Wrestling with God to Win: A Literary Reading of the Story of Jacob at Jabbok in Honor of Don Williams," *Stone-Campbell Journal* 15 (2012): 59.

this, Jacob's reference to a divine promise that his descendants would be "like the sand of the sea" recalls what God swore to Abraham in 22:17.[696]

32:13–20. Fearful of Esau, Jacob prepares an exceptionally generous gift of domesticated animals for Esau.[697] These he divides into three herds, which will be sent ahead of the rest of Jacob's household and property. As he did previously, Jacob instructs his servants to refer to Esau as "my lord" (v. 18) and Jacob as "your servant" (vv. 18, 20; cf. vv. 4–5). Jacob's deference to Esau is noteworthy in the light of earlier statements about Esau serving Jacob (27:37; cf. 25:23; 27:29, 40). Jacob hopes that the gift will "appease Esau" (v. 20); the verb translated "appease" is כִּפֵּר (*kipper*), which can be translated "to atone/make amends." Interestingly, the Hebrew text of verse 20 [Heb. 21] contains four uses of the noun "face,"[698] twice with the pronominal suffix "his" and twice with the pronominal suffix "my." The noun "face" becomes an important motif, linking together the events of this passage with those that follow (see 32:30 [Heb. 31]; 33:10).

32:21–23. Sending the gift ahead, Jacob camps for the night to the north of the Jabbok River. The river flows into the Jordan valley from the east about twenty miles to the north of the Dead Sea. Then, during the night, Jacob crosses the river with his family and possessions.

Bridge

The content of Jacob's prayer strongly suggests that he is no longer the self-centered Jacob of preceding episodes. The deceiver, who seized every opportunity to gain an advantage over his older brother, humbles himself as he petitions God for help. As Long comments, "Becoming 'small' (that is, exhibiting humility) turns out to be the basis for a healthy relationship with the God of Israel."[699] Fearful of what may happen, Jacob takes practical steps to protect his family.

---

[696] The wording is slightly different; 22:17 refers to the seashore. Genesis does not record specifically God's promising Jacob that his descendants would be like the sand of the sea. However, God speaks of Jacob's offspring being as "the dust of the earth" (28:14), a promise made also to Abraham (13:16).

[697] Many scholars observe a wordplay involving the terms מַחֲנֶה (*maḥăneh*, "camp") and מִנְחָה (*minḥâ*, "gift"). Apart from aesthetic reasons, it is difficult to see why a wordplay is introduced here.

[698] One of these uses involve the preposition "before," which etymologically means "to the face of."

[699] Long, "Wrestling with God to Win," 60n55.

Despite his desire to be reconciled to his brother, he cannot be certain that Esau will not attack him and his family. Drawing on God's promises, Jacob trusts that God will transform his brother's attitude toward him. Those who humbly place their trust in God are not disappointed. Reconciliation rarely occurs easily.

M. Jacob Encounters God at Peniel (32:24–32)

> [24] Jacob was left alone, and a man wrestled with him until daybreak. [25]
> When the man saw that he could not defeat him, he struck Jacob's hip
> socket as they wrestled and dislocated his hip. [26] Then he said to Jacob,
> "Let me go, for it is daybreak."
>
> But Jacob said, "I will not let you go unless you bless me."
>
> [27] "What is your name?" the man asked. "Jacob," he replied.
>
> [28] "Your name will no longer be Jacob," he said. "It will be Israel because you have struggled with God and with men and have prevailed."
>
> [29] Then Jacob asked him, "Please tell me your name."
>
> But he answered, "Why do you ask my name?" And he blessed him there.
>
> [30] Jacob then named the place Peniel, "For I have seen God face to face," he said, "yet my life has been spared."
>
> [31] The sun shone on him as he passed by Penuel—limping because of
> his hip. [32] That is why, still today, the Israelites don't eat the thigh
> muscle that is at the hip socket: because he struck Jacob's hip socket
> at the thigh muscle.

Context

In this incident, which recalls Jacob's dream at Bethel (28:10–22), Jacob experiences a nighttime encounter with God. The two accounts balance each other in the symmetry of the narrative that composes 25:19–35:29.[700] Whereas the previous experience took place as he was leaving Canaan, this one occurs as he is about to reenter the promised land. Importantly, this nighttime encounter is also closely tied to the immediately surrounding episodes in chapters 32–33 and should be read in conjunction with them.[701] While the description of the incident leaves many questions

---

[700] See Fishbane, "Composition and Structure," 15–38.

[701] Steve L. McKenzie, "'You Have Prevailed': The Function of Jacob's Encounter at Peniel in the Jacob Cycle," *Restoration Quarterly* 23 (1980): 227, observes, "Genesis 32:23–33 represents a sophisticated literary piece with intricate connections with the passages which surround it." McKenzie lists various wordplays that link 32:23–33 with its immediate context.

unanswered, one important element of this event is the renaming of Jacob as Israel. This underscores a transformation that takes place in his life. He returns to Canaan a different man, and this underpins his subsequent reconciliation with Esau.

Comments

32:24–26. With a minimum of detail, the narrative introduces a stranger who wrestles with Jacob in the dark prior to daybreak. The darkness adds to the mystery of what is happening. Like Jacob, the reader must wait for daybreak to discover the identity of the unexpected opponent. This is revealed first in verse 28 and confirmed in verse 30; the assailant is none other than "God." While it is perhaps surprising that God should appear in human form to wrestle with Jacob, in the preceding Genesis narrative God appeared as a man and participated in a meal hosted by Abraham (18:1–15).[702]

The struggle is protracted, but little is said about it. The verb וַיֵּאָבֵק (*wayyēʾābēq*, "and he wrestled") which occurs only in this passage in the Old Testament, creates a wordplay with the names יַעֲקֹב (*yaʿăqōb*, "Jacob") and יַבֹּק (*yabbōq*, "Jabbok"). While Jacob is injured, he tenaciously refuses to release his opponent, demanding that his opponent should bless him. This specific request makes best sense in the light of Jacob's desire to be heir to the divine promise of blessing given to Abraham and Isaac (see Biblical and Theological Themes §2).

32:27–29. Jacob's desire to be blessed is greeted with the question, "What is your name?" This could be interpreted as implying that the stranger is ignorant of Jacob's identity,[703] but the question is more likely rhetorical, designed to remind Jacob of his past nature.[704] The name "Jacob" is associated with cheating and supplanting, a point highlighted by Esau (see 27:36). The renaming of Jacob as "Israel" signals a radical

---

[702] Although the present passage does not mention the concept of "the angel of God" or "the angel of the Lord," this is how God's appearance in human form to Jacob is understood in Hos 12:3–4. The idea of someone seeing God is also present in Hagar's encounter with "the angel of the Lord" (16:7–14).

[703] Alter, *Genesis*, 181, remarks, "The stranger exercises no divine privilege of omniscience and must ask Jacob to tell him his name." However, it seems highly unlikely that this assault on Jacob, which is clearly attributed to God (v. 30), took place without God knowing Jacob's identity.

[704] Allen P. Ross, "Studies in the Life of Jacob, Part 2: Jacob at the Jabbok, Israel at Peniel," *BSac* 142 (1985): 345.

transformation of his life.[705] This conversion paves the way for Jacob's reconciliation with Esau (see 33:1–20). Regarding the name Israel, the usual protocol with Hebrew names would suggest that it means "God will prevail/strive" or "may God prevail/strive."[706] This gives emphasis to what God does, rather than what Jacob does.

The reference to Jacob having prevailed after struggling with God and men (v. 28) in the present context highlights Jacob's tenacity. Despite his injury, he has not been prepared to let his assailant go free, without being blessed. Previously, he was prepared to exploit Esau's hunger and Isaac's blindness to obtain the firstborn birthright and its associated paternal blessing. While these actions were inappropriate, Jacob was tempted to do this by a desire for the benefits of the divine blessing given to Abraham and Isaac. He must learn, however, that this blessing is not something that can be grasped by force; it is a gift from God to those who trust in his ability to deliver rather than in their own ability to achieve through purely human effort.

When Jacob asks to know his assailant's name, he is told, "Why do you ask My name?" Most likely, this implies that Jacob's request is unnecessary; he should know his opponent's name already.[707] Having struggled tenaciously, Jacob is finally rewarded by being blessed (v. 29).[708] This is God's final action in this episode.

32:30–32. Capturing the significance of what has occurred, Jacob names the location Peniel, which means "face of God." The name confirms

---

[705] Sarna, *Understanding Genesis*, 206, comments, "The major significance of the episode derives ... from the change of name that resulted. This ... portends a new destiny, effectuates a decisive break with the past and inaugurates a fresh role, all symbolized here by the substitution of Israel for Jacob."

[706] The name "Israel" is composed of אֵל (*ʾēl*, "God") and ישׂר (*yśr*), which probably derives from the root שׂרה (*śrh*, "to contend/strive"), although some scholars favor the root שׂרר (*śrr*, "to rule"). Normally, in names combining a theophoric element with a *yiqtol* verb, the deity is the subject of the verb. See William Foxwell Albright, "The Names 'Israel' and 'Judah' with an Excursus on the Etymology of *tôdâh* and *tôrâh*," *JBL* 46 (1927): 159–60. Some scholars take Jacob to be the implied subject of the verb because of the explanation given in v. 28 [Heb. 29], where the verb שָׂרִיתָ (*śārîtā*, "you have striven") is used with Jacob as subject and God as object. However, this may be another example of a wordplay that draws on the etymology of "Israel," which means "God contends/strives"; it is not intended to explain the actual etymology of the name "Israel."

[707] Hamilton, *Genesis: Chapters 18–50*, 336, rephrases the question: "Jacob, don't you realize who I am?"

[708] Speiser, *Genesis*, 254–55, minimizes the significance of this remark by understanding it as a valediction.

that "Jacob understood his adversary as God himself." [709] The expression "face-to-face" conveys the intimacy of what has occurred. The same expression appears in Exodus 33:11, in a passage that records how Moses regularly dialogued with YHWH at a tent erected outside the Israelite camp (Exod 33:7–11). Although Moses speaks face to face with YHWH, the curtains of the tent prevent him from seeing God's face directly.[710] Darkness probably limits Jacob's vision of God's face. Nevertheless, Jacob's proximity to God is highly significant, for he speaks of his life having been rescued/delivered (v. 30). In saying, "I have been delivered," Jacob uses the verb נָצַל (*nāṣal*), which he used in his prayer in verse 11 [Heb. 12] in asking for protection from his brother Esau. When the brothers meet, Jacob's remarks in 33:10 strongly imply a connect between their reconciliation and Jacob's encounter with God at Peniel.[711]

After his extraordinary encounter with God, Jacob journeys on to meet Esau. The night has passed and, as Sarna observes, "the radiance of the sun greets the patriarch as he crosses back into his native land."[712] However, Jacob's experience lives with him, for he now limps due to the injury caused by God in the struggle. Jacob's limp is memorialized by his descendants, who refrain from eating the thigh muscle at the hip joint. By doing so, they associate themselves with the transformed Jacob.

Bridge

Jacob's time in Paddan-aram is framed by two accounts in which God encounters him (28:10–22; 32:22–32). Taken together, these events underline that throughout his time away from the land of Canaan, God has been with Jacob, ensuring that he will return in safety to the promised land. Despite Laban's attempts to keep Jacob in Paddan-aram, God had other plans. Jacob, however, is a different person on his return to Canaan. An inner conversion has occurred. With humility he expresses his dependence upon God (32:9–12). In the past Jacob manipulated others to be

---

[709] Curtis, "Structure, Style and Context," 135.

[710] No contradiction exists between Exod 33:11 and 33:20; see Alexander, *Exodus*, 636, 644–45.

[711] Penuel in v. 31 is a variant spelling of Peniel.

[712] Sarna, *Genesis*, 213. Sarna contrasts this with the brief comment about the sun setting when Jacob was leaving the land of Canaan (28:11): "Jacob's ignominious flight from home was appropriately marked by the setting of the sun."

blessed. Powerless at Peniel, he tenaciously holds on to God, pleading to be blessed. The prophet Hosea summarizes Jacob's experience:

> In the womb he (Jacob) grasped his brother's heel,
> and as an adult he wrestled with God.
> Jacob struggled with the angel and prevailed;
> he wept and sought his favor (Hos 12:3–4).

Jacob becomes Israel through an experience that involves more than receiving a new name. Jacob is weakened physically, but he sees the face of God, and this guarantees him deliverance as he anticipates meeting his estranged brother Esau. As Curtis observes, "The incident at Jabbok brought him to the awareness that the fulfillment of the promise must be the work of God rather than the work of Jacob. He came to see the difference between receiving the inheritance as a gift and gaining the inheritance through his own powers."[713]

N. Jacob Meets Esau (33:1–20)

> 1 Now Jacob looked up and saw Esau coming toward him with four hun-
> dred men. So he divided the children among Leah, Rachel, and the two
> slave women. 2 He put the slaves and their children first, Leah and her
> children next, and Rachel and Joseph last. 3 He himself went on ahead
> and bowed to the ground seven times until he approached his brother.
>
> 4 But Esau ran to meet him, hugged him, threw his arms around him,
> and kissed him. Then they wept. 5 When Esau looked up and saw the
> women and children, he asked, "Who are these with you?"
>
> He answered, "The children God has graciously given your servant." 6
> Then the slaves and their children approached him and bowed down.
> 7 Leah and her children also approached and bowed down, and then
> Joseph and Rachel approached and bowed down.
>
> 8 So Esau said, "What do you mean by this whole procession I met?"
>
> "To find favor with you, my lord," he answered.
>
> 9 "I have enough, my brother," Esau replied. "Keep what you have."
>
> 10 But Jacob said, "No, please! If I have found favor with you, take this
> gift from me. For indeed, I have seen your face, and it is like seeing
> God's face, since you have accepted me. 11 Please take my present that

[713] Curtis, "Structure, Style and Context," 135.

was brought to you, because God has been gracious to me and I have everything I need." So Jacob urged him until he accepted.

12 Then Esau said, "Let's move on, and I'll go ahead of you."

13 Jacob replied, "My lord knows that the children are weak, and I have nursing flocks and herds. If they are driven hard for one day, the whole
herd will die. 14 Let my lord go ahead of his servant. I will continue on slowly, at a pace suited to the livestock and the children, until I come to my lord at Seir."

15 Esau said, "Let me leave some of my people with you."

But he replied, "Why do that? Please indulge me, my lord."

16 That day Esau started on his way back to Seir, 17 but Jacob went to
Succoth. He built a house for himself and shelters for his livestock; that is why the place was called Succoth.

18 After Jacob came from Paddan-aram, he arrived safely at Shechem
in the land of Canaan and camped in front of the city. 19 He purchased
a section of the field where he had pitched his tent from the sons of
Hamor, Shechem's father, for a hundred pieces of silver. 20 And he set
up an altar there and called it God, the God of Israel.

Context

The narrative moves toward a dramatic climax as Esau and his 400 men draw ever nearer to Jacob. Having held out an olive branch to Esau, Jacob hopes that his brother's hostile attitude toward him will have lessened. Transformed by his own experience in exile, Jacob waits to see if his brother has also changed in the intervening years.

Comments

33:1–2. In the light of their antagonistic separation twenty years previously, the sight of Esau with 400 men must have filled Jacob with dread. The brief report about how Jacob arranges his family for the encounter with Esau mentions Leah, Rachel, and Joseph. By deliberately naming only one of Jacob's sons, the narrator highlights Joseph, anticipating later developments in the Genesis narrative. The designation of Bilhah and Zilpah as "slave women" (better designated "female servants" as in ESV and NIV) recalls their initial status as maidservants to Rachel and Leah respectively (29:24, 29).

33:3–4. Having arranged his family in order of ascending importance, we might have expected Jacob, as head of the family, to come at the very rear of the procession. He goes in front, however, possibly signaling that he is the least important member of the group. This perspective is also emphasized by his sevenfold act of deference toward Esau. By bowing down Jacob expresses submission to Esau, reversing the earlier oracle that the older would serve the younger (25:23). The vivid description of Esau's exuberant welcome of Jacob conveys well the warmth and sincerity of the reconciliation. The image of Esau running (an uncharacteristic action for an older man in Middle Eastern culture) and embracing Jacob may well have influenced Jesus's description of the father welcoming home his lost son (Luke 15:20).

33:5–7. Jacob had separated from Esau as a single man. He now introduces his brother to his family, emphasizing God's role in providing for them. Joseph is named before Rachel, whereas in verse 2 the order is reversed. In both instances, the chosen order gives priority to Joseph.

33:8–11. Jacob had arranged for a very substantial quantity of domesticated animals to be sent ahead as a gift to Esau, with specific instructions to his servants on how they should greet Esau (32:13–21). Everything Jacob does conveys his deference to Esau.[714] Esau calls Jacob "my brother" (v. 9), but Jacob consistently addresses Esau as "my lord" and speaks of himself as "your servant." As Blum observes, "The blessed one, as he bows to the unblessed one, gives up any triumphant claim to his superior status."[715] Through his words and actions, Jacob portrays himself as being inferior to Esau, despite having grounds for claiming to be Esau's equal: he has vast possessions (Gen 30:43); he can give a substantial gift to appease Esau (Gen 32:14–22 [Heb. 13–21]); and he has already held his own against his uncle, who also had sufficient manpower to enforce his demands on Jacob (31:22–24, 42).[716]

Jacob intentionally lowers himself before Esau. He treats Esau with the utmost respect, drawing a remarkable parallel between his encounters with God and with Esau. At Peniel Jacob saw God face to face. He now compares seeing Esau's face to seeing the face of God (v. 10). Esau

---

[714] Commenting on Jacob's actions, Fishbane claims that Jacob "is ever yet the trickster. He arranges his camp to deceive his brother ... he rushes to him and kisses him ... Jacob offers a gift to Esau ..." ("Composition and Structure," 27–28). While Jacob may possibly be disingenuous, the overall tone of the narrative suggests that he displays a genuine desire to be reconciled to Esau.

[715] Blum, "The Jacob Tradition," 185.

[716] Edward J. Bridge, "The 'Slave' Is the 'Master': Jacob's Servile Language to Esau in Genesis 33.1–17," *JSOT* 38 (2014): 278.

graciously embraces Jacob, just as God had done. In the light of this, Curtis suggests, that "the acceptance of Jacob which he saw on the face of Esau recalled for him the events at Peniel and confirmed for him that it was God who had changed Esau's heart to make it friendly."[717] Emphasizing how God has abundantly blessed him, Jacob urges Esau to accept his gift. Significantly, Jacob refers to this gift as בִּרְכָתִי (*birkātî*, "my present"), which could be translated "my blessing" (see ESV). Although Jacob does not have the authority to reinstate Esau as "firstborn," he seeks to make reparation for his past actions by blessing Esau.[718]

33:12–17. Esau's invitation to accompany Jacob to Seir suggests that the brothers are now fully reconciled. Jacob, however, graciously refuses his brother's offer, pointing to the weariness of his family and flocks. Having already traveled about 500 miles from Paddan-aram, the journey to Seir would require Jacob's family to travel at least another 100 miles. Although Jacob intimates that he will eventually follow Esau to Seir, there is no record of this happening. Instead, the subsequent narrative describes how Jacob moves to Succoth, before relocating to Shechem, Bethel, and then (via Bethlehem) Hebron, locations that reflect a southward journey. From what is said, it is not necessary to conclude that Jacob deliberately deceived Esau when he said that he would follow him to Seir. Nor is it necessary to accept Bridge's suggestion that Jacob "puts himself in the role of social inferior to Esau" in order to "have as little to do with Esau as he possibly can."[719] While Esau returns to Seir, Jacob journeys about five miles westward to Succoth in the Jordan Valley, where he camps for a period of time.

33:18–20. From Succoth, Jacob moves westward again out of the Jordan Valley to Shechem, the first place associated with Abraham's arrival in Canaan (12:6). Confirming his status as heir to the Abrahamic promises, Jacob buys land (cf. 23:3–20) and sets up an altar, as Abraham did (12:6–7).[720] This is the first altar associated with Jacob and its name, "God, the God of Israel," recalls how God changed Jacob's name to Israel

---

[717] Curtis, "Structure, Style and Context," 136.

[718] Bridge rightly rejects the "common interpretations that Jacob gives back to Esau the stolen blessing and that Jacob negotiates a treaty with Esau" ("The 'Slave' Is the 'Master,' " 263).

[719] Bridge, "The 'Slave' Is the 'Master,' " 277.

[720] The Hebrew verb used to describe the making of the altar is not the one usually associated with altar building.

at Peniel (32:28–30). The naming of the altar confirms that the God of Abraham and Isaac has now become the God of Jacob in a meaningful way. Prior to his encounter with God at Peniel, Jacob does not appear to have grasped fully the nature of true faith in God. The naming of Hamor and Shechem anticipates the events that will dominate the next chapter.

Bridge

The theme of reconciliation dominates this passage. Although Jacob has the birthright, he humbles himself to be reconciled with his brother Esau. The image of alienated brothers being reunited will reappear later in Genesis when Joseph is reconciled with his brothers, who sold him into slavery in Egypt. Since fratricide is one of the earliest sins recorded in Genesis, it is noteworthy that those who belong to the central patriline play a part in restoring harmonious relationships between estranged brothers. The restorative activity of the divinely promised vicegerent, undertaken with true humility, will involve the reconciliation of people to both God and others.

O. Dinah and Shechem (34:1–31)

> [1] Leah's daughter Dinah, whom Leah bore to Jacob, went out to see some of the young women of the area.
>
> [2] When Shechem—son of Hamor the Hivite, who was the region's chieftain—saw her, he took her and raped her.
>
> [3] He became infatuated with Jacob's daughter Dinah. He loved the young girl and spoke tenderly to her. [4] "Get me this girl as a wife," he told his father.
>
> [5] Jacob heard that Shechem had defiled his daughter Dinah, but since his sons were with his livestock in the field, he remained silent until they returned. [6] Meanwhile, Shechem's father Hamor came to speak with Jacob. [7] Jacob's sons returned from the field when they heard about the incident and were deeply grieved and very angry. For Shechem had committed an outrage against Israel by raping Jacob's daughter, and such a thing should not be done.
>
> [8] Hamor said to Jacob's sons, "My son Shechem has his heart set on your daughter. Please give her to him as a wife. [9] Intermarry with us; give your daughters to us, and take our daughters for yourselves. [10] Live with us. The land is before you. Settle here, move about, and acquire property in it."
>
> [11] Then Shechem said to Dinah's father and brothers, "Grant me this favor, and I'll give you whatever you say. [12] Demand of me a high com-

pensation and gift; I'll give you whatever you ask me. Just give the girl
to be my wife!"

[13] But Jacob's sons answered Shechem and his father Hamor deceit-
fully because he had defiled their sister Dinah. [14] "We cannot do this
thing," they said to them. "Giving our sister to an uncircumcised man
is a disgrace to us. [15] We will agree with you only on this condition: if
all your males are circumcised as we are. [16] Then we will give you our
daughters, take your daughters for ourselves, live with you, and become
one people. [17] But if you will not listen to us and be circumcised, then
we will take our daughter and go."

[18] Their words seemed good to Hamor and his son Shechem. [19] The young
man did not delay doing this, because he was delighted with Jacob's
daughter. Now he was the most important in all his father's family. [20]
So Hamor and his son Shechem went to the gate of their city and spoke
to the men of their city.

[21] "These men are peaceful toward us," they said. "Let them live in our
land and move about in it, for indeed, the region is large enough for
them. Let us take their daughters as our wives and give our daughters
to them. [22] But the men will agree to live with us and be one people only
on this condition: if all our men are circumcised as they are. [23] Won't
their livestock, their possessions, and all their animals become ours?
Only let us agree with them, and they will live with us."

[24] All the men who had come to the city gates listened to Hamor and his
son Shechem, and all those men were circumcised. [25] On the third day,
when they were still in pain, two of Jacob's sons, Simeon and Levi, Di-
nah's brothers, took their swords, went into the unsuspecting city, and
killed every male. [26] They killed Hamor and his son Shechem with their
swords, took Dinah from Shechem's house, and went away. [27] Jacob's
sons came to the slaughter and plundered the city because their sister
had been defiled. [28] They took their flocks, herds, donkeys, and whatever
was in the city and in the field. [29] They captured all their possessions,
dependents, and wives and plundered everything in the houses.

[30] Then Jacob said to Simeon and Levi, "You have brought trouble on
me, making me odious to the inhabitants of the land, the Canaanites
and the Perizzites. We are few in number; if they unite against me and
attack me, I and my household will be destroyed."

[31] But they answered, "Should he treat our sister like a prostitute?"

Context

Some years have elapsed since Jacob and his family returned to Canaan. Having purchased a plot of land near Shechem (32:18–19),

Jacob's family resides near the city. Over time, his daughter Dinah, whom Leah bore (30:21), associates with some of the young woman of the area. This results in Shechem, the son of Hamor, a local Hivite chieftain, having an inappropriate premarital sexual encounter with Dinah. Following on from this liaison, Shechem desires to marry Dinah because he loves her. However, Dinah's brothers deceitfully arrange for the men of the city to be circumcised as a prerequisite to Shechem's marrying Dinah. Taking revenge for Shechem's mistreatment of Dinah, as the men are still recovering from the effects of circumcision, two of Dinah's full brothers, Simeon and Levi, attack them, killing all the adult males in the city. When their father Jacob disapproves of their actions, Simeon and Levi remain defiant that they have acted appropriately. Ultimately, the inclusion of this episode in Genesis is about Jacob's relationship with his sons Simeon and Levi. Due to their actions, each is excluded from being the next person in the unique patriline traced throughout Genesis (see 49:5–7).

Comments

34:1–4. The events of this chapter begin by focusing on Jacob's daughter Dinah. However, the narrator says almost nothing about her feelings regarding what happens. As we shall see, the primary issue in this episode is the relationship between Jacob and his sons Simeon and Levi, who usurp their father's authority by killing the men of Shechem. While they justify their actions on the basis that Hamor's son Shechem has mistreated their sister Dinah, their behavior endangers all of Jacob's family.

Much recent discussion regarding Genesis 34 centers on the issue of what happened to Dinah. Was she raped? Was she seduced? Is this an example of abduction marriage? Scholarly opinion is divided on the nature of this relationship.[721] The narrator's description of what occurs between Shechem and Dinah is sufficiently ambiguous for scholars to disagree on how the Hebrew text should be understood. While there is a trend toward interpreting the series of verbs at the end of verse. 2 as indicating rape (e.g., CSB, NET, NIV, NJB, NLT, NJPS),[722] the verbs lack suf-

---

[721] Angela B. Wagner, "Considerations on the Politico-Juridical Proceedings of Genesis 34," *JSOT* 38 (2013): 145–61, offers a brief survey of different interpretations.

[722] Yael Shemesh, "Rape Is Rape Is Rape: The Story of Dinah and Shechem (Genesis 34)," *ZAW* 119 (2007): 2–21, argues that Shechem raped Dinah.

ficient semantic precision that they may denote inappropriate consensual premarital sex (e.g., ESV, JPS, KJV, RSV).[723] As Wagner notes,

> The legal consequences of the action in Gen. 34.2, for both Dinah and Shechem, would appear to be unaffected by distinctions between rape and consensual sex. Accordingly, this particular aspect of the action described in Gen. 34.2 is not the linchpin of the narrative that it is often supposed to be. The concern with which this aspect has been discussed, therefore—at least for understanding the narrative—seems to be misplaced.[724]

Even if it is consensual on the part of Dinah, her premarital sexual encounter with Shechem is unacceptable in a society where the virgin status of a bride is considered important. The fact that Dinah is living in Shechem's house when Simeon and Levi attack the men of the city (v. 26) suggests that Shechem did not assault Dinah in a violent sexual manner against her will. As modern readers, influenced by current discussions regarding sexual exploitation and rape, we run the risk of reading into this chapter more than the original narrator intended. What matters is that in the ANE premarital sex between unbetrothed individuals was "a misdeed regardless of the either forcible or non-forcible nature of the sexual encounter."[725] In such circumstances, the woman is viewed as having been defiled because she can no longer claim to be a virgin.

34:5–17. Although Jacob becomes aware that Shechem has mistreated Dinah, he is reluctant to say anything until his sons return from grazing their livestock. However, subsequent events portray Jacob's sons as acting without any regard for their father, despite his standing as head of the clan. Jacob plays no part in the negotiations that take place, when Hamor seeks to arrange for Dinah to become Shechem's wife. By way of reparation for having premarital sex with Dinah, Shechem offers a large betrothal-gift[726] and another gift to marry Dinah. In the ANE it was customary for a husband-to-be to give a betrothal-gift (sometimes

---

[723] Some translations deliberately choose English equivalents for Hebrew terms that emphasize the violent nature of what Shechem did (e.g., "seize" rather than "took"). The Hebrew text is less specific than some English translations imply; it uses terms that have a broad semantic range.

[724] Wagner, "Considerations," 155.

[725] Wagner, "Considerations," 154.

[726] CSB translates מֹהַר (*mōhar*) as "high compensation." However, it is better to think of מֹהַר (*mōhar*) as a dowry (KJV, NTL, JPS) or marriage present (RSV, NRSV).

called unhelpfully the "bride-price"). Shechem appears to offer more than that was normally the case. Jacob's sons, however, exploit the situation and request that Shechem and all the men of the city be circumcised as a prerequisite for intermarriage between the two communities. Their deceptive use of circumcision is significant because of its association with Abraham being the father of many nations (17:4–5). Whereas circumcision was meant to bring divine blessing to those who acknowledge the importance of the unique patriline associated with Abraham, Jacob's sons use circumcision to enable them to harm the men of Shechem.

34:18–24. Out of his strong desire to marry Dinah, and with his father's support, Shechem persuades all the men of the city to be circumcised. Unsuspectingly, Hamor and Shechem tell the men that Jacob's sons "are peaceful toward us" (v. 21). They have no sense of being deceived by Jacob's sons. To gain support for their request, Hamor and Shechem suggest that a closer association with Jacob's family will bring financial rewards for all the men of Shechem.

34:25–29. Simeon and Levi's slaughter of the men of Shechem goes far beyond any retribution that might be expected for Shechem's mistreatment of Dinah. While Simeon and Levi take the lead in killing all the men of Shechem, their brothers participate in the looting of the city. As Noble observes, "The brothers' true motives are shown by the way the narrative lingers over the booty they capture (vv. 27–29), which is listed in far greater detail than the story line would otherwise require. The actions of these brothers, then, have degenerated into a self-interested plundering of the defenceless."[727] The treachery of Jacob's sons is all the greater because they use circumcision, which is associated with the blessing of the nations in Genesis 17, to weaken their opponents.

34:30–31. Jacob confronts Simeon and Levi concerned that their slaughter of the men of Shechem will cause others to attack his household. His sons, however, justify their behavior by arguing that Shechem treated Dinah like a prostitute. Their accusation suggests that they did not view Shechem's treatment of Dinah as falling into the category of a man being sexually violent toward a woman, what we might classify as rape.

---

[727] Paul R. Noble, "A 'Balanced' Reading of the Rape of Dinah: Some Exegetical and Methodological Observations," *BibInt* 4 (1996): 193.

Bridge

In a book that is especially interested in tracing a unique patriline over many generations, the present episode contributes important information that will have a bearing on the future status of Simeon and Levi within Jacob's family. Despite being two of his oldest sons, their slaughter of the men of Shechem places them at odds with their father. On his deathbed Jacob expresses his negative assessment of them, highlighting their impulsive and violent nature (49:5–7). In Jacob's eyes, their actions at Shechem—exploiting circumcision, the very sign of God's covenant with Abraham, for evil ends—exclude them from being suitable members of the patriline that is intended to bring God's blessing to all the families of the ground. Within the balanced structure of the Isaac *tôlĕdôt*, this episode stands in sharp contrast to chapter 26, where Isaac is portrayed as blessing others by making a friendship treaty or covenant with Abimelech the king of Gerar.[728]

P. Jacob at Bethel (35:1–15)

> 1 God said to Jacob, "Get up! Go to Bethel and settle there. Build an altar there to the God who appeared to you when you fled from your brother Esau."
>
> 2 So Jacob said to his family and all who were with him, "Get rid of the foreign gods that are among you. Purify yourselves and change your clothes. 3 We must get up and go to Bethel. I will build an altar there to the God who answered me in my day of distress. He has been with me everywhere I have gone."
>
> 4 Then they gave Jacob all their foreign gods and their earrings, and Jacob hid them under the oak near Shechem. 5 When they set out, a terror from God came over the cities around them, and they did not pursue Jacob's sons. 6 So Jacob and all who were with him came to Luz (that is, Bethel) in the land of Canaan. 7 Jacob built an altar there and called the place El-bethel because it was there that God had revealed himself to him when he was fleeing from his brother.
>
> 8 Deborah, the one who had nursed and raised Rebekah, died and was buried under the oak south of Bethel. So Jacob named it Allon-bacuth.
>
> 9 God appeared to Jacob again after he returned from Paddan-aram, and he blessed him. 10 God said to him, "Your name is Jacob; you will no longer be named Jacob, but your name will be Israel." So he named

[728] See Provan, *Discovering Genesis*, 169.

him Israel. [11] God also said to him, "I am God Almighty. Be fruitful and multiply. A nation, indeed an assembly of nations, will come from you, and kings will descend from you. [12] I will give to you the land that I gave to Abraham and Isaac. And I will give the land to your future descendants." [13] Then God withdrew from him at the place where he had spoken to him.

[14] Jacob set up a marker at the place where he had spoken to him—a stone marker. He poured a drink offering on it and anointed it with oil. [15] Jacob named the place where God had spoken with him Bethel.

Context

As Jacob observes, the slaughter of the men of Shechem puts Jacob's family in great danger. Other ethnic groups living in the area around Shechem were likely to become fearful that they too would be attacked. Against this background, God instructs Jacob to relocate southward to Bethel. Jacob will subsequently move his family further south, eventually arriving at Hebron where his father Isaac is living. Several incidents associated with Jacob's journey from Shechem to Hebron are recorded briefly in chapter 35. These either bring closure to previous episodes or anticipate future developments in Genesis.[729] The narrative section that begins in 25:19 with the *tôlĕdôt* heading of Isaac is concluded by a brief description of Isaac's death and burial (35:29).

Comments

35:1–4. God tells Jacob to go to Bethel, reminding him that this is the location where he encountered God when leaving Canaan during his flight to Paddan Aram (28:11–22). At Bethel God had promised to protect Jacob and bring him back safely to the land of Canaan. As a location, Bethel was special for Jacob; he had named it Bethel, which means "house of God" (28:19). In the light of the location's sacred associations with God, and as a clear signal of Jacob's personal commitment to serve only YHWH, Jacob instructs his household to rid itself of all foreign gods. These cannot be brought to Bethel. Rachel had stolen her father's idols and hidden them in her camel's saddlebag (31:19, 34–35). Other members of the household may have had similar items. All of these, along with earrings,[730] are buried

---

729 Cf. Steinmann, *Genesis*, 326–27.

730 The mention of earrings suggests that they were of religious significance, possibly indicating that the wearer worshiped a particular deity.

by Jacob, sending out a strong message that these gods are impotent and worthless; they are to be considered dead.

Additionally, in preparation for coming to the "house of God," Jacob instructs his household to purify themselves and change their clothing. Such actions are more fully explained in connection with the Sinai covenant, when God comes to dwell among the Israelites. Jacob, however, has some appreciation of the importance of being ritually clean before approaching God. In marked contrast to the idols that are buried, Jacob speaks of building an altar at Bethel where God spoke to him. While many in the ANE believed that gods manifested their presence in idols, Jacob associates God's presence with the locations where God has appeared and spoken to him. In Genesis such locations are normally marked through the construction of sacrificial altars, although previously at Bethel Jacob had only set up a stone pillar (28:18–22).

35:5–8. After Jacob speaks of God's presence with him wherever he went (v. 3), God continues to protect Jacob's family as they journey from Shechem to Bethel. The term חִתַּת (*ḥittat*), translated "terror," comes only here in the whole of the Old Testament. It appears to denote a sense of fear, recalling how God is referred to as "the Fear of Isaac" in 31:42 and "the Fear of his father Isaac" in 31:53. After arriving at Luz (cf. 28:19),[731] Jacob constructs an altar, which he names El-Bethel, meaning "God of the house of God." The name is somewhat similar in form to the one given to the altar that Jacob makes at Shechem (see 33:20). In verse 7 the narrator underlines once again the importance of Bethel as the location where God revealed himself to Jacob (cf. v. 1), recalling the events of 28:11–22.

Somewhat unexpectedly, verse 8 describes how Rebekah's nurse, Deborah, is buried below the canopy of a large tree that was to the south of Bethel. This results in the tree being known as Allon-bacuth, "the Oak of Weeping." Rebekah's nurse is mentioned previously in 24:59, but without being named. No reason is given to explain why Deborah is with Jacob's household; possibly she has been sent by Rebekah with news about Esau (see 27:45) or perhaps she had returned to Paddan-aram years previously and then journeyed back to Canaan with Jacob's household. Deborah's burial near Bethel is perhaps mentioned here briefly to draw out a contrast between the burials at Shechem (v. 4)

---

[731] Bethel appears to have been located very close to the city of Luz (see Josh 16:2; 18:13).

and Bethel. Whereas Deborah's death is marked by weeping, there is no sense of grief over the loss of the foreign gods at Shechem.

35:9–15. Jacob's return to Bethel is marked by God's speaking to him again, as he had done previously at this location (28:13–15). This speech, which is the last divine utterance recorded in the *tôlĕdôt* section of Isaac (25:19–35:29), is an important statement of divine blessing regarding Jacob/Israel's inclusion within the patriline traced throughout Genesis. The narrator's comment that God "blessed" Jacob (v. 9; cf. 32:29) places him on a par with Abraham (24:1) and Isaac (25:11; 26:12).

God's initial words recall his announcement at Peniel that Jacob's name would be changed to Israel (32:28). Alongside this confirmation of a transformation in Jacob's nature and status in God's eyes, God also asserts in verses 11–12 that the divine promises given to Abraham and Isaac are now transferred to Jacob/Israel. God's words echo previous divine speeches in Genesis, underlining the importance of what is said here. The statement, "I am God Almighty" echoes how God addresses Abraham in 17:1. It is also the divine name used by Isaac when he says to Jacob, "May God Almighty bless you and make you fruitful and multiply you so that you become an assembly of peoples. May God give you and your offspring the blessing of Abraham so that you may possess the land where you live as a foreigner, the land God gave to Abraham" (28:3–4). God's assurances in verses 11–12 recall closely what Isaac hopes for Jacob in 28:3–4, hopes that draw upon God's covenant promises to Abraham (cf. 17:5–8). The concept of being fruitful and multiplying, which may be traced back to the creation mandate in 1:28 (cf. 9:1, 7), is also prominent in God's repeated promises to Abraham (13:16; 15:5; 17:2, 6; 22:17).

Although CSB translates the expression גּוֹי וּקְהַל גּוֹיִם יִהְיֶה מִמֶּךָּ (*gôy ûqĕhal gôyim yihye mimmekkā*) as "a nation, indeed an assembly of nations, will come from you," the Hebrew is better rendered "a nation and an assembly of nations will come from you." As Lee observes, God's remarks in verse 11 draw a distinction between "a nation and a company of nations" coming from Jacob/Israel.[732] This distinction recalls God's covenant with Abraham that he would be the father of many nations (17:4–6), one of which will be his biological offspring (15:1–21). The

---

[732] Chee-Chiew Lee, "גים in Genesis 35:11 and the Abrahamic Promise of Blessings for the Nations," *JETS* 52 (2009): 467–82.

reference to kings coming from Jacob's body (v. 11) recalls God's promise of royal descendants made to Abraham and Sarah in 17:6 and 17:16. The allusion to future kings reinforces the expectation that the patriline highlighted in Genesis will lead to a perfect vicegerent who will rule over the earth on God's behalf.[733]

As previously at Bethel (see 28:18), Jacob sets up a stone pillar and pours oil on it. On this occasion he also pours a drink offering over the pillar. This is the only mention of a drink offering in Genesis. References to drink offerings elsewhere suggest that wine may have been used (e.g., Exod 29:40; Lev 23:13).

Bridge

As the *tôlĕdôt* section that focuses on Isaac's immediate offspring comes to an end, Jacob's inclusion within the patriline of Abraham and Isaac is confirmed by God when he addresses Jacob at Bethel. This event takes on special significance in the light of God's earlier appearance to Jacob at Bethel. The intervening years have witnessed a transformation in Jacob's character, and he is now a more worthy recipient of the divine promises given to Abraham and Isaac. Importantly, God's speech to Jacob underlines that kings will come from him (v. 11). This is a further indication that the unique patriline set out in Genesis will lead to a vicegerent who will rule over the earth of God's behalf.

Q. The Deaths of Rachel and Isaac (35:16–29)

> [16] They set out from Bethel. When they were still some distance from
> Ephrath, Rachel began to give birth, and her labor was difficult. [17]
> During her difficult labor, the midwife said to her, "Don't be afraid,
> for you have another son." [18] With her last breath—for she was dy-
> ing—she named him Ben-oni, but his father called him Benjamin. [19]
> So Rachel died and was buried on the way to Ephrath (that is, Beth-
> lehem). [20] Jacob set up a marker on her grave; it is the marker at
> Rachel's grave still today.
>
> [21] Israel set out again and pitched his tent beyond the Tower of Eder. [22]
> While Israel was living in that region, Reuben went in and slept with his
> father's concubine Bilhah, and Israel heard about it. Jacob had twelve sons:
>
> > [23] Leah's sons were Reuben (Jacob's firstborn),
> > Simeon, Levi, Judah,

[733] See Diffey, "Royal Promise in Genesis," 313–16.

Issachar, and Zebulun.
[24] Rachel's sons were
Joseph and Benjamin.
[25] The sons of Rachel's slave Bilhah
were Dan and Naphtali.
[26] The sons of Leah's slave Zilpah
were Gad and Asher.

These are the sons of Jacob, who were born to him in Paddan-aram.

[27] Jacob came to his father Isaac at Mamre in Kiriath-arba (that is, He-
bron), where Abraham and Isaac had stayed. [28] Isaac lived 180 years. [29]
He took his last breath and died, and was gathered to his people, old
and full of days. His sons Esau and Jacob buried him.

Context

After journeying from Shechem to Bethel, Jacob continues to move in a southward direction, relocating via Bethlehem to Hebron. Before he arrives at Hebron, two significant events take place. First, Rachel, the wife whom Jacob loved the most, dies as a result of giving birth to Benjamin. Benjamin is the last son to be born to Jacob. Second, Reuben, the first son to be born to Jacob, inappropriately sleeps with Bilhah, the mother of Jacob's sons Dan and Naphtali. Jacob learns of Reuben's intimate relationship with Bilhah, which has important consequences for Reuben's status as Jacob's firstborn. As becomes evident in the rest of Genesis, the birthright of the firstborn is taken from Leah's eldest son and given to Rachel's eldest son, Joseph (see 1 Chr 5:1–3). Although the births of all Jacob's sons have been recorded previously in Genesis, verses 22b–26 provide a short summary, which is organized under the names of Jacob's wives. The final sentences of the *tôlĕdôt* section of Isaac record his death and burial. This brings closure to the carefully composed narrative that begins in 25:19.

Comments

35:16–20. Jacob's southward journey is interrupted by the death of Rachel shortly after she gives birth to Benjamin. Before she dies, she names her son Ben-oni, which means "son of my sorrow," although it could also be understood to mean "son of my strength" (see ESV footnote). Jacob, however, names his youngest son Benjamin, meaning "son of my right hand," suggesting that even from birth Benjamin enjoyed his father's favor in a special way. Subsequent events underscore Jacob's affection for Benjamin, especially after his full brother Joseph is spitefully sold into slavery in Egypt by his older brothers. No doubt the unfortunate circumstances surrounding Benjamin's birth added to Jacob's concern for

Benjamin. Although other family members are buried at Hebron, Jacob buries Rachel somewhere between Shechem and Bethlehem. Jeremiah 31:15 possibly locates Rachel's tomb to the north of Jerusalem, but Jewish tradition places the burial south of Jerusalem.

35:21–22a. Attention switches from Jacob's youngest son to his firstborn son, Reuben (see v. 23). Reuben's intimate relationship with Bilhah implies a total disregard for his father's status as head of the clan. Reuben's actions result in his exclusion from the unique patriline traced in Genesis (see 49:4; cf. 1 Chr 5:1–2). His subsequent plan to rescue Joseph from the pit (37:21–22, 29) may have been motivated by a desire to win back his father's favor. Due to Reuben's inappropriate behavior, he forfeits his birthright as firstborn, a birthright that Jacob subsequently bestows on Joseph.[734] The מִגְדַּל־עֵדֶר (*migdal-ʿēder*, "tower of Eder") was probably located somewhere between Bethlehem and Hebron. A similar Hebrew expression is found in Micah 4:8, where it is translated "watchtower for the flock." The name suggests that it was a tower used by shepherds.

35:22b–26. Jacob's sons are listed under the names of their mothers, with priority being given to Leah, who was first to bear Jacob a son (see 29:31–30:24). The general statement that these were the sons born to Jacob in Paddan-aram does not apply to Benjamin, who is born to Rachel in Canaan.

35:27–29. The brief account of Isaac's death concludes the narrative section that commences in 25:19 with a *tôlĕdôt* heading. Like Abraham and Sarah, Isaac is buried in the cave at Machpelah close to Hebron (see 49:30–31). On the expression "gathered to his people," see Comments on 25:8. Isaac's death occurs twenty years after Jacob's return from Paddan-aram.

Bridge

The final paragraphs of the *tôlĕdôt* section devoted to Isaac's immediate offspring ends fittingly with a reference to Isaac's death and burial. At this point, Jacob succeeds as the next head or *paterfamilias* of the unique

---

[734] According to Chapman, *The House of the Mother*, 236n17, "a man's *bĕkôr* was his first-born son ... This would be the social norm and professed ideal." She rejects the suggestion of Frederick E. Greenspahn, *When Brothers Dwell Together: The Preeminence of Younger Siblings in the Hebrew Bible* (Oxford: Oxford University Press, 1994), 56–69, 81–82, that the Hebrew term *bĕkôr* should be translated "designated heir" rather than "firstborn son." Greenspahn dismisses the concept of primogeniture, arguing that the concept of *bĕkôr* is "an assigned rather than an automatic status." While it was normal for the birthright to be given to the firstborn son, a father could assign it to another son (see 1 Chr 5:1–2). This occurs on various occasions in Genesis, all of which have a bearing on the membership of the unique patriline that begins with Adam and Eve.

patriline that will eventually lead to a divinely appointed vicegerent, who will succeed where Adam and Eve failed. Although Jacob is not Isaac's firstborn son, he inherits the birthright of the firstborn and so becomes heir to the divine promises given to Abraham and Isaac. By way of anticipating future developments in Genesis, the *tôlĕdôt* section of Isaac concludes by mentioning briefly Reuben's inappropriate relationship with Bilhah, Rachel's maid whom she gave to Isaac as a wife (30:3–8). This brief report signals the possibility that the birthright inherited by Jacob will not pass automatically to Reuben, his eldest son. This sets the scene for the *tôlĕdôt* section devoted to Jacob's offspring that begins in 37:2.

X. The Offspring of Esau (36:1–37:1)

1 These are the family records of Esau (that is, Edom). 2 Esau took his
wives from the Canaanite women: Adah daughter of Elon the Hittite,
Oholibamah daughter of Anah and granddaughter of Zibeon the Hivite,
3 and Basemath daughter of Ishmael and sister of Nebaioth. 4 Adah bore
Eliphaz to Esau, Basemath bore Reuel, 5 and Oholibamah bore Jeush,
Jalam, and Korah. These were Esau's sons, who were born to him in
the land of Canaan.

6 Esau took his wives, sons, daughters, and all the people of his house-
hold, as well as his herds, all his livestock, and all the property he had
acquired in Canaan; he went to a land away from his brother Jacob. 7 For
their possessions were too many for them to live together, and because
of their herds, the land where they stayed could not support them. 8 So
Esau (that is, Edom) lived in the mountains of Seir.

9 These are the family records of Esau, father of the Edomites in the
mountains of Seir.

> 10 These are the names of Esau's sons:
> Eliphaz son of Esau's wife Adah,
> and Reuel son of Esau's wife Basemath.
> 11 The sons of Eliphaz were
> Teman, Omar, Zepho, Gatam, and Kenaz.
> 12 Timna, a concubine of Esau's son Eliphaz,
> bore Amalek to Eliphaz.
> These were the sons of Esau's wife Adah.
> 13 These are Reuel's sons:
> Nahath, Zerah, Shammah, and Mizzah.
> These were the sons of Esau's wife Basemath.
> 14 These are the sons of Esau's wife Oholibamah
> daughter of Anah and granddaughter of Zibeon:

She bore Jeush, Jalam, and Korah to Edom.
15 These are the chiefs of Esau's sons:
the sons of Eliphaz, Esau's firstborn:
Chiefs Teman, Omar, Zepho, Kenaz,
16 Korah, Gatam, and Amalek.
These are the chiefs of Eliphaz
in the land of Edom.
These are the sons of Adah.
17 These are the sons of Reuel, Esau's son:
Chiefs Nahath, Zerah, Shammah, and Mizzah.
These are the chiefs of Reuel
in the land of Edom.
These are the sons of Esau's wife Basemath.
18 These are the sons of Esau's wife Oholibamah:
Chiefs Jeush, Jalam, and Korah.
These are the chiefs of Esau's wife Oholibamah
daughter of Anah.
19 These are the sons of Esau (that is, Edom),
and these are their chiefs.
20 These are the sons of Seir the Horite,
the inhabitants of the land:
Lotan, Shobal, Zibeon, Anah,
21 Dishon, Ezer, and Dishan.
These are the chiefs of the Horites,
the sons of Seir, in the land of Edom.
22 The sons of Lotan were Hori and Heman.
Timna was Lotan's sister.
23 These are Shobal's sons:
Alvan, Manahath, Ebal, Shepho, and Onam.
24 These are Zibeon's sons: Aiah and Anah.
This was the Anah who found the hot springs in the wilderness
while he was pasturing the donkeys of his father Zibeon.
25 These are the children of Anah:
Dishon and Oholibamah daughter of Anah.
26 These are Dishon's sons:
Hemdan, Eshban, Ithran, and Cheran.
27 These are Ezer's sons:
Bilhan, Zaavan, and Akan.
28 These are Dishan's sons: Uz and Aran.
29 These are the chiefs of the Horites:
Chiefs Lotan, Shobal, Zibeon, Anah,
30 Dishon, Ezer, and Dishan.
These are the chiefs of the Horites,

according to their divisions, in the land of Seir.
31 These are the kings who ruled in the land of Edom
before any king ruled over the Israelites:
32 Bela son of Beor ruled in Edom;
the name of his city was Dinhabah.
33 When Bela died, Jobab son of Zerah from Bozrah became
king in his place.
34 When Jobab died, Husham from the land of the
Temanites became king in his place.
35 When Husham died, Hadad son of Bedad became king
in his place.
He defeated Midian in the field of Moab;
the name of his city was Avith.
36 When Hadad died, Samlah from Masrekah became king
in his place.
37 When Samlah died, Shaul from Rehoboth on the Euphra-
tes River became king in his place.
38 When Shaul died, Baal-hanan son of Achbor became
king in his place.
39 When Baal-hanan son of Achbor died, Hadar became
king in his place.
His city was Pau, and his wife's name was Mehetabel
daughter of Matred daughter of Me-zahab.
40 These are the names of Esau's chiefs,
according to their families and their localities,
by their names:
Chiefs Timna, Alvah, Jetheth,
41 Oholibamah, Elah, Pinon,
42 Kenaz, Teman, Mibzar,
43 Magdiel, and Iram.
These are Edom's chiefs,
according to their settlements in the land they possessed.
Esau was father of the Edomites.
1 Jacob lived in the land where his father had stayed, the
land of Canaan.

Context

The death and burial of Isaac recorded in 35:29 brings to a conclusion the *tôlĕdôt* section that begins in 25:19. Before focusing on Jacob's family in the final *tôlĕdôt* section of Genesis (37:2–50:26), some information is recorded concerning Esau's family and their association with the hill country of Seir, south of the Dead Sea, later called Edom. As happens elsewhere in Genesis, the author writes about less significant figures, in this case Esau, before focusing on the main participants of the unique patriline. The material on Esau involves the use of two *tôlĕdôt* headings, which distinguish verses 1–8 from verses 9–43. Verses 1–8 address Esau's time in Canaan, whereas verses 9–43 describe in the main how Esau's descendants gain prominence in the territory of Seir/Edom. The use of the two *tôlĕdôt* headings draws attention to Esau's relocation from Canaan to the hill country of Seir/Edom. Jacob, however, remains in Canaan. Significantly, Esau marries a great granddaughter of Seir the Horite, whose descendants form important clans in the land of Seir. Details regarding Seir's family are recorded in verses 20–30. While the region of Seir is initially populated by Horites, Esau's descendants eventually assume control of the region and rename it Edom. We also witness in this passage the creation of minor kingdoms, a development that will be paralleled later by the establishment of a monarch in Israel.

Comments

36:1–8. A new phase in the Genesis narrative is marked by the *tôlĕdôt* heading in verse 1. While verses 2–5 provide details of Esau's wives and the sons born to him when he was living in the land of Canaan, verses 6–8 explain why Esau moves from Canaan to the mountains of Seir. The reason given recalls the earlier story of Lot's separation from Abraham (13:6–7). In all, five sons and some daughters are born to Esau in Canaan. On the origin of Esau's alternative name Edom, see Comments on 25:30.

According to 26:34, Esau married Judith, the daughter of Beeri, and Basemath, the daughter of Elon. He later married Mahalath, the daughter of Ishmael (28:9). In the present passage, Esau's wives are named as "Adah daughter of Elon," "Oholibamah daughter of Anah and granddaughter of Zibeon" and "Basemath daughter of Ishmael." The author of Genesis offers no explanation to explain why the names of Esau's wives appear to be inconsistent. Possibly, two of the women were known by two different names: Basemath may also have been known as Adah, since both names denote a daughter of Elon, and Mahalath may have been known as Basemath, since both names refer to a daughter of Ishmael. Perhaps Judith is omitted from the details recorded in 36:1–5 because she had no children, and Esau takes Oholibamah as a fourth wife. In listing Esau's wives, Oholibamah is described as "the daughter of Anah and granddaughter of Zibeon" (cf. v. 14) in order to distinguish her from another Oholibamah whose father is also called Anah (see vv. 20, 25).

36:9–19. These verses record the names of the five sons and ten grandsons that were with Esau in the hill country of Seir. Esau's sons and grandsons create a number of clans in the hill country of Seir, over which they rule as chiefs. Whereas Esau's offspring establish fourteen clans,[735] Seir's descendants form only seven clans (see vv. 20–21, 29–30). This suggests that Esau's descendants dominate the population of Seir/Edom (see Deut 2:12, 22).

36:20–30. Verses 20–30 provide information about the descendants of Seir. Various individuals, who are close relatives, share similar names. Seir has a son called Anah (v. 20), who fathers a daughter called Oholibamah (v. 25). Seir also has a grandson called Anah (the son of Zibeon; v. 24); he in turn has a daughter who is called Oholibamah (cf. vv. 2, 14). The unexpected information about Anah and the hot spring alerts the careful reader to the presence of two different men called Anah, one being the uncle of the other. Anah the son of Zibeon is the one who finds the hot spring in the wilderness (v. 24), and his daughter is the Oholibamah, who marries Esau. The Oholibamah mentioned in verse 25 is not Esau's wife.[736]

36:31–39. Verses 15–19 and 20–30 list the chiefs descended from Esau and Seir respectively, who established various clans. Alongside these tribal chiefs, verses 31–39 highlight the existence of kings who rule in the land of Edom. These Edomite kings are linked to different cities and probably belong to different tribes. The repeated expression "in his place" implies that these kings succeed one another but their association with different locations suggests that they do not belong to a single dynasty. Significantly, no king is directly linked to Esau, revealing that his patriline does not lead to royalty. Importantly, verse 31 contains the striking observation that there were kings in Edom before there was any king in Israel. The author of Genesis either anticipates the creation of a monarchy in Israel or is writing after the establishment of kingship in Israel.

---

[735] The seven chiefs linked to Eliphaz, Esau's firstborn, who are listed in vv. 15–16, include an extra individual (Korah) not included with the sons of Eliphaz mentioned in vv. 11–12.

[736] Wenham, *Genesis 16–50*, 339, mistakenly states that she is Esau's wife.

36:40–43. These verses list eleven Edomite chiefs, who are descendants of Esau, according to their clans and dwelling places (v. 40). These chiefs are linked to regions in Edom that possibly bear their names. Most of the names in verses 40–43 do not appear earlier in the chapter. This information possibly reflects the situation in Edom long after the time when Esau settled there. 1 Chronicles 1:51–54 repeats this list of Edomite chiefs.

37:1. Verse 1 provides a transition to the final tôlĕdôt section in Genesis, which will focus on Jacob's offspring. Van Peursen helpfully notes a "correlation" between 36:8 and 37:1, with both verses preceding a *tôlĕdôt* heading. [737] Whereas Esau in located in the hill country of Seir (36:8), Jacob remains in the land of Canaan (37:1). The *tôlĕdôt* section on Esau's offspring in Edom in 36:9–37:1 will now be followed by another focusing on Jacob's descendants in Canaan (37:2–50:26).

Bridge

As the Genesis narrative traces the patriline descended from Adam and Eve, it reveals in chapter 36 that Esau's descendants live outside Canaan in the land of Seir/Edom. In addition, Esau's patriline does not establish a monarchy despite the presence of kings in Edom. These factors confirm that the divine promises made to Abraham and Isaac do not find their fulfilment in Esau and his descendants. Having established this fact, the Genesis narrative focuses on Jacob's offspring in 37:2–50:26. By noting that there were kings in Edom prior to the establishment of a monarchy in Israel (v. 31), the text signals that the patriline of Abraham, Isaac, and Jacob will eventually lead to the appointment of a king. With this in view it is noteworthy that the opening verses of the next *tôlĕdôt* section introduce the theme of royalty through the dreams that Joseph experiences (37:5–11).

XI. The Offspring of Jacob (37:2–50:26)

A. Joseph Is Sold into Slavery (37:2–36)

[2] These are the family records of Jacob.

---

[737] Wido Th. van Peursen, "Delimitation Markers, Chapter Division, Syntax and Literary Structure: The Case of Genesis 37:1–2," in *Textual Boundaries in the Bible: Their Impact on Interpretation*, ed. M. C. A. Korpel and P. Sanders (Leuven: Peeters, 2017), 99.

At seventeen years of age, Joseph tended sheep with his brothers. The
young man was working with the sons of Bilhah and Zilpah, his father's
wives, and he brought a bad report about them to their father.

3 Now Israel loved Joseph more than his other sons because Joseph was
a son born to him in his old age, and he made a robe of many colors for
him. 4 When his brothers saw that their father loved him more than all
his brothers, they hated him and could not bring themselves to speak
peaceably to him.

5 Then Joseph had a dream. When he told it to his brothers, they hated
him even more. 6 He said to them, "Listen to this dream I had: 7 There
we were, binding sheaves of grain in the field. Suddenly my sheaf stood
up, and your sheaves gathered around it and bowed down to my sheaf."

8 "Are you really going to reign over us?" his brothers asked him. "Are
you really going to rule us?" So they hated him even more because of
his dream and what he had said.

9 Then he had another dream and told it to his brothers. "Look," he
said, "I had another dream, and this time the sun, moon, and eleven
stars were bowing down to me."

10 He told his father and brothers, and his father rebuked him. "What
kind of dream is this that you have had?" he said. "Am I and your
mother and your brothers really going to come and bow down to the
ground before you?" 11 His brothers were jealous of him, but his father
kept the matter in mind.

12 His brothers had gone to pasture their father's flocks at Shechem. 13
Israel said to Joseph, "Your brothers, you know, are pasturing the flocks
at Shechem. Get ready. I'm sending you to them."

"I'm ready," Joseph replied.

14 Then Israel said to him, "Go and see how your brothers and the flocks
are doing, and bring word back to me." So he sent him from the Hebron
valley, and he went to Shechem.

15 A man found him there, wandering in the field, and asked him, "What
are you looking for?"

16 "I'm looking for my brothers," Joseph said. "Can you tell me where
they are pasturing their flocks?"

17 "They've moved on from here," the man said. "I heard them say,
'Let's go to Dothan.' " So Joseph set out after his brothers and found
them at Dothan.

18 They saw him in the distance, and before he had reached them, they
plotted to kill him. 19 They said to one another, "Oh, look, here comes

that dream expert! 20 So now, come on, let's kill him and throw him into
one of the pits. We can say that a vicious animal ate him. Then we'll see
what becomes of his dreams!"

21 When Reuben heard this, he tried to save him from them. He said,
"Let's not take his life." 22 Reuben also said to them, "Don't shed blood.
Throw him into this pit in the wilderness, but don't lay a hand on him"—
intending to rescue him from them and return him to his father.

23 When Joseph came to his brothers, they stripped off Joseph's robe,
the robe of many colors that he had on.

24 Then they took him and threw him into the pit. The pit was empty,
without water.

25 They sat down to eat a meal, and when they looked up, there was a
caravan of Ishmaelites coming from Gilead. Their camels were carrying
aromatic gum, balsam, and resin, going down to Egypt.

26 Judah said to his brothers, "What do we gain if we kill our brother
and cover up his blood? 27 Come on, let's sell him to the Ishmaelites
and not lay a hand on him, for he is our brother, our own flesh," and
his brothers agreed. 28 When Midianite traders passed by, his brothers
pulled Joseph out of the pit and sold him for twenty pieces of silver to
the Ishmaelites, who took Joseph to Egypt.

29 When Reuben returned to the pit and saw that Joseph was not there,
he tore his clothes. 30 He went back to his brothers and said, "The boy is
gone! What am I going to do?" 31 So they took Joseph's robe, slaughtered
a male goat, and dipped the robe in its blood. 32 They sent the robe of
many colors to their father and said, "We found this. Examine it. Is it
your son's robe or not?"

33 His father recognized it. "It is my son's robe," he said. "A vicious an-
imal has devoured him. Joseph has been torn to pieces!" 34 Then Jacob
tore his clothes, put sackcloth around his waist, and mourned for his
son many days. 35 All his sons and daughters tried to comfort him, but
he refused to be comforted. "No," he said. "I will go down to Sheol to
my son, mourning." And his father wept for him.

36 Meanwhile, the Midianites sold Joseph in Egypt to Potiphar, an officer
of Pharaoh and the captain of the guards.

Context

The statement, "These are the family records of Jacob," (37:2) introduces the final major narrative section of Genesis, which continues to trace the family line that has been followed closely throughout Genesis 4–36. Prominence is given to Joseph, who is the central character in chapter

37 and whose death concludes Genesis (50:26). Standing apart from his older brothers, Joseph is distinguished as a man of integrity and wisdom, who is used by God to bring salvation to many (cf. 47:25; 50:20). Although he is the eleventh son born to Jacob, Joseph receives the birthright of the firstborn, a status that is subsequently transferred to his younger son Ephraim (see Comments on 48:1–22; cf. 1 Chr 5:1–2).[738] Joseph's preeminence reflects a recurring motif within the patriarchal narratives whereby the principle of primogeniture is set aside in favor of a younger sibling (see Biblical and Theological Themes §1). Coinciding with Joseph's status as firstborn, he is also associated with royalty and experiences God's blessing (see Biblical and Theological Themes §2). The convergence of these concepts takes on special significance in the light of preceding chapters of Genesis where the blessing of the nations is associated with a future descendant of Abraham.

In the light of how the plot of Genesis develops, the prominence given to Joseph is significant, especially when it is associated with the theme of royalty. Since the narratives in Genesis 12–36 link future kingship with a unique line descended from the patriarchs, the manner of Joseph's introduction in Genesis 37 is significant. Everything points to the "royal" line being continued through him. This is reinforced by his dreams. Moreover, throughout chapters 12–36, the birthright of the firstborn is consistently given to a younger brother to whom the divine promises are reaffirmed.[739] This pattern appears to continue into chapters 37–50, with Joseph being favored by his father over other brothers who have acted inappropriately (e.g., Reuben, Simeon and Levi). Ironically, there are twenty-one references to "brothers" throughout chapter 37, which serves to underline the inappropriateness of how Joseph is treated. Jacob's sons form a divided and dysfunctional family. Hostility between brothers is a continuing theme within Genesis.

---

[738] Joseph's firstborn status is also reflected by that fact that he receives, through his sons Ephraim and Manasseh, a double portion of the Promised Land in comparison to all his brothers.

[739] Various studies have picked up on the motif of the eldest son being overshadowed by a younger brother: e.g., Judah Goldin, "The Youngest Son or Where Does Genesis 38 Belong," *JBL* 96 (1977): 27–44; Everett Fox, "Stalking the Younger Brother: Some Models for Understanding a Biblical Motif," *JSOT* 60 (1993): 45–68; Greenspahn, *When Brothers Dwell Together*.

Comments

37:2. Verse 2 introduces the final section of Genesis (see Comments on 2:4).[740] The translation "family records" is somewhat misleading if it is taken to mean written documents; the Hebrew term *tôlĕdôt* refers to what comes forth from Jacob.

Joseph is deliberately given pride of place in the narrative. None of Jacob's other sons is named until verse 21, despite opportunities to do so. Skillfully the narrator sets the scene for subsequent events by indicating that Joseph is someone of integrity unlike his brothers. By stating that Joseph brought a bad report to his father concerning the sons of Bilhah (i.e., Dan and Naphtali) and Zilpah (i.e., Gad and Asher),[741] the narrator hints that there will be hostility between Joseph and his half-brothers.[742] As the story develops the distance between Joseph and his brothers increases.

37:3–4. Joseph is especially favored by his father. The unusual Hebrew expression בֶּן־זְקֻנִים (*ben-zĕqunîm*), translated "a son born to him in old age," may imply that Joseph was a "born leader."[743] The Hebrew phrase כְּתֹנֶת פַּסִּים (*kĕtōnet passim*, "a robe of many colors") is used elsewhere in the Old Testament only for a garment worn by King David's daughter, Tamar (see 2 Sam 13:18–19, where CSB translates the same phrase as a "long-sleeved robe").[744] Does the narrator possibly imply that Joseph was dressed as a

---

[740] See van Peursen, "Delimitation Markers," 3–18.

[741] Chapman, *The House of the Mother*, 45, observes that by using the label "the sons of Bilhah and Zilpah, his father's wives" the narrator distances them relationally from Joseph. She writes, "The narrator describes their link to Jacob's house through maternally mediated pathways, the less valued, peripheral means thought which to claim belonging with a named foundational house."

[742] According to Hamilton, *Genesis: Chapters 18-50*, 406, the Hebrew expression translated "Joseph tended sheep with his brothers" could imply that Joseph shepherded his brothers; cf. Ron Pirson, *The Lord of the Dreams: A Semantic and Literary Analysis of Genesis 37–50*, JSOTSup 355 (London: Sheffield Academic, 2002), 28–30. For a critique of this view, see Samuel Emadi, *From Prisoner to Prince: The Joseph Story in Biblical Theology*, NSBT (Downers Grove: InterVarsity Press Academic, 2022), 54n62.

[743] While it is true that Joseph is born when Jacob is 91 years old, making him a son of Jacob's old age, all ten of Joseph's older brothers were born to Jacob after he had reached the age of 84. It is, therefore, difficult to see why Joseph should be distinguished as the son of his old age. Eric I. Lowenthal, *The Joseph Narrative in Genesis: An Interpretation* (New York: Ktav, 1973), 167n7, suggests that בֶּן־זְקֻנִים (*ben-zĕqunîm*) denotes someone of maturity, wise beyond their years. This assessment of Joseph is very different to that of Waltke and Fredricks, *Genesis*, 496, 98, who consider Joseph to be immature; cf. Sternberg, *Poetics of Biblical Narrative*, 98; Alter, *Genesis*, 208. Alternatively, בֶּן־זְקֻנִים (*ben-zĕqunîm*) may be an allusion back to how Isaac is described in 21:2, 7; see Emadi, *From Prisoner to Prince*, 53–54.

[744] The cloak's design is uncertain; the translators of the LXX designated it ποικίλον (*poikilon*, "many-colored"), but other possibilities exist (e.g., long-sleeved).

"prince"?[745] Jacob's love for Joseph intensifies his brothers' jealousy and hatred of him.

37:5–11. The brothers' animosity toward Joseph is increased when he shares with them his dreams.[746] Previously in Genesis dreams have been sources of divine revelation (20:3; 28:12; 31:10–11). The wording of the brothers' response in verse 8 emphasizes their skepticism.[747] Even his father rebukes him. But unlike his brothers, who become increasingly jealous of Joseph, his father ponders the significance of the dreams, possibly recalling the content of the blessing he received from his father Isaac: "Be master over your relatives; may your mother's sons bow in worship to you" (27:29). Jacob's reference to "your mother" (v. 10) may refer to Leah, since by this stage Rachel is probably already dead (cf. 35:16–19; the mention of eleven stars in v. 9 implies that Benjamin has been born). Joseph's brothers eventually bow down to him (42:6; 43:26; 44:14) and his father may have done so (47:28–31). In the light of the overall plot of Genesis, Joseph's dreams signal strongly that the "royal line of seed" will continue through him (cf. 49:26; Deut 33:16; see Biblical and Theological Themes §1).

37:12–17. Jacob may well have been concerned about his sons pasturing the flocks in the region of Shechem given the events of chapter 34. After traveling to Shechem, Joseph journeys about thirteen miles further north to Dothan. Walton helpfully observes that Joseph's encounter with the stranger at Shechem, who has "by chance" overheard the plans of his brothers, is an example of how the narrator subtly draws attention to the providential activity of God.[748] God intends for Joseph to find his brothers, despite the harm that awaits him (cf. 45:4–8; 50:20).

37:18–30. Human history begins with fratricide when Cain kills his brother Abel (4:8), threatening the continuation of the line of seed. This line is now threatened again (cf. 27:41). Hatred and jealousy motivate the brothers' desire to kill Joseph. The brothers' sarcastic description of

---

[745] Waltke and Fredricks, *Genesis*, 500.

[746] This pair of dreams indirectly prepares for the dreams, also in pairs, which are recorded later in chs. 40 and 41. Since dreams are used as a medium of revelation in Gen 37 prior to Joseph's enslavement, his ability to interpret first the prisoners' and then the pharaoh's dreams comes as no surprise within the story.

[747] Infinitive absolutes, translated by "really," are used to give emphasis to how they challenge Joseph. A similar construction comes in Jacob's second question in v. 10.

[748] Walton, *Genesis*, 689–90.

Joseph as "that dream expert" (v. 19) is ironic given his ability to interpret dreams later in Egypt (40:12–15, 18–19; 41:25–36).

Reuben's intervention, which temporarily saves Joseph from death (vv. 21–22),[749] is possibly motivated by his desire to win his father's favor. Having previously dishonored his father (35:22), Reuben had forfeited his birthright as firstborn (cf. 49:3–4). Later, when he is unable to rescue Joseph, Reuben's reaction is difficult to interpret (vv. 29–30). He may be genuinely disturbed by Joseph's disappearance, but he has also lost the opportunity to regain his firstborn status.

With utter callousness, the brothers imprison Joseph in a dried-up cistern at a distance from human habitation. As if totally oblivious to what they have done, they sit down to eat (v. 25). However, with the arrival of traders Judah seizes the opportunity to benefit financially from their plan to kill Joseph. With great irony, Judah promotes his heartless plan by emphasizing how Joseph is their "brother," their "own flesh" (v. 27). Judah manipulates the situation to his own advantage, not that of Joseph.[750] Although Reuben is the eldest brother, Judah controls what happens to Joseph. As next in line after Reuben, Simeon, and Levi, who have all offended their father, Judah may possibly have hoped that he would replace Joseph as the one favored by Jacob to be his "firstborn" heir.

The traders are variously referred to as Ishmaelites (vv. 25, 27) and Midianites (v. 28, 36).[751] While some scholars have exploited these different names to argue that the present narrative is an amalgam of once

---

[749] Richard C. Steiner, "'He Said, He Said': Repetition of the Quotation Formula in the Joseph Story and Other Biblical Narratives," *JBL* 138 (2019): 473–95, helpfully suggests that in v. 21 Reuben speaks to himself, before speaking to the brothers in v. 22.

[750] Richard J. Clifford, "Genesis 37–50: Joseph Story or Jacob Story?," in Evans, Lohr, and Petersen, *The Book of Genesis*, 217, writes, "Even prior to ch. 37, then, the three oldest of the four primary sons of Leah—Reuben, Simeon, and Levi—have attempted to wrest family leadership from their father. One has to assume that the fourth son of Leah, Judah, was fully aware that he was the only unsullied candidate left among the primary Leah sons. Hence, Judah's persuading his brothers to sell Joseph into slavery in 37:25–27 and foiling Reuben's plan to restore Joseph to his father should be viewed as, respectively, eliminating the most likely candidate for firstborn status, and frustrating Reuben's attempt to repair his relationship with his father by saving Joseph."

[751] Chapman, *The House of the Mother*, 45, makes the interesting observation that the Ishmaelites and Midianites are descendants of Abraham's concubines, Hagar and Keturah (21:10–21; 25:1–6). Their sons were sent away eastward from the land promised by God to Abraham (25:6). Having been excluded from the unique line of designated heirs, they now play a part in taking Joseph away from the land of Canaan.

disparate accounts, this is unnecessary.[752] The precise relationship between Ishmaelites and Midianites is unclear, but the two designations are also linked in Judges 8:22–26.[753] On "camels," see 12:16. Since slaves could be sold for up to thirty shekels, the Midianite traders would hope to make a profit from their purchase of Joseph.

37:31–35. The brothers' deception of Jacob, using Joseph's distinctive cloak and the blood of a slaughtered goat, recalls how Jacob deceived his father Isaac by dressing in Esau's cloak and covering his arms with goatskins (see 27:15–16). For the reader, Jacob's reference to "a vicious animal" underscores ironically the inner nature of the brothers. As Kruschwitz observes, "They themselves resemble 'a wicked beast' in their inhuman act against their brother."[754] Beginning with Adam and Eve's failure to rule over the serpent, human nature has resembled closely that of wild animals (see Comments on 3:21). Jacob's despair is underlined by his reference to "Sheol," the Hebrew name for an underworld for the dead, almost always associated with the wicked.[755] The intensity of references to Jacob's mourning in verses 34–35 underlines the depth of his grief at the loss of Joseph.

37:36. Potiphar is designated "the captain of the guards," the Hebrew expression possibly denoting that he is Pharaoh's chief executioner. This would explain why Joseph is later placed in a prison that houses prisoners under threat of death for displeasing the king (see 40:1–3).

---

[752] McKeown, *Genesis*, 165; cf. Robert E. Longacre, *Joseph: A Story of Divine Providence: A Text Theoretical and Textlinguistic Analysis of Genesis 37 and 39–48* (Winona Lake: Eisenbrauns, 1989), 31; Hamilton, *Genesis: Chapters 18–50*, 423; Waltke and Fredricks, *Genesis*, 503.

[753] Walton, *Genesis*, 665, speculates that the caravan was made up of both Midianite merchants and Ishmaelite businessmen: "The Midianites are the negotiators and buyers fronting for their Ishmaelite bosses, who provide them with the capital." A comparable view is expressed by Murphy, *Genesis*, 444, who writes, "They [the Midianites] seem to have been the actual purchasers, though the caravan takes its name from the Ishmaelites, who formed by far the larger portion of it." Adopting a different approach, Barbara Green, *What Profit for Us? Remembering the Story of Joseph* (Lanham: University Press of America, 1996), 49–50, suggests that the wording of v. 28 allows for the possibility that, unknown to the brothers, Midianite traders took Joseph from the pit and sold him to the Ishmaelites.

[754] Jonathan Kruschwitz, "The Type-Scene Connection between Genesis 38 and the Joseph Story," *JSOT* 36 (2012): 400.

[755] T. Desmond Alexander, "The Old Testament View of Life after Death," *Themelios* 11 (1986): 41–46; cf. Johnston, *Shades of Sheol*, 69–85.

Bridge

This passage provides a further illustration in Genesis of perverted human nature, as brotherly affection is replaced by jealousy and hatred. It also contributes to the ongoing plot of Genesis that traces the "offspring of the woman" (3:15; see Biblical and Theological Themes §1). Joseph becomes the next member of the unique lineage that will eventually lead to Jesus Christ. The story of Joseph continues the theme of opposition to the "offspring of the woman," as Joseph is rejected by his brothers. This theme is later echoed when Jesus is rejected by his own (cf. John 1:10–11).

B. Judah and Tamar (38:1–30)

> 1 At that time Judah left his brothers and settled near an Adullamite named Hirah. 2 There Judah saw the daughter of a Canaanite named Shua; he took her as a wife and slept with her. 3 She conceived and gave birth to a son, and he named him Er. 4 She conceived again, gave birth to a son, and named him Onan. 5 She gave birth to another son and named him Shelah. It was at Chezib that she gave birth to him.
>
> 6 Judah got a wife for Er, his firstborn, and her name was Tamar. 7 Now Er, Judah's firstborn, was evil in the Lord's sight, and the Lord put him to death. 8 Then Judah said to Onan, "Sleep with your brother's wife. Perform your duty as her brother-in-law and produce offspring for your brother." 9 But Onan knew that the offspring would not be his, so whenever he slept with his brother's wife, he released his semen on the ground so that he would not produce offspring for his brother. 10 What he did was evil in the Lord's sight, so he put him to death also.
>
> 11 Then Judah said to his daughter-in-law Tamar, "Remain a widow in your father's house until my son Shelah grows up." For he thought, "He might die too, like his brothers." So Tamar went to live in her father's house.
>
> 12 After a long time Judah's wife, the daughter of Shua, died. When Judah had finished mourning, he and his friend Hirah the Adullamite went up to Timnah to his sheepshearers. 13 Tamar was told, "Your father-in-law is going up to Timnah to shear his sheep." 14 So she took off her widow's clothes, veiled her face, covered herself, and sat at the entrance to Enaim, which is on the way to Timnah. For she saw that, though Shelah had grown up, she had not been given to him as a wife. 15 When Judah saw her, he thought she was a prostitute, for she had covered her face.
>
> 16 He went over to her and said, "Come, let me sleep with you," for he did not know that she was his daughter-in-law.
>
> She said, "What will you give me for sleeping with me?"

[17] "I will send you a young goat from my flock," he replied.

But she said, "Only if you leave something with me until you send it."

[18] "What should I give you?" he asked.

She answered, "Your signet ring, your cord, and the staff in your hand."
So he gave them to her and slept with her, and she became pregnant by
him. [19] She got up and left, then removed her veil and put her widow's
clothes back on.

[20] When Judah sent the young goat by his friend the Adullamite in order
to get back the items he had left with the woman, he could not find her.
[21] He asked the men of the place, "Where is the cult prostitute who was
beside the road at Enaim?"

"There has been no cult prostitute here," they answered.

[22] So the Adullamite returned to Judah, saying, "I couldn't find her, and be-
sides, the men of the place said, 'There has been no cult prostitute here.' "

[23] Judah replied, "Let her keep the items for herself; otherwise we will
become a laughingstock. After all, I did send this young goat, but you
couldn't find her."

[24] About three months later Judah was told, "Your daughter-in-law,
Tamar, has been acting like a prostitute, and now she is pregnant."

"Bring her out," Judah said, "and let her be burned to death!"

[25] As she was being brought out, she sent her father-in-law this message:
"I am pregnant by the man to whom these items belong." And she added,
"Examine them. Whose signet ring, cord, and staff are these?"

[26] Judah recognized them and said, "She is more in the right than I,
since I did not give her to my son Shelah." And he did not know her
intimately again.

[27] When the time came for her to give birth, there were twins in her
womb. [28] As she was giving birth, one of them put out his hand, and the
midwife took it and tied a scarlet thread around it, announcing, "This
one came out first." [29] But then he pulled his hand back, out came his
brother, and she said, "What a breakout you have made for yourself!"
So he was named Perez. [30] Then his brother, who had the scarlet thread
tied to his hand, came out, and was named Zerah.

Context

The narrator abandons Joseph in Egypt to focus the reader's attention on Judah, the brother who proposed selling Joseph into slavery. Chapter 38 is often viewed as unnecessarily "interrupting" the account of Joseph's life,[756] but this digression is an integral part of the entire story in chapters 37–50.[757] Judah will play an important role later, especially when the brothers go to Egypt; he selflessly offers to become a slave in Egypt in place of Benjamin, Joseph's younger brother (44:33–34). The transformation in Judah's character from a self-seeking conspirator to a self-sacrificing brother can only be explained by the life-changing events of chapter 38.[758]

Not only is chapter 38 significant for the coherence of the Joseph story, but also it has an important role to play within Genesis as regards the continuation of the patriline. For the alert reader, the contents of chapter 38 center on the issue of the continuation of the line of the "offspring of the woman." The episode focuses on the "firstborn" line of Judah and the keyword זֶרַע (*zeraᶜ*, "offspring/seed") appears three times in verses 8–9. When the chapter concludes with the birth of twins, the narrator records the bizarre scene of Perez breaking out in front of his twin brother, whose

---

[756] E.g., von Rad, *Genesis*, 351; Vawter, *On Genesis*, 389; Speiser, *Genesis*, 299. Brueggemann, *Genesis*, 307, writes, "This peculiar chapter stands alone, without connection to its context. It is isolated in every way and is most enigmatic. It does not seem to belong with any of the identified sources of ancestral tradition. It is not evident that it provides any significant theological resource. It is difficult to know in what context it might be of value for theological exposition." Jacques Berlinerblau, "The Bible as Literature?," *HS* 45 (2004): 18, remarks, "Genesis 38 seems completely incongruous with its surroundings."

[757] See J. A. Emerton, "Some Problems in Genesis 38," *VT* 25 (1975): 338–61; Alter, *The Art of Biblical Narrative*, 3–11; Steven D. Mathewson, "An Exegetical Study of Genesis 38," *BSac* 146 (1989): 384–87; Aaron Wildavsky, "Survival Must Not Be Gained through Sin: The Moral of the Joseph Stories Prefigured through Judah and Tamar," *JSOT* 19 (1994): 37–48; Alter, *Genesis*, 217; Paul R. Noble, "Esau, Tamar, and Joseph: Criteria for Identifying Inner-Biblical Allusions," *VT* 52 (2002): 232–43; Friedemann W. Golka, "Genesis 37–50: Joseph Story or Israel-Joseph Story?," *CurBR* 2 (2004): 153–77; Judy Fentress-Williams, "Location, Location, Location: Tamar in the Joseph Cycle," *The Bible and Critical Theory* 3 (2007): 201–8; Clifford, "Genesis 37–50," 213–29; Hans-Georg Wünch, "Genesis 38—Judah's Turning Point: Structural Analysis and Narrative Techniques and Their Meaning for Genesis 38 and Its Placement in the Story of Joseph," *Old Testament Essays* 25 (2012): 777–806; Provan, *Discovering Genesis*, 43–44, 185–86. Kruschwitz, "Type-Scene Connection," 392–93, proposes that Genesis 38 models a distinctive type-scene that "includes an act of deception, an act of counter-deception, some sort of confession or acknowledgment of wrongdoing, and a final *anagnorisis* [a recognition by one character of the true identity of another character]." He contends that this model is repeated in the chapters surrounding ch. 38 involving Joseph.

[758] Anthony J. Lambe, "Judah's Development: The Pattern of Departure-Transition-Return," *JSOT* 24 (1999): 53–68; Bryan Smith, "The Central Role of Judah in Genesis 37–50," *BSac* 162 (2005): 160–65; Yong Zhao, "The Story of Judah, the Hero: An Analysis of Genesis 38," *JBQ* 42 (2014): 238–43.

wrist bears a scarlet cord marking him as firstborn. For those who are genealogically aware, the mention of Perez is exceptionally significant, for from him comes the Davidic dynasty (cf. Ruth 4:18–22).[759]

While modern readers may well be dismayed by the sexually oriented contents of chapter 38, the account of Judah's relationship with Tamar adds an important, if unexpected, dimension to the central plot of Genesis. The nature of the events in chapter 38 argues against the chapter being merely a digression to create suspense regarding Joseph's fate in Egypt. The transformation of Judah's character has an important bearing on the content of the concluding chapters of Genesis, and the continuation of his family line plays an important role in the larger narrative running to the end of Kings.[760] While there are strong indicators that royalty in Israel will be associated with the line of Joseph/Ephraim, the story of Jacob's sons also links kingship with the descendants of Judah.[761]

Comments

38:1–5. The brief report of Judah's separation from his brothers conveys a negative picture; he appears to have no desire to be associated with the divine promises given to Abraham, Isaac, and Jacob. Additionally, his marriage to a Canaanite is ominous in the light of prior passages in Genesis that present Canaanites in a negative light (9:24–27; 24:3; 28:1; cf. 26:34–35).

38:6–11. These verses are framed by comments about Judah's dealings with Tamar; he initially gives her as a wife to Er, but later he sends her back as a widow to her father's family. Tamar's ethnic background is not stated, but she is most likely a Canaanite. Through no fault of her own, Tamar is widowed twice, and both of her husbands are punished by God.[762] While no explanation of his wickedness is given in the case of Er, Onan's death comes as a result of his blatant refusal to fulfil his "levirate" duty. In the ANE it was customary for a brother to marry a widowed sister-in-law, who was childless (see Deut 25:5–10; Ruth 1:11–13; Matt 22:24–25; Luke 20:28).

---

[759] Dohyung Kim, "The Structure of Genesis 38: A Thematic Reading," *VT* 62 (2012): 550–60

[760] See Dalrymple, "Ephraim or Judah," 50–73.

[761] Dohyung Kim, "Genesis 37–50: The Story of Jacob and His Sons in Light of the Primary Narrative (Genesis–2 Kings)," *ExpTim* 123 (2012): 486–93, rightly notes that chs. 37–50 are not simply about Joseph, but feature all of Jacob's sons, as reflected in the heading in 37:2.

[762] The case for Tamar being married to Onan is made by Eryl W. Davies, "Inheritance Rights and the Hebrew Levirate Marriage, Part 1," *VT* 31 (1981): 143, rejecting the position of George W. Coats, "Widow's Rights: A Crux in the Structure of Genesis 38," *CBQ* 34 (1972): 461–66.

The narrator mentions twice in quick succession that Er is the firstborn, a noteworthy feature given the narrator's interest in tracing carefully a patriline from Adam onwards. Onan's actions are best understood as *coitus interruptus*.[763] His repeated behavior indicates that he acts deliberately, probably motivated by self-interest. If Er is heirless, Onan will become "firstborn," entitling him to a double portion of Judah's inheritance.[764] After losing two sons, Judah is determined to protect his remaining, youngest son, Shelah. His treatment of his twice-widowed daughter-in-law Tamar is reprehensible; he makes no provision for her and humiliates her by sending her back to her father.[765] Once again, Judah is portrayed as heartless toward one of his close relatives.

38:12–23. The story jumps forward some years. Shelah is now old enough to marry Tamar, but Judah reneges on his promise to his daughter-in-law. Judah, who has deceived Tamar by falsely promising her Shelah, is now deceived by his daughter-in-law.[766] When Judah's wife dies, Tamar—presumably to continue the family line of Judah—takes the highly unusual step of seducing Judah. Disguising herself as a "prostitute" and wearing a veil, Tamar encounters Judah at the aptly named Enaim.[767] Although Tamar has dressed like a prostitute, it is Judah who propositions her regarding sexual intercourse. Once more, the narrative portrays Judah as a man who seeks to gratify his own desires; he is prepared to buy sex for the price of a young goat. Knowing that Judah cannot be trusted, Tamar asks for Judah's seal, staff and cord as a pledge. According to Alter, these are the "instruments of Judah's legal identity and social standing," the ancient equivalent of "a person's driver's license and credit cards."[768] By the time Judah sends Hiram to retrieve the pledge, Tamar has disappeared. Judah perceived Tamar as a "prostitute" (זֹנָה, *zônāh*), but Hiram

[763] The distinctive form of the Hebrew verbs indicates that Onan *repeatedly* avoided ejaculating within Tamar so that he would not make her pregnant (see GKC § 159o).

[764] Eryl W. Davies, "Inheritance Rights and the Hebrew Levirate Marriage: Part 2," *VT* 31 (1981): 257–58.

[765] See Susan Niditch, "The Wronged Woman Righted: An Analysis of Genesis 38," *HTR* 72 (1979): 145–46; Kim, "The Structure of Genesis 38," 550–60. Throughout the Old Testament, frequent comments underscore that widows, who are more vulnerable to exploitation than other women, are not to be mistreated (e.g., Exod 22:22; Isa 1:17, 23).

[766] Kruschwitz, "Type-Scene Connection," 396–404.

[767] The name means "two wells" or "two eyes." On the one hand, all that Judah can see of Tamar's face is her two eyes. On the other hand, the phrase, "entrance to Enaim" could be interpreted "the opening of the eyes"; what happens here will open Judah's eyes to the truth about himself.

[768] Alter, *Genesis*, 221.

describes her as a "shrine prostitute" (קְדֵשָׁה, *qĕdēšāh*), perhaps wishing to imply that Judah's actions were motivated by religious factors and, from Hiram's perspective, honorable.[769] Ironically, it is Tamar's actions, and not Judah's, that appear to be driven by religious considerations.

38:24–26. Paradoxically, Judah claims legal authority over Tamar, although he has refused as her father-in-law to provide materially for her or to give Shelah to her in marriage. With only two words in Hebrew, Judah pronounces judgment on Tamar: for her sexual promiscuity she deserves to be burned alive. Judah's hypocrisy, however, is soon revealed when Tamar produces his seal, cord, and staff.[770] As Waltke and Fredricks notes, Judah is "a profane fornicator who is quick to condemn another for the same crime."[771]

To his credit, Judah readily confesses his own guilt. The expression "She is more in the right than I" is best understood as a comparison of exclusion: "She is in the right, not I."[772] "It is when Judah truly looks that he recognizes Tamar's true worth as a woman in need who is more righteous than he, not a prostitute but a daughter-in-law, who ought to have been protected and provided for by her household and community."[773] Apart from a brief note that Judah had no further sexual contact with Tamar, nothing more is said about Judah. The reader must wait for Judah to reappear in later episodes to witness how this event transforms his character.[774]

---

[769] The Old Testament only mentions "shrine prostitutes" elsewhere in Deut 23:17 and Hos 4:14. Fertility rituals had no place in Israelite worship, although they were an accepted part of Canaanite religious practices. The term קְדֵשָׁה (*qĕdēšāh*) implies a "holy woman."

[770] Kruschwitz, "Type-Scene Connection," 391, observes that Tamar's "Examine them" (v. 25) and Judah's subsequent recognition echo what happens in 37:32–33 concerning Jacob's recognition of Joseph's cloak.

[771] Waltke and Fredricks, *Genesis*, 508.

[772] *IBHS*, §14.4e.

[773] L. Juliana M. Claassens, "Resisting Dehumanization: Ruth, Tamar, and the Quest for Human Dignity," *CBQ* 74 (2012): 670; cf. Niditch, "Wronged Woman Righted," 143–49. Richard J. Clifford, "Genesis 38: Its Contribution to the Jacob Story," *CBQ* 66 (2004): 531, comments, "Verse 26 marks a turning point in Judah's attitude. After his courageous acknowledgement, he rises to a level of moral behavior from which he will never deviate. Gone forever is the Judah who conspired against his brother, scorned endogamy, neglected a widow, associated with a prostitute, and recklessly condemned a family member."

[774] R. J. Clifford, "Genesis 38," *CBQ* 66 (2004): 532, helpfully remarks, "Judah's conversion is a paradigm, told quickly and completely before the Joseph story unfolds at its more leisurely pace, so that readers might learn at the very outset that it is possible for the sons to change—*just possible*. ... As might happen with the larger-than-life characters in a Flannery O'Connor

38:27–30. To avoid any confusion at the birth of the twins, the midwife ties a scarlet thread to Zerah's wrist so that she can easily identify him as the firstborn. But before Zerah fully emerges, his twin brother comes out, leading the midwife to give him the name Perez, which means "the one who breaks through."[775] In the light of previous incidents in Genesis, the inclusion of this unusual birth narrative is hardly a coincidence.[776] Once again a younger brother takes precedence over an older sibling. Since the patriarchal narratives anticipate the coming of a king, the birth of Perez is highly significant; from his descendants will come the royal line of David (Ruth 4:18–22).

Bridge

Chapter 38 contributes a vital element to the plot of Genesis, which is centered on identifying the "offspring of the woman" who will overcome the serpent. In Genesis 49:8–12, Jacob will associate future kingship with Judah, and the line of Perez will eventually lead to King David (cf. Ruth 4:18–22). However, this association of Judah with the future Davidic monarchy needs to be reconciled with the emphasis given in Genesis to Joseph as "firstborn," and the fact that Joseph's youngest son, Ephraim, will be given priority over his older brother, Manasseh (48:17–20). Additionally, Jacob's blessing of Joseph in 49:22–26 leaves open the possibility that kingship may come from the line of Joseph (see Biblical and Theological Themes §1). Various factors point to the tribe of Ephraim as the tribe linked to future kingship up to the time of

---

story, the outlandish Tamar and her bizarre deed shock Judah into seeing divine purpose at work in the world and enable him to become an example to his brothers." Thomas L. Brodie, *Genesis as Dialogue: A Literary, Historical & Theological Commentary* (Oxford: Oxford University Press, 2001), 354–55, calls ch. 38 a "conversion story." Cf. Wenham, *Genesis 16-50*, 363–65.

[775] Eran Viezel, "The Influence of Realia on Biblical Depictions of Childbirth," *VT* 61 (2011): 685–89, assumes that this birth account describes both Zerah and Perez as being fully born with arms emerging first from the womb. While the description of the midwife tying a scarlet thread to Zerah's arm may imply that he was born with arms emerging first, insufficient information is given to confirm this. For an explanation of the birth, see John Makujina, "'Behold, There Were Twins in Her Womb' (Gen. 25:24–26; 38:27–30): Medical Science and the Twin Births in Genesis," *TynBul* 68 (2017): 49–57.

[776] Esther Marie Menn, *Judah and Tamar (Genesis 38) in Ancient Jewish Exegesis: Studies in Literary Form and Hermeneutics* (Leiden: Brill, 1997), 90–91, observes that there are only two accounts of twins being born in the Bible. The other concerns Esau and Jacob (25:22–26). Both accounts come in Genesis and have an important bearing on the continuation of the special family line.

Samuel (e.g., Joshua is an Ephraimite).[777] In the light of later developments, the image of Perez breaking out ahead of the apparent firstborn may prefigure how the tribe of Judah will ultimately gain priority over the tribe of Ephraim in the time of David (see Ps 78:67–72).[778]

In recognition of her role in sustaining the patriline, Tamar, along with Rahab, Ruth, and Uriah's wife (Bathsheba), gains a noteworthy place in Matthew's genealogy of Jesus (Matt 1:3, 5–6).[779] Tamar's persistence and unorthodox behavior is rewarded. Tellingly, she is the one who causes Judah to acknowledge publicly his wickedness. Judah's acknowledgement of his own sinful nature is a vital step in the process that leads to a change of heart.

C. Joseph in Egypt (39:1–23)

> 1 Now Joseph had been taken to Egypt. An Egyptian named Potiphar,
> an officer of Pharaoh and the captain of the guards, bought him from
> the Ishmaelites who had brought him there. 2 The Lord was with Jo-
> seph, and he became a successful man, serving in the household of his
> Egyptian master. 3 When his master saw that the Lord was with him and
> that the Lord made everything he did successful, 4 Joseph found favor
> with his master and became his personal attendant. Potiphar also put
> him in charge of his household and placed all that he owned under his
> authority. 5 From the time that he put him in charge of his household
> and of all that he owned, the Lord blessed the Egyptian's house because
> of Joseph. The Lord's blessing was on all that he owned, in his house and
> in his fields. 6 He left all that he owned under Joseph's authority; he did
> not concern himself with anything except the food he ate.
>
> Now Joseph was well-built and handsome. 7 After some time his master's
> wife looked longingly at Joseph and said, "Sleep with me."
>
> 8 But he refused. "Look," he said to his master's wife, "with me here
> my master does not concern himself with anything in his house, and
> he has put all that he owns under my authority. 9 No one in this house
> is greater than I am. He has withheld nothing from me except you,

---

777 For more on this, see Alexander, "The Regal Dimension of the תלדות־יעקב," 207–10.

778 Walton, *Genesis*, 690–91, arrives at a different conclusion, suggesting that the birth incident anticipates how Joseph will "emerge on top," despite Judah occupying "a privileged position in the family." Walton's proposal, however, is undermined by the fact that Joseph is clearly the privileged one in ch. 37, and Judah separates from the rest of his family at the start of ch. 38.

779 It can hardly go unnoticed that all these women are non-Israelites or linked to a non-Israelite, in the case of Bathsheba, and all are associated to differing degrees with sexual behavior that is inappropriate or could be perceived as inappropriate.

because you are his wife. So how could I do this immense evil, and how
could I sin against God?"

10 Although she spoke to Joseph day after day, he refused to go to bed
with her. 11 Now one day he went into the house to do his work, and
none of the household servants were there. 12 She grabbed him by his
garment and said, "Sleep with me!" But leaving his garment in her
hand, he escaped and ran outside. 13 When she saw that he had left
his garment with her and had run outside, 14 she called her household
servants. "Look," she said to them, "my husband brought a Hebrew
man to make fools of us. He came to me so he could sleep with me, and
I screamed as loud as I could. 15 When he heard me screaming for help,
he left his garment beside me and ran outside."

16 She put Joseph's garment beside her until his master came home. 17
Then she told him the same story: "The Hebrew slave you brought to
us came to make a fool of me, 18 but when I screamed for help, he left
his garment beside me and ran outside."

19 When his master heard the story his wife told him—"These are the
things your slave did to me"—he was furious 20 and had him thrown
into prison, where the king's prisoners were confined. So Joseph was
there in prison.

21 But the Lord was with Joseph and extended kindness to him. He grant-
ed him favor with the prison warden. 22 The warden put all the prisoners
who were in the prison under Joseph's authority, and he was respon-
sible for everything that was done there. 23 The warden did not bother
with anything under Joseph's authority, because the Lord was with him,
and the Lord made everything that he did successful.

Context

By reminding the reader of what was said in 37:36, the narrator picks up the story of Joseph's enslavement in Egypt. Chronologically, the narrative jumps back in time, for the births of Perez and Zerah recorded in chapter 38 probably took place over twenty years after Joseph arrived in Egypt.[780] In spite of Joseph's tragic misfortune, the narrator emphasizes that YHWH is with him (v. 2). Joseph's success is attributed to YHWH who through Joseph blesses Potiphar's household. By associating Joseph with blessing, the narrator recalls how God's blessing is linked to the unique lineage traced in Genesis (see Biblical and Theological Themes §2). Joseph brings prosperity to Potiphar's house, but events take an unexpected twist when

[780] U. Cassuto, "The Story of Tamar and Judah," in *Biblical and Oriental Studies* (Jerusalem: Magnes, 1973), 29–40.

Joseph is vindictively accused of sexual impropriety by Potiphar's wife.[781] This results in further misfortune for Joseph, but once again the narrator highlights that YHWH is with him (v. 21).[782] Joseph's transition from slave to prisoner might suggest that YHWH is not watching over him; however, the ongoing story will bring about a surprising reversal of fortune.

Comments

39:1. By echoing closely 37:36, this verse continues the story of Joseph after the digression concerning Judah and Tamar in chapter 38.

39:2–6a. The divine name YHWH, translated "Lord," is used sparingly throughout 37:2–50:26, but verses 2–6 mention YHWH five times.[783] This concentration is highly significant, emphasizing that despite his brothers' actions Joseph has an important role to play in the outworking of God's redemptive plan. YHWH's providential care of Joseph makes him a source of divine blessing to others, recalling how Genesis associates the divine blessing of the nations with both Abraham and the unique line of offspring descended from him (e.g., 12:3; 18:18; 22:17; 30:27; see Biblical and Theological Themes §2). Joseph's rapid rise to the most senior position of responsibility in Potiphar's household is remarkable, especially given his youth; Joseph is probably in his early twenties at this stage of his life.

39:6b–9. While verses 3–6a emphasize Potiphar's positive relationship with Joseph, verses 6b–9 concentrate on how Potiphar's wife is sexually attracted to Joseph. For this reason, the narrator informs the reader that "Joseph was well-built and handsome" (v. 6), words that echo closely what is said concerning his mother Rachel (29:17) and his great-grandmother Sarah (12:11). Potiphar's wife's short, seductive instruction to Joseph to sleep with her (v. 7)—two words in Hebrew—contrasts sharply with Joseph's words of

---

[781] Various scholars note interesting parallels between the actions of Tamar in ch. 38 and those of Potiphar's wife in ch. 39. See Shemaryahu Talmon, "The Presentation of Synchroneity and Simultaneity in Biblical Narrative," *Scripta Hierosolymitana* 27 (1978): 18n21; McKeown, *Genesis*, 167.

[782] Alter, *Genesis*, 224, views this chapter as having been carefully structured with the opening frame (vv. 1–6) being balanced by a similar closing frame (vv. 20–23); he notes the repetition of the phrases: "God was with Joseph," "granted him favor in the eyes of," "placed in Joseph's hands," "all," "succeed" (228). Waltke and Fredricks, *Genesis*, 516, adopt a somewhat different approach, analyzing chs. 39–40 into two parallel scenes (39:1–20; 39:21–40:23), each having a pattern of exaltation and humiliation. In Waltke and Fredricks's approach, 39:1–6 is paralleled by 39:20–23.

[783] Apart from three occurrences in 39:21, 23, which mirror the present passage, there is only one occurrence of the divine name "Lord" in chs. 40–50, in 49:18.

rebuff—35 words in Hebrew.[784] Joseph's refusal to "sleep" with Potiphar's wife distinguishes him from his brothers Reuben and Judah, who seek sexual gratification (35:22; 38:15–18). Joseph refuses to betray Potiphar by committing adultery, which he considers to be a "sin against God" (cf. Ps 51:4a).

39:10–15. Potiphar's wife is persistent and attempts by force to compel Joseph to sleep with her. Leaving his garment behind, Joseph flees. Potiphar's wife then uses Joseph's clothing to persuade those within her household to side with her. For a second time a garment belonging to Joseph is used to deceive others (cf. 37:31–33). Adeptly, Potiphar's wife manipulates those around her by implying that (a) her husband is guilty of bringing Joseph into the household, (b) Joseph is a foreigner, and (c) Joseph's actions are against the entire household. The Hebrew verb translated "make a fool of," is used elsewhere in Genesis with the sense "mocking" (21:9) and "caressing" (26:8).

39:16–19. Potiphar's wife skillfully exploits the situation by implying that her husband is partially to blame by having brought Joseph into the household; speaking to her husband, she intentionally refers to Joseph as "your slave" (v. 19). On this occasion, she emphasizes how the "Hebrew slave" has made a "fool of me" (contrast "fool of us" in v. 14).

39:20–23. As captain of the guards (v. 1), Potiphar is well placed to have Joseph imprisoned. Verses 21–23 recall what is said in verses 2–6, with the narrator emphasizing that YHWH was with Joseph (vv. 21, 23; cf. v. 2; Acts 7:9). Even in prison, Joseph is treated favorably and given authority over everything that happens there. By mentioning that the prison houses "the king's prisoners" the narrative anticipates later developments in the story.

Bridge

The report of Joseph's time in Egypt emphasizes how God is with him, enabling him to use his gifts of administration and management to help others. The theme of Joseph's bringing God's blessing to others (v. 5) is significant; divine blessing is intimately tied to the members of the unique line of descendants. Yet, Joseph's personal integrity and righteousness is challenged by his master's wife, who is willing to commit adultery. With good reason, the book of Proverbs warns of the danger posed by yielding to the seductive words of the adulteress (Prov 6:23–29; 7:1–27; cf. 9:13–18 where Folly is compared to an adulteress). Joseph's refusal to betray his

---

[784] Alter, *Genesis*, 225, observes how the dialogue is skillfully used to disclose the fundamentally different natures of the two characters.

master engenders opposition (cf. Gen 37:2). Those who adhere to God's moral standards are likely to be persecuted by the wicked (Matt 5:10).

D. Joseph and the King's Prisoners (40:1–23)

1 After this, the king of Egypt's cupbearer and baker offended their
master, the king of Egypt. 2 Pharaoh was angry with his two officers,
the chief cupbearer and the chief baker, 3 and put them in custody in
the house of the captain of the guards in the prison where Joseph was
confined. 4 The captain of the guards assigned Joseph to them as their
personal attendant, and they were in custody for some time.

5 The king of Egypt's cupbearer and baker, who were confined in the
prison, each had a dream. Both had a dream on the same night, and
each dream had its own meaning. 6 When Joseph came to them in the
morning, he saw that they looked distraught. 7 So he asked Pharaoh's
officers who were in custody with him in his master's house, "Why do
you look so sad today?"

8 "We had dreams," they said to him, "but there is no one to interpret them."

Then Joseph said to them, "Don't interpretations belong to God? Tell
me your dreams."

9 So the chief cupbearer told his dream to Joseph: "In my dream there
was a vine in front of me. 10 On the vine were three branches. As soon
as it budded, its blossoms came out and its clusters ripened into grapes.
11 Pharaoh's cup was in my hand, and I took the grapes, squeezed them
into Pharaoh's cup, and placed the cup in Pharaoh's hand."

12 "This is its interpretation," Joseph said to him. "The three branches
are three days. 13 In just three days Pharaoh will lift your head and
restore you to your position. You will put Pharaoh's cup in his hand
the way you used to when you were his cupbearer. 14 But when all goes
well for you, remember that I was with you. Please show kindness to
me by mentioning me to Pharaoh, and get me out of this prison. 15 For
I was kidnapped from the land of the Hebrews, and even here I have
done nothing that they should put me in the dungeon."

16 When the chief baker saw that the interpretation was positive, he said
to Joseph, "I also had a dream. Three baskets of white bread were on
my head. 17 In the top basket were all sorts of baked goods for Pharaoh,
but the birds were eating them out of the basket on my head."

18 "This is its interpretation," Joseph replied. "The three baskets are
three days. 19 In just three days Pharaoh will lift your head—from

off you—and hang you on a tree. Then the birds will eat the flesh from your body."

[20] On the third day, which was Pharaoh's birthday, he gave a feast for all
his servants. He elevated the chief cupbearer and the chief baker among
his servants. [21] Pharaoh restored the chief cupbearer to his position as
cupbearer, and he placed the cup in Pharaoh's hand. [22] But Pharaoh
hanged the chief baker, just as Joseph had explained to them. [23] Yet the
chief cupbearer did not remember Joseph; he forgot him.

Context

Joseph's time in prison brings him into contact with two men who hold positions close to the king of Egypt. Both, however, are imprisoned for having offended the king. Joseph's ability to interpret correctly their dreams prepares the way for him to be summoned later to interpret Pharaoh's dreams (41:9–36).

Comments

40:1–4. Joseph encounters two important royal officials, who have displeased the king of Egypt. Their standing as officials within the royal court appears to be similar to that of Potiphar. The "captain of the guards," who appoints Joseph to serve the chief cupbearer and the chief baker, could be Potiphar (cf. 37:36; 39:1) or an official of similar status. As Joseph served Potiphar (39:4), he now serves the imprisoned royal officials (v. 4).

40:5–8. Dreams were often considered by ancients to be a medium of divine revelation. Due to their imprisonment, the royal officials have no access to sorcerer-priests or wise men, who might have provided an interpretation of their dreams (cf. 41:8). Joseph's question, "Don't interpretations belong to God?" (40:8) is a further indication of his own personal devotion to God and his belief in God's presence with him.

40:9–19. The dreams of the imprisoned officials correspond to each man's occupation within the royal court. While their duties differ, their dreams share common features. The similarities in the dreams suggest that they have some special significance. As corresponding dreams, they recall Joseph's own pair of dreams in 37:5–11. Although Joseph predicts a positive outcome for the cupbearer, the opposite is true for the chief baker. Both outcomes, however, are linked by a common idiom that is repeated in verses 13 and 19 (cf. v. 20): "Pharaoh will lift up your head." For the cupbearer, this idiom implies restoration to his position of responsibility in the royal household; for the chief baker, the additional words "from off you" (v. 19) imply that he will be executed, possibly by decapitation, after which his body will be impaled on a stake.

After interpreting the first dream, Joseph asks the cupbearer to remember him before Pharaoh (vv. 14–15). In doing so, Joseph underlines his innocence, recalling how he was wrongly taken from "the land of the Hebrews" and how he was imprisoned unjustly in Egypt. Joseph's request that the cupbearer should show him חֶסֶד (*ḥesed*, "kindness") recalls how God has shown Joseph חֶסֶד (*ḥesed*, "kindness") (39:21).

40:20–23. As Joseph predicted, both dreams are fulfilled. The heads of both men are "lifted up" (v. 20; cf. vv. 13, 19), with the cupbearer being restored to Pharaoh's court and the chief baker being executed. The timing of this coincides with Pharaoh's "birthday," which probably refers to the anniversary of his ascension and coronation to the throne.[785] Despite Joseph's request (v. 14), the cupbearer forgets him.

Bridge

Joseph uses his God-given ability to interpret the dreams of the chief cupbearer and chief baker. This is a further indication that God is with him. Although Joseph's social status has changed from being a cherished son, loved by his father, to being a slave in a foreign prison, God has not abandoned him. Moreover, God has gifted him with the ability to interpret dreams. Joseph's special abilities recall how God gives a variety of grace-gifts to individuals for the benefit of others (Rom 12:3–8; 1 Cor 12:4–31; 1 Pet 4:10–11).

E. Joseph Interprets Pharaoh's Dream (41:1–57)

> [1] Two years later Pharaoh had a dream: He was standing beside the Nile,
> [2] when seven healthy-looking, well-fed cows came up from the Nile and
> began to graze among the reeds. [3] After them, seven other cows, sickly
> and thin, came up from the Nile and stood beside those cows along the
> bank of the Nile. [4] The sickly, thin cows ate the healthy, well-fed cows.
> Then Pharaoh woke up. [5] He fell asleep and dreamed a second time:
> Seven heads of grain, plump and ripe, came up on one stalk. [6] After them,
> seven heads of grain, thin and scorched by the east wind, sprouted up. [7]
> The thin heads of grain swallowed up the seven plump, ripe ones. Then
> Pharaoh woke up, and it was only a dream.

[785] Hoffmeier, *Israel in Egypt*, 89–91.

8 When morning came, he was troubled, so he summoned all the magi-
cians of Egypt and all its wise men. Pharaoh told them his dreams, but
no one could interpret them for him.

9 Then the chief cupbearer said to Pharaoh, "Today I remember my
faults. 10 Pharaoh had been angry with his servants, and he put me and
the chief baker in the custody of the captain of the guard. 11 He and I had
dreams on the same night; each dream had its own meaning. 12 Now a
young Hebrew, a slave of the captain of the guards, was with us there.
We told him our dreams, he interpreted our dreams for us, and each had
its own interpretation. 13 It turned out just the way he interpreted them
to us: I was restored to my position, and the other man was hanged."
14 Then Pharaoh sent for Joseph, and they quickly brought him from
the dungeon. He shaved, changed his clothes, and went to Pharaoh.

15 Pharaoh said to Joseph, "I have had a dream, and no one can interpret
it. But I have heard it said about you that you can hear a dream and
interpret it."

16 "I am not able to," Joseph answered Pharaoh. "It is God who will give
Pharaoh a favorable answer."

17 So Pharaoh said to Joseph: "In my dream I was standing on the bank
of the Nile, 18 when seven well-fed, healthy-looking cows came up from
the Nile and grazed among the reeds. 19 After them, seven other cows—
weak, very sickly, and thin—came up. I've never seen such sickly ones
as these in all the land of Egypt. 20 Then the thin, sickly cows ate the first
seven well-fed cows. 21 When they had devoured them, you could not
tell that they had devoured them; their appearance was as bad as it had
been before. Then I woke up. 22 In my dream I also saw seven heads of
grain, full and good, coming up on one stalk. 23 After them, seven heads
of grain—withered, thin, and scorched by the east wind—sprouted up.
24 The thin heads of grain swallowed the seven good ones. I told this to
the magicians, but no one can tell me what it means."

25 Then Joseph said to Pharaoh, "Pharaoh's dreams mean the same thing.
God has revealed to Pharaoh what he is about to do. 26 The seven good
cows are seven years, and the seven good heads are seven years. The
dreams mean the same thing. 27 The seven thin, sickly cows that came
up after them are seven years, and the seven worthless, scorched heads
of grain are seven years of famine.

28 "It is just as I told Pharaoh: God has shown Pharaoh what he is about
to do. 29 Seven years of great abundance are coming throughout the
land of Egypt. 30 After them, seven years of famine will take place, and
all the abundance in the land of Egypt will be forgotten. The famine will
devastate the land. 31 The abundance in the land will not be remembered
because of the famine that follows it, for the famine will be very severe.

[32] Since the dream was given twice to Pharaoh, it means that the matter
has been determined by God, and he will carry it out soon.

[33] "So now, let Pharaoh look for a discerning and wise man and set him
over the land of Egypt. [34] Let Pharaoh do this: Let him appoint overseers
over the land and take a fifth of the harvest of the land of Egypt during
the seven years of abundance. [35] Let them gather all the excess food
during these good years that are coming. Under Pharaoh's authority,
store the grain in the cities, so they may preserve it as food. [36] The food
will be a reserve for the land during the seven years of famine that will
take place in the land of Egypt. Then the country will not be wiped out
by the famine."

[37] The proposal pleased Pharaoh and all his servants, [38] and he said to
them, "Can we find anyone like this, a man who has God's spirit in him?"
[39] So Pharaoh said to Joseph, "Since God has made all this known to you,
there is no one as discerning and wise as you are. [40] You will be over my
house, and all my people will obey your commands. Only I, as king, will
be greater than you." [41] Pharaoh also said to Joseph, "See, I am placing
you over all the land of Egypt." [42] Pharaoh removed his signet ring
from his hand and put it on Joseph's hand, clothed him with fine linen
garments, and placed a gold chain around his neck. [43] He had Joseph
ride in his second chariot, and servants called out before him, "Make
way!" So he placed him over all the land of Egypt. [44] Pharaoh said to
Joseph, "I am Pharaoh and no one will be able to raise his hand or foot in
all the land of Egypt without your permission." [45] Pharaoh gave Joseph
the name Zaphenath-paneah and gave him a wife, Asenath daughter of
Potiphera, priest at On. And Joseph went throughout the land of Egypt.

[46] Joseph was thirty years old when he entered the service of Pharaoh
king of Egypt. Joseph left Pharaoh's presence and traveled throughout
the land of Egypt.

[47] During the seven years of abundance the land produced outstanding
harvests. [48] Joseph gathered all the excess food in the land of Egypt
during the seven years and put it in the cities. He put the food in every
city from the fields around it. [49] So Joseph stored up grain in such abun-
dance—like the sand of the sea—that he stopped measuring it because
it was beyond measure.

[50] Two sons were born to Joseph before the years of famine arrived.
Asenath daughter of Potiphera, priest at On, bore them to him. [51] Joseph
named the firstborn Manasseh and said, "God has made me forget all
my hardship and my whole family." [52] And the second son he named
Ephraim and said, "God has made me fruitful in the land of my affliction."

[53] Then the seven years of abundance in the land of Egypt came to an
end, [54] and the seven years of famine began, just as Joseph had said.
There was famine in every land, but in the whole land of Egypt there

> was food. 55 When the whole land of Egypt was stricken with famine,
> the people cried out to Pharaoh for food. Pharaoh told all Egypt, "Go
> to Joseph and do whatever he tells you." 56 Now the famine had spread
> across the whole region, so Joseph opened all the storehouses and sold
> grain to the Egyptians, for the famine was severe in the land of Egypt.
> 57 Every land came to Joseph in Egypt to buy grain, for the famine was
> severe in every land.

Context

After about thirteen years as a slave in Egypt, including at least two years in prison, Joseph experiences an extraordinary change in fortune, becoming Egypt's second most powerful person. Only Pharaoh, the king of Egypt, surpasses Joseph in rank. This chapter describes the events surrounding Joseph's meteoric promotion, based on his ability to interpret Pharaoh's two dreams. Joseph, however, readily acknowledges that his ability to do this comes from God. Pharaoh's dreams also set the scene for subsequent events, when famine will cause Joseph's brothers to travel to Egypt in search of food. Joseph's unexpected promotion leads to the fulfilment of his own dreams, when his brothers bow before him (42:6; 43:26; 44:14).

Comments

41:1–7. Joseph is now thirty years old (see 41:46), having been in Egypt about thirteen years (see 37:2). The imagery in Pharaoh's dreams reflects strongly the Egyptian context. The shared pattern of healthy cows and heads of grain being swallowed up by thin cows and heads of grain conveys powerfully the idea that both dreams communicate the same message. This is the third time within chapters 37–41 that dreams have been paired together. Understandably, Pharaoh is anxious to have his dreams explained.

41:8–13. Initially Pharaoh seeks an explanation from those who would normally be called upon to interpret dreams. The reference to "magicians" may create a misunderstanding for modern readers, who normally associate this term with illusionists. According to Hoffmeier, the Hebrew noun חַרְטֹם (*ḥarṭōm*, "magician") perhaps best translated "sorcerer-priest," is derived from an abbreviation of an Egyptian expression meaning "chief lector priest."[786] Religious practices in ancient Egypt often involved magic performed by priests, who studied ritual and magical texts

786 Hoffmeier, *Israel in Egypt*, 88.

in libraries attached to temples. In the story of the Israelites' exodus from Egypt, Moses and Aaron confront "sorcerer-priests," who are capable of replicating some of the miraculous signs sent by God (Exod 7:11, 22; 8:7). When the "magicians" and "wise men" fail to interpret Pharaoh's dreams, the chief cupbearer recalls how Joseph was able to interpret dreams accurately.

41:14–16. With a minimum of narrative detail, the narrative describes how Joseph is brought into Pharaoh's presence. The brief description of Joseph's shaving and changing clothes is sufficient to capture the significance of his transfer from prison to Pharaoh's court. The Hebrew term בּוֹר (*bôr*), translated here "dungeon," recalls the pit into which Joseph was thrown by his brothers (37:23–24). At that time, he was stripped of his robe. Now he is taken from a "pit" and clothed. This marks the beginning of a momentous reversal in Joseph's fortune. By denying that he has the innate ability to interpret dreams, Joseph rightfully acknowledges God as the ultimate interpreter of dreams. In doing so, he confirms what has been implicit in chapters 37–41: the recorded dreams are a source of divine revelation and as such are trustworthy (cf. 41:25, 28, 32).

41:17–24. By repeating almost word-for-word the narrator's initial report of Pharaoh's dreams (vv. 1–8), Pharaoh's account underscores their importance. Their fulfilment will be a vital element in the ongoing story. However, as Sternberg observes, "What distinguishes the narrator's telling from Pharaoh's retelling is not so much that the king interpolates subjective or emotive expressions ('I have never seen their likes for poorness,' 'no one would have known that they had consumed them') as that he unmakes the symmetry that the narrator has taken such care to make. Within each vision, Pharaoh blurs the contrast between the units; and within the pair of visions as a whole, he blurs the similarity."[787]

41:25–36. Joseph emphasizes, through repetition in verses 25, 28, and 32, how God has revealed to Pharaoh what will happen in the coming years. The duplication in the dreams underlines that God has determined to do this. After explaining the dreams, Joseph proceeds to instruct Pharaoh regarding what should now be done to prepare for the years of famine. To oversee the preparations, Pharaoh should appoint a "discerning and

[787] Sternberg, *Poetics of Biblical Narrative*, 399.

wise man."[788] The person needs to be more than merely intelligent; he needs to be perceptive and skilled in relating to other people.

41:37–45. By interpreting Pharaoh's dreams, Joseph sets himself above all the sorcerer-priests and wise men of Egypt (cf. v. 8). Pharaoh recognizes this, readily acknowledging that Joseph's ability comes from God. While the Hebrew expression רוּחַ אֱלֹהִים (*rûaḥ ʾĕlōhîm*) could be translated "spirit of gods," the same expression appears in Exodus 31:3 and 35:31 in connection with Bezalel, who is specifically equipped by God to supervise the construction of the portable sanctuary. Elsewhere in the Old Testament, the Spirit of YHWH empowers individuals as leaders (e.g., Judg 3:10; 11:29; 13:25; 1 Sam 10:6; 16:13).[789]

From being an imprisoned slave, Joseph is given responsibility over Pharaoh's "house" (v. 40). This marks the third time in Egypt that Joseph has been given this type of duty (cf. 39:4, 22–23). In the light of this, it is noteworthy that when Jacob bestows on Joseph the status of firstborn, Joseph is given authority over Jacob's household, which includes his brothers. Joseph's ability to govern others is very much in keeping with the idea that the unique line of offspring traced in Genesis should continue through Joseph.

Fittingly, Joseph is appropriately clothed by Pharaoh, recalling how his father had also given him an ornate cloak.[790] Pharaoh's clothing of Joseph stands in contrast to the actions of his brothers and Potiphar's wife, all of whom disrobed Joseph. As Joseph travels about on Pharaoh's second chariot, the people call out אַבְרֵךְ (*ʾabrēk*), a term that possibly has the sense "kneel down" or "make way" in Egyptian, but interestingly the word resembles the Hebrew term for "blessing." As Joseph brought blessing to Potiphar's house (39:5), so now he brings blessing to Pharaoh's domain.

---

[788] Various scholars have discussed links between the Joseph Story and other parts of the Old Testament that are often categorized as Wisdom Literature (e.g., the book of Proverbs). For assessments, see George W. Coats, "The Joseph Story and Ancient Wisdom: A Reappraisal," *CBQ* 35 (1973): 285–97; Michael V. Fox, "Joseph and Wisdom," in Evans, Lohr, and Petersen, *The Book of Genesis*, 231–62.

[789] Wilf Hildebrandt, *An Old Testament Theology of the Spirit of God* (Peabody: Hendrickson, 1995), 104–50.

[790] Walton, *Genesis*, 691, notes that the "Egyptianization" of Joseph will disguise him from his brothers. Furthermore, although Pharaoh gives Joseph "office, status, privilege, name, wife—everything," "Joseph is not first and foremost Pharaoh's man, but God's man. ... He is God's instrument of salvation."

By way of integrating Joseph into Egyptian society, Pharaoh names him Zaphenath-paneah and gives him an Egyptian wife. Scholars consider the various names listed in verse 45 to be Egyptian in character.[791] Unlike some names in Genesis, these Egyptian names do not appear to contribute thematically to the story, although they provide evidence that the narrative is based on actual events.

41:46–52. During the seven years of abundance, Joseph stores up grain in Egypt. These years also witness the birth of two sons to Joseph. Both are given Hebrew names that appropriately reflect Joseph's new circumstances. Manasseh means "he who makes [someone] forget." Joseph indicates that the birth of Manasseh enables him to forget his past hardships that began with his brothers' selling him into slavery, but it is somewhat ironic that the act of naming implicitly recalls what has happened. The name Ephraim is linked to the Hebrew verb פָּרָה (*pārāh* "to be fruitful"). The mention of fruitfulness recalls how this is a recurring motif in the divine promises given to the patriarchs (17:6, 20; 26:22; 28:3; 35:11; cf. 48:4); it is also a prominent motif in Jacob's deathbed blessing of Joseph (49:22).[792] Joseph associates both names with what God has done for him. By doing so, the naming of the boys suggests that Joseph has not abandoned his Hebrew roots, despite being married to the daughter of an Egyptian priest.

41:53–57. As predicted, famine strikes Egypt and the surrounding region, including Palestine where Joseph's family reside. There is no compelling reason to suppose, as some modern commentators do,[793] that by selling grain to the Egyptians Joseph exploited the situation. Joseph may well have bought the grain from the people in the first place; verses 48–49 say nothing about how Joseph acquired the grain. There is no evidence to confirm that Joseph acquired the grain without payment.

Bridge

As the story develops, God's providential care of Joseph continues to be evident. Despite being victimized by his brothers and Potiphar's wife and being forgotten by the chief cupbearer, Joseph is not abandoned by God. For his part, Joseph remains faithful to God and willingly serves others

---

[791] See Hoffmeier, *Israel in Egypt*, 84–87; Kitchen, *On the Reliability of the Old Testament*, 345–47.

[792] See Biblical and Theological Themes §3.

[793] E.g., Provan, *Discovering Genesis*, 180–81.

with absolute integrity regardless of his unjust circumstances. After thirteen years of enslavement, God enables Joseph to interpret Pharaoh's dreams, opening the door for him to become responsible for the future well-being of Egypt and its neighboring nations. At the age of thirty, Joseph rises from obscurity to be given authority over Pharaoh's house, which includes governing the whole land of Egypt. As famine strikes the nations, Joseph is a source of divine blessing, giving life to many people (47:25; 50:20). In doing so, he partially fulfills the divine promise of blessing to the nations given to Abraham and his offspring (12:3; 22:18; see Biblical and Theological Themes §2), and he foreshadows a greater descendant of Abraham who, as a servant, will bring eternal life to the world (John 3:16–17; Phil. 2:7–8; see Biblical and Theological Themes §1).

F. Joseph's Brothers' First Journey to Egypt (42:1–38)

> 1 When Jacob learned that there was grain in Egypt, he said to his sons,
> "Why do you keep looking at each other? 2 Listen," he went on, "I have
> heard there is grain in Egypt. Go down there and buy some for us so that
> we will live and not die." 3 So ten of Joseph's brothers went down to buy
> grain from Egypt. 4 But Jacob did not send Joseph's brother Benjamin
> with his brothers, for he thought, "Something might happen to him."
>
> 5 The sons of Israel were among those who came to buy grain, for the famine
> was in the land of Canaan. 6 Joseph was in charge of the country; he sold
> grain to all its people. His brothers came and bowed down before him with
> their faces to the ground. 7 When Joseph saw his brothers, he recognized
> them, but he treated them like strangers and spoke harshly to them.
>
> "Where do you come from?" he asked.
>
> "From the land of Canaan to buy food," they replied.
>
> 8 Although Joseph recognized his brothers, they did not recognize him.
> 9 Joseph remembered his dreams about them and said to them, "You
> are spies. You have come to see the weakness of the land."
>
> 10 "No, my lord. Your servants have come to buy food," they said. 11 "We
> are all sons of one man. We are honest; your servants are not spies."
>
> 12 "No," he said to them. "You have come to see the weakness of the
> land."
>
> 13 But they replied, "We, your servants, were twelve brothers, the sons
> of one man in the land of Canaan. The youngest is now with our father,
> and one is no longer living."

14 Then Joseph said to them, "I have spoken: 'You are spies!' 15 This is
how you will be tested: As surely as Pharaoh lives, you will not leave
this place unless your youngest brother comes here. 16 Send one from
among you to get your brother. The rest of you will be imprisoned so
that your words can be tested to see if they are true. If they are not,
then as surely as Pharaoh lives, you are spies!" 17 So Joseph imprisoned
them together for three days.

18 On the third day Joseph said to them, "I fear God—do this and you will
live. 19 If you are honest, let one of you be confined to the guardhouse,
while the rest of you go and take grain to relieve the hunger of your
households. 20 Bring your youngest brother to me so that your words
can be confirmed; then you won't die." And they consented to this.

21 Then they said to each other, "Obviously, we are being punished
for what we did to our brother. We saw his deep distress when he
pleaded with us, but we would not listen. That is why this trouble
has come to us."

22 But Reuben replied: "Didn't I tell you not to harm the boy? But you
wouldn't listen. Now we must account for his blood!"

23 They did not realize that Joseph understood them, since there was
an interpreter between them. 24 He turned away from them and wept.
When he turned back and spoke to them, he took Simeon from them
and had him bound before their eyes. 25 Joseph then gave orders to fill
their containers with grain, return each man's silver to his sack, and
give them provisions for their journey. This order was carried out. 26
They loaded the grain on their donkeys and left there.

27 At the place where they lodged for the night, one of them opened
his sack to get feed for his donkey, and he saw his silver there at the
top of his bag. 28 He said to his brothers, "My silver has been returned!
It's here in my bag." Their hearts sank. Trembling, they turned to one
another and said, "What is this that God has done to us?" 29 When they
reached their father Jacob in the land of Canaan, they told him all that
had happened to them: 30 "The man who is the lord of the country spoke
harshly to us and accused us of spying on the country. 31 But we told
him: We are honest and not spies. 32 We were twelve brothers, sons
of the same father. One is no longer living, and the youngest is now
with our father in the land of Canaan. 33 The man who is the lord of the
country said to us, 'This is how I will know if you are honest: Leave one
brother with me, take food to relieve the hunger of your households,
and go. 34 Bring back your youngest brother to me, and I will know that
you are not spies but honest men. I will then give your brother back to
you, and you can trade in the country.'"

[35] As they began emptying their sacks, there in each man's sack was his bag of silver! When they and their father saw their bags of silver, they were afraid.

[36] Their father Jacob said to them, "It's me that you make childless. Joseph is gone, and Simeon is gone. Now you want to take Benjamin. Everything happens to me!"

[37] Then Reuben said to his father, "You can kill my two sons if I don't bring him back to you. Put him in my care, and I will return him to you."

[38] But Jacob answered, "My son will not go down with you, for his brother is dead and he alone is left. If any-thing happens to him on your journey, you will bring my gray hairs down to Sheol in sorrow."

Context

When the famine impacts Joseph's family in Canaan, Jacob sends his ten oldest sons to Egypt to buy food. Once there they encounter Joseph, who recognizes them. Joseph, however, hides his identity from them. Joseph's reluctance to make himself known is highly understandable given his brothers' previous readiness to sell him into slavery. Reconciliation cannot be rushed. Through a slow process involving testing, Joseph seeks to discern if his brothers' hearts have changed for the better.

Comments

42:1–5. The final verse of chapter 41 prepares the reader for a change of scene. The narrative moves to Canaan, where Jacob's family is threatened by famine. Not surprisingly, Jacob instructs his sons to go to Egypt. However, he keeps at home Benjamin, Joseph's younger brother, fearing that something terrible might happen to him. Jacob's protection of Benjamin plays an important role in the developing story.

42:6–17. Alongside others, Joseph's brothers come to buy grain in Egypt. Their journey brings them into contact with Joseph. However, about twenty years have passed, and Joseph has become fully integrated into Egyptian society. Consequently, the brothers have no reason to suppose that this high-ranking Egyptian official is their younger brother. Joseph, on the other hand, recognizes them. When they bow before him (v. 6) he recalls his dreams (v. 9; cf. 37:5–11), which are now being fulfilled, partially at least.

Joseph's interaction with his brothers, conducted through an interpreter (cf. v. 23), is deliberately designed to disclose something of their inner disposition.[794] By accusing them of being "spies" (vv. 9, 12, 14), Joseph begins a dialogue that concentrates on the identity of the brothers. He knows them and is well placed to judge if they are honest. Will their responses be truthful? Kruschwitz helpfully observes that Joseph's deception of his brothers is reminiscent of how Tamar deceives Judah; as the victim of deception, Joseph "initiates his own act of counter-deception."[795]

The brothers' situation is perilous; if found guilty of being spies, they will be executed. As the brothers seek to convince Joseph that they are not spies, they gradually disclose details about their family, briefly mentioning the existence of Benjamin and alluding to the death of Joseph (v. 13). For the reader, knowing who Joseph is, the dialogue contains several ironies. The brothers say to Joseph, "We are all sons of one man." They then briefly add that "one is no longer living" (v. 13). Joseph knows otherwise. Eventually, to test the brothers' honesty, Joseph challenges them to bring their youngest brother to Egypt.[796] Only one of them, however, will return to Canaan; all the rest will remain in prison (vv. 15–16).

42:18–26. Addressing his brothers three days later, Joseph intentionally juxtaposes a statement about fearing God with the instruction "do this and you will live."[797] Joseph's words possibly prompt the brothers to consider their present situation as divine punishment for their past cold-blooded treatment of Joseph. As Clifford observes, "Sending back *all* the brothers except one to the father recreates in a single stroke the brothers' long-ago crime. It signals to them that their

---

[794] The Hebrew root נכר (*nkr*) comes four times in vv. 7–8, three times in the *hiphil*, meaning "to recognize" and once in the *hithpael*, translated here "treated them like strangers." The *hithpael* form of נכר (*nkr*) is rare in the Old Testament, occurring elsewhere in 1 Kgs 14:5–6 and Prov 20:11. On the basis of how נכר (*nkr*) is used in Prov 20:11, it is possible that in 42:7 it conveys the idea that Joseph looks to disclose who they are. In other words, v. 7 says that Joseph recognized them and then proceeded to have them disclose who they were. This would account for how he questions them (v. 7) and why he subsequently accuses them of being spies with evil intent (v. 9).

[795] Kruschwitz, "Type-Scene Connection," 394.

[796] Kruschwitz, "Type-Scene Connection," 404, remarks:

When he says, "Your words will be tested [whether there is] truth with you" (Gen. 42.16), his brothers hear only of a trial of their purpose in coming to Egypt. Now acting as ironist, however, Joseph speaks of more than a mere test of his brothers' motivation for coming to Egypt. His words insinuate rather, on a deeper level, his concern with the overall integrity of the brothers whose deceptive betrayal had sent him to Egypt in the first place.

[797] The Hebrew text has the more striking order "do this and you will live" followed by "I fear God."

present distress is *divine* vengeance because of the perfect symmetry between crime and punishment: one brother who does not return to his father for one brother who does not return to his father."[798] According to Alter, verses 21–22 are a "remarkable instance of withheld narrative exposition";[799] only now do we learn of Joseph's plea for help and Reuben's warning against harming Joseph. These details move Joseph to tears, possibly because the brothers are now beginning to acknowledge the terrible consequences of their actions (v. 24). In the light of Reuben's comment about saving Joseph, Joseph possibly chooses Simeon to remain in Egypt. Next to Reuben, Simeon is the second eldest brother, and he would have had a major say when Joseph was sold into slavery.[800] The use of donkeys as beasts of burden is in keeping with the historical setting.[801]

42:27–28. When the money appears inexplicably at the top of a sack, the brothers' guilty consciences fill them with considerable apprehension. They are gradually sensitized to the idea that God may be punishing them for their past actions.

42:29–38. Returning to Jacob, the brothers give an accurate report of what happened in Egypt (vv. 30–34). They then discover to their shock that the money given by them to buy the grain is present in their sacks. This unexpected occurrence fills them and Jacob with fear. It is an ominous sign. Jacob's response (v. 36) strongly implies that his sons are responsible for the misfortune that has come upon his family. Reuben's callous offer does little to help the situation; Jacob is unlikely to entrust Benjamin to someone who is willing to kill his own two sons. Strikingly, Jacob's words strongly imply that only Rachel's two sons really matter to him (cf. 44:27); he makes no reference to his other sons.[802] Jacob's fearful comments about possibly losing Benjamin (v. 38) recall what he said when he was deceived into believing that Joseph was dead (37:35). On the meaning of Sheol, see Comments on 37:35.

---

798 Clifford, "Genesis 37–50," 223.

799 Alter, *Genesis*, 247.

800 Waltke and Fredricks, *Genesis*, 548, notes that Simon has a "reputation for being cruel."

801 A nineteenth-century BC tomb painting from near Beni Hasan in Egypt has an illustration of donkeys being used for transportation between Egypt and Canaan.

802 Chapman, *The House of the Mother*, 46, observes, "The loss of Simeon occasions no words of mourning and no plan of rescue."

Bridge

Joseph could have identified himself to his estranged brothers. However, he chooses rather to discern if they have any sense of regret regarding their callous treatment of him some twenty years previously.[803] If there is to be a genuine reconciliation, Joseph must witness sincere remorse on the part of his brothers. By accusing them of being spies, Joseph can gauge their honesty. Previously they sold him into slavery for money. Joseph now returns their money so that later he will be able to assess if greed still has the upper hand. By unusual means, Joseph pricks the consciences of his brothers, perhaps to remind them that God is the "judge of all the earth," a truth that they would have known from their great-grandfather Abraham (18:25). Ultimately, we shall all stand in judgment before Jesus Christ (Matt 25:31–46; Rev 20:11–15).

The brothers' guilty consciences trouble them. As McKeown observes, "The debilitating effect of guilt is clearly illustrated in the stories. Every time the brothers face a crisis, it is not faith that comes into play but guilt. Guilt destroys their ability to face life's crises positively, and they helplessly wallow in feelings of self-pity and regret."[804] Only atonement brought by Jesus Christ cleanses guilty consciences (Heb 9:14; 10:22).

G. Joseph's Brothers Return to Egypt (43:1–34)

> [1] Now the famine in the land was severe. [2] When they had used up the
> grain they had brought back from Egypt, their father said to them, "Go
> back and buy us a little food."
>
> [3] But Judah said to him, "The man specifically warned us: 'You will not
> see me again unless your brother is with you.' [4] If you will send our
> brother with us, we will go down and buy food for you. [5] But if you will

---

[803] Some scholars interpret Joseph's failure to reveal himself to his brothers as evidence of a serious flaw, claiming that he cold-heartedly causes additional agony to his father. See, for example, Mark A. O'Brien, "The Contribution of Judah's Speech, Genesis 44:18–34, to the Characterization of Joseph," *CBQ* 59 (1997): 439–40, who describes Joseph as a "deeply flawed character" (440). Cf. Hyun Chin Paul Kim, "Reading the Joseph Story (Genesis 37–50) as a Diaspora Narrative," *CBQ* 75 (2013): 226. However, Everett Fox, *Genesis and Exodus: A New English Rendition* (New York: Schocken, 1991), 185, answers well this criticism of Joseph:

> Some have questioned the morality of Yosef's actions, seeing that the aged Yaakov might well have died while the test was progressing, without ever finding out that Yosef had survived. But that is not the point of the story. What it is trying to teach (among other things) is a lesson about crime and repentance. Only by recreating something of the original situation—the brothers are again in control of the life and death of a son of Rahel—can Yosef be sure that they have changed. Once the brothers pass the test, life and covenant can then continue.

[804] McKeown, *Genesis*, 173.

not send him, we will not go, for the man said to us, 'You will not see
me again unless your brother is with you.'"

6 "Why have you caused me so much trouble?" Israel asked. "Why did
you tell the man that you had another brother?"

7 They answered, "The man kept asking about us and our family: 'Is
your father still alive? Do you have another brother?' And we an-
swered him accordingly. How could we know that he would say, 'Bring
your brother here'?"

8 Then Judah said to his father Israel, "Send the boy with me. We will
be on our way so that we may live and not die—neither we, nor you,
nor our dependents. 9 I will be responsible for him. You can hold me
personally accountable! If I do not bring him back to you and set him
before you, I will be guilty before you forever. 10 If we had not delayed,
we could have come back twice by now."

11 Then their father Israel said to them, "If it must be so, then do this:
Put some of the best products of the land in your packs and take them
down to the man as a gift—a little balsam and a little honey, aromatic
gum and resin, pistachios and almonds. 12 Take twice as much silver
with you. Return the silver that was returned to you in the top of your
bags. Perhaps it was a mistake. 13 Take your brother also, and go back
at once to the man. 14 May God Almighty cause the man to be merciful
to you so that he will release your other brother and Benjamin to you.
As for me, if I am deprived of my sons, then I am deprived."

15 The men took this gift, double the amount of silver, and Benjamin.
They immediately went down to Egypt and stood before Joseph.

16 When Joseph saw Benjamin with them, he said to his steward, "Take
the men to my house. Slaughter an animal and prepare it, for they will
eat with me at noon." 17 The man did as Joseph had said and brought
them to Joseph's house.

18 But the men were afraid because they were taken to Joseph's house.
They said, "We have been brought here because of the silver that was
returned in our bags the first time. They intend to overpower us, seize
us, make us slaves, and take our donkeys." 19 So they approached Jo-
seph's steward and spoke to him at the doorway of the house.

20 They said, "My lord, we really did come down here the first time only
to buy food. 21 When we came to the place where we lodged for the night
and opened our bags of grain, each one's silver was at the top of his
bag! It was the full amount of our silver, and we have brought it back
with us. 22 We have brought additional silver with us to buy food. We
don't know who put our silver in the bags."

> 23 Then the steward said, "May you be well. Don't be afraid. Your God and the God of your father must have put treasure in your bags. I received your silver." Then he brought Simeon out to them. 24 The steward brought the men into Joseph's house, gave them water to wash their feet, and got feed for their donkeys. 25 Since the men had heard that they were going to eat a meal there, they prepared their gift for Joseph's arrival at noon. 26 When Joseph came home, they brought him the gift they had carried into the house, and they bowed to the ground before him.
>
> 27 He asked if they were well, and he said, "How is your elderly father that you told me about? Is he still alive?"
>
> 28 They answered, "Your servant our father is well. He is still alive." And they knelt low and paid homage to him.
>
> 29 When he looked up and saw his brother Benjamin, his mother's son, he asked, "Is this your youngest brother that you told me about?" Then he said, "May God be gracious to you, my son." 30 Joseph hurried out because he was overcome with emotion for his brother, and he was about to weep. He went into an inner room and wept there. 31 Then he washed his face and came out. Regaining his composure, he said, "Serve the meal."
>
> 32 They served him by himself, his brothers by themselves, and the Egyptians who were eating with him by themselves, because Egyptians could not eat with Hebrews, since that is detestable to them. 33 They were seated before him in order by age, from the firstborn to the youngest. The men looked at each other in astonishment. 34 Portions were served to them from Joseph's table, and Benjamin's portion was five times larger than any of theirs. They drank and became drunk with Joseph.

Context

The predicted seven-year famine continues to impact Jacob's family. Lack of food forces the patriarch to permit his sons to return to Egypt with Benjamin. To their surprise, they are hosted for a meal in Joseph's house. This sets the scene for Joseph to accuse Benjamin of theft, an event that leads to the disclosure of Joseph's true identity to his brothers.

Comments

43:1–14. When the grain runs out, Jacob has little choice but to send his sons back to Egypt. Judah, however, reminds his father that they cannot return to Egypt without Benjamin. Judah underlined this condition by repeating what the "man" said: "You will not see me again unless your brother is with you" (vv. 3–4). Judah takes the lead in speaking to Jacob. Although he has not been named since chapter 38, from this point on

Judah becomes spokesman for the brothers (cf. 43:8–10; 44:14–34; 46:28; cf. 37:26). And in marked contrast to Reuben, who offers his sons (42:37), Judah pledges his own life for Benjamin's safety (v. 9).[805] This is the first indication that Judah has undergone an inner transformation;[806] further evidence will follow. Jacob also instructs his sons to take back the money that was returned to them,[807] as well as other gifts for the "man."[808] Jacob's reference to God in verse 14 reveals that he still believes in God's sovereignty despite all that has happened; his prayer will be answered. On the designation "God Almighty," see 17:1; cf. 28:3; 35:11. Whereas Jacob names Benjamin in verse 14, he merely refers to Simeon as "your other brother." A subtle distinction is made here between the sons of Jacob's favorite wife, Rachel, and his other sons

43:15–28. On seeing Benjamin with his brothers, Joseph arranges for them to be taken to his house for a midday meal. Not surprisingly, the brothers are apprehensive. Remembering the money that was returned to them in their sacks, they fear that they will be enslaved, the very thing that they did to Joseph for money (v. 18). Joseph's steward speaks reassuringly to them. When Joseph appears, his brothers bow before him, on this occasion twice (vv. 26, 28; cf. 42:6). Joseph's first dream is fulfilled (see 37:6–7).

43:29–34. After over twenty years, Joseph's reunion with Benjamin is charged with emotion, but Joseph hides this. Joseph's prayer that God should show grace to Benjamin recalls how God gave Joseph grace/

---

[805] See James S. Ackerman, "Joseph, Judah, and Jacob," in *Literary Interpretations of Biblical Narratives*, ed. Kenneth R. R. Gros Louis, with James S. Ackerman, vol. 2 (Nashville: Abingdon, 1982), 105; Waltke and Fredricks, *Genesis*, 544. Judah Kraut, "The Literary Roles of Reuben and Judah in Genesis Narratives: A 'Reflection Complex,' " *JSOT* 43 (2019): 205–27, suggests that the actions of both Reuben and Judah recall previous episodes in Jacob's life.

[806] Clifford, "Genesis 37–50," 221, emphasizes that ch. 38 explains "the extraordinary change in Judah's character." Kim, "Reading the Joseph Story," 235, captures well how Judah changes: "The episodes skillfully insinuate how Judah has been transformed: from the cold-blooded mastermind (compared to Reuben), to the mortified but empathetic father-in-law (through Tamar), and finally to the authentically caring, compassionate brother (toward Benjamin)."

[807] Alter, *Genesis*, 254, contends that the brothers were to take with them three times the original amount of money: double what they took first time, plus the money that was returned. He discounts the view of Sarna, *Genesis*, 276, that the total amount taken back was only double the original. Verse 15, which mentions double the money, would appear to undermine Alter's interpretation.

[808] The list of items in v. 11 includes those mentioned in 37:25: aromatic gum, balsam, and resin.

favor in the eyes of others (see 39:4, 21). For a second time, the narrator records that Joseph wept (v. 30; cf. 42:24; see also 45:2, 14–15; 46:29; 50:17); the fuller description given here, compared to 42:24, reveals how Benjamin's presence impacts Joseph emotionally.[809] Joseph avoids recognition by eating separately, which due to existing cultural expectations does not raise any suspicion. The brothers, however, are surprised when they are seated by age; this is yet another occurrence that unsettles them. By concluding this episode with a reference to Joseph's drinking with his brothers the possibility is created for charging Benjamin with the theft of Joseph's silver cup.

Bridge

The unfolding events begin to show Joseph's brothers in a more positive light. Importantly, Judah takes responsibility for the safe return of Benjamin, a commitment that will be tested in the next episode. The brothers also demonstrate integrity by offering back the money that was found in their sacks. Joseph, however, continues the process of assessing his brothers' inner disposition. Even the presence of Benjamin does not cause him to disclose his identity. One further test awaits the brothers. The true nature of people is revealed by their fruit (Matt 7:16).

By doing unorthodox things, like putting the money into his brothers' sacks, Joseph causes them to reflect on the supernatural. Even the comment of his steward underlines this point: "Your God and the God of your father must have put treasure in your bags" (Gen 43:23). As Waltke observes, "Joseph's privileged knowledge and his control over his brothers functions as a microcosm of God's omniscience and his ultimate control over all."[810]

H. Benjamin Is Accused of Stealing (44:1–34)

> [1] Joseph commanded his steward, "Fill the men's bags with as much food as they can carry, and put each one's silver at the top of his bag. [2] Put my cup, the silver one, at the top of the youngest one's bag, along with the silver for his grain." So he did as Joseph told him.
>
> [3] At morning light, the men were sent off with their donkeys. [4] They had not gone very far from the city when Joseph said to his steward,

[809] Philip Y. Yoo, "Why Does Joseph Wash His Face?," *JSOT* 38 (2013): 3–14, suggests that the brief comment about Joseph's face-washing is designed to reflect the Egyptian background of the Joseph story.

[810] Waltke and Fredricks, *Genesis*, 557.

"Get up. Pursue the men, and when you overtake them, say to them,
'Why have you repaid evil for good? [5] Isn't this the cup that my master
drinks from and uses for divination? What you have done is wrong!'"

[6] When he overtook them, he said these words to them. [7] They said
to him, "Why does my lord say these things? Your servants could
not possibly do such a thing. [8] We even brought back to you from the
land of Canaan the silver we found at the top of our bags. How could
we steal silver or gold from your master's house? [9] If it is found with
one of us, your servants, he must die, and the rest of us will become
my lord's slaves."

[10] The steward replied, "What you have said is right, but only the one
who is found to have it will be my slave, and the rest of you will be
blameless."[11] So each one quickly lowered his sack to the ground and
opened it. [12] The steward searched, beginning with the oldest and
ending with the youngest, and the cup was found in Benjamin's sack.
[13] Then they tore their clothes, and each one loaded his donkey and
returned to the city.

[14] When Judah and his brothers reached Joseph's house, he was still
there. They fell to the ground before him. [15] "What is this you have
done?" Joseph said to them. "Didn't you know that a man like me could
uncover the truth by divination?"

[16] "What can we say to my lord?" Judah replied. "How can we plead?
How can we justify ourselves? God has exposed your servants' iniquity.
We are now my lord's slaves—both we and the one in whose possession
the cup was found."

[17] Then Joseph said, "I swear that I will not do this. The man in whose
possession the cup was found will be my slave. The rest of you can go
in peace to your father."

[18] But Judah approached him and said, "My lord, please let your servant
speak personally to my lord. Do not be angry with your servant, for you
are like Pharaoh. [19] My lord asked his servants, 'Do you have a father
or a brother?' [20] and we answered my lord, 'We have an elderly father
and a younger brother, the child of his old age. The boy's brother is
dead. He is the only one of his mother's sons left, and his father loves
him.' [21] Then you said to your servants, 'Bring him to me so that I can
see him.' [22] But we said to my lord, 'The boy cannot leave his father.
If he were to leave, his father would die.' [23] Then you said to your
servants, 'If your younger brother does not come down with you, you
will not see me again.'

[24] "This is what happened when we went back to your servant my fa-
ther: We reported to him the words of my lord. [25] But our father said,
'Go again, and buy us a little food.' [26] We told him, 'We cannot go down
unless our younger brother goes with us. If our younger brother isn't

> with us, we cannot see the man.' [27] Your servant my father said to us, 'You know that my wife bore me two sons. [28] One is gone from me—I said he must have been torn to pieces—and I have never seen him again. [29] If you also take this one from me and anything happens to him, you will bring my gray hairs down to Sheol in sorrow.'
>
> [30] "So if I come to your servant my father and the boy is not with us—his life is wrapped up with the boy's life—[31] when he sees that the boy is not with us, he will die. Then your servants will have brought the gray hairs of your servant our father down to Sheol in sorrow. [32] Your servant became accountable to my father for the boy, saying, 'If I do not return him to you, I will always bear the guilt for sinning against you, my father.' [33] Now please let your servant remain here as my lord's slave, in place of the boy. Let him go back with his brothers. [34] For how can I go back to my father without the boy? I could not bear to see the grief that would overwhelm my father."

Context

This chapter "carries forward the great theme of moral restitution,"[811] as Joseph, through one final test, deliberately manipulates circumstances to discern the inner disposition of his brothers. By accusing Benjamin of stealing his silver cup, Joseph presents his older brothers with a stark choice. This takes them back to a choice they made years previously with Joseph. Like Joseph, Benjamin is Jacob's favorite son. When the opportunity presents itself, will his brothers leave Benjamin as a slave in Egypt and return to their father in Canaan? Will they repeat the past, seeing this as an opportunity to rid themselves of their youngest brother, as they did with Joseph? Or, will they decide otherwise, demonstrating a radical change of heart? In this context, Judah's lengthy speech (44:18–34) contrasts sharply with his earlier plea to his brothers to sell Joseph into slavery (37:26–27).

Comments

44:1–2. For a second time, Joseph directs that each man's money should be placed in his sack. In addition, his silver cup is to be put into Benjamin's sack. As Alter notes, "Joseph's scheme ... is to make the brothers feel they are trapped in a network of uncanny circumstances they can neither control nor explain."[812]

---

[811] Alter, *Genesis*, 261.

[812] Alter, *Genesis*, 259.

44:3–13. Although the steward is instructed to say that Joseph uses his silver cup for divination (v. 5), this comment is part of a clever ruse designed to reveal the inner character of Joseph's older brothers.[813] Joseph intentionally wants them to believe that he has supernatural insight (v. 15). Quite naturally, believing themselves to be entirely innocent of theft, the brothers deny the steward's charge. They even propose that anyone guilty should be put to death and the rest enslaved (v. 9). However, Joseph's steward is less severe, stating that only the guilty person should be enslaved (v. 10). As Joseph intended, the silver cup is found in Benjamin's sack. Devastated by this discovery, the brothers tear their clothing in mourning, as Jacob had previously done over Joseph (37:34).

44:14–17. At Joseph's house, Judah takes the initiative. When challenged by Joseph, Judah makes no attempt to argue that the brothers are innocent. Rather, he bluntly states, "God has exposed your servant's iniquity," concluding that all the brothers should become Joseph's slaves (v. 16).[814] Judah's words suggest that the brothers have interpreted all that has happened to them as God's way of punishing them for having malevolently sold Joseph into slavery. On the basis of moral equivalence, their punishment—being enslaved—matches their crime—enslaving Joseph. Yet, in a masterful stroke, Joseph presents his older brothers with an opportunity to escape slavery, but this comes at the cost of leaving Benjamin behind (v. 17). By returning the grain money to his brothers, Joseph tests their integrity. Will they put this money and their own personal safety before their younger brother? While the circumstances are different, once again the brothers are confronted with the choice of condemning a younger brother to a life of slavery.[815] Previously, Judah callously advocated selling Joseph into slavery (37:26–27). How will he and the other brothers respond on this occasion? After years apart Joseph is now well placed to judge if his brothers have changed.

44:18–34. Deliberately, Judah looks to speak personally to Joseph. In one of the longest human speeches in Genesis, he selflessly offers to

---

[813] Waltke and Fredricks, *Genesis*, 566, write, "Joseph's description of his goblet to his brothers as a divining cup is as much a part of the ruse as putting the silver in their sacks and accusing them of burglary."

[814] Kruschwitz, "Type-Scene Connection," 407, finds in Judah's remark about "justify ourselves" (v. 16) an echo of his remark that "she [Tamar] is more in the right than I" in 38:26. The same Hebrew root צדק (*ṣdq*) comes in both verses.

[815] Sternberg, *Poetics of Biblical Narrative*, 294, describes this as "role-duplication."

take the place of Benjamin. Speaking deferentially, he petitions Joseph to let Benjamin return to Canaan to prevent his father Jacob from suffering the loss of another son.[816] Previously, Judah had cared little about how his father would be devastated by the loss of his favorite son. Years later, Judah's entire speech "is at once a moving piece of rhetoric and the expression of a profound inner change."[817] Even within the speech, as Sternberg notes, Judah moves from speaking about the brothers collectively to taking personal responsibility for what has happened.[818]

> With this speech, it is clear that Joseph has managed in the course of Genesis 42–44 to bring all of his brothers to a degree of understanding of their guilt and of Joseph's own experience at their hands, and that he has to some extent changed them. Where there was once only jealousy, hatred and a willingness to sacrifice a favoured younger brother (a son of Rachel) in order to be rid of an annoyance, now we see a desire to sacrifice on behalf of a favoured younger brother (and another son of Rachel) in order to save him from slavery, and to save their father from further grief.[819]

Understandably, Wenham describes Judah's speech as one of most moving examples of "true contrition and repentance ... to be found in Scripture."[820]

Bridge

The brothers stand on the verge of being reconciled to Joseph due to Judah's passionate and sacrificial offer to become a slave in Egypt in place of Benjamin. The transformation evident in Judah can best be explained by what happens to him in chapter 38, when he is confronted by his own hypocrisy in judging Tamar (38:26).[821] Judah's change of heart undoubtedly explains why he receives an exceptionally positive blessing from his father Jacob, associating his lineage with future royalty (49:8–12; see

---

[816] Waltke and Fredricks, *Genesis*, 561, note that "father" is a key word in Judah's speech, coming fourteen times. This underlines Judah's concern for the well-being of his father.

[817] Alter, *Genesis*, 265. Alter observes, "Judah, who conceived the plan of selling Joseph into slavery, now comes around 180 degrees by offering himself as a slave in place of Benjamin."

[818] Sternberg, *Poetics of Biblical Narrative*, 308. Cf. Alter, *Art of Biblical Narrative*, 174–75.

[819] Provan, *Discovering Genesis*, 183.

[820] Wenham, *Genesis 16-50*, 431. On the persuasive nature of Judah's speech, see Jan Joosten, "Biblical Rhetoric as Illustrated by Judah's Speech in Genesis 44.18–34," *JSOT* 41 (2016): 15–30; Edward J. Bridge, "Polite Rhetoric: Judah's Plea to Joseph in Genesis 44.18–34," *JSOT* 43 (2019): 571–87.

[821] Kim, "Reading the Joseph Story," 233. Cf. Noble, "Esau, Tamar, and Joseph," 241–42.

Biblical and Theological Themes §1).[822] Perceptively, Waltke and Fredricks observe that Judah "stands as a witness to God's amazing grace. He fails as a son of the covenant (i.e., intermarrying with Canaanites and behaving like them), as a father (i.e., his sons are wicked), and as a father-in-law (i.e., deceiving Tamar). Even the worst sort of sinners can enter heaven by God's redemptive grace."[823] Judah's transformation comes through repentance, which in his case is evident when the "slave-trader" offers to become a "slave" in order to set his youngest brother free. As the first person mentioned in Scripture to offer his life for another, Judah's willingness to sacrifice his life for that of his brother prefigures Christ's willingness to give his life as "a ransom for many" (Mark 10:45).

I. Joseph Reveals His Identity (45:1–28)

> 1 Joseph could no longer keep his composure in front of all his attendants, so he called out, "Send everyone away from me!" No one was with him when he revealed his identity to his brothers. 2 But he wept so loudly that the Egyptians heard it, and also Pharaoh's household heard it. 3 Joseph said to his brothers, "I am Joseph! Is my father still living?" But they could not answer him because they were terrified in his presence.
>
> 4 Then Joseph said to his brothers, "Please, come near me," and they came near. "I am Joseph, your brother," he said, "the one you sold into Egypt. 5 And now don't be grieved or angry with yourselves for selling me here, because God sent me ahead of you to preserve life. 6 For the famine has been in the land these two years, and there will be five more years without plowing or harvesting. 7 God sent me ahead of you to establish you as a remnant within the land and to keep you alive by a great deliverance. 8 Therefore it was not you who sent me here, but God. He has made me a father to Pharaoh, lord of his entire household, and ruler over all the land of Egypt.
>
> 9 "Return quickly to my father and say to him, 'This is what your son Joseph says: "God has made me lord of all Egypt. Come down to me without delay. 10 You can settle in the land of Goshen and be near me—you, your children, and your grandchildren, your flocks, your herds, and all you have. 11 There I will sustain you, for there will be five more years of famine. Otherwise, you, your household, and everything you have will become destitute."' 12 Look! Your eyes and the eyes of my brother

[822] Waltke and Fredricks, *Genesis*, 567, comment, "Jacob will crown Judah with kingship because he demonstrates that he has become fit to rule according to God's ideal of kingship that the king serves the people, not vice versa."

[823] Waltke and Fredricks, *Genesis*, 515.

> Benjamin can see that I'm the one speaking to you. 13 Tell my father about all my glory in Egypt and about all you have seen. And bring my father here quickly."
>
> 14 Then Joseph threw his arms around his brother Benjamin and wept, and Benjamin wept on his shoulder.
>
> 15 Joseph kissed each of his brothers as he wept, and afterward his brothers talked with him.
>
> 16 When the news reached Pharaoh's palace, "Joseph's brothers have come," Pharaoh and his servants were pleased. 17 Pharaoh said to Joseph, "Tell your brothers, 'Do this: Load your animals and go on back to the land of Canaan. 18 Get your father and your families, and come back to me. I will give you the best of the land of Egypt, and you can eat from the richness of the land.' 19 You are also commanded to tell them, 'Do this: Take wagons from the land of Egypt for your dependents and your wives and bring your father here. 20 Do not be concerned about your belongings, for the best of all the land of Egypt is yours.'"
>
> 21 The sons of Israel did this. Joseph gave them wagons as Pharaoh had commanded, and he gave them provisions for the journey. 22 He gave each of the brothers changes of clothes, but he gave Benjamin three hundred pieces of silver and five changes of clothes. 23 He sent his father the following: ten donkeys carrying the best products of Egypt and ten female donkeys carrying grain, food, and provisions for his father on the journey. 24 So Joseph sent his brothers on their way, and as they were leaving, he said to them, "Don't argue on the way."
>
> 25 So they went up from Egypt and came to their father Jacob in the land of Canaan. 26 They said, "Joseph is still alive, and he is ruler over all the land of Egypt!" Jacob was stunned, for he did not believe them. 27 But when they told Jacob all that Joseph had said to them, and when he saw the wagons that Joseph had sent to transport him, the spirit of their father Jacob revived.
>
> 28 Then Israel said, "Enough! My son Joseph is still alive. I will go to see him before I die."

Context

Over time, Joseph has astutely manipulated circumstances to discover the inner character of his brothers. This culminates in Benjamin being condemned to be a slave in Egypt for stealing Joseph's silver cup. At this point, Judah intervenes voluntarily, offering to sacrifice his own future so that Benjamin may go free (44:18–34). The scene is set for an emotional reunion. The story of Joseph's separation from his brothers comes full circle as Joseph is reconciled to them. After years of being apart, their reunion is a highly sensitive occasion, especially given that his brothers had callously sold Joseph into slavery in Egypt.

Comments

45:1–15. Judah's self-sacrificing speech (44:18–34) is too much for his estranged brother; it shatters Joseph's composure and his emotions overcome him. For a third time, Joseph weeps, but on this occasion he does so openly in front of his brothers (cf. 42:24; 43:30), revealing his true feelings to them.[824] To the utter bewilderment of his unsuspecting brothers, Joseph reveals his identity.[825] Understandably, they are filled with terror, expecting Joseph justifiably to take revenge by enslaving them.

With the utmost magnanimity, Joseph looks to reassure his shocked brothers. To reduce their sense of guilt Joseph attributes all that has happened to the providential activity of God. Twice he affirms that God sent him ahead of his brothers to preserve their lives (v. 5, 7; cf. v. 8). Not only did God send Joseph to Egypt, but he also made him "father to Pharaoh, lord of his entire household, and ruler over all the land of Egypt" (v. 8). Joseph's exalted status not only fulfills his dreams (37:5–11) but also more importantly links back to how God promised Abraham that he would be the "father of many nations" (17:4–5). As their "father," Abraham was to be a source of blessing to the nations. This role continues through the unique patriline descended from Abraham, as the firstborn members of the lineage mediate God's blessing to others (see Biblical and Theological Themes §2). Through providing food during the years of famine, Joseph is the epitome in Genesis of someone mediating blessing to the nations. With five years of famine still to come, Joseph encourages his brothers to bring Jacob and the rest of their family down to Egypt. The location of Goshen (v. 10) is uncertain. It was probably a region in the eastern delta of the River Nile, near the city of Rowaty, which in subsequent centuries was known as Avaris, then Peru-Nefer and eventually Pi-Ramesses (see 47:11) prior to its demise.

45:16–28. With Pharaoh's full support Joseph sends his brothers back to Canaan laden with gifts. Joseph's gift of clothing to his brothers is a

---

[824] Waltke and Fredricks, *Genesis*, 562.

[825] Observing a parallel with the events recorded in Gen 38 involving Tamar and Judah, Kruschwitz, "Type-Scene Connection," 395, remarks, "In a progression of events comparable to those of Genesis 38, the antagonists come to recognize the true identity of the person whom they wronged only after they have come to acknowledge their own wrongdoing."

fitting symbol of their reconciliation in the light of how they de-robed Joseph to deceive their father (37:31–33).[826] His generosity not only underlines the genuineness of the reconciliation that has taken place but also provides evidence to support the brothers' testimony that Joseph is alive. Joseph's gift of 300 shekels of silver to Benjamin is extravagant, especially when we recall that his brothers sold him as a slave for twenty shekels (37:28). Understandably, Jacob is reluctant to believe that his favorite son is not only alive but also ruler of all Egypt.

Bridge

The Joseph story is a remarkable account of reconciliation in practice. Joseph's wisdom is underlined by his ability to transform alienation into affection, potential fratricide into genuine fraternal love. Through the circumstances created by Joseph, his brothers are made to confront their past actions. When their remorse becomes evident, the process of reconciliation moves forward.

Although Joseph's behavior could be interpreted as callous and uncaring, causing his brothers considerable discomfort and extending unnecessarily his father's grief, his actions result in the fractured family being fully reconciled. Whereas the deceit of Joseph's older brothers was designed to cover up their wrongdoing and brought profound grief to their father, Joseph's ruse causes his brothers to confess their crime, resulting in the restoration of family unity. Joseph has the opportunity and the motive to reap revenge, but Genesis says nothing to suggest that he has a vindictive spirit. As Waltke and Fredricks observe,

> When Judah gives impeachable evidence of the brothers' complete transformation, with intense emotions of love Joseph gives up his power over them by revealing his identity (45:1–3). He weeps over his brothers and kisses them (45:14–15). Right to the end of the book, he refuses to hold a grudge against his brothers; he forgives them and speaks kindly to them (50:21). Neither the narrator nor the protagonists at any time suggest that Joseph is angry with them or motivated by revenge.[827]

In response to his brothers, Joseph willingly attributes all that has happened to him to divine providence. This strongly held conviction enables

---

[826] Sarna, *Genesis*, 284.

[827] Waltke and Fredricks, *Genesis*, 544.

him to resist the temptation to bear a grudge against his brothers. In spite of his unjust circumstances, Joseph remains convinced that his life is in God's hands. His attitude recalls the apostle Paul's remarks in Romans 8:38–39:

> [38] For I am persuaded that not even death or life,
> angels or rulers,
> things present or things to come, hostile powers,
> [39] height or depth, or any other created thing
> will have the power to separate us
> from the love of God that is in Christ Jesus our Lord!

J. Jacob's Family Relocates to Egypt (46:1–27)

> [1] Israel set out with all that he had and came to Beer-sheba, and he of-
> fered sacrifices to the God of his father Isaac. [2] That night God spoke to
> Israel in a vision: "Jacob, Jacob!" he said. And Jacob replied, "Here I am."
>
> [3] God said, "I am God, the God of your father. Do not be afraid to go
> down to Egypt, for I will make you into a great nation there. [4] I will go
> down with you to Egypt, and I will also bring you back. Joseph will close
> your eyes when you die."
>
> [5] Jacob left Beer-sheba. The sons of Israel took their father Jacob in the
> wagons Pharaoh had sent to carry him, along with their dependents
> and their wives. [6] They also took their cattle and possessions they had
> acquired in the land of Canaan. Then Jacob and all his offspring with
> him came to Egypt. [7] His sons and grandsons, his daughters and grand-
> daughters, indeed all his offspring, he brought with him to Egypt.
>
> [8] These are the names of the sons of Israel who came to Egypt—Jacob
> and his sons:
>
> Jacob's firstborn: Reuben.
> [9] Reuben's sons: Hanoch, Pallu, Hezron, and Carmi.
> [10] Simeon's sons: Jemuel, Jamin, Ohad, Jachin, Zohar, and
> Shaul, the son of a Canaanite woman.
> [11] Levi's sons: Gershon, Kohath, and Merari.
> [12] Judah's sons: Er, Onan, Shelah, Perez, and Zerah; but Er
> and Onan died in the land of Canaan.
> The sons of Perez were Hezron and Hamul.
> [13] Issachar's sons: Tola, Puvah, Jashub, and Shimron.
> [14] Zebulun's sons: Sered, Elon, and Jahleel.

> [15] These were Leah's sons born to Jacob in Paddan-aram, as
> well as his daughter Dinah. The total number of persons:
> thirty-three.
> [16] Gad's sons: Ziphion, Haggi, Shuni, Ezbon, Eri, Arodi,
> and Areli.
> [17] Asher's sons: Imnah, Ishvah, Ishvi, Beriah, and their
> sister Serah.
> Beriah's sons were Heber and Malchiel.
> [18] These were the sons of Zilpah—whom Laban gave to his
> daughter Leah—that she bore to Jacob: sixteen persons.
> [19] The sons of Jacob's wife Rachel: Joseph and Benjamin.
> [20] Manasseh and Ephraim were born to Joseph in the land
> of Egypt. They were born to him by Asenath daughter of
> Potiphera, a priest at On.
> [21] Benjamin's sons: Bela, Becher, Ashbel, Gera, Naaman,
> Ehi, Rosh, Muppim, Huppim, and Ard. [22] These were
> Rachel's sons who were born to Jacob: fourteen persons.
> [23] Dan's son: Hushim.
> [24] Naphtali's sons: Jahzeel, Guni, Jezer, and Shillem.
> [25] These were the sons of Bilhah, whom Laban gave to his
> daughter Rachel. She bore to Jacob: seven persons.
> [26] The total number of persons belonging to Jacob—his
> direct descendants, not including the wives of Jacob's
> sons—who came to Egypt: sixty-six.
> [27] And Joseph's sons who were born to him in Egypt: two
> persons.
> All those of Jacob's household who came to Egypt: seventy
> persons.

Context

After learning that Joseph is alive (45:26–28), Jacob takes his entire family to Egypt, where he is reunited with Joseph. Jacob's journey brings him to Beer-sheba, where in a vision God reassures him that he will be present with him in Egypt. This intervention is significant, because previously God had prohibited Jacob's father, Isaac, from going to Egypt during a time of famine (26:1–6). The relocation of Jacob's whole family to Egypt sets the scene for all that is recorded in the book of Exodus.

Comments

46:1–4. Jacob's southward journey to Egypt brings him to Beer-sheba, where his grandfather Abraham and his father Isaac both resided for a limited period (21:22–34; 26:23–33). At Beer-sheba YHWH had appeared to Isaac at night, promising to be with him and to bless him (26:23–24). In response, Isaac had built an altar there. Possibly returning to this altar at Beersheba, Jacob offers sacrifices to the God of his father Isaac. God then speaks to Jacob at night, assuring him that he need not be fearful about going to Egypt. This assurance is important because previously during a time of famine God had stopped Isaac from going to Egypt (26:1–6). Jacob may also have recalled with apprehension Abraham's troubled visit to Egypt during another famine (12:10–20). The promise that Jacob will become a great nation (v. 3) recalls God's promise to Abraham (12:2), subsequently repeated to Jacob (28:13–15; see Biblical and Theological Themes §1). God's words assure Jacob that his journey to Egypt will not hinder the fulfilment of the divine promises to the patriarchs, especially those involving the gift of Canaan to Abraham's descendants. Like Abraham and Isaac, Jacob will be buried in Canaan (see 49:29–50:13). The Hebrew text of verse 4 does not imply that the promises are listed in chronological order of fulfilment. We learn later that Jacob dies in Egypt, where Joseph closes his eyes (49:33), and after this Jacob's body is transported to Canaan for burial (see 50:1–14).

46:5–27. Reassured by God, Jacob leaves Beer-sheba, taking his entire family and all their possessions to Egypt.[828] Although 46:7 mentions Jacob's sons, daughters, grandsons, and granddaughters, the heading in verse 8 refers specifically to the "names of the sons of Israel."[829] The list of sons, grandsons, and great-grandsons is arranged by the names of Jacob's wives: Leah (vv. 8–15), Zilpah (vv. 16–18), Rachel (vv. 19–22), and Bilhah (vv. 23–25). A summary comes in verses 26–27. Two women, Dinah and Serah, are also named.

Some of the numbers associated with the lists of names present minor difficulties, perhaps due to scribal errors in the process of transmission.[830] Verses 8–15 list six sons, one daughter, twenty-five grandsons, and two

---

[828] Brian O. Sigmon, "Shadowing Jacob's Journey: Gen 47:13–26 as a Sideshadow," *BibInt* 19 (2011): 454–70, notes that although Jacob's journey to Egypt involves a number of inherent dangers, the contents of Gen 46–47 confirm that Jacob's family maintains its distinctive identity and autonomy, preserving the patriarchal promises.

[829] The Hebrew phrase בְּנֵי־יִשְׂרָאֵל (*bĕnê-yiśrāʾēl*) often refers elsewhere to the "Israelites" as a people. In this context, however, it denotes Israel's sons.

[830] The listing of Jacob's descendant in vv. 8–27 differs in minor ways from that found in Num 26:5–50; see Hamilton, *Genesis: Chapters 18–50*, 599. Understanding the reasons for these differences is not straightforward, for different rationales may have played a part in the construction of the lists; see Walton, *Genesis*, 685.

great-grandsons, giving a total count of thirty-four. Yet, verse 15 gives a total of thirty-three. To reconcile the number of names with the total of thirty-three, Dinah, as the only daughter mentioned, could be omitted from the final count; this would leave the names of thirty-three males.[831] However, not all of those named traveled with Jacob to Egypt. Two of Jacob's grandsons, Er and Onan, died in Canaan (cf. 38:2–10) and for chronological reasons it is unlikely that Hezron and Hamul were born to Perez before he arrived in Egypt. Of the thirty-three males named, possibly only twenty-nine would have journeyed with Jacob to Egypt. This may explain why in verse 15, the Hebrew text preceding the number thirty-three mentions "his sons and his daughters."[832] As regards the sons associated with Zilpah, only fifteen males are named, but the total is given as sixteen.[833] The numbers given in verses 15, 18, 22, and 25, respectively thirty-three, sixteen, fourteen,[834] and seven add up to seventy.[835]

Verse 27 also states that all those belonging to Jacob's household numbered seventy, but this count probably includes Jacob himself, as well as Joseph and his sons Ephraim and Manasseh, who are already in Egypt.[836] If we take from this total, Jacob, Joseph, Ephraim, and Manasseh, the resulting number of sixty-six equates with what is given in verse 26 for those belonging to Jacob, who went with him to Egypt.

Bridge

The detailed list of the names of Jacob's "sons" underscores that his entire family migrates to Egypt. No one remains in Canaan. Although Jacob leaves the territory promised to Abraham and Isaac, God reveals that the divine promises associated with the patriarchs will still be fulfilled. Jacob's family will be in Egypt for several centuries before God brings them back to the land of Canaan. Their dramatic deliverance

---

[831] Alternatively, Ohad's name might possibly be removed from v. 10 as it does not appear in comparable lists in Num 26:12–13 and 1 Chr 4:24.

[832] The CSB translation reads: "The total numbers of persons."

[833] If Serah, the only woman in the list, is included, there are sixteen names in all.

[834] LXX reads eighteen, not fourteen.

[835] The total based on the LXX figures of thirty-three, sixteen, eighteen, and seven is seventy-four.

[836] The LXX makes the total number of Jacob's household seventy-five (cf. Acts 7:14). To reach this higher total, the LXX states in v. 27 that Joseph had seven male descendants; the MT says two.

from slavery in Egypt will provide an important paradigm for how God redeems his people from the power of evil.

K. Jacob's Family Settles in Egypt (46:28–47:12)

> [28] Now Jacob had sent Judah ahead of him to Joseph to prepare for his arrival at Goshen. When they came to the land of Goshen, [29] Joseph hitched the horses to his chariot and went up to Goshen to meet his father Israel.
>
> Joseph presented himself to him, threw his arms around him, and wept for a long time.
>
> Then Israel said to Joseph, "I'm ready to die now because I have seen your face and you are still alive!"
>
> Joseph said to his brothers and to his father's family, "I will go up and inform Pharaoh, telling him, 'My brothers and my father's family, who were in the land of Canaan, have come to me. [32] The men are shepherds; they also raise livestock. They have brought their flocks and herds and all that they have.' [33] When Pharaoh addresses you and asks, 'What is your occupation?' [34] you are to say, 'Your servants, both we and our fathers, have raised livestock from our youth until now.' Then you will be allowed to settle in the land of Goshen, since all shepherds are detestable to Egyptians."
>
> [47:1] So Joseph went and informed Pharaoh: "My father and my brothers, with their flocks and herds and all that they own, have come from the land of Canaan and are now in the land of Goshen."
>
> [2] He took five of his brothers and presented them to Pharaoh. [3] And Pharaoh asked his brothers, "What is your occupation?"
>
> They said to Pharaoh, "Your servants, both we and our fathers, are shepherds." [4] And they said to Pharaoh, "We have come to stay in the land for a while because there is no grazing land for your servants' sheep, since the famine in the land of Canaan has been severe. So now, please let your servants settle in the land of Goshen."
>
> [5] Then Pharaoh said to Joseph, "Now that your father and brothers have come to you, [6] the land of Egypt is open before you; settle your father and brothers in the best part of the land. They can live in the land of Goshen. If you know of any capable men among them, put them in charge of my livestock."
>
> [7] Joseph then brought his father Jacob and presented him to Pharaoh, and Jacob blessed Pharaoh. [8] Pharaoh said to Jacob, "How many years have you lived?"

> [9] Jacob said to Pharaoh, "My pilgrimage has lasted 130 years. My years have been few and hard, and they have not reached the years of my fathers during their pilgrimages." [10] So Jacob blessed Pharaoh and departed from Pharaoh's presence.
>
> [11] Then Joseph settled his father and brothers in the land of Egypt and gave them property in the best part of the land, the land of Rameses, as Pharaoh had commanded. [12] And Joseph provided his father, his brothers, and all his father's family with food for their dependents.

Context

After listing the names of the male descendants of Jacob (46:8–25) and noting that Jacob's household numbered seventy (46:26–27), the narrative describes Jacob's emotional reunion with Joseph in the land of Goshen. Joseph deliberately selects this region of Egypt for his family to prevent their assimilation into the nation of Egypt. This was a very real danger given the relatively small size of Jacob's family and Joseph had already experienced the pressure of such integration. Joseph wisely ensures that the Egyptian king grants their request to settle in Goshen with their livestock.

Comments

46:28–34. Having played a vital role in the reconciliation of Joseph to his brothers, Judah is trusted by his father Jacob to make arrangements with Joseph for the family's arrival in Egypt. Judah's leadership role at this stage will later be rewarded by a substantial blessing pronounced upon him by his father, Jacob (see 49:8–12). When Jacob arrives, Joseph swiftly sets off to meet him. After decades apart, their reunion is charged with great emotion.

Anticipating that his brothers will be summoned by Pharaoh, Joseph carefully advises them to ensure that Pharaoh will settle them in the land of Goshen, previously mentioned in 45:10. By emphasizing that they are pastoralists, the brothers will ensure for Jacob's family an independent existence in Egypt. Although Joseph states that "all shepherds are abhorrent to Egyptians" (v. 34), no specific reason is offered to explain this antipathy.[837] Possibly the flocks of seminomadic shepherds, espe-

---

[837] Gen 43:32 states that Egyptians did not eat with Hebrews, perhaps because of their dislike of pastoralists. Exod 8:26 mentions an Egyptian abhorrence of Hebrews based on their sacrificial practices.

cially foreigners, were viewed as a dangerous threat by Egyptians who cultivated crops in open fields without fences.

47:1–6. Having primed his brothers for their audience with Pharaoh, Joseph ensures that the Egyptian king grants them permission to settle in the land of Goshen. The precise location of Goshen is uncertain. It probably lay in the northeastern region of the Nile Delta in the area of Wadi Tumilat.[838] In the book of Exodus the Israelites are associated with the cities of Pithom and Rameses (Exod 1:11), the remains of which are located near to the modern-day locations of Tell el-Retaba and Qantir/Tell el-Dabᶜa respectively.[839]

47:7–10. The description of Jacob's encounter with Pharaoh is framed by two brief statements that record how Jacob blessed Pharaoh (vv. 7, 10). At one level, these may simply refer to how Jacob greeted and said farewell to Pharaoh. On another level, the idea of Jacob blessing Pharaoh recalls how the members of the patriline in Genesis are to be a source of blessing to others.[840] Pharaoh's positive attitude toward Joseph's family results in blessing (see Biblical and Theological Themes §2). The irony of Jacob being the one who blesses Pharaoh is captured by Waltke and Fredricks: "The Pharaoh is secure, royal, and condescending yet dependent on Jacob for blessing. Jacob, precarious and completely dependent on Pharaoh's goodwill, is the honorable benefactor of divine blessing."[841]

According to the chronology of Genesis, Jacob is 130 years old, and he will live a further seventeen years (cf. 47:28). Not surprisingly, Pharaoh enquires about Jacob's age. The patriarch's response is striking, especially his twofold use of the relatively rare term "pilgrimage" or "sojourn" (מָגוֹר, *māgôr*) to describe his life and that of his fathers (cf. 17:8; 28:4; 37:1; Exod 6:4). Jacob's use of מָגוֹר (*māgôr*) may have influenced the author of Hebrews when he remarks that the patriarchs "confessed that they were foreigners and temporary residents on the earth" (Heb 11:13). At this stage of his life, Jacob's 130 years does not match the 175 and 180 years of Abraham and Isaac respectively. Within Genesis, longevity is clearly a sign of divine favor.

838 Walton, *Genesis*, 686.

839 Alexander, *Exodus*, 47–48.

840 See Brian Alexander McKenzie, "Jacob's Blessing on Pharaoh: An Interpretation of Gen 46:31–47:26," *WTJ* 45 (1983): 393. Cf. Alter, *Genesis*, 280.

841 Waltke and Fredricks, *Genesis*, 586.

The name Rameses (v. 11) was the last name given to an ancient city located at Qantir/Tell el-Dab^{c}a. The city was abandoned toward the end of the twelfth century BC when a distributary of the Nile dried up. During the second millennium BC, the name of this city appears to have changed from Rowaty to Avaris to Peru-Nefer to Pi-Ramesse. From the thirteenth century BC onwards, Rameses would have been the most natural name for Hebrews to use for this location. The use of Rameses as the name for the city in the time of Joseph is anachronistic.[842]

Bridge

Jacob's brief encounter with the king of Egypt reinforces the idea that God's blessing will come to the nations of the earth through the unique patriline that descends from Abraham. Moreover, Jacob's description of his own life and that of his fathers as a "pilgrimage" is striking. The author of Hebrews draws on this when affirming that the patriarchs Abraham, Isaac, and Jacob lived in tents, looking forward to inhabiting in the life to come a "city that has foundations, whose architect and builder is God" (Heb 11:10).

L. Joseph Oversees the Famine in Egypt (47:13–26)

> 13 But there was no food in the entire region, for the famine was very severe. The land of Egypt and the land of Canaan were exhausted by the famine. 14 Joseph collected all the silver to be found in the land of Egypt and the land of Canaan in exchange for the grain they were purchasing, and he brought the silver to Pharaoh's palace. 15 When the silver from the land of Egypt and the land of Canaan was gone, all the Egyptians came to Joseph and said, "Give us food. Why should we die here in front of you? The silver is gone!"
>
> 16 But Joseph said, "Give me your livestock. Since the silver is gone, I will give you food in exchange for your livestock." 17 So they brought their livestock to Joseph, and he gave them food in exchange for the horses, the flocks of sheep, the herds of cattle, and the donkeys. That year he provided them with food in exchange for all their livestock.
>
> 18 When that year was over, they came the next year and said to him, "We cannot hide from our lord that the silver is gone and that all our livestock belongs to our lord. There is nothing left for our lord except our bodies and our land. 19 Why should we die here in front of you—both us and our land? Buy us and our land in exchange for food. Then we

842 Walton, *Genesis*, 686. Compare the use of the name Dan in 14:14.

with our land will become Pharaoh's slaves. Give us seed so that we can live and not die, and so that the land won't become desolate."

[20] In this way, Joseph acquired all the land in Egypt for Pharaoh, because every Egyptian sold his field since the famine was so severe for them. The land became Pharaoh's, [21] and Joseph moved the people to the cities from one end of Egypt to the other. [22] The only land he did not acquire belonged to the priests, for they had an allowance from Pharaoh. They ate from their allowance that Pharaoh gave them; therefore they did not sell their land.

[23] Joseph said to the people, "Understand today that I have acquired you and your land for Pharaoh. Here is seed for you. Sow it in the land. [24] At harvest, you are to give a fifth of it to Pharaoh, and four-fifths will be yours as seed for the field and as food for yourselves, your households, and your dependents."

[25] "You have saved our lives," they said. "We have found favor with our lord and will be Pharaoh's slaves." [26] So Joseph made it a law, still in effect today in the land of Egypt, that a fifth of the produce belongs to Pharaoh. Only the priests' land does not belong to Pharaoh.

[27] Israel settled in the land of Egypt, in the region of Goshen. They acquired property in it and became fruitful and very numerous.

Context

The Genesis narrative turns away from Jacob's family to consider the severe impact of the ongoing famine upon the people of Egypt. This digression serves several purposes. First, it creates a hiatus in the flow of the narrative concerning Jacob's family. When the narrative returns to focus on Jacob in 47:28, the story jumps forward seventeen years; verses 13–27 create a sense of time passing. Second, the passage underlines that Joseph's preparations enabled the Egyptians to survive what would otherwise have been a devastating famine, resulting in many deaths. Third, verses 13–27 enable the narrator to compare the effect of the famine upon Jacob's family with its impact upon the Egyptian population. Whereas Jacob's family prosper in the land of Goshen, acquiring property (v. 27), the Egyptians of necessity sell themselves and their land to become debt-slaves to Pharaoh (v. 19).[843]

[843] Sigmon, "Shadowing Jacob's Journey," 455, describes this episode as a "sideshadow" (a literary device to show what might have but did not take place): "As a sideshadow, the episode of Joseph enslaving the Egyptians portrays their situation as a set of circumstances that were not realized for Jacob and his family, thereby illuminating the conditions under which Israel went down to Egypt at the end of the patriarchal period." Waltke and Fredricks,

Comments

47:13–17. The devastating impact of the famine requires the Egyptians and others to buy food from Joseph. When their money (that is, "silver") runs out, the people trade their livestock for food. The livestock includes horses, sheep, cattle, and donkeys. In marked contrast, prior events concerning Jacob's family have resulted in them receiving from Joseph money/silver (42:25; 44:1; 45:22) and donkeys (45:23).

47:18–27. When other sources of funding for food are exhausted, the Egyptians have nothing left to sell apart from themselves and their land. Rather than face death by starvation, they voluntarily become debt-slaves to Pharaoh. While this offers them security from starvation, they do not become fully dependent upon Pharaoh. Joseph requires them to sow seed and harvest the crop, with the incentive that they may keep four-fifths of all that is produced. Given the severity of the situation, Joseph could have compelled the people to give even more of their time and energy in serving the Egyptian king.

Although some scholars contend that Joseph unfairly exploits the famine to enslave the Egyptians,[844] the people's response in verse 25 suggests that they are grateful to Joseph for saving them from death. As Skinner observes, Joseph merely responds positively to the people's proposal to buy them and their land.[845] Given their dire circumstances, Joseph could have demanded much more from the starving Egyptians.[846]

In verse 27 the narrator turns the reader's attention back to Jacob and his family, picking up the story from verses 11–12. Despite the famine, which has had a devastating impact upon the Egyptians, the Israelites prosper. Importantly, they preserve their identity as Israelites and do not assimilate to become one with the Egyptians. The brief comment that the Israelites "became fruitful and very numerous" implies divine blessing, a motif first introduced in 1:28 concerning people. It comes frequently in Genesis in conjunction with divine blessing (e.g., 9:1, 7; 17:20; 28:3; 35:11; 48:4; see Biblical and Theological Themes §2).

Genesis, 589, remark: "Israel's increase and acquisition of land stands in striking contrast to the Egyptians' loss of land and freedom."

[844] Turner, *Genesis*, 196–97; W. Sibley Towner, *Genesis*, Westminster Bible Companion (Louisville: Westminster John Knox, 2001), 273–74.

[845] Skinner, *Genesis*, 499–500.

[846] von Rad, *Genesis*, 406, notes that there are examples from the ANE of interest being imposed at forty or even sixty percent.

Bridge

The contrast created between the experience of the Israelites and the Egyptians prefigures the opening chapter of Exodus, which emphasizes, like verse 27, the remarkable growth of the Israelite population (Exod 1:7). However, Joseph's gracious treatment of the Egyptians contrasts sharply with what transpires later for Jacob's descendants. Under a Pharaoh, who does not know Joseph, the Israelites are harshly exploited as slaves (Exod 1:8–11).

M. Jacob Requests to Be Buried in Canaan (47:27–31)

> [28] Now Jacob lived in the land of Egypt 17 years, and his life span was
> 147 years. [29] When the time approached for him to die, he called his son
> Joseph and said to him, "If I have found favor with you, put your hand
> under my thigh and promise me that you will deal with me in kindness
> and faithfulness. Do not bury me in Egypt. [30] When I rest with my fathers,
> carry me away from Egypt and bury me in their burial place."
>
> Joseph answered, "I will do what you have asked."
>
> [31] And Jacob said, "Swear to me." So Joseph swore to him. Then Israel
> bowed in thanks at the head of his bed.

Context

The storyline moves forward some seventeen years, leaving behind the seven years of famine that brought Jacob's family to Egypt. Jacob is now 147 years of age, and he perceives that death is imminent. Requesting that he should be buried in Canaan, Jacob affirms his belief that the divine promises given to the patriarchs will be fulfilled. For Jacob, his family's sojourn in Egypt is merely temporary. Jacob's request in 47:28–31 is fulfilled in 49:29–50:14, with both passages framing the final section of Genesis (47:28–50:14), leaving only two brief episodes involving Joseph to conclude the book (50:15–21 and 50:22–26).

Comments

47:28–31. As death approaches, Jacob seeks a solemn pledge from Joseph that he will be buried with his fathers in Canaan. On the instruction "put your hand under my thigh" (v. 29), see Comments on 24:9. Jacob's reference to finding favor with Joseph recalls what the Egyptians say in 47:25. To find favor in the eyes of someone has positive connotations in Genesis, usually associated with life (e.g., 6:8; 18:3; 19:19). Jacob's request to be shown favor by Joseph is reinforced by his desire to be treated with "kindness and faithfulness." This latter expression brings together the Hebrew words חֶסֶד (*ḥesed*) and אֱמֶת (*ʾemet*), which are later used by God in Exodus 34:6 when he describes himself as "abounding in faithful love (חֶסֶד, *ḥesed*) and truth (אֱמֶת, *ʾemet*)." "Faithful love" is a much better translation of חֶסֶד (*ḥesed*) than "kindness," which is a rather weak description for this type of love.

On receiving Joseph's solemn assurance, Jacob bows at the head of his bed. CSB adds "in thanks," but the Hebrew text is not so specific. Jacob may have bowed in gratitude or in recognition of Joseph's special status, thus fulfilling Joseph's dream in 37:9–10. Alternatively, he may have bowed in worship. Influenced by the LXX translation, the NIV reads "worshiped as he leaned on the top of his staff."[847]

Bridge

The relocation of the Israelites to another country is part of God's plan (see 15:13–16). Jacob's desire to be buried in Canaan, and not Egypt, reflects his strong belief that God will fulfil his promises to the patriarchs that they will inherit the land of Canaan as a "permanent possession" (17:8). This expectation is highlighted by the author of Hebrews when he affirms that the patriarchs died without receiving what God had promised (Heb 11:13–16, 39–40). Nevertheless, by faith they believed that God's promises to them would be fulfilled in the life to come.

N. Jacob's Blessing of Joseph and His Sons (48:1–22)

> [1] Some time after this, Joseph was told, "Your father is weaker." So he set out with his two sons, Manasseh and Ephraim. [2] When Jacob was told, "Your son Joseph has come to you," Israel summoned his strength and sat up in bed.

---

[847] Perhaps due to the influence of Heb 11:21, the NIV translation of 47:31 reads "staff" (מַטֶּה, *maṭṭeh*) rather than "bed" (מִטָּה, *miṭṭāh*), as found in most English versions. The MT reads מִטָּה (*miṭṭāh*, "bed"); the Hebrew for staff is מַטֶּה (*maṭṭeh*). The difference between these terms is small in Hebrew; only the vowels differ, and these were not written in the earliest form of the text. In addressing the question of which reading is original—"bed" or "staff"—it is worth observing that Heb 11:21 refers to Jacob "leaning on the top of his staff" after he had "blessed each of the sons of Joseph." Gen 48:31, however, describes Jacob's bowing at the head/top of the bed/staff prior to Joseph's sons being blessed. It is possible that the author of Hebrews is not alluding to the event described in Gen 48:31 but has in view what Jacob did after blessing Joseph's sons, something not specifically mentioned in Genesis.

3 Jacob said to Joseph, "God Almighty appeared to me at Luz in the land
of Canaan and blessed me. 4 He said to me, 'I will make you fruitful and
numerous; I will make many nations come from you, and I will give
this land as a permanent possession to your future descendants.' 5 Your
two sons born to you in the land of Egypt before I came to you in Egypt
are now mine. Ephraim and Manasseh belong to me just as Reuben and
Simeon do. 6 Children born to you after them will be yours and will
be recorded under the names of their brothers with regard to their
inheritance. 7 When I was returning from Paddan, to my sorrow Rachel
died along the way, some distance from Ephrath in the land of Canaan.
I buried her there along the way to Ephrath" (that is, Bethlehem).

When Israel saw Joseph's sons, he said, "Who are these?"

And Joseph said to his father, "They are my sons God has given me here."

So Israel said, "Bring them to me and I will bless them." 10 Now his eye-
sight was poor because of old age; he could hardly see. Joseph brought
them to him, and he kissed and embraced them. 11 Israel said to Joseph,
"I never expected to see your face again, but now God has even let me
see your offspring." 12 Then Joseph took them from his father's knees
and bowed with his face to the ground.

13 Then Joseph took them both—with his right hand Ephraim toward
Israel's left, and with his left hand Manasseh toward Israel's right—and
brought them to Israel. 14 But Israel stretched out his right hand and put
it on the head of Ephraim, the younger, and crossing his hands, put his
left on Manasseh's head, although Manasseh was the firstborn. 15 Then
he blessed Joseph and said:

> The God before whom my fathers Abraham and Isaac walked,
> the God who has been my shepherd all my life to this day,
> 16 the angel who has redeemed me from all harm—
> may he bless these boys.
> And may they be called by my name
> and the names of my fathers Abraham and Isaac,
> and may they grow to be numerous within the land.

17 When Joseph saw that his father had placed his right hand on
Ephraim's head, he thought it was a mistake and took his father's hand
to move it from Ephraim's head to Manasseh's. 18 Joseph said to his
father, "Not that way, my father! This one is the firstborn. Put your
right hand on his head."

19 But his father refused and said, "I know, my son, I know! He too will
become a tribe, and he too will be great; nevertheless, his younger
brother will be greater than he, and his offspring will become a pop-

> ulous nation." [20] So he blessed them that day, putting Ephraim before Manasseh when he said, "The nation Israel will invoke blessings by you, saying, 'May God make you like Ephraim and Manasseh.' "
>
> [21] Israel said to Joseph, "Look, I am about to die, but God will be with you and will bring you back to the land of your fathers. [22] Over and above what I am giving your brothers, I am giving you the one mountain slope that I took from the Amorites with my sword and bow."

Context

Jacob's request to be buried in Canaan in 47:28–31 and its fulfilment in 50:29–50:14 forms a frame around a long episode that describes how on his deathbed Jacob blesses his sons.[848] This single episode, running from 48:1 to 49:28, however, falls into two parts with 48:1–22 focusing on Joseph and his sons, Ephraim and Manasseh, and 49:1–28 recording a series of blessings pronounced by Jacob on all of his twelve sons.

When Jacob is close to death, Joseph comes to him with his sons, Manasseh and Ephraim. Taking the initiative, Jacob announces his intention to give Joseph's two sons a special status. Although in reality they are only Jacob's grandsons, they are to be treated as his sons, on a par with Joseph's brothers. However, in the process of bestowing this special status upon them, Jacob intentionally disregards the principle of primogeniture, promoting the younger brother Ephraim over his older brother Manasseh. This action is highly significant in the light of how Genesis traces a unique patriline, anticipating a future "offspring of the woman" who will reverse the consequences of Adam and Eve's betrayal of God (see Biblical and Theological Themes §1).

Comments

48:1–2. The opening words of this episode suggest that Joseph does not come with the intention of getting his father's blessing for either himself or his sons.

48:3–7. Jacob recalls how God appeared to him at Bethel.[849] There YHWH promised Jacob that he would inherit the divine promises given to Abraham and Isaac (35:11–12; cf. 28:13–15). Underlying Jacob's remarks about the divine promises made to him at Luz is his desire to see these

---

[848] Waltke and Fredricks, *Genesis*, 593, refer to 48:1–49:28 as "one unit."

[849] Luz was the name of the location before it was renamed Bethel. See Comments on 28:18-22.

pass from Joseph to Ephraim. Jacob's brief recollection of what God said to him recalls how the covenant of circumcision is established with the members of the patriline.[850] This is underlined by his use of the divine name God Almighty (see comments on 17:1, 28:3 and 35:11).

Although the narrator speaks of "Manasseh and Ephraim" in verse 1, reflecting their order of birth (see 41:51–52), Jacob deliberately refers to them as "Ephraim and Manasseh" (v. 5), anticipating how he will promote Ephraim to the status of firstborn over Manasseh (vv. 13–20). By adopting both Ephraim and Manasseh as "sons" (v. 5), Jacob underlines Joseph's status as firstborn (see 1 Chr 5:1–2). When Canaan is later divided among Jacob's descendants, Joseph, through his descendants, receives a double portion because his sons, Ephraim and Manasseh, are each given one-twelfth of the land. By mentioning Ephraim and Manasseh alongside Reuben and Simeon (v. 5), "Jacob explicitly equates Joseph's two sons with his own firstborn and secondborn, intimating that the former are to have as good an inheritance, or better, as the latter, and thus once more invokes the great Genesis theme of the reversal of primogeniture."[851] Jacob's reference to the death of Rachel, which coincided with her giving birth to Benjamin (35:16–20), may imply that he views Ephraim and Manasseh as replacements for sons that Rachel might have borne to him had she lived.

48:8–20. Jacob's question regarding the identity of Joseph's sons may be part of the adoption ceremony, but it is more likely that Jacob cannot identify them at a distance due to his poor eyesight (v. 10; cf. 27:1 which highlights how Isaac had poor eyesight due to his age).[852] However, when they come close enough for Jacob to touch them, he distinguishes Ephraim from Manasseh (vv. 17–19).[853] In a highly sig-

---

[850] Verse 4 contains the key terms "fruitful," "numerous," "nations," "land," "permanent possession," "future descendants," all of which go back to Gen 17.

[851] Alter, *Genesis*, 287. The mention of Reuben and Simeon is striking, because both have been linked previously in Genesis with actions that suggest they are unsuitable candidates for the status of firstborn (see 34:30; 35:22).

[852] Wenham, *Genesis 16–50*, 460, highlights various parallels between this occasion and Isaac's blessing of Jacob in chs. 27–28. Similar motifs include deathbed scene, blindness, primogeniture reversal, protest and reaffirmation of the blessing.

[853] Jacob requests in v. 9 that Joseph's sons should be brought near to him so that he can lay his hands on them to bless them. The CSB translation reads: "Bring them to me and I will bless them." A better rendering would be: "Bring them to me so that I may bless them." The verbal sequence of imperative followed by cohortative, but not with *wayyiqtol*, indicates purpose (cf., e.g., ESV, NIV, RSV, NJPS).

nificant way, Jacob proceeds to give the blessing of the firstborn to Ephraim, promoting him over his older brother Manasseh. Despite Joseph's intervention, Jacob insists on rejecting the principle of primogeniture.[854] Subsequent events recorded in the books of Exodus to Kings underscore the importance of the tribe of Ephraim. It is noteworthy that Joshua, an Ephraimite, leads the Israelites into the promised land. Yet, after the time of Joshua the Ephraimites become increasingly corrupt morally until they, as the tribe associated with leadership, are eventually replaced by Judah (see Ps 78:67–71).[855]

Unlike the CSB, which follows the MT, some English versions translate the start of verse 15 "he blessed them." While this latter reading reflects the LXX and Vg, there is no compelling reason to say that the MT does not preserve the earliest and best reading.[856] Joseph and his sons, Ephraim and Manasseh, are intimately connected;[857] by blessing Ephraim and Manasseh, Jacob blesses Joseph. Jacob's blessing of Joseph and his sons recalls how his elderly father, Isaac, blessed him (27:27–29).

Jacob's blessing of Joseph, via Ephraim and Manasseh, in verses 15–16 begins with three statements regarding God. These draw attention to different aspects of what has been recorded in Genesis already concerning the patriarchs' relationship with God. In the first statement, Jacob observes that his grandfather, Abraham, and father, Isaac, "walked" before God, a concept that implies a close and harmonious relationship with God.[858] Jacob's second description of God highlights God's constant care of Jacob. God has been his shepherd, an image with which Jacob, as a shepherd himself, would be especially familiar. Jacob's third description of God as "the angel who has redeemed me from all harm" is striking, for in this context the term "angel" clearly

---

[854] This recalls how Jacob himself received the blessing of the firstborn over his older brother Esau (27:27–29; 28:1–4). See Biblical and Theological Themes §1 and §2.

[855] See Alexander, "The Regal Dimension of the תלדות־יעקב" 207–12; Dalrymple, "Ephraim or Judah," 50–73.

[856] Mathews, *Genesis 11:27–50:26*, 878; *pace* Alter, *Genesis*, 289.

[857] This is underlined by what Jacob says in v. 6. His comments there probably imply that Joseph's descendants will be listed under the tribes of Ephraim and Manasseh.

[858] This expression uses the distinctive *hithpael* verbal form. In Genesis this concept is linked to Enoch (5:22, 24), Noah (6:9) and Abraham (17:1; 24:40; cf. 13:17). In 17:1 CSB translates "Walk before me" as "Live in My presence," with a footnote offering "Walk" as an alternative to "Live." See comment of 5:22–24.

denotes God himself and not another creature. This use resembles how the expression "angel of the Lord" designates God on various occasions.[859] While Jacob does not specify how God has redeemed him, "he is probably referring in a general sense to God's intervention on his behalf to protect him from his enemies."[860] The Hebrew verb גָּאַל *gaʾal* "to redeem" is often used of someone who rescues a relative because he or she is a victim of injustice or harsh circumstances. The concept of the angel redeeming Jacob from harm or evil anticipates how God will later redeem the Israelites from oppression in Egypt (cf. Exod 6:6; 15:13).

By putting Ephraim ahead of Manasseh, Jacob continues a pattern that runs through the patriarchal narratives. Importantly, Jacob confirms that Ephraim will be greater than his older brother. Although the CSB reads "his offspring will become a populous nation" at the end of verse 19, the Hebrew text refers to "nations" (see CSB footnote which offers the alternative translation "a multitude of nations," recognizing that the Hebrew expression has the sense "a fullness of nations.") Other English versions have "a multitude of nations" (ESV, KJV, NLT, NRSV); NIV reads "a group of nations." A similar idiom appears in Isaiah 31:4 involving shepherds and English versions render מְלֹא (*mĕlōʾ*) as "band" (CSB, ESV, NIV, NRSV) or "multitude" (KJV, JPS). Rather than referring to one nation, Jacob is alluding to what God said to him in 35:11 regarding "an assembly of nations." The concept of nations finds its roots in God's promise to Abraham that he would be "a father of many nations" (17:4–6).

48:21–22. Jacob anticipates that his entire family will return to Canaan from Egypt; the pronouns "you" and "your" in verse 21 are plural in the original Hebrew text. As for Joseph, Jacob gives him שְׁכֶם אַחַד (*šĕkem ʾaḥad*), which CSB renders "one mountain slope" (cf. ESV, RSV). Other translations are possible. NIV reads, "one more ridge of land," implying that Joseph gets an extra portion of the land of Canaan because he has the status of firstborn. The term שְׁכֶם (*šĕkem*) can be read as a common noun meaning "shoulder" or "mountain ridge"; it can also be viewed as a proper noun, "Shechem." This is the location where Joseph is buried in

[859] E.g., Gen 16:7–14; 21:15–21; 22:11–18; 31:11–13; Judg 6:11–24; for a fuller discussion, see Alexander, *Exodus*, 82–83.

[860] McKeown, *Genesis*, 183. Apart from Esau threatening to kill him (27:41–45), Jacob also found himself in difficult situations involving Laban (31:22–55) and the inhabitants of Shechem (34:1–31).

territory belonging to the tribe of Ephraim (Josh 24:32). Jacob's remark that he took this ridge of land from the Amorites by force is noteworthy. There is no mention of this forceful action elsewhere in Genesis.

Bridge

Joseph's encounter with his father is highly significant in the light of the patriline that runs throughout Genesis. When Jacob blesses Ephraim ahead of his older brother Manasseh, he creates the expectation that a future king will arise from the tribe of Ephraim, the younger of Joseph's sons.[861] Subsequent events recorded in the books of Exodus to Samuel underline the tribe of Ephraim's prominence within Israel. However, as the book of Judges reveals, after the time of Joshua, who is himself an Ephraimite, the tribe of Ephraim becomes increasingly corrupt. This eventually results in God's rejection of the patriline of Ephraim and his choice of David from the tribe of Judah to be king over the Israelites. This radical step is summarized in Psalm 78:67–72:

> He (God) rejected the tent of Joseph
> and did not choose the tribe of Ephraim.
> 68 He chose instead the tribe of Judah,
> Mount Zion, which he loved.
> 69 He built his sanctuary like the heights,
> like the earth that he established forever.
> 70 He chose David his servant
> and took him from the sheep pens;
> 71 he brought him from tending ewes
> to be shepherd over his people Jacob—
> over Israel, his inheritance.
> 72 He shepherded them with a pure heart
> and guided them with his skillful hands.

With this movement from Ephraim to Judah, which is narrated in the books of Samuel, the patriline traced in Genesis shifts from the descendants of Joseph to those of Judah.[862] This transition from Joseph's

---

861 In all probability Jacob's intentional blessing of Ephraim gives rise to the later Jewish tradition that there will be a future Messiah descended from Joseph, through Ephraim. See Mitchell, *Messiah ben Joseph*.

862 For a fuller discussion, see Alexander, "The Regal Dimension of the תלדות־יעקב," 196–212; Dalrymple, "Ephraim or Judah," 50–73.

patriline to Judah's patriline reflects the special interest that the author of Genesis gives to both Joseph and Judah within the *tôlĕdôt* section of Genesis devoted to Jacob's offspring (37:2–50:26).

O. Jacob Blesses His Twelve Sons (49:1–28)

1 Then Jacob called his sons and said, "Gather around, and I will tell you
what will happen to you in the days to come.

2 Come together and listen, sons of Jacob;
listen to your father Israel:
3 Reuben, you are my firstborn,
my strength and the firstfruits of my virility,
excelling in prominence, excelling in power.
4 Turbulent as water, you will not excel,
because you got into your father's bed
and you defiled it—he got into my bed.
Simeon and Levi are brothers;
their knives are vicious weapons.
6 May I never enter their council;
may I never join their assembly.
For in their anger they kill men,
and on a whim they hamstring oxen.
7 Their anger is cursed, for it is strong,
and their fury, for it is cruel!
I will disperse them throughout Jacob
and scatter them throughout Israel.
8 Judah, your brothers will praise you.
Your hand will be on the necks of your enemies;
your father's sons will bow down to you.
9 Judah is a young lion—
my son, you return from the kill.
He crouches; he lies down like a lion
or a lioness—who dares to rouse him?
10 The scepter will not depart from Judah
or the staff from between his feet
until he whose right it is comes
and the obedience of the peoples belongs to him.
11 He ties his donkey to a vine,
and the colt of his donkey to the choice vine.
He washes his clothes in wine
and his robes in the blood of grapes.
12 His eyes are darker than wine,
and his teeth are whiter than milk.
13 Zebulun will live by the seashore

and will be a harbor for ships,
and his territory will be next to Sidon.
14 Issachar is a strong donkey
lying down between the saddlebags.
15 He saw that his resting place was good
and that the land was pleasant,
so he leaned his shoulder to bear a load
and became a forced laborer.
16 Dan will judge his people
as one of the tribes of Israel.
17 Dan will be a snake by the road,
a viper beside the path,
that bites the horses' heels so that its rider falls backward.
I wait for your salvation, Lord.
Gad will be attacked by raiders,
but he will attack their heels.
Asher's food will be rich,
and he will produce royal delicacies.
Naphtali is a doe set free
that bears beautiful fawns.
Joseph is a fruitful vine,
a fruitful vine beside a spring;
its branches climb over the wall.
23 The archers attacked him,
shot at him, and were hostile toward him.
24 Yet his bow remained steady,
and his strong arms were made agile
by the hands of the Mighty One of Jacob,
by the name of the Shepherd, the Rock of Israel,
25 by the God of your father who helps you,
and by the Almighty who blesses you
with blessings of the heavens above,
blessings of the deep that lies below,
and blessings of the breasts and the womb.
26 The blessings of your father excel
the blessings of my ancestors
and the bounty of the ancient hills.
May they rest on the head of Joseph,
on the brow of the prince of his brothers.
27 Benjamin is a wolf; he tears his prey.
In the morning he devours the prey,
and in the evening he divides the plunder."

[28] These are the tribes of Israel, twelve in all, and this is what their father said to them. He blessed them, and he blessed each one with a suitable blessing.

Context

Immediately after blessing Joseph and his sons, Jacob summons all his sons and makes pronouncements regarding the future of their descendants. The order in which the sons are addressed appears to be influenced by a mixture of various factors, none of which alone can explain the arrangement: their age, the identity of their mother, geography.[863] Jacob links the destiny of each son's descendants with his perception of the moral character of each son.[864] Consequently, some announcements are positive and others negative; all are described as "suitable" blessings in verse 28. Expressed in poetry using vivid imagery and metaphors, elements of Jacob's pronouncements have a measure of ambiguity as to what will happen in the future. The archaic nature of the poetry, including the use of wordplays, adds to the difficulty of interpreting clearly all that Jacob says.[865] Occasionally, Jacob highlights certain attributes by comparing his sons with various animals (i.e., lion, donkey, snake, doe, wolf). The narrator of Genesis undoubtedly views Jacob's pronouncements as prophetic and as having an important role in confirming the future direction of the patriline that is traced throughout Genesis. Strikingly, Jacob's remarks regarding the descendants of Judah and Joseph far exceed, both in extent and nature, what is said concerning their brothers.

---

[863] According to 29:31–30:24; 35:16–18, the birth order is Reuben, Simeon, Levi, Judah, Dan, Naphtali, Gad, Asher, Issachar, Zebulun, Joseph, and Benjamin. The first six sons listed in ch. 49 all belong to Leah, but Zebulun is placed before Issachar. Provan, *Discovering Genesis*, 184, suggests that the sons may be grouped by geography, with a southern group (Reuben, Simeon, Levi and Judah), a northern group (Zebulun, Issachar, Dan, Gad, Asher, Naphtali), and a central group (Joseph and Benjamin). However, the initial allocation of land places Dan and Gad alongside the central group, and the tribe of Levi is dispersed throughout all the tribal regions.

[864] Strong links with the preceding narrative are evident from what is said about Reuben, Simeon, Levi, Judah, and Joseph. For this reason, Brueggemann, *Genesis*, 365–66, is quite mistaken when he claims that ch. 49 has no "important connection with its context." For the remaining sons Jacob's remarks are brief and largely neutral, neither commending nor condemning each person.

[865] For a detailed study of Jacob's blessing, see Raymond de Hoop, *Genesis 49 in Its Literary and Historical Context*, Oudtestamentische Studien 39 (Leiden: Brill, 1999). Wenham, *Genesis 16–50*, 468–71, helpfully addresses issues of form and date.

Comments

49:1–2. Jacob gathers his sons around to tell them about their descendants. Jacob is not simply predicting what will happen; his pronouncements, as blessings, will shape what happens (see Comments on 9:25–27), but the future is also determined to some extent by the nature of each ancestor.[866] The Hebrew expression translated "in the days to come" (CSB) elsewhere is rendered "in the last days" (e.g., Isa 2:2).

49:3–4. Jacob emphasizes Reuben's privileged position as firstborn, but stresses his lack of reliability, recalling his inappropriate liaison with Bilhah, one of Jacob's wives (see Comments on 35:22–23). As 1 Chronicles 5:1–2 confirms, Reuben's birthright as firstborn is given to Joseph. Like Reuben, his descendants lack the qualities necessary to exercise authority over all of Jacob's descendants. As many commentators observe, no judge, king, or prophet comes from the tribe of Reuben.[867]

49:5–7. Jacob's remarks concerning Simeon and Levi underline their aggressive nature, recalling how together they took the lead in massacring the male inhabitants of Shechem (34:25–26).[868] Jacob distances himself from their cruel anger, announcing that their descendants should be scattered throughout Israel to prevent the two tribes joining forces. Consequently, the tribe of Simeon is allocated territory within a region occupied by the tribe of Judah (Josh 19:1–9) and the tribe of Levi is given forty-eight cities located across all the tribal areas (Num 18:23–24; 35:1–8; Josh 21:1–45). Keeping the two tribes apart dissipates their power. In the light of Jacob's comments, it is worth observing that Moses, from the tribe of Levi, in defending Hebrew slaves resorts to violence and kills an Egyptian (Exod 2:11–12). Later, the tribe of Levi takes up swords to punish apostate Israelites (Exod 32:25–29).

49:8–12. Compared to the blessings of Reuben, Simeon, and Levi, Jacob's blessing of Judah is much longer and considerably more positive

[866] Already in Genesis, there are illustrations of how descendants resemble their ancestors. As early as Gen 4, Lamech is portrayed as following closely in the footsteps of Cain (see Biblical and Theological Themes §1).

[867] Jacob, *The First Book of the Bible: Genesis*, 330; von Rad, *Genesis*, 418; Wenham, *Genesis 16–50*, 473; Waltke and Fredricks, *Genesis*, 605.

[868] Calum M. Carmichael, "Some Sayings in Genesis 49," *JBL* 88 (1969): 435–37, suggests that Jacob's comment, "they hamstring oxen" in 49:6 involves a wordplay with his remark that they "have brought trouble on me" in 34:30; the Hebrew roots of the words are עקר (*ʿqr*) and עכר (*ʿkr*) respectively.

in outlook. Jacob associates kingship with Judah's descendants. This reflects the high regard that Jacob has for Judah, which results from the transformation that took place in Judah's life after Tamar confronted him regarding his hypocrisy (38:26). After this life-changing experience Judah has an influential leadership role within Jacob's family (43:3, 8; 44:14, 16, 18; 46:28).[869] Although the wording of Jacob's announcement seems to be about Judah himself, it is meant to be interpreted as referring to a future "Judah," a descendant who resembles Judah. His brothers will praise this future "Judah" and bow down to him in homage (v. 8).[870] Using the imagery of a lion, Jacob underlines the concept of leadership (v. 9).[871] Importantly, the influence of this future "Judah" will extend beyond Israel, for peoples will obey him (v. 10).[872] The idea of Judah ruling over peoples echoes a recurring theme in Genesis that builds upon the concept of Abraham being a source of blessing to the nations (12:3; cf. 17:4–5; 27:29; see Biblical and Theological Themes §2).

The meaning of verse 10 is much debated, especially the phrase translated in CSB as "until he whose right it is comes." NIV reads "until he to whom it belongs shall come" (cf. ESV footnote, NAS footnote, RSV). Alternative readings are "until Shiloh come" (KJV; cf. ESV footnote, NAS, NRSV footnote) and "until tribute comes to him" (ESV, NJB, NRSV).[873] To

---

[869] Lambe, "Judah's Development," 67; Clifford, "Genesis 38," 522; Martin Pröbstle, "'Lion of Judah': The Blessing on Judah in Genesis 49:8–12," in *"For You Have Strengthened Me": Biblical and Theological Studies in Honor of Gerhard Pfandl in Celebration of His Sixty-Fifth Birthday*, ed. Martin Pröbstle (St. Peter am Hart: Seminar Schloss Bogenhofen, 2007), 34; Wünch, "Genesis 38," 784.

[870] Jacob's comment involves a wordplay on the name Judah (יְהוּדָה, *yĕhûdh*) and "praise you" (יוֹדוּךָ, *yôdûkâ*).

[871] In Rev 5:5, Jesus Christ is designated "the Lion from the tribe of Judah, the Root of David"; Heb 7:14 also links Jesus Christ with the tribe of Judah, as does the genealogy in Matt 1:2–16.

[872] Claus Westermann, *Genesis 37–50: A Commentary*, trans. John J. Scullion (Minneapolis: Augsburg, 1986), 230, associates the fulfilment of Jacob's predictions with the period of David and Solomon. Yet, this period did not experience the "golden age" described by Jacob. E. Jenni, "Messiah, Jewish," *IDB*, 3:362, views the expectations of 49:10–12 as referring "to a new messianic ruler in a new era of paradisaical fruitfulness." Ancient Jewish exegetes linked the fulfilment of Jacob's pronouncement to Judah to a messianic age. See Moses Aberbach and Bernard Grossfeld, *Targum Onkelos to Genesis: A Critical Analysis Together with an English Translation of the Text* (New York: Ktav, 1982), 286–91. Ps 72:8–11, associated with David, looks forward in hope to the coming of a future king who will rule the nations.

[873] Support for this latter reading comes from Richard C. Steiner, "Poetic Forms in the Masoretic Vocalization and Three Difficult Phrases in Jacob's Blessing: יֶתֶר שְׂאֵת (Gen 49:3),

these possibilities, Frolov adds "until he [sc. Judah] comes to Shiloh."[874] Of these possibilities, "until Shiloh comes" fits well with the fact that actual kingship does not come to the tribe of Judah until God appoints David to reign in Jerusalem/Zion, having rejected Shiloh as the location for his presence (Ps 78:60–72; see Biblical and Theological Themes §1). This development in the future may explain why the first part of verse 10 refers to the scepter and staff not departing "from between his feet until Shiloh comes." Kingship does not come immediately to Judah. If Jacob's announcement is interpreted as alluding to the appointment of David as king, his subsequent comments clearly anticipate much more than what was achieved in the time of David.[875] This becomes especially evident in verse 11, which speaks of an extravagant harvest with so many grapes that a donkey can be tied to a vine without the owner being concerned that it will eat the whole crop. The grapes are so plentiful that "wine can be substituted for wash water."[876] Agricultural prosperity is associated with a unique, future Davidic king in Psalm 72:16 (cf. Ezek 34:23–31; Amos 9:11–15). With dark eyes and white teeth (v. 12), the king's appearance befits his special status.[877]

49:13. Jacob's remarks concerning Zebulun convey little, either positive or negative, about the nature of his character.[878] The brief comment seems to imply that the tribe will be located close to the Mediterranean Sea with Sidon lying to the north. According to Joshua 19:10–16, the western border of Zebulun's territory lay about ten miles from the coast in Lower Galilee.[879]

יְצוּעַי עָלָה (49:4), and יָבֹא שִׁילֹה (49:10)," *JBL* 129 (2010): 219–26, 233–235.

[874] Serge Frolov, "Judah Comes to Shiloh: Genesis 49:10bα, One More Time," *JBL* 131 (2012): 417–22; cf. footnotes in ESV; NRSV; NAB.

[875] *Pace* Westermann, *Genesis 37-50*, 230, who claims that the reference to the ruler to come who wins the obedience of the nations "corresponds exactly to the historical reality under David and Solomon."

[876] Mathews, *Genesis 11:27-50:26*, 896.

[877] McKeown, *Genesis*, 187, considers the description as reflecting "good diet and healthy lifestyle." Waltke and Fredricks, *Genesis*, 609, suggest that "sparkling" would be a better translation of חַכְלִילִי (*ḥaklîlî*) than "darker."

[878] Provan, *Discovering Genesis*, 185, suggests that Jacob's remarks are "a rebuke regarding aspirations for sea commerce."

[879] Richard S. Hess, *Joshua*, TOTC (Leicester: Inter-Varsity Press, 1996), 296–97; David M. Howard, *Joshua*, NAC 5 (Nashville: Broadman & Holman, 1998), 368–70; David G. Firth, *Joshua*, Evangelical Biblical Theology Commentary (Bellingham: Lexham Academic, 2021), 318–19.

49:14–15. Jacob's pronouncement appears to imply that the tribe of Issachar, like a donkey, will fulfil the role of serving others. McKeown suggests that Issachar is "like a lazy donkey that remains inactive when there is work to be done."[880]

49:16–17. Jacob's remarks begin by involving a wordplay on the name Dan, which means "he judged" (see Gen 30:6).[881] The image of Dan as a snake attacking the heels of a horse carries negative connotations. There is no reason to think that Jacob has in view any single event, but his comments resonate with what is said in Judges 18, which condemns the tribe of Dan for its brutal attack on the unsuspecting residents of Laish. Verse 16 contains the first reference in the Old Testament to the "tribes of Israel" (cf. 49:28).

49:18. This brief prayer interrupts the pronouncements. Jacob's hope rests not on the achievements of his descendants, but on YHWH.

49:19. Jacob's brief comments about Gad (גָּד, *gād*) involve a repeated wordplay involving the Hebrew root גוד (*gwd*), meaning "to raid." The Gadites settled to the east of the Jordan River, south of the Sea of Galilee (see Josh 13:24–27). The Mesha Stele, a Moabite inscription from the ninth century BC, illustrates the kind of threat posed by surrounding nations to the tribe of Gad.[882] Jacob seems to suggest that the Gadites will attack foreign raiders as they retreat.

49:20. Jacob pronounces that the tribe of Asher will have a prosperous future. When the land of Canaan is allocated by lot (Josh 19:24–30), the tribe of Asher is given part of the coastal plain of Acco, a rich agricultural region.

49:21. Jacob compares the tribe of Naphtali to a graceful doe that enjoys freedom to raise beautiful offspring. This positive image may anticipate later developments when the tribe of Naphtali receives fertile territory to the northwest of the Sea of Galilee (Josh 19:32–38).

49:22–26. Jacob's longest blessing confirms Joseph's preeminent status among the brothers. The twofold reference to Joseph's fruitfulness in

---

880 McKeown, *Genesis*, 188.

881 Alter, *Genesis*, 297, takes Dan to be the object of the verb "judge," with "his people" being the subject. This would imply that the Israelites will judge or rule over the tribe of Dan despite its more remote location in the north. While attractive, the word order in Hebrew weighs against this interpretation.

882 McKeown, *Genesis*, 189, notes that Gad is named by Mesha, the king of Moab, in an inscription that extols the king's military success. Mesha states: "And the men of Gad lived in the land of Ataroth from ancient times, and the king of Israel built Ataroth for himself, and I fought against the city, and I captured it."

verse 22 recalls both the naming of Ephraim, which means "fruitful" (see Comments on 41:50–52), and the motif of fruitfulness that recurs throughout Genesis (cf. 48:4; see Biblical and Theological Themes §4).[883] Jacob implies that Joseph's descendants will resemble "a prodigious tree whose enclosure cannot accommodate the thriving plant."[884] Although his brothers attacked him (v. 23), the Mighty One of Jacob, the Rock of Israel, protected Joseph (v. 24). Both of these epithets underline God's omnipotence.

Looking to the future, Jacob prays that God's multifaceted blessings will rest on Joseph's descendants, far exceeding those given to Abraham and Isaac (vv. 25–26). This emphasis upon blessing brings to mind how God blessed Joseph during his time in Egypt (39:5), but more importantly it emphasizes that the blessing associated with the divine promises given to Abraham pass through Joseph to his descendants (see Comments on 12:1–3; see Biblical and Theological Themes §2). Strikingly, of all Jacob's pronouncements, only this one mentions God specifically, a fact that fits well with Jacob's decision to give to Joseph the birthright of the firstborn (see Biblical and Theological Themes §1).

Jacob's concluding remarks about Joseph refer to him as "the prince of his brothers," a comment that both acknowledges Joseph's status and confirms that leadership will be associated with Joseph's descendants.[885] Centuries later, Moses will announce a similar blessing on Joseph, echoing much of what Jacob says and adding more (cf. Deut 33:13–17, esp. v. 16).

49:27. As with some of his other sons, Jacob associates Benjamin with an animal. By comparing Benjamin to a wolf, Jacob indicates that his descendants may be violent predators. This expectation is reflected later in the behavior of the men of Gibeah, who assault and rape a woman from Bethlehem (Judg 19:12–30).

---

[883] Most English versions translate the unusual Hebrew expression בֵּן פֹּרָת (*bēn pōrāt*) as "fruitful vine/bough" (e.g., CSB, ESV, KJV, NET, NIV, NJB, NRSV), but a few view the expression as denoting an animal (i.e. NAB "a wild colt"; NLT "foal of a wild donkey"; NJPS "a wild ass"; cf. Speiser, *Genesis*, 367–68). This latter rendering of the MT is perhaps less likely, despite animal imagery being used in other pronouncements in vv. 2–27.

[884] Mathews, *Genesis 11:27-50:26*, 903.

[885] While some English versions adopt the translation "prince" (e.g., CSB, NIV), others give the alternative "him who was set apart from" (ESV; cf. KJV, NJB, RSV). The Hebrew word that lies behind these translations is the term נָזִיר (*nāzir*). This same term is used in the Old Testament to denote those who become Nazirites (e.g., Samson). It may also be this term that the apostle Matthew has in mind when he writes of Jesus being called a Nazarene (Matt 2:23).

49:28. The narrator's concluding remark underlines that Jacob's pronouncements are about the tribes created by the descendants of his twelve sons. Joseph will later be represented by the tribes of Ephraim and Manasseh. While the pronouncements convey a wide range of expectations, both positive and negative, those linked to Judah and Joseph stand out as exceptional, emphasizing that these two tribes will have significant roles in providing leadership for Jacob's descendants. This reflects the portraits of Joseph and Judah in chapters 37–47 and is consistent with how these tribes are portrayed in the books of Exodus to Kings (see Biblical and Theological Themes §1).

Bridge

Jacob's pronouncements concerning his sons move the book of Genesis toward a conclusion by underscoring how future leadership of the tribes is linked to Judah-Perez and Joseph-Ephraim. This expectation mirrors what is recorded regarding Joseph and Judah in chapters 37–47, where their leadership qualities are evident.[886] The prominence given to both Judah and Joseph leaves open the future direction of the unique lineage traced in Genesis.[887] Subsequent events provide clarity as the line of Ephraim is eventually rejected by God and replaced by the line of Judah in the time of David (Ps 78:67–72). God's commitment to the Davidic dynasty, which is a significant development in the ongoing story of Israel, resonates with Jacob's pronouncement regarding Judah, but the initial establishment of the Davidic dynasty does not fulfil all that Jacob anticipates. The "obedience of the peoples" awaits the coming of Jesus Christ, the preeminent "son of David" (cf., e.g., Matt 1:1; 28:18–20).

P. The Death and Burial of Jacob (49:29–50:14)

> 29 Then he commanded them: "I am about to be gathered to my people.
> Bury me with my fathers in the cave in the field of Ephron the Hethite. 30
> The cave is in the field of Machpelah near Mamre, in the land of Canaan.
> This is the field Abraham purchased from Ephron the Hethite as burial
> property. 31 Abraham and his wife Sarah are buried there, Isaac and his
> wife Rebekah are buried there, and I buried Leah there. 32 The field and

886 In the case of Judah, this involves a radical transformation that is brought about by Tamar (38:1–30, esp. v. 26).

887 For a helpful analysis of the relationship between Joseph and Judah, see Twiss, "Tale of Two Brothers," 255–67.

> the cave in it were purchased from the Hethites." [33] When Jacob had
> finished giving charges to his sons, he drew his feet into the bed, took
> his last breath, and was gathered to his people.
>
> [50:1] Then Joseph, leaning over his father's face, wept and kissed him.
> [2] He commanded his servants who were physicians to embalm his
> father. So they embalmed Israel. [3] They took forty days to complete
> this, for embalming takes that long, and the Egyptians mourned for
> him seventy days.
>
> [4] When the days of mourning were over, Joseph said to Pharaoh's house-
> hold, "If I have found favor with you, please tell Pharaoh that [5] my father
> made me take an oath, saying, 'I am about to die. You must bury me
> there in the tomb that I made for myself in the land of Canaan.' Now
> let me go and bury my father. Then I will return."
>
> [6] So Pharaoh said, "Go and bury your father in keeping with your oath."
>
> [7] Then Joseph went to bury his father, and all Pharaoh's servants, the
> elders of his household, and all the elders of the land of Egypt went
> with him, [8] along with all Joseph's family, his brothers, and his father's
> family. Only their dependents, their flocks, and their herds were left in
> the land of Goshen. [9] Horses and chariots went up with him; it was a very
> impressive procession. [10] When they reached the threshing floor of Atad,
> which is across the Jordan, they lamented and wept loudly, and Joseph
> mourned seven days for his father. [11] When the Canaanite inhabitants
> of the land saw the mourning at the threshing floor of Atad, they said,
> "This is a solemn mourning on the part of the Egyptians." Therefore the
> place is named Abel-mizraim. It is across the Jordan.
>
> [12] So Jacob's sons did for him what he had commanded them. [13] They
> carried him to the land of Canaan and buried him in the cave at Mach-
> pelah in the field near Mamre, which Abraham had purchased as burial
> property from Ephron the Hethite. [14] After Joseph buried his father, he
> returned to Egypt with his brothers and all who had gone with him to
> bury his father.

Context

This section brings the account of Jacob's earthly life to a conclusion. From his birth in 25:19–26 through to his death in 49:29–33, Jacob's life has featured throughout almost half of Genesis, although chapters 37–50 concentrate attention mainly on his sons. The brief description of Jacob's death in verses 29–33 is followed by a fuller report that highlights how he is buried near Hebron, alongside other members of his family, including Abraham and Isaac. Jacob's wish to be buried with them confirms his belief that his descendants will live in the land of Canaan in fulfilment of the divine promises given initially to Abraham. His family's time in Egypt will be limited.

Comments

49:29–33. Jacob's dying request is to be buried with his fathers near Hebron, where Abraham bought a field and cave (23:1–20). Both Abraham and Isaac were buried there (25:8–10; 35:27–29). Although it is not stated elsewhere in Genesis, Jacob mentions that Rebekah and Leah were also buried in this cave.

Strikingly, Jacob speaks of being gathered to his people (v. 29; cf. 25:8, 17; 35:29), a concept that is linked to dying and not to burial, as verse 33 confirms. While it is difficult to be certain, this expression conveys a sense of being reunited with others in the life to come.[888] Alter suggests that Jacob's description of the cave underlines that it belongs legally to Jacob and his family. By emphasizing this fact, Jacob indicates "that Abraham's offspring are legitimately bound to the land God promised them, and that the descent into Egypt is no more than a sojourn."[889]

50:1–3. In order that Jacob's corpse may be taken to Hebron, Joseph has it embalmed. He calls on the help of Egyptian physicians because mummification was not a Hebrew practice. By mourning for Jacob for seventy days, the Egyptians display their respect for Jacob.[890] It is not clear from the text of Genesis whether the seventy days begin with the death of Jacob or after he has been embalmed. Most likely, the mourning begins with his death.

50:4–6. Ever respectful of Pharaoh's status as king, Joseph asks permission to bury his father in Canaan. As Alter suggests, Joseph tactfully asks Pharaoh's household to speak on his behalf to the king to lessen any apprehension that Joseph might be planning to return to Canaan permanently.[891]

50:7–11. In recognition of Joseph's standing in Egypt, many prominent Egyptian officials and civic representative accompany the funeral cortege to Canaan. To the Canaanites living near "the threshing floor of Atad," the cortege had the appearance of being Egyptian. A seven-day period of mourning by Egyptians at this location must have appeared very strange to the local population. It is not surprising, therefore, that the threshing floor was named "Abel-mizraim," which means "the mourning of the Egyptians."[892] The location of the threshing floor is

---

888 See Comments on 25:8.

889 Alter, *Genesis*, 301.

890 By comparison, Deut 34:8 records that the Israelites mourned thirty days for Moses.

891 Alter, *Genesis*, 303.

892 The Hebrew word אָבֵל (*ʾābēl*) can mean a "stream," but it also sounds like the verb אָבַל (*ʾābal*, "to mourn").

uncertain, although the expression "across the Jordan" (vv. 10, 11) would imply that it was located to the east of the Jordan River. If the funeral cortege arrived at Hebron by traveling through Transjordan, this route mirrors that taken centuries later by the Israelites at the time of the exodus from Egypt.

50:12–14. Jacob's sons fulfill their father's dying request (cf. 49:29–32). The identity of the cave is precisely given by naming Abraham, Ephron, Machpelah, and Hebron (cf. 23:1–20). This is the only parcel of ground that Abraham acquired as a permanent possession in the land of Canaan. With Jacob's passing, Joseph becomes the head of the family; by referring to Joseph by name in verse 14, the narrator sets him apart from his brothers.

Bridge

Jacob's desire to be buried in the land of Canaan is his testimony to the importance of the divine promises given to the patriarchs. While the text of Genesis is restrained in speaking about life after death, the author of Hebrews 11:8–16 emphasizes that the patriarchs died expecting to experience resurrected life as citizens of the city of God. This expectation is developed throughout the Old Testament and is reflected in the eschatological hope that is associated with a new Jerusalem (see Biblical and Theological Themes §4).[893]

Q. Joseph's Brothers Bow Before Him (50:15–21)

> [15] When Joseph's brothers saw that their father was dead, they said to one another, "If Joseph is holding a grudge against us, he will certainly repay us for all the suffering we caused him."
>
> [16] So they sent this message to Joseph, "Before he died your father gave
> a command: [17] 'Say this to Joseph: Please forgive your brothers' trans-
> gression and their sin—the suffering they caused you.' Therefore, please forgive the transgression of the servants of the God of your father." Joseph wept when their message came to him.
>
> [18] His brothers also came to him, bowed down before him, and said, "We are your slaves!"
>
> [19] But Joseph said to them, "Don't be afraid. Am I in the place of God?
> [20] You planned evil against me; God planned it for good to bring about

[893] Gowan, *Eschatology in the Old Testament*.

the present result—the survival of many people. [21] Therefore don't be afraid. I will take care of you and your children." And he comforted them and spoke kindly to them.

Context

With the death of Jacob, authority over his entire family passes to Joseph. Recalling how they had treated Joseph shamefully selling him into slavery in Egypt (37:26–28), his brothers dread that he will now seize the opportunity to take revenge.

Comments

50:15. Joseph has shown no signs of animosity toward his brothers since their reunion, but they are fearful that with Jacob's death Joseph will repay them for what they did to him years previously. Their past continues to haunt them.

50:16–17. Unsure of Joseph's feelings toward them, the brothers send a message hoping that it will prevent him from taking revenge. Invoking the memory of Jacob, they hope that Joseph will respect the wishes of their deceased father.[894] Whether genuine or otherwise, the message moves Joseph deeply, causing him to weep yet again (cf. 42:24; 43:30; 45:2). Joseph's reaction probably reflects his disappointment that his brothers do not believe that he has forgiven them fully (cf. 45:1–15).

50:18–21. Following up on their message to Joseph, his brothers come and fall before him. Their actions and words recall what was predicted in Joseph's dreams (37:5–10). The brothers, who had sold Joseph into slavery out of hatred, now offer themselves to him as slaves (cf. 44:9, 33). Joseph, however, stresses that, despite their evil intentions, God has ensured a positive outcome (cf. 45:4–8).

Joseph is not claiming that God caused the brothers to act in an evil way. Rather, he contrasts the actions of the brothers, which were intended to bring harm, with those of God, which bring salvation. Joseph's brief assessment mirrors the story of Genesis itself: God acts to reverse the evil done

---

[894] Waltke and Fredricks, *Genesis*, 622, suggest that this instruction is a "fabrication." This is a possibility since there is no previous reference to such an instruction. However, given the selective nature of what is recorded in Hebrew narrative, Jacob may have said this, but the narrator reports it only now. There is no evidence to suggest that Joseph challenged the veracity of the message. See Matthew Michael, "The Dead Trickster and His Shrewd Children? The Persuasive Use of the Double Quotations of a Dead Patriarch in Genesis 49:29–50:21," *JSOT* 43 (2018): 186–89.

by humans. Joseph speaks reassuringly to his brothers, treating them with respect and promising to care for them and their families. The evil of the past is forgotten as Jacob's family is united under Joseph's gracious leadership.

Bridge

Joseph's willingness to forgive his brothers paves the way for family members to be reconciled to each other. As with Jacob and Esau, sibling envy and hatred is eventually replaced by affection and harmony. Importantly, this process of reconciliation is engineered by God, who overcomes the human propensity to do evil at every possible turn. As the Joseph story reveals, God has the power to rescue alienated humanity from the power of evil, reversing malevolent intentions and bringing good out of evil. Moreover, Joseph foreshadows Jesus Christ, who willingly submits to the humiliation of being a servant and even to death itself to reconcile sinful people to God (cf. Phil 2:7–8; cf. Acts 3:13–26; Rom 8:28).

R. The Death of Joseph (50:22–26)

> 22 Joseph and his father's family remained in Egypt. Joseph lived 110
> years. 23 He saw Ephraim's sons to the third generation; the sons of
> Manasseh's son Machir were recognized by Joseph.
>
> 24 Joseph said to his brothers, "I am about to die, but God will certainly
> come to your aid and bring you up from this land to the land he swore
> to give to Abraham, Isaac, and Jacob." 25 So Joseph made the sons of
> Israel take an oath: "When God comes to your aid, you are to carry my
> bones up from here."
>
> 26 Joseph died at the age of 110. They embalmed him and placed him
> in a coffin in Egypt.

Context

The concluding verses of Genesis record the death of Joseph. This occurs some sixty years after the burial of Jacob (50:1–14). Although the seven years of famine have passed, the Israelites continue to reside in Egypt, where they will remain for some four centuries (cf. 15:13–16; Exod 12:40–41).[895] Almost nothing is said about the events that occur during the sixty years that Joseph outlives Jacob, apart from a brief comment about Joseph's relationship to his grandchildren. The book of Genesis concludes here, but this final passage anticipates events yet to come. This future orientation is

---

[895] For more information on the length of the Israelites' stay in Egypt, see Alexander, *Exodus*, 239, 243–44.

reinforced by Joseph's assertion that God will fulfill his promise to Abraham, Isaac and Jacob that their descendants will possess the land of Canaan (15:18–21; 17:8; 26:3; 28:13; 48:21; see Biblical and Theological Themes §4).

Comments

50:22–23. The book of Genesis has traced a patriline that begins with Adam and ends with Joseph. However, Joseph's family line continues as children and grandchildren[896] are born to Ephraim and Manasseh. The naming of Ephraim before Manasseh recalls how Jacob gave the birthright blessing of the firstborn to the younger of the boys (48:13–20; see Biblical and Theological Themes §1).

50:24–26. In confident expectation of what God will do, Joseph makes the sons of Israel swear that they will take his bones from Egypt to the land of Canaan. With this in view, Joseph's corpse is embalmed and preserved in a coffin.[897] Centuries later, recalling this instruction, Moses takes Joseph's coffin from Egypt to Canaan (Exod 13:19). Unlike Abraham, Isaac, and Jacob, who are all entombed at Machpelah near Hebron, Joseph is interred at Shechem, in territory allocated to the tribe of Ephraim (Josh 24:32; see Gen 33:18–20). Joseph's burial at Shechem confirmed that this part of Canaan belonged permanently to his descendants.

Bridge

Genesis concludes with expectations that the Israelites will eventually leave Egypt and settle in the land of Canaan, in fulfilment of God's promises to the patriarchs. For the author of Hebrews, Joseph's instructions to the Israelites exemplify faith that trusts God for something that cannot yet be seen: "By faith Joseph, as he was nearing the end of his life, mentioned the exodus of the Israelites and gave instructions concerning his bones" (Heb 11:22). Joseph confidently believes that God will bring the Israelites out of Egypt. This becomes the focus of the book of Exodus, where God redeems the Israelites from the power of a malevolent dictator. However, the author

---

[896] The expression "Ephraim's sons to the third generation" probably denotes Joseph's great-grandchildren, taking Ephraim to be the first generation (cf. Job 42:16 which speaks of Job seeing a fourth generation). Mathews, *Genesis 11:27–50:26*, 929, tentatively suggests that the expression could possibly refer to Joseph's great-great-grandchildren.

[897] The use of a coffin is a distinctively Egyptian practice and not one adopted by the Hebrews when they lived in the land of Canaan. Verse 26 has the only use in the Old Testament of the Hebrew term אֲרוֹן (*ʾărôn*) to denote a coffin.

of Hebrews may well have in view the idea that Joseph anticipates a bodily resurrection. The whole thrust of what is said in Hebrews 11:8–22 concerns the patriarchs inheriting the city that God has prepared for them, an outcome that the author clearly sees as still to come (Heb 11:39–40; 12:22; 13:14).

BIBLIOGRAPHY

Aalders, G. Ch. *A Short Introduction to the Pentateuch*. London: Tyndale, 1949.
Aberbach, Moses, and Bernard Grossfeld. *Targum Onkelos to Genesis: A Critical Analysis Together with an English Translation of the Text*. New York: Ktav, 1982.
Abernethy, Andrew T., and Gregory Goswell. *God's Messiah in the Old Testament: Expectations of a Coming King*. Grand Rapids: Baker Academic, 2020.
Ackerman, James S. "Joseph, Judah, and Jacob." Pages 85–113 in *Literary Interpretations of Biblical Narratives*, edited by Kenneth R. R. Gros Louis, with James S. Ackerman. Vol. 2. Nashville: Abingdon, 1982.
Albright, William Foxwell. *Archaeology and the Religion of Israel*. Baltimore: Johns Hopkins University Press, 1942.
———."The Names 'Israel' and 'Judah' with an Excursus on the Etymology of *tôdâh* and *tôrâh*." *JBL* 46 (1927): 151–85.
Alexander, P. S. "The Targumim and Early Comments on 'Sons of God' in Genesis 6." *JJS* 23 (1972): 60–71.
Alexander, T. Desmond. *Abraham in the Negev: A Source-Critical Investigation of Genesis 20:1–22:19*. Carlisle: Paternoster, 1997.
———. "Are the Wife/Sister Incidents of Genesis Literary Compositional Variants?" *VT* 42 (1992): 145–53.
———. "Authorship of the Pentateuch." Pages 61–72 in *Dictionary of the Old Testament: Pentateuch*, edited by T. Desmond Alexander and David W. Baker. Downers Grove: InterVarsity Press, 2003.
———. *The City of God and the Goal of Creation*. Short Studies in Biblical Theology. Wheaton: Crossway, 2018.
———. *Exodus*. Apollos OT Commentary 2. London: Apollos, 2017.
———. *Face to Face with God: A Biblical Theology of Christ as Priest and Mediator*. Essential Studies in Biblical Theology. Downers Grove: InterVarsity Press, 2022.
———. "From Adam to Judah: The Significance of the Family Tree in Genesis." *EvQ* 61 (1989): 5–19.
———. *From Paradise to the Promised Land: An Introduction to the Pentateuch*, 4th ed. Grand Rapids: Baker Academic, 2022.

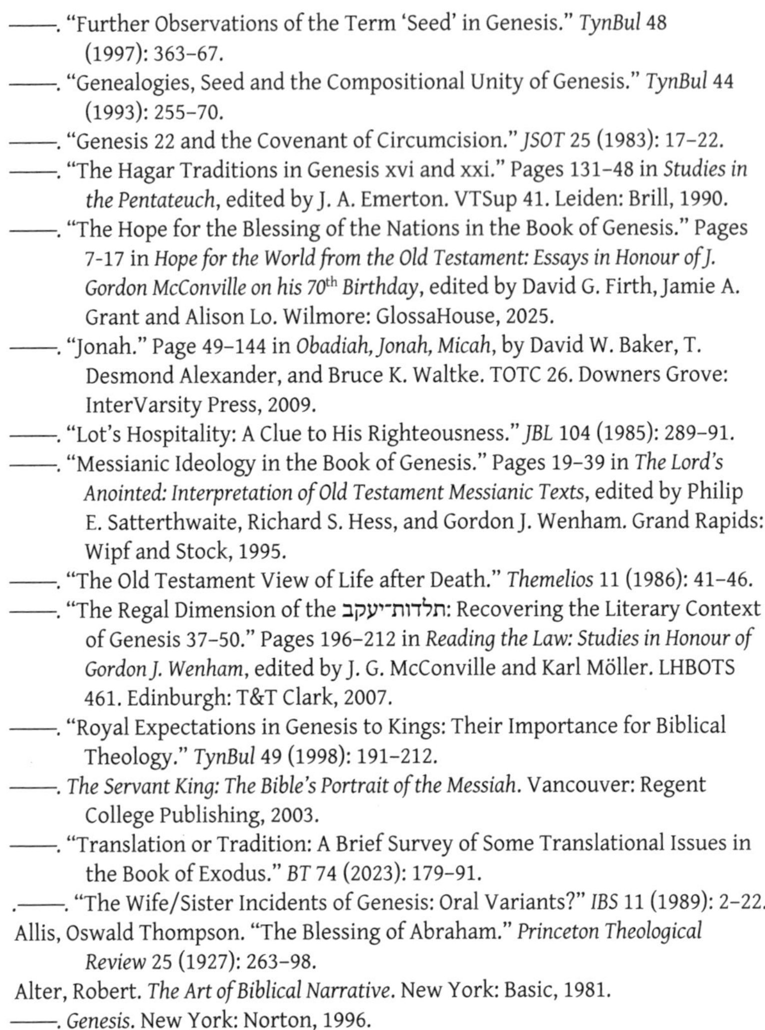

———. "Further Observations of the Term 'Seed' in Genesis." *TynBul* 48 (1997): 363–67.

———. "Genealogies, Seed and the Compositional Unity of Genesis." *TynBul* 44 (1993): 255–70.

———. "Genesis 22 and the Covenant of Circumcision." *JSOT* 25 (1983): 17–22.

———. "The Hagar Traditions in Genesis xvi and xxi." Pages 131–48 in *Studies in the Pentateuch*, edited by J. A. Emerton. VTSup 41. Leiden: Brill, 1990.

———. "The Hope for the Blessing of the Nations in the Book of Genesis." Pages 7-17 in *Hope for the World from the Old Testament: Essays in Honour of J. Gordon McConville on his 70th Birthday*, edited by David G. Firth, Jamie A. Grant and Alison Lo. Wilmore: GlossaHouse, 2025.

———. "Jonah." Page 49–144 in *Obadiah, Jonah, Micah*, by David W. Baker, T. Desmond Alexander, and Bruce K. Waltke. TOTC 26. Downers Grove: InterVarsity Press, 2009.

———. "Lot's Hospitality: A Clue to His Righteousness." *JBL* 104 (1985): 289–91.

———. "Messianic Ideology in the Book of Genesis." Pages 19–39 in *The Lord's Anointed: Interpretation of Old Testament Messianic Texts*, edited by Philip E. Satterthwaite, Richard S. Hess, and Gordon J. Wenham. Grand Rapids: Wipf and Stock, 1995.

———. "The Old Testament View of Life after Death." *Themelios* 11 (1986): 41–46.

———. "The Regal Dimension of the תלדות־יעקב: Recovering the Literary Context of Genesis 37–50." Pages 196–212 in *Reading the Law: Studies in Honour of Gordon J. Wenham*, edited by J. G. McConville and Karl Möller. LHBOTS 461. Edinburgh: T&T Clark, 2007.

———. "Royal Expectations in Genesis to Kings: Their Importance for Biblical Theology." *TynBul* 49 (1998): 191–212.

———. *The Servant King: The Bible's Portrait of the Messiah*. Vancouver: Regent College Publishing, 2003.

———. "Translation or Tradition: A Brief Survey of Some Translational Issues in the Book of Exodus." *BT* 74 (2023): 179–91.

.———. "The Wife/Sister Incidents of Genesis: Oral Variants?" *IBS* 11 (1989): 2–22.

Allis, Oswald Thompson. "The Blessing of Abraham." *Princeton Theological Review* 25 (1927): 263–98.

Alter, Robert. *The Art of Biblical Narrative*. New York: Basic, 1981.

———. *Genesis*. New York: Norton, 1996.

Amit, Yairah. "Progression as a Rhetorical Device in Biblical Literature." *JSOT* 28 (2003): 3–32.

Anderson, Bernhard W. "From Analysis to Synthesis: The Interpretation of Genesis 1 -11." *JBL* 97 (1978): 23–39.

———. *From Creation to New Creation: Old Testament Perspectives*. Minneapolis: Fortress, 1994.

Anderson, John E. "Jacob, Laban, and a Divine Trickster? The Covenantal Framework of God's Deception in the Theology of the Jacob Cycle." *PRSt* 36 (2009): 3–23.

Armgardt, Matthias, Benjamin Kilchör, and Markus Zehnder, eds. *Paradigm Change in Pentateuchal Research*. Beihefte zur Zeitschrift für Altorientalische und Biblische Rechtsgeschichte 22. Wiesbaden: Harrassowitz, 2019.

Arnold, Bill T. *Genesis*. Cambridge: Cambridge University Press, 2009.

Arnold, Bill T., and John H. Choi. *A Guide to Biblical Hebrew Syntax*. 2nd ed. Cambridge: Cambridge University Press, 2018.

Asselin, David Tobin. "Notion of Dominion in Genesis 1–3." *CBQ* 16 (1954): 277–94.

August, Jared M. "The Messianic Hope of Genesis: The Protoevangelium and Patriarchal Promises." *Themelios* 42 (2017): 46–62.

——. "The *Toledot* Structure of Genesis: Hope of Promise." *BSac* 174 (2017): 267–82.

Augustine. *The City of God*. Translated by Marcus Dods. In vol. 2 of *The Nicene and Post-Nicene Fathers*, Series 1. Edited by Philip Schaff. 1886–1889. 14 vols. Repr. Peabody: Hendrickson, 1994.

Averbeck, Richard E. "A Literary Day, Inter-Textual, and Contextual Reading of Genesis 1–2." Pages 7–34 in *Reading Genesis 1-2: An Evangelical Conversation*, edited by J. Daryl Charles. Peabody: Hendrickson, 2013.

Azevedo, Joaquim. "At the Door of Paradise: A Contextual Interpretation of Gen 4:7." *Biblische Notizen* 100 (1999): 45–59.

"Babel, Tower of." Pages 66–67 in *Dictionary of Biblical Imagery*, edited by Leland Ryken, James C. Wilhoit, and Tremper Longman III. Downers Grove: InterVarsity Press, 1998.

Baden, Joel S. *The Composition of the Pentateuch: Renewing the Documentary Hypothesis*. New Haven: Yale University Press, 2012

——. "Why Is the Pentateuch Unreadable? Or, Why Are We Doing This Anyway?" Pages 243–51 in *The Formation of the Pentateuch: Bridging the Academic Cultures of Europe, Israel and North America*, edited by Jan C. Gertz, Bernard M. Levinson, Dalit Rom-Shaloni, and Konrad Schmid. FAT 111. Tübingen: Mohr Siebeck, 2016.

Baker, David W. "Diversity and Unity in the Literary Structure of Genesis." Pages 189–205 in *Essays on the Patriarchal Narratives*, edited by A. R. Millard and Donald J. Wiseman. Leicester: Inter-Varsity Press, 1980.

Barker, Margaret. *The Gate of Heaven: The History and Symbolism of the Temple in Jerusalem*. London: SPCK, 1991.

Bartholomew, Craig G. "The Theology of Place in Genesis 1–3." Pages 173–95 in *Reading the Law: Studies in Honour of Gordon J. Wenham*, edited by J. G. McConville and Karl Möller. LHBOTS 461. Edinburgh: T&T Clark, 2007.

Bateman, Herbert W. IV, Darrell L. Bock, and Gordon Johnston. *Jesus the Messiah: Tracing the Promises, Expectations, and Coming of Israel's King*. Grand Rapids: Kregel, 2010.

Beale, Gregory K. "Eden, the Temple, and the Church's Mission in the New Creation." *JETS* 48 (2005): 5–31.

———. "The Final Vision of the Apocalypse and Its Implications for a Biblical Theology of the Temple." Pages 191–209 in *Heaven on Earth: The Temple in Biblical Theology*, edited by T. Desmond Alexander and Simon Gathercole. Carlisle: Paternoster, 2004.

———. *The Temple and the Church's Mission: A Biblical Theology of the Dwelling Place of God*. NSBT 17. Leicester: Apollos, 2004.

Bembry, Jason A. "Justifying Slavery Via Genesis 9:20–27: The Vicious Legacy of Racist Interpretation of the Bible." *Stone-Campbell Journal* 23 (2020): 69–82.

Berlinerblau, Jacques. "The Bible as Literature?" *HS* 45 (2004): 9–26.

Berman, Joshua A. *Inconsistency in the Torah: Ancient Literary Convention and the Limits of Source Criticism*. New York: Oxford University Press, 2017.

Blenkinsopp, Joseph. "The 'Covenant of Circumcision' (Gen 17) in the Context of the Abraham Cycle (Gen 11:27–25:11): Preliminary Considerations." Pages 145–56 in *The Post-Priestly Pentateuch: New Perspectives on Its Redactional Development and Theological Profiles*, edited by Federico Giuntoli and Konrad Schmid. FAT 101. Tübingen: Mohr Siebeck, 2015.

———. *Creation, Un-Creation, Re-Creation: A Discursive Commentary on Genesis 1–11*. London: T&T Clark, 2011.

Blocher, Henri. *In the Beginning: The Opening Chapters of Genesis*. Leicester: Inter-Varsity Press, 1984.

Block, Daniel I. *The Book of Ezekiel: Chapters 1–24*. NICOT. Grand Rapids: Eerdmans, 1997.

———. "Eden: A Temple? A Reassessment of the Biblical Evidence." Pages 3–29 in *From Creation to New Creation: Biblical Theology and Exegesis*, edited by Daniel M. Gurtner and Benjamin L. Gladd. Peabody: Hendrickson, 2013.

———. "My Servant David: Ancient Israel's Vision of the Messiah." Pages 17–56 in *Israel's Messiah in the Bible and the Dead Sea Scrolls*, edited by Richard S. Hess and M. Daniel Carroll. Grand Rapids: Wipf and Stock, 2003.

Blum, Erhard. "The Jacob Tradition." Pages 181–211 in *The Book of Genesis: Composition, Reception, and Interpretation*, edited by Craig A. Evans, Joel N. Lohr, and David L. Petersen. VTSup 152. Leiden: Brill, 2012.

Bompiani, Brian A. "Is Genesis 24 a Problem for Source Criticism?" *BSac* 164 (2007): 403–15.

———. "Style Switching in the Jacob and Laban Narratives." *HS* 55 (2014): 43–57.

———. "Style Switching in the Speech of Transjordanians." *HS* 57 (2016): 51–71.

Booij, Th. "Hagar's Words in Genesis xvi 13b." *VT* 30 (1980): 1–7.

Boyd, Samuel L. "The Flood and the Problem of Being an Omnivore." *JSOT* 43 (2018): 163–78.

Breasted, James Henry. *Ancient Records of Egypt: The Nineteenth Dynasty*. 4 vols. Chicago: University of Chicago Press, 1906.

Bridge, Edward J. "Polite Rhetoric: Judah's Plea to Joseph in Genesis 44.18–34." *JSOT* 43 (2019): 571–87.

———. "The 'Slave' Is the 'Master': Jacob's Servile Language to Esau in Genesis 33.1–17." *JSOT* 38 (2014): 263–78.

Bright, John. *Covenant and Promise: The Prophetic Understanding of the Future in Pre-Exilic Israel*. London: SCM, 1977.

Brodie, Thomas L. *Genesis as Dialogue: A Literary, Historical & Theological Commentary*. Oxford: Oxford University Press, 2001.

Bruce, F. F. "Sin, Redemption, and Sacrifice: A Biblical and Patristic Study." *Biblica* 54 (1973): 115–18.

Brueggemann, Walter. *Genesis*. Interpretation. Atlanta: John Knox, 1982.

Burlet, Dustin G. *Judgment and Salvation: A Rhetorical-Critical Reading of Noah's Flood in Genesis*. Eugene: Pickwick, 2022.

Burnett, Joel S. "Transjordan: The Ammonites, Moabites, and Edomites." Pages 309–52 in *The World around the Old Testament: The People and Places of the Ancient Near East*, edited by Bill T. Arnold and Brent A. Strawn. Grand Rapids: Baker Academic, 2016.

Carmichael, Calum M. "Some Sayings in Genesis 49." *JBL* 88 (1969): 435–44.

Carroll R., M. Daniel. "Blessing the Nations: Toward a Biblical Theology of Mission from Genesis." *BBR* 10 (2000): 17–34.

Cassuto, U. *A Commentary on the Book of Exodus*. Jerusalem: Magnes, 1967.

———. *A Commentary on the Book of Genesis: Part I: From Adam to Noah*. Jerusalem: Magnes, 1961.

———. *A Commentary on the Book of Genesis: Part II: From Noah to Abraham*. Jerusalem: Magnes, 1964.

———. "The Story of Tamar and Judah." Pages 29–40 in *Biblical and Oriental Studies*. Jerusalem: Magnes, 1973.

Cefalu, Rita F. "Royal Priestly Heirs to the Restoration Promise of Genesis 3:15: A Biblical Theological Perspective on the Sons of God in Genesis 6." *WTJ* 76 (2014): 351–70.

Chapman, Cynthia R. *The House of the Mother: The Social Roles of Maternal Kin in Biblical Hebrew Narrative and Poetry*. AYBRL. New Haven: Yale University Press, 2016.

Charles, J. Daryl, ed. *Reading Genesis 1–2: An Evangelical Conversation*. Peabody: Hendrickson, 2013.

Charles, R. H. *The Apocrypha and Pseudepigrapha of the Old Testament*. Vol. 2, *Pseudepigrapha*. Oxford: Clarendon, 1913.

Chase, Mitchell L. "The Genesis of Resurrection Hope: Exploring Its Early Presence and Deep Roots." *JETS* 57 (2014): 467–80.

Cheek, Jonathan M. "Recent Developments in the Interpretation of the Seed of the Woman in Genesis 3:15." *JETS* 64 (2021): 215–36.

Childs, Brevard S. *Biblical Theology of the Old and New Testaments: Theological Reflection on the Christian Bible*. London: SCM, 1992.

Chung, Il-Seung. "Hagar and Ishmael in Light of Abraham and Isaac: Reading Gen. 21:8–21 and Gen. 22:1–19 as a Dialogue." *ExpTim* 128 (2017): 573–82.

Claassens, L. Juliana M. "Resisting Dehumanization: Ruth, Tamar, and the Quest for Human Dignity." *CBQ* 74 (2012): 659–74.

Clark, W. Malcolm. "A Legal Background to the Yahwist's Use of 'Good and Evil' in Genesis 2–3." *JBL* 88 (1969): 266–78.

Clements, Ronald E. *Abraham and David: Genesis XV and Its Meaning for Israelite Tradition*. Studies in Biblical Theology, Second Series 5. London: SCM, 1967.

———. "*goy*." *TDOT*, 2:426–33.

Clifford, Richard J. "Genesis 37–50: Joseph Story or Jacob Story?" Pages 213–29 in *The Book of Genesis: Composition, Reception, and Interpretation*, edited by Craig A. Evans, Joel N. Lohr, and David L. Petersen. VTSup 152. Leiden: Brill, 2012.

———. "Genesis 38: Its Contribution to the Jacob Story." *CBQ* 66 (2004): 519–32.

Clines, David J. A. "אדם, the Hebrew for 'Human, Humanity': A Response to James Barr." *VT* 53 (2003): 297–310.

———. "The Image of God in Man." *TynBul* (1968): 53–103.

———. *The Theme of the Pentateuch*. JSOTSup 10. Sheffield: JSOT Press, 1978.

———. "What Does Eve Do To Help? And Other Irredeemably Androcentric Orientations in Genesis 1–3." Pages 25–48 in *What Does Eve Do To Help? And Other Readerly Questions to the Old Testament*. JSOTSup 94. Sheffield: JSOT Press, 1990.

Coats, George W. *From Canaan to Egypt: Structural and Theological Context for the Joseph Story*. CBQ Monograph Series 4. Washington: Catholic Biblical Association of America, 1976.

———. *Genesis with an Introduction to Narrative Literature*. FOTL 1. Grand Rapids: Eerdmans, 1983.

———. "The Joseph Story and Ancient Wisdom: A Reappraisal." *CBQ* 35 (1973): 285–97.

———. "Widow's Rights: A Crux in the Structure of Genesis 38." *CBQ* 34 (1972): 461–66.

Cody, Aelred. "When Is a Chosen People Called a Gôy?" *VT* 14 (1964): 1–6.

Collins, C. John. "Galatians 3:16: What Kind of an Exegete Was Paul?" *TynBul* 54 (2003): 75–86.

———. *Genesis 1-4: A Linguistic, Literary, and Theological Commentary*. Phillipsburg: P&R, 2006.

———. "Reading Genesis 1–11 with the Grain: Analogical Days." Pages 73–92 in *Reading Genesis 1-2: An Evangelical Conversation*, edited by J. Daryl Charles. Peabody: Hendrickson, 2013.

———. "A Syntactical Note (Genesis 3:15): Is the Woman's Seed Singular or Plural?" *TynBul* 48 (1997): 139–48.

Condren, Janson C. "Toward a Purge of the Battle of the Sexes and 'Return' for the Original Meaning of Genesis 3:16b." *JETS* 60 (2017): 227–45.

Currid, John D. "Genesis." Pages 37–63 in *A Biblical-Theological Introduction to the Old Testament: The Gospel Promised*, edited by Miles V. Van Pelt. Wheaton: Crossway, 2016.

Curtis, Edward M. "Structure, Style and Context as a Key to Interpreting Jacob's Encounter at Peniel." *JETS* 30 (1987): 129–37.

Dalrymple, Sarah. "Ephraim or Judah: Divine Sovereignty and the Potential for Kingship in Joshua-Judges." Pages 50–73 in *The Seed of Promise: The*

Sufferings and Glory of the Messiah: Essays in Honor of T. Desmond Alexander, edited by Paul R. Williamson and Rita F. Cefalu. GlossaHouse Festschrift Series 3. Wilmore: GlossaHouse, 2020

Davidson, Richard M. "Earth's First Sanctuary: Genesis 1–3 and Parallel Creation Accounts." *AUSS* 53 (2015): 65–89.

——. *Flame of Yahweh: Sexuality in the Old Testament*. Peabody: Hendrickson, 2007.

——. "The Genesis Account of Origins." Pages 59–129 in *The Genesis Creation Account and Its Reverberations in the Old Testament*, edited by Gerald A. Klingbeil. Creation in the Bible Series. Berrien Springs: Andrews University Press, 2015.

Davies, Eryl W. "Inheritance Rights and the Hebrew Levirate Marriage, Part 1." *VT* 31 (1981): 138–44.

——. "Inheritance Rights and the Hebrew Levirate Marriage: Part 2." *VT* 31 (1981): 257–68.

Day, John. "Noah's Drunkenness, the Curse of Canaan, Ham's Crime, and the Blessing of Shem and Japheth (Genesis 9:18–27)." Pages 31–44 in *Leshon Limmudim: Essays on the Language and Literature of the Hebrew Bible in Honour of A. A. Macintosh*, edited by David A. Baer and Robert P. Gordon. London: T&T Clark, 2013.

Dean, David Andrew. "Covenant, Conditionality, and Consequence: New Terminology and a Case Study in the Abrahamic Covenant." *JETS* 57 (2014): 281–308.

Deenick, Karl. *Righteous by Promise: A Biblical Theology of Circumcision*. NSBT 45. London: Apollos, 2018.

Dempster, Stephen G. "The End of History and the Last Man." Pages 113–41 in *The Seed of Promise: The Sufferings and Glory of the Messiah: Essays in Honor of T. Desmond Alexander*, edited by Paul R. Williamson and Rita F. Cefalu. GlossaHouse Festschrift Series 3. Wilmore: GlossaHouse, 2020

——. "'He Believed the Lord': The Pedigree of Justification in the Pentateuch." Pages 37–62 in *The Doctrine on Which the Church Stands or Falls: Justification in Biblical, Theological, Historical, and Pastoral Perspectives*, edited by Matthew Barrett. Wheaton, IL: Crossway, 2019.

DeRouchie, Jason S. "The Blessing-Commission, the Promised Offspring, and the Toledot Structure of Genesis." *JETS* 56 (2013): 219–47.

——. "Circumcision in the Hebrew Bible and Targums: Theology, Rhetoric, and the Handling of Metaphor." *BBR* 14 (2004): 175–203.

——. "Counting Stars with Abraham and the Prophets: New Covenant Ecclesiology in OT Perspective." *JETS* 58 (2015): 445–85.

——. "Father of a Multitude of Nations: New Covenant Ecclesiology in OT Perspective." Pages 7–38 in *Progressive Covenantalism: Charting a Course between Dispensational and Covenant Theologies*, edited by Stephen J. Wellum and Brent E. Parker. Nashville: B&H Academic, 2016.

DeRouchie, Jason S., and Jason C. Meyer. "Christ or Family as the 'Seed' of Promise? An Evaluation of N. T. Wright on Galatians 3:16." *SBJT* 14 (2010): 36–48.

Diamond, J. A. "The Deception of Jacob: A New Perspective on an Ancient Solution to the Problem." *VT* 34 (1984): 211–13.

Diffey, Daniel S. "The Royal Promise in Genesis: The Often Underestimated Importance of Genesis 17:6, 17:16 and 35:11." *TynBul* 62 (2011): 313–16.

Dörnyei, Zoltan. *Progressive Creation and the Struggles of Humanity in the Bible: A Canonical Narrative Interpretation*. Eugene: Pickwick, 2018.

Driver, S. R. *The Book of Genesis*. London: Methuen, 1905.

———. *A Treatise on the Use of the Tenses in Hebrew and Some Other Syntactical Questions*. 10th ed. London: Methuen, 1916.

Dumbrell, William J. *Covenant and Creation: An Old Testament Covenantal Theology*. Exeter: Paternoster, 1984.

———. "Genesis 2:1–17: A Foreshadowing of the New Creation." Pages 53–65 in *Biblical Theology: Retrospect and Prospect*, edited by Scott J. Hafemann. Downers Grove: InterVarsity Press, 2002.

Eberhart, Christian A. "A Neglected Feature of Sacrifice in the Hebrew Bible: Remarks on the Burning Rite on the Altar." *HTR* 97 (2004): 485–93.

Ehrlich, Carl S. "Philistia and the Philistines." Pages 353–77 in *The World around the Old Testament: The People and Places of the Ancient Near East*, edited by Bill T. Arnold and Brent A. Strawn. Grand Rapids: Baker Academic, 2016.

Elgvin, Torleif. *Warrior, King, Servant, Savior: Messianism in the Hebrew Bible and Early Jewish Texts*. Grand Rapids: Eerdmans, 2022.

Emadi, Samuel. *From Prisoner to Prince: The Joseph Story in Biblical Theology*, NSBT. Downers Grove: InterVarsity Press Academic, 2022.

Emerton, J. A. "An Examination of Some Attempts to Defend the Unity of the Flood Narrative in Genesis: Part I." *VT* 37 (1987): 401–20.

———. "An Examination of Some Attempts to Defend the Unity of the Flood Narrative in Genesis: Part II." *VT* 38 (1988): 1–21.

———. "The Origin of the Promises to the Patriarchs in the Older Sources of the Book of Genesis." *VT* 32 (1982): 14–32.

———. "Some Problems in Genesis 38." *VT* 25 (1975): 338–61.

Eslinger, Lyle M. "A Contextual Identification of the *bene ha'elohim* and *benoth ha'adam* in Genesis 6:1–4." *JSOT* 4 (1979): 65–73.

Fensham, F. Charles. "Son of a Handmaid in Northwest Semitic." *VT* 19 (1969): 312–21.

Fentress-Williams, Judy. "Location, Location, Location: Tamar in the Joseph Cycle." *The Bible and Critical Theory* 3 (2007): 201–8.

Finkelstein, J. J. "The Ox That Gored." *Transactions of the American Philosophical Society* 71 (1981): 5–47.

Firth, David G. *Joshua*. Evangelical Biblical Theology Commentary. Bellingham: Lexham Academic, 2021.

Fishbane, Michael A. *Text and Texture. Close Readings of Selected Biblical Texts*. New York: Schocken, 1979.

Foh, Susan T. "What is the Woman's Desire." *WTJ* 37 (1975): 376–83.

Fokkelman, J. P. *Narrative Art in Genesis: Specimens of Stylistic and Structural Analysis*. 2nd ed. Eugene: Wipf and Stock, 2004.

Fox, Everett. *The Five Books of Moses: Genesis, Exodus, Leviticus, Numbers, Deuteronomy; a New Translation with Introductions, Commentary, and Notes*. The Schocken Bible. New York: Schocken, 1995.

———. *Genesis and Exodus: A New English Rendition*. New York: Schocken, 1991.

———. "Stalking the Younger Brother: Some Models for Understanding a Biblical Motif." *JSOT* 60 (1993): 45–68.

Fox, Michael V. "Joseph and Wisdom." Pages 231–62 in *The Book of Genesis: Composition, Reception, and Interpretation*, edited by Craig A. Evans, Joel N. Lohr, and David L. Petersen. VTSup 152. Leiden: Brill, 2012.

Fretheim, Terence E. *God and World in the Old Testament: A Relational Theology of Creation*. Nashville: Abingdon, 2005.

———. "Violence and the God of the Old Testament." Pages 108–27 in *Encountering Violence in the Bible*, edited by Markus Zehnder and Hallvard Hagelia. The Bible in the Modern World 55. Sheffield: Sheffield Phoenix, 2013.

Frolov, Serge. "Judah Comes to Shiloh: Genesis 49:10bα, One More Time." *JBL* 131 (2012): 417–22.

Frymer-Kensky, Tikva S. "Atrahasis Epic and Its Significance for Our Understanding of Genesis 1–9." *BA* 40 (1977): 147–55.

Fuller Dow, Lois K. *Images of Zion: Biblical Antecedents for the New Jerusalem*. New Testament Monographs 26. Sheffield: Sheffield Phoenix Press, 2010.

Futato, Mark D. "Because It Had Rained: A Study of Gen 2:5–7 with Implications for Gen 2:4–25 and Gen 1:1–2:3." *WTJ* 60 (1998): 1–21.

Gentry, Peter J. and Stephen J. Wellum. *Kingdom through Covenant: A Biblical-Theological Understanding of the Covenants*. Wheaton: Crossway, 2012.

Gesenius, H. F. W. *Gesenius' Hebrew Grammar*. Edited by E. Kautzsch. Translated by A. E. Cowley. 2nd ed. Oxford: Clarendon, 1910.

Gilbert, Pierre. *God Never Meant for Us to Die: The Emergence of Evil in the Light of the Genesis Creation Account*. Eugene: Wipf and Stock, 2020.

Goldenberg, David M. *Black and Slave: The Origins and History of the Curse of Ham*, Studies of the Bible and Its Reception 10. Berlin: de Gruyter, 2017.

———. *The Curse of Ham: Race and Slavery in Early Judaism, Christianity, and Islam*. Princeton: Princeton University Press, 2003.

Goldin, Judah. "The Youngest Son or Where Does Genesis 38 Belong." *JBL* 96 (1977): 27–28.

Goldingay, John. *Old Testament Theology: Israel's Gospel*. Downers Grove: InterVarsity Press Academic, 2003.

———. "The Patriarchs in Scripture and Tradition" Pages 11–42 in *Essays on the Patriarchal Narratives*, edited by A. R. Millard and Donald J. Wiseman. Leicester: Inter-Varsity Press, 1980.

Golka, Friedemann W. "Genesis 37–50: Joseph Story or Israel-Joseph Story?" *CurBR* 2 (2004): 153–77.

Gooding, David W. *The Riches of Divine Wisdom: The New Testament's Use of the Old Testament*. Coleraine: Myrtlefield House, 2013.

Gordis, Daniel H. "Lies, Wives and Sisters: The Wife-Sister Motif Revisited." *Judaism* 34 (1985): 344–59.

Gordon, Cyrus H. "Biblical Customs and the Nuzu Tablets." *BA* 3 (1940): 1–12.

Gordon, Robert P. "The Ethics of Eden: Truth-Telling in Genesis 2–3." Pages 11–33 in *Ethical and Unethical in the Old Testament: God and Humans in Dialogue*, edited by Katharine J. Dell. LHBOTS 528. London: T&T Clark, 2010.

———. "Evensong in Eden: As It Probably Was Not in the Beginning." Pages 17–30 in *Leshon Limmudim: Essays on the Language and Literature of the Hebrew Bible in Honour of A. A. Macintosh*, edited by David A. Baer and Robert P. Gordon. London: T&T Clark, 2013.

———. "The Week That Made the World: Reflections on the First Pages of the Bible." Pages 228–41 in *Reading the Law: Studies in Honour of Gordon J. Wenham*, edited by J. G. McConville and Karl Möller. LHBOTS 461. Edinburgh: T&T Clark, 2007.

———. "Who 'Began to Call on the Name of the Lord' in Genesis 4:26b? The MT and the Versions." Pages 57–68 in *Let Us Go up to Zion: Essays in Honour of H. G. M. Williamson on the Occasion of His Sixty-Fifth Birthday*, edited by Iain W. Provan and Mark J. Boda. Leiden: Brill, 2012.

Gowan, Donald E. *Eschatology in the Old Testament*. Philadelphia: Fortress, 1986.

Green, Barbara. *What Profit for Us? Remembering the Story of Joseph*. Lanham: University Press of America, 1996.

Green, William Henry. "Primeval Chronology." *BSac* 47 (1890): 285–303.

Greenberg, Moshe. "Another Look at Rachel's Theft of the Teraphim." *JBL* 81 (1962): 239–48.

———. "Some Postulates of Biblical Criminal Law." Pages 5–28 in *Yehezkel Kaufmann Jubilee Volume*, edited by Menahem Haran. Jerusalem: Magnes, 1960.

Greengus, Samuel. "Sisterhood Adoption at Nuzi and the 'Wife-Sister' in Genesis." *Hebrew Union College Annual* 46 (1975): 5–31.

Greenspahn, Frederick E. *When Brothers Dwell Together: The Preeminence of Younger Siblings in the Hebrew Bible*. Oxford: Oxford University Press, 199.

Gunkel, Hermann. *Genesis*. Translated by Mark E. Biddle. Mercer Library of Biblical Studies. Macon: Mercer University Press, 1997.

Habel, Norman C. *Literary Criticism of the Old Testament*. Philadelphia: Fortress, 1971.

Hahn, Scott W. *Kinship by Covenant: A Canonical Approach to the Fulfillment of God's Saving Promises*. AYBRL. New Haven: Yale University Press, 2009.

Hamilton, James M. "The Seed of the Woman and the Blessing of Abraham." *TynBul* 58 (2007): 253–73.

Hamilton, Victor P. *The Book of Genesis: Chapters 1-17*. NICOT. Grand Rapids: Eerdmans, 1990.

———. *The Book of Genesis: Chapters 18-50*. NICOT. Grand Rapids: Eerdmans, 1995.

———. "Genesis: Theology of." *NIDOTTE*, 4:663–75.

Han, Jin H. "The Role of 'an Audience' in Isaac's Blessing in Genesis 27." *PRSt* 42 (2015): 5–10.

Harper, G. Geoffrey. *"I Will Walk among You": The Rhetorical Function of Allusion to Genesis 1-3 in the Book of Leviticus*. BBRSup 21. University Park: Eisenbrauns, 2018.

Hart, Ian. "Genesis 1:1–2:3 as a Prologue to the Book of Genesis." *TynBul* 46 (1995): 315–36.

Hasel, Gerhard F. "The Meaning of 'Let Us' in Gn 1:26." *AUSS* 13 (1975): 58–66.

———. "The Meaning of the Animal Rite in Gen. 15." *JSOT* 19 (1981): 61–78.

———. "The Polemic Nature of the Genesis Cosmology." *EvQ* 46 (1974): 81–102.

Haynes, Stephen R. *Noah's Curse: The Biblical Justification of American Slavery*. New York: Oxford University Press, 2002.

Hays, J. Daniel. *The Temple and the Tabernacle: A Study of God's Dwelling Places from Genesis to Revelation*. Grand Rapids: Baker, 2016.

Heide, Martin. "The Domestication of the Camel: Biological, Archaeological and Inscriptional Evidence from Mesopotamia, Egypt, Israel and Arabia, and Literary Evidence from the Hebrew Bible." *Ugarit Forschungen* 42 (2010): 331–84.

Henry, Matthew. *An Exposition of the Old Testament: Wherein Each Chapter is Summed up in Its Contents: The Sacred Text Inserted at Large, in Distinct Paragraphs, Each Paragraph Reduced to Its Proper Heads: The Sense Given, and Largely Illuminated: With Practical Remarks and Observations. Old Testament*. Vol. 1. London: James Nisbet, 1857.

Hess, Richard S. "Adam, Father, He: Gender Issues in Hebrew Translation." *BT* 56 (2005): 144–53.

———. *Joshua*. TOTC. Leicester: Inter-Varsity Press, 1996.

———. "Lamech in the Genealogies of Genesis." *BBR* 1 (1991): 21–25.

———. "The Roles of the Woman and the Man in Genesis 3." *Themelios* 18 (1993): 15–19.

———. "Second-Millennium BC Cuneiform from the Southern Levant and the Literature of the Pentateuch." Pages 66–72 in *Exploring the Composition of the Pentateuch*, edited by L. S. Baker Jr., Kenneth Bergland, Felipe A. Masotti, and A. Rahel Wells. BBRSup 27. University Park: Eisenbrauns, 2020.

———. "The Slaughter of the Animals in Genesis 15: Genesis 15:8–21 and Its Ancient Near Eastern Context." Pages 55–65 in *He Swore an Oath: Biblical*

Themes from Genesis 20–50, edited by R. S. Hess, G. J. Wenham, and P. R. Satterthwaite. 2nd ed. Grand Rapids: Wipf and Stock, 1994.

———. "Splitting the Adam: The Usage of ʾādām in Genesis i-v." Pages 1–15 in *Studies in the Pentateuch*, edited by J. A. Emerton. VTSup 41. Leiden: Brill, 1990.

———. *Studies in the Personal Names of Genesis 1–11*. Alter Orient und Altes Testament. Kevelaer: Butzon & Bercker, 1993.

Hiebert, Theodore. "The Tower of Babel and the Origin of the World's Cultures." *JBL* 126 (2007): 29–58.

Hildebrandt, Wilf. *An Old Testament Theology of the Spirit of God*. Peabody: Hendrickson, 199.

Ho, Andrew Chinpeng. "A Paragon of Faith? Doubting Abraham." *Themelios* 42 (2017): 452–64.

Hoekema, Anthony A. *Created in God's Image*. Grand Rapids: Eerdmans, 1986.

Hoffmeier, James K. *Israel in Egypt: The Evidence for the Authenticity of the Exodus Tradition*. New York: Oxford University Press, 1997.

Holmgren, F. C. "Looking Back on Abraham's Encounter with a Canaanite King: A Reversal of Expectations (Genesis 20:1–18)." *Currents in Theology and Mission* 37 (2010): 366–77.

Hom, Mary Katherine Y. H. "'... A Mighty Hunter before YHWH': Genesis 10:9 and the Moral-Theological Evaluation of Nimrod." *VT* 60 (2010): 63–68.

Hoop, Raymond de. *Genesis 49 in Its Literary and Historical Context*. Oudtestamentische Studien 39. Leiden: Brill, 1999.

Houtman, C. "What Did Jacob See in His Dream at Bethel? Some Remarks on Genesis xxviii 10–22." *VT* 27 (1977): 337–51.

Howard, David M. *Joshua*, NAC 5. Nashville: Broadman & Holman, 1998.

———. "Philistines." *NIDOTTE*, 4, 1048–52.

———. "Philistines." Pages 231–50 in *Peoples of the Old Testament World*, edited by Alfred J. Hoerth, Gerald L. Mattingly, and Edwin M. Yamauchi. Cambridge: Lutterworth, 1996.

Hutter, M. "Adam als Gärtner und König (Gen 2:8,15)." *Biblische Zeitschrift* 30 (1986): 258–62.

Jackson, Bernard S. *Wisdom-Laws: A Study of the Mishpatim of Exodus 21:1–22:16*. Oxford: Oxford University Press, 2006.

Jacob, Benno. *The First Book of the Bible: Genesis*. Translated by Ernest I. Jacob and Walter Jacob. New York: Ktav, 1974.

Janzen, J. Gerald, and John T. Noble. "Did Hagar Give Ishmael up for Dead? Gen. 21.14–21 Re-Visited." *JSOT* 44 (2020): 517–31.

Jenni, E. "Messiah, Jewish." *IDB*, 3:360–65.

Johnson, Sylvester A. *The Myth of Ham in Nineteenth-Century American Christianity: Race, Heathens, and the People of God*. Black Religion, Womanist Thought, Social Justice. New York: Palgrave Macmillan, 2004.

Johnston, J. Derek. "Setting the Book of Ruth in Its Literary Context with Special Reference to the Epilogue of the Book of Judges." *IBS* 27 (2009): 156–62.

Johnston, Philip S. *Shades of Sheol: Death and Afterlife in the Old Testament.* Leicester: Apollos, 2002.

Jónsson, Gunnlaugur A. *The Image of God: Genesis 1:26–28 in a Century of Old Testament Research.* ConBOT 26. Stockholm: Almqvist & Wiksell, 1988.

Joosten, Jan. "Biblical Rhetoric as Illustrated by Judah's Speech in Genesis 44.18–34." *JSOT* 41 (2016): 15–30.

Joüon, Paul. *A Grammar of Biblical Hebrew.* Translated and revised by T. Muraoka. 2nd ed. Subsidia Biblica 27. Rome: Pontifical Biblical Institute, 2006.

Kaminski, Carol M. *Was Noah Good? Finding Favour in the Flood Narrative.* LHBOTS 563. London: Bloomsbury T&T Clark, 2014.

Kang, Hwagu. *Reading the Wife/Sister Narratives in Genesis: A Textlinguistic and Type-Scene Analysis.* Eugene: Pickwick, 2018.

Kapelrud, Arvid. S. "Temple Building: A Task for Gods and Kings." *Orientalia* 32 (1963): 56–62.

Kawashima, Robert S. "Literary Analysis." Pages 83–104 in *The Book of Genesis: Composition, Reception, and Interpretation,* edited by Craig A. Evans, Joel N. Lohr, and David L. Petersen. VTSup 152. Leiden: Brill, 2012.

Keil, C. F., and F. Delitzsch. *The Pentateuch.* Biblical Commentary on the Old Testament. Edinburgh: T&T Clark, 1869.

Keiser, Thomas A. "The Divine Plural: A Literary-Contextual Argument of Plurality in the Godhead." *JSOT* 34 (2009): 131–46.

Kidner, Derek. *Genesis: An Introduction and Commentary.* TOTC. Leicester: Inter-Varsity Press, 1967.

Kikawada, Isaac. "The Shape of Genesis 11:1–9." Pages 18–32 in *Rhetorical Criticism: Essays in Honor of James Muilenburg,* edited by Jared J. Jackson and Martin Kessler. Pittsburgh: Pickwick, 1974.

Kim, Dohyung. "Genesis 37–50: The Story of Jacob and His Sons in Light of the Primary Narrative (Genesis–2 Kings)." *ExpTim* 123 (2012): 486–93.

———. "The Structure of Genesis 38: A Thematic Reading." *VT* 62 (2012): 550–60.

Kim, Hyun Chin Paul. "Reading the Joseph Story (Genesis 37–50) as a Diaspora Narrative." *CBQ* 75 (2013): 219–38.

Kitchen, Kenneth A. *On the Reliability of the Old Testament.* Grand Rapids: Eerdmans, 2003.

Kline, Meredith G. *By Oath Consigned: A Reinterpretation of the Covenant Signs of Circumcision and Baptism.* Grand Rapids: Eerdmans, 1968.

———. "Divine Kingship and Genesis 6:1–4." *WTJ* 24 (1962): 187–204.

Knoppers, Gary N. "Ancient Near Eastern Royal Grants and the Davidic Covenant: A Parallel?" *JAOS* 116 (1996): 670–97.

Kramer, Samuel Noah. *The Sumerians: Their History, Culture, and Character.* Chicago: University of Chicago Press, 1963.

Kraut, Judah. "The Literary Roles of Reuben and Judah in Genesis Narratives: A 'Reflection Complex.'" *JSOT* 43 (2019): 205–27.

Kruschwitz, Jonathan. "The Type-Scene Connection Between Genesis 38 and the Joseph Story." *JSOT* 36 (2012): 383–410.

Lacocque, André. "Whatever Happened in the Valley of Shinar? A Response to Theodore Hiebert." *JBL* 128 (2009): 29–41.

Lambdin, Thomas O. *Introduction to Biblical Hebrew*. London: Darton, Longman and Todd, 1973.

Lambe, Anthony J. "Judah's Development: The Pattern of Departure-Transition-Return." *JSOT* 24 (1999): 53–68.

Larsson, Gerhard. "Septuagint Versus Massoretic Chronology." *ZAW* 114 (2002): 511–21.

Lawton, Robert B. "Genesis 2:24: Trite or Tragic?" *JBL* 105 (1986): 97–98.

Lee, Chee-Chiew. "גים in Genesis 35:11 and the Abrahamic Promise of Blessings for the Nations." *JETS* 52 (2009): 467–82.

———. "Once Again: The Niphal and the Hithpael of ברך in the Abrahamic Blessing for the Nations." *JSOT* 36 (2012): 279–96.

Lehmann, Manfred R. "Abraham's Purchase of Machpelah and Hittite Law." *BASOR* 129 (1953): 15–18.

Limburg, James. "The Responsibility of Royalty: Genesis 1–11 and the Care of the Earth." *Word & World* 11 (1991): 124–30.

Livingston, David P. "Location of Biblical Bethel and Ai Reconsidered." *WTJ* 33 (1970): 20–44.

———. "Traditional Site of Bethel Questioned." *WTJ* 34 (1971): 39–50.

Lohr, Joel N. "Sexual Desire? Eve, Genesis 3:16 and תשוקה." *JBL* 130 (2011): 227–46.

Long, Jesse. "Wrestling with God to Win: A Literary Reading of the Story of Jacob at Jabbok in Honor of Don Williams." *Stone-Campbell Journal* 15 (2012): 47–61.

Longacre, Robert E. *Joseph: A Story of Divine Providence: A Text Theoretical and Textlinguistic Analysis of Genesis 37 and 39–48*. Winona Lake: Eisenbrauns, 1989.

———. "Weqatal Forms in Biblical Hebrew Prose: A Discourse-Modular Approach." Pages 50–98 in *Biblical Hebrew and Discourse Linguistics*, edited by Robert D. Bergen. Winona Lake: Eisenbrauns, 1994.

Longman, Tremper III. *How to Read Genesis*. Downers Grove: InterVarsity Press, 2005.

———. "What Genesis 1–2 Teaches (and What It Doesn't)." Pages 103–28 in *Reading Genesis 1–2: An Evangelical Conversation*, edited by J. Daryl Charles. Peabody: Hendrickson, 2013.

Lowenthal, Eric I. *The Joseph Narrative in Genesis: An Interpretation*. New York: Ktav, 1973.

Mabee, Charles. "Jacob and Laban: The Structure of Judicial Proceedings (Genesis xxxi 25–42)." *VT* 30 (1980): 192–207.

Makujina, John. "'Behold, There Were Twins in Her Womb' (Gen. 25:24–26; 38:27–30): Medical Science and the Twin Births in Genesis." *TynBul* 68 (2017): 39–58.

Malul, M. "'āqēb 'Heel' and 'āqab 'To Supplant' and the Concept of Succession in the Jacob-Esau Narratives." *VT* 46 (1996): 190–212.

Mann, Steven T. "Let There Be Cain: A Clash of Imaginations in Genesis 4." *JSOT* (2021): 79–95.

Martens, Elmer A. *Plot and Purpose in the Old Testament*. Leicester: Inter-Varsity Press, 1981.

Martin, R. A. "The Earliest Messianic Interpretation of Genesis 3:15." *JBL* 84 (1965): 425–27.

Mason, Steven D. *"Eternal Covenant" in the Pentateuch: The Contours of an Elusive Phrase*. LHBOTS 494. New York: T&T Clark, 2008.

Mathews, Kenneth A. *Genesis 1–11:26*. NAC 1A. Nashville: Broadman & Holman, 1995.

———. *Genesis 11:27–50:26*. NAC 1B. Nashville: Broadman & Holman, 2005.

Mathewson, Steven D. "An Exegetical Study of Genesis 38." *BSac* 146 (1989): 373–92.

Mattingly, Gerald L. "Moabites." Pages 317–34 in *Peoples of the Old Testament World*, edited by Alfred J. Hoerth, Gerald L. Mattingly, and Edwin M. Yamauchi. Cambridge: Lutterworth, 1996.

McCartney, Dan G. "*Ecce Homo*: The Coming of the Kingdom as the Restoration of Human Vicegerency." *WTJ* 56 (1994): 1–21.

McComiskey, Thomas E. *The Covenants of Promise: A Theology of the Old Testament Covenants*. Nottingham: Inter-Varsity Press, 1985.

McConville, J. Gordon. "Abraham and Melchizedek: Horizons in Genesis 14." Pages 93–118 in *He Swore an Oath: Biblical Themes from Genesis 20–50*, edited by R. S. Hess, G. J. Wenham, and P. R. Satterthwaite. 2nd ed. Grand Rapids: Wipf and Stock, 1994.

———. "Jerusalem in the Old Testament." Pages 21–51 in *Jerusalem Past and Present in the Purposes of God*, edited by P. W. L. Walker. Croydon: Deo Gloria Trust, 1992.

McKenzie, Brian Alexander. "Jacob's Blessing on Pharaoh: An Interpretation of Gen 46:31–47:26." *WTJ* 45 (1983): 386–99.

McKenzie, Steve L. "'You Have Prevailed': The Function of Jacob's Encounter at Peniel in the Jacob Cycle." *Restoration Quarterly* 23 (1980): 225–31.

McKeown, James. "Blessings and Curses." Pages 83–87 in *Dictionary of the Old Testament: Pentateuch*, edited by T. Desmond Alexander and David W. Baker. Downers Grove: InterVarsity Press, 2003.

———. *Genesis*. Two Horizons Old Testament Commentary 1. Grand Rapids: Eerdmans, 2008.

———. "Messianic Trajectories in Ruth—A Redeemer and Great Name." Pages 74–89 in *The Seed of Promise: The Sufferings and Glory of the Messiah: Essays in Honor of T. Desmond Alexander*, edited by Paul R. Williamson and Rita F. Cefalu. GlossaHouse Festschrift Series 3. Wilmore: GlossaHouse, 2020.

Menn, Esther Marie. *Judah and Tamar (Genesis 38) in Ancient Jewish Exegesis: Studies in Literary Form and Hermeneutics*. Leiden: Brill, 1997.

Merrill, Eugene H. "The Book of Ruth: Narration and Shared Themes." *BSac* 142 (1986): 130–39.

Meyers, Carol L. "Gender Roles and Genesis 3:16 Revisited." Pages 337–54 in *The Word of the Lord Shall Go Forth: Essays in Honor of David Noel Freedman*, edited by Carol L. Meyers and M. O'Connor. Winona Lake: Eisenbrauns, 1983.

———. *The Tabernacle Menorah: A Synthetic Study of a Symbol from the Biblical Cult*. ASOR Dissertation Series. Missoula: Scholars, 1976.

Miano, David. *Shadow on the Steps: Time Measurement in Ancient Israel*. Resources for Biblical Study 64. Atlanta: SBL, 2010.

Michael, Matthew. "The Dead Trickster and His Shrewd Children? The Persuasive Use of the Double Quotations of a Dead Patriarch in Genesis 49:29–50:21." *JSOT* 43 (2018): 179–90.

Middleton, J. Richard. "The Blessing of Abraham and the *Missio Dei*: Reframing the Purpose of Israel's Election in Genesis 12:1–3." Pages 44–64 in *Orthodoxy and Orthopraxis: Essays in Tribute to Paul Livermore*, edited by Douglas R. Cullum and J. Richard Middleton. Eugene: Pickwick, 2020.

———. *The Liberating Image: The Imago Dei in Genesis 1*. Grand Rapids: Brazos, 2005.

Millard, A. R. "The Etymology of Eden." *VT* 34 (1984): 103–6.

———. "The Meaning of the Name Judah." *ZAW* 86 (1974): 216–18.

———. "Where Was Abraham's Ur? The Case for the Babylonian City." *Biblical Archaeology Review* 27 (2001): 52–53, 57.

Millard, A. R., and P. Bordreuil. "A Statue from Syria with Assyrian and Aramaic Inscriptions." *BA* 45 (1982): 124–43.

Millard, A. R., J. K. Hoffmeier, and D. W. Baker, eds. *Faith, Tradition, and History: Old Testament Historiography in Its Near Eastern Context*. Winona Lake: Eisenbrauns, 1994.

Millard, A. R. and Donald J. Wiseman, eds. *Essays on the Patriarchal Narratives*. Leicester: Inter-Varsity Press, 1980.

Miller, Patrick D. Jr. "Syntax and Theology in Genesis xii 3a." *VT* 34 (1984): 472–76.

Mitchell, David C. *Messiah ben Joseph*. Newton Mearns: Campbell, 2016.

Moberly, R. W. L. "Abraham's Righteousness (Genesis xv 6)." Pages 103–30 in *Studies in the Pentateuch*, edited by J. A. Emerton. VTSup 41. Leiden: Brill, 1990.

———. *From Eden to Golgotha: Essays in Biblical Theology*. South Florida Studies in the History of Judaism. Atlanta: Scholars, 1992.

Möller, Karl. "Images of God and Creation in Genesis 1–2." Pages 3–29 in *A God of Faithfulness: Essays in Honour of J. Gordon McConville on His 60th Birthday*, edited by Jamie A. Grant, Alison Lo, and Gordon Wenham. LHBOTS 538. New York: T&T Clark, 2011.

Morales, L. Michael. *Exodus Old and New: A Biblical Theology of Redemption*. Essential Studies in Biblical Theology. Downers Grove: InterVarsity Press Academic, 2020.

Moran, W. L. "The Scandal of the 'Great Sin' at Ugarit." *JNES* 18 (1959): 280–81.

Moskala, Jiri. "Interpretation of *bereʾšît* in the Context of Genesis 1:1–3." *AUSS* 49 (2011): 33–44.

Muilenburg, James. "Abraham and the Nations: Blessing and World History." *Int* 19 (1965): 387–98.

Murphy, James Gracey. *A Critical and Exegetical Commentary on the Book of Genesis with a New Translation*. Edinburgh: T&T Clark, 1863.

Newsom, Carol A. "Angels." *ABD*, 1:248–53.

Nicol, George G. "Story-Patterning in Genesis." Pages 215–33 in *Text as Pretext: Essays in Honour of Robert Davidson*, edited by Robert P. Carroll. JSOTSup 138. Sheffield: JSOT Press, 1992.

Niditch, Susan. *Underdogs and Tricksters: A Prelude to Biblical Folklore*. New Voices in Biblical Studies. San Francisco: Harper & Row, 1987.

———. "The Wronged Woman Righted: An Analysis of Genesis 38." *HTR* 72 (1979): 143–49.

Niehaus, Jeffrey J. *God at Sinai*. Grand Rapids: Zondervan, 1995.

———. "In the Wind of the Storm: Another Look at Genesis iii 8." *VT* 44 (1994): 263–67.

———. *When Did Eve Sin? The Fall and Biblical Historiography*. Bellingham: Lexham, 2020.

Noble, Paul R. "A 'Balanced' Reading of the Rape of Dinah: Some Exegetical and Methodological Observations." *BibInt* 4 (1996): 173–204.

———. "Esau, Tamar, and Joseph: Criteria for Identifying Inner-Biblical Allusions." *VT* 52 (2002): 219–52.

Noegel, Scott B. "Sex, Sticks, and the Trickster in Gen 30:31–43." *Journal of the Ancient Near Eastern Society* 25 (1997): 7–17.

Noonan, Benjamin J. "Abraham, Blessing, and the Nations: A Reexamination of the Niphal and Hitpael of ברך in the Patriarchal Narratives." *HS* 51 (2010): 73–93.

O'Brien, Mark A. "The Contribution of Judah's Speech, Genesis 44:18–34, to the Characterization of Joseph." *CBQ* 59 (1997): 429–47.

Oden, Robert A. "Jacob as Father, Husband, and Nephew: Kinship Studies and the Patriarchal Narratives." *JBL* 102 (1983): 189–205.

Ollenburger, Ben C. "Creation and Peace: Creator and Creature in Genesis 1–11." Pages 143–58 in *The Old Testament in the Life of God's People: Essays in Honor of Elmer A. Martens*, edited by Jon M. Isaak. Winona Lake: Eisenbrauns, 2009.

———. *Zion, City of the Great King: A Theological Symbol of the Jerusalem Cult*. JSOTSup 41. Sheffield: JSOT Press, 1987.

Orlinsky, H. M. "The Plain Meaning of Genesis 1:1–3." *BA* 46 (1983): 207–09.

Osborn, Ronald E. *Death before the Fall : Biblical Literalism and the Problem of Animal Suffering*. Downers Grove: InterVarsity Press Academic, 2014.

Osborne, W. "Babel." Pages 73–75 in *Dictionary of the Old Testament: Pentateuch*, edited by T. Desmond Alexander and David W. Baker. Downers Grove: InterVarsity Press, 2003..

Palmer, E. H. *The Survey of Western Palestine: Arabic and English Name-Lists Collected by Lieutenants Conder and Kitchener, R.E. Transliterated and Explained by E. H. Palmer*. London: Committee of the Palestine Exploration Fund, 1881.

Park, Song-Mi Suzie. "Transformation and Demarcation of Jacob's 'Flocks' in Genesis 30:25–43: Identity, Election, and the Role of the Divine." *CBQ* 72 (2010): 667–77.

Parunak, H. Van Dyke. "A Semantic Survey of NḤM." *Biblica* 56 (1975): 512–32.

Patterson, Todd L. *The Plot-Structure of Genesis: "Will the Righteous Seed Survive?" in the* Muthos-*Logical Movement from Complication to Dénouement*. Biblical Interpretation Series 160. Leiden: Brill, 2018.

Payne, J. B. "אבה (ʾbh)." *TWOT*, 1:5–6.

Peleg, Y. "Was the Ancestress of Israel in Danger? Did Pharaoh Touch (נגע) Sarai?" *ZAW* 118 (2006): 197–208.

Person, Raymond F., and Robert Rezetko. "Introduction: The Importance of Empirical Models to Assess the Efficacy of Source and Redaction Criticism." Pages 1–35 in *Empirical Models Challenging Biblical Criticism*, edited by Raymond F. Person and Robert Rezetko. AIL 25. Atlanta: SBL, 2016.

Peterson, Thomas V. *Ham and Japheth: The Mythic World of Whites in the Antebellum South*. ATLA Monograph 12. Metuchen: Scarecrow, 1978.

Peursen, Wido Th. van. "Delimitation Markers, Chapter Division, Syntax and Literary Structure: The Case of Genesis 37:1–2." Pages 3–18 in *Textual Boundaries in the Bible: Their Impact on Interpretation*, edited by M. C. A. Korpel and P. Sanders. Leuven: Peeters, 2017.

Pirson, Ron. *The Lord of the Dreams: A Semantic and Literary Analysis of Genesis 37–50*, JSOTSup 355.London: Sheffield Academic, 2002.

Plantinga, Cornelius. *Not the Way It's Supposed to Be: A Breviary of Sin*. Grand Rapids: Eerdmans, 1995.

Polzin, Robert. "'The Ancestress of Israel in Danger' in Danger." *Semeia* 3 (1975): 81–97.

Pope, Marvin H. "Enigmatic Bible Passages: The Timing of the Snagging of the Ram, Genesis 22:13." *BA* 49 (1986): 114–17.

Poythress, Vern S. *Christian Interpretations of Genesis 1*, Christian Answers to Hard Questions. Phillipsburg: P&R, 2013.

Premsagar, P. V. "Theology of Promise in the Patriarchal Narratives." *Indian Journal of Theology* 23 (1974): 112–22.

Pritchard, James B., ed. *Ancient Near Eastern Texts*. 3rd ed. Princeton: Princeton University Press, 1969.

Pröbstle, Martin. "'Lion of Judah': The Blessing on Judah in Genesis 49:8–12." Pages 23–49 in *"For You Have Strengthened Me": Biblical and Theological Studies in Honor of Gerhard Pfandl in Celebration of His Sixty-Fifth Birthday*, edited by Martin Pröbstle. St. Peter am Hart: Seminar Schloss Bogenhofen, 2007.

Propp, William H. C. *Exodus 19–40: A New Translation with Introduction and Commentary*, AB 2B. New York: Doubleday, 2006.

Provan, Iain. *Discovering Genesis: Content, Interpretation, Reception*, Discovering Biblical Texts. London: SPCK, 2015.

Rabinowitz, Jacob J. "The 'Great Sin' in Ancient Egyptian Marriage Contracts." *JNES* 18 (1959): 73–73.

Rad, Gerhard von. *Genesis: A Commentary*. 2nd ed. OTL. London: SCM, 1972.

———. *The Theology of Israel's Historical Traditions*. Vol. 1 of *Old Testament Theology*. Edinburgh: Oliver and Boyd, 1962.

Radday, Yehuda T. "Chiasmus in Hebrew Biblical Narrative." Pages 50–115 in *Chiasmus in Antiquity: Structures, Analyses, Exegesis*, edited by John W. Welch. Hildesheim: Gerstenberg, 1981.

Rainey, Anson F., and R. Steven Notley. *The Sacred Bridge: Carta's Atlas of the Biblical World*. Jerusalem: Carta, 2006.

Reddish, Mitchell G. "Heaven." *ABD*, 3, 90–91.

Rendsburg, Gary A. *The Redaction of Genesis*. Winona Lake: Eisenbrauns, 1986.

———. "Some False Leads in the Identification of Late Biblical Hebrew Texts: The Cases of Genesis 24 and 1 Samuel 2:27–36." *JBL* 121 (2002): 23–46.

Revell, E. J. "Concord with Compound Subjects and Related Uses of Pronouns." *VT* 43 (1993): 69–87.

Riccardi, Michael. "The Seed of Abraham: A Theological Analysis of Galatians 3 and Its Implications for Israel." *MSJ* 25 (2014): 51–64.

Rickett, Dan. "Rethinking the Place and Purpose of Genesis 13." *JSOT* 36 (2011): 31–53.

Ringgren, Helmer. "בָּבֶל *bābhel*." *TDOT*, 1:466–69.

Robinson, Edward, and Eli Smith. *Biblical Researches in Palestine, Mount Sinai, and Arabia Petræa: A Journal of Travels in the Year 1838*. Boston: Crocker & Brewster, 1841.

Robinson, Robert D. "Literary Functions of the Genealogies of Genesis." *CBQ* 48 (1986): 595–608.

Rogland, Max. "Interpreting אד in Genesis 2.5–6: Neglected Rabbinic and Intertextual Evidence." *JSOT* 34 (2010): 379–93.

Ross, Allen P. "Studies in the Book of Genesis, Part 2: The Table of Nations in Genesis 10—Its Structure." *BSac* 137 (1980): 340–53.

———. "Studies in the Book of Genesis, Part 4: The Dispersion of the Nations in Genesis 11:1–9." *BSac* 138 (1981): 119–38.

———. "Studies in the Life of Jacob, Part 2: Jacob at the Jabbok, Israel at Peniel." *BSac* 142 (1985): 338–54.

Russell, Stephen C. "Abraham's Purchase of Ephron's Land in Anthropological Perspective." *BibInt* 21 (2013): 153–70.

Rydelnik, Michael A. *The Messianic Hope: Is the Hebrew Bible Really Messianic?* NAC Studies in Bible and Theology 9. Nashville: Broadman & Holman, 2010.

Ryle, Herbert Edward. *The Book of Genesis: The Cambridge Bible for Schools and Colleges*. Cambridge: Cambridge University Press, 1914.

Sandmel, Samuel. "Parallelomania." *JBL* 81 (1962): 1–13.

Sarna, Nahum M. "Abraham." Pages 111–20 in *Encyclopaedia Judaica*. Vol. 2. Jerusalem: Keter, 1972.

———. "The Anticipatory Use of Information as a Literary Feature of the Genesis Narratives." Pages 76–82 in *The Creation of Sacred Literature: Composition and Redaction of the Biblical Text*, edited by Richard Elliot Friedman. Berkeley: University of California, 1981.

———. *Exodus*. JPS Torah Commentary. Philadelphia: Jewish Publication Society, 1991.

———. *Genesis: The Traditional Hebrew Text with the New JPS Translation*. JPS Torah Commentary. New York: Jewish Publication Society, 1989.

———. *Understanding Genesis*, The Heritage of Biblical Israel 1. New York: Jewish Theological Seminary of America, 1966.

Satterthwaite, Philip E. "Genealogy in the Old Testament." *NIDOTTE*, 4:654–63.

Satterthwaite, Philip E., Richard S. Hess, and Gordon J. Wenham, eds. *The Lord's Anointed: Interpretation of Old Testament Messianic Texts*. Grand Rapids: Baker Academic, 1995.

Schmutzer, Andrew J. "Did the Gods Cause Abraham's Wandering? An Examination of םיהלא יתא ועתה in Genesis 20.13." *JSOT* 35 (2010): 149–66.

Schreiner, Thomas R. *Commentary on Hebrews*. Nashville: B&H, 2015.

Schultz, R. "Servant, Slave." *NIDOTTE*, 4:1183–98.

Schwartz, Sarah. "Isaac's Dual Test in the Blessings Narrative: A New Reading of Gen 27:18–29." *JSOT* 43 (2019): 693–711.

———. "Narrative Toledot Formulae in Genesis: The Case of Heaven and Earth, Noah and Isaac." *Journal of Hebrew Scriptures* 16 (2016): 1–36.

Scobie, Charles H. H. "Israel and the Nations: An Essay in Biblical Theology." *TynBul* 43 (1992): 283–305.

Selman, Martin J. "Comparative Customs and the Patriarchal Age." Pages 93–138 in *Essays on the Patriarchal Narratives*, edited by A. R. Millard and Donald J. Wiseman. Leicester: Inter-Varsity Press, 1980.

———. "The Social Environment of the Patriarchs." *TynBul* 27 (1976): 114–36.

Shead, Andrew G. "Sabbath." Pages 745–50 in *New Dictionary of Biblical Theology*, edited by T. Desmond Alexander and Brian S. Rosner. Leicester: InterVarsity Press, 2000.

Shemesh, Yael. "Rape Is Rape Is Rape: The Story of Dinah and Shechem (Genesis 34)." *ZAW* 119 (2007): 2–21.

Sigmon, Brian O. "Shadowing Jacob's Journey: Gen 47:13–26 as a Sideshadow." *BibInt* 19 (2011): 454–70.

Ska, Jean-Louis. "Genesis 18:6—Intertextuality and Interpretation: 'It All Makes Flour in the Good Mill,' " in *The Comments on the Pentateuch: Exegetical*

Studies and Basic Questions, edited by Jean-Louis Ska. FAT 66. Tübingen: Mohr Siebeck, 2009, 89–96.

———. "The Tree and the Tent: The Function of the Scenery in Gen 18:1–15." Pages 82–88 in *The Comments on the Pentateuch: Exegetical Studies and Basic Questions*, edited by Jean-Louis Ska. FAT 66. Tübingen: Mohr Siebeck, 2009.

Skinner, John. *Genesis*. 2nd ed. ICC. Edinburgh: T&T Clark, 1930.

Smith, Bryan. "The Central Role of Judah in Genesis 37–50." *BSac* 162 (2005): 158–74.

Smith, Gary V. "Structure and Purpose in Genesis 1–11." *JETS* 20 (1977): 307–19.

Smith, Mark S. *The Priestly Vision of Genesis 1*. Minneapolis: Fortress, 2010.

Sommer, Benjamin D. "Dating Pentateuchal Texts and the Perils of Pseudo-Historicism." Pages 85–108 in *The Pentateuch: International Perspectives on Current Research*, edited by Thomes B. Dozeman, Konrad Schmid, and Baruch J. Schwartz. FAT 78. Tübingen: Mohr Siebeck, 2011.

———. Review of *The Pentateuch in the 20th Century: The Legacy of Julius Wellhausen*, by Ernest Nicholson. *Review of Biblical Literature* 2 (2000): 184–89.

Sonek, Kris. "The Abraham Narratives in Genesis 12–25." *CurBR* 17 (2019): 158–83.

Speiser, E. A. *Genesis*, 2nd ed. AB 1. Garden City: Doubleday, 1964.

———. "'People' and 'Nation' of Israel." *JBL* 79 (1960): 157–63.

———. "The Wife-Sister Motif in the Patriarchal Narratives." Pages 62–88 in *Oriental and Biblical Studies: Collected Writings of E. A. Speiser*, edited by J. J. Finkelstein and Moshe Greenberg. Philadelphia: University of Pennsylvania Press, 1967.

Spina, Frank A. "Babel (Place)." *ABD*, 1:561–63.

Steiner, Richard C. "Poetic Forms in the Masoretic Vocalization and Three Difficult Phrases in Jacob's Blessing: יֶתֶר שְׂאֵת (Gen 49:3): 49:4 (יְצוּעִי עָלָה): and 49:10 (יָבֹא שִׁילֹה)." *JBL* 129 (2010): 209–35.

———. "'He Said, He Said': Repetition of the Quotation Formula in the Joseph Story and Other Biblical Narratives." *JBL* 138 (2019): 473–95.

Steinmann, Andrew E. "Gaps in the Genealogies in Genesis 5 and 11?" *BSac* 174 (2017): 141–58.

———. *Genesis: An Introduction and Commentary*. TOTC 1. Downers Grove: InterVarsity Press, 2019.

———. "Jesus and Possessing the Enemies' Gate (Genesis 22:17–18; 24:60)." *BSac* 174 (2017): 13–21.

Stek, John H. "What Says the Scripture?" Pages 203–65 in *Portraits of Creation: Biblical and Scientific Perspectives on the World's Formation*, edited by Howard J. Van Till. Grand Rapids: Eerdmans 1990.

Sternberg, Meir. *The Poetics of Biblical Narrative: Ideological Literature and the Drama of Reading*. Bloomington: Indiana University Press, 1985.

Stordalen, Terje. "Man, Soil, Garden: Basic Plot in Genesis 2–3 Reconsidered." *JSOT* 53 (1992): 3–26.

Storkey, Elaine. *Scars Across Humanity: Understanding and Overcoming Violence Against Women*. London: SPCK, 2015.

Stuart, Douglas K. *Exodus*. NAC 2. Nashville: Broadman & Holman, 2006.

Stuhlmiller, Wayne J. H. "One Flesh: In the Old and New Testaments." *Consensus* 5 (1979): 3–9.

Talmon, Shemaryahu. "The Presentation of Synchroneity and Simultaneity in Biblical Narrative." *Scripta Hierosolymitana* 27 (1978): 9–26.

Thomas, D. Winton. "Consideration of Some Unusual Ways of Expressing the Superlative in Hebrew." *VT* 3 (1953): 209–24.

Thomas, Matthew A. *These Are the Generations: Identity, Covenant, and the Toledot Formula*. LHBOTS 551. London: T&T Clark, 2011.

Thompson, R. J. *Moses and the Law in a Century of Criticism since Graf*. VTSup 19. Leiden: Brill, 1970.

Thompson, Thomas L. *The Historicity of the Patriarchal Narratives*. BZAW 133. Berlin: de Gruyter, 1974.

———. *The Literary Formation of Genesis and Exodus 1–23*. Vol. 1 of *The Origin Tradition of Ancient Israel*. JSOTSup 55. Sheffield: JSOT Press, 1987.

Tigay, Jeffrey H. "The Documentary Hypothesis, Empirical Models and Holistic Interpretation." Pages 116–43 in *Modernity and Interpretations of Ancient Texts. The Collapse and Remaking of Traditions*, edited by J. Ikeda. Kizugawa-City, Kyoto, Japan: International Institute of Advanced Studies, 2012.

Timmer, Daniel C. *Creation, Tabernacle, and Sabbath: The Sabbath Frame of Exodus 31:12–17; 35:1–3 in Exegetical and Theological Perspective*. Forschungen zur Religion und Literatur des Alten und Neuen Testaments 227. Göttingen: Vandenhoeck & Ruprecht, 2009.

Toorn, K. van der, and P. W. Van der Horst. "Nimrod before and after the Bible." *HTR* 83 (1990): 1–29.

Towner, W. Sibley. *Genesis*. Westminster Bible Companion. Louisville: Westminster John Knox, 2001.

Tsevat, M. "*bek̲ôr*." *TDOT*, 2:126.

Tsumura, David Toshio. *Creation and Destruction: A Reappraisal of the Chaoskampf Theory in the Old Testament*. Winona Lake: Eisenbrauns, 2005.

Tucker, Gene M. "The Legal Background to Genesis 23." *JBL* 85 (1966): 77–84.

Turner, Laurence A. *Announcements of Plot in Genesis*. JSOTSup 96. Sheffield: JSOT Press, 1990.

———. *Genesis*. Readings: A New Biblical Commentary. Sheffield: Sheffield Academic, 2000.

Twiss, Paul. "A Tale of Two Brothers: The Messiah in Genesis 49." *MSJ* 33 (2022): 255–67.

Uffenheimer, B. "Genesis 18–19, A New Approach." Pages 145–53 in *Mélanges André Neher*, edited by E. A. Levy-Valense. Paris: A. Maisonneuve, 1975.

Ullendorff, Edward. "Construction of Noah's Ark." *VT* 4 (1954): 95–96.

VanGemeren, Willem A. "The Sons of God in Genesis 6:1–4 (An Example of Evangelical Demythologization)." *WTJ* 43 (1981): 320–48.

Van Leeuwen, Raymond C. "ברא." *NIDOTTE*, 1:728–35.
Van Seters, John. *Abraham in History and Tradition*. New Haven: Yale University Press, 1975.
Vawter, Bruce. *On Genesis: A New Reading*. Garden City: Doubleday, 1977.
Vermeulen, Karolien. "The 'Song' of the Servant—Gen 24:23." *VT* 61 (2011): 499–504.
Viberg, Åke. *Symbols of Law: A Contextual Analysis of Legal Symbolic Acts in the Old Testament*. ConBOT 34. Stockholm: Almqvist & Wiksell, 1992.
Viezel, Eran. "The Influence of Realia on Biblical Depictions of Childbirth." *VT* 61 (2011): 685–89.
Wagner, Angela B. "Considerations on the Politico-Juridical Proceedings of Genesis 34." *JSOT* 38 (2013): 145–61.
Walsh, Jerome T. *Old Testament Narrative: A Guide to Interpretation*. Louisville: Westminster John Knox, 2009.
Waltke, Bruce K., and Cathi J. Fredricks. *Genesis: A Commentary*. Grand Rapids: Zondervan, 2001.
Waltke, Bruce K., and Michael O'Connor. *An Introduction to Biblical Hebrew Syntax*. Winona Lake: Eisenbrauns, 1990.
Walton, John H. "Creation." Pages 155–69 in *Dictionary of the Old Testament: Pentateuch*, edited by T. Desmond Alexander and David W. Baker. Downers Grove: InterVarsity Press, 2003.
———. "Creation in Genesis 1:1–2:3 and the Ancient Near East: Order out of Disorder after *Chaoskampf*." *Calvin Theological Journal* 43 (2008): 48–63.
———. "Eden, Garden of." Pages 202–7 in *Dictionary of the Old Testament: Pentateuch*, edited by T. Desmond Alexander and David W. Baker. Downers Grove: InterVarsity Press, 2003.
———. *Genesis*. NIV Application Commentary. Grand Rapids: Zondervan, 2001.
———. *The Lost World of Genesis One: Ancient Cosmology and the Origins Debate*. Downers Grove: InterVarsity Press Academic, 2009.
Walton, John H., and J. Harvey Walton. *The Lost World of the Israelite Conquest: Covenant, Retribution, and the Fate of the Canaanites*. Downers Grove: InterVarsity Press, 2017.
Watson, Rebecca S. *Chaos Uncreated: A Reassessment of the Theme of "Chaos" in the Hebrew Bible*. BZAW 341. Berlin: Walter de Gruyter, 2005.
Weaks, Joseph A. "Limited Efficacy in Reconstructing the Gospel Sources for Matthew and Luke." Pages 331–54 in *Empirical Models Challenging Biblical Criticism*, edited by Raymond F. Person and Robert Rezetko. AIL 25. Atlanta: SBL, 2016.
Webb, Barry G. "Zion in Transformation: A Literary Approach to Isaiah." Pages 65–84 in *The Bible in Three Dimensions*, edited by D. J. A. Clines, Stephen E. Fowl, and Stanley E. Porter. JSOTSup 87. Sheffield: JSOT Press, 1990.
Weinfeld, Moshe. "The Covenant of Grant in the Old Testament and in the Ancient Near East." *JAOS* 90 (1970): 184–203.
Welker, Michael. "Creation and the Image of God: Their Understanding in Christian Tradition and the Biblical Grounds." *Journal of Ecumenical Studies* 34 (1997): 436–48.

Wenham, Gordon J. "The Coherence of the Flood Narrative." *VT* 28 (1978): 336-48.
——. *Genesis 1–15*. WBC 1. Waco: Word, 1987.
——. *Genesis 16–50*. WBC 2. Waco: Word, 1994.
——. *Rethinking Genesis 1–11: Gateway to the Bible: The Didsbury Lectures 2013*. Didsbury Lecture Series. Eugene: Cascade, 2015.
——. "Sanctuary Symbolism in the Garden of Eden Story." Pages 399–404 in *"I Studied Inscriptions before the Flood": Ancient Near Eastern, Literary, and Linguistic Approaches to Genesis 1–11*, edited by Richard S. Hess and David Toshio Tsumura. Winona Lake: Eisenbrauns, 1994.
——. "The Symbolism of the Animal Rite in Genesis 15: A Response to G. F. Hasel, *JSOT* 19 (1981) 61–78." *JSOT* 22 (1982): 134–37.
Westbrook, Raymond. "The Female Slave." Pages 214–38 in *Gender and Law in the Hebrew Bible and the Ancient Near East*, edited by Bernard M. Levenson, Tikva Frymer-Kensky, and Victor H. Matthews. JSOTSup 262. Sheffield: Sheffield Academic, 1998.
——. "Purchase of the Cave of Machpelah." *Israel Law Review* 6 (1971): 29–38.
Westermann, Claus. *Blessing: In the Bible and the Life of the Church*. Philadelphia: Fortress, 1978.
——. *Genesis 1–11: A Commentary*. Translated by John J. Scullion. Minneapolis: Augsburg, 1984.
——. *Genesis 12–36: A Commentary*. Translated by John J. Scullion. Minneapolis: Augsburg, 1985.
——. *Genesis 37–50: A Commentary*. Translated by John J. Scullion. Minneapolis: Augsburg, 1986.
——. *The Promises to the Fathers: Studies on the Patriarchal Narratives*. Translated by David E. Green. Philadelphia: Fortress, 1980.
White, Lynn. "The Historical Roots of Our Ecological Crisis." *Science* 155 (1967): 1203–7.
Whitford, David M. *The Curse of Ham in the Early Modern Era: The Bible and the Justifications for Slavery*. St. Andrew's Studies in Reformation History. Farnham: Ashgate, 2009.
Whybray, R. Norman. "Genesis." Pages 38–66 in *The Oxford Bible Commentary*, edited by John Barton and John Muddiman. Oxford: Oxford University Press, 2001.
——. "The Joseph Story and Pentateuchal Criticism." *VT* 18 (1968): 522–28.
——. *The Making of the Pentateuch: A Methodological Study*. JSOTSup 53. Sheffield: JSOT Press, 1987.
Wildavsky, Aaron. "Survival Must Not Be Gained through Sin: The Moral of the Joseph Stories Prefigured through Judah and Tamar." *JSOT* 19 (1994): 37–48.
Williamson, Paul R. *Abraham, Israel and the Nations: The Patriarchal Promise and Its Covenantal Development in Genesis*. JSOTSup 315. Sheffield: Sheffield Academic, 2000.

———. "Covenant." Page 419–29 in *New Dictionary of Biblical Theology*, edited by T. Desmond Alexander, Brian S. Rosner, D. A. Carson, and Graeme Goldsworthy. Leicester: Inter-Varsity Press, 2000.

———. *Death and the Afterlife: Biblical Perspectives on Ultimate Questions*. NSBT 44. London: Apollos, 2017.

———. *Sealed with an Oath: Covenant in God's Unfolding Purpose*. NSBT 23. Downers Grove: InterVarsity Press, 2007.

———. "Snakes and Dragons: A Neglected Theological Trajectory of Genesis 3:15 in Scripture?" Pages 332–52 in *The Seed of Promise: The Sufferings and Glory of the Messiah: Essays in Honor of T. Desmond Alexander*, edited by Paul R. Williamson and Rita F. Cefalu. GlossaHouse Festschrift Series 3. Wilmore: GlossaHouse, 2020.

Wilson, Robert R. *Genealogy and History in the Biblical World*. New Haven: Yale University Press, 1977.

Wolff, Hans Walter. "Kerygma of the Yahwist." *Int* 20 (1966): 131–58.

Wright, Christopher J. H. "אב (ʾab)." *NIDOTTE*, 1:219–23.

———. *The Mission of God: Unlocking the Bible's Grand Narrative*. Nottingham: Inter-Varsity Press, 2006.

———. "Reading the Old Testament Missionally." Pages 107–23 in *Reading the Bible Missionally*, edited by Michael W. Goheen. The Gospel and Our Culture. Grand Rapids: Eerdmans, 2016.

Wünch, Hans-Georg. "Genesis 38—Judah's Turning Point: Structural Analysis and Narrative Techniques and Their Meaning for Genesis 38 and Its Placement in the Story of Joseph." *Old Testament Essays* 25 (2012): 777–806.

Yarchin, William. "Imperative and Promise in Genesis 12:1–3." *Studia Biblica and Theologica* 10 (1980): 164–78.

Yoo, Philip Y. "Hagar the Egyptian: Wife, Handmaid, and Concubine." *CBQ* 78 (2016): 215–35.

———. "Why Does Joseph Wash His Face?" *JSOT* 38 (2013): 3–14.

Younker, Randall W. "Ammonites." Pages 293–316 in *Peoples of the Old Testament World*, edited by Alfred J. Hoerth, Gerald L. Mattingly, and Edwin M. Yamauchi. Cambridge: Lutterworth, 1996.

Zehnder, Markus. "Cause or Value: Problems in the Understanding of Gen 9,6a." *ZAW* 122 (2010): 81–89.

Zhao, Yong. "The Story of Judah, the Hero: An Analysis of Genesis 38." *JBQ* 42 (2014): 238–43.

Zucker, David J. "The Deceiver Deceived: Rereading Genesis 27." *JBQ* 39 (2011): 46–58.

SCRIPTURE INDEX

OLD TESTAMENT

2 Chronicles

Ezra

Nehemiah

Job

Psalms

Proverbs

Ecclesiastes

Song of Songs

Isaiah

NEW TESTAMENT

DEUTEROCANONICAL BOOKS

OTHER ANCIENT LITERATURE

EVERY PAGE IS THE LONG STORY SHORT

The Evangelical Biblical Theology Commentary (EBTC) series locates each biblical book within redemptive history and illuminates its unique theological contributions. All EBTC volumes feature informed exegetical treatment of the biblical book and thorough discussion of its most important theological themes in relation to the canon—in a style that is useful and accessible to students of Scripture.

LexhamPress.com/EBTC